Freethought Across The Centuries

Dedication

*To my students, past and present,
with gratitude for helping to provide
an academic environment for
the growth of freethought
and
for giving me hope for the future
through anticipation of the
contributions they will make to
the new enlightenment during
the 21st century.*

Freethought Across the Centuries

Toward a New Age of Enlightenment

by

Gerald A. Larue

HUMANIST PRESS

AMHERST, NEW YORK 14226

Objectivity, Accuracy and Balance in Teaching About Religion, Inc. (OABITAR), P.O. Box 567, Burlingame, CA 94011-0567; (415) 343-0222, FAX (415) 343-0922. OABITAR is a nonprofit public benefit corporation organized in the State of California, #1828425 on April 14, 1993. Its purpose is promotion of objectivity, accuracy and balance in teaching about religion.

Published 1996 by Humanist Press

Humanist Press is a division of the American Humanist Association, 7 Harwood Drive/P.O. Box 1188, Amherst, NY 14226-7188, (800) 743-6646, FAX (716) 839-5079.

Library of Congress Catalog Card Number: 94-74348

ISBN 0-931779-04-9 Cloth cover
ISBN 0-931779-03-0 Paperback

Printed in the United States of America on acid-free paper.

Contents

Preface

As a professional educator, I have long been troubled by the many students who enter university without ever having been educationally challenged to engage in critical thinking — in fact they seem to be afraid to do so! I assign an article and ask each student to independently evaluate the writer's presentation or argument. So fearful and uncertain are they of expressing their own points of view or insights that they submit essays telling me what the writer has written. I explain that I already know what the writer has expressed, now I want their opinion and evaluation of the essay. The answer, over and over again, is "We have never been asked to do that before!"

I find it difficult to believe that independent thinking in the public school system is discouraged — or at least not encouraged! What is happening in our public schools? Are students being provided only with rote learning, with the mastery of bland book data to provide answers to book-data-questions on examinations? Where is critical thinking being encouraged in the curricula? Why should students be surprised, even startled, to discover that human progress has taken place because individuals have dared to think for themselves, have dared to re-evaluate and to challenge established ideas and the thinking of others?

For more than thirty years I have taught in the field of history of religions, specializing in biblical and Near-Eastern studies. My classes have included men and women of many different faiths, ordained clergy and their spouses, and many who, embracing no religion, were either classified by others or by themselves as unbelievers, skeptics, agnostics, or atheists. The mix has made for lively in-class discussion and, I hope, for student awareness of the diversity of human thought and the legitimacy of challenges to stubbornly held positions. It has also served to introduce the importance of the mastery of rational and logical thought and argument as well as the importance of testing using the scientific method. As a consequence, many have learned to say something like: "This is what we think we know or what we believe in the light of the evidence in hand. In the future new evidence may cause us to modify or change this conclusion just as new evidence has caused us to abandon concepts once held by our ancestors."

This mode of thinking touches the history of thought, from the way society once embraced the notion that the world was the center of the universe around which the sun and moon and stars revolved to our new information about the cosmos and space, to old beliefs about wood-sprites inhabiting the forests or that drought ensued because the rain god was held captive by the god of death, to our new appreciation of ecology and our satellite information about jet streams and the movement of high and low areas of air pressure. Whether or not any students abandoned previously held belief patterns, I can't say. I do know that the students left the classes with an awareness that their own particular faith or non-faith position could be challenged and critically evaluated; that the diversity of belief or non-belief systems called for respect and understanding; and that to be a thoughtful and contributing citizen in the twentieth (and now the coming twenty-first century) required understanding of others, the ability and willingness to challenge ideas on the basis of logic, reason and science, as well as mastery of the best and most up-to-date information on a given subject.

In our present public school system, at least in California, students are introduced to the major religions of the world in grades seven, eight and nine. Unfortunately, these religions are not presented as humans wrestling with their understanding of their place in the cosmos in terms of what they knew about their world, but rather blandly as something that happened to develop in history. They are not taught that each new religion constituted a rejection of a previously held belief system and that within each religion there have been and there are those who challenge basic precepts, ethics and the scientific validity of the claims of the faith and of those in authority. The absence of the role of skeptics, freethinkers, atheists and doubters is ignored as if they never existed and never brought about change and development within the human family.

It was out of awareness of this tremendous educational gap that OABITAR (*Objectivity, Accuracy and Balance In Teaching About Religion*) was born. The aim of this unique, innovative and pioneering effort is to attempt to encourage public educators to recognize the important roles and contributions of skeptics, freethinkers, rationalists, agnostics, atheists and doubters who embraced what might be called "nonreligion." Further, the hope is that by introducing freethought into the curricula, students will be made aware of the diversity of human reasoning and behavior and be encouraged to engage in critical thinking and evaluation in all dimensions of life and learning. Certainly, if as educators we believe that the use of reason, logic and the scientific method are the finest tools we humans have developed for the testing of ideas and claims, then our task must be to lead our students into ways of appreciating how these critical and analytical tools were developed, how their use has contributed to human progress, and how they are to be employed to evaluate present-day ideas.

The progenitor of OABITAR has been John B. Massen who has devoted time, energy and money as coordinator of the program he brought into being. His deep concern and commitment to enlarging the educational vision and horizons and to the encouragement of critical thinking and diversity in the educational programs is inspiring, to say the least. When he invited me to participate and to create this book, I was pleased to become involved, even though I am still teaching at the University of Southern California (now in the field of ethics in Gerontology) and involved in research and writing. The OABITAR project, which touched on some of my deepest concerns as an educator, was too important to ignore. The content of the book has been enriched by insights from Jack Massen and he has been responsible for the format, editing, and the preparation of the detailed Index. In every respect he has been a dedicated associate throughout this enterprise.

The production of this book has been a long and arduous task, and as it draws to conclusion I am still not satisfied that I have done all that could be done to explore and present the important dimensions of freethought in human history and development.

From time to time I have called on colleagues for insight, including Joseph E. Barnhart, Professor of Philosophy, North Texas State University in Denton, Texas; and Edd Doerr, Executive Director, Americans For Religious Liberty. Adolph Surtshin M.D., of the Ethical Culture Society of Los Angeles, read portions of the early form of the manuscript and offered helpful suggestions. My sons, Dr. Gerald A. Larue, Jr. who is Director of Support Programs in the Downey Unified School District, California, and Dr. David K. Larue, a geologist with Exxon Corporation have, from time to time, provided insights. In the formatting stages of the book, my student assistant in the School of Gerontology of the University of Southern California, Miss Jennifer Sherwood, has been my right hand, enabling me to bring the manuscript into readable and publishable condition. Finally, my wife Emily P. Larue has kept her promise to keep my study out-of-bounds so far as housekeeping is concerned and has cheerfully endured my tendency to have piles of paper here, there and everywhere (research materials!) in my office. Moreover, despite her own demanding professional and administrative responsibilities, she has found time to listen to some of my at-home discussions of the work in progress. To each of these special people, I wish to say "thank you."

Note to the reader: In keeping with international scholarly practice, I have used the abbreviations B.C.E. (Before the Common Era) and C.E. (Common Era) in place of the usual B.C. (Before Christ) and A.D. (*Anno Domini*).

Gerald A. Larue, February, 1996

1

Concerning Freethought

This book is about freethought. It is concerned with critical thinking and independent reasoning. It recognizes brave men and women who dared to question, to challenge, and even to upset the claims, opinions and beliefs of crown and church. It deals with the human quest for understanding the meaning and purpose of life and living. And, finally, it bears upon the kind of thinking and responding that has given birth to democracy and the rights of men and women to be themselves, to rise to their greatest potential while at the same time granting to others the freedom to be different and to express themselves openly and without fear of reprisal.

Freethought is not based on groundless speculation or credulity. It involves conjecture based on reason, logic, analysis and testing. Ideas that just float in the air so to speak, or that consist of "maybes" and "perhapses," do not constitute freethought. Freethought demands disciplined thinking, careful evaluations, and openness to change and growth whenever new information becomes available. Freethought involves the inquirer in an exciting adventure that keeps the mind and spirit open and alive — always probing, questioning, seeking and always with the awareness that "final" answers will never truly be final, and that whatever "ultimate truth" is will always be just beyond our grasp. Freethought is constantly on the cutting edge and in the forefront. It is open to the future with an awareness and an appreciation of the past, but without accepting what has been said in the past simply because it is "old" or "revered." It is cognizant and appreciative of what has been proclaimed as an "orthodox" or final authoritative statement without the need to accept that particular claim.

The term "freethought" came into existence in England towards the end of the seventeenth century. The *Oxford English Dictionary* defines a freethinker as "one who refuses to submit his reason to the control of authority in the matters of religious belief; a designation claimed *especially* by the deistic and other rejecters of Christianity at the beginning of the eighteenth century." *Webster's New Collegiate Dictionary* splits the term into two words as "free thought" and defines it as "free thinking or unorthodox thought" and defines a "free-thinker" as "one that forms opinions on the basis of reason independently of authority; *esp*: one who doubts or denies religious dogma, *syn*. See ATHEIST." Other American dictionaries employ similar language. Freethought is, therefore, closely related to "critical thinking" and, perhaps also, to "independent thinking" — each of which calls upon the individual to "think for one's self," to reach conclusions based on reason and open inquiry and not to accept blindly the dogma and opinions espoused by others. Freethought engenders basic questions such as "How do we know this is true?", "What is the evidence supporting this conclusion?", "What are the basic presuppositions underlying this belief and how do we test their validity?", and so forth. Today, in freethought, we employ reason and logic in analysis and utilize a scientific approach which calls for independent testing and re-testing. These approaches automatically leave the door open to change based on new findings.

What this present study will make clear is that both critical and independent thinking are as old as the human race. In every culture where we find written material, there is evidence of challenges made to prevailing concepts and dogmas, and we can assume that such questioning went on for millennia before beliefs were put in written form. What is demonstrated, over and over again, is that, out of the refusal to accept what those in power and authority have claimed to be the ultimate truth, has come ever-widening knowledge of the natural world, as well as human progress in ethics, morals, human behavior, human relations, freedom and the quality of life.

Unfortunately, today many are not ready to exercise free thinking or critical thinking in all areas of life. All too easily we become locked in to what our particular branch of American culture may proclaim as right, proper and the ultimate truth. The results of uncritical acceptance of attitudes and beliefs are bigotry, racism, dogmatism, anti-science postures, and a lack of compassion or understanding that endorses limiting the rights and freedoms of others. Thus, dogmas, attitudes, beliefs, behavior, life styles, endorsed or condemned by church or state are accepted without critical examination or judgment, no matter what their effect on society or on human freedom may be. It is at this point that the freethought movement stands apart. Freethought maintains that *any* theory or thesis or concept is open to challenge and can be accepted or rejected on the basis of logic, reason and scientific investigation and on the basis of its effect on human well-being and human freedom.

Looking Backwards

How do ideas, beliefs and attitudes become the norm? We can only conjecture about the origins of beliefs. We can imagine one of our ancient ancestors on a hunting expedition. Suddenly a rock falls from an adjacent cliff and startles a small antelope that had been standing quietly out of sight. The hunter makes a kill and returns to his camp with the animal slung across his shoulders. In his hand is the rock that frightened the antelope. He relates the story of the hunt and states that the rock obviously has magical powers to affect the hunt. Two days later he sets out once again. Before leaving camp he strokes the rock and calls upon the power in it to help him in his search for food. He returns with a brace of rabbits. It is clear to him that the stone's magic is working. On the days when the hunt fails, he assumes it is because he or one of the group did something to offend the stone's power. Perhaps he thinks that he should share the benefits of the hunt and put animal fat on the stone. By now the stone has become an icon, an object of uncritical devotion.

If there had been a freethinker in the group, that person might have suggested that the stone did not fall of its own accord. Recent rains had loosened the soil in which it was embedded and the stone broke loose and fell (we would say due to gravity). A critical thinker might have pointed out that a few weeks before the falling stone frightened the antelope, the same hunter had been just as successful in bringing home game from the hunt, and that perhaps the falling of the stone was nothing more than a fortunate happenstance. In other words, freethinking would challenge the basic presupposition of magical power in the stone. Questions about the validity of the hunter's conjectures needed to be raised. Finally, his thesis required testing by engaging in a series of hunts that ignored the stone. We will never know whether or not such critical questioning ever occurred in the hunting-gathering era. What we will find is that, time and again in human history, whenever and wherever men and women engaged in independent freethought and challenged the established notions endorsed by the clergy and the crown, superstitious and irrational beliefs were either abandoned or transformed.

Even where we do have written records, we have no way of knowing the thinking of individuals whose ideas were not recorded or have been lost. For example, when King Hammurabi of Babylon had the laws of the land carved on a stele of black diorite (it is now in the Louvre), he claimed that he, personally, had received the engraved legislation from Shamash, the sun god, the patron of justice. Indeed, in the top panel of the stone slab, Hammurabi is pictured standing before the seated sun god. Presumably, the monarch is being given divine authorization to enact the laws. It would have been most daring for a freethinker to question whether or not the sun was really a god or whether Shamash had actually given the laws to the monarch. To do so would have been to question the authority of both the state and the temple. A critical thinker might have observed that the laws embodied little more than the traditional legal practices now being given divine sanction. That same person might have noted that Hammurabi's laws reflected prescriptions that earlier monarchs had endorsed, each claiming that they had come from some deity other than Shamash. An independent ethical thinker might have questioned whether it was fair that the code should endorse one set of laws for the rich and powerful and another set for the common laborer and slave. But those were different times. Challenges could be dangerous and engender risk of punishment, ostracism or death. Today, scholars raise all of these questions. We know that the motif of gods giving laws to humans was common throughout the ancient world. We know that the sun is simply a small star, that it has no personality and that only by the wildest stretch of modern imagination could it be considered to be a god. Archaeological research has produced older law codes than that of Hammurabi, and we know that some of his laws reflect older legislation. We have rejected the authority of one person, no matter what his or her claims to divine authority might be, to make and impose laws on the populace, just as we reject the injustice of one set of rules for the rich and another for the poor. We believe in justice for all.

Today, we would not accept the notion that the constitution of the United States was somehow handed supernaturally to the founding fathers by God. We also deny both the claims of the divine right of kings and rulers and of the divine right of one people to enslave another. Our government and laws are of the people, for the people and by the people and, as we all know, making that ideal a reality has been a slow and painful process.

What we will learn from this book is that, although the term "freethought" is recent, freethinking is really much older than the seventeenth century and our heritage of freethought is much richer than the products of a couple of centuries. Throughout human history there have been those who have challenged the authority of dogmas and questioned the reasonableness of belief in the supernatural. Some raised doubts about the validity of the proclamations of those who claimed to have had experiences of the supernatural or who stated that as prophets or priests they spoke on behalf of some supernatural being or beings.

Queries were raised concerning the effectiveness of prayers, rituals, offerings and pleadings that were supposed to be based on knowledge of what a deity or deities required of human beings. The authority of those who claimed to hold their office as a god-given right or because they were particularly chosen by a god was challenged. As a consequence, claims by kings, emperors, and those who claimed to be incarnate gods, and of high priests and shamans who claimed to be functionaries of one deity or another, were opened to doubt and inquiry. Even the idea of a people or a nation to be particularly chosen by a supreme deity came to be questioned. Some who raised doubts about a particular dogma or supernaturalistic claim, substituted another similar but different authority as a guide for life. Still others focused on the human dimension and on what human beings could accomplish without relying on gods or goddesses. Consequently, instead of labeling humans as inferior or sinful creatures, they rejoiced in their humanity and exalted the human potential.

Freethought: An Expanded Definition

As I began my research, it became clear that I needed to define freethought a bit more broadly than the definitions given in dictionaries and not neglect independent, rational thought that was manifested long before the seventeenth and eighteenth centuries. While it is clear that in culture after culture we have evidence of secular thinking and of deistic thinking and of the presence of doubters and atheists, much independent thought occurred *within* the context of religious belief systems. Therefore, when the Buddha rejected Hinduism with its multitude of gods and began his independent quest for the meaning of human existence, he became a freethinker or an independent thinker within the social and religious context of ancient India. When Muhammad broke from the multi-god religion of ancient Arabia and established Islam, he was, in a sense, a freethinker and certainly an independent thinker within the context of the sixth century of the Common Era. And when, within Islam, sects arose and philosophers and poets expressed ideas that conflicted with those expressed in traditional Islam, they were, in a broad sense, freethinkers. When Martin Luther broke with the authority of the Church of Rome, he functioned as an independent thinker, free of the traditional authority and dogma of the Roman Church. Of course, he substituted one external authority (the Bible) for another (the Church), but the break he initiated opened the door for further deviations, contributing to the development of deism and modern empiricism.

Such expanded defining of freethought will not please everyone. In defense, I must point out that today we live in a time and place different from our early ancestors. We have in hand, for the interpretation of our world, tools that they never knew, and this fact calls upon us to appreciate who we are and how we have arrived at where we are.

Today, even as free and open inquiry continues to expand upon what we think we know and at times discredits currently held ideas and beliefs, and even as by using reason and science we move away from and break with the old, there are among us those who continue to cling to the past — perhaps for security, perhaps for other reasons. They find comfort in the familiar; they are discomfited by the new. This is their right as free people. However, it must never be assumed that it is their right to compel others to accept or conform to their particular beliefs and life patterns. It is important that we understand the reasoning and the rationale for the break-away ideas that developed in the past. Let me explain what I am getting at by once again going back in time.

Our forebears looked at their world with their feet planted firmly on the ground. They attempted to understand, to comprehend, to define what they observed. They sought to appreciate and explain their place in the cosmos as they understood it. For example, it is clear to all of us that the sky *appears* to touch the earth at the horizons. As we look toward the horizons, the earth *appears* to be a relatively flat plate with an overarching dome or roof. It is obvious that each morning the sun appears over the horizon in the east and descends below the horizon in the west each evening. Those who believed in a flat world with an overarching heaven asked, "How does the sun get from the west to the east?" Their answer made sense in terms of their understanding of the cosmos: the sun travels under the earth, perhaps through a tunnel, to reach the eastern horizon. The optical illusion of "sunrise" and "sunset" (terms we still employ) was based on what *seemed* to be happening and on limited understanding of the cosmos. These conjectures, founded on what human beings saw as they stood on the surface of the earth, mark the beginnings of the kind of speculation and inquiry that have led, in our day, to the adventuring into outer space with machines and with human beings.

Today, we view our world from a different perspective. As the first generation to see the world from outer space, we are able to sit in the comfort of our homes and witness on the television screen men landing on the surface of the moon. We are the first to watch live visual transmissions of how men and women function in space and live in a space station. We can demonstrate that the earth is spherical, not flat, and that there is no overarching heaven above. We can demonstrate that we exist on a relatively small planet circling a relatively small star in a cosmos so immense that it staggers our imagination. Our ancestors were wrong and the life-perspectives and faiths they developed that incorporated and supported these notions about the world were wrong. Still, we dare not laugh at or condemn their interpretations. They were men and women like ourselves who lived in a different time and in a different space-world. Nor, I hope, will men and women of the future mock our limited twentieth century understanding of science and our cosmos, which will probably appear to them as naive.

With these facts in mind, I propose to look at freethought as embracing the efforts of human beings who, like ourselves, locked into a particular space-time world, attempted to define and understand their universe and their place in it. They were aware, as we are, of powerful forces and energy in nature that lie outside of human beings and human communities. They knew, as we do, that they had no control over the sun and the moon and the stars, nor over the wind and the rain, the snow and the sleet, the flooding of rivers, the earthquakes and the tidal waves. Regardless of where they were on the face of the earth, they experienced, just as we do, forces that impacted directly on daily existence.

To deal with these external powers, they did what we do today: they studied them and learned about them. They charted the cycles of nature. They knew that winter was followed by spring which would give way to summer and fall. They knew there was a seasonal cycle. They developed calendars and could determine when the nights would be shortest and the days would be the longest and when the days would be shortest and the nights longest. They learned to follow the movement of the stars. They found a rhythm in nature and knew that the rhythm affected their wellbeing. And they sought to explain why these patterns occurred — why there were seasons, why the Nile River rose according to a regular schedule each year, why the moon went through its phases, and so forth. They saw themselves as one with nature. What they observed in their human interacting, they read into nature. The forces or powers or energies external to themselves were given names and personalities and were regarded as superior beings. The wind was not just an impersonal force of nature; it had personality and, like some individuals, it could be unpredictable. The sun, on the other hand, followed a set pattern and could be relied upon not to deviate. Rains, like some people, could generally be relied upon, but not always. How could our ancestors know of jet streams or be forewarned by satellite observations to prepare for advancing storms? They were practical people and the fundamental question they raised was practical: how do we deal with these superhuman powers? Once again, their answers developed from what they knew: one deals with superhuman powers as one deals with powerful human beings. If humans can be cajoled, bought, begged, bribed and affected by all sorts of acts, so could the humanized superhuman powers. In time, experts developed among those who studied the sun and the stars, the cycle of seasons and the forces of nature. The shaman came into being together with the priest, the prophet, the seer and others who claimed some sort of ability to deal with the unseen forces. And all sorts of rituals and protocols were designed to affect these external forces — magically or otherwise.

As recognition was given to the cycle of the seasons, celebrations came into being, based on the myths or stories that developed to explain the nature and activities of the god creatures who regulated seasonal patterns. Magical rituals were developed to affect and influence seasonal changes. When the power of the sun waned at the time of the winter solstice, some human beings employed magic to revitalize it. They kindled yule logs and celebrated festivals of lights. The myths, or stories about the god or gods, explained why the natural forces acted as they did. For example, because light appeared to be opposed to darkness or because rain rescued the land from drought, the myths told about conflicts or interactions among the gods who represented these natural forces. In Palestine, the Canaanite father god, El, had among his many children two sons. One was Ba'al, the god of fertility and the life-giving rains; the other was Mot, the god of aridity, death and the underworld. To explain why the rains did not fall during the summer months, a myth explained that Ba'al was in the realm of death in the underworld, a captive of his brother Mot. In the fall, when the autumnal and winter rains began, the Canaanites began their new year and celebrated the resurrection of Ba'al from the realm of the dead. During the ritual, as a priest opened the windows of the temple, this magical act would influence Ba'al to open the windows of the heavens and let the waters above the firmament pour down as rain. When the rains came and they heard his voice in the thunder, the people knew Ba'al had been resurrected and was alive. The imagery of the windows in the firmament of the heavens is echoed in the biblical flood story (Gen. 7:11). The time of the Jewish new year, Rosh Hashannah, in the fall of the year, was borrowed from Canaanite predecessors.

In Babylon, the new year was celebrated at the time of the vernal equinox, because the seasonal pattern differed from that of Palestine. According to Babylonian mythology, the god Tammuz was in the underworld, and the Akitu Festival, held in March-April, celebrated his ascent. Echoes of this ancient myth can be found in the Christian Easter observances. In Egypt there were no rain myths. Egyptians relied on the annual flooding of the Nile to bring the sedimentary deposits that refreshed the land. For them, the Nile was their special gift from the gods; for other nations the gods had provided a less reliable Nile-in-the-sky.

Unfortunately, the beginnings of these wonderful myths are, for the most part, lost to us. We know them only from the times when they were recorded in written form and by that time they were fully developed. The gods and goddesses had attained full personalities. Thus a goddess like Ishtar, whose symbol was the star Venus, could be depicted as a passionate lover in one myth, as a vicious female warrior in another, and as a petulant and demanding daughter in still another. Her roles and her personality are revealed in the myths. Nor can we know the details of all the rituals performed to appease her anger or win her support and influence. In Egypt, the sun could be worshipped under a number of different names, and the personality of this powerful god could range from that of an aging male who in a rage decided to destroy humankind, to that of a benevolent life-giver. So it was that our ancestors sought to come to terms with the complexities of human existence and endeavored to make sense out of life and living.

Do these explanations seem amusing in their naivete? Then, ask how you might have dealt with your place world, your topocosm, several thousand years ago? These men and women of a different era are our forebears and their stories are part of our rich human heritage. We have moved far beyond them in our understanding of our cosmos and their ideas can no longer govern our lives. We marvel when we look at the pyramidal structures in the Yucatan or in Egypt or at the stepped towers in Iraq. These architectural wonders were erected by our ancestors and are directly related to their efforts to come to grips with life, living, nature, meaning and death, just as much as the magnificent cathedral of St. Peter's in Rome or of Santa Sophia in Istanbul are efforts to relate human beings to the energy and power in the universe which Christians personify and call "God."

As we look at the evolution of these concepts, it is equally important that we recognize the men and women who challenged the authority, the claims, and the explanations of the clerics and rulers who demanded obedience to their authority as representatives and interpreters of the will of the deity. As we shall see, over and over again, out of such challenges have come progress in the understanding of our world and in the recognition of human rights and human freedom. Indeed, in our discussion of the development of America, we will look at the ways in which freethinking individuals have contributed to our liberty, our democracy and our growth.

Therefore, because "freethought" is a relatively recent term, it is necessary, in our discussion of *Freethought Across The Centuries*, to broaden it to embrace the independent thinking of men and women who lived millennia before the term came into being. We will give recognition to independent thought and to the rejection of a particular kind of authority as a form of freethinking.

Freethought Movements

Freethought *movements* are of recent date. In 1853 the Leicester Secular Society was formed in Leicester, England, and in 1866 the National Secular Society came into being in London. Similar organizations developed in France, Germany, the Netherlands, and also in America. The Appendix on pp. 486-490 lists principal membership organizations and sources of literature in the broad freethought field in the U.S., and a sample of freethought organizations outside the U.S. which indicates the extensive worldwide network of freethinkers.

2

On Teaching About Religion

"Congress shall make no law respecting an establishment of religion, or prohibiting the free exercise thereof . ."

These words, which were ratified in December, 1791, form the opening of the Federal Constitution's First Amendment, and comprise what is known as the "establishment clause" and the "free exercise clause." The language reflects the founding fathers' deep concerns for individual liberty — a concern that grew out of awareness of English and European edicts that often had imposed on the general populace religious beliefs and morality that had to be adhered to on pain of punishment. The commitments to freedom, which were to become part of the development of what was, for Europeans, "the new world," were not won easily.

The study of American history makes it clear that those who came from Europe did not come religiously unencumbered. Nor did they always bring with them a religious tolerance that would admit the validity of other similar, but different, faith systems. If, perhaps, those whose religious history included memories of persecution under tyrannical state-endorsed religious systems entertained some interest in supporting the formation of a governing system whereby no single religion could ever ally itself with government to enforce any single dogma, that concern was seldom evident.

Separation of Church and State

The importance of the separation of church and state became clear to James Madison who has often been called, "Father of the Constitution." In June, 1785, he opposed a bill sponsored by Patrick Henry that would have placed a tax on all Virginians for the nondiscriminatory support of religion — that is, each taxpayer might designate the church to which his tax money would go. The taxes of the non-religious would be used to support secular education. Madison's broadside, titled "Memorial and Remonstrance Against Religious Assessments," was published in Alexandria and quickly spread. He wrote, in part:

Religion can be directed only by reason and conviction, not by force or violence. The religion, then, of every man, must be left to the conviction and conscience of every man; and it is the right of every man to exercise it as these may dictate. In matters of religion no man's right is abridged by the institution of civil society; and religion is wholly exempt from its cognizance . . .

Who does not see that the same authority which can establish Christianity, in exclusion of all other religions, may establish, with the same ease, any particular sect of Christians, in exclusion of all other sects? That the same authority that can call for each citizen to contribute three pence only of his property for the support of only one establishment, may force him to conform to any other establishment, in all cases whatsoever?

If "all men by nature are equally free and independent," they are to be considered as retaining an "equal right to free exercise of religion, according to dictates of conscience." While we assert for ourselves a freedom to embrace, to profess, and to observe, the religion which we believe to be of divine origin, we cannot deny an equal freedom to those whose minds have not yet yielded to the evidence which has convinced us. . . .

Experience witnesseth that ecclesiastical establishments, instead of maintaining the purity and efficacy of religion, have had contrary operation. During almost fifteen centuries has the legal establishment of Christianity been on trial. What have been its fruits? More or less, in all places, pride and indolence in the clergy, ignorance and servility in the laity; in both, superstition, bigotry, and persecution. Enquire of the teachers of Christianity for the ages in which it appeared in its greatest lustre; those of every sect point to the ages prior to incorporation with civil policy. Propose a restoration of this primitive state, in which its teachers depended on the voluntary rewards of their flocks; many of them predict its downfall. . . .

What influences, in fact, have ecclesiastical establishments had on civil society? In some instances they have been seen to erect a spiritual tyranny on the ruins of civil authority; in many instances they have been seen upholding the thrones of political tyranny; in no instance have they been seen the guardians of liberties of the people. Rulers who wish to subvert the public liberty may have found an established clergy convenient auxiliaries. A just government instituted to secure and perpetuate it, needs them not.

It was out of a combination of deism and reason that recognition of the importance of a free society was to emerge — a society composed of a free people who could not be compelled to accept or to live by any given set of religious beliefs. According to historian Henry Steele Commager, the decision was "perhaps the most important decision reached in the New World. Everywhere in the western world of the eighteenth century, church and state were one; and everywhere the state maintained the established church and tried to force conformity to its dogma." As a consequence of that decision, Commager notes: "Thus the United States took the lead among the nations of the earth in the establishment of religious freedom. That is one reason America has never had any religious wars or religious persecutions." (Menendez and Doerr, p. 21f)

The Amendment provides for freedom from any religion as well as freedom of religion. This means that Americans are free to belong to the religious organization of their choice, thereby rejecting the claims of any other faith system. Simultaneously, they are free from the need to accept another's beliefs. At the same time, they are free to create new religions, thereby rejecting all other established religions. They are also free to choose not to belong to or believe in any religion. No matter what the choice, each and every American maintains full status as a citizen. These rights have been widely recognized and acclaimed, not only by those in the legal profession, but also by Protestant and, on occasion, Roman Catholic churches.

For example, the American Baptist Churches have had a long history supporting individual human rights. In a Policy Statement on Human Rights adopted by the General Board of the American Baptist Churches in December, 1976 (Reference # 7021:12/76), it was stated that:

> Baptist history is rooted in concern for conscience and freedom for persons to believe, to choose, to live unregimented, whether by religious dogma and institution or by social and political structures. John Bunyan in prison and Roger Williams driven from Massachusetts, reflect commitment to these ideas, as did Martin Luther King, in his witness to human dignity and the rights of minority groups. Resolutions by the American Baptist Churches over the years have particularly sought to reflect the denomination's basic principles of freedom of thought and belief, the right of dissent, and the responsibility to speak prophetically to church and society and support human dignity and social justice.

As the report continues, the first statement relates to freedom of and freedom from religion:

> As American Baptists we declare the following rights to be basic human rights, and we will support programs and measures to assure these rights:
>
> 1. The right of every person to choose a religion freely, to maintain religious belief or unbelief without coercion; the right for communities of faith to meet together to engage in public worship, to witness publically to others, to speak prophetically from religious conviction to government and society, to live out religious beliefs, and to be free from governmental intrusion, coercion, and control in the free exercise of conscience and religion . . .

It is important to note that the Resolution recognizes the rights of persons who endorse "unbelief" in religion as a basis for life. The rights that the resolution claims for those who "maintain religious belief" are the same rights afforded to those who choose not to maintain such beliefs.

On May 26, 1988, Joseph Cardinal Bernardin addressed the Center for Clinical Medical Ethics, University of Chicago Hospital. His subject was "Euthanasia: Ethical and Legal Challenge." He began his address as follows:

> One of the hallmarks of our democratic system of government and our social environment here in the United States is the fact that a plurality of views informs our public discourse regarding fundamental human questions. At times, these views flow from religious beliefs. At other times, they derive from philosophical or pragmatic judgments about the meaning and purpose of life.
>
> This pluralism is the result of the free speech accorded by the Constitution to each citizen as well as the right both to freely exercise one's religion and to practice *no* religion. (italics his). But this constitutionally protected pluralism has not been bought at the price of excluding religious or moral values from the public life of the nation. On the contrary, the goal of the American system has been to provide space for moral or religious substance in our society.
>
> Indeed, in our pluralistic society we must decide how those who have such beliefs or ethical principles may appropriately participate in the development of public policy. In my view,

> positions that are informed by particular religious beliefs or philosophical assumptions need to be translated into commonly agreed upon language, arguments, and categories before they can become the moral or ethical foundations for key public policy choices.

As one might expect, Cardinal Bernardin's guiding principles will be derived from his Roman Catholic faith. However, the Cardinal, like those of the Baptist faith, recognized and acknowledged the rights of others to accept no religion and to base their guiding principles on a philosophy or on philosophies. This idea has important overtones regarding the responsibilities of both government and education.

Because the government may not engage in the promotion or endorsement of any particular belief system, it is automatically required by law to honor and respect all of the varying forms of belief and non-belief expressed by the people. What the First Amendment created was, in the words of Thomas Jefferson in his letter to the Danbury (Connecticut) Baptist Association, "a wall of separation between church and state." The protections of freedom guaranteed by this wall of separation include both the individual right to free choice and to privacy of choice. That is to say that not only is the individual free to make a personal choice regarding belief or disbelief in any or all religions, but that the person cannot be required to disclose that choice or have that choice used against him or her as a basis for discrimination. We are all equal under the law of the land, no matter in what we choose to believe or disbelieve. This concept was reinforced in Justice Black's decision in the *Everson* case:

> The "establishment of religion" clause of the First Amendment means at least this: Neither a state nor the Federal Government can set up a church. Neither can pass laws which aid one religion, aid all religions, or prefer one religion over another. Neither can force nor influence a person to go to or to remain away from church against his will or force him to profess a belief or disbelief in any religion. No person can be punished for entertaining or professing religious beliefs or disbeliefs, for church attendance or non-attendance. No tax in any amount, large or small, can be levied to support any religious activities or institutions, whatever they may be called, or whatever form they may adopt to teach or practice religion. Neither a state nor the Federal Government can, openly or secretly, participate in the affairs of any religious organization or groups and *vice*

versa. In the words of Jefferson, the clause against establishment of religion by law was intended to erect "a wall of separation between church and state."

The "wall" that was erected pertains not only to the establishment of a religion, but also to the establishment of religious codes of morality. For example, a given religion may believe that divorce is acceptable only on the grounds of adultery. Civil codes cannot be limited by what that particular religion accepts as right and proper. Civil morality must be secular morality, which is to say that the acceptable reasons for legal divorce cannot be restricted by what a religious group claims to be proper. Therefore *legal* divorce becomes possible on other grounds ranging from incompatibility to infidelity. Any given religious organization may have its own grounds for *acknowledging* the divorce, but that policy remains within the faith system and has no legitimacy or significance for the general populace.

Some religious groups may condemn homosexuality on the basis of an interpretation of what is, for them, authoritative or revealed divine commands. Other religious groups, using the same sources, may provide a different interpretation that accepts homosexuality. For example, the Metropolitan Community Churches are Christian churches whose membership is composed largely of Christian homosexuals. Governments may not pass legislation based solely on religious morality; and although legislation may be cognizant of the varying belief systems, the legislation must embrace the social, political and personal rights of all people, including homosexuals. In other words, civil laws that formulate communal moral and ethical standards must be secular — not derived solely from a religious belief system.

Similarly, although the teaching and promulgation of a particular faith system is accepted as appropriate in educational institutions founded and funded solely by individual religious organizations, it is both inappropriate and illegal for any public school or any public school teacher to teach or to endorse in any way the concepts or dogmas associated with any specific religion or belief system. However, in courses where teaching *about* religion is authorized by the state educational system, it is proper and it is legal to teach *about* religions. Teaching *about* religions automatically includes recognition of the rights of people living in a free society to choose between the various faith systems as well as their right to reject any one or all of such faith systems. Teaching *about* religions requires the recognition of the legitimacy of lives lived according to varying belief systems as well as the legitimacy of lives committed to a non-religious life style. That is to say, that teaching about religions must include teaching about the beliefs of those who reject a religion or religions.

What is "Religion"?

Educators who teach about religion immediately face the problem of defining the subject. Is a "religion" to be regarded as another form of human thought or opinion covered by guarantees of freedom of speech, assembly, press and so on? Or does religion always imply supernaturalism? Should the definition simply refer to those who feel that they are in a particular relationship to God (however defined) with an obligation to fulfill divinely revealed law? For example, Judaism is always listed as a "religion," but what about Humanistic Judaism, which focuses on persons and humanity without reference to a deity? According to its founder, Dr. Sherwin Wine, "Humanistic Judaism is a secular religion" (p. 242). Many secular Humanists tend to eschew the term "religion" because, in its popular interpretation, it carries with it overtones of a supernaturalism that they reject. This raises the questions: what does the word "religion" mean, and what is religion and what is non-religion?

The root of the word "religion" is usually traced to the Latin *religare* (*re*: back, and *ligare*: to bind), so that the term is associated with "being bound." The idea may reflect a concept prominent in biblical literature. Israel was said to be in a "covenant" (*berith*) relationship with its God (Yahweh). In a sense the nation was "covenanted" or "bonded" to the deity. But what does being bound or bonded mean? Is a slave who is bound or bonded to his or her master in a "religious" relationship? Is a business agreement which binds partners in a legal covenant a form of "religious" binding? At one time, in human history, such "bindings" may have had religious sanction, but today, in America, slavery is outlawed and business contracts are made in legal settings. This particular notion of religion as "binding" doesn't really fit and therefore this interpretation of the root meaning of the term proves not to be particularly helpful.

On the other hand, one might argue that the religious person is one "bound" by choice or by commitment to the tenets of a particular faith system. Once again, the parameters of this definition can be broadened to include any commitment to a particular way of life. Such an expansion would embrace concepts like "philosophy" or "psychology" or even any chosen way of living. One's religion then becomes "how one lives one's life" or "how one lives in the light of a particular commitment" or, in popular vernacular, one's "life style." Obviously, while the term "commitment" may provide some insight into the concept of "being bound," it is far too inclusive to be acceptable.

Religion may embrace the notion of "faith" and it is not uncommon to find mention of the "faiths of humankind." The reference is generally to that to which individuals or groups are loyal, to that in which trust is placed. Theologian H. Richard Niebuhr pointed out that, when a patriotic nationalist might claim

> "I was born to die for my country" he is exhibiting the double relationship that we now call faith. The national life is for him the reality whence his own life derives its worth. He relies on the nation as source of his own value. He trusts it; first, perhaps, in the sense of looking constantly to it as the enduring reality out of which he has issued, into whose ongoing cultural life his own actions and being will merge. His life has meaning because it is part of that context, like a word in a sentence. It has value because it fits into a valuable whole. His trust may also be directed toward the nation as a power which will supply his needs, care for his children, and protect his life. But faith in the nation is primarily reliance upon it as an enduring value-center. Insofar as the nation is the last value-center to which the nationalist refers, he does not raise the question about its goodness to him or about its rightness or wrongness. Insofar as it is value-center rightness and wrongness depend on it. This does not mean in any Hobbesian sense that for such faith the national government determines what is right and what is wrong but rather that the rightness of all actions depends on their consonance with the inner constitution of the nation and on their tendency to enhance or diminish national life, power, and glory. (Niebuhr, p. 17)

"Value-center," "trust," "loyalty," "meaning" are intertwined to provide the definition of "faith" or "a faith." It is not difficult to understand that, whereas a theist may express such a faith in a god, an atheist or a humanist may also claim to have such a value-center that gives meaning and direction to life. This value-center would be a faith in the possibilities and potentials of "humanity." Inasmuch as many religions have humanistic concerns and dimensions, there will be overlaps in outreach to those in need and in the interpretation of meaningful response. Whereas the religious person may respond to human need because his or her faith system calls for such response, the humanist will respond out of the well-springs of compassion. The responses may be the same or paralleled, but the motivations will emerge from different value-centers.

Those who accept and those who do not accept supernaturalistic beliefs will enjoy the same or similar feelings of awe and wonder as they view a sunset, a magnificent forest, or the broad rolling prairies; or as they listen to the quieting murmur of a brook, the lapping of waves of a lake or ocean, or the soughing of wind in the tree tops; or as they witness the fury of an electric storm, a hurricane, or a tidal wave. The difference will be in the interpretations. The supernaturalist will interpret these experience with reference to a deity, the non-supernaturalists will see them as manifestations of nature. The experiences will be the same or paralleled; the interpretations will differ. Perhaps both can be interpreted as "spiritual" experiences — in one case with supernaturalistic overtones; in the other resonating with wonder and awe, but without the supernatural.

It is not surprising to discover that most present day scholars tend to avoid definitions when they discuss religions. The reasons for evasion become obvious as we look at some of the many earlier efforts to define the term. For example, in his Gifford Lectures (1902), the psychologist William James defined religion as "the feelings, acts, and experiences of individual men in their solitude, so far as they apprehend themselves to stand in relation to whatever they may consider the divine" (p. 42). Obviously, this definition is too limited; religion is more than affect and more than what people do in their solitariness. As William Newsman pointed out: "regardless of what else may be said of religion, it is also a social phenomenon — it is something that people do in groups." (p. 3) Mircea Eliade, the Roman Catholic historian of religions, rejected the study of religions solely from psychological or sociological perspectives and sought to examine the patterns or forms of religious expression. He would separate the sacred from the profane, even though he recognized that religion has the capacity to transform the profane into the sacred. (1963, p. 30) The Protestant theologian, Paul Tillich, wrote of religion in terms of "ultimate concern" within which he would include secularism: "For secularism is never without ultimate concern." (p. 124) The sociologist, Emile Durkheim, linked religion to the concept of "church:" "A religion is a unified system of beliefs and practices relative to sacred things, that is to say, things set apart and forbidden — beliefs and practices which unite into one single moral community called a Church, all those who adhere to them." (p. 47) Obviously, this definition runs counter to the recognition of the ascetics who express their beliefs outside of a community.

Into this struggle for definition, others have introduced a number of special terms. From his studies among the Melanesians, Bishop Codrington imported the words *mana*, meaning power, and *tabu* which reflected the negative aspects of *mana*. Rudolph Otto in *The Idea of the Holy* produced a battery of Latin terms that suggest aesthetic dimensions in religion. He wrote of human confrontation with the "numinous," which is "wholly other" or outside normal experience and which is indescribable, terrifying, fascinating, characterized by dread and awe. The experience is of a *mysterium tremendum et fascinosum*, an "awe-filled and fascinating mystery." He wrote of the *numen tremendum*, which refers to the sense of the uncanny or that which renders a person "awestruck." All of these feeling responses he associated with religion. However, these terms refer to reactions not unlike those expressed by astronomers as they are awestruck, fascinated and moved by the immensity of space; or by our cosmonauts when, with deep emotion and fascination, they viewed the earth from space; or by poets and artists as they struggle to articulate the wonder they experience in everything from nature to human technological creativity; and by paleontologists and other scientists as they confront the mysterious beginnings of life on planet earth. As we noted above, some of us experience similar feelings as we view the majesty of the mountains, the beauty of a sunset, the power of the ocean, the deepest chasm in the crust of the earth, or the shaking of the earth during an earthquake or violent storm. These are human aesthetic responses to the wonders of our cosmos. They are not limited to "true believers" nor are they necessarily to be defined as "religious," although some would accept the term "spiritual," indicating the deep emotional stirrings evoked, but without any supernaturalistic implications.

Nor is it possible to link religion in a singular way to values, as Ames has done in his definition of religion as "the consciousness of the highest social values" (Braden, p. 11). As we shall see, values rise out of society and can exist quite apart from religion. Religion is not alone in seeking meaning for existence. Joseph Gaer described religion as a person's thoughtful response to the question "why?" This implies that religion alone seeks meaning for existence. But philosophy, psychology and the sciences also pose this question. Nor can religion be linked simply to "impulse directed to the conservation and preservation of life," as Jane Harrison phrased it. And the list goes on and on. The question arises: How does one handle this problem? Perhaps the answer lies in "no definition."

John A. Hutchinson, in his book *Paths of Faith,* acknowledged the difficulty in defining religion. He wrote:

> Formal definitions of religion are as numerous, as various, and often as mutually conflicting as there are students of religion. Often such definitions illustrate the oriental parable of the blind men describing the elephant, each taking hold of part of the beast and defining the whole in terms of this part. Like the elephant, religion is a large and complex phenomenon. In this connection, some historians of religion question or reject the word *religion* as a distortion of the form of experience it seeks to communicate. Several of the world's major languages lack any word that can be adequately translated as "religion." The common noun *religion* imputes a unity or homogeneity of experience that many observers believe does not exist. (pp. 3-4)

He goes on to point out that substituted words do not work, then settles on the word "value" and defines religious experience as "ultimate valuation" (p. 4). As indicated above, even this terminology is inadequate.

We begin by recognizing that the development of religion is a peculiarly human endeavor. In this book, we will follow a pattern set by other writers who simply discuss "religions" without becoming entangled in debates over precise definitions. Religions include aspects of all of the themes mentioned above. Many, if not most, religions have supernaturalistic overtones. However, those groups that label themselves a "religion" but reject supernaturalism will also be acknowledged.

Our *basic* concern will be with the recognition of those who have not only rejected standard faith or belief systems, but have also excluded any form of supernaturalism. These persons and groups define themselves in different ways. They include skeptics, freethinkers, humanists, agnostics, atheists, secularists, naturalists, unbelievers, rationalists, materialists, and so forth. They have been present throughout history up to and including our present time. What is their place in human history and in American life? What are their contributions to a free society? How do they help to create and maintain the constitutional wall of separation between church and state? As a beginning, it is necessary to clarify some of the labels that identify those who do not accept religious belief systems.

Who are the Nonreligious?

The nonreligious are those who have moved away from what was once defined as *homo religiosus* — the religious man who lived in a world permeated with the sacred — to become *homo saecularis* —

secular man, living in a *mundus saecularis* — a secular, non-sacred, world. Inasmuch as secular humans are, in part, products of their past, they cannot entirely escape or abolish the past. For them, the cultic rites, beliefs and myths of the past are treated as just that — relics of the past, even as token acknowledgment of their existence is made. For example, even though secularists no longer celebrate Christmas or Hanukkah, they may participate in a winter solstice festival that immediately links them to ancient religious observances of seasonal change. They may light yule logs, not in any attempt to re-kindle the sun, but simply to warm the home during the festive season. Celebrations and partying take place for the sake of getting together to affirm life and to have fun. The central ritual will be a commensality rite (*com*: together, *mensa*: table) — a gathering about the table — in which the sharing of food and drink have no mystical overtones other than those of companionship (*com*: together, *panis*: bread) or bread-togetherness. Mircea Eliade described this new sense of secular personhood in his book *The Sacred and the Profane* as follows:

> Modern nonreligious man assumes a new existential situation; he regards himself solely as the subject and agent of history, and he refuses all appeal to transcendence. In other words, he accepts no model for humanity outside the human condition as it can be seen in the various historical situations. Man *makes himself*, and he only makes himself completely in proportion as he desacralizes himself and the world. The sacred is the prime obstacle to his freedom. He will become himself only when he is completely demysticized. He will not be truly free until he has killed the last god. (p. 203)

The labels by which nonreligious humans identify themselves are numerous and include the following:

Skeptics are those who question, who doubt, who challenge the claims of factuality in accepted beliefs and faith statements. Paul Kurtz puts it simply: "Briefly stated, a skeptic is one who is willing to question any claim to truth, asking for clarity in definition, consistency in logic, and adequacy of evidence." (Kurtz, p. 9) The Greek term *skeptikos* simply meant "to inquire, to examine, to consider." Indeed, at one time a school of skeptics existed in ancient Greece led by Pyrrho of Elis (c. 320-c. 270 B.C.E.). Pyrrho claimed that real knowledge of things was impossible and therefore truth was unattainable and the search for truth was a vain exercise. This form of what has been called "systematic skepticism" leads nowhere, is logically untenable, and is to be separated from the present day approach of what is known as "methodological skepticism."

Modern methodological skeptics are not cynics. However, they do insist that claims of factuality, both religious and non-religious, must be tested by reason employing the rules of logic and by the best tools of scientific investigation. Skeptics are concerned with reliability. Thus, when an individual claims to be a "channel" for knowledge provided by some creature living on an unknown planet in some distant galaxy, the skeptic challenges and questions the factuality of the claim on the basis of our best scientific knowledge and on the basis of the validity of the allegedly transported information. As philosopher Mario Bunge of McGill University in Canada has pointed out, those who adopt methodological skepticism

> believe that it is foolish, imprudent, and morally wrong to announce, practice, or preach important ideas or practices that have not been put to the test or, worse, that have been shown in a conclusive manner to be utterly false, inefficient or harmful. (Note the restriction to *important* beliefs; by definition, trivialities are harmless even when false.) Because we trust research and action based on research findings, we are not systematic skeptics. We disbelieve falsity and suspend judgment concerning whatever has not been checked, but we believe, at least temporarily, whatever has passed the requisite tests. At the same time, we are willing to give up whatever beliefs prove to be groundless. In sum, methodological skeptics are constructive. (p. 378)

Dr. Bunge went on to point out that the methodological skeptic presupposes "that scientific theories and methods satisfy certain philosophical requirements." These include the following:

- *(a) materialism:* everything in the universe is concrete or material, though not necessarily corporeal, and everything behaves lawfully;
- *(b) realism:* the world exists independently of those who study it, and moreover it can be known at least partially and gradually;
- *(c) rationalism:* our ideas ought to be internally consistent and they should cohere with one another;

(*d*) *empiricism:* every idea about real things should be empirically testable; and
(*e*) *systemism:* the data and hypotheses of science are not stray but constitute a system . . . (p. 379)

Dr. Bunge noted that:

> The methodological skeptics uphold many principles and, above all, they trust humans to advance even further in the knowledge of reality. Their faith is critical, not blind; it is the explorer's faith not the believer's. They do not believe anything in the absence of evidence, but they are willing to explore bold new ideas if they find reasons to suspect that they have a chance. . . They are open-minded but not blank-minded; they are quick to filter out intellectual rubbish. (p. 380)

Skeptical thinking and inquiry go back as far as our earliest recorded human history. In fact, skepticism is a supremely human quality that, by posing challenges to accepted notions, gives rise to progress. For example, the second century C.E. mathematician and astronomer Ptolemy taught that the earth was immovable and that the sun moved across the heavens and under the earth daily to rise again the next day. This assumption was based on an optical illusion — on an interpretation of what *seemed* to be happening. As we have noted, because the earth was believed to be a flat disc, the interpretation of what the sun *appeared* to do was accepted as reality. The notion was endorsed and supported by the Roman Catholic Church. In the 16th century, the Polish astronomer, Nicolaus Copernicus (1473-1543), challenged that belief and argued that the earth and planets revolved about the sun. Copernicus' approach was scientific. He was not concerned with fighting against the Catholic church; he was interested in following the leads of his research.

Copernicus' hypothesis was supported and demonstrated by the Italian physicist and astronomer, Galileo Galilei (1564-1642), who used a telescope to corroborate the new theory. Galileo was persecuted and prosecuted by the Roman Catholic Church, forced to recant and confined to his home for life. Later, writing in his own defence, Galileo quoted Copernicus' dedication of his work to the Pope. Copernicus had written:

> If there should chance be any Mataeologists, who though ignorant in all the Mathematicks, yet pretending a skill in those

> Learnings, should dare, upon the authority of some place of Scripture wrested to their purpose, to condemn and censure this my Hypothesis, I value them not, but shall slight their inconsiderate Judgement. For it is not unknown, that Lactantius (otherwise a Famous Author, though mean Mathematician) writeth very childishly touching the Form of the Earth, when he scoffs at those who affirm the Earth to be in the Form of a Globe. So that it ought not seem strange to the Ingenious, if any should likewise now deride us. The Mathematicks are written for Mathematitians, to whom, (if I deceive not myself) these Labours of mine shall seem to add something, as also to the Commonweale of the Church, whose Government is now in the hands of Your Holiness. (quoted in Ulich, p. 327)

Like Copernicus, Galileo saw himself as a Christian Roman Catholic. It was not his intention to disrupt religious thought. Like Copernicus, he followed where his research led him. He even sought to harmonize his findings with biblical thought by suggesting that the Bible was not, in many places, to be interpreted literally but metaphorically. For example, in a letter to the Grandduchess of Tuscany, he pointed out that if one took seriously biblical anthropomorphisms relating to God:

> we should be forced to assign God feet, and hands, and eyes, yea more corporal and human affections, as of Anger, of Repentance, of Hatred, nay and sometimes the Forgetting of things past, and Ignorance of those to come . . .

He argued that the critics of Copernicus had never read Copernicus' theses and therefore spoke from ignorance. He suggested that:

> . . . methinks that in the Discussion of Natural Problemes, we ought not to begin at the authority of places of Scripture; but at Sensible Experiments and Necessary Demonstrations . . (quoted in Ulich, pp. 328-9)

How close his concepts were to those that lie behind modern science! Despite his wise comments, Galileo's books were placed on the Index of Prohibited Books until 1835. It was not easy to be a skeptic nor to oppose accepted religious teachings, even with the support of new scientific instruments. Nevertheless, the reasoned skepticism of Copernicus and Galileo regarding the Ptolemaic theory ultimately prevailed. The work of those seekers-after-truth gave rise to a new hypothesis concerning the relationship of the earth to the sun and the planets that has been corroborated over and over and is today accepted without argument. Obviously the Bible, Ptolemy and the Church were wrong. Their assumptions concerning the relationship of the earth and the sun have been proven to be false by scientific research and by the theories based on scientific investigations. Indeed, the Roman Catholic Church, after a thirteen year investigation of the case against Galileo, has finally acknowledged that the 17th century astronomer had been wronged by the Church in what Pope John Paul II was content to describe as "a sad misunderstanding" (Montalbano). The Catholic Church does not acknowledge its errors easily and only when a situation develops where, in Pope John Paul II's words, the failure to do so resulted in "an incomparability between the spirit of science and its rules of research on the one hand, and the Christian faith on the other" (Montalbano).

Skepticism thrives best in societies that encourage open inquiry unhampered by authorities, religious or civil, who might seek to curtail challenges to, or evaluations of, accepted beliefs. On the other hand, the fruits of healthy skepticism, resulting from freethought and open inquiry into accepted "truths," will continue to find expression, even in situations and societies that seek to control the minds of the people.

Freethinkers are those who reach judgments based on critical thinking and independent reasoning without regard to prevailing authority and tradition. Freethought, to be truly "free," requires a setting providing both the environment and opportunity for expression — a setting in which the results of open inquiry, including doubts or counter-theories, may be published without threat of persecution or prosecution. In properly functioning free, democratic societies, religious and political suppressions cannot easily occur. Consequently, the results of skeptical inquiry or freethought receive a respectable hearing without threats of violence or efforts to repress.

Recently, when Salman Rushdie published a volume titled *The Satanic Verses*, he was threatened with death by fundamentalist Muslims who found his writing distasteful, blasphemous and heretical. Rushdie has been compelled to seek asylum, protection and anonymity in the free society of England to safeguard his own life and the well-being of his family. Clearly, there are those among us who would deny to others the right to express openly what they believe or what their research and scholarship or creative artistry has produced. In such a climate freethought and open inquiry become difficult and almost impossible.

Agnostics are those who say, with regard to a given subject, "we are without knowledge concerning it." The term "agnostic," coined by Thomas Huxley in the late 19th century, is formed from two Greek words: the root *gnosis* means "knowledge," and the Greek prefix *a* means "without." An agnostic, therefore, neither affirms nor denies the existence of God. She or he simply says that, despite all the arguments pro and con, one does not know and perhaps cannot know whether or not there is a God. Huxley put it this way:

> Agnosticism, in fact, is not a creed, but a method, the essence of which lies in the rigorous application of a single principle. That principle is of great antiquity; it is as old as Socrates, as old as the writer who said, "Try all things, hold fast by that which is good;" it is the foundation of the Reformation, which simply illustrated the axiom that every man should be able to give a reason for the faith that is in him; it is the great principle of Descartes; it is the fundamental axiom of modern science. Positively the principle may be expressed: In matters of the intellect, follow your reason as far as it will take you, without regard to any other consideration. And negatively, In matters of the intellect do not pretend that conclusions are certain which are not demonstrated or demonstrable. (Huxley, 1894)

Scientists often profess religious agnosticism. They choose to embrace a posture of openness concerning the possibility of the existence of a supernatural deity in the conviction that this is a proper scientific stance. They claim that, because they cannot prove or demonstrate whether or not some god-power or form may exist, they should, theoretically, leave the door open. Despite what they may affirm in the name of logic or science, agnostics live their lives as if there is no God. They do not regularly attend worship services, nor engage in prayer, nor in any way acknowledge the presence or the reality of the supernatural. Their mental and scientific commitment is to agnosticism and open inquiry; their way of life is committed to atheism (defined below).

Deists represent a skepticism that is not far removed from agnosticism. They are impressed by the complexity and organization of the universe from the immensity of space to the infinitesimal smallness of the atom. They reason that the laws governing nature presuppose a supreme law-maker or a God, but they do not seek to define that deity nor do they believe that this God is presently involved in nature. Their God is regarded as transcendent; God is apart from and above "his" creation. The Creator God has done "his" work, there is nothing left to do. "Creation" is complete. Deists reject claims of supernatural revelation. Some belong to organizations like the American Ethical Union, where the focus is on the importance of ethical growth and development in personal, interpersonal and ecological relationships rather than on the supernatural. Once again, the life pattern is atheistic, for even as they discuss ethics, there is no acceptance of, or belief in, or appeal to, divinely revealed rules for ethical conduct.

Atheists are those who do not believe in the existence of a god or gods or in any supernatural power. The label is formed from the Greek *theos* meaning "god" and the prefix *a* meaning "without", so that atheists are those without any deity. Atheists do not seek to "prove" there is no God; they are not concerned with disproof. They simply say that, because there is no proof of the existence of God and no acceptable or known way to prove that God exists they are, therefore, "without God" or "without a god." They comprise the polar opposite to "theists" who believe in a God or who claim that a God exists. Atheists include secularists and naturalists who base their attitudes, their thinking, and their conclusions on scientific explanations of nature, and whose life-commitment is to the world of the human without any acceptance of supernaturalism.

Igtheists are those who argue that theistic language makes no sense and therefore they cannot understand what theists are talking about. The term was introduced by Dr. Paul Kurtz in *The New Skepticism* (1992). He moves away from atheism, which denies that there is any evidence to prove or demonstrate that God exists, to a position where one is ignorant (hence *ig*) of what is meant by theists. He points out that theological language tends to be murky, and that the God language in particular ranges from the symbolic terms used by the theologian Paul Tillich (God is the "ground of being") to the metaphorical (God is "creator" of the universe) to the anthropomorphic (as in the Bible). These God concepts are made more confusing by the arguments that God is "unknowable" or "transcends" human knowledge but is "revealed" to specific humans from time to time in history. He states that "To talk about God in a transcendent sense is to utter indefinable, even nonsensical language." (p. 196) Therefore, he states, "That is why I can maintain, as a skeptic, that I am an *igtheist*, for I do not understand what the theist is talking about." (p. 197) He concludes, "The question that we will have to deal with is a second one, whether such a being exists (whatever "God" refers to), or whether it is reasonable to disbelieve in such a being." (p. 198) Because the term is newly created, it will be used sparingly in this book.

Secularists focus on secular issues, in particular on human well-being. They reject the notions of a deity and supernaturalism. As noted above, some secular groups are willing to classify themselves as "religions;" others absolutely refuse the label because they find that the word "religion" carries supernaturalistic overtones in its popular usage.

Naturalists believe that, inasmuch as there are no non-natural objects, events or causes, all objects and events are to be accounted for scientifically and explained in terms of natural "laws" or natural causes. There is no need to attribute religious or spiritual or supernatural influence or significance to the happenings or phenomena in our universe. Naturalists recognize and stress the affinity of the human and nature. Human beings are a product of nature and are therefore not above or apart from nature. Naturalists reject the concept of human dualism — body and soul — and therefore also reject any belief in an afterlife.

Materialists accept a philosophy of materialism, that states that physical matter in its modifications and movements is the only reality. All processes and phenomena (everything) in the universe, including thought, feeling and mind, are to be explained in terms of physical laws and as resulting from material agencies. To understand the materialistic universe in which we live, materialists rely upon the scientific method of examining, testing and re-testing. Obviously, such a philosophy discounts the significance and validity of spiritual claims and constitutes a form of atheism. The term "materialism" has acquired a different and somewhat negative connotation in popular speech, namely, implying greed for material "things." To avoid confusion, this important philosophical term will be used sparingly in this book.

Rationalists reject the supernatural and argue that reason is the prime source of knowledge. Reason, not spiritual or supernatural revelations, provides the only valid basis for ethics and beliefs. Some rationalists are deists, others are atheists or agnostics.

Humanists. Basic to each freethought group is a humanistic emphasis. Each is concerned with the human dimension, with the affairs of life on planet earth without reference to supernatural interference or direction.

Many established religions have humanistic concerns. They reach out to feed the poor, aid the sick, and help the forgotten and unwanted. These noble acts accord with the humanistic interests of freethinkers. The difference lies in the motivation. *Religious humanism* looks to its scriptures for the motivation and authority to act on behalf of others and for the rules to guide the outreach. As we have noted above, because religious teachings insist that the believer should or must act on behalf of others, the outreach becomes part of the faith pattern and can be recognized as a faith requirement. Often the humane responses are accompanied by efforts at religious indoctrination. In other words, the free meal follows or is accompanied by indoctrination.

These same religious groups that are involved in humanistic outreach may simultaneously be limited in the ways they think about the role of women or the issue of sexual preferences. Their attitudes and behavior which tend to limit the freedoms and rights of women and homosexuals are based on accepted authoritative teachings or dogmas. This means that, even as they do good works, they limit some dimensions of human life for some of their followers in ways that are foreign to *secular humanism*.

The secular or freethinking humanist looks into the self for guidance. Response to need comes from deep human feelings of compassion, concern for others and a desire to help. The freethinker is not motivated by a divine command to act, but rather by personal humanistic response to pain, loneliness, hunger and homelessness. Benevolent actions are not accompanied by a need to convert or indoctrinate, but rather flow from deep human wellsprings of empathy and a desire to improve the condition of the world by improving the lives of those near at hand. The secular humanist places no limitations on human freedom to achieve. The secular humanist seeks to provide an environment in which each individual, regardless of race, color, creed, sex or sexual orientation, may have the opportunity to achieve his or her highest potential.

Humanism is concerned with the well-being of all humans. There is no desire to shut the door of compassion on someone because he or she belongs to a different race or embraces a different creed. This attitude is reflected in the humanistic poem "Outwitted" by Edwin Markham:

He drew a circle that shut me out
Heretic, rebel, a thing to flout;
But Love and I had the wit to win:
We drew a circle that took him in.

This inclusive regard for all human beings marks the essence of freethought humanism at its best — an interest and concern that characterizes most non-religious persons who describe themselves as skeptics, agnostics, atheists, secularists, naturalists, materialists, rationalists, ig-theists, humanists and secular humanists. Some religious groups would exclude and ignore freethinkers from their areas of concern; freethinkers will not ignore or exclude those others from their areas of concern.

* * * * *

These, then, are the groups that will constitute the focus of this book. Arguments supporting each of these different labels or positions can become exhaustive and will not concern us here, anymore than we will be concerned about why one chooses to be a Baptist rather than a Roman Catholic or a Buddhist. Our interests will focus on how, in a world dominated by supernaturalistic beliefs, persons and groups that reject supernaturalism respond to and contribute to life, to living, to their world and to society in general. Because rationalist and skeptical thinking and ideas often stand outside of mainstream patterns of belief, just as those of Galileo did, those who embrace such approaches often come under condemnation even as they introduce profoundly important changes in human life, thought, and behavior. Fortunately, this is not always so. Once in a while, some public acknowledgment gives recognition to the profound contributions freethought has made to culture.

In March, 1991, Arne Carlson, Republican governor of the State of Minnesota, issued the following proclamation:

> WHEREAS: The pledge of religious liberty is contained in the First Amendment to the United States Constitution, which states that "Congress shall make no law respecting the establishment of religion, or prohibiting the free exercise thereof"; and
>
> WHEREAS: The right of free expression is part of the cornerstone of that same Constitution; and
>
> WHEREAS: Freethinkers, Humanists, skeptics, atheists, and agnostics all have made major contributions in the various fields of science, law, medicine, art, and government; and
>
> WHEREAS: Recognition and entitlement to the same rights, opportunities, benefits, and obligations are inalienable and guaranteed to all citizens;
>
> NOW THEREFORE, I, ARNE H. CARLSON, Governor of the State of Minnesota, do hereby proclaim and call upon all

Minnesotans to respect the rights and dignity of all fellow citizens.

IN WITNESS THEREOF, I have hereto set my hand and caused the Great Seal of the State of Minnesota to be affixed at the State Capitol this first day of March in the year of our Lord, one thousand nine hundred and ninety-one, and of the State the one hundred thirty second.

This important statement honors and recognizes those who stand outside of current religious belief systems. The final clause, which includes the phrase "in the year of our Lord," seems, in the eyes of some, to stand in contradiction to the intent of the proclamation. It has produced some amusement for both freethinkers and religious believers. One of the emphases in this book will be the recognition of the contributions of those mentioned by the governor.

References

Braden, *The World's Religions*. Nashville, Tenn.: Abingdon, 1939.

Bunge, Mario, "The Scientist's Skepticism," *The Skeptical Inquirer,* Vol. 16, No. 4, 1992, p. 377f.

Durkheim, Emile, *The Elementary Forms of the Religious Life*. (Trans. by Joseph Ward Swain). London: George Allen & Unwin, Ltd. 1915. (6th edition, 1968).

Earles, Beverley, "The Faith Dimension of Humanism," *Humanism Today*, Vol. 6, 1991, pp. 87-99.

Eliade, Mircea, *The Sacred and the Profane*. Trans. by Willard R. Trask. New York: Harcourt, Brace and Company, 1959.

Eliade, Mircea, *Patterns in Comparative Religion*. Trans. by Rosemary Sheed. New York: The World Publishing Company (Meridian), 1963.

Gaer, Joseph, *How the Great Religions Began*. New York: Signet, 1958.

Harrison, Jane, *Themis*. London: Cambridge University Press, 1912.

Hutchinson, John A. *Paths of Faith*. New York: McGraw-Hill Book Company, 1981.

Huxley, Thomas Henry, "Agnosticism," *Science and the Christian Tradition*. London: Macmillan & Co., 1894. Reprinted in Gordon Stein, *An Anthology of Atheism and Rationalism*. Buffalo, New York: Prometheus Books, 1980, pp. 42-45.

James, William, *The Variety of Religious Experience*. New York: Collier Books, 1961.

Kurtz, Paul, *The New Skepticism*. Buffalo, New York: Prometheus Books, 1992.

Menendez, Albert J., and Edd Doerr, *The Great Quotations on Religious Freedom*. Long Beach, Calif: Centerline Press, 1991.

Montalbano, William D., "Earth Moves for the Vatican in Galileo Case," *The Los Angeles Times*, Nov. 1, 1992, p. A8.

Newsman, William M, editor, *The Social Meanings of Religion*. Chicago: Rand McNally College Publishing Company, 1974.

Niebuhr, H. Richard, *Radical Monotheism and Western Culture*. New York: Harper and Row, 1943, 152, 1955, 1960 (A Harper Torchbook).

Otto, Rudolph, *The Idea of the Holy*. London: Oxford University Press, 1923.

Tillich, Paul, *The Dynamics of Faith*. New York: Harper and Row (Torchbook), 1958.

Ulich, Robert, edit., *Three Thousand Years of Educational Wisdom: Selections From Great Documents*. Cambridge, Mass.: Harvard University Press, second edition, 1954.

Wine, Sherwin, *Judaism Beyond God*. Farmington Hills, Mich: Society for Humanistic Judaism, 1985.

3

In the Beginning

According to some recent controversial studies in human evolution, all of us, all human beings — Negroid, Pygmanoid, Bushmanoid, Caucasoid and Mongoloid — are members of a single human family and Africa is our motherland. Mitochondrial DNA studies have suggested that all human beings may be descended from a common stock and from one mother whom anthropologists have named "Eve." In other words, while there were other females in existence, only the African Eve's mitochondrial line survived. Just how differences in skin tones, hair texture, eye shape, height and so forth developed continues to provide subjects for research and discussion among scholars. As in any given family, each child is unique and different but is still part of the family, thus we are, with all our differences, according to this theory which has been contested, members of a single human family, descended from one African mother: Eve.

It was Darwin who proposed that the origin of the human species might be found in Africa. In 1871, following a study of the distribution of the great apes, he conjectured in his *Descent of Man*:

> It is therefore possible that Africa was formerly inhabited by extinct apes closely allied to the gorilla and chimpanzee; and as these two species are now man's nearest allies, it is somewhat probable that our earliest progenitors lived on the African continent than elsewhere. But it is useless to speculate on this subject.

Of course he was attacked by the clergy as denigrating humankind and because his theories clashed with the Genesis stories of creation. His suggestion that Africa was the originating place for humans was rejected also by scholars who argued that human origins lay in Asia. It was not until 1924 that the Asian theory was finally abandoned, largely due to the investigations and discoveries by anthropologists Mary Leakey and her husband L.S.B. Leakey, Raymond A. Dart, Robert Broom and Donald Johanson, among others.

Now, recent studies have added to the possibility of a common human ancestor. According to microbiological studies made some 25 years ago by Vincent Sarich of the University of California, Berkeley, "the ancestors of apes and humans had split from one another between seven and five million years ago." (Fagan, p. 18) But the research did not stop with this conclusion. Mitochondrial DNA, which is inherited from the mother alone, became the tool for the study of genetic relationships and matrilineal lineages of living people throughout the world. The conclusion, based on the studies by the late Alan Wilson of the University of California, Berkeley, and Linda Vigilant of the University of Pennsylvania, is that "all modern humanity originated in Africa about 200,000 years ago, later migrating to Europe and Asia." (Fagan, p. 19) Therefore, according to this particular study, *Homo sapiens* originated in Africa. Linda Vigilant "traced, and statistically tested, a genealogical tree for *Homo sapiens* that has 15 branches. The 14 deepest branches led only to Africans while the last branch leads to both additional Africans and to all non-African lineages." (Fagan, p. 19)

Not all scholars accept these conclusions. Some paleontologists oppose the theory, arguing that "there was only one population movement out of Africa, archaic *Homo erectus* spreading into Europe and Asia about a million years ago. Thereafter modern humans evolved separately in several areas." (Fagan, p. 20) That is to say, that according to paleontological interpretations of the fossil records, *Homo sapiens* developed multiregionally about 400,000 years ago. However, because DNA research is providing a new scientific approach to the study of human origins, it is possible that fossil studies may have to be re-appraised.

What has become clear from genetic studies is that the concept of race has no biological basis. Thus, judging human beings on the basis of skin color, hair, or facial features is meaningless, inasmuch as these are merely surface distinctions and have nothing to do with the basic biology of human differences. As University of Pennsylvania anthropologist Solomon H. Katz stated at the meeting of the American Association for the Advancement of Science in February, 1995: "Biologically, we are saying in essence that race is no longer a valid scientific distinction." (Hotz, p. A3) Claims of racial superiority are, therefore, spurious. They represent attempts to employ a biological basis for mistreatment of people by using concocted or artificial theory designed to cover social bias or to explain behavior differences stemming from culture. The new emerging theories do not deny human diversity. Creative people in differing environments will always develop varying life patterns and the study of these differences will continue to engage sociologists and anthropologists. What is important is the potential for exploring and reconstructing "the genetic evolution of humankind and a new appreciation for how humanity has developed genetic diversity as it spreads around the globe." (Hotz, p. A10)

It is not in our interest to attempt to try to trace our complex human evolutionary pattern as it is becoming known to us today. As we shall see, some aspects of the development of the awareness of the self, of the family and of the community in terms of relationships to the non-human world will become evident. In the following discussion we will deal with the earliest evidence of humans attempting to manipulate fate and fortune.

No one is sure just when or how religion or belief in supernatural forces originated or when our ancient ancestors began to think about spirits and occult powers or gods and goddesses. We know that about 70,000 years ago, humans began to bury their dead. This custom further distanced human beings from their animal predecessors from whom they were already distinct by virtue of their advanced mental and physical abilities and skills. Unlike other life forms, humans had developed the ability to use language for communication, they had mastered the control of fire, and they could manufacture an amazing variety of weapons and tools. And, unlike animals, humans expressed feelings for the dead that were, ultimately, to develop into beliefs about the after-life.

Cave Paintings and Sculptures

Then, about 25,000 years ago, when ice still covered large sectors of northern Europe, gifted artists painted stirring polychrome images of animals and humans in the dark recesses of the caves at Altamira and elsewhere in Spain and France. Why? Anthropologists suggest that the paintings in those remote hard-to-reach places may have been associated with rites designed to increase the possibility of a successful hunt. What those rituals might have included, or what those who performed them may have thought, cannot be known, for there are no written records. We depend on insights from anthropologists who reach conclusions based on comparisons with isolated groups that today live in what might be recognized as comparable settings.

Some cave paintings at Altamira and Lescaux portray wounded bison with their backs pierced by darts. Were these paintings the work of a reportorial artist? Are they nothing more than pictorial representations of what took place during a hunt? Were they, perhaps, teaching tools for young hunters, providing a visual image of what they would encounter during a hunt? Or were they associated with religious pre-hunting magical rites? The crouching bear, modelled in clay, found in a cave at Montespan, Haute Garonne, held a real bear skull between its clay paws. Actual stab wounds were found in the figure's back and it has been hypothesized that perhaps the clay bear was covered with a bear's hide and success in the hunt was symbolized and anticipated by an attack on the animal figure. E.O. James concluded that:

> It is now certain that early man in the Old Stone Age had sacred places to which he resorted, primarily to exercise supernatural control over his food supply by the performance of mimetic rites. (p. 15)

If such interpretations are correct or even nearly correct, then 25,000 years ago our ancestors were involved in highly developed magico-religious rites that included the performance of acts and perhaps the reciting of words believed to have power. The rituals were designed to affect that which lay ahead, namely, the acquisition of food necessary for survival. Perhaps, by dramatizing the hunt in a ritual of sympathetic magic, they hoped to guarantee success. Through tapping unseen powers or primal sources of energy, they hoped to compel events to occur as they wished them to happen.

The paintings in the cave at Ariege in the French Pyrenees, known as Les Trois Freres, include the depiction of a dancing, bearded human who wears a mask and antlers of a deer and the skin of another animal with a long, bushy tail — perhaps belonging to a wolf. This figure has been popularly labeled "the sorcerer." Was this an individual who was believed to possess exceptional conjuring skills, so that by incantation and dance he could produce magical power for the hunt? Does he mark the beginnings of what was to become the priesthood in the religions that were to develop later? Was his dance part of a religious rite designed to invoke supernatural powers and prepare hunters for their tasks? These questions are still unanswered.

In another cave in the French Pyrenees (Tuc d'Audoubert), a circular chamber has been found with two clay statues of bison propped against a stone in the center. What is most intriguing is the circle of some 50 small heel imprints in the clay floor surrounding the figures. Just what may have taken place here cannot be known, but it is as if children had been engaged in a round-about dance. If this interpretation is accurate, were these young people participating in a maturation rite through which young men were admitted to the role of hunter? Or were the footprints made by women, as some anthropologists have suggested? Could the rituals have been designed to promote fertility? Did some form of music accompany the dance? The discovery of flutes and whistles made from hollowed bird bone, plus animal bones and ivory that could have formed parts of ancient rattles, indicate that sound variants in the form of rhythmic beats and perhaps even some variant tones may have been part of the rituals performed within the cave sanctuaries.

Are the ancient cave paintings to be associated with the beginnings of religion? If they are, they suggest that already, 25,000 years ago, deep in the remote darkness of caves which may be the forerunners of present day cathedrals and places of worship, our ancestors expressed beliefs, performed rituals, followed formulae, and portrayed in art, concepts that were already well developed and widespread. The use of colors, the discovery of ornaments and of carvings in bone and ivory reflect an aesthetic maturity, a response to nature and a concern for survival that must have been the culmination of an earlier history which, at this time, we cannot know. In other words, the origins of human religions are at least 25,000 years old and perhaps much older and appear to be deeply entrenched in rites of "sympathetic magic" — a term employed by Sir James G. Frazier (p. 11f). In sympathetic magic it is believed that like produces like. If one acts out a desired result involving animals and humans, then one can induce the desired action.

Among the thousands of artifacts from this very early period are hundreds of female figurines. They are only a few inches in height and are made of baked clay or carved from bone or ivory. Usually, there is no attempt at portraiture. Often the heads are simply featureless knobs and the arms and legs are poorly represented. The emphasis is on sexual features. The breasts are full and pendulous, the buttocks are large and there are clear signs of pregnancy. The suggestion that these art forms represent the beginnings of a cult of the mother goddess has not been widely accepted. What seems to be obvious is that the female figurines are associated with human procreation and with birth. Perhaps they were amulets designed to increase group fertility or to provide magical help in childbirth. In any case, they mark the beginnings of the human effort to express the invisible, the unknown and hidden powers that lie behind life in terms of the natural, the tangible, the known.

Ancient hunters and gatherers who depended on the capture of game and the finding of roots, herbs, fruit and grain to sustain life continued to evolve technically and socially, so that about 15,000 years later humans had learned to exercise control over their means of survival. They had evolved from hunters and gatherers to herders. Now they raised the animals that provided them with wool and hides for clothing and other necessities, milk and meat for food, and antlers and bones that could be shaped into weapons and tools. Each year they migrated with these herds from lowland winter pasturage to the highlands of the mountains in the summer. Remains of their ancient camps have been excavated in the Near East. Indeed, echoes of their life patterns are evident today among certain Kurdish tribes, the Bakhtiari, in the Zagros mountains of Iran. But we cannot learn about the ancient herders' beliefs from their modern counterparts who are Muslims. Nor do we have collections of ancient religious artifacts to stir our imaginations because migrants carry with them only what they can use in their daily sojourn.

Towns and Cities

Ten thousand years ago, some human beings became agriculturists. No longer did they have to hunt for wild grains; now they grew their own. They did not migrate with their herds from the lowlands to the highlands; they pastured their domesticated animals on nearby hillsides. Hay and grains were harvested and stored (often in caves) for the animals' survival. This new way of life made possible existence in large settled communities near perennial sources of water. One of their earliest locales was at Jericho in the Jordan valley where the spring, Ain es Sultan, provided an abundance of water essential for communal survival. At this site, some of the environmental dimensions of the earliest settlers have been exposed through excavations by John Garstang and Kathleen Kenyon.

Neolithic (new stone age) Jericho was a highly developed village community. The well-built houses had their fine plaster floors covered with woven reed mats which left the patterned imprints found by archaeologists. The massive stone wall with a ditch or moat in front of it that surrounded the city was enhanced by a huge stone tower with well-made steps running through a central shaft that led from ground level to the top. The control of the waters of Ain es Sultan and the cooperative efforts that would be required for the construction of the defense wall, moat and tower, reflect a highly developed social pattern that will be commented on later.

What is most interesting was the discovery of three lime plaster representations of human figures — a bearded male, a female and a child. These almost life-sized figures were molded in thin, flattened forms with hair and other features painted on and with eyes of inlaid shells. Although it has been suggested that this triad formed the basis for what was to become father, mother and son divinities in later times (Anati, p. 256), the discovery of four similar life-sized clay statues from the same period at Ein Ghazzi near Amman, Jordan, makes this claim hard to accept.

Even more startling was the discovery at Jericho of seven human skulls, the lower parts of which had been covered with plaster to model a human face with eyes of inlaid shells. No satisfactory explanation of this art form has been presented. It has been suggested that they may have been the skulls of enemies and were, therefore, trophies of war. On the other hand, in view of the care that appears to have been taken in the modeling of the skulls, perhaps they were the skulls of ancestors, which could imply a cult of ancestor worship. At this moment, any interpretation must be handled with caution.

A small rectangular room with a semicircular niche that may have been a shrine was uncovered at Jericho. In nearby debris, a one-and-a-half foot oval-shaped pillar of volcanic rock from the Dead Sea area was discovered. This stone fitted precisely into the niche in the room. It has been surmised that the pillar may be a forerunner of the standing pillars, known as *mazzeboth*, found in later Semitic sanctuaries. Just what the Jericho pillar may have symbolized cannot be known. It is hardly likely that it was a memorial stone (cf. Gen. 35:20; 2 Sam. 18:18). Perhaps it was an object of worship associated with belief that it contained an in-dwelling spirit (cf. Gen. 35:14). Again, it may have had phallic significance.

Archaeological records make it clear that, as humans learned to live together in larger and larger social groups, they must have established rules and regulations for the preservation of harmony within the group, for the sharing of goods, responsibilities and labor, and for dealing with others who might be outsiders.

Whether or not there was ever, as some would claim, a golden era of peace and harmony, when women were in control and the deities worshipped were overwhelmingly female while men were engaged in hunting, building and navigating, is a matter of controversy. What is important is to recognize that the rules for human interaction and the morals and ethics that govern any society, grow out of community. To survive, ancient families had to learn to live together and function as cooperating units.

When families expanded to become clans or tribes, the relationships and responsibilities between the emerging groups had to be prescribed. When villages and towns developed, rules for the governance of the community had to be made. How the rules were determined, whether by the influence of the most powerful, or the most persuasive, or by democratic vote cannot be known. As we shall see, when some human beings began to live in large cities, they developed law codes which they claimed were divinely revealed and which had, therefore, supernatural authority that superseded individual wishes and desires. What is clear from this pattern is that, having produced and agreed upon the moral and ethical standards that would govern their particular society, the community projected these same laws into the realm of their deities so that they could claim to have received them back as divine prescriptions.

As towns and cities developed and multiplied, so did shrines and temples and gods, priesthoods and rituals. With the growing complexity of society, it became essential for humans to keep records and hence writing was invented. It is through the discovery and deciphering of these written records that we are able to grasp essentials of ancient religious beliefs which we will be discussing in subsequent chapters.

References

Anati, Emmanuel, *Palestine Before the Hebrews*. New York: Alfred A. Knopf, 1963.

Fagan, Brian, "All About Eve," *Archaeology*, November/December, 1992, pp. 18-24.

Frazier, Sir James George, *The Golden Bough*. New York: The Macmillan Company, 1941. One volume abridged edition.

Harding, Lankester, *The Antiquities of Jordan*. New York: Thomas Crowell Company, 1959.

Hotz, Robert Lee, "Scientists Say Race Has No Biological Basis," *The Los Angeles Times*, February 20, 1995, pp. A3,10.

James, E.O., *From Cave to Cathedral*. London: Thames and Hudson, 1963.

Kenyon, Kathleen, *Archaeology of the Holy Land* (third edition). New York: Praeger Publishers, 1970.

Pfeiffer, John E., *The Emergence of Man*. New York: Harper and Row, Publishers, 1969.

Piggot, Stuart, editor, *The Dawn of Civilization*. New York: McGraw-Hill Book Company, 1961.

Young, Louise B., editor, *The Evolution of Man*. New York: Oxford University Press, 1970.

4

The Birth of the Gods

Through the ancient written records we learn the identity of the gods of our ancestors. It is not surprising to find that they were usually associated with natural phenomena, for as humans began to live in permanent settled communities and learned, through agriculture, to control the basic needs for survival, they had to contend with natural forces that seemed to possess whimsical moods. At one moment, air movement might provide cooling breezes during the heat of summer, but at another could mount to tornado force to destroy homes and crops. Beneficial rains could feed the thirsty soil to ensure a good harvest or could come as flood storms that washed away whole villages and denuded the soil. Rivers that were the source of fresh water, fish and nourishing plants could overflow their banks with devastating results. Why did these changes occur and how could humans cope with these natural forces? They did not have the resources we have today with weather predictions to forecast storms, dams to control water flow and so forth; they interpreted what they could see and hear, taste, smell, touch and experience, in terms of themselves as persons.

By the time written records were made, natural forces had been personified. There were gods and goddesses of the earth, the sky, the wind, the rain, the sun, the moon and the stars, the rivers, the springs — in fact, supernatural forces were everywhere and they had to be respected. Having personified the life-affecting aspects of their place-world, humans created stories or myths that explained why things were the way they were and why events, both beneficial and destructive, happened. The gods and goddesses who participated in or triggered these events were given human personalities. Like humans they experienced varying moods. Some were prone to anger and were primarily destructive, others were frivolous and their pranks could either benefit or harm humans. Into each divinity, their human creators projected human feelings and responses. The gods reacted in accordance with their feelings — they could quarrel among themselves, feel jealousy, sulk or withdraw, they could strike out and punish, they could bless and reward. Like humans, they could be appealed to, cajoled, appeased and influenced through pleas or by rituals that expressed praise and adoration. Humans could purchase divine support through offerings and sacrifices. Scholars have labelled the purposeful presentation of gifts to the gods as a *do ut des* ("I give so that thou mayest give") relationship.

The Gods of Babylon

Each city, each state had its own chief deity, just as each city or state had its own human leader or lord or king. The personalities of the gods reflected human personalities and the organization of the gods reflected human organizations. Human rulers had their own palaces or precincts and the gods, likewise, had their own houses or shrines or temples. In any given city, a number of holy places, each dedicated to a particular god or goddess, could be found, in addition to the central shrine of the chief deity. For example, in Mesopotamia, when Hammurabi, the sixth king of the first dynasty of Babylon was in power (1728-1686 B.C.E.), Marduk, the supreme god of the city-state was considered by his worshippers to be king of kings and lord of lords. During the annual new year festival (the *Akitu*) held each year during the month of Nisanu (March-April), sacred statuary, the images of the gods of the city states under the control of Babylon, were brought to the capitol to pay homage to Marduk as the supreme god, in the same way that rulers and envoys from the subject states came to pay homage to Hammurabi. Within the walls of Babylon there were, in addition to the temple tower (the ziggurat) associated with Marduk, shrines to other deities including Ishtar, the goddess of love and fertility, Ninurta, the god of the hunt and Ninmah the mother goddess.

The sun, named Shamash, which could penetrate all dark places to reveal that which was hidden, was the god of justice. According to Babylonian religious mythology, it was Shamash who gave Hammurabi the laws by which the land was to be governed. Babylonian artists depicted in bas-relief on the upper portion of a stele of black diorite the divine commissioning of Hammurabi as recorder and enactor of the divinely endorsed laws. Shamash is shown as a bearded male, seated on a raised bench with a three-tiered footstool. The god's flowing, flounced garment leaves his right shoulder bare and from his shoulders come the shimmering rays or flames of the sun. He wears a coiled headdress with horns and with his right hand he extends to Hammurabi a rod and ring, the symbols of authority. The bearded monarch stands before the god with his right hand raised to his lips in supplication. Below the empowering scene, the laws of the land are inscribed.

The law code implies that the Babylonian laws are unique and original, but it is clear from comparisons with older law codes that many prescriptions reflect regulations that had been commonly observed long before Hammurabi's time. Indeed, some of Hammurabi's laws appear to be borrowed directly from older codes such as that of Lipit-Ishtar, the king of Eshnunna, who ruled over a century before Hammurabi and who claimed that his laws came from Anu, the sky god and Enlil, the wind god. Obviously, there could be no separation of church and state in ancient Babylon; the temple and the palace were in league and were part of the same ruling system. The notion that the leader received the laws directly from the god was commonplace and continued down to the development of the Hebrew kingdoms where it was taught that Moses received the rules for governing Israel directly from the Hebrew deity, Yahweh.

Myths are stories about the gods concerning their interactions with one another and with humans. Some myths told of the creation of the world and its inhabitants, others related stories concerning tensions among the divine families the effects of which could impact on humans. The Babylonian creation myth, *enuma elish*, portrayed the god Marduk as the creator of the cosmos following his conquest of other deities. The myth, which stated that humans were created for the purpose of serving the gods, enhanced the power and wealth of the state (as god endorsed), and the temple with its staff which served in the god's shrine. Once again, the world of human life is projected into the realm of the divine, for as captured slaves were considered to be persons of lesser worth and therefore destined to serve their conquerors, so citizens as creatures of lesser status than divinities were designed to be servants of the gods.

The multiplicity of gods with their specific fields of expertise was further expanded by family deities who, like persons of influence in human life, might, in the divine realm, have access to high gods on behalf of their client worshippers. At times occasions arose when the misfortunes that plagued life became overwhelming and the suffering person could not determine which deity he had offended and needed to be appeased. The following prayer demonstrates the plight of such a worshipper. He had been taught that suffering resulted from some infraction of the divine law, but he does not know what he has done or which god he has provoked. The prayer, often called "Prayer to Every God," is a "to whom it may concern" appeal for surcease:

May the anger in my lord's heart toward me be assuaged.
May the unidentified god be assuaged regarding me.

> May the unidentified goddess be assuaged regarding me.
> May the god whom I know or do not know be assuaged regarding me
> May the goddess whom I know or do not know be assuaged regarding me.

The prayer continues in this vein and the worshipper complains:

> Although I continue to seek help, no one takes my hand;
> When I weep they do not come to me.

He sums up his confusion:

> Man is stupid, what does he know?
> Mankind, everyone who exists — what does he know?
> He doesn't even know whether or not he is committing a sin or doing good. (Stephens, pp. 391-2)

So he pled with the god whom he either knew or did not know and with the goddess whom he either knew or did not know to let go of anger and to act towards him as a caring parent (Stephens, p. 392). The prayer constitutes a pitiful cry for surcease and demonstrates the difficulties that can arise when human good fortune or misfortune are attributed to supernatural powers. The prayer also represents a confused worshipper's challenge to current theology — a challenge growing out of the failure of the divine-human system to function in a reasonable way.

Divine-human relationships could be complicated when a country under the aegis of one god was conquered by a country belonging to another god. Sometimes the conquered god became a subject deity paying homage to the more powerful god as in the time of Hammurabi. When, during the sixth century B.C.E., leading Jews were transported as prisoners of war to Babylon where the god Marduk was in control, one captive wrote "How can we sing Yahweh's song in a foreign land?" (Ps. 137) They were far away from Israel, the territory they believed belonged to Yahweh. Shortly afterward, the idea of monotheism was developed and belief in a single god became the new faith. (see below)

Of course life in ancient Mesopotamia entailed much more than simply following laws. Laws were designed to provide order within the nation. The temple served as the city hall where litigations were settled, usually at the temple gate, but on occasion by oaths taken before the statue of the god. Temple priests constituted, among other things, what today would be called the "Department of Public Health," for they diagnosed illnesses and prescribed both the medicines and the rituals required for divine healing. There was no developed belief in life after death; indeed, in Babylon the descriptions of the place of the dead were horrifying. Therefore, within the requirements of the law, and the need to observe annual festivals and make offerings to the gods, there was a way of life recommended that would today be called "existential."

A story was told about the adventures of Gilgamesh, king of the ancient city of Uruk. According to the legend, he sought to defeat death and become immortal. As he journeyed to the realm of the gods, he paused for refreshments at an inn, where the serving maid offered him some practical advice:

> Gilgamesh, where are you running?
> You will not find the immortal life you seek.
> When the gods created man
> They ordained death for man
> And kept immortality for themselves.
> You, Gilgamesh, let your belly be full.
> Make merry by day and by night.
> Let every day be a festival of joy.
> Dance and play, day and night.
> Wear sparkling, fresh clothing,
> Bathe your head. Refresh yourself with water.
> Cherish the child who takes your hand.
> Let your wife rejoice in your bosom
> For this is the fate of man.

The poem does not define life in terms of the worship of the gods or with regard to duties to the gods; it has a lot to say about the enjoyment of life apart from rules, regulations and temple duties.

The Gods of Egypt

Meanwhile, in Egypt a different religious pattern developed. Egypt was not dependent upon rain, but upon the Nile river which flowed as a central thoroughfare uniting the country from north to south and bearing with it from its headwaters in central Africa the rich humus and minerals that nourished the soil. Consequently, unlike Mesopotamia, there were no rain or storm gods; the beneficent Nile was deified and its rising on July 19th with the appearance of Sothis (Sirius), the Dog

Star, was a time for celebration. The other life-giving power was the sun and it too was an object of worship. In Egypt the sky deity was female and the beautiful body of Nut, with her outstretched arms, arched over the earth to form the heavens. Immediately below her was the air god which separated Nut from her lover, the earth god, Geb. Earth and sky were the progenitors of the line of kings descended from Osiris, who became the god of the afterlife.

Egyptian mythology abounds in gods and more than eighty are known by name. In the earliest times, Egypt was composed of a series of small independent communities or nomes clustered along the banks of the life-giving Nile, each with its own family of gods and goddesses. In time, through conquest, they were united, and some gods that had parallel functions were merged, others were simply adopted into an ever-expanding divine family or hierarchy. Although the gods were conceived in human form, they could also be represented as animals, birds or insects. For example the god Horus was often portrayed as a hawk, Thoth, the ancient moon god of the delta, could be depicted as the dog-faced baboon or with the head of an ibis, and so forth.

Different cosmological theologies were espoused at different centers of worship. For example, at Memphis, the god Ptah was worshipped as the sole creator who, by his word, brought into being all that exists, including the other gods. At the city of On (called Heliopolis by the Greeks) the sun god Atum, who later merged with Ra to become Atum-Ra, was believed to be the creator. At Hermopolis, it was the ibis-headed Thoth, the moon god, who laid the primeval cosmic egg from which the sun god emerged; and at Thebes Amon, who later merged with Ra to become Amon-Ra, was recognized as the creator god because Amon, as a goose, laid the cosmic egg. The parallels and differences in the theologies appear to have caused no great problems but seem to have been accepted as variations or as similar-but-different aspects of whatever "reality" might be. It was only when Amenophis IV (1370-1352 B.C.E.) changed his name to Akhenaton and declared that the sun disc Aton was to be worshipped as the sole god of Egypt that discord erupted. When Akhenaton created a new worship center called Akhetaton in the inhospitable desert in Middle Egypt, he ran into opposition from the other centers of worship, particularly those of Amon-Ra. His intent was, in part, to break the power of the Theban priesthood. He installed himself as the high priest of Aton but, when he died, his new faith system died with him. Aton went back to his divine role as one of the many manifestation of the sun, and religion returned to what was normal for Egypt.

Church and state were allied in Egypt in an unusual pattern. The pharaoh was recognized as a deity, a god incarnate. Temple mythology told of the divine birth of the first pharaoh and the concept of the holy family was recognized: the pharaoh was the incarnate father god, his queen was the wife of the god and mother of the next divine pharaoh, her son. The pattern is reflected in the myth of Osiris, the first god-king, his divine wife, Isis, and their son Horus. The incarnate god participated in key festivals and made his wishes known through his court and temple administrators.

So far no law codes, no revealed once-for-all-time divinely revealed proclamations, have been discovered in Egypt. It has been suggested that because of pharaonic god-in-the-flesh-dwelling-among-his-people theology, such a law code would have been a denial of pharaonic divinity. The pharaoh, as a god representing the divine court, dwelt among men, hence a law code was unnecessary. There are, in the ancient texts, many references to trials and punishments, but the legal codes on which judgements were based are, so far, unknown.

The divine-human status of the pharaoh was the basis for a rich mythology of the afterlife. Through mummification, through rites and rituals, the buried pharaoh was believed to become one with the divine Osiris in the world beyond death. In time, the privilege of immortality was extended to the nobility and ultimately to the common man. Not everyone was persuaded of the validity of the reality of the afterlife. A fourteenth century B.C.E. papyrus records a skeptical song by a harpist, one of those employed to entertain at banquets (see also pp. 98-100). He sang:

Since the time of our ancestors
Generations have come and gone and been replaced.
The gods who lived in former times, rest in their pyramids,
The dead nobles too are buried in their pyramids
And those who built the tombs — the places have disappeared
What has happened to them?
I have heard the words of Imhotep and Hordedef [sages]
Whose sayings men recite.
What has happened to their places today?
The walls are crumbled, and their places are gone
And it is as if they had never been.
No one ever comes back from over there [the grave]
To inform us about their condition
Or to tell us about their needs
Or to calm our hearts [minds].

Until the time comes when we go where they have gone
Let your desire [for life] be strong
Let your heart [mind] forget funerary rites.
Follow your desires so long as you live.
Anoint your head with myrrh and wear fine linen
Anoint yourself with the wondrous gifts of god.
Heap up joys, don't let your spirits flag.
Follow your wishes and your desires.
Let your heart direct your earthly needs
Until the time of your day of mourning comes.
Osiris doesn't listen to their mourning
And wailing saves no man from the grave.

The song ended with a refrain:

Rejoice! and don't become weary,
For no one can take his goods with him
And no one, once departed, can return.

An equally skeptical poem derided the validity of belief in an afterlife and extolled the writers of literature as the only ones who achieved immortality. Miriam Lichtheim, the translator, suggests that the writer is "voicing a rationalist skepticism which surpasses that of the Harper's Song in boldness and radicalism" (Lichtheim: Vol.II, p. 176). The poet wrote:

Man decays, his corpse is dust,
All his kin have perished;
But a book makes him remembered
Through the mouth of its reciter.

He points out that the writers' homes have crumbled away, the priests who guaranteed perpetual care and liturgies at their burial places are dead and the tombs have been abandoned and forgotten. But, the literary work lives on:

Death made their names forgotten
But books made them remembered!

Polytheism, Monolatry, Monotheism.

Although it would be possible to discuss in detail animism in which spiritual powers are read into natural objects (rocks, springs, trees, etc) it is only important to recognize the movement towards monotheism in the ancient Near Eastern world. As we have seen, the great centers of culture were polytheistic—that is to say that many gods were recognized and families of gods were worshipped. The belief in one chief god for one people also developed. The god was the god of the nation and of the territory claimed by that nation. This is known as monolatry. Thus Chemosh was the god of the Moabites just as Yahweh was the god of the Hebrews. There is no denial of the existence of other gods, but a recognition of a sole god for a particular people (Gen. 17:8).

Monotheism requires not only the recognition of a single god for a single people, but a claim that this god is the only god and that all other deities are non-existent or false. This belief system was first proclaimed in the Jewish scriptures in writings from the sixth century B.C.E. found in Isaiah 40-56 in the much repeated phrase "I am God, there is no other" (cf. 45:5,6,18,21,22; 46:9, etc.).

References

Larue, Gerald A., *Ancient Myth and Modern Life*. Long Beach, Calif.: Centerline Press, 1988.

Larue, Gerald A., "Ancient Ethics" in: Peter Singer, edit., *A Companion to Ethics*. Oxford, England: Basil Blackwell, 1991.

Stephens, Ferris J., "Prayer to Every God" in: James B. Pritchard, edit., *Ancient Near Eastern Texts Relating to the Old Testament*. Princeton, New Jersey: Princeton University Press, 1950, pp. 391-392.

For translations of the "Song of the Harper," see:

Breasted, James H., *The Dawn of Conscience*. New York: Charles Scribner's Sons, 1933, pp. 163-164.

Lichtheim, Miriam, *Ancient Egyptian Literature*. Berkeley, Calif.: University of California Press, 1975. Vol. I, pp. 196-197; Vol. II, 1976, pp. 175-178.

Wilson, John. A., "A Song of the Harper" in: James B. Pritchard, edit., *Ancient Near Eastern Texts Relating to the Old Testament*. Princeton, New Jersey: Princeton University Press, 1950, p. 467.

5

Mesopotamia

❖

About 10,000 years ago, when the great ice fields began to shrink, our human ancestors began to move from nomadism into settled communal life in the great river valleys of the Tigris and Euphrates rivers. Near the Caspian Sea and in the upper reaches of the Tigris River, Paleolithic (before 9,000 B.C.E.), Mesolithic (between 9,000 and 7,000 B.C.E.) and pre-pottery Neolithic (7,000 to 6,500 B.C.E.) materials have been recovered, largely from caves. At Mesolithic sites below Lake Urmia (Karim Shahir, Zawi Chemi, Shanidar), circular dwelling foundations of stone together with hearths, storage bins, grinding stones and other implements, plus the bones of sheep, cattle and dogs, indicate the beginnings of settled culture. These sites may have been occupied only seasonally.

It is from Neolithic Jarmo in eastern Iraq, a site that was sporadically excavated between 1948 and 1955 by Professor R.J. Braidwood of the University of Chicago, that evidence of the transition to year-round living was uncovered. No pottery vessels were found. Pressed or pounded clay was used to construct dwellings and ovens. Animal bones were fashioned into tools and utensils, and limestone was shaped to form vases or implements that included mortars and pestles, axes and saddle-querns. There is clear evidence of the domestication of animals, including sheep, cattle, pigs and dogs, and of the growing of wheat and barley. Aesthetic interests were manifest in the necklaces of stone and clay beads, marble bracelets and shell pendants. Pregnant-female figurines of unbaked clay may have been associated with childbirth or perhaps with some early form of the worship of the mother goddess.

At Tell Hassuna, south of Mosul, further evidence of settled living patterns were uncovered. Adobe buildings were built around central courts. Crude pottery from the earliest levels gave way to fine hand-painted vessels. Human interment was in jars in which food was also placed, suggesting some belief in an afterlife.

During the late Chalcolithic age (*chalcos*, copper; *lithos*, stone) which extended from the middle of the fifth to near the end of the fourth millennium B.C.E., the art of smelting and molding copper was developed, and stone and bone tools were augmented by a limited supply of implements made from this new substance. At Tell Halaf on the Khabour River, a tributary of the Euphrates, hard, thin pottery, with a beautiful finish produced by high firing at controlled heat, was found. This pottery, from the middle of the fifth millennium, was decorated with geometric designs in red and black on a buff slip background. Some vessels had human and animal depictions. One figure is shown in a chariot, indicating that the wheel had been invented. Houses were made of mud brick, but reeds, bundled and plastered with mud, were also used in home construction. Cones of clay, painted in red or black or left plain, were often inserted into the mud walls to form mosaics and to prevent weathering.

Temple Beginnings

Early evidence of religious structures was found at Eridu. A small, mud brick shrine from the middle of the fourth millennium B.C.E. was uncovered. Only foundations and a plastered floor remain, but it is surmised that the upper structure had plastered and painted walls. Subsequently, this shrine was covered over with earth and a second temple was built above it, thereby raising the new building considerably above the surrounding plateau. This elevation of the shrine may have been one of the first steps that led, ultimately, to placing temples on the top of huge man-made mounds.

A more pretentious structure from the beginning of the fourth millennium was found at Tepe Gawra, near modern Mosul. Three large buildings of sun-baked brick were built on an acropolis and designed to frame three sides of an open court. Inner rooms were painted in red-purple, and the exterior walls were red on one building, white on another, and brown on the third.

The fourth millennium temple at Uruk was built on a staged, elevated mound, 140 by 150 feet at the base and 30 feet high. This man-made, mountain-top home for the gods was constructed out of pounded clay with layers of sun-dried brick and asphalt. It was surmounted by a white-washed temple (65 x 150 x 14 feet) and approached by a steep stairway and a ramp. The mound-structure, known as a ziggurat (from the Assyrian-Babylonian *ziqquratu*, meaning "to be raised up" and hence "a high place"), is the prototype of loftier and more magnificent ziggurats of later periods — one of which was called in the Bible "the tower of Babel" (Gen.11).

The Beginning of Writing

To cope with the fallibility of human memory, the Mesopotamians invented writing. They did not write on parchment or papyrus but on the ever abundant clay. The first writing rose out of the need to record business transactions. Small tokens made of clay or stone were placed in round or spherical-shaped balls of clay which scholars have called *bulla* (plural: *bullae*) — a term borrowed from the seal used to sign papal bulls or documents. Once the damp clay hardened, no one could alter the contents without breaking the clay. To indicate the nature of the contents, symbols were pressed into the bullae before clay hardened. It is believed that this primitive method of keeping records led to the use of clay tablets and cuneiform symbols to keep records.

Using a stylus, scribes pressed cone-shaped or wedge-shaped symbols into soft clay tablets. Once the inscribed tablet was baked, the record was forever preserved without any possibility of alteration. The earliest tablets, from about 3500 B.C.E., used pictographic symbols — that is to say, that the signs for a head or a foot or a hand or a tool were simply outline depictions of the object. Later the patterns were stylized to include some 600 symbolic forms using combinations of some 30 wedge-patterns.

As we have noted, the subject-matter of the earliest tablets was primarily related to business and concerned with property rights and exchange of goods. But the contents of the tablets were soon expanded to include treaties, records of battles and wars, poetry and mythology. Subsequently, documents recording the history and myths of Mesopotamian culture were copied and recopied, then stored in royal or temple libraries to await discovery by archaeologists.

The first real historical records appeared during the second millennium. Much research remains to be done to help us understand just what took place in earlier times. What we have learned is that two separate and distinct human groups occupied southern Mesopotamia. They were the Sumerians and the Semites — two different peoples of two different races speaking two different languages.

The Sumerians

The origins of the Sumerians, who called themselves "the black-headed people," are unknown, although the region of the Caspian sea has been suggested (Kramer, 1963, p. 42). It has been determined that they were neither Semites nor Indo-Europeans. Sometime after the middle of the fourth millennium they occupied an area between the Tigris and Euphrates rivers that corresponds roughly to today's Iraq (from just north of Baghdad to the mouth of the Persian gulf). This southern area, which is known as Sumer (as opposed to Akkad, the northern region), possessed the rich soil deposited annually over the millennia by the Tigris and Euphrates rivers. This soil could be worked, fertilized and watered by canals to produce grains, grapes and orchards with figs, date palms and olives. The rivers provided an abundance of fish and wild fowl. Flocks and herds could be pastured.

Linguistic studies suggest that the Sumerians displaced earlier settlers. For example, by examining the names of some Sumerian towns, it is clear that these identifications did not originate in the Sumerian language even though Sumerians continued to employ them. Just who the predecessors to the Sumerians were is not known; but in the hot, dry climate where the soil, composed of river deposit, had supported only marshes, the first newcomers made their homes, tilled the soil, fished the streams, and raised their cattle. Scholars identify them only as the Ubaid people — named after the site al-Ubaid, where evidence of their presence was first uncovered by archaeologists.

By virtue of their superior technological skills, the Sumerians converted the land into a productive, life-supporting garden. Irrigation canals channeled rich, silt-laden waters through fields and orchards. The clay (there is virtually no stone in the area) was formed into bricks that were sun-dried or baked for the construction of walls and buildings, or was shaped into pottery. Marsh reeds were woven into mats or tied in bundles, coated with mud and stacked to form walls for huts. The inventive Sumerians produced new tools including the plow and the wheel (of solid wood). Their sail boats moved from the waters of the rivers and the Persian Gulf to the Mediterranean Sea. Their builders discovered the arch and the dome. They learned to work with copper and bronze, silver and gold. And when they invented writing, they wrote on the ever-present clay using cuneiform symbols. They also invented cylinder seals, which are small stone cylinders with distinctive patterns carved into the surface. Each seal was a unique personal possession and, when rolled into the soft clay of the inscribed tablet, the seal impressions served as a personal signature to an agreement. Sometimes the seals were used as amulets or talismans and were believed to have magical power.

The high point of Sumerian culture was between 3000 and 2000 B.C.E., a period characterized by wealth, power and a richly expressed artistic and religious life. Some dimensions of the incredible wealth and the amazing skills of artists and artisans were revealed in the excavation of the royal tombs of Ur (c. 2650 B.C.E.) by Sir Leonard Woolley. The graves consisted of huge pits in which tombs of imported stone housed the body of the royalty and closest retainers. Figurines, headdresses, jewelry, and so forth were placed in chests in the tombs. Magnificent harps testify to the love of music. Immediately outside the tomb proper were the bodies of servants and soldiers who appear to have been buried alive. Ox-drawn carts had also been moved into the pits and the animals were also covered with earth. Although there is some problem in placing the buried kings in the history of ancient Ur and Sumer, there is little doubt that they belong in the earliest years of the third millennium, probably from the First Dynasty of Ur about 2650 B.C.E.

From Democracy to Monarchy

It is quite possible that, before there were kings, the most ancient Sumerian societal structure may have been a democracy that was both urban and agricultural. Some acreage was owned by the temple, administered by the priests, and worked by tenants who paid a portion of the harvest as rental. The remaining land was held as private property by freemen, some controlling large estates and others small plots. Some people raised livestock, some were hunters or fishermen, some were artisans and merchants, some were traders, importing and exporting by land and water routes, and some were professionals — scribes and doctors. The business of the city was conducted by an *ensi*, an appointed city manager who was considered to be of equal status with the freemen — not above them. Crucial decisions concerning civic welfare and security were made by a council of elders and freemen.

However, this democratic system was to undergo change. Social, economic, and political pressures, largely from the outside, threatened the survival of the people and led to the development of military leadership which was subsequently transformed into an hereditary monarchy. Thus a new class structure emerged: kings, nobles, priests, commoners who were freemen, laborers who were freemen, and slaves who had been reduced through poverty into selling themselves and their families into servitude or who were prisoners of war from surrounding areas. The king, although not treated as a god, was recognized as the agent of the god, subservient to the divine will. The god was the real king, and there appears to have been no way in Mesopotamian thought for the ruler to claim for himself the kind of divinity accorded the Egyptian pharaoh.

The gods of Sumer, which under different names became the gods of subsequent Mesopotamian people, were human in every way — in their moods, their temperaments, their actions and so forth. At the head of the heavenly pantheon was the sky god An, who was recognized as God the Father or as King of the Gods. His wife, the mother goddess, was Inanna, who was called "the Great Lady." Their son, Enlil, the wind or air god, was lord of the earth and his consort was Ninlil. Enki was lord of the subterranean regions, Ea was the god of water. The moon god was Nanna, Utu was the sun god, and Innin was the star we call Venus. Each deity had his or her own role, priesthoods and temples, and each was appealed to by a multitude of ordinary citizens who accepted the mythology as a means to make sense out of existence.

The structure of the earthly society was supposed to be modelled on the heavenly system. As the gods met in council to decide on proper action, so the earthly royal court employed the same procedures. Of course, in reality, the opposite actually took place — heavenly society was portrayed by the priests in terms of the established earthly patterns. As royalty and leaders met in council to formulate policy and make decisions, this pattern was projected into the mythological realm of the gods. Through theology or mythology, the earthly was made to mirror the heavenly and, simultaneously, through theology/mythology tremendous powers became vested in the priesthood and in the state. Mesopotamian society recognized itself as responsible both to the gods and to the human councils (Speiser, 1954).

The basic social unit was the family, and both monogamy and polygamy were accepted. Marriages usually developed out of contractual arrangements between the fathers of the two families, not out of courtship. Property was passed through the males, but women controlled the dowry given by the father at the time of marriage. In a case of divorce, the woman retained her inheritance. A man could divorce his wife for failing in what are vaguely described as "wifely duties," which included bearing children. Thus, a woman who did not bear could be dismissed with her dowry and her marriage price or with a cash settlement and then replaced with another woman.

Some women became devotees or hierodules of the mother goddess, who represented the procreative and reproductive forces in the universe. It is important to remember that the focus in Mesopotamian society was on plenteous well-being for all the inhabitants, and this required fertility of the land, the crops, the flock and herds, the rivers and the family. In the annual new year festival, a sacred marriage rite was performed in which the ruling monarch assumed the role of the god and copulated with the fertility goddess represented by a high priestess. The goddess' devotees not only served within the temple as slaves but were also sexually active in encouraging fertility. The role was not considered degrading but sacred. Some of the beautiful love songs employed in the rituals may have served as models for the language of romance and love-making among the populace. Samuel Noah Kramer has published much of the material in his book, *The Sacred Marriage Rite*.

Obviously the Sumerians wrote no "history" in the modern sense of the word. Like other ancient people, they recorded human memories and human fanciful interpretations of the past. The earliest "historical" document, a Sumerian King List, was copied and recopied by scribes and thus passed on faithfully year after year. Royal names do not help us very much nor do the records of events, because the persons cannot always be traced and the happenings, whether political or religious, often provide inadequate clues for dating. What is provided is a sense of the struggles that ensued between communities and efforts at growth and expansion.

The length of the lives of some of the monarchs named in the King List stagger the imagination. We learn, for example, that Kings Alulim and En-men-gal-Anna each ruled for 28,000 years, that Kings Alalgar and Dumuzi each reigned for 36,000 years, and so on. As the list approached the time of recording, the length of reigns dropped so that Gilgamesh ruled for 126 years, his son Ur-Nungal for 15 years and Balulu for 36 years (Oppenheim, 1950). How can these records of long-lived monarchs be explained in the light of what we know of the brief history of the Sumerians?

Scholars believe that the length of reigns was extended incredibly to cover immense periods between the time of the creation of the world as recorded in their myths and the time of the priestly scribes who were composing the "history." The Sumerians had little or no recollection of what took place during the eons of time before they settled in Mesopotamia; therefore they filled the time slot with the names of monarchs, providing each ruler with a reign of many millennia but with few accomplishments. Exactly the same pattern was followed by the Hebrew writers of the biblical record. Pre-flood heros lived incredibly long lives and seemed to have done little that was noteworthy during the time period. For example, Seth lived 912 years, Methuselah, 969 years and so on. Noah, who lived for 950 years, did build the ark (cf. Gen. 5-9). Obviously the Hebrew temple priests wished to fill the interval between the time of creation of the world as told in their mythology and the time of writing. Like their Mesopotamian predecessors, they used names and long lives as historical tools.

The Flood Story

The King List also reflects the unpredictable potential for river floods. It notes that, "After the Flood had swept over (the earth) (and) when kingship was lowered (again) from heaven, kingship was (first) in Kish" and Alulim was the first ruler (Oppenheim, 1950). Excavations have revealed that from time to time the great rivers swept over their banks and waters inundated established settlements. It is logical to assume that experience of these local floods lie behind the Mesopotamian flood legends that were to provide the source for the biblical flood story.

The idea of a world-wide flood that covered the earth rests upon the optical illusion that the arch of heaven meets the surface of the flat earth at the horizon. The dome of heaven was believed to be of hard material. The world of humans was, therefore, believed to be something like a modern cheese-dish, with its glass dome over the flat cheese-board. Above the dome of heaven and below the flat earth were the primeval waters. In terms of this imagery, the enclosed earth could be flooded by opening the "windows of heaven" and the sluice gates of the subterranean waters, to use the language of the Bible (Gen. 7:11).

Unfortunately, only one fragmented tablet recording the Sumerian flood story has been found. The Babylonian account, which provides greater detail, will be discussed below. According to the Sumerian myth, when the gods decided to destroy humankind by flood, their intention was transmitted to Ziusudra, a human priest-king. Although the information is missing, but on the basis of the Babylonian flood story, it assumed that Ziusudra built a huge boat and saved himself, his family and animals and birds. In any case, the story picks up after the flood had raged for seven days and seven nights and the sun god, Utu, broke forth from the clouds to warm the earth. It should be noted that the number seven will appear over and over again in Near Eastern literature where it serves as a symbol of completion. After Ziusudra prostrated himself and made sacrificial offerings of sheep and cattle to the gods, he was given "life like a god" (immortality) and was transported to Dilmun, the earthly paradise where the "sun rises." It has been suggested that Dilmun is, perhaps, the island Bahrein (Bibby) or perhaps the region of the Indus river valley (Kramer, 1963, p. 281) where the Harrapan culture had developed (see chapter 13 on India). The identification of this paradise remains conjectural.

The flood story was later retold with a new hero in the epic story of Gilgamesh, the fifth king of the dynasty of Uruk according to the Sumerian King List. The story relates the royal search for meaning and purpose in life — a search for human identity. According to the King List, Gilgamesh ruled for 126 years — a figure that is obviously exaggerated but, in terms of the long reigns given to other monarchs, relatively short! Present translations of the myth are based on fragmented tablets found in the seventh century B.C.E. library of the Assyrian King Ashur-banipal at Nineveh, supplemented by texts found at Boghazkoy, a Hittite site in Asia Minor, and at Megiddo in Israel. It is clear that the story had wide circulation for centuries.

According to the epic, Gilgamesh, king of Uruk (ancient Erech), was the offspring of a goddess (Aruru) and a human father. He violated his regal role as shepherd of the people and abused his subjects. When they appealed to the gods, Aruru created an alter ego named Enkidu. Enkidu was a man of the wilds who ran with the animals and freed them from the hunters' traps. His activities interfered with the work of the trappers and hunters who complained to Gilgamesh. Gilgamesh dispatched a temple harlot to woo Enkidu away from his animal associations. After spending seven days and seven nights with the woman (again the symbolic number seven appears), Enkidu found that he was no longer acceptable to the animals; he had joined the human family. When he learned of Gilgamesh's bullying behavior, he was incensed and decided to go to Uruk to confront the king. The temple prostitute clothed him with part of her skirt and taught him how to eat as a human.

After a dramatic physical encounter, Gilgamesh and Enkidu became friends and decided to find meaning in life by engaging in heroic ventures. On one occasion they offended the gods by violating the gods' sacred garden, a cedar grove, by killing the monster Huwawa that guarded the sacred precincts and by insulting Ishtar, the goddess of love. The gods met in council and it was decided that as punishment Enkidu would die. The image of the place of the dead, revealed to Enkidu in a dream, was a dreary, desolate underworld kingdom, where bodies hung like carcasses in a butcher shop, where the dead ate mud and could be compared to bedraggled birds dwelling eternally in darkness. The grave was no place of joy.

Enkidu did not die a hero's death, but suffered a lingering demise. For seven days and seven nights Gilgamesh held the dead body of his friend in his arms until a maggot dropped from Enkidu's nostrils. Horrified, Gilgamesh suddenly became aware of his own mortality. What Enkidu had become would happen to him. His aggressive response to life had not forsaken him and he determined to set out on a new heroic venture and seek ways to conquer death. He knew of an ancestor named Utnapishtim who had been granted immortality by the gods, so he decided to journey to the realm of the gods to see if such a gift could be his.

On his journey to the edge of the world where the dome of heaven met the edge of the flat earth, he paused for refreshment at an ale house. When he told of his quest, the bar maid commented that his mission was impossible, that death was the fate of all mortals, for when the gods created humans, they had retained immortality for themselves. Gilgamesh would be wise to accept that fact. She advised him: "Make merry night and day and make each day a day of joy . . . dance, play, day and night, wear dazzling clothes . . . cherish the child who takes your hand" and "hold close your wife." "This," she observed, "is the fate of man." (see p. 46)

A philosophy that recommended enjoyment of life did not fit Gilgamesh's heroic mind-set. He continued his journey to the edge of the flat world where he was able to enter the place where Utnapishtim lived eternally. He asked his ancient relative how he had achieved immortality and was told in great detail the story of the flood.

According to this version, the gods were angry with humans and decided to eliminate them by a flood. Fortunately for humankind, the earth god, Ea, revealed their intention to Utnapishtim, advised him to build a ship and to take aboard "the seed of all living things."

Utnapishtim's boat was a bit larger than that of Noah and was in the form of a cube — 120 cubits or 180 feet in height, length and width. It had seven floors divided into nine compartments providing a total floor space of 226,800 square feet (Larue, 1988, p. 150f). The storm raged for seven days and seven nights. The ark came to rest on Mount Nisir. Utnapishtim sent out a dove that returned, then a swallow that returned and finally a raven which did not return, signifying that the earth was dry enough for Utnapishtim to disembark. Utnapishtim prepared a burnt offering for the gods and they gathered "like flies" drawn by the scent. As a reward for preserving the numerous life-forms, Utnapishtim and his wife were awarded immortality. Inasmuch as no similar flood was in the planning, there was no hope for immortality for Gilgamesh.

Utnapishtim did offer a consolation prize. He told Gilgamesh of a plant growing at the bottom of the ocean that "makes the old man young again." Gilgamesh recovered the plant, but delayed eating it. He set it aside while he bathed and it was consumed by a serpent. Thus the tale provided a folkloric explanation of why the snake could shed its old skin and seemingly become young again, while mortals must age, wrinkle and die.

Gilgamesh, thwarted in his efforts to defeat death and old age, now accepted his role as monarch, sought the well-being of his people and, apparently, fulfilled his destiny through following the work ethic (Larue, 1991, pp. 29-33). The futility in attempting to thwart the divine determination concerning human life and death are obvious. If a superhuman like Gilgamesh could not defeat death, the ordinary human should not even consider the effort. The parallels with the biblical flood story are obvious and suggest that neither the biblical nor the Gilgamesh accounts were original works but drew upon older (probably Sumerian) traditions. Here, as in the biblical story of the Garden of Eden, a serpent is involved in preventing humans from acquiring eternal life or longevity.

The Development of Law Codes

With kingship came the organization of the laws of the land. In Sumer, as elsewhere, laws developed out of communal living but were attributed to the gods. According to this scheme, any violation could be seen as something more than non-compliance with societal patterns and became a blasphemous offense against the gods. Lawlessness risked engendering divine retribution and could bring disaster upon the person or upon the community that permitted persons to ignore the law. One of the earliest codes was promulgated in the name of King Ur Nammu, founder of the third dynasty of Ur during the twenty-first century B.C.E. There can be little question that there were earlier codes which probably used the same mythic interpretation of the rules for societal living, but so far they have not been found.

According to the prologue of the Ur Nammu Code, the sky god An and the wind/storm god Enlil assigned responsibility for the city of Ur to the moon god Nanna. Nanna, in turn, chose Ur Nammu, who is described as a child of the goddess Ninsun, to be ruler. Ur Nammu developed his law code in accord with the will of Utu, the sun god, child of Nanna and patron of justice. Regulations dealt with business ethics such as standardizing weights, with familial rights including the protection of widows, orphans and the poor, and with sexual issues including adultery, rape and divorce. In case of conflicting evidence, trial by river ordeal was employed to determine guilt or innocence. The river god was considered to have sacral judicial power.

What the code provided was a religiously endorsed basis for society. It outlined what was acceptable or good behavior and what was unacceptable or bad behavior. It also recognized the classes of people as a god-given arrangement. The king was a divinely selected individual. Priests and temple personnel were separated from the ordinary citizens and accorded special status as interpreters of divine will within society. The code also set forth the responsibilities of citizens for their mutual welfare. Obviously, such a document that combined the forces of religion and state exercised powerful control over the life and behavior of the community. To deviate, to suggest other behavior or other classifications as acceptable, was to act against the will of the gods. In other words, freethought was not and never is encouraged in such settings.

Over the centuries, subsequent monarchs developed similar law codes, each claiming sponsorship by one god or another. Depicting the monarch as a child of a goddess or as divinely chosen person became the forerunner of what was to become "the divine right of kings." The Lipit Ishtar Code, developed by the fifth king of Isin dynasty during the first half of the nineteenth century B.C.E., pointed out that King Lipit Ishtar had been chosen by the gods Anu and Enlil and that the regulations were in accord with the will of Enlil.

The Semites

From the best archaeological evidence available, it is clear that there had been a long history of movement of Semites from the Arabian and Syrian deserts into the Tigris-Euphrates areas. The earliest newcomers appear to have settled in small enclaves, particularly in the northern region. However, starting about 2400 B.C.E., Semitic patterns impacted more and more on Sumerian communities until by 2,000 B.C.E. the Sumerian culture had been completely absorbed and replaced. Akkadian, the Semitic tongue, became the language of business, religion and the state. Clay tablets and cuneiform continued to be the tools for recording.

Whereas Sumerian political life was centered in a city-state concept which often included dominion over neighboring cities, the Semitic pattern was that of a territorial state (Oppenheim, p. 58). Tribal-family connections enabled the establishment of a clan network among rulers.

The first Semitic king in Mesopotamia, Sharrum-kin, who is best known as Sargon of Agade (2371-2316 B.C.E.), began his career in the royal court of Sumerian King Ur-Zababa. He rose through the ranks to become a military leader and ultimately a king whose conquests were chronicled on clay tablets. As with many ancient heroes, a wondrous birth-story attested to his being chosen and protected by remarkable events from the very beginning of his life. According to the legend,

Sargon's mother constructed a basket made of rushes and waterproofed it with tar. She placed the baby in the basket and set it afloat on the Euphrates river. The infant Sargon was rescued and raised by Akki, the water-carrier, whom he ultimately served as gardener. Then the goddess Ishtar granted Sargon her love and he became king of "the black-headed people" (Speiser, 1950, p. 119). The parallels to the much later birth legend about Moses are obvious (Exod. 2).

Historically, Sargon's first conquest was the city of Uruk which he took during the absence of the Sumerian king Lugal-zagesi. Once again Sargon claimed supernatural support for his success, and this time he employed a political strategy by using the name of a Sumerian god. He stated that the victory came because Enlil, the Sumerian wind and storm god, favored him, a Semite, over the Sumerian ruler.

According to the Sumerian King list, kingship in Mesopotamia was now transferred to Agade (Akkad). City after city fell before Sargon's forces until he controlled the entire Mesopotamian basin. Through trade and commerce, he reached westward to the Mediterranean Sea. The dynasty he founded lasted for more than a century (2371-2230 B.C.E.) and his successors extended the trade outreach to India and Saudi Arabia.

Sargon's governmental pattern favored a centralized administrative pattern anchored in Agade. Citizens of Agade were placed in office in the subjugated cities and prominent families from subject cities were held as hostages in Agade. In 2250 B.C.E., fierce warriors, known as Gutians, swept down from the Zagros mountains to plunder, rape and enslave. Agade was destroyed and government moved to the city of Lagash. Inscriptions from the Gutian period, particularly under the reign of King Gudea, boast of wide-spread trade, of the restoration of temples and of military campaigns. But the people were restless and the Gutian period ended by 2120. Once again Sumerians were in control, but their supremacy was short-lived. Semitic peoples continued to migrate into the Mesopotamian region from the west — some peacefully, some in waves that took the form of raids on cities. By 1894 B.C.E., Babylon, which had heretofore been a small city under a local governor, assumed status as the center of a Semitic dynasty that is known as the First Dynasty of Babylon (1894-1595 B.C.E.).

Absolutely nothing is known about the founding of Babylon or about its earliest history. The Akkadian creation myth, *enuma elish*, provides a mythological account. It claims that Babylon was the first city to come into existence after the creation of the world and that it was manually constructed by the gods who built its shrines as their personal dwelling places. Disregarding the mythology, it is clear that

Babylon was, at first, a Sumerian settlement known as Ka-Dingirak which, when translated into Akkadian, is *Bab-ilim*; both terms mean "gate of god." This same designation appears in the biblical story of the tower (ziggurat) of *Babel* (gate of god) in Shinar (Sumer) — a Hebrew temple tale designed to explain how peoples who had descended from one family (Noah's) ended up speaking different languages (Gen. 11).

There are few literary references to the early history of Babylon. According to the "Sargon Chronicle," which is known only in a sixth century, Neo-Babylonian version, but which probably originated in the 24th century B.C.E., Babylon was recognized as a holy city under the protection of the god Marduk as early as the third millennium. Sharkalisharri, king of Agade in the twenty-third century B.C.E., is reported to have laid the foundation of one of Babylon's temples. During the twenty-first century Third Dynasty of Ur, mention was made of Esagila, the temple of Marduk in Babylon (Larue, 1969, p. 19f). But it is under the rule of Sumu-abum that Babylon began to grow in importance. Sumu-abum's name is West Semitic, but it is impossible to know whether he came to Babylon from the desert or from a neighboring city such as Isin, or whether he was born and raised in the city. Nor can we know much about his rise to power. He appears to have recognized Babylon's strategic location as a trade center. He encouraged the development of trade up the Euphrates into the interior and down the river to ports that could be reached through the Persian Gulf. Growth was limited northward by the presence of the Assyrians who controlled the area north of Baghdad on the Tigris River. Four kings succeeded Sumuabum before the most famous ruler in that dynasty, Hammurabi (c. 1792-1750 B.C.E.) came to the throne.

With Hammurabi, the golden age of ancient Babylon began. As a brilliant administrator and governor he transformed the city-state of Babylon into a leading Mesopotamian power. His military exploits extended Babylonian holdings from the Persian gulf into Syria. He conquered Assyria to the north and ultimately ruled all of Mesopotamia.

Thousands of cuneiform tablets from his reign include official letters from other monarchs and court officials. It is clear that Hammurabi maintained a strong centralized government with tight control over the cities in his far-flung empire. Babylon itself changed and grew. Irrigation canals improved agriculture. A single language, Akkadian, was adopted for economic and business exchange; Sumerian was reserved for liturgies. Taxes were universal and temples were not exempt. Public work programs thrived with cheap labor available through captive slaves.

The Law and Humankind

Semitic rulers followed the Sumerian custom of ascribing laws to the gods. Indeed, once the pattern of god-given laws became established it was followed throughout the Near East. Therefore, it is not surprising to find that, centuries later in the Hebrew tradition, Moses was chosen by the Hebrew god, Yahweh, to give divinely transmitted laws to the Hebrew people. The prescriptions in the Christian scriptures also indicate that the Mosaic laws and the teachings of Jesus are of divine origin. Later Mohammed was to claim he was chosen by Allah to reveal the prescriptions of the Koran. Some of the laws in the Mosaic code echo those of the Hammurabi code.

What changed in the Semitic law codes was the names of the gods. The sky god was now called Anu, but his authority as the chief of the gods was replaced by Marduk, the chief god of Babylon, who had possession of the "Tablets of Destiny" that governed the shape of things to come. Anu's consort was Ishtar or Inanna-Ishtar. Enlil remained as the wind/storm god, but the moon god was called Sin, the sun god was Shamash and the evening star was the star of Ishtar. These changes resulted from the fusion of cultures and the reforming of myths to enhance the roles of Semitic deities. Something of the change can be seen in the Hammurabi code of laws.

The Hammurabi code is the best known of Near Eastern laws. Today, an eight-foot stele or slab of black diorite bearing these laws, recovered by archaeologists, stands in the Louvre in Paris. As noted earlier (p. 43), the top panel portrays the king standing before the Semitic sun god Shamash, the patron of justice, who is portrayed as a seated bearded man. From this god, Hammurabi received the commission to establish justice through the proclamations of the law code. Below the portraiture, is a prologue which explains the king's divine appointment. Hammurabi's code follows the format of his predecessors. He claimed that he was chosen for kingship by the Semitic sky god Anu and by the storm god Enlil and that he had been commissioned by Marduk, the god of the city of Babylon, to promote human welfare. The royal task was to relieve the poor conditions of the weak, to destroy evil and to establish justice. Four columns relate Hammurabi's accomplishments and extol his role as both shepherd and savior of the people and as a great ruler and warrior.

Below the king's assertion of his task are the 282 laws of Babylon. Presumably, such steles were set up at key points throughout the empire so that any person could read the laws and understand his or her rights as a citizen. An analysis of the laws reveals dependence upon older law codes as well as the development of new laws.

Law under Hammurabi was harsh. The code opens with regulations designed to protect individuals against false accusations. For falsely accusing another of murder, the accuser was killed. A charge of sorcery was tested by the river ordeal and if the charge proved to be false, the accuser was put to death and his estates went to the accused. On the other hand, if the accused drowned (indicating guilt) his estates went to the accuser. In cases where the false accusations involved money or grain, the perjurer paid a fine. Crimes of theft were severely punished with some fines calling for a ten-fold restitution. Because men, women and children could be bought and sold as property, stealing a slave or helping a slave to escape were property violations punishable by death.

There was no true equality under the law. Three distinct god-endorsed social classes were recognized: the upper class person (*awilum*), the freeman (*mushkenum*) and the slave (*wardum*). Social stratification produced legal stratification. Among men of equal rank, the *lex talionis* or law of retaliation called for an eye for an eye and so on. Should a man of rank injure a person from a lower social stratum, legal responsibilities could be met with a fine. Should the injured person be a *wardum*, a slave, reparation was made to the slave owner for damage to property. On the other hand, should a *wardum* strike an *awilum*, the slave might forfeit an ear. The death penalty was frequently invoked.

Although the bulk of Hammurabi's code dealt with business matters including the buying, selling and renting of property, some laws dealt with the family. A family consisted of the father, one or more wives and perhaps concubines, and the children by wives or servant women. Without a contract, cohabitation did not constitute marriage, but once a marriage was legally consummated, the woman was subject to severe punishment for any violation of the contract. A man could divorce his wife by saying "you are not my wife" and paying a separation fee. If a woman should say to her husband, "You are not my husband," she would be bound and thrown into the water. Obviously, there was no equality between sexes, but women could own property and conduct business. There are references in the code to women involved in land holding and wine selling. Children were under the absolute control of their parents and could be sold into slavery to pay debts (Larue, 1988, p. 80).

The numerous temples mentioned in the records together with references to festivals, plus the many prayers and incantations that have been found, suggest that the Semites, like the Sumerians, were deeply involved in religion. In addition to the many gods that had to be appeased, there were demonic spirits that could affect human well-being. For example, the demon Pazuzu, the evil wind-demon who brought fever and sickness, was portrayed as a horned, scaly winged man with a lion's face, a scorpion's tail and feet that were claws (Larue, 1991, p. 71). To ward off this demon, the priests provided inscribed magical amulets, and should possession occur, they had the magical incantations and rituals to expel the demon. Pazuzu's frightful image has been used in modern movies that engage in depictions of Satanic possession. Pazuzu's equally terrifying mate, the demon Lamashtu, also had a lion's head and bird's feet and was believed to cause stillbirths. In other words, illnesses that most of us today recognize as caused by everything from stress, to infections, to inherited genetic disorders were attributed to demonic powers. It must be admitted that the ancient fantasies of sorcery and demonic possession are still current in some parts of our world and the same magical techniques of exorcism and amulets are employed by religious practitioners to "cure" the affected person.

One other facet of Mesopotamian religious and social life is worthy of mention. Like other ancient people, and like some modern individuals, the Babylonians were addicted to belief in omens. For example, if a man was building a house and black ants were seen on the foundations, it was a good sign foretelling the completion of the building and long life for the owner. White ants, however, augured the fall of the house, yellow ants meant the house would not be built and red ants signified an early death for the owner. A snake crossing the path of a man from left to right gave forewarning that the man would have a bad name; however, should the snake be moving from right to left, the man was promised a good name. On what may seem to us a more humorous level, it was taught that if a white dog urinated on a man it foretold bad times, but if the dog was red there was a promise of happiness! There were no references to black cats or to walking under ladders, but it is clear that, despite efforts to induce critical thinking into school programs and to teach logic and a rational approach to life, the superstitions of the past have their modern counterparts.

Fortunately, the priests provided ways to undo or forestall the potential evils predicted by omens. The householder would hire a *Mashmashu* (incantation) priest who would kill the ants by sprinkling them with oil and putting a mixture of gypsum and alkali in their holes. The priest would undo the power of the omen by sprinkling a mixture of boat dust with dust from the city gate with clay and water over the threshold and by burning incense. This combination of the practical, which eliminated the ants, with the magical, would undo the evil predicted by the omen. Such superstitions accorded the priesthood possession of what were believed to be magical formulae, rites and incantations to deal with the negative ways that the supernatural could impinge on the natural. No formulae were given for undoing the action of the dogs. (cf. Saggs, p. 308f)

Hammurabi's kingdom began to crumble after his death. The actual end of the first dynasty occurred in 1595 B.C.E. when the Hittites swept out of Syria and sacked Babylon as well as other cities controlled by the Semites. When the Hittites withdrew, Cassites swept down from the Zagros mountains and took control of the empire. The Cassites exercised a liberal and open ruling formula, utilizing the language and cuneiform script of Babylon in their widespread trading and political adventures. To the north the kingdom of Assyria which had been part of Sargon's empire began to develop as a trading and warring nation.

Assyria

With the collapse of the first dynasty, the Babylonian hold on Assyria disintegrated. Now, an Indo-European people known as the Mitanni took control of the area. By the middle of the fifteenth century, these people, whose rulers bore Aryan names and who worshipped the old gods of Indra, Mitra and Varuna, had established a Mitanni kingdom. Their rule was short-lived and during the fourteenth century, the Assyrian king Ashur-Uballit (1365-1330 B.C.E.) began the rebuilding of the Assyrian empire. Much important information about the development of Assyria has come from the discovery of a clay prism on which the exploits of King Tiglath Pileser I (1115-1077 B.C.E.) were recorded.

Now Assyrian gods were assumed to be in control of the nation. Assyrian conquests and Assyrian business grew. The chief national god was Ashur or Assur who exercised a role not unlike that of Marduk of Babylon. When the Assyrians went to war, their god Ashur led the armies against the foe. He is depicted in a fiery disc as a bearded, helmeted and winged male, whose lower body appears as a feathered tail. Ashur's bow is drawn and is ready to launch an arrow. The goddess Ishtar was given an Assyrian designation as Ishtar of Nineveh. Other gods were similarly assimilated into the Assyrian pantheon.

Assyrian military control pressed into Syria and Asia Minor where Hittite power had collapsed about 1200 B.C.E. The Assyrians engaged in trade with Egypt and held Babylonian expansion in check. It is not important at this time to trace the fluctuations in Assyrian rule. However, it is worthwhile to note that in 724, the kingdom of Israel that had been paying taxes to Assyria as a subject state, decided to rebel. The Assyrian response was swift. King Shalmaneser V moved his armies into the northern kingdom and, by the time Shalmaneser died in 722, Israel was conquered. Shalmaneser's successor, Sargon II initiated a deportation policy and twenty percent of the population of Israel was removed and scattered throughout the Assyrian empire. At the same time conquered people from other areas were imported into Israel. Thus the northern kingdom disappeared from history and is presently represented only by a handful of remnant Israelites known as the Samaritans. To the south, the kingdom of Judah, under King Ahaz, survived by continuing to pay tribute to the Assyrian overlords.

Assyrian control of the ancient Near East was not secure. Although their armies had entered Egypt and a ruler chosen by the Assyrians was placed on the throne, once the Assyrians withdrew their armies, the Egyptians deposed the ruler and enthroned their own monarch. The rise of Persia (see below) posed a threat on Assyria's southeastern flank. Desert Arabs contributed to the unrest in Babylon and forced the Assyrian ruler Ashurbanipal (669-626) to attack the city and place a puppet ruler on the throne. When Ashurbanipal died, a Chaldean named Nabopolassar seized the throne of Babylon, formed an alliance with the Median tribes and declared independence. Meanwhile, Scythians, from what is today southern Russia, pressed southward and threatened Assyrian holdings in Syria. In 612, the Babylonian king, Nabopolassar, attacked and destroyed Nineveh, the chief city of Assyria, and Assyrian control of Mesopotamia ended.

The Neo-Babylonian Period

It was Nabopolassar's son Nebuchadnezzar II (605-602), the Nebuchadnezzar of the Bible, who re-established the Babylonian empire. Under his brilliant leadership and statesmanship, the nation was unified and trade routes were established. Military might ensured acceptable relationships with surrounding powers and provided national protection. A massive building program made Babylon one of the most beautiful cities in the Near Eastern world.

The city of Babylon straddled the Euphrates river. The main city was surrounded by a massive wall eleven miles long, sixty-five feet high and eighty-five feet thick. Huge defense towers, which served as reinforcement, were spaced at sixty-five foot intervals. The city was further protected by an encircling moat that tapped the waters of the Euphrates. The second half of the city, which did not have such elegant protection, was linked to the first by a bridge resting on boat-shaped piers.

Entrance to the central city was through any one of eight gates, each named after a Babylonian deity: Ishtar, the goddess of fertility and battle; Sin, the moon god; Marduk, the creator god and patron of the city; Ninurta, the god of the hunt and warfare; Urash, the patron god of the city of Dilbat; Enlil, the god of the wind and the sky; Shamash, the sun god and patron of justice; and Adad, the storm god. The most important gateway was that of Ishtar which opened through flanking towers onto Marduk's way, the chief processional route. Marduk's way was flanked by high walls faced with blue enameled brick decorated with rows of white lions with yellow manes and yellow lions with red manes, each over six feet long. Behind the walls on one side was the temple of Ishtar, while on the other side were the famous hanging gardens of Babylon and the royal palace. Just beyond the gardens was the sacred precinct of the god Marduk where the most important sacred rituals were held.

In Babylon, as in other nations, there was constant concern that the sins of the people would upset the gods and bring disaster upon the nation. Each year, as part of the New Year festival, a purification rite was performed to rid the city of its accumulated evil. The New Year celebration, known as the Akitu Festival, was held at the time of the vernal equinox from the first to the twelfth days of the month Nisanu. This period corresponds to the Hebrew month of Nisan (March-April), the time of the observance of Jewish Passover and of Christian Easter.

Akitu rites began with the observance of patterns of privation that symbolized the death of the old year. Unleavened bread and unfermented wine were consumed. No new business contracts were made and no marriages performed. It was as if the vitality of the nation had come to a standstill.

Ceremonial activities centered around Marduk's temple called Esagila (House of the Uplifted Head), which stood in the precincts of the great ziggurat called E-temen-an-ki (House of the Platform of Heaven and Earth). This massive structure with its three hundred foot square base rose in a series of seven successive stages or levels to a height of three hundred feet. Each stage was painted in a different color. Although precise details are conjectural and all measurements are not available, it has been calculated that the first stage was colored white; the second, which was two hundred and sixty feet square and sixty feet high, was black; the third was two hundred feet square and twenty feet high and was painted blue; the fourth was one hundred and seventy feet square and was painted yellow; the fifth was one hundred and forty feet square, twenty feet high and was colored silver; no information is available regarding the sixth level, but the seventh stage was ninety by seventy feet and fifty feet high and may have had a golden hue. On the topmost level was a temple (cf. Larue, 1969, p. 62). The three hundred foot multi-colored ziggurat must have towered magnificently above the flat countryside and have been visible for miles as it rose above the city walls.

At the center of the Akitu ritual was the recital of the ancient myth of creation, which recounted Marduk's victory over the forces of chaos, the creation of the world and the bringing of life into being. It's recitation symbolized the annual recreation of the world and the annual re-establishment of the nation under the god, Marduk. The myth related how Marduk fought and defeated the primeval powers of chaos symbolized by the monster Tiamat. He then created the world out of Tiamat's body. One half of her body was formed into the arch of heaven, the other half became the earth. Out of her eyes flowed the Tigris and Euphrates rivers. Above and below the body were the primeval waters. The gods built the city of Babylon and Marduk created humans out of clay to be the servants of the gods.

The pageantry associated with the Akitu Festival included colorful processionals marking the arrival and departure of gods (represented by their images) and their individual priesthoods from the various cities of the empire. Each group came on its own day and, having entered the city through the Ishtar gate, proceeded along Marduk's way to the sacred precincts to pay homage to Marduk as the chief god of the empire, and of course to recognize the king as Marduk's chosen representative.

Ritual purification ceremonies cleansed Marduk's temple. To symbolize the death of the year, the king temporarily abdicated the throne and was humiliated before the statue of the god. Following a royal confession of faith and a profession of innocent behavior, the king was again recognized as monarch as he took "the right hand" of the god (Marduk's statue). Each facet of the ritual symbolized the death and rebirth of the nation, the supremacy of the god and the king's role as a servant of the god. There is some argument among scholars concerning the possible death and resurrection of Marduk, who may have descended briefly into the underworld of death before returning to the world of the living. Such mythic notions would further underscore the emphasis on death and rebirth.

One purification ritual is worthy of mention. To rid the city of accumulated sin, a sin-bearer was chosen — perhaps a felon or deformed person. As this man was forced to walk through the city, he symbolically drew to himself the sins of the city. Then, sin laden, he was taken beyond the city walls, perhaps to die, perhaps to await the conclusion of the ceremonies.

During the 6th century B.C.E., a Jewish prophet, who was among the Jews exiled in Babylon, witnessed this ceremony. He employed the imagery of the sin-bearer to give mythic significance to the role of the exiled Jews. According to his interpretation, just as the Babylonian sin bearer was the suffering servant of the god Marduk, so the exiled Jews were the suffering servant of the Jewish god, Yahweh. Their exile was tantamount to bearing the sins of others (Larue, 1985). The prophet's words, preserved in Isaiah 52:13 to 53:12, portray the misery of the Babylonian sin-bearer as a despised, rejected and mocked individual in whom the writer saw a parallel to the position of the Jews in exile. Later, Christians applied the prophet's imagery to interpret the role of Jesus as sin-bearer.

The Babylonian ceremony concluded with a fertility rite, a sacral marriage, symbolizing the sexual uniting of Marduk with his consort Zarpanit. The participants may have been the monarch and the high priestess who would consummate the marriage in the sanctuary at the top of the ziggurat. Now the city, cleansed of guilt and sin and re-energized by the god, brought the Akitu Festival to a climax in joyous celebration of the new year. The tablets of destiny held by Marduk were consulted by the temple priests to predict the good and bad days of the coming year. The enjoyment of once again eating leavened bread and drinking fermented wine plus the return to normal sexual and business relationships gave promise for the days ahead.

National purification rites may have rendered the nation temporarily free from sin, but the people were normal human beings and when misfortune came it was assumed that some sin had been committed. One can only imagine the power of the priesthood who controlled the means for the expiation of sin and the appeasement of the god or goddess whose will or wishes may have been violated.

Nebuchadnezzar died in 562 B.C.E. and, after seven years of unrest in which four different monarchs occupied the Babylonian throne, Nabonidus or Nabu-na'id was enthroned by officers of the court. He was the son of an Assyrian nobleman and a high priestess of the moon god Sin, whose temple at Haran had been destroyed in 610 B.C.E. Although Nabonidus' Assyrian lineage did not, apparently, interfere with his political advancement to ruler, his efforts to restore the moon cult of Sin at Haran did. He succeeded in retaking Haran from the Medes, but when his interest in the Sin cult became apparent, the priests of Marduk, the chief god of Babylon, disapproved. Perhaps Nabonidus envisioned making Sin the chief god of the empire, which would have won the approval of the Arabian worshippers of Sin, among whom Nabonidus was developing commercial relationships. Perhaps the the priesthood and court officials were disturbed by the fact that Nabonidus spent too much of his time in the desert regions in cultivating the Arab relationships. Due to his absences, for ten years he failed to participate in the annual Akitu rites which were considered essential to the national welfare. Spiraling inflation resulting from a famine also provoked the impatience of the people. In any case, when he finally returned to Babylon in 545 B.C.E., perhaps to campaign against the Elamites in southern Babylon, he was faced with new threats to his security. These threats were associated with the growth of Persian power under Cyrus the Great.

The Persians

Among the migratory groups that formed part of the Median empire was the tribe from Parsua, the land west of Lake Urmia. These people had settled near the Persian Gulf in a territory they named Parsa after their native homeland. By the middle of the seventh century B.C.E., they had expanded their tribal holdings and incorporated an area known as Anshan which lay to the north of the gulf. At the beginning of the sixth century, King Cambyses I, known as the "King of Anshan," a petty prince within the Median empire, married the daughter of the emperor, King Astyges of Medea. The son born of this union was named Cyrus, destined to become "the Great."

Cyrus became king of Anshan in 559 B.C.E. Astyges became aware of Cyrus' intent to revolt and was prepared to attack Anshan. A rebellion within the Median army frustrated Astyges' plans and by 550 Cyrus was in control of the Persian-Mede empire.

Nabonidus of Babylon nervously watched the growth of Persian power. To forestall any attack on his kingdom, he entered into alliances with King Croesus of Lydia (560-546) in Asia Minor and with the Pharaoh Amasis of Egypt (569-525). Cyrus did not attack Babylon. He moved his forces across northern Mesopotamia, wresting Syria from Babylonian control. In a brilliant military move, Cyrus ignored usual assault patterns whereby hostilities ceased during winter months. He attacked King Croesus in his winter palace at Sardia. Croesus was completely unprepared and Lydia became part of Cyrus' expanding empire. Now the Babylonian-Egyptian pact dissolved. Cyrus conquered Afghanistan and prepared to move on Babylon.

Babylon was ready for Cyrus. Persian fifth-columnists had been at work within the capital city spreading pro-Persian propaganda. Nabonidus had offended much of the populace with his long absences. The monarch's religious deviations caused dissent within the temple hierarchy. The reports of the liberal-minded Persian ruler fell on willing ears and Cyrus entered Babylon without opposition. Indeed, it has been suggested that the Babylonians opened the gates of the city to welcome the Persians.

Cyrus' report of the occasion, recorded on the Cyrus cylinder (Oppenheim, "Cyrus," p. 315f), followed a familiar political strategy. He claimed that he came to Babylon at the invitation of the Babylonian god Marduk. His report states that the army strolled toward the city, weapons sheathed to be welcomed by the entire countryside. Cyrus forbade plunder, began a program of urban renewal, permitted captive peoples (including the Jews, cf. Isa. 45:1) to return to their homelands, restored sanctuaries and returned sacred implements to their respective shrines. It cannot be known for sure whether or not he was a follower of the Persian prophet Zoroaster; but it is clear that, with the coming of the Persians, Zoroastrian religion was introduced throughout the Near East. Hence once again we see the alliance between the state and the representatives of the national gods.

The Religion of Zoroaster

Zoroaster is the Greek form of the name of Zarathushtra. The date of his birth is not known, but it is most probable that it was during the seventh century B.C.E. According to tradition, he was born in northeastern Iran, perhaps near Lake Urmia. Legends tells of his miraculous escapes from enemies who sought to destroy him and of his spiritual pilgrimage. Apparently he was originally a priest of the old Aryan religion who became a prophet and independent thinker preaching a new gospel.

He was supposed to have been led by Vohu Manah (Good Thought) to an assemblage of spirits where he was instructed by Ahura Manu in the true or pure religion. His initial efforts to reach his countrymen with his religious message were unsuccessful, but eventually he converted King Vishtaspa, the ruler of a small tribal federation. With royal support, the religion spread and efforts were made to forcefully convert neighboring tribes through a series of holy wars. In one of these battles, Zoroaster died.

Zoroastrian religion introduced ethical monotheism. It postulated the idea of a single god of goodness and truth. According to Zoroaster, Ahura Mazda was the all-knowing creator and sustainer of the world of good. From this god emerged all the good and positive factors of the universe including light and wisdom and truth. Then, how could one account for evil? The answer introduced the concept of cosmic dualism. Evil came from the "Hostile Spirit," Angra Mainyu (also called Ahriman), the epitome of evil who was the opposing spirit and the symbol of darkness and the lie. These two counterforces became personified and their attributes became personalities or opposing angelic and demonic identities who were part of heavenly versus satanic hierarchies. Here truth struggles with the lie, light with darkness. Surrounding Ahura Mazda were Good Thought, Correct Action, Wisdom, Piety, Salvation and Immortality. Ahriman's forces included Evil Thought or Deceit, Pride, Disease, Irreverence and Desecration.

Manifestations of the cosmic conflict could be seen in nature in the seasonal cycles, in the shortening and lengthening of night and day, in the sown land versus the desert and, ultimately, in life versus death. Humans were personally involved in the struggle. Each individual was free to choose which side he or she would support. Every act, every thought testified either to allegiance to Ahura Mazda or to Ahriman. Zoroastrian myth called humans to a life of rigid discipline in support of the good, the truth and the proper, despite the ever present pressure from the cohorts of Ahriman that tempted them to betray the commitment.

What was the reward for good behavior? What advantage was there if one followed the way of Ahura Mazda but suffered nothing but misfortune? The answer lay in the future and in the afterlife. Within the cosmic bipolarity, Zoroaster envisioned history moving toward an ultimate goal. As time moved through its various periods — from the age of gold, to the age of silver, then to bronze and iron — it approached closer and closer to end time. Ultimately there would be a final conflict in which the powers of good and truth and light would overcome the forces of evil, the lie and darkness. Then, (according to later Zoroastrian mythology) in the eschaton, a savior would come to renew all existence, produce a new cosmos, resurrect the dead and unite body and soul.

Meanwhile, at death, each human soul approached a bridge called *Civat* or "The Bridge of the Separator" over which the righteous could pass to paradise. The wicked, the foolish followers of the lie, would be turned back for punishment. They would go to the house of the lie, the place of evil thought, to dwell throughout the ages in darkness, misery and suffering. Finally, at the end of time, following the final conflict, all would be resurrected, judged and tested by passing through a flood of molten metal. For the followers of Ahura Mazda the passage would be as going through a warm bath. They would then enter the realm of the righteous, the house of song, the dwelling place of good thought where they would behold the divine throne of Ahura Mazda. As for the wicked, they would be utterly destroyed (although some texts suggest that, after terrible suffering that would purge them of evil, they too would be admitted to paradise).

Worship practices called for prayer five times per day (a practice later followed by the Muslims) and sacrifices of meat and *haoma*, a drink that produced feelings of exhilaration. The sacred symbol was fire, but earth and water were also sacred. Priests, known as Magi, were descendants of a Median priestly tribe.

As we have noted, it was after the Persians had conquered the ancient Near Eastern world that Zoroastrian religion was to make its impact. One of the religions that borrowed from Zoroaster's teachings was Judaism and, through Judaism, some aspects of Persian thought became part of Christianity (see chapters 7 on Israel and 10 on Christianity). Later, worship of the Vedic sky god Mitra or Mithra became an important religion in the Mediterranean world. When Mithra was identified with the Semitic sun-god Shamash, his worship spread throughout the Roman empire where the god was known as *Deus Sol Invictus Mithras*, whom we shall meet again in chapter 10 on Christianity.

The Greeks

The Persian empire fell before the Greeks in the fourth century. Alexander the Great defeated Darius III, the last Persian or Achaemenian king in 331 B.C.E. When Alexander died in Babylon, his general Seleucis I (312-281 B.C.E.) controlled most of what had been the Persian empire. The capital city was Seleucis on the Tigris river and Seleucis' kingdom reached from the borders of India to the Mediterranean Sea in Lebanon. Under Seleucis, Greek thought and culture impacted on the Mesopotamian world.

When Rome grew to power and sought to control the Middle east, battles were fought over a period of several hundred years. The Sassanian monarchy ruled Iran or Persia from 226 C.E. to 651 C.E. During that period, Jewish and Christian congregations sprang up throughout the empire. The final religious conversion of Persia came with Islam. Although Zoroastrianism was tolerated by the Muslims, pressures compelled Zoroaster's followers to move to India where a small colony remains today in the city of Goa (see chapter 13 on India).

For a long time, a certain amount of freethought was tolerated under Islam (see chapter 11 on Islam). However, when fundamentalist Shiite Muslims came into power during the twentieth century all free-thinking was outlawed. Non-conformists fled or were killed. Followers of religions deemed deviant were tortured and killed. The union of mosque and state smothered democracy, critical thinking and free-thought in Iran. Meanwhile, although a more liberal form of Islam developed in Iraq, during the twentieth century the religion and the state focussed on conquest of surrounding territories. Military intervention by the United Nations curtailed the growth.

References

Bibby, Geoffrey, *Looking for Dilmun*. New York: Alfred A. Knopf, Inc., 1969. Paperback edition by The New American Library (Signet), New York, 1974.

Burn, A.R., *Persia and the Greeks*. New York: Minerva Press, 1962.

Champdor, Albert, *Babylon*. trans. by Elsa Coult, New York: G.P. Putnam's Sons, 1958.

Cottrell, Leonard, *The Anvil of Civilization*. New York: The New American Library, 1957 (a Mentor Book).

Frankfort, Henri, et al., *The Intellectual Adventure of Ancient Man*. Chicago: The University of Chicago Press, 1946 (Phoenix Paperback edition, 1977).

Frye, Richard N., *The Heritage of Persia*. London: Weidenfeld and Nicolson, 1962.

Frye, Richard N. *The Golden Age of Persia*. London: Weidenfeld and Nicolson, 1975.

Gadd, C.J., *History and Monuments of Ur*. New York: Benjamin Blom, Inc., 1972.

Kramer, Samuel Noah, *History Begins at Sumer*. Garden City, New York: Doubleday & Company, Inc., 1959 (Anchor edition).

Kramer, Samuel Noah, *Sumerian Mythology*. Philadelphia: University of Philadelphia Press, 1961.

Kramer, Samuel Noah, *The Sumerians*. Chicago: The University of Chicago Press, 1963.

Kramer, Samuel Noah, *The Sacred Marriage Rite*. Bloomington, Ind.: Indiana University Press, 1969.

Lansing, Elizabeth, *The Sumerians: Inventors and Builders*. New York: McGraw-Hill Book Company, 1978.

Larue, Gerald A., *Babylon and the Bible*. Grand Rapids, Mich.: Baker Book House, 1969.

Larue, Gerald A., *Humanism and Easter* (pamphlet). Amherst, New York: The American Humanist Association, 1985.

Larue, Gerald A., *Ancient Myth and Modern Life*. Long Beach, Calif.: Centerline Press, 1988.

Larue, Gerald A., " Ancient Ethics" in: Peter Singer, edit., *A Companion to Ethics*. Oxford and Cambridge, MA: Basil Blackwell, 1991, pp. 29-40.

Lloyd, Seton, *Foundations in the Dust*. Harmondsworth, Middlesex: Penguin Books, Ltd. 1955.

Olmstead, A.T., *History of the Persian Empire*. Chicago: University of Chicago Press, 1970.

Oppenheim, A. Leo, "The Sumerian King List" in: James B. Pritchard, edit., *Ancient Near Eastern Texts Relating to the Old Testament*. Princeton, NJ: Princeton University Press, 1950, pp. 265-266.

Oppenheim, A. Leo, "Cyrus" in: James B. Pritchard, edit., *Ancient Near Eastern Texts Relating to the Old Testament*. Princeton, NJ: Princeton University Press, 1950, pp. 315-316.

Roux, Georges, *Ancient Iraq*. New York: The World Publishing Company, 1964.

Saggs, H.W.F., *The Greatness That Was Babylon*. New York: Hawthorn Books, Inc., 1962.

Speiser, E. A., "Akkadian Myths and Epics" in: James B. Pritchard, edit., *Ancient Near Eastern Texts Relating to the Old Testament*. Princeton, NJ: Princeton University Press, 1950, pp. 60-119.

Speiser, E. A., "Authority and Law in Mesopotamia," *Journal of the American Oriental Society*, Supplement 17, "Authority and Law in the Ancient Orient," July-September, 1954, p. 8.

Stephens, Ferris J., "Sumero-Akkadian Hymns and Prayers" in: James B. Pritchard, edit., *Ancient Near Eastern Texts Relating to the Old Testament.* Princeton, NJ: Princeton University Press, 1950, pp. 383-392.

Wiseman, D.J., *Cylinder Seals of Western Asia*. London: Batchworth Press, n.d.

Woolley, Sir Leonard, *Excavations at Ur*. New York: Barnes and Noble, Inc., 1963.

6

Egypt

❖

There is but one main street in Egypt and it is the Nile. This mighty river originates with snows and rains in the Mountains of the Moon in central Africa which drain into lakes Victoria, Albert, and Edward. It flows northward over a 4,000 mile circuitous course toward the Mediterranean Sea. Its tributaries are the White Nile, which is fed almost daily by the tropical rains of equatorial Africa, and the Blue Nile, which originates in the mountains of Ethiopia. As the Nile flows through the granite ridges of Nubia (ancient Kush), where its six cataracts characterize the area that came to be known as Upper Egypt, the river is single strip of water separating the Libyan and the Arabian deserts. Just above modern Cairo, at the ancient city of Memphis, the Nile divides into a number of streams that provide life to the fertile delta known as Lower Egypt. To the ancient Egyptians, the strips of agriculturally productive soil on either side of the Nile were known as "the black land;" the deserts that extended endlessly beyond the black land constituted "the red land." The black land constituted Egypt proper and the main street that linked the nation was the Nile river.

During the Upper and Middle Paleolithic periods (300,000 to 35,000 B.C.E.), the Nile valley was marshy and inhospitable. Human habitation was established on terraces overlooking the river, at oases, and on the shores of ancient nearby lakes. The dwellings were simple structures made from mud and reeds. Flint and stone artifacts indicate that these people lived by hunting, fishing and the gathering of wild edible plants. "Early paleolithic strata yield bones which indicate the presence in these early times of hippopotami, buffalo, aurochs, wild asses, gazelles and ostriches" (Kees, p. 18). Rock drawings and grave excavations from the Mesolithic period (12,000 to 10,000 B.C.E.) provide limited information about cultural development.

The Tasian period, which was named for the site called Deir Tasa in Middle Egypt, began between 10,000 and 7,000 B.C.E. and initiated the Neolithic era. Oval shaped homes were built of unbaked mud bricks. The variety of grain crops included wheat, barley, and flax. A large central granary gave evidence of the development of co-operative enterprise. Woven plant fibers and ornaments of shell, ivory, and bone reflect artistic skills. Bodies were buried wrapped in animal skins and interred with household items, but there is no way of knowing the reasoning that lay back of the custom.

The next archaeologically designated period is the Chalcolithic (*chalcos*, copper; *lithos*, stone), which extends from the middle of the fifth to the end of the fourth millennium B.C.E. In Egypt, this period is known as "Badarian" because the first evidence was discovered at al Badari. Now, tools and ornaments resulting from the mastering of techniques for smelting and molding copper augmented stone and bone implements. Green malachite ore, so important for the beautification of the eyes, was ground to powder on slate palates. The skeletal remains reveal that the Badarians, a stocky people, buried their dead in a partially flexed or sleeping posture accompanied by food and artifacts.

The next period, which began at the start of the fourth millennium, is known as Amratian, after the site el-Amreh near Abydos. A new people — tall and slender — appeared on the scene. Some of their artifacts indicate borrowing from the Badarians, but the extensive use of copper, the magnificent flint work, and the artistic expressions in slate, ivory, and clay mark their uniqueness. Amratian dead were buried in oval pits in tightly flexed positions with the knees brought up against the chest beneath the chin. The usual grave furnishings, enriched by the inclusion of ivory and clay figurines of women and slaves, have led some scholars to suggest that these human-form items might be substitutes for an earlier practice of sacrificing living individuals to serve the dead in an afterlife.

About the middle of the fourth millennium, the Gerzean period began, and for the first time written documents are found in Egypt. Local towns or districts (later called "nomes" by the Greeks) came into existence. Each had its own distinctive symbol, which was often displayed on Nile ships to indicate district of origin. During this period, nomes were sometimes united by conquest to form larger districts.

Gerzean tombs were elaborate. The poor were buried in oblong graves with a ledge at one side to hold funerary offerings. The rich were interred in tombs lined with mud bricks. Gold and silver objects appear along with those fashioned from meteoritic iron.

During the next half millennium, important administrative changes took place. Gerzean districts of Upper Egypt (Egypt above Memphis/Cairo) united under a single ruler who wore a tall, white helmet as a crown. Nomes in the delta region or Lower Egypt also united; their ruler wore a crown of red wicker-work. By 2900 B.C.E., the two areas had become unified under a single ruler who wore both red and white crowns and who was known as "King of Upper and Lower Egypt."

Egyptian religion abounds in gods. As noted earlier (p. 47), more than eighty are known by name. In numerous instances divine functions and identities overlap. Each of the forty-two nomes or provinces that were to combine and form the united kingdoms of Upper and Lower Egypt had its own official deity. Sometimes the same god or goddess was important in more than one district. Battles between nomes were regarded as battles between the representative deities. When one district was conquered or absorbed by another, the god of the defeated area was often taken into the pantheon of the victor and sometimes melded with another god. Because local deities were often symbolized in animal and human form, thc fusions of dcitics resulted in their depiction in a variety of human, animal and insect forms. A single deity might assume several different appearances. For example, Thoth, the god of wisdom, could be seen in the form of the ibis or the dog-headed ape, or in a human body with a bull's head surmounted with a disk and ureas (the sacred asp).

United Egypt: A Brief Overview

After Egypt was united, specific locales emerged from time to time as national cult centers. The chief god of that place would assume cosmic dimensions and perhaps be given qualities that had belonged to the deity whose status had been preempted. The results of this political and religious history made it possible for Egypt to exhibit a lack of dogmatism and an openness to, or toleration of, contradictions. There was no single basic revelation, no unique dogma, no sacred scripture or fundamental creed. Rather, the presence of unharmonized beliefs led away from systematized theology. As explained above (p. 47), parallels and duplications constituted no problem, but were treated as similar but individual aspects of whatever "reality" might be.

It was during the third century B.C.E. that Manetho, an Egyptian priest-historian, wrote about Egyptian history in terms of dynasties. Modern historians utilize Manetho's pattern but prefer designations such as Protodynastic, Old, Middle, and New Kingdoms, to mark periods of outstanding prosperity and development. They use the term "Intermediate Periods" to designate eras of socio-political weakness.

During the Protodynastic period (2900-2200 B.C.E.) Egypt developed widespread commercial contacts with Syria and Mesopotamia. What is most important is that a new concept of monarchy developed. The king or pharaoh was recognized as a god; consequently Egyptian government became a pharaoh- or god-centered bureaucracy with a powerful priesthood. The concept of divinity was fluid. When it was determined that kings could be gods, the cult center at Heliopolis produced a myth explaining how the royal divinity came about. It was taught that the sun god, Ra, chose the wife of the high priest to bear divine offspring. The god assumed the identity of the husband and copulated with woman to produce three sons who were to be the first three pharaohs of the First Dynasty. From that point on, all pharaohs were accepted as sons of Ra and were assumed to be divine and immortal. Later, viziers and wise men were believed to be able to become gods after death. Subsequently, mortuary religion, originally designed for the pharaoh, was extended to include queens and nobles.

Memphis, which is located near the junction of Upper and Lower Egypt, became the capital; nearby Heliopolis was the headquarters of the priesthood. Because godship and immortality are closely linked concepts, the burial of the pharaoh assumed great importance. Royal tombs of the first dynasty were underground pits, lined with brick and roofed with timber and matting. Small offering rooms were clustered around the central chamber. Adjacent to the tomb were the graves of servants, sacrificed to accompany the god-king into the afterlife. Later, rectangular shells with sloping sides and a flat table-top were erected above the tombs. These were known as mastabas (platforms).

During the Old Kingdom (c. 2700-2200 B.C.E.), which includes the IIIrd to VIth dynasties, mastabas underwent change. The gifted magician-priest-engineer-architect Imhotep erected the first pyramid for the entombment of King Djoser, the first pharaoh of the period. Five mastabas, each diminishing in size, were imposed one upon the other to form the famous step-pyramid. Succeeding monarchs built both larger and smaller pyramid tombs.

The First Intermediate Period is marked by an invasion of Amoritic people, perhaps from Syria (c. 2200-1900 B.C.E.). Little history — and none that is important for our study — emerges from this period that covers the VIIth to XIth dynasties.

The Middle Kingdom (c. 1990-1786 B.C.E.), which embraces the XIIth dynasty, was controlled by Theban rulers. This was a period of Egyptian splendor, marked by such engineering marvels as the construction of a canal linking the Nile river and the Red Sea so that trade would be enhanced. It was a time of artistic and literary creativity. This magnificent period was brought to an end by an invasion of a people of mixed stock called the Hyksos.

Once again, Egypt entered a darkened time known as the Second Intermediate Period. What the Hyksos brought to Egypt were new military skills, including the use of the horse and chariot for the fast movement of troops, and a superior weapon — the composite bow and arrow.

The New Kingdom (XVIIIth to XXth dynasties) began with Ahmose and lasted from approximately 1570 to 1290 B.C.E. This was a period of Egypt's greatest glory. Ahmose, using the new weapons introduced by the Hyksos, extended Egypt's borders from the fourth cataract of the Nile to the Euphrates river. Art, architecture, and religion flourished. Intermarriage with foreign princesses helped to secure foreign policies and extend trade.

It was during this same period that Amenhotep IV (c. 1370-1353) changed his name to Akhenaton. Sun worship, which had always been central in Egypt, had employed a number of different sun symbols. For example, at Thebes, the sun was known as Amon or Amun. Akenaton insisted that the sun symbol be limited to one form only — the sun disc, called Aton. To emphasize the new religious format, Akhenaton had a new worship center built at El Amarna, which he called Akhetaten (Horizon of Aton). By shifting the center of worship and government from traditional sites, he robbed ancient shrines of power, prestige, and wealth, and roused the anger and animosity of the priests.

At his new center, Akhenaton composed a beautiful hymn to the sun that has striking echoes in the biblical Psalm 104. Many scholars are convinced that the biblical writer borrowed directly from the Egyptian hymn. When Akenaton died, his el-Amarna capital was demolished and abandoned. Government returned to Thebes and once again religion focussed on the god Amon. Something of the wealth and grandeur of pharaonic life of that period has been revealed in the more than 5,000 objects found in the tomb of King Tutankhamon, the boy king who came to the throne shortly after Akhenaton's death.

For twelve years after Akhenaton's death, Egypt was ruled by weak and ineffective monarchs: Smenkhkare, Tutankhamon and Ay. Smenkhkare died shortly after attaining the throne. Tutankhamon was nine years old when he became pharaoh by virtue of his marriage to Akhenaton's daughter Ankhespaaten (who a few years earlier had married her father). Tutankhamon died at age eighteen. His widow wrote to the king of the Hittites asking for his son in marriage, promising the young man the throne of Egypt. But the Hittite prince was murdered as he journeyed to Egypt, the princess disappeared from history, and Ay, a priest of Amon, who had been in Akenaton's court, seized the throne. At Ay's death, a military commander, Haremheb, took control, claiming that he was appointed by the god Amon. Haremheb established law and order and engaged in temple building. He was the last ruler of the XVIIIth dynasty.

The XIXth or Ramessid Dynasty (c. 1340-1200 B.C.E.) was characterized by a series of powerful rulers. Seti 1, the second pharaoh in the dynasty, sought to regain control of the Asian empire which had been lost during Akhenaton's reign. He battled the Bedouin of Palestine and defeated a powerful Hittite army in a battle near the Orontes river in Syria. He was aided in battle, so he recorded, by the god Amon. He reigned for sixty-seven years and was succeeded in 1232 by Mernephtah, who put down a minor revolt in Palestine. In his record of the battle, he wrote that "Israel is laid waste and has no seed, Palestine has become a widow for Egypt." This is the only mention of the name "Israel" in any Egyptian inscription and its meaning is not clear. The sign associated with the name "Israel" indicates a foreign people; the sign with the name Palestine indicates a foreign land. Certainly the term "Israel" does not connote what it later came to mean in the Hebrew Bible where it signifies a fusion of tribes into a national entity. In his fifth year (1227 B.C.E.), Mernephtah battled the Libyans, who came as part of an invasion of the delta region.

The most important ruler of the XXth dynasty (1197-1085 B.C.E.) and the last great ruler of the New Kingdom in Egypt, was Ramesses III (1195-1164). The twelfth century marked the beginning of the Iron Age in the Middle East, and the mastery of molding this new, hard metal provided superior tools and weapons.

Ramesses faced continuing invasions by Libyans and Bedouin, but his greatest threat came from the Sea People — a sea-faring, migratory group seeking a new homeland following their movement out of Southern Greece. Now, for the first time, Egypt moved into military conflict with Europeans. The naval battle that kept the Sea People out of Egypt did not prevent them from establishing themselves on the Palestinian coastline. There they developed the Philistine nation (see chapter 7 on Israel).

From 1085 to 663 B.C.E., Egypt was in a state of decline. Dynasty XXI (1085-950 B.C.E.), which is also known as the Tanite Dynasty, was ruled by priest-kings in Thebes. In Dynasty XXII, the Bubastite Dynasty (950-730 B.C.E.), Libyan Kings were on the throne. We mention only one, Sheshonq I (950-929), who, after the death of King Solomon, made a quick raid into Palestine when the Hebrew kingdom was in a state of disruption. Sheshonq attacked Jerusalem and raided the temple (see I Kings 14:25-26, where Sheshonq's name is given as "Shishak").

The XXVth Dynasty (751-656 B.C.E.) was ruled by Kushite/Ethiopian kings (see chapter 12 on Africa). This was a time when Assyrian power was at its greatest. In 671, the Assyrian King Esarhaddon sacked Memphis; and in 663, King Ashurbanipal sacked Thebes.

Persian control in Egypt began with conquest by Cambyses in 525. It ended with Darius III, in 330 B.C.E., when the Greeks, under Alexander the Great, assumed control. Then, for three hundred years, the Ptolemies ruled Egypt. They yielded to the Romans who remained in control from 30 B.C.E. to 324 C.E. The accession of King Constantine introduced the Byzantine or Coptic period. When the Muslims swept across North Africa in 640 C.E., Egypt became an Islamic nation.

Obviously, this brief survey does not do justice to the intricacies of Egyptian history. For example, it should be noted that during the Coptic period, Egyptian Christians engaged in a systematic despoiling of Egyptian carvings that depicted mythological themes — particularly those that had sexual connotations. Under Islam, the importance of Egypt's past was negated. What counted was what had happened since the revelation of Allah to Muhammad.

Egyptian Cosmological Myths

We now return to a discussion of ancient Egyptian religion. Egyptian mythology centered in two natural phenomena: the Nile river and the sun. The Nile sustained life along the narrow strips of black land that were its borders. Soil fertility depended on the rising of its waters which began each year when the Dog Star, Sothis (Sirius), appeared on the horizon, just before sunrise (July 19). Fed by rains and the melting snows, the headwaters flowed in a mighty torrent from the equator, carrying humus and essential minerals for enriching the soil of Egypt. The alluvium-bearing waters were channeled into fields along the Nile and captured behind dams for later use. The earliest literature described the milky flow as coming from the phallus of Osiris who, as a fertility god, was at one time depicted as the fructiferous earth.

The sun, which shines on Egypt throughout the year from an almost always cloudless sky, was recognized as the other life-sustaining force. Manifestations of the sun god ranged from the eye of the falcon to the sun disc Aton which, as we have noted, King Akhenaton espoused as the sole acceptable representation of the god. The course of the sun was given earthly manifestations. In the morning, the sun was Kephri, the scarab or dung-beetle that rolled the dung ball (the sun) with its hind legs toward the zenith of the heavens. At noon, it was Re or Ra, the vigorous young god of Heliopolis. By evening, it had become the old man, Atum, descending in the west. During the night it traveled through the underworld to rise again as Kephri. In another representation, the sun was born each day as a golden calf from the celestial cow, or as a child from the vagina of the celestial woman who swallowed it again at evening. No matter what the symbolic manifestation, the sun was the most important factor in Egyptian mythology.

According to Egyptian cosmological myth, in the beginning there was only the primeval surfaceless water, the all-encompassing abyss, called Nun. Nun was without form and void and complete darkness permeated the deep. The cosmos was a hollowed-out chamber within the deep, protected from the waters above by a firmament, and from the waters below by the earth. The sky, the hemisphere above the earth, was sometimes depicted as a cow supported by its four legs, or as an arched female figure supported by extended arms and legs, or as a shell, held up by four mountains at the cardinal compass points. In the beginning, the sun, described at times as self-created and at other times as the child of the sky-goddess, pushed back the abysmal darkness, just as each day the new-born sun's rays pushed away the darkness of the night.

Creation was attributed to several deities, sometimes through sexual activity, at other times through the spoken word which was the projection of thought. There were five different cosmologies associated with cult centers at Memphis, Heliopolis, Hermopolis, Thebes and Elephantine.

Memphite Cosmology

The city of Memphis was built about 2900 B.C.E. by the pharaoh Menes (Narmer) who, according to the third century B.C.E. Egyptian priest-historian Manethos, was the first ruler of permanently united Egypt. Memphis, located at the apex of the Nile delta and at the junction of Upper and Lower Egypt, was the center of government and religion. Memphis mythology was augmented by the city's claim to exceptional status.

Basic information about the myth has come from the Shabaka stone, which was produced during the reign of the Ethiopian or Kushite Pharaoh, Shabaka (Shabako) about 700 B.C.E. However, that inscription is based on sources that may go back to the fourth millennium B.C.E. The account appears to represent some form of dialogue between the gods, and was probably designed for a dramatized ritual enactment of the myth.

Ptah, the high god of Memphis was the creator of the world and master of destiny. He brought into being all that existed, including the other gods, their cults, and the offerings made to them. His creation came through his "word," which was the activation of the thoughts of his "heart" (mind), uttered by his "tongue." The heart was the symbol of mind or intelligence; the tongue, the symbol of command or power. The god spoke, his words took form and became reality. All other gods were projections of his will and his command; all that exists was recognized as a manifestation of his mind and his creative word. The Shabaka account states that the gods entered into their forms in all kinds of wood, minerals, soils, and growing things. Everywhere, within and without, the Egyptians encountered the divine. It is not surprising, therefore, to discover that the Egyptian artisans depicted gods in various human and animal forms and in combinations of these. In all that existed there was a manifestation of the sacred.

The Shabaka account provides no information about the cosmological process. There is no reference to the creation of the earth, the sky, the seas, the rivers or growing things. All was presupposed. Ptah caused the divine, the gods, to infuse the world. It can be assumed that Ptah created the cosmos in the same way that he created everything else — by his word.

Heliopolitan Cosmology

The ancient city of On, named Heliopolis by the Greeks, was located just across the river from Memphis. Here the sun god, sacred to Egyptians from predynastic times, was worshipped under the name of Atum, later Atum-Ra or Atum-Re, when the two manifestations of the god were linked.

Atum was a self-generated god who emerged from the primeval waters of Nun by an act of will. The seventeenth chapter of the Book of the Dead, which is a compilation of coffin texts that go back to the third millennium B.C.E., refers to Atum as being "alone in Nun." Self-generation, an idea found also in Hermopolitan and Theban myths, conferred unique authority on Atum. He was his own first cause. His mythic history began in and with himself. Other gods had predecessors. Atum had none. He was the beginning of the creative process. Without him nothing was made that was made. Consequently, his power and authority were unsurpassed. All other gods and all created things were destined to function and respond to their existence in given ways. Atum was above all that he created, therefore he was not under any controls. He was embodied in and through his creation and was, thus, both imminent and transcendent.

In the beginning, because Atum had nowhere to stand, he brought into being the primeval hillock or mound on which the Heliopolitan temple was said to have been built. The notion of the primeval mound may have originated in the observation of the muddy hillocks that emerge as the Nile recedes after innundation. The temple represented sacred space, a holy site, the house of the god. Rituals conducted in its precincts were divine rituals, including the re-enactment of cosmic beginnings on the very foundation place of the universe.

The Memphite account of creation by the god Ptah may have been too abstract for worshippers. Heliopolitan mythology described the formation of the gods and goddesses in a manner more easily comprehended. Some early texts describe Atum as the great He-She, a bisexual implication, but it is clear that in the creation mythology the god is exclusively male. Because Atum's devotees conceived of creation in sexual terms, and because Atum was alone and without a mate, it is recorded that he created by masturbation. The primary creations, according to the Shabaka inscription, were the Ennead, the first gods. They were created by Atum "by his semen and his fingers." A variant form of the myth was found in a dedicatory text carved inside a Sixth Dynasty pyramid from about the middle of the third millennium B.C.E. (Budge, Vol 1, p. 308f) The name Atum is linked with Kephri, and Atum-Kephri is said to have taken the semen from the masturbatory act into his mouth and to have spat forth Shu, the air god, and Tefnut, the moisture goddess, who was both sister and wife to Shu. Clearly, life-giving is associated with the male semen, thus the woman might be interpreted as the vessel in which life developed rather than being recognized as a vital contributor to the life-form conceived within her. Atum-Re also created the "names" of his body parts. In the very naming, divine beings representing the world came into existence. These included:

Geb, the earth god and his sister-wife Nut, the sky goddess
Osiris, the fertility god who was to become the chief deity in the mortuary cult, and his sister-wife, Isis
Seth or Set, the rival of Osiris, and his twin sister-wife Nephthys

Shu and Tefnut were said to have been the parents of Geb and Nut. Nut (the sky) and Geb (the earth) were at one time sexually united, until the air god came between them. The products of their union were Osiris, Isis, Seth and Nephthys. In this variant form of the myth, Atum is the "All," and all gods are extensions or parts of Atum.

Humans were formed from the tears of Atum. It appears that the god had but one eye which was physically and ideationally independent. Once, when Shu and Tefnut were lost in the murkiness of Nun, Atum sent his eye to look for them. During its absence, he replaced it with a substitute eye. When the original eye returned with the missing gods, it was furious at being replaced. As appeasement, it was given a place in the forehead of Atum, where it would be able to rule the world that was shortly to come into being. Atum shed tears of joy over the return of his missing offspring and the tears became human beings. Then, according to this interpretation, Atum created the world.

Hermopolitan Cosmology

At Hermopolis in Upper Egypt, Thoth, the ancient moon god of the delta, was recognized as the supreme deity and the embodiment of divine wisdom, intelligence, and omniscience. His chief manifestation was in the form of an ibis or an ibis-headed man, although he is also depicted as a dog-faced baboon.

Thoth was self-begotten, emerging in a lotus flower in the primeval waters of Nun. According to one myth, the ibis god laid the cosmic egg out of which Re, the sun god, appeared. A variant version depicted Re emerging as a child when the lotus flower opened its petals and the sun, in the form of a scarab beetle, was revealed. The scarab was transformed into a boy (Re), whose tears were to became humankind.

Associated with Thoth were the Ogdoad, a group of eight divinities — four males and their consorts. They were said to have created the world and ruled it in a golden age. Following their death, they journeyed to the underworld from whence they caused the Nile river to flow. The names of the four male deities personify four aspects of formless pre-creation chaos. The names of their consorts are simply feminine forms of the male appellations. Nun and Naunet represent the primeval waters, the abyss; Huh and Hauhet, the formless, endless expanse of chaos; Kuk and Kauket the primeval darkness, the obscure; and Amon and Amonet, the air that moved over the primeval waters.

The holy city of Hermopolis was located on the primeval hillock that appeared first in Nun as "the Island of Two Flames." The sacred lake in the temple's park represented Nun and was called "the Sea of the Two Knives." The temple itself was believed to have been the primeval dwelling place of the Ogdoad.

Many aspects of Thoth mythology are obscure. In the New Kingdom, which began about the middle of the sixteenth century B.C.E., a new cult center, which borrowed some aspects of Hermopolitan mythology, began in Thebes. According to a fourteenth century B.C.E. text, Thoth, as the moon god, was recognized as Re's vizier. Ultimately, as a god of wisdom, Thoth was prominent in the Osirian cult of the dead.

Theban Cosmology

When Thebes, in Upper Egypt, became the seat of government in the New Kingdom (c. 1570-1085 B.C.E.), Amon, the chief god of the city, assumed national importance. His early role, as the goose that laid the cosmic egg, or as the fertile ram god, became less prominent, and Amon was fused with Re to become Amon-Re, the solar deity. Theban mythology borrowed from Memphite, Heliopolitan and Hermopolitan mythology. Like Atum, Amon was self-created. As god of the air, he was invisible and symbolized the dynamic, creative power of the moving atmosphere or wind, or even the quality of the breath of life in humans and animals. Amon was said to have brought everything into being, beginning with the Ogdoad of Hermopolis, and then continuing with other gods. As it was said of Ptah, so was it said of Amon, that all deities were manifestations of different aspects of his nature. Having created the gods, Amon left the earth to be manifested in the heavens as Re, the light-giver. At night, he could be recognized in Thoth, the moon. Amon ruled his creation, sailing above the world in a boat during the day.

A fourteenth century B.C.E. account (which has been preserved in a thirteenth century document) extols Thebes, the holy city of Amon, as the first city ever created. A statement carved on the doorpost of the second pylon at Karnak, describes the emergence of the primeval hillock out of Nun. Like the mythology of Hermopolis and Heliopolis, this account testifies that the sacred domain of the god Amon was located on that mound. Human beings were created to construct other cities modelled on Thebes.

The world of Egypt was a unity. Societal patterns harmonized with nature and to disturb one was to disturb the other. Order (*ma'at*) had to prevail over disorder and disharmony. The pharaoh was the embodiment of order and power (Amon) and the transmitter of divine stability.

The Cosmology of Elephantine and Philae

The two small islands of Elephantine and Philae are located in the Nile river at the southernmost boundary of Upper Egypt, just below the first cataract. Here, from earliest times, the ram-headed god, Khnum, was worshipped. According to the local mythology, Khnum created the heavens, the earth, and the underworld. He brought the Nile up from Nun by way of two caverns, one of which supplied the waters to the south of the islands and the other the waters to the north. Thus, Khnum controlled the life-giving waters of Egypt. From Nile mud, Khnum fashioned human beings on a potter's wheel. Indeed, every child was said to have been molded by Khnum. Under the name Khnum-re, the god was associated with the sun as the living soul of the sun. Thus Khnum became a fertility god linked to the two life-giving and life-sustaining resources of Egypt, the Nile river and the sun.

The Cult of the Dead

One of the most interesting dimensions of Egyptian religious thought was the refusal to accept the finality of death. In Mesopotamia, the story of Gilgamesh demonstrated that death was the end of life and that there was no joy to be had in an afterlife. For the most part, the Egyptians remained in a constant state of denial. Perhaps their environment contributed to their thinking.

The Egyptians knew that bodies buried in the desert, the red land that bordered the black land, would not decay. Body fluids simply evaporated, leaving only skin and bones. Archaeologists have found perfectly preserved desiccated bodies that were buried before the Dynastic period. As Egyptian communities developed, the need to prevent the decay of the body became a major concern and a cult of the dead came into being. From the study of ancient inscriptions we have learned a great deal about their mortuary beliefs.

The earliest Egyptian texts concerning the dead are the Pyramid texts of the third millennium B.C.E. The sophisticated nature of these writings suggest that they reflect much older, well thought through, concepts. Included are hymns, prayers, incantations and innumerable mythic themes. Two distinct mythological patterns were dominant. The first was Heliopolitan and linked to the sun god Ra. The other was from Abydos and was Osirian. These two patterns not only existed side by side but at many points melded with one another.

Because great emphasis was placed on body preservation, the art of mummification was highly developed as part of priestly responsibilities in the cult of the dead. Priests would make an incision in the left groin of the cadaver, through which they extracted the vital organs — liver, lungs, stomach and intestines. Each organ was cleansed and placed in one of four canopic jars, each under the protection of one of the sons of the god Horus. The heart, which was considered to be the organ of intelligence, was left in the body. The brain, which we recognize as the organ of intelligence, was sometimes left intact, but during the Middle Kingdom (c. 2000-1780 B.C.E.) was withdrawn through the nostrils by using an iron hook. Body cavities were filled with linen balls or sometimes with mud to preserve physical features.

The embalming or mummifying process required seventy days. The body was desiccated by being soaked in natron. Tissue was preserved through anointing with oils and resins. The entire corpse was then wrapped with linen bandages. The greater the stature and wealth of the individual, the more elaborate and costly the mummification rites. For example, wealthier clients were wrapped in bandages on which incantations had been written; for poorer clients plain linen strips were used.

According to the Heliopolitan myth, the pharaoh was the incarnation of Horus the Elder, the physical son of the god Ra, and was, therefore, a divine being. According to the Ra mythology, which we outlined above, the sun was born anew each morning, reached full maturity at noon, and declined into old age at eventide. As it entered the underworld, the sun was named Auf. As Auf, it passed through the twelve provinces (hours) of darkness where it overcame serpent-like, demonic powers, before it could be born anew the next morning.

At death, the pharaoh joined or was identified with Ra. The accounts of his translation varied. For example, according to one myth, he was ferried across the Lake of Lilies by a boatman who demanded that he prove his royal identity. In other texts, the pharaoh became a falcon and winged his way into heaven. In still others, he ascended a ray of the sun, as if it were a staircase, to assume his place among the immortals. The story of Si-nuhe, which was composed during the twentieth century B.C.E., records the death of King Amen-em-het and states that the divine monarch "ascended to heaven and merged with the sun disc, the divine body became one with his creator" (Wilson, p. 18f). On arrival in heaven, the pharaoh underwent purification rites in the sacred celestial lake. Food in heaven came from offerings that were supposed to be offered through perpetuity at the sepulchral shrines, or which came by sucking the breasts of the goddesses associated with Ra, or from the harvests of the celestial fields.

Stellar myths, as old as the solar myths, presented a somewhat different interpretation of the afterlife. The multitude of the stars became associated with the dead who had risen to heaven. The entrance to the Great Pyramid of King Cheops was designed so that it pointed directly toward the polestar — perhaps to guide the stellar flight of the monarch.

The Osirian cult, with its completely different mythological pattern, merged with the solar-stellar rites and ultimately dominated them. The most complete and unified version of the Osiris myth was preserved by Plutarch (first century C.E.). Unfortunately, Plutarch could not read ancient Egyptian and was, therefore, dependent upon what priests, who were not particularly interested in the most ancient traditions, told him. Nevertheless, comparison with references to the myth in ancient texts suggests that what Plutarch recorded is substantially accurate.

According to the myth, Geb, the earth god, and Nut, the sky goddess, were the parents of Isis, Osiris, Nephthys and Set. Set and Nephthys were paired, but Nephthys remained barren until one night when she managed to get Osiris drunk and embraced him sexually. The child born of the union was Anubis, the jackal god, who presided at embalming rites and was popularly known as "the master of mummy wrapping."

Set was represented as an adversary, the embodiment of evil. He was born prematurely, emerging from his mother's womb through an opening he tore in it. He had white skin and his red hair was despised by the Egyptians who compared it to the hide of an ass. Set was jealous of Osiris and plotted his brother's death. Some scholars have suggested that Set may have been a representation of the fringe area of the desert, which always seemed to be pressing in to take control of the rich black land.

The key figures in the myth are the divine triad — Isis, Osiris, and their son Horus. Isis, the mother goddess, represented the Egyptian ideal of womanhood. It was she who imparted the essence of domesticity to women and revealed techniques for grinding grain and weaving linen. It was she who domesticated men by educating them in the concept of marriage, and revealed to them the secrets of curing illness and disease. When Osiris, who was king of Egypt, went abroad, she ruled in his place. When he was murdered and dismembered, she gathered his scattered body parts, reconstituted them, and with the help of Anubis, mummified the body. As Osiris' devoted companion, she sought always to protect her mate against evil. When he was killed, her mourning rites provided a model for mourning women in Egypt. She was the magician goddess, the sorceress and the model mother-wife.

She symbolized the rich alluvial plains made fertile by the inundation of the Nile (Osiris).

Osiris, the father god figure, may have been an historical king who, through folklore, became the ideal monarch and who, ultimately, was deified. In the earliest texts he is a fertility god and identified with the soil and vegetation — with the corn that springs to life from a dead seed, and with the Nile, which was depicted as flowing from his penis. He was associated with regenerative life forces, and thus combined in himself fecundity and kingship.

However, it was as a god of the dead that Osiris made the greatest impact on Egyptian life. According to legend, he was born at Thebes on the first of the five intercalary days created for the sky goddess, Nut, by Thoth. At the moment of his birth, a voice was heard in the temple, crying out that a great and good king was born, and that the lord of all was entering the world of light. As an adult, he was supposed to have been tall, handsome, and dark-skinned. When his father, the earth god Geb "retired," Osiris became lord of Egypt and Isis was his queen. He taught men such agricultural skills as the growing of grain and grapes. He showed them how to manufacture implements. He instituted the cult of the gods. Because he wished to spread his divine gifts among all nations, he left his throne in the hands of Isis and, with Thoth, his grand vizier, set out to win Asia. As an advocate of non-violence, he overcame opposition with gentleness, and won allegiance from people by playing various musical instruments and by singing.

When he returned to Egypt, he fell victim to a plot. According to Plutarch's account, Set and seventy-two co-conspirators prepared a banquet to which they invited Osiris. The centerpiece was a magnificently wrought casket, designed to fit the form of Osiris. Set offered to give the casket to the one whose body would conform to its pattern. One by one the conspirators tried and failed to fit into the coffin. Of course, when Osiris lay down in the casket, he fitted perfectly. The conspirators slammed the lid shut, sealed it and hurled the chest into the Nile. It was carried into the Mediterranean and floated to Byblos.

After a desperate search, Isis recovered the chest, returned it to Egypt and concealed it in the Nile marshes. Set discovered and dismembered the body, then scattered the fourteen severed parts throughout the countryside. Isis gathered thirteen of the body parts, failing only to recover the phallus which had been devoured by the Oxyrhyncus crab. She made the body whole, constructed a clay penis, transformed herself into a vulture and by the beating of her wings animated the corpse. She then returned to her female form, copulated with the resuscitated Osiris and gave birth to a son, the divine Horus, the third member of the triad.

The basis for this myth may lie in Osiris' origin as a fertility god through whom the inert earth received the seed that became a living plant. The physical evidence of this symbolism has been found in tombs. In the early dynastic era, corn kernels were placed in Osiris boxes within the tombs of the dead. Indeed, in the tomb of Tutankhamon, there was found:

> . . . a long narrow box containing a frame outlining the mummiform silhouette of the god Osiris. It contained alluvial Nile mud sown with corn. The grains had germinated in the darkness of the tomb, and had thus recreated a sprouting and new-born outline of Osiris, symbol of resurrection. Of human size, it had been wrapped in linen like a mummy. (Desroches-Noblecourt, p. 84)

The Tutankhamon Osirian box is presently on display in the Cairo museum. The dead king became Osiris, monarch of the realms of the dead. The divine son, Horus, reigned as pharaoh on earth. The fusion of myths preserved the notion of the divinity of the king as established in the Ra mythology, but extended it into the afterworld in a different way than in the Heliopolitan cult.

At first, only the pharaoh was believed to become one with Ra or with Osiris in the afterworld. During the First Intermediate Period (c. 2250-2000), when nobles and princes were in control of the country, the privilege was extended to the nobility. During the New Kingdom, when merchants and farmers — the common people — acquired wealth, they too enjoyed the immortality once reserved for the monarch.

The emotional appeal of the Osirian cult is obvious. Osiris had lived as a human — a king, to be sure, but human. He was a good person, betrayed to death by the envious conspirator, Set. Osiris' sister-wife, Isis, had mourned her loss, just as in all ages the living have mourned the beloved dead. She was the mourning mother-goddess who understood human pain and suffering. But Osiris had conquered death and achieved immortality, and to his followers he offered the same victory over the grave. His son Horus, who was god incarnate, carried on his father's earthly responsibilities. Thus we have what is perhaps the earliest holy family — father, mother and son.

Furthermore, the Osirian myths provided models for all people. For the ruler, the myth pointed back to the ideal ruler. For the citizen, the myth portrayed ideal family relationships as well as the responsibilities of husband and wife, parent and child. The images of Isis cradling the infant Horus on her knee or suckling him at her breast "formed the foundation for Christian figures of the Madonna and Child" (Budge, pp. 220-221; Larue, 1990, pp. 184-187). The priestly mummification of the body paralleled Isis' reconstruction and preservation of Osiris' body. As Osiris overcame death and was portrayed as a mummy-wrapped form with a green or black visage, so other dead bodies, wrapped as mummies with darkened skin, would, through the enactment of sacred burial rituals and the pronouncement of incantations, transcend death and achieve immortality.

The form assumed by the deceased in the afterlife is not really clear. There was the *ba*, which is often interpreted as the soul, which seems to have come into existence at the moment of death, possessing both material and immaterial form. It is usually depicted as a human-headed falcon or as a stork, but it could assume the form of other creatures if it so desired. Although it had freedom of movement, it often sought the protection of the tomb at night. Then there was the *ka*, which was more closely related to the physical body. It came into existence when the person was born, and it seems to have been regarded as a protective genius. It was represented in the tomb by statues that were almost life-size. At the moment of death, the *ka* separated from the body and did not die. It travelled to the west where it was welcomed by the goddess Hathor, then strengthened before returning to the mummy. The tomb was known as the house of the *ka*. Offerings made at the tomb sustained the *ka*; when offerings ceased, the *ka* perished. It is not hard to understand why monarchs sought to protect their tombs containing their *ka* statues from pillage and violation. It is also clear why the officials of the cult of the dead promised eternal protection of the tombs and the continual offering of food for the *ka*.

After magical rituals (including the opening-of-the-mouth rite) were performed to promote "life" in the afterworld, the body was entombed and the sepulchre was sealed. From this point on, the deceased was on his or her own in the realm of the dead. Armed with spells and talismans to protect against evil or to influence the gods, and with passwords and statements from the Book of the Dead, the deceased travelled the space between the living and the dead. Led by Anubis, he was brought to a tribunal of deities in the Hall of Two Judgments, where Osiris presided as chief justice. Forty-two judges representing the forty-two nomes of Egypt, each in mummy-form and each holding a knife, were seated around the hall. In addition, the gods and goddesses of the Heliopolitan hierarchy were present, each seated on a throne. Thanks to the Book of the Dead, the deceased knew the proper address to be made to each deity and was able to recite the "negative confession" through which was made a denial of guilt, evil action and sin. A second judgment, involving the weighing of the heart of the deceased (the seat of volition) against the feather of truth, was conducted by Thoth. Standing beside Thoth was the fearsome devourer — a creature part crocodile, part hippopotamus and part lion. Presumably, those who failed to pass the test were consumed on the spot. Those who passed the second judgment were led by the god Horus to the throne of Osiris and enabled to enter the sacred realm as an *akh* — a glorified being — to enjoy the association of friends and to be sustained by regular funerary offerings.

Of course rites varied, depending on the ability to pay. What was promised in the myth and by the priesthood was a future in eternity wherein the joys surpassed those of the one's earthly sojourn. When it became apparent that the guarantee of perpetual mortuary care failed and the promised offerings were not being made, tombs began to carry inscriptions begging passersby to make offerings to the dead, promising in return that the deceased would commend the donor to the gods. Sometimes magical formulae were employed to aid the dead. When tombs were violated and their contents stolen, inscriptions promising curses that would befall the robbers were added.

Ancient Egyptian Wise Men and Skeptics.

No doubt, many Egyptians accepted literally the symbolic animal and human representations of the divine. Sophisticated worshippers, whose beliefs we are slowly beginning to understand, recognized qualities of divinity in these symbolic figures, and moved beyond the physical to recognize and appreciate a sacred oneness that permeated all life. As Henri Frankfort has expressed it, the Egyptians saw the universe "suffused with life" and human life "integrated with the life of nature." (p. 28f) At the same time, within this notion of sacredness, there was a practical, secular wisdom and a daring skepticism. Perhaps the variety of religious beliefs moved Egyptians away from the formulation of dogmatic, once-for-all-time-revealed theology. Such an atmosphere may have encouraged the exchange of ideas, the questioning of sacred "truth," and the freedom to exercise some form of critical thinking.

Secular wisdom was taught in the schools of the wise. Although the teachers told their students that the moral and ethical life patterns they espoused were favorable to the gods, they did not claim that their wisdom was revealed or god-given. Their teachings were drawn from what they experienced and witnessed in life, and their instruction was designed to maintain a balanced, perhaps even a serene, society. For example, from the fragments of the teachings of Prince Hor-dedef, the son of the fourth dynasty pharaoh Khufu (Cheops), we learn that he advised his son to take a wife, beget a son, and to prepare a place for the son and a burial place for himself — all patterns accepted as normal and proper at that time. The aged Ptah-hotep, the vizier of King Izezi of the fifth dynasty (25th century B.C.E.), looked back over his lifetime and offered advice for meaningful leadership. He taught students how to play the socio-political games so necessary to gain approval, win favors and get ahead politically. For example, one should bend one's back and bow before a superior, look down in humility when he spoke and laugh after he laughed, so that he might feel good. He believed that the responsible man would have a family, with a carefully chosen wife for whom he would provide food, clothing, and ointments to keep her happy. Students were warned to avoid legal disputes with a wife, and to keep away from other men's wives. One should never be puffed up with wisdom, but be open to insights, even from those deemed ignorant, because no single individual could know everything. Justice was to be pursued, and all fraud or dishonesty eschewed.

The list of wisdom teachings could be extended to include the "Instructions for Meri-ka-re" provided by his father sometime after the twenty-second century, or the words of Amen-em-opet from the fourteenth century, and those of Ani, given during the thirteenth or twelfth century B.C.E. It is enough to recognize that these teachings were practical guides to successful living. They were taught in schools to the sons of men of influence. They gave guidance regarding what to avoid and what to pursue. They were not theological instructions; they were purely secular.

From that same school of thinking came the songs of the harpists. These musicians performed at the funerary banquets which were part of the mortuary ceremonies. What is unique is that, on occasion, they brought their critical thinking into their presentation. Their songs have been found inscribed in tombs, such as that of Pa-Aton-em-heb at Sakkarah, from about 1375-1360 B.C.E., and that of Nefer-hotep at Thebes, from about 1350-1320 B.C.E. The British Museum's Papyrus Harris 500, from about 1300 B.C.E., also contains a version (Wilson, p. 467).

As noted on pp. 48-49, the harpist sang that he had listened to the practical teachings of the wise men including the words of Imhotep and Hor-dedef. But, he asked, what has happened to these wise men and teachers? He had seen the tombs of the god-pharaohs and noted that their houses of eternity, like those of the wise men, had been pillaged and lay in ruins. The promise of perpetual tomb care given in burial rituals had been negated. He sang:

> Their places are gone
> As though they had never existed.

His comments on beliefs in the afterlife raised the question of how can one know the facts for sure, or how does one test the theology? Concerning the promised afterlife, he noted:

> No one ever returns from there,
> To tell of their conditions,
> To tell about their needs
> Or to comfort our hearts (minds)
> Until we go where they have gone.

How, then, does one live in the face of the uncertainty concerning the validity of accepted beliefs? He recommended:

> Follow your wishes as long as you live.
> Put myrrh on your head,
> Dress in fine linen,
> Anoint yourself with perfumes fit for a god!
> Add to the joys that you have
> And don't be faint-hearted
> Follow your desires and be good to yourself!

In the refrain which followed, the harpist added:

> Spend the day in happiness
> And don't weary of it!
> Look! no one can take his goods with him.
> And look! no one who has departed ever returns!

The harpist did not outrightly deny the existence of the gods. He was a skeptic who raised legitimate and thoughtful questions about beliefs and theology. His focus was on the present, not on the hope for a future existence. His recommendation concerning how life could and should be lived is reminiscent of the advice of the barmaid to Gilgamesh, which we discussed in chapter 5 on Mesopotamia.

To what degree the men and women of the various strata of Egyptian society actually accepted theological dogmas, or how many raised the kind of thoughtful questions found in the harper's song, we cannot know. What is important is to recognize the presence of skeptics in the ancient kingdoms of the Nile.

References

Breasted, James H., *The Dawn of Conscience*. New York: Charles Scribner's Sons, 1933.

Budge, E.A. Wallis, *The Gods of the Egyptians*. 2 Volumes. New York: Dover Publications, 1969. Reprint of 1904 edition).

Carter, Howard and A.C. Mace, *The Discovery of the Tomb of Tutankhamen*. New York: Dover Publications, 1977. Reprint of 1923 edition published by Cassell and Company, London.

Daniel, Glyn, *The First Civilizations*. New York: Thomas Y. Crowell Company, 1968.

Desroches-Noblecourt, Christiane, *Tutankhamen*. Boston: New York Graphic Society, 1963.

Fairservis, Walter A. *The Ancient Kingdoms of the Nile*. New York: The New American Library (A Mentor Book), 1962.

Finegan, Jack, *Light From the Ancient Past*. Princeton, New Jersey: Princeton University Press, 1959.

Frankfort, Henri, *Kingship and the Gods*. Chicago: University of Chicago Press, 1978 (Phoenix Edition).

Harrell, James A. and V. Max Brown, "The World's Oldest Surviving Geological Map: The 1150 B.C. Turin Papyrus From Egypt," *Journal of Geology*, 1992, Vol. 100, pp. 3-18.

Kaster, Joseph, *Wings of the Falcon*. New York: Holt, Rinehart and Winston, 1968.

Kees, Hermann, *Ancient Egypt*. Chicago: University of Chicago Press, 1977 (Phoenix Edition).

Larue, Gerald A., *Old Testament Life and Literature*. Boston: Allyn and Bacon, Inc., 1968.

Larue, Gerald A., *Ancient Myth and Modern Life*. Long Beach, Calif.: Centerline Press, 1988.

Larue, *The Supernatural, the Occult and the Bible*. Buffalo, New York: Prometheus Books, 1990.

Lichtheim, Miriam, *Ancient Egyptian Literature. Vol II, The New Kingdom*. Berkeley, Calif.: University of California Press, 1976.

Maugh, Thomas H., "Ancient Bakery May be Clue to Egypt's History," *Los Angeles Times*, March 20, 1992 p. A5.

Moscati, *The Face of the Ancient Orient*. Garden City, New York: Doubleday and Company, Inc., 1962 (Anchor Edition).

Murray, Margaret A., *The Splendor That Was Egypt*. New York: Hawthorn Books, Inc. 1963.

Piankopff, Alexandre, *The Shrines of Tutankhamon*. New York: Bollingen Foundation, Inc., 1955. Harper Torchbook edition, 1962.

Smith, William Stevenson, *Ancient Egypt*. Boston: Museum of Fine Arts, 1960.

Steindorff, George and Keith C. Seele, *When Egypt Ruled the East*. Chicago: University of Chicago Press, 1957.

Wilson, John A., trans., "The Story of Si-nuhe" in: James B. Pritchard, edit., *Ancient Near Eastern Texts Relating to the Old Testament*. Princeton, New Jersey: Princeton University Press, 1950, pp. 18-22.

Wilson, John A., "A Song of the Harper" in: James B. Pritchard, edit., *Ancient Near Eastern Texts Relating to the Old Testament*. Princeton, New Jersey: Princeton University Press, 1950, p. 467.

7

Israel and Judaism

Human life in ancient Palestine can be traced back as far as the Paleolithic period (70,000-35,000 years ago). Excavations at Mount Carmel and in the region of the Sea of Galilee have produced evidence of the presence of Carmel Man and Galilee Man who were prototypes of the Neanderthals. As we noted earlier, one of the earliest human villages has been found at Jericho and dated to some 10,000 years ago.

Long before the coming of the Hebrew people, Palestine was occupied by those who spoke a northwest-semitic language, who were known as Canaanites. But the land of Canaan did not develop in isolation. The strategic location of Palestine as a land-link between the great river civilizations of Mesopotamia and Egypt both enriched its cultural development and made it subject to invasion.

To the north was the Hittite nation, which came into being during the second millennium when Indo-Europeans swept into Anatolia (modern Turkey), took control of the existing native population, and established a feudal nobility under a monarch with limited powers. During the 16th century, as the Hittites pushed into Syria and Upper Mesopotamia, they clashed with the Egyptians who were, at that time, in control of Palestine. Hittite documents indicate that their conflicts were usually settled by treaties. One Hittite contribution to the local culture was the discovery of the techniques of working with iron. Until the twelfth century they held a virtual monopoly on the production and use of iron for weapons and tools.

To the northeast of Palestine were the peoples who had settled in Mesopotamia, in the valleys of the Tigris and Euphrates rivers. They are known to us as Sumerians, Chaldeans, Babylonians and Assyrians and each impacted on the Palestinian area through trade and military campaigns. To the south was the desert and Egypt. Whenever Egypt expanded its holdings northward, Palestine was embraced in the expansion. Therefore, long before the Hebrew people moved into the area, resident Palestinians were in active communication with the outside world.

The Sea People

During the twelfth century, bands of people associated with Mycenaeans began to roam the seas in search of new places to live. Mycenaean beginnings go back to the nineteenth century when waves of Indo-Europeans (related to those whom we will note entered India) invaded Greece. Some disturbance appears to have taken place (perhaps an earthquake) which disrupted normal Mycenaean life. These "Sea People," as they are called in Egyptian literature, first threatened the Egyptian delta during the reign of Ramesses III (c. 1184-1153 B.C.E.). Ramesses was able to contain their invasion. The invaders are called Danaoi (Danuna or Denyen in Egyptian sources) and Achaeans — both names were used by Homer to designate Greeks. It has been suggested that the Hebrew tribe of Dan, which does not appear to have been part of the early Hebrew federation (Gen. 49:16-17), may have been connected with the Sea People as the Danoi. (Raban and Stieglitz, p. 41)

A second wave of Sea People broke into two parts. One group, the Tjikal or Tjeker, attacked Syria. The second, known as the Peleste or Pulusatu, attacked Egypt. After a bitter land and sea battle, the Peleste were held to an area along the Mediterranean coast to which they gave their name so that it was known as the Philistine Plain; today it includes the Gaza strip. The Peleste or Philistine people established themselves in five major cities: Ashkelon, Ashdod, Ekron, Gath and Gaza, but their influence extended far inland. The northern group, the Tjikal, settled around Tyre and Sidon where they merged with the resident Canaanites and came to be known as the Phoenicians. Their attacks on an internally weak Hittite empire broke the power of that people, so that the Hittites were never again a threatening force in the ancient Near East.

The Peleste, the Sea People, the Philistines, gave the name "Palestine" to the area (Peleste-land = Palestine). So far, none of their literary materials have been found in the excavation of their cities and the few seal inscriptions that have been recovered remain undeciphered. We know that the cult of Dagon (the name means "corn"), one of their deities, was well established and associated with fertility and productivity in the ancient Near East long before the Philistine invasion. As the Hebrew nation began to develop, the Philistines constituted a threatening power on their western flank.

The Canaanites

At the time the Hebrews began to make their presence felt in ancient Canaan, and when the Philistines established themselves on the sea coast, there was already a well-developed, centuries old, Canaanite culture in existence. Large cities, surrounded by massive protective walls built of huge stones, were located throughout the land. There was active trade with Syria and with Egypt. Indeed, Egypt controlled many of the central cities.

Because the culture was primarily agricultural, Canaanite deities tended to reflect the survival needs of farmers and herdsmen. El was the father god, Asherah, the mother goddess, and their children included Ba'al, the god of the fertilizing rains, Yam, the sea god, Mot, the god of death and the harvest, Anat, a fertility goddess who was the consort of Ba'al, and so on. Important information concerning Canaanite mythology has come from inscribed clay tablets found during the excavation of Ras es-Shamrah in northern Syria. It is now clear that existing Canaanite customs impacted directly on the developing Hebrew culture.

For example, the Canaanite new year began in the fall of the year when the god Ba'al, having been released from the power of Mot (death), was resurrected to bring the fertilizing autumnal rains so important to local agriculture. Present day Jewish observations of Rosh Hashannah, which means "Head of the Year," occur in the autumnal period, because the new year festival date was, apparently, borrowed from the Canaanites. Canaanite tripartite temples, with two free-standing pillars in front, provided the model for the Hebrew temple which Solomon built in Jerusalem. In the Canaanite shrines offerings were made, sacrifices performed and fertility rites associated with their deities enacted. When the Hebrew kingdom was established, Canaanite religion with its strong fertility emphasis afforded a supplement, or an alternative, to Hebrew religion. I Kings 18 relates a dramatic story of the conflict between followers of the Canaanite god of fertility, Ba'al, and followers of the Hebrew god, Yahweh, to determine which deity provided the life-sustaining rain. At a sacred site on Mount Carmel, the Hebrew prophet Elijah contested the priests of Ba'al. Of course, because the account is a Hebrew story, Yahweh was the winner.

The Hebrews

The real origins of the Hebrew people are lost in the mists of history. There is absolutely no way that historians can fix dates for Hebrew heroes like Abraham and Moses nor authenticate stories told about them. The name "Hebrew" (*'ibri*) has been associated with the name of a people called *habiru* mentioned in cuneiform documents from the 20th to the 11th centuries. These people are variously described as hired mercenaries, servants bound to masters, or as settled people. The El Amarna (14th century) tablets from Egypt refer to the *'apiru*, a group invading Palestine. It has been suggested that the terms *'apiru*, *habiru* and "Hebrew" (*'ibri*) all relate to groups that had renounced a relationship to an existing society and who, by a deliberate action, withdrew from some organization or rejected some authority. Through such action, they became freebooters, slaves, employees or mercenaries. Some scholars suggest that many of these people had settled in the hill areas of ancient Palestine.

In the Bible, the word "Hebrew" becomes an ethnic term used interchangeably with "Israelite." Scholars identify the Hebrews of the Bible with one branch of a Northwest Semitic group, related linguistically to Canaanites, Edomites, and Moabites. During the late Bronze or early Iron age, the Hebrews moved into settled life. Hebrew history begins in the late 12th century, when tribal groups began to move aggressively into the Canaanite communities. Stories about events prior to that migration must be categorized as legend and myth. Nor is there any way to corroborate the anecdotal accounts of the invasion of Palestine by the Hebrews as recorded in Joshua and Judges.

The enthronement of the first Hebrew king, Saul, marked the beginning of a transition from tribal federations to monarchy. There are several stories associated with his coming to power. The one that scholars find fits the cultural context best, and which is believed to be the earliest and perhaps the most reliable, is found in I Samuel 11: 1-11, 15. The Trans-Jordan city of Jabesh-Gilead was under siege by the Ammonites. Unable to cope with their powerful attackers and desirous of saving the city from siege, the citizens of Jabesh-Gilead offered to surrender the city and become Ammonite slaves (11:1). The Ammonite commander, Nahash, agreed, but demanded as a symbol of servitude that the right eye of each inhabitant be gouged out. During the grace period before the sealing of this dehumanizing contract, word of the situation reached Saul.

Saul, a huge man, became violently angered, experienced what was described as a divine seizure (to designate his charismatic role), and summoned the various Hebrew tribes to come to the rescue of the Jabesh-Gileadites on the threat of violent retaliation should they fail to respond. The besieged city was delivered and Saul was crowned king. Other stories, including that which tells of Samuel's selection of Saul (I Sam. 9-10:6), were composed and added later. These additions can be recognized as religious fiction.

Biblical writers almost ignored Saul's role as king. Despite the fictional account which records his divine selection, Hebrew writers who exalted the regal line stemming from David, Saul's successor, found it necessary to create a tale explaining how Yahweh realized that his divine choice of Saul was an error. The first king was rejected in favor of the second.

The story of David's rise to power, as recorded in what is recognized by scholars as "the early source," appears to have been written by someone who knew him personally. According to this tradition, Saul suffered from a depressing mental illness which was eased by music. David, a shepherd, played the lyre for the ailing king, won his affection (I Sam. 16:14-23), became a bosom friend of Saul's son, Jonathan (18:3ff), married Saul's daughter, Michel (18:20ff), and became a popular hero (18:7). Rivalry developed between Saul and David and when Saul died, David became king.

Under David's military rule, the Hebrew kingdom reached its greatest strength. As David aged and became impotent, his eldest son, Absalom made a bid for the throne (I Kings 1:1-5ff). Absalom was killed and Solomon became co-ruler with David. The diarchy ended with David's death. Solomon reigned as an oriental despot, lavishly spending the wealth of the kingdom, enslaving the people through forced labor gangs, and in a multitude of ways paving the way for the split of the nation into the two separate states of Israel and Judah, which occurred after his death.

The Jewish scriptures are called Tanak (Torah: Law; Nebhiim: Prophets; Kethubhim: Writings). They are also known by the Christian designation as "The Old Testament." This Christian label obviously denigrates the Jewish writings by placing the Jewish writings in a lesser position as the *Old* Testament to the Christian scriptures, the *New* Testament.

It is important to remember that Roman Catholic and Eastern Orthodox versions of the Old Testament contain some Jewish writings not accepted as authoritative by Jews and Protestants. These latter groups place these writings in a collection called "the Apocrypha" — a designation which means "hidden" or "concealed."

Tanak began as temple literature at the time of the construction of the temple in Jerusalem during the reign of King Solomon (late 10th century B.C.E.). At that time, the earliest sections of the Torah, certain Psalms and Wisdom Sayings (Proverbs) and the beginnings of the history of the Hebrew kingdom, were composed. Later, each writing was expanded and in some cases rewritten.

Like the temple literature of Mesopotamia and Egypt, Hebrew temple writings contained an account of creation, the divine giving of the laws, and defined the basis for the relationship between temple and state. As in other cultures the chief god of a people was said to be responsible for creation, so in Hebrew scriptures it was claimed that the Hebrew god, Yahweh, brought the cosmos into existence.

The earliest Hebrew creation story (Gen 2:4b-3:24) points out that freethought, independent thinking and the ability to make moral choices is a factor that lifts the human above the animal. According to the story, the Hebrew deity, Yahweh, created a man to be a gardener in the divine orchard. The man (*adam*) was formed out of clay (*adamah*) as a potter might hand-fashion a vessel. This notion was not uniquely Hebrew and appears in Mesopotamian and Egyptian creation stories. To animate this clay figure, Yahweh blew into the image's nostrils, in the same way that Arab mid-wives initiate life in a newborn infant. As the clay figure began to breath, it became a live human being. This breath that animated the figurine should not be interpreted as a "soul;" such an idea was foreign to early Israelite thought. What is clear is the Hebrew notion of the relationship of breath to life.

Because the man was alone, Yahweh decided to create a helper for him. His earliest efforts were failures. Yahweh molded creature after creature from the same clay that was used to form the man. After animation (presumably in the same way the man had been given breath) each new creature was presented to the man to be named or given an identity. Of the multitude of creatures presented, none was acceptable as the required helper. Finally, the deity put the man to sleep and extracted a rib from his side from which he formed a woman (*isshah*). This creature was accepted. The man and woman were to live together in Yahweh's garden with the animal companions and work the divine estate.

Within the orchard were two trees, one of which was forbidden to the couple, namely, "The Tree of the Knowledge of Good and Evil." Despite the divine prohibition, the woman, prompted by a serpent (a creature which had been formed as a companion for the man and one that was more astute than other life forms), made an independent decision and ate the fruit, sharing some with her husband. That act immediately separated the human from the animal, for, as Yahweh was to admit to the heavenly court, "Now the man has become like one of us, knowing good and evil" (Gen. 3:22). In other words, the ability to make moral choices, to think for oneself and act on personal decisions, had up to that moment been reserved only for divinities. The woman, who was later named Eve (Hebrew: *Chavah* = life giver) had, by her act of free will, forever broken the barrier that would have kept human beings on an animal level and unable to make moral choices. She and her husband Adam (named after the female earth from which he had been formed) became the first thinking and choosing creatures.

Only one thing now separated the human and the divine: immortality. Out of fear that Adam or Eve might eat of the tree of immortality and achieve divinity, Yahweh expelled them from the sacred garden. Their re-entry was prevented by cherubim, monstrous human-animal figures like the *kerubim* that protected the entries to Assyrian precincts, and by a magical, flaming sword. As in the story of Gilgamesh, a snake was blamed for the failure of humans to gain immortality.

Unfortunately, the importance of the acquisition of the free, independent, right to choose was ignored by later writers, particularly Christian. The role of Eve as liberator was also ignored. Emphasis was placed on the loss of paradise and on Eve's "sin." Ancient Hebrew writers, however, never lost sight of what was implied in this mythic tale of beginnings. The temple priests would have preferred that all Israelites obey the laws which they claimed Moses had received from Yahweh. At the same time, they recognized that, by their very nature, human beings could and would make choices that would affect the weal or the woe of the individual, the family and the nation. They threatened that choices that did not harmonize with the divine laws brought disaster and they attempted to trace every historical downfall to some individual or group who made the wrong choice. But the freedom of rational or irrational choice was a human freedom, and as we shall see, provoked some freethinkers to challenge the authority of the revealed faith.

Just as Hammurabi and other Mesopotamian rulers claimed to promulgate laws of state endorsed by one god or another, so Hebrew temple literature claimed that Yahweh had given their laws to Moses. Analytical and linguistic studies by modern scholars have demonstrated that, over the one thousand years during which Tanak was composed, the laws were written, re-written and over-written. Changing times, changing events called for new thinking. What seemed to remain constant were laws requiring sacrifice and offerings to the temple, by which the priesthood was fed, rewarded and maintained.

The close relationship between the temple and the palace that was common in other nations was obvious in the Hebrew state from the side-by-side location of palace and temple in Jerusalem. Solomon's royal palace was built right next to the temple and, as ruler, he had immediate access to the innermost shrine.

The early Hebrew kingdom was religiously pluralistic. It acknowledged the existence of other gods. It was also monolatrous (*not* monotheistic), which is to say that, without denying the existence of other deities, the primacy of Yahweh was affirmed. Hebrew law stated that Yahweh was to be recognized as the chief deity: "You shall have no other gods before (ahead of) me" (Exod. 20:3). When Solomon built the temple of Yahweh in Jerusalem, he also built cultic centers on the nearby Mount of Olives, where he paid homage to the chief fertility deities of Sidon, Moab and Ammon (I Kings 11).

Rivalry between the various cults continued long after the time of Solomon in the divided kingdoms of Judah and Israel. Temple worship in Jerusalem was cluttered with rituals and artifacts not associated with Yahwistic religion (II Kings 23). For example, when Assyria took control of the area, accouterments associated with Assyrian gods were added to or replaced vessels used in Yahweh worship (2 Kings 16). The serpent mounted on a pole, which temple literature associated with Moses and the wilderness period (Num. 21:6-9), was recognized as coming from a non-Yahwistic source. Thus, when King Hezekiah sought to purge temple worship and return it to what he deemed to be purified Yahwism, the serpent idol was destroyed as a non-Yahwistic artifact (II Kings 18:4).

In the seventh century, prior to the conquest of the Kingdom of Judah by the Babylonians, the prophet Jeremiah complained that Judean families cooperated in the worship of the fertility goddess Ishtar (Jer. 7:16-18), that Jews who fled to Egypt argued that the goddess was a better provider than Yahweh (Jer. 44:15-19), and that sacrificial offerings to the Canaanite deity Ba'al and the burning of incense to other gods was rampant (Jer. 19:1-6). In other words, the religion of ancient Israel was monolatrous, recognizing Yahweh as the central deity, without denying the reality or the existence of other gods. It was during this same time that King Josiah, seeking to centralize Judahite worship at the Jerusalem temple, destroyed local Yahwistic cult centers and came into conflict with the *bamah* priests (local cult center officiants) who declined to participate in the Temple rites (2 Kings, 23).

Judaism

It was not until the time of the exile (6th century B.C.E.) that the Jews became monotheists and claimed that their deity was the *only* God and that all others were, therefore, false. It happened this way. When Nebuchadnezzar, king of Babylon, conquered Judah at the beginning of the sixth century B.C.E., he took leaders of the Jewish community into exile. Just before Cyrus of Persia conquered Babylon and freed the Jews later in the sixth century, there emerged from among the Jewish captives a prophet whose name is not known, but whose words have been appended to the writings of Isaiah of Jerusalem (chs. 40-55). This man, whom scholars name "Deutero-Isaiah" or "Second Isaiah" or "Isaiah of Babylon," proclaimed the uniqueness of Yahweh and provided the first clear statement of monotheism to be found in the Bible (45:5, etc.). He denied the existence of other gods and proclaimed Yahweh as the only deity. From that time on, monotheism became a dominant theme in Judaism, separating it from other contemporary religions. Shortly after this prophet made his proclamations, Cyrus released the Jews and permitted those who wished, to return to Jerusalem and reestablish their temple and religion. Judah became a satrap of Persia. The developing religion was Judaism.

Deutero-Isaiah made a unique interpretation of the Babylonian sojourn. As he witnessed the scapegoat ritual of the Babylonian Akitu or New Year festival (see chapter 5 on Mesopotamia), he envisioned captive Israel as a scapegoat bearing the suffering for the sins of others. In the magnificent poetry of chapters 52:13 to 53:12, he depicted captive Israel in the role of the Akitu human scapegoat who bore the accumulated evil of the city on his shoulders and healed and cleansed the sin-laden city with his suffering. So for Deutero-Isaiah, exiled Israel had become the suffering servant "despised and rejected by men" who was "wounded for our transgressions and bruised for our iniquities." Exiled Israel bore "the chastisement that made us whole and with his stripes we are healed."

Later, in Judean religion, the official scapegoat ritual became a temple ceremony. Two goats were presented to the high priest on the Day of Atonement (Lev. 16). One was killed as a sin offering and its blood was sprinkled in the innermost shrine of the temple. Over the head of the other goat, the "goat for Azazel," the high priest confessed the sins of Israel. Then, the sin-laden goat was driven into the wilderness where it was killed by the demon of waste places, Azazel. Much later, this scapegoat rite, together with that of the sin-bearer role in the

Akitu festival, provided a basis for the Christian interpretation and explanation of the death of Jesus as the sin-bearer for the world.

Zoroastrianism

When the religion of Zoroaster was adopted by Persian rulers, the influence of this faith system impacted upon nations under Persian control. The prophet Zoroaster had proclaimed a single deity, Ahura Mazda, in control of the world. Ahura Mazda was the god of justice, truth, integrity. The presence of evil in the world was explained in terms of an anti-god force (Ahriman). Zoroastrianism pictured world history in decline, moving from a golden age toward a day of final judgment. Ultimately, all history would cease and rewards and punishments based on individual behavior would be meted out to the living and the dead. This theology impacted on developing Judaism. Up to this time, Hebrew religion had taught that death separated humans from Yahweh (Pss. 6:5, 88:5-6) and that good and evil were punished in this life (cf. Pss. 27, 35, 37, etc.). The book of Daniel, which was written about 167 B.C.E., reflects the Persian-Zoroastrian points of view. It emphasizes the declining stages of history, the proximity of the end of time (12:5-13), and a resurrection of the dead with judgment in the afterlife (12:2-3).

At the time when Daniel was written, the Jews were under severe persecution from the Greeks who had defeated Persia and were in control of Palestine. Daniel's message, with its counsel of passive perseverance in the face of the most destructive opposition, constituted a failure of nerve. The Jews who accepted the idea set forth in Daniel, no longer believed in the possibility of humans to overcome the evils of the world and develop a peaceful and wholesome society. They abandoned faith in humanity in the conviction that the end of the age was at hand, and that the faithful would, ultimately and automatically, be victors and be rewarded.

The power of Persia was broken by Alexander the Great. Between 334 and 323 B.C.E. Greek armies took control of Egypt, Palestine, Syria and Mesopotamia and extended Greek authority up to the borders of India. This take-over initiated the Hellenistic period in Judea. Alexander's successors sought to force Greek culture on its conquered peoples. A group of Jews known as the *hasidim* (a label derived from the Hebrew word *hesed* which signifies "loyalty") came into being. They were "the pious" whose loyalty to the Torah never wavered during the most horrendous persecution.

It was about this time, perhaps shortly after the collapse of Persian rule, that the secular book of Esther was composed (it contains no reference to a deity). It is not an historical document, but is a short story exalting the role of a Jewish heroine, Esther, who saves the people from persecution. Esther is not a model orthodox Jewess. She does not keep kosher food laws. Mordecai, her uncle, is named after the Babylonian god, Marduk. The story contains entertaining exaggerations. For example, the gallows built by Haman, the villain in the story, was 50 cubits (75 feet) high! Money that was to be raised by confiscating Jewish property was estimated at 10,000 talents or the equivalent of 25 million dollars or more today! The story is really a grim reminder to a people buffeted by great powers, of the ever-present danger of perecution by a tyrant — not necessarily a king, but rather the power-hungry, attention-loving, minor official whose uneasy ego could be threatened when a single man of conviction refuses to conform to the tyrant's demands for public esteem. The book of Esther is a humanistic statement, exalting the individual who stands up for what he or she perceives to be the right. The story provides the basis for the Jewish festival of Purim.

The Sects of Judaism

Some Jews fought against the Greek oppressors. The Maccabean revolt (168-165 B.C.E.) pitted Jews, who followed their rebel leaders, against the powers of one of Alexander's successors, the Greek Antiochus IV, who ruled from Syria. These Jews rejected the passivity expressed in the book of Daniel and refused to wait for divine rescue at the end of time. Led by Judas Maccabeus, they were ultimately victorious. Subsequent struggles for power within Judea weakened the success of their bid for independence. It was only when Simon, one of the Maccabean brothers, took control (141-135 B.C.E.) that the Jews really breathed the pure air of freedom. It was during this troubled period that the Jewish religious community began to splinter into varying schools of interpretation or thought. Sects known as the Sadducees, the Pharisees, the Essenes, the Sicarii, the Zealots, the Therapeutae and ultimately, the Christians, came into being.

The Sadducees were pro-Greek, aristocratic temple priests, experts in the Torah and in rituals of sacrifice. Their name may have been derived from Zadok, the famous priest in the time of David and Solomon (II Sam. 8:17, 15:24; I Kings 1:34). Because at times the offices of high priest and governor were combined, the Sadducees tended to be involved in high-level politics. Politically, they were committed to independence and to the concept of a theocratic state, as were most Jews. Although they were opposed to foreign domination, they did not object to the introduction of foreign elements into Jewish life. They retained what might be called the "old religion" with belief in Sheol as the place of the dead. They rejected the Pharisaic beliefs in an afterlife and in the existence of angels. When confronted by situations not covered in the Torah, they enacted new laws.

The Pharisees, whose name may have meant "separatists," were a group of lay leaders committed to the purification of Judaism through meticulous observance of moral and ceremonial laws. They supported the temple cult but were uneasy about the relationship between the temple priests and the government. Most often they were identified with synagogues, which were the local, autonomous gathering places for worship, where prayers and scriptural study took place. In addition to the study of the Jewish scriptures, the Pharisees emphasized the teachings of the elders or what was called "the oral tradition" (rejected by the Sadducees). They professed belief in ideas borrowed from Persia, such as the resurrection of the body, and a future life where rewards and punishments would be meted out in accordance with behavior in this earthly life. They also believed in angels through whom revelations would come. Later, they developed a belief in a Messiah who, like David, would be a military leader who would set the Jews free.

The Essenes, whose name may have meant "the pious ones" or "the holy ones," may have developed out of the *hasidim*. For some unknown reason, perhaps to separate themselves from the Pharisees or the Sadducees, they felt compelled to withdraw to the shore of the Dead Sea. The discovery and excavation of a Jewish religious settlement at Qumran, and the recovery of numerous scrolls and thousands of manuscript fragments, have led many scholars to identify the Qumran sectarians with the Essenes, despite the fact that nowhere in the manuscript materials is such an identification made. The scrolls come from several different centuries and therefore may provide evidence of the evolving concepts of the wilderness community.

The Dead Sea Essenes (if such they were) appear to have been motivated by some religious ideas that we have recognized as originating in Persia. Like the author of Daniel, they believed they were living in the last days before a final battle would establish the kingdom of the righteous Jews. Because they felt they were being misled by temple authorities (Sadducees), they withdrew to the wilderness to live according to the Torah and to prepare God's way in fulfillment of Isaiah 40:3

("In the wilderness prepare Yahweh's way"). The proper or right way to live appears to have been expounded by an unknown "Right Teacher" or "Teacher of Righteousness." The "right way" required living in a wilderness community composed of those who, having yielded up their private possessions to the group, had been formally initiated. The community was structured with various authoritative ranks and required strict obedience to regulations. They were waiting for the coming of the end of time and the final battle between the Sons of Light and the Sons of Darkness. This war of the end would culminate in victory and rewards for the Sons of Light (with which they identified themselves). They appear to have believed in the coming of a messiah who would suffer and perhaps die in accordance with an interpretation of the suffering servant passages in Isaiah 52:12-53:13. The discovery of what have been recognized as "ink wells" and desks suggests, that among other activities, these monastics engaged in copying accepted Jewish scriptures (no evidence of the secular book of Esther was found). They also created their own religious documents, which are now known as "The Dead Sea Scriptures." Some of their teachings parallel those that were to appear later in Christian documents.

The Sicarii, or dagger men, were revolutionary **Zealots** who did not hesitate to use violence in their opposition to the Roman control of Palestine. **The Therapeutae** were healers, located primarily in the huge Jewish community in Alexandria, Egypt. The **Christians** were followers of Jesus.

Ancient Jewish Skeptics

Among the ancient religious thinkers in Israel, there were skeptics, but whether these skeptics can be classified as atheists is a matter of debate. A number of the Psalms echo a believer's feelings of abandonment by Yahweh. For example, the author of Psalm 13 asks,

> How long, O Yahweh? Will you forget me for ever?
> How long will you turn your face away from me?

The speaker is obviously in trouble and feels abandoned by his God. The Psalm ends with a statement of assurance that Yahweh will rescue or perhaps has rescued the believer. The same pattern appears in other psalms: Psalm 22 ("My God, why have you abandoned me?"), Psalm 31:10 ("Have pity on me, O Yahweh for I am in distress"), Psalm 38:22 ("Do not forsake me, O Yahweh, my God, do not be far from me!"),

Psalm 102:2 ("Do not hide your face from me in the day of my distress!") as well as Psalms 6, 55, and 69. Sometimes the sense of being forsaken takes on a national overtone. In Psalm 10, the writer asks: "Why, O Yahweh do you stand so far off, and hide yourself in time of trouble?" He then delineates the success of the wicked over the righteous and calls on the deity to physically abuse evil persons (10:15) — a wish or prayer that is echoed elsewhere (Pss. 11:6; 57:6-10; 137:9, etc). Often the Psalmist makes promises of what he will do to repay Yahweh for his deliverance (Pss. 22:22; 71:17-14; 79:13; 106:47, etc.). The sense of divine abandonment does not imply rejection of the idea of a god; it does reflect feelings of lack of contact with the deity, and some question about the relationship of the deity to the well-being of the nation or the individual. The true believer, on the other hand, does not hesitate to suggest that because of his good behavior he has earned and deserves divine protection (Pss. 17; 18:23-24; 26, etc.).

In each instance, the Psalmist is in a miserable state and feels abandoned by his God. The hopeful endings may signify the belief that rescue has come (Pss. 30; 32; 34, etc.), or express the hope that somehow rescue will come from the deity (Pss. 27:13; 31:14ff; 54; 55, etc.). In such straits the believer was vulnerable and there were those skeptics who asked, "Where is your God when you need him?" One Psalmist writes (Psalm 3:2) that his adversaries suggest that "there is no help for him in God," which might suggest that the pious ones find him unworthy of divine help.

An accusation of non-belief that appears in two versions of a psalm (one from a Judah collection, Psalm 14:1, and one from an Israel collection, Psalm 53:1) does not refer to intellectual atheism. Rather, the concern is with corrupt or unethical behavior that the believer can only attribute to one who acts as if there were no God. The passage reads: "The fool says in his heart, 'there is no God.'" The poem then goes on to describe the asocial behavior of an evil cabal that preys on the people. What the writer is saying is that these persons act as if there were no deity. They do not call upon Yahweh and they ignore the possibility of divine punishment. Although the passage cannot be taken as proof of the existence of atheists in ancient Israel, Robert H. Pfeiffer wrote that "According to the Pious, this attitude of the ungodly amounted to rank atheism." (p. 638)

There is, however, clear evidence of the presence of secularism and skepticism in ancient Israel. The courts of the ancient Near Eastern world entertained what have been called "wisdom schools." These learning centers were led by men who taught what today would be labelled "courses in pragmatic ethics." The Hebrew term for the teachings is *hokmah*, a word that "is related to a root meaning 'skill' or 'care' and came to imply 'skill in living'" (Larue, 1968, 1970, p. 389). The instructor was a wise man (*hakam*) who often presented a lesson in the form of a proverb (*mashal*). The Hebrew proverbs are similar to, or parallel, the collections of wisdom teachings from Egypt and Mesopotamia. These latter sayings were preserved in many forms. Some have been recognized as student copies, others are formally preserved documents (Larue, 1988, pp. 70-73, 81-85).

The ancient wise men were secularists. Their practical (as opposed to theoretical) teachings drew insights from observations on life. They taught by directing their students to what could be seen and recognized in everyday life. Then, adding their own interpretations, they encouraged the reaching of conclusions that would demonstrate that it was preferable to be wise than foolish.

When the Hebrew monarchy began in Israel (10th century B.C.E.) the custom of having wise men instruct potential leaders was well established throughout the ancient world. The Hebrew royal court followed that trend. It is clear that Hebrew wisdom writers did not hesitate to borrow from international sources. For example, the Bible contains one collection of wisdom sayings titled simply "Words of the Wise" that are drawn, in part, from an Egyptian collection by Amen-em-ope (Prov. 22:17-24:22). As Robert Pfeiffer noted (p. 652), "The blunt statements about using the rod in bringing up children which we read in 22:13f" is "taken from the Wisdom of Ahikar" — a 7th century B.C.E. Assyrian folk tale (Larue, 1988, p. 82f).

In the beginning, the schools were run as secular institutions by the palace, not by the temple. As Pfeiffer put it, "We know positively that among the Israelites the secular school flourished before the pious" (p. 650). One example from an early wisdom teaching in Proverbs illustrates the practical, non-theological nature of the instruction. An instructor is telling his students about his personal observation of a young man who was about to become involved with a seductive married woman whose husband was away on a business trip:

> For as I looked from the window of my house
> And peered out through the lattice,
> Watching the simpletons,
> I observed among them a foolish young man,
> Crossing over on the street near her corner,
> Walking toward her house,
> In the twilight, as evening came on,
> At the beginning of night and darkness.

A woman comes to meet him,
Dressed up like a prostitute and just as persuasive,
Boisterous and bold,
Her feet do not stay at home
Now in the street, now in the market square
Lurking at every corner.
She grabs him and kisses him
And brazenly says to him,
I have sacrificial food on hand
For today I fulfilled my (religious) vows;
And now I have come out to meet you,
I was looking for you and now I have found you.
I have spread my couch with sheets of gaily colored Egyptian linen.
I have perfumed my bed with myrrh, aloes and cinnamon.
Come, let us drink our fill of love until morning,
Let us revel in our mutual love-making.
For my husband is not at home,
He has gone on a long journey,
He took his moneybag with him
And he won't return until the moon is full.
She persuades him with her seductive charm
And compels him with her enticing words.
Suddenly he goes with her
Like an ox being led to the slaughter
Like a stag moving towards a trap
Until an arrow pierces its heart,
Like a bird fluttering into a net
Without being aware his life is in danger. (Prov. 7:6-23)

The teacher concludes with a warning that the woman's house is the open door to death (vs. 27). There are no religious overtones in the account. There is no reference to a divine command: "You shall not commit adultery" (Exod. 20:14; Deut. 5:18). The message is nothing more than straightforward practical advice designed to keep young pupils out of trouble. The wisdom is based on what the teacher had observed, and was, no doubt, reinforced by what the young men had already witnessed of life in their community. Religious admonitions were developed later and added to the secular counsel.

Pfeiffer demonstrated just how the infusion into the secular by the religious occurred:

> That wisdom originally had nothing to do with religion and could even be regarded as antagonistic to piety is also shown by the prophetic denunciations against the wise (Is. 5:21; 10:13; 28:9; 29:14; 31:2; Jer. 4:22; 8:8f; 9:23; 18:18). The early idea of wisdom as technical skill is still found in Proverbs side by side with the new religious idea of wisdom (6:6; 21:22; 24:3-6; 30:24-28, etc.), and such human wisdom is contrasted with religion and morals (3:7; cf. particularly Pss. 119:97-104).
>
> Another proof of the gradual identification of secular wisdom with religion and morals is furnished by the growing legend of the wisdom of Solomon, traditional author of two large sections of Proverbs. In the earliest stage (I Kings 5:12; cf. 5:7), Solomon's wisdom consisted of diplomatic skill in making a commercial agreement with Hiram king of Tyre. In a second stage, he was identified with the anonymous king of an Oriental folk tale, in which his wisdom became that of a shrewd judge (I Kings 3:16-28). In the third stage, presented in the post-exilic story of his dream at Gibeon (I Kings 3:4-15), his wisdom contrasts with riches and power and acquires a religious aspect by being divinely bestowed. In his interviews with the Queen of Sheba (10:4-8), Solomon's wisdom was typically Oriental: the ability to propound and solve riddles. Finally, Solomon's wisdom was identified with scholarship (4:29-34) and he was said to be the author of 3,000 proverbs, 1005 songs, and disquisitions on botanical and zoological subjects — a scholarly production far in excess of the extant books attributed to him in later ages (Prov., Eccl., Song of Songs, Pss. 72 and 127, The Wisdom of Solomon, the Psalms of Solomon, and the Odes of Solomon). (p. 651)

Obviously, the process of overwriting the secular with the religious took place over a long period of time. The pattern traced by Pfeiffer in the tradition of Solomon as a wise man occurred also (as Pfeiffer went on to demonstrate) in the wisdom sayings of the book of Proverbs — a discussion too lengthy for consideration here.

Proverbs does contain one unique collection: the words of Agur, son of Yakeh, from Massa (Prov. 30). Agur is truly a seeker whose words Pfeiffer described as "the confessions of a skeptic unable to understand God and his creation" (p. 649). My translation, which follows, draws directly from the scholarly interpretations of William McKane and R.B.Y. Scott. Agur opens with a statement reflecting his weariness in the search for answers. He is despondent because he feels that he lacks the authoritative insights usually associated with wise teachers. He begins in what must surely be a mocking tone:

> There is no God, there is no God,
> and I am at the end (of my resources).
> Surely, I am more beast than man
> and human insight eludes me.
> I have neither learned wisdom
> nor been given knowledge of the Holy One.

He is a skeptic and he challenges his listeners with the skeptic's request for evidence. After all, he asks ironically,

> Who has ascended to heaven and come down again?
> Who has held the wind in his fists?
> Who has wrapped up the waters in a garment?
> Who has established the ends of the earth?
> What is his name? and his son's name?
> If, indeed, you know?

His challenge, which I interpret as confrontive but which McKane suggests "must be taken as a cry of despair and not as a militant dogmatic atheism" (p. 647), evokes a response by an orthodox teacher. The respondent, immersed in the security of his own faith, argues that the revelation of the divine is demonstrated and "confirmed in the experience of the religious man" (Scott, p. 177). He says:

> Every saying of God has stood the test!
> He is the shield of those who trust him.
> Don't add to his words
> Lest he correct you and prove you to be a liar!

The poem then moves away from the dialogue to a prayer (Prov. 30: 7-9) and finally on to wisdom teachings. Agur's words make clear the presence of those who, through their search for validation of the claims of Judaic faith, question, challenge and disbelieve the claims of divine revelation.

A different form of challenge and inquiry can be found in the book of Job. This document was probably written during the sixth century B.C.E. when the Jews were in exile in Babylon. In the Prologue, the writer sets the stage for the central portion of the book. The reader is introduced to Job as a man who dutifully fulfills all the requirements of faith and is judged to be fully "righteous" by the writer of the story, by the Jewish God and by God's son who was named "Satan" — a term which means "adversary" or "challenger."

The reader is introduced to a scene in heaven where the father God glows with approval as he contemplates Job's righteousness. His son, Satan, like sons everywhere, challenges his parent's interpretation. He suggests that the basis for Job's good behavior and dutiful execution of the requirements of the faith rested solely on the rewards he received for being good. If Job were to lose the blessings that accrued from good behavior, he would curse God. The father God agreed to a test. Consequently, Job lost all his possessions in one disaster after another, and all his children died. Job did not curse god.

In the next heavenly scene, Satan is confronted by his father who, perhaps a bit smugly, pointed out that, despite having lost everything, Job had not cursed his God. Satan suggested that, because Job had lost only property and family but had not personally been affected, the test was incomplete. The father and son agreed to submit Job to physical suffering without killing him.

In the next earthly scene, Job still did not curse his God. The poor afflicted man is pictured sitting in misery, using a shard of broken pottery to press pus out of sores that covered his body from head to foot. He is visited by three friends who came to comfort him.

The body of this dramatic story deals with Job's challenge to divine fairness. He asks, "Why is this happening to me?" and "What have I done to deserve this treatment?" In the name of justice he calls for a response from his God. His attitude and his questioning horrify his comforters who seek to justify traditional Jewish theology by suggesting that Job must have done something to warrant this treatment, that his children probably did something to offend the deity, that Job is probably not getting what he really deserves, and so on. Job responds to each accusation and continues to cry out for an answer and for some understanding of divine justice (cf. 27:1; 30:20, etc).

Finally, the deity responds (ch. 38). The response provides no answer to Job's anguished questions. Indeed, God's response has been labelled that of a "bully." He calls Job "ignorant." He contrasts the limitations of Job's human knowledge with divine wisdom and power. He compels Job to repent.

In the Epilogue, we are told that Job's fortunes are restored, that he raises more sons and daughters and, in a fairy-tale ending, we are led to presume that "he lived happily ever after." The theologizing by his comforters (who really brought no comfort but only arguments) was discredited and Job was asked to intercede for them.

The book of Job challenged the current Jewish theology that taught that suffering resulted from violation of divine commands, and that the good life was earned by obedience to what was considered to be revealed truth. What the writer of Job was claiming was that no one knew what went on in the realm of the divine and that human suffering could be recognized as nothing more than a divine whim to test the endurance of a human being. Indeed, in something of the same spirit as that of Agur from Masseh, the writer was questioning the validity of Jewish theology. He demonstrated that, because humans could not know or understand the nature of divine justice, the best one could do was to live the good, righteous, and proper life as best one could, in full knowledge that no answer would be coming from the realm of the supernatural.

The same challenging, skeptical spirit appears in Ecclesiastes, which scholars believe was written during the fourth century B.C.E. The speaker is Qoheleth, a term that means "teacher" (not "preacher"). The setting is the schoolroom where the wise master is instructing his students. He poses as Solomon who, because of status and wealth, had the opportunity to explore and taste the best that the world could offer.

Two questions trouble Qoheleth. The first is: how does one find meaning in what appears to be a meaningless existence? The second comes as response to the conclusion of the book of Job: how does one live when the heavens are silent and there are no answers to basic human questions of meaning?

His opening statement employs the Hebrew word *hebel* which means "vapor" or "breath" and signifies that which is unsubstantial or empty or meaningless. His introduction could be translated either:

Vapor of vapor, everything is vaporous
or
Meaninglessness of meaninglessness, everything is meaningless

Several facets of life have impressed Qoheleth: the constancy of the natural cycle, the fragility of life and knowledge, and the emptiness of the desperate human search for meaning. In his role as Solomon, he claims to have sought meaning through wisdom, humor, possessions, the creation of buildings and parks, and in wine, women and song — but all to no avail.

Qoheleth is a realist. He recognizes that in life some human conditions are to be preferred over others. Companionship is preferable to loneliness. Wisdom is better than folly even though both the fool and wise man end up in the same place, the grave. He is aware that good and evil coexist but, he notes, ultimately both the evil man and the good man also end up in the grave. He is no atheist; indeed he cautions against efforts to deceive the deity by making vows which one will subsequently ignore (Eccles. 5). He does not believe that human beings have any real knowledge of God or of the ways of the deity. Nor does humankind have any clue as to what the meaning of life might be, other than that which they themselves give to it:

> I have seen the God-given tasks with which men busy themselves and that God makes each happening acceptable for its time, and also that, although he has put in men's minds the quest for that which is hidden, man can not comprehend what God has been doing from start to finish (Eccles. 3:10-11).

How does one live in the face of this enigma? He answers:

> I know that there is nothing better for men than to be happy and enjoy themselves so long as they live and that when men can eat, drink and find enjoyment in their work, this is a gift from God (Eccles. 3:12-13).

He rejects claims that humans have revealed knowledge of the afterlife and, indeed, he questions whether an afterlife even exists. He observes:

> The fate of men and the fate of animals is the same; as one dies so dies the other for all have the same breath of life. Man has no superiority over the animal, both are void of meaning. Both go to the same place; all are from the dust and all return to dust. Who knows whether the life of man ascends upward and the life of beasts descends to the underworld? (Eccles. 4:19-21).

What humans do know for certain is that they will die. As for the dead:

> they know nothing at all, and they experience no rewards and (ultimately) they are not remembered. Their love, their hate, their passions have completely perished, and never more do they have any part in what happens beneath the sun. (Eccles. 9:5-6).

What does one do in the light of this finality? His response is like that given to Gilgamesh by the barmaid and that sung by the Egyptian harpist:

> So go, eat your bread with enjoyment and drink your wine with pleasure, inasmuch as God has already accepted what you do. Let your garments be white, and let there be no lack of oil for your head. Enjoy life with the woman you love all the days of the meaningless life God has granted you under the sun, for this is your compensation for your work and your toil in this world. Whatever your hand undertakes, do it with your might, for there is neither work nor thought nor knowledge nor wisdom in Sheol (the grave) for which you are bound (Eccles. 9:7-10).

The pragmatic dimensions of his teaching fit the life patterns of the modern unbeliever. Without faith in an afterlife or belief in judgment by a deity, one seeks to enjoy life to the full, finding meaning in the work that sustains existence. At the same time, one recognizes that, inasmuch as all other humans are, whether or not they acknowledge it, in the same existential situation, the skeptic seeks to help them to enjoy this one life to the fullest. The Teacher is skeptical of current Jewish belief. He denies the claims of revealed religion and questions the reality of the afterlife which was part of the new theology derived from Persia.

Ancient Humanistic Concerns

Humanistic concerns emerge in the words of some prophets who dismiss the efficacy and significance of standard temple worship with its rituals of prayer and sacrifice. These men are not atheists or agnostics. They represent a religious humanism that acknowledges the existence of a deity, but insist that the core of the religion is to be found in human concern for fellow humans. For example, the 8th century prophet, Amos of Tekoa, announced what he claimed were the words of Yahweh:

> I hate, I despise your feasts.
> I find no pleasure in your sacred rituals.
> I will not accept your grain offerings
>   nor your burnt offerings

nor your fatted animal peace offerings.
Get rid of your noisy chanting.
I will not listen to your harp music.
Rather, let justice roll like a mighty river
And righteousness like an everflowing stream. (5:22-24)

The Prophet Isaiah of Jerusalem echoed Amos' thought:

Yahweh says: What do I care about the number of your sacrifices?
I am sickened with the excess of whole burnt ram offerings
And animal fats.
I take no pleasure in bull blood or lamb blood or goat blood.
Who asked that you do these things when you come trampling
my courts to visit me?
Bring no more meaningless offerings.
The stench of your sacrifices is unbearable.
I detest your new moon and sabbath festivals.
They bore me. I can no longer tolerate them.
Your hands are covered with blood!
Wash yourselves and cleanse yourselves!
Take your evil doings out of my sight.
Stop doing evil and learn to do good.
Make justice your aim.
Set things right for those who are wronged.

His contemporary, Micah of Moresheth, put the humanistic concerns in simple but positive terms:

What does Yahweh ask of you?
Only to act justly, to love (humanity) loyally
And to walk cautiously with your God. (6:8).

The parenthetical insertion of the term "humanity" reflects the research of Nelson Glueck (p. 61) and reinforces the humanistic elements of the prophetic rejection of standard Hebrew temple religion.

The Formation of the Jewish Canon

The development of a Jewish canon of scriptures took place over a long period of time (Larue, 1968, pp. 433-442). It was not until the Persian period (5th century B.C.E.) that the final additions were made to the Torah and those five books became the primary guide for Jewish life and worship. By the first century of the Common Era, there was deep concern among Jewish leaders as to which of the many other Jewish religious documents should be accepted as authoritative. By this time, Christianity had come into being and some Christian writers were quoting as scripture writings that Jewish leaders did not accept as authoritative (for example, cf. Jude 14 which quotes from the Book of Enoch, 1:9). Moreover, the Jewish scriptures had been translated from Hebrew into Greek for the Greek-speaking Jews of Alexandria, Egypt, and the Alexandrian collection (now known as the Septuagint) contained writings that were later to be excluded from the Jewish canon and included in the "Apocrypha." The Jews of Qumran not only utilized the generally accepted Jewish scriptures, but were producing their own authoritative writings (up until 70 C.E. when the Romans destroyed the community). Finally, the Samaritan Jews had their own canon of scriptures which included only the Torah because they rejected the prophetic books and writings. Clearly, it was time for the defining of books authoritative for Jewish faith and guidance.

Meetings were held in Jamnia, Israel, between 90 C.E. and about 120 C.E. There were no arguments about the inclusion of the Torah and most of the prophetic books (questions were raised about Ezekiel), but the authority of some writings was debated. For example, the Song of Songs was troublesome because of its fertility overtones and lack of mention of the deity. Today, the contents can be recognized either as secular love poems associated with wedding rituals or, perhaps, as a non-Hebrew ritual piece originating in fertility rites associated with the marriage of a god and goddess. The book was finally included as sacred scripture because Rabbi Akiba insisted that it was really an allegory, representing Yahweh's love for Israel. Later, the Christian Church interpreted the poem as symbolic of Christ's love for his Church (Larue, 1968, p. 393f). The forced nature of these interpretations can be easily discerned by reading the book and interpreting the male's clearly sexual statements as those of the deity.

The final decisions of this council resulted in the inclusion of the books of the Jewish scriptures as we have them today. However, the developing Christian group accepted what we might label as "the Alexandrian canon." This includes some books rejected as authoritative by the Jews (cf. chapter 10 on Christianity).

Critical Inquiry

The claims of the Jewish canon were to come under analysis and discussion. Although it was accepted as fact that the Torah was the product of Moses, about 500 C.E. one Jewish savant wrote in the Talmud that the last eight verses of the book of Deuteronomy, which tell of Moses' death and burial, obviously could not have been written by Moses. Therefore, he concluded, "Joshua wrote . . . eight verses of the Law" (*Baba Bathra*, 14b-15a).

Cautious critical inquiry into the Torah by a Spanish Jewish scholar, Abraham ibn Ezra (c. 1088-1167), produced other problems concerning the claims of divine revelation to Moses. It became clear to ibn Ezra that Moses could not have written the entire Torah, but only parts of it. As we shall see, the undermining of belief in the divine gift of the Jewish scriptures would continue as both Jewish and Christian scholars continued their critical analyses. These inquirers were not skeptics or agnostics. They were devout believers seeking to understand contradictions in their scriptures. Through their studies, they became skeptical of the claims of the Jewish tradition even as they remained devout Jews.

The far-reaching impact of ibn Ezra's research can be seen in the critical work of Baruch (Benedict) Spinoza, a Dutch Jewish philosopher (1632-1677). In the late 15th century, during the Inquisition, Jews in Portugal and Spain were persecuted by Christians and were compelled to convert or to leave the Iberian Peninsula. Those who converted were called "Marranos," but many continued to practice their ancient faith in secret. Spinoza's family did not convert but fled to Amsterdam.

Despite the fact that he was raised in Orthodoxy, Spinoza rejected the Torah and its message. He pointed to the inconsistencies in the Torah, argued that Moses could only have authored certain parts, and suggested that the final compiler of the completed work was Ezra (about 450 B.C.E.) — a position held by many scholars today. He questioned biblical miracles and the divinity of Jesus. Although he had been educated for the rabbinate, Spinoza's rationalist views caused him to be excommunicated. He has been labelled "the God-intoxicated" and his intellectual love of God cannot be contested, but his concept of God was quite different from that of traditional Judaism. He denied that God was either purposeful or personal and claimed that both spirit and matter were attributes of the one substance, nature, that underlies all. He was, therefore a pantheist (Greek: *pan* = all, *theos* = god) — an idea that is at least as old as 3rd millennium B.C.E. Egyptian theology concerning the god Ptah. Ptah was said to have created the cosmos by first conceiving the idea in his mind and then speaking his thought which became reality. Therefore everything, including the other gods (which he also created), were manifestations of the divine Ptah. In other words, the god was in everything and everything was tinged with divinity. Spinoza's pantheism was expressed in his words: "All is in God; all lives and moves in God."

Spinoza called for a secular state, free from ecclesiastical pressures or interference. His rational-critical approach to the Bible reflected opinions and research that were current among biblical scholars of his era.

Almost in reaction to Spinoza, during the eighteenth century, a popular mystical movement known as Hasidism developed among the Jews of Poland. By the nineteenth century, it had spread throughout Eastern Europe. The term "Hasid" was derived from the Hebrew word *hesed* which, as previously noted, has the basic meaning of "loyalty," but which can embrace other expressions such as "graciousness," (Larue, 1967) and perhaps also "pious." Hence, the Hasidim were known as "the pious ones." The tales of the Hasidim are largely legendary but they embrace the kinds of teachings associated with the leaders of the movement. For example, a Hasidic tale (Newman, p. 494), about Rabbi Moshe Lieb of Sasov who claimed that God created everything for a purpose, records his response to the query of why God would create atheists:

> There is no quality and there is no power of man that was created to no purpose . . . But to what end can the denial of God have been created? This too can be uplifted through deeds of charity. For if someone comes to you and asks your help, you shall not turn him away with pious words, saying: "Have faith and take your troubles to God!" You shall act as if there was no God, and as if there were only one person in all the world who could help this man — only yourself.

The question reveals the presence of atheists who engaged in "denial of God" in the Jewish community. The rabbi's response echoes classical atheistic humanism. Atheists are committed to self help and to coming to the aid of others out of the conviction that, because there is no supernatural assistance available, the only possible help must come from other humans. According to the rabbi, the proper response of the "pious" person to human need was to act as the atheist would act in the assurance that this was the most acceptable or best way to respond.

The critical examination of Jewish scriptures by Jewish scholars is on-going. Each Jewish scholar utilizes the best and latest critical and analytical tools which, by their very nature, effectively remove the idea of divinely revealed scriptures. Thus Jewish scholars, without saying so, endorse a position held by non-believers. The Jewish scholar, Samuel Sandmel, in his thoughtful analysis of the Jewish scriptures, employed modern criticism. He observed that the Torah "is still central to Jewish worship, however modified Judaism has become, and however much of the literal has become a whisper rather than a full voice" (p. 535f).

In 1947, the State of Israel came into being and in subsequent years Jews from all parts of the world became part of the population. Here again, the alliance of church and state has demonstrated the ways in which such unions can limit and control human freedom. Up until 1994, the rules and regulations of Orthodox Judaism were dominant in the state. Indeed, prior to the six-day-war in 1967, all business activity, all public transportation, all sources of public entertainment, ceased to operate at sundown on Friday evenings; silence enveloped the communities until sundown on Saturday. Sabbath-day laws were strictly enforced. However, with the acquisition of West-bank territory, the State of Israel had to contend with the rights of Muslims and Christians, particularly in the "Old City" of Jerusalem. The compromise reached provided that Christian businesses would close on Sunday, the Christian holy day; Muslims would close shops on Fridays, the Muslim holy day; and Jews would continue to follow the Sabbath closing regulations. This meant that the city was virtually wide-open for business, travel, restaurant dining and entertainment. What was more interesting was that now Jews could shop at non-Jewish establishments in the Old City. On "pork days" in the Christian Armenian meat-markets, shops were crowded with Jewish patrons who could purchase openly what they previously could only buy surreptitiously before the war. Thus, the control by the Orthodox was somewhat limited.

However, Reform and Conservative Judaism were still denied a voice. It was not until January, 1994, that the Supreme Court in Israel gave official recognition to rabbis from these branches of Judaism by overruling objection by the Orthodox chief rabbinate to the appointment of a Reform Rabbi to the religious council in Tel Aviv. The court ruled: "Banning candidates because of their world-view constitutes discrimination and contradicts the principles of equality." (Kampeas, 1994) The Orthodox establishment continues to refuse recognition of marriages, divorces and other services performed by Conservative and Reform rabbis.

In late 1995, Orthodox political parties demanded that the Labor Party seek adoption by Israel's Knesset of a law requiring that only Israelis born to a Jewish mother or Jews who have converted according to Orthodox standards can have the word "Jew" stamped on their identity card in the "Nationality" box. The Orthodox power over which marriages are accepted as legal affects citizens' tax status and ability to receive social welfare benefits. The law demanded by the Orthodox seeks to close a loophole that allows people converted by Reform or Conservative rabbis in foreign countries to be registered as Jews. The current system is a headache for Israel's Reform Jews as well as for those Jews who wish to marry Christians or Muslims or who do not want to be married in religious ceremonies. Also affected are the 150,000 immigrants from the former USSR who are not technically Jews by Orthodox criteria. Many Israelis oppose the proposed law and vow to fight it. This divisive national problem is rooted in the fact that Israel does not have a written constitution, and hence no clear separation of religion and the state. At the annual conference of the International Jewish Reform Movement, held in Georgia in December 1995, an Israeli couple were married before 5,000 people to highlight the plight of Israelis who cannot marry in Israel. (Shiloh)

Orthodoxy also denies equality to Jewish women who wish to pray at the Western Wall in Jerusalem — perhaps Judaism's holiest site in that it is the only visible remnant of King Solomon's temple. Some Jewish women wish to wear prayer shawls and sing ancient songs of praise to God at the Western Wall. They have not challenged the women-only and men-only sectioning of the wall; they only request equality in worship. Their appeals have been turned down. Once again, the potential restrictions that can arise from the union of church and state become apparent; one segment of a religious faith is endowed with power to limit freedom of expression by another segment of that same faith. (Fineman, p. A2)

Interest in the past has generated several generations of Israeli archaeologists who, although they use the Bible as a guide book for the location of sites and so on, tend be secular and atheistic, rather than religious, Jews. They are not interested in demonstrating that the Bible is accurate in all of its claims nor in proving that it is a divine revelation. The Bible is simply one tool among others to be used as part of their research. They focus on ancient cultures and look at the ancient Jewish religion as one part of the culture. Further, within Israel there is a Humanist group composed of atheistic and agnostic Jews who have no interest in the religion of Judaism and are committed to the separation of Church and State insofar as that is possible within Israel.

In the United States, non-theistic movements have developed out of traditional Judaism. The oldest of these is the American Ethical Union (Ethical Culture), the most recent is Humanistic Judaism.

Ethical Culture

The Ethical Culture movement was started in 1876 by Felix Adler, a Reformed Rabbi. His intent was to create a society that focussed on ethics and ethical behavior rather than on creedal statements. He was keenly aware of the theologies that separated people even as these same theologies embraced the ethical principles that should have united them. The new organization excluded both rituals and prayer from meetings, and Adler stressed "Diversity in creed, unanimity in the deed. This is that common ground where we may clasp hands as brothers, united in mankind's common cause." He was not an atheist and his organization has welcomed both those who believed in a deity and those who do not believe. For Adler, theological concepts were not the issue; ethical religion was. As a consequence, the society is composed of persons who were raised in various faith systems as well as those who come from atheistic or secular backgrounds.

From the beginning, the Society was active in social outreach. In 1877-78, it established the first free kindergartens in New York and San Francisco, the District Nursing Service which developed into the Visiting Nurse Service, and the Tenement House Building Company for families and orphaned children. In none of these enterprises were any efforts made to proselytize or indoctrinate the beneficiaries. The list of other social activities is extensive and includes the founding of the Workingman's School (1880) which was to become the Ethical Culture School (1895), the Visiting and Teaching Guild for Crippled Children (1889), and the Bureau of Justice in Chicago (1888) which was to become part of the Legal Aid Society (1905). Ethical Culture was also active in the formation of the National Association for the Advancement of Colored Peoples (1909). The various societal involvements are far too numerous and complex for mention here, but are all associated with ethical expression and with humanistic concern and outreach, not with theological issues. The movement spread to Europe and soon an international association of Ethical societies came into being which continues today as The International Humanist and Ethical Union. The headquarters for the American Ethical Union is located in New York.

Ethical Societies have formulated statements of purpose which express their basic commitments and concerns. The one that follows is endorsed by the Ethical Culture Society of Los Angeles:

> Ethical Culture is a humanistic religious and educational movement inspired by the ideal that the supreme aim of human life is working to create a more humane society. Our faith is in the capacity and responsibility of human beings to act in their personal relationships and in the larger community to help create a better world. Our commitment is to the worth and dignity of thc individual and to the treatment of each human being so as to bring out the best in him or her. Members join together in ethical societies to assist each other in developing ethical ideas and ideals, to celebrate life's joys and support one another through life's crises, to work together to improve our world and the world of our children.

The Death of God Movement in Judaism

During the 1960s, a movement titled "The Death of God" came into being. The Jewish scholar, Richard L. Rubenstein, wrote a powerful book titled *After Auschwitz* in which this idea became explicit. The death of the deity, he wrote, was both a cultural event and a cultural fact. For Rubenstein, God died at Auschwitz. When millions of Jews went to their death, calling on the traditional God of history to intervene and to save, and the only response was silence, the Jewish God became alien to the Jewish community — God was dead. The statement is, of course, symbolic, signifying the movement of society away from the sacred toward the secular. According to Rubenstein, the implications are tragic: humans are left alone in the wasteland.

The movement faded. Traditional Judaism continues to function without reference to Rubenstein's insights and claims. But there are Jews who have turned away from the ancient Jewish God concept and who do not find life a tragic existence in the wasteland.

The Death of God arguments provoked controversy but produced no organized following. It reflected the impotency of the ancient Jewish God-notions for contemporary society, but left atheistic and agnostic Jews without any sense of historic bonding and with only the exuberance many felt in the freedom from the restrictive beliefs of the past.

Humanistic Judaism

In 1959, Emil Weitzner published a book titled *Meditations of a Humanist.* In the Preface he made reference to a small group of Jews who had been meeting for two years. These individuals had abandoned the historic Jewish belief in a deity:

> They are religious in their sense of mystery and wonder and of man's limitations, insignificance and oneness. But having no faith in deity, they can pray neither to a Thou nor a Him nor a Whom, whether conceived as an existent entity or as a partner in an I-Thou dialogic relation or as process, force, intelligence, Eternal or principle. These persons nevertheless have need — as do those who profess faith in a personified deity, a "personal God" — for articulating their identification with and amazement at the mystery and their sense of unity.

In partial response to this sense of need, Weitzner composed a set of meditations in which he paraphrased certain biblical Psalms, omitting or replacing God-images and God-language with humanistic and naturalistic phrases. His work represented the plight of Jews who found no comfort or meaning in traditional Judaism since it was out of touch with the modern scientific world. Old ideas no longer evoked response. Something new was needed.

Almost in response to Weizner's plight, The Society for Humanistic Judaism came into being in 1969. Initiated by Sherwin Wine, a rabbi trained in the Reform tradition, the Society was composed of Jews who recognized their Jewish heritage but who were far removed from the religion of Judaism. They did not attend synagogue, they did not pray or express any interest or belief in a deity and they refused to be bound by what they perceived as the parochial interests of Judaism found in Orthodox, Conservative and Reform congregations. They were progressive Jews, involved in the cutting edge of research, literature, entertainment and thought in America and in the world at large. They had been born into Jewish families and hence by birth and familial tradition were Jews, but Jews devoid of the traditions and the authority of the faith. They were not prepared to compromise their intellectual convictions.

The new organization is avowedly humanistic, which is to say that it "affirms the power" of humans and "glorifies the beauty and possibilities of the human mind" in the conviction that humans have the power and ability to solve their own problems and meet their own needs (Wine, 1978, p. 115f). Such a stance does not negate the potential for destructiveness and hurtfulness in humans, but affirms the conviction that humans have the potential of rising to the highest levels of human interaction and cooperation. The new society emphasizes the importance of individual self-respect and autonomy without negating the significance of community. Humanistic Judaism's approach to truth and to life underscores rationality as opposed to authoritarianism, and affirms what might be recognized as situation ethics as opposed to rule book ethics.

The congregations, composed of both Jews and non-Jews, find "meaning in the celebration of life as expressed through the historic Jewish calendar," seeking to "interpret this calendar in a naturalistic way" — which is to say that the rituals are interpreted in a secular manner. There is no "God" language, no prayer, no appeal to the traditional Jewish concept of God, which is considered religiously irrelevant along with the authority of the Jewish scriptures. Nevertheless, "A humanistic Jew, because of a common history and shared religious practices, feels a strong bond to Jews throughout the world. He also feels an important tie with all men who seek to promote individual self-esteem" (Wine, 1978, p. 121). Humanistic Judaism has developed centers in communities where there are large populations of Jews and where Jews have broken from traditional Judaism.

Some Jewish Freethinkers

Individual Jewish thinkers and philosophers have wrestled with the relationship of their traditional beliefs to the developing rationalist and scientific modes of inquiry. Some sought to harmonize the ancient and the modern. Others departed from traditional Judaism — some to become Pantheists, some to become Deists and some to become Atheists and Agnostics.

Moses Mendelssohn (1729-1786), the Jewish thinker and philosopher believed that Judaism and rationalism could be harmonized. For him Judaism was not a revealed religion, it was a revealed law — and it is here that his dependence upon reason is abandoned. General religious tenets, such as belief in God, could, he argued, be established by reason without revelation; but Jewish law was the uniquely "revealed" essence of Judaism and was for Jews alone. He, therefore, represents those who sought to embrace rationalism and accept certain aspects of Deism, while continuing to hold fast to the non-rational acceptance of a special revelation. He was an early advocate of freedom of conscience and freedom of choice as he pled for religious tolerance and the separation of church and state. He argued that the state could neither "control nor regulate the ideas or convictions of its citizens, and must not be allowed to favor one religion over another or to require its citizens to hold particular beliefs as a condition of citizenship" (Jospe, p. 29).

Louis D. Brandeis (1856-1941) was a humanistic Jew whose magnificent contributions to American life lay in the fields of law and justice (in 1916, he became the first Jew to serve on the Supreme Court of the United States), social policy (for example, he pioneered the idea of collective bargaining between employers and labor unions), education (he sought to make business a profession with professional schools) and Zionism (he supported the movement for a homeland for the Jews). He was committed to scientific management in industry, to the use of reason and logic in reaching judicial decisions, and to the protection of the rights to free speech. His Judaism, which did not develop until he was 58 years old, was not related to theological belief but to ethnicity. He was, in all things, a humanistic Jew.

When **Albert Einstein** (1879-1955), the Jewish physicist and mathematician and winner of the Nobel Prize (1922), was asked about his religious beliefs, he refrained from mentioning "God" but talked of "the sense of mystery" which lies at the "root of religion and beauty." When challenged by a rabbi, he responded, "I believe in Spinoza's God who reveals Himself in the orderly harmony of what exists, not in a God who concerns Himself with fates and actions of Human beings" (Franquiz, p. 65). This would suggest that he was a pantheist. Other challenges from Roman Catholics prompted him to speak of his belief in a "great Power" which is the source of order and beauty in the universe, but he rejected anthropomorphic images of deity. His deep social concerns led him to passionate involvement in cultural causes including the defense of African Americans, Jews, minorities and refugees. Science, he believed, should be employed for the benefit of humans: "Concern for man himself and his fate must always form the chief interest of all technical endeavors" (Franquiz, p. 69). Based on his delight and wonder at the basic uniformity of the universe in all of its dimensions, his recognition of unifying principles and his deep concern for and commitment to the world of human beings, perhaps Einstein is best recognized as a pantheist, an agnostic, and a Humanist. A number of his thoughts have been brought together in a collection titled *Essays in Humanism*.

Richard P. Feynman, a Nobel prize-winning scientist who was born into a Jewish family, recounted an episode that dramatizes the gap that can exist between the concerns of conservative Judaism and modern scientific thought. He attended a conference in New York and was housed in the Jewish Theological Seminary. He wrote that he was approached by several young rabbis who said:

> "We realize that we can't study to be rabbis in the modern world without knowing something about science, so we'd like to ask you some questions."
>
> Of course there are thousands of places to find out about science, and Columbia University was right near there, but I wanted to know what kind of questions they were interested in.
>
> They said, "Well, for instance, is electricity fire?"
>
> "No," I said, "but . . . what is the problem?"
>
> They said, "In the Talmud it says you are not supposed to make a fire on Saturday, so our question is, can we use electrical things on Saturday?"
>
> I was shocked. They weren't interested in science at all. The only way science was influencing their lives was so they might be able to interpret better the Talmud! They weren't interested in the world outside, in natural phenomena; they were only interested in resolving some question brought up in the Talmud. (p. 259-260)

As one contemplates this story, it becomes clear that the findings and methods of science and the study of religion can, for some, only meet tangentially. Consequently, popular conservative efforts to modify or water down the teaching of critical thinking and scientific analysis in the public schools will continue.

The list of Jewish freethinkers could be extended. It is enough to show that within the Jewish tradition there are free minds that move away from the binding restrictions of religion to free inquiry, preferring to be led by reason, logic, and scientific inquiry rather than by a dogmatic faith. For an extended discussion see the article by Sherwin T. Wine, "Unbelief in Judaism," which is listed below on p. 137.

References

Adler, Felix, *The Reconstruction of the Spiritual Ideal.* New York: Ethical Press, 1929.

Einstein, Albert, *Essays in Humanism.* New York: Philosophical Library, 1950.

Einstein, Albert, *Out of My Later Years.* New York: Philosophical Library, 1950.

Feynman, Richard P., *Surely you're Joking, Mr. Feynman!* New York: W.W. Norton, 1985, Bantam edition, 1986.

Fineman, Mark, "Israeli Group Chips Away at Walls of Religion," *Los Angeles Times,* Jan. 29, 1994, p. A2.

Franquiz, J.A., "Albert Einstein's Philosophy of Religion," *Journal For the Scientific Study of Religion*, Vol. IV, No. 1, 1964, pp. 64-70.

Friess, Horace L., *Felix Adler and Ethical Culture: Memories and Studies*. New York: Columbia University Press, 1981.

Gaster, Theodor H., *The Dead Sea Scriptures*. Garden City, New York: Anchor Press/Doubleday, 1976.

Glueck, Nelson, *Hesed in the Bible*. Trans. by Alfred Gottschalk. Cincinnati: Hebrew Union College Press, 1967.

Gordis, Robert, *Koheleth: The Man and His World*. New York: Jewish Theological Seminary of America, 1951.

Gordis, Robert, *The Song of Songs*. New York: Jewish Theological Seminary of America, 1954.

Jospe, Alfred, "Moses Mendelssohn" in: Simon Noveck, edit., *Great Jewish Personalities in Modern Times*. Clinton, Mass.: Clinton Press Inc., 1960, pp. 11-36.

Kampas, Ron, "Israeli High Court Grants Recognition to All Rabbis," *Los Angeles Times*, Jan. 29, 1994, p. B10.

Konvitz, Milton R. "Louis D. Brandeis" in: Simon Noveck, edit., *Great Jewish Personalities in Modern Times*. Clinton, Mass.: Clinton Press Inc., 1960, pp. 295-315.

Larue, Gerald A., "Recent Studies in *Hesed*" in: Nelson Glueck, *Hesed in the Bible*, trans. by Alfred Gottschalk. Cincinnati: The Hebrew Union College Press, 1967, pp. 1-32.

Larue, Gerald A., *Old Testament Life and Literature*. Boston: Allyn and Bacon, 1968, 1970.

Larue, Gerald A. *Ancient Myth and Modern Life*. Long Beach, Calif.: Centerline Press, 1988.

McKane, William, *Proverbs*. Philadelphia: The Westminster Press, 1970.

McKenney, John L., "Spinoza, Baruch or Benedict" in: Gordon Stein, edit., *The Encyclopedia of Unbelief*. Buffalo, New York: Prometheus Books, 1985. Vol. 2, pp. 653-654.

Morgenstern, Julian, *Amos Studies*. Cincinnati: Union of American Hebrew Congregations, 1941.

Morgenstern, Julian, *The Message of Deutero-Isaiah in its Sequential Unfolding*. Cincinnati: University Publishers, Inc., 1961.

Nakhai, Beth Alpert, "What's a *Bamah*?" *Biblical Archaeology Review*, Volume 20, No. 3, May/June 1994, pp. 19-29, 77-78.

Newman, Louis I., *The Hasidic Anthology: Tales and Teachings of the Hasidim*. New York: Scribner's, 1934.

Pfeiffer, Robert H., *Introduction to the Old Testament*. New York: Brothers Publishers, 1948.

Raban, Avner, and Robert R. Stieglitz, "The Sea People and Their Contribution to Civilization," *Biblical Archaeology Reader*, November-December, 1991, Vol. XVII, No. 6, pp. 34-52.

Radest, Howard B., *Toward Common Ground: The Story of the Ethical Societies in the United States*. New York: Frederick Ungar Publishing Co., 1969.

Rubenstein, Richard L., *After Auschwitz*. Indianapolis: Bobbs-Merrill, 1966.

Sandmel, Samuel, *The Hebrew Scriptures*. New York: Oxford University Press, 1978.

Scott, R.B.Y., *Proverbs, Ecclesiastes*, The Anchor Bible, Vol. 18. Garden City, New York: Doubleday & Company, 1965.

Shiloh, Dina, "'Who is a Jew' Returns as Israeli Flash Point," San Francisco Chronicle, December 13, 1995, pp. B1, B8,

Vermes, G., *The Dead Sea Scrolls in English*. Baltimore, Maryland: Penguin Books Ltd. 1968 and subsequent years.

Weitzner, Emil, *Meditations of a Humanist*. New York: Behrman House, Inc., 1959.

Wine, Sherwin T., *Humanistic Judaism*. Buffalo, New York: Prometheus Books, 1978.

Wine, Sherwin T., *Judaism Beyond God*. Farmington Hills, Michigan: Society for Humanistic Judaism, 1985.

Wine, Sherwin T., "Unbelief within Judaism" in *The Encyclopedia of Unbelief*, edit. by Gordon Stein. Buffalo, New York: Prometheus Books, 1985. Vol. 1, pp. 369-373.

8

Greece

No other ancient people have contributed more to freethought in the western world than Greece. It was here, in Greece, that philosophy, humanism, and the spirit of critical inquiry came to fullest flower. And it was here that, as never before in human history, the questing spirit was nurtured and blossomed.

Ancient Greece

The settlement of ancient Greece was directly related to geography. Some time between the end of the sixth and the beginning of the fourth millennium B.C.E., the first settlers, men and women of the stone-age, came overland from the east, perhaps from Asia Minor. They did not come in a single migratory movement, but infiltrated slowly over the centuries. Although there appear to have been a few paleolithic and mesolithic communities in existence prior to their arrival, these Neolithic intruders do not seem to have encountered opposition. In the Greek peninsula, with its central mountains, sea-indented shorelines and sea-girt islands, they found a homeland. The climate was pleasant. Hot summers were tempered by cool winds; winters were moderated by the effects of the seas. Fertile, well-watered soil produced crops of wild olives and grapes. The sea abounded in fish, the forests in wild game.

The newcomers built homes on foundations of rough stone with walls of mud bricks and roofs of mud-plastered reeds. Their domesticated animals included cattle, sheep, goats and pigs, and they grew barley, wheat, figs, pears and peas. Their weapons were the sling with clay pellets and the bow with arrows tipped with flint and obsidian points.

Since no place on mainland Greece is more than 40 miles from the sea, overland routes were soon augmented by sea travel. As navigational skills developed, the sea became a major thoroughfare for exchange of products as well as for communication. Ultimately, the naval outreach was to develop contact with Egyptians, Phoenicians, Persians, and others.

Very little can be known of Neolithic notions about deities or their theological beliefs. Clay female figurines may point to beliefs in mother or female goddesses. As time passed, each community developed its own collection of gods and goddesses and each had its own priesthood and sacred locales. The emphases were on the seasonal cycle, fertility, war, and so forth. Intercommunication between settlements may have produced overlapping religious themes, but communal independence negated the growth of what might have become a national theology. In other words, in ancient Greece there were no universally accepted sacred scriptures, no dogmatic theologies, no written codes of divinely revealed moral law. There were, of course, theological writings that included hymns and oracles and prayers, and there were the cultic patterns of the mystery religions — but none of these attained status as a required belief. Such an atmosphere negated the rise of a controlling or all-powerful priesthood and, ultimately, made possible open discussions by philosophers, rationalists and freethinkers.

By its very nature, Greece seems to have encouraged the development of independent communities. During the Bronze Age (c. 2800-1200 B.C.E.), large walled cities and the city-state concept developed. About 2000 B.C.E., hordes of Aryan or Indo-Europeans swept down from northern Greece with their horses and chariots to become masters of the previous inhabitants. They brought with them their gods who joined existing deities. The chief god, Dyaus Pitar, was replaced by the Greek god Zeus. Zeus was the sky god, the father god, the rain-maker. Demeter was the earth mother, whose cult was at a peak of popularity during the formative years of Christianity. Hestia (whom the Romans called Vesta) was Zeus' sister and the virgin goddess of the hearth. Other gods included Rhea, who may have been of Minoan origin, Athena who appears to have been Mycenean, Hermes and Hera who came from the Aegean, Apollo from Ionia, Aphrodite from Cyprus, and Dionysius and Ares from Thrace. Ultimately, all of these deities were to meet on Mount Olympus. As we contemplate what occurred, three major cultural groups will be recognized: the Minoans, the Mycenaeans, and the Dorians.

The Minoans (c. 2000 - 1450 B.C.E.)

Sometime, perhaps as early as the seventh millennium, the first settlers came to Crete and established independent Neolithic settlements. How they crossed the seventy or so miles of troubled waters that separate the island from mainland Greece is hard to imagine. But they were the first, and other settlers were to follow. There, on an island about 160 miles long and 30 miles wide, a land without any imposing rivers, they found springs to water grazing land and orchards. Their house structures were similar to those found on the mainland, but the pottery was unique, decorated with inscribed chevrons, triangles and zigzag lines. Vases were often black and shiny. Weapons and tools were made of polished stone.

From a period after 4000 B.C.E., migrants arrived from Asia Minor, from Egypt and from the Lebanese coastland. With the coming of the Bronze age, tools and weapons were fashioned from this new material. Clay female figurines were fiddle-shaped, with extremely narrow waist lines. Men were portrayed with broad shoulders. Cretan caves appear to have been used for inhumation by families or perhaps by entire villages. Cremation was practiced and human ashes have been found in burial pits and, from a later period, in jars.

Sometime between 3000 and 2000 B.C.E. a tremendous cultural development took place — a development that was to impact on Greece. Legend has it that the key figure in this civilizing period, known as the Minoan age, was a conqueror and law-giver known as King Minos. Under his rule the people were united and three great cities came into existence: Knossos, Cydonia and Phoestos.

Minos was said to be the first law-giver. According to legend, every nine years the king visited a sacred cave where Zeus would reveal laws for governing society — obviously a variant of the religious fictions about divine law-giving we have previously encountered in Sumeria, Babylonia, Assyria and Israel. Indeed, according to Greek mythology, Crete was the birthplace of Zeus, the king of the gods. The laws were supposed to have maintained the equality of all citizens (although there are those who claim that this notion did not come into being until the time of the Dorians — see below). Slaves worked the land. In time of war the royal power was supreme, but in times of peace a senate governed the state. Minos was supposed to have developed naval power and put down the raids of pirates. Minos also encouraged the colonization of the islands of Thrace and Rhodes and of the Asian mainland. These traditions must be placed in the category of legend, but there are some things that can be said, without contradiction, concerning the Minoans.

The Minoans were sea-faring people whose great power impacted on the early history of Greece. Minoans traded with Egypt, Phoenicia and Mesopotamia. On Crete, they constructed magnificent palaces with maze-like rooms surrounding a central courtyard. These buildings were equipped with piped, running water, bathing rooms and underground plumbing. Palace walls were richly adorned with murals depicting scenes of ordinary life. During the excavation of Knossus by Sir Arthur Evans, tablets were found using two different forms of writing known as Linear A and Linear B. Linear B appears to have developed from linear A. The Knossus Linear B tablets have been translated and are now dated about 1375 B.C.E. Linear A tablets still defy decipherment.

What cannot be known, as yet, from the excavations are the exact nature of the relationships between independent towns and cities. There can be no question that each town or city controlled the immediate surrounding area, but the nature of that control is not clear. From the frescoes and from the fact that their cities were not walled, it is assumed that the Minoans were a relatively peaceful people. It was not until the end of the 15th century, with the coming of peoples from the Greek mainland and the destruction of Knossos, that the face of society underwent change. Now military tombs and literary references to military equipment and titles are found. These appear to be a contribution from the Mycenaeans who were engaging in military outreach. Consequently the city-state pattern was adopted in Crete.

The Mycenaeans (c. 1450 - 1100 B.C.E.)

Even as the Minoan civilization was flourishing on the island of Crete, Mycenaean culture was developing on the mainland. The Mycenaean period, named after Mycenae, the first and most important site to be excavated, was characterized by small city-states united in a loose federation under kings of Mycenae, Thebes, Athens, Tiryns and Pylos, among others. The geography of Greece negated closer unions so that each district developed its own government and character. Mycenaean civilization reached its zenith during the final stages of the Bronze Age in the early thirteenth century. Mycenaeans destroyed Knossus and controlled Crete, but by the end of the thirteenth century Mycenaean culture was collapsing.

The Mycenaean center for government, justice, handicrafts, trade and so on, was the walled city. Beyond lay fertile plains and small villages. Sea-faring trade was common. Although the city-state did not always promote democracy, it did embrace a kind of freedom in which individuals were able to be themselves and develop their own personalities. Consequently there was no elevation or sacralizing of rulers.

Sometime during the thirteenth century, the Mycenaean civilization began to deteriorate. Exactly what brought about the change is still under debate. Theories of decline include pestilence, famine, and war.

Cities were destroyed — by whom, it is not clear. Internecine struggles and over-extension abroad may have weakened the economy. The end of the Mycenaean world ushered in a time period known as "the dark ages" in Greece. The next several hundred years, from the eleventh to the eighth centuries, provide us with little information about what occurred in Greece apart from what has been called the "miserable contents of simple tombs" (Chadwick, p. 193).

The Dorians (c. 1200 - 800 B.C.E.)

The decline and ultimate collapse of Mycenaean civilization made it possible for a people known as the Dorians to move into Mycenaean territory. Sometime during the late thirteenth or early twelfth century B.C.E., these Indo-European speaking peoples came out of the north into Greece and filtered down to the southernmost parts of the peninsula. A few Mycenaean cities, including Athens, appear to have been able to maintain independence, but were not unaffected. Mycenaean shrines, such as the one at Delphi, continued to function.

The Dorian invasion initiated the displacement of peoples. Some Mycenaean Greeks fled across the Aegean to regions known as Aeolis and Ionia. This area with its small fortified cities had long been familiar to the Greeks. There the newcomers developed the city-state pattern known as the *polis* and from which the Western world developed its pattern of defined separate territorial units or states. Others built cities in Crimea to the north and at Marseilles on the west and in Sicily and southern Italy. The migrants did not lose contact with their homeland and they retained the same gods.

In the discussions on Egypt and Israel, it was pointed out that some migrating Mycenaeans came to be known as the Sea People who attempted to invade Egypt. Others were the Philistines who established themselves on the coast of Palestine.

During the Dorian period trade diminished and writing moved into decline. This was the time when the Hittites learned the mastery of iron. During the Dorian period, the use of this new metal was greatly expanded. Sparta, already noted for its bronze work, had readily exploited nearby iron mines, but during the Dorian dark-ages, the enterprises declined.

Change came about 800 B.C.E. A new system of writing, using an alphabet based on a Phoenician system, was introduced. During the eighth century the works of Homer and Hesiod came into being and the dark ages were past.

The Homeric Epics

As we have noted, the Greeks produced no sacred documents providing divinely revealed rules for human life. We learn of Greek theology or religion through the works of poets, philosophers, story tellers and artists. Like other contemporary nations, the ancient Greeks entertained a variety of gods, goddesses, shrines and cult centers — but there was a difference. As the writings of Homer make plain, gods and goddesses were clearly projections of the human. They displayed all the strengths and weaknesses found in human beings. They could be loyal, supportive, kind and benign. They could also be capricious, malicious, deceitful, deceptive and manipulative. They fought among themselves. They took sides in human battles. In the *Iliad*, Homer relates that, in the battle between Hector and Achilles, the goddess Athena deceives Hector, ensuring his death.

However, if the gods were like humans, humans might become god-like, but with a difference: humans were not divine. As divinities, the gods did not experience old age and death; humans did. The physical forms and the lives of the gods, despite their human qualities, remained always beautiful and vigorous; humans would age and grow feeble. Finally, the gods possessed power unavailable to humans, although at times the gods bestowed power on individual humans. Human beings could appeal to the gods for help and sometimes the gods responded. For example, as we have noted, according to Homer, gods and goddesses actually participated in the battles of the Trojan war. Thus, while the Greeks knew full well they could never enjoy the power and privileges that were the unique possessions of the gods, they knew that at times, there were occasions when, as individuals and even as a people, they enjoyed some dimensions of the happiness and freedom and power they assigned to their deities.

The earliest Greek records come from about 1400 B.C.E., but understanding of Greek life, thought and history begins with the writings of Homer in the 8th century. Homer purports to record history, but the history he presents is history as a story mingling memory, legend, myth, and tradition. His records of life in the Mycenaean period enable us to peer into early Greek communities and into Greek thought to discern the paramount importance of the individual.

The great man, the hero, was one who, having been naturally endowed with superior qualities of body and mind, made the most of these qualities to surpass others and gain respect and applause. Personal honor was a prime quality of the heroic ideal and any affront or challenge had to be met head-on — a characteristic found in heroes from Achilles to Alexander. Homeric heros were warriors and chieftains embodying the noble ideals of virtue or morality (*arete*) and justice (*dike*) as they confronted and conquered a hostile world. These virtues imposed moral constraints on human behavior, that were augmented by the concepts of *Nemesis* or the anger that avenges, and by *Moira*, the supreme power of the universe that places limits upon what one may do without crossing the borders of *Nomos* or law, thereby triggering *Nemesis*. To be blinded or carried away by one's own ambitions or infatuations (*Ate*) was to forsake responsibility or duty (*Aidos*) and to be guilty of arrogance or false pride (*Hubris*) which again rendered the individual subject to *Nemesis*. To appreciate how these powerful moral forces functioned in society, one might think of the Oriental notion of "loss of face," the shame that dishonor brings.

The honor-system, which forbade the heroic individual to do that which brought shame or dishonor, established a moral pattern in which the positive outweighed the negative and obligations outweighed prohibitions. The heroic person was never satisfied, but always strove to better himself, to go beyond. Honor was that which enhanced life. Heroic ideals placed high value on war.

Achilles is portrayed as beautiful, valiant, the strongest and swiftest, the most eloquent, gentle, courteous, and generous of men. He sought to fulfil his father's will. He embodied the true essence of the heroic warrior, the true excellence (*arete*) of humanity. He was one who fought not only for his own glory but for the glory of the state.

What about women? Generally speaking Greek women were without power. They moved easily in the world of men, but did not, ordinarily, engage in war or participate in male-dominated ceremonies. They had their own sphere and were often involved in serious decision making.

Did people really believe the Homeric tales? Perhaps "belief" is too strong a term. As Veyne has pointed out:

> . . . there were people who did not believe in the existence of the gods, but never did anyone doubt the existence of heroes. And with reason. The heroes were only men, to whom credulity had lent supernatural traits, and how could one doubt that human beings now exist and have always existed? (Veyne, p. 42)

Critical thinking will not be found in the Homeric accounts. Therefore, the hero was not the model for philosophers who favored contemplation and the acquisition of knowledge.

The Gods of Ancient Greece

The story of creation is related in Hesiod's *Theogony* which was written about 700 B.C.E. Hesiod begins with primeval Chaos — a pattern we have seen in both ancient Mesopotamia and Egypt. Chaos had existence. Then came Gaia or Mother Earth, from whom all else derives. She was manifested in the mystery religions as Demeter, the earth mother. Her presence in Hesiod may point back to much earlier beliefs about the coming into being of life — perhaps manifested in the pregnant female figures that abound in the Neolithic period. From Gaia came the gods of Mount Olympus and of the underworld and, most important of all, Eros, the god of love. Gaia brought forth the starry heavens above, the undulating hills with their glens and groves, and the rivers that welled up from the earth. From Chaos came Erebus or Night, and from Erebus came Day and Air (*Aether*). Gaia copulated with Heaven to produce the oceans. Much more could be said, for Hesiod names a multitude of deities including Apollo, Athena, Aphrodite, Hermes and so on.

What the writings of Homer and Hesiod introduce is one facet of Greek religion, namely, the gods who were believed to live on Mount Olympus. Traditionally, twelve deities were recognized: seven males: Zeus, Poseidon, Hermes, Ares, Apollo, Hephaistos and Dionysus; and five females: Hera, Artemis, Aphrodite, Athena and Demeter. Each had its own territorial jurisdiction. Zeus was the god of the heavens and Hera was his wife; Poseidon was the god of the sea, and so forth. Each deity was in charge of rewarding or punishing those who ventured into his or her particular area of control.

Olympian religion was a state religion that celebrated the magnificence of Greek culture. Temples to Olympian gods dotted the Greek countryside. Zeus, like other gods, absorbed whatever duties local deities might have had. As John B. Noss notes:

> Not only was he Zeus of Olympus, but Zeus Lykaios in Arcadia, Zeus Laphystios in southern Thessaly, and Zeus Kithairon in Boetia. But he also assumed other, down-to-earth duties. He was the god of fertility in many districts, and in at least three places a deity of the underworld. As Zeus Polieus he was the guardian of several city-states. As Zeus Aphiktor he was the united cry of the suppliants, itself become deity and forcibly beating its way to heaven. At Athens he was Zeus Phratrios, and received on his altar the votes cast by members of the phratry when a father brought his child for enrollment. At

> Dedona he spoke oracles through the murmuring leaves of the sanctuary oak. Generally, of course, he was the Cloud-Compeller, the Rain-Maker, carrying his bright thunderbolt, hurled amid earthshaking tremors, but the thunderbolt sometimes had the judicial use of punishing the wickedness of men. (p. 56)

Nor was he alone in the assimilation of various duties. The other gods also assumed multiple roles.

In attitudes and behavior, the gods were little more than divinely anthropomorphized embodiments of the ideals found in Homeric heros. Thus, Olympian religion was this-life oriented and affirmed the destiny of Greeks as that of bringing about the triumph of Greek culture. Olympian religious confidence in the Greek way of life as the supreme way of life tended to move Greeks away from fears of chaos and meaninglessness in life. The national religion of Olympian gods enabled Greeks to see themselves and their way of life as the finest and best — a conviction that encouraged Alexander the Great to seek the Hellenization of the territories he conquered.

Thus, Greeks not only shared a common language with several dialects, but, generally speaking, a common religion centered in the Olympian gods and their shrines. The temple of Zeus at Olympia and Apollo at Delphi were visited by Greeks from all parts of the country, which demonstrates that the humanistic dimensions of Greek religion did not remove Greeks from some feelings of dependency on the supernatural. Olympian games served to harmonize aspects of culture as Greeks came together to compete. This sense of oneness was emphasized in the term used to designate foreigners: *barbaros*, from which our word "barbarian" is derived. In ancient Greece the term was not hostile or contemptuous; it simply signified that which was different or foreign. However, after the Persian wars and the experience of destruction wrought by Persians, the term *barbaros* acquired some of its modern connotation.

The Mystery Religions

The Greek world was not dominated by demonic spirits, lying in wait to pounce upon mortals, but in the minds of some there was belief in dark powers that needed to be thwarted by magic. There were always shamans who were prepared to respond to the needs of the gullible. What were much more important were the vegetation cults, such as that at Eleusis.

The gods of Olympus were distant and, for the most part, involved in their own affairs. True, at the Apollo shrine at Delphi and at the Zeus shrine at Dodona, where it was believed that secret knowledge was available, oracles were given. A petitioner might appeal to the high gods for healing from some ailment. But there were other gods who were close, near at hand, involved in the well-being of human life and often closely associated with nature. The religions associated with these deities are known as *mystery religions* because the details of beliefs and rites were held to be secret and known only to members (much like certain lodges in our present society). Because of the secrecy, only some facets of the religions are known.

There were three parts to the mystery religions. The first was the myth or the story of the gods or goddesses involved. For example, in the Eleusinian myth, which was centered at Eleusis near Athens, the story focused on Demeter, the ancient corn goddess, an agricultural deity, intimately related to the productivity of the region. According to the myth, one day as her daughter Persephone, the corn maiden, was gathering flowers, she was seized and taken to the underworld by Pluto, the god of that dark region. In desperation Demeter began a search for her missing child. Part of the myth recounted the pain of the loss and the mourning by the mother.

Day and night, far and wide, Demeter searched, carrying a torch to enable her to peer into dark recesses where Persephone may have disappeared. Disguised as an old woman, she came to Eleusis. Here she met the royal family and became a nurse to the infant son of the queen. She began magic rituals to make the child immortal. The rites included feeding the boy the food of the gods (ambrosia) by day, and by night ridding him of his mortality by fire. When she was discovered by the horrified queen, the goddess disclosed her true identity, abandoned the immortality rituals for the infant prince, and took up residence in a sanctuary built for her by the people of Eleusis. There she would teach those who came to her, initiate them into her Mysteries, and bestow on them immortality.

According to the myth, during the period when the fertility goddess was involved in her mourning rites, drought and famine plagued the land and the corn crops failed. Zeus intervened and it was agreed that Persephone would spend only one-third of the year in the underworld with Pluto and two-thirds of the year in the upper world with her mother. Of course the myth was directly related to the seasonal cycle and to agricultural pursuits such as planting and harvesting.

The second part of the religion was the ritual. The rites began in the fall of the year with the tilling of the soil and the sowing of seed in anticipation of the autumnal rains. They continued through spring into the growing period of the crops. At harvest time, when the ripened crops were gathered, Persephone entered the underworld and was with Pluto, the god of the dead. At sowing and growing time, Persephone was resurrected and once again was reunited with her mother.

Each year the cycle was repeated and each year worshippers reenacted the story. The way between Athens and Eleusis was a sacred way (*via sacra*), the way of sorrows (*via dolorosa*), along which worshippers made their devotional journey, stopping at central stations where some particular part of the story was supposed to have taken place. At the close of the ritual, worshippers would rejoice in the resurrection of Persephone from the underworld, in her triumphant reunion with the mother goddess, in the assurance of immortality for themselves, and in the promise of a rich corn harvest as they began the sowing of seed.

The third part of the religion involved the initiation of worshippers (*mystae*). The initiation took place near Eleusis where the neophytes underwent a course of instructions in the secrets of the faith system. The ceremonial began with a solemn proclamation: "Let no one enter whose hands are not clean and whose tongue is not prudent." (Hatch, p. 285) Next, the initiant made a confession of sins. Hatch notes that:

> Confession was followed by a kind of baptism. The candidates for initiation bathed in the pure waters of the sea. The manner of bathing and the number of immersions varied with the degree of guilt which they had confessed. They came from the bath new men. It was a *catharsis a loutron*, a layer of regeneration. They had to perform certain forms of abstinence; they had to fast, and when they ate they had to abstain from certain kinds of food. (p. 287)

The next part of the initiation was called *soteria* or a sacrifice of salvation. "Each candidate sacrificed a pig for himself." (p. 287) Other sacrificial rituals took place over a period of several days.

Later the initiants would take the spiritual journey along the *via sacra*. At key stations, where some part of the myth was supposed to have taken place, they would pause and worship. With torches they reenacted and joined in Demeter's search for Persephone. Then, having come to the shrine at Eleusis, they engaged in other rites.

Now, physically and spiritually cleansed, they entered the darkness of the hall of initiation where they were privileged to behold sacred sights and receive the secret information (*musterion*) of the faith which were never to be revealed to others. The best estimates of what took place, based on scraps of information from ancient writers, is that the drama of the seizure and rape of Persephone by Pluto was recited and perhaps enacted symbolically, and that the resurrection of Persephone from the underworld was also dramatized. It seems that an ear of grain, the symbol of rebirth, and statuettes of men and women engaged in acts of sexual intimacy, plus models of genital organs were displayed (Grant, 1987, p. 45). What mattered most to the worshipper was that he was there, with the goddesses, participating in the sacred drama. He was no onlooker, he was personally involved — emotionally, physically, spiritually. In the words of Walter F. Otto,

> the Eleusinian mystes lived the miracle of intimacy with the goddesses, he experienced their presence. He was received into the sphere of their acts and sufferings, into the immediate reality of their sublime being. His famous vision was no mere looking on. It was sublimation to a higher existence, a transformation of his being. What wonder then that the beholder of this vision should have been confident of a higher destiny in life, and in death, where Persephone was queen. (p. 30)

The annual ceremony dramatized the seasonal change of summer, winter and spring, of sowing and harvest, and ultimately of life and death. Hatch wrote:

> It was a drama also of human life. It was the poetry of the hope of the world to come. Death gave place to life. It was the *purgatio animae*, by which the soul might be fit for the presence of God. Those who had been baptized and initiated were lifted into a new life. Death had no terrors for them. The blaze of light after darkness, the symbolic scenery of the life of the gods, were a fore-shadowing of the life to come. (p. 289)

In other words, the participants felt that they had been born anew and that this rebirth gave promise of rewards in the afterlife.

But there were still other dimensions to the mystery religions. Demeter was not a goddess far removed from the life and experiences of her followers. She, the mother goddess, knew the grief and pain of loss as did human parents. Like them, she grieved for her missing child. This was no Olympian deity, far removed on Mount Olympus and involved in her own affairs. This was the mother figure who knew and understood pain and loss and grief so familiar to humans and who could, as humans would, rejoice when her daughter was resurrected and returned to her. The myth linked the goddess to the world of human experiences even as it explained the seasonal cycle.

Another important aspect of these ancient cults was that the mystery religions enabled human beings, who felt lost in the world, who were burdened by evil and desirous of escape, to find salvation in the rites and teachings of the cult. It was during the sixth century B.C.E. that a wave of what Martin P. Nilsson has called an "epidemic of psychopathic religiosity" swept across the nation (Nilsson, p. 205). From Thrace came the cult of the god Dionysus. In the stories about the god, we learn that at first he was despised, but as time went on he was cherished as he exerted himself in power. As an alien import, he stood apart from the Olympian gods, for his cult involved practices which were abhorrent to the Greeks, including frantic and obscene dancing by women (*maenads* or *Bacchae*) maddened by divine possession, the tearing apart of living animals such as the bull and the devouring of raw flesh in the omophagia rite, and even human sacrifice. In the processionals, males (Sileni and satyrs), dressed in animal skins, wore crowns of ivy and carried phalluses which were symbols of fertility (Grant, 1987, p. 303). Dionysus began as a fertility power and as his cult was Hellenized, some of its more extreme behaviors were reduced to symbolic gestures. His power became more narrowly associated with wine and with intellectual, spiritual and physical release — all symbolized in wine. In the *Bacchae*, Euripedes concludes one of the odes praising Dionysius (p. 416f) with these words:

> Our deity, Zeus' son, rejoices in festivals. He loves goddess Peace, who brings prosperity and cherishes youth. To rich and poor he gives in equal measure the blessed joy of wine. But he hates the man who has no taste for such things — to live a life of happy days and sweet and happy nights, in wisdom to keep his mind and heart aloof from overbusy men. Whatever the majority, the simple folk, believe and follow, that way will I accept. (quoted in Hadas and Smith, p. 21)

The Dionysian cult offered escape from the routine burdens of life, ecstatic communication with the god and strengthening of the divine element within through partaking of the sacred food and drink. Finally, as Dionysus was associated with the death and resurrection patterns of the fertility cult, adherents were offered a share in the better world that lay beyond death.

The Persian Invasion

During the sixth century the Persian empire continued the pattern of expansion to which we alluded in chapter 5 on Mesopotamia. Darius I succeeded Cyrus the Great in 530 B.C.E. All of ancient Persia, Mesopotamia, Palestine, Asia Minor and Egypt had come under Persian domination.

Darius then turned his attention to Europe. He defeated the Scythians who lived beside the Black Sea and then directed his forces towards Greece. His progress was stopped at the famous battle of Marathon in 490 B.C.E. When Darius died (486), his successor, Xerxes, initiated a naval attack on Greece. He was repulsed by the Greeks at the battle of Salamis in 480. By now it had become clear to Greek leaders that they were truly at the mercy of the sea, for the sea marked their territorial boundaries. Consequently, after the battles with Persia, they were to develop a powerful navy for protection as well as for commerce.

As the Persian Empire entered a period of declining strength, the Greeks moved towards a new unity which became a reality under Philip of Macedon. The final collapse of the Persian Empire came about through the leadership and the armies of Alexander the Great, who pushed the outreach of the Greek world to the borders of India.

Following Alexander's death in 323 B.C.E., his empire was divided among his generals, the diodochoi or successors: Ptolomy was in control of Egypt; Lysimachus became ruler of Thrace; Selucis I ruled Babylon; Antipater, succeeded by his son Cassander, got Macedonia and Greece; Antigonus took Phrygia; and Eumenes controlled the area to the south of the Black Sea. It was an uneasy partition. Greedy Antigonus brought about Eumenes' death and took control of Eumenes' territory. Out of fear of Ptolomy with whom he disputed control of Palestine, Antigonus formed a coalition with the other leaders. After his death in 301, a new partition took place. Alexander's once united empire was now divided under four rulers: Lysimachus continued to hold Thrace but also ruled over a part of Asia Minor; Cassander controlled Greece and Macedon; Selucis held everything from northern Palestine to the Indus river; and Ptolomy ruled over Egypt and southern Palestine.

What is most important is that each of these men, like Alexander himself, was imbued with belief in the superiority of the Greek way of life and was bound to infuse it into whatever cultures he commanded. In other words, Alexander's vision of a united Greek world was continued under a process of Hellenization. Greek culture flourished. The

Greek language was the language of the empire and of the world of trade, business and diplomacy.

Greek Democracy

Hesiod reminds his readers that there was a time when aristocracies controlled the cities. The prime responsibility for law and order and for public service was in the hands of the rich and powerful. In some instances, an oligarchic form of government prevailed, in others the rule was autocratic. Of course some form of legal code must have been developed in each case and the seeds of what was to become democracy were present.

In Sparta, if traditions are correct, probably during the eighth century B.C.E., the Great Rhetra or enactment, quoted by Plutarch (who wrote during the second or third centuries C.E.), came into being. A council of thirty elders, which included kings or leaders, was established. Each season at the festival of Apollo, the council was to submit proposals to the *demos* (people). The *demos* then had the right to criticize and express a final vote. However, should the elders decide that the people had not evaluated correctly, they could decide to accept the original formulation. Just how factual this account is, cannot be known.

Democracy was to develop, in part, through the unification of Greece which was brought about by the Persian invasion. Greek city-states tended to be independent units under the control and governance of powerful men. As the city-states grew in population, territorial controls expanded over surrounding areas where farming was done, resulting in boundary disputes between rulers. On occasion, new communities would be founded so that, during the seventh and sixth centuries (the so called "Age of Expansion"), the city-state pattern was greatly extended.

City-state government involved rule by a monarch, and succession to the throne was generally passed to the eldest son. As nobles gained power and wealth, they challenged the exclusive rule by one family and an oligarchic system of government developed whereby rule of the city-state was by a group of powerful men. As many as several hundred of the rich and powerful could be involved, but the actual governing was generally in the hands of a small council of ten or fifteen. The shared control has been recognized as a first step towards democracy. The expansion of territorial holdings during the sixth century exhausted the potential of many of the surrounding farms to support the needs of the city. Food shortages produced discontent. Small land holders lost their property to the wealthy and some were forced to sell themselves and their families into slavery.

Now, a new form of leadership was developed by men who seized power by force and who won the support of the people with promises of reform. Some of these new leaders or tyrants, as they were called, were cruel and greedy for power. They developed luxurious courts and ignored the needs of the people. Some engaged in public projects to aid the city-state. Others, like those in Athens, cancelled debts and redistributed the land. No longer were the rich and powerful the sole arbiters of justice and law. Indeed, it was clear that uprisings of the people could overthrow and replace an unpopular tyrant. This is what happened in Athens.

One of the key figures in Athenian politics was Solon (c. 658-c. 558). Through his advocacy of the principles of a just society in Athens, he brought Greece one step closer to democracy. Under Solon, about 560 B.C.E., unity of culture ultimately resulted in "the establishment of a citizen's government based upon citizen-made laws." (Wilbur & Allen, p. 2) Solon's contribution was the fusion of the concept of the city-state (*Polis*) with that of justice (*dike*) so that the city-state centralized the highest qualities of the Greek spirit. Individuals had the responsibility to exercise good judgment, to embody the essence of individual freedom coupled with allegiance to the *Polis*. Ultimately, even the gods were made to accommodate to these ideals:

> The gods took on new functions — Apollo at Delphi becoming a god of the aristocratics; Athena symbolizing the state as an organ of reconciliation; Hermes, the god of the merchants and patron of commerce. (Winspear, p. 62)

Out of this unique culture there was to develop the idea of the human potential and of the human ideal of a healthy mind in a healthy body. Testing, to determine the best of the body-mind combination, gave rise to the games, the theater, Greek poetry, Greek art and Greek philosophy.

Rivalry between Greek clans and the seizure of control of government in Athens by clan leaders produced conflict with tradesmen. The constant struggle clashed with Athens' image as a growing trade and marketing center. Ultimately, through collusion, Peisistratus seized power in 546 B.C.E. He took control of the Acropolis and imprisoned and held hostage the sons of leading families. After his death, his son

Hippias assumed control. Between the two, they ruled Athens for some thirty-six years.

Hippias, tyrant of Athens, was a harsh ruler. In 510, with military help from the city-state of Sparta, he was driven from the city. He was not replaced with a successor; instead, the first European democracy came into being. It is customary to call the Athenian democracy the "first" democratic system, but in view of what we have noted in the discussion of early Sumerian rule, it is quite possible that the earliest democracy was in Mesopotamia. What is most important about Athenian democratic government is that, even though it was later replaced by a monarchy, through Greek literature the democratic concept remained alive in the minds of men and women. Ultimately, the idea and the ideal would be translated into the reality it is in America and in other democracies.

Democracy did not suddenly emerge with the departure of Hippias. First there was a power struggle out of which Cleisthenes was empowered to carry out reform and it was out of this reform that Greek democracy was born.

Cleisthenes was called upon to draw up a new constitution. Involvement in communal affairs had always been part of Greek culture. One of the rights of citizenship had been participation in the public meetings in the market place. In Athens, this Assembly, or Ecclesia, was open to all adult citizens (18 years of age and older) who were free to speak should they choose. Stobart has commented on the Ecclesia:

> It was, of course, an ignorant, fickle, excitable body, especially in conducting a war or a piece of foreign policy. But it was a wonderful instrument of education, and it gave the Athenian citizen that sense of direct participation in the affairs of his state which alone could satisfy the political aspirations of a Greek. (p. 112)

Cleisthenes sought to make common people more responsible and more influential in government. Much of what he was to organize he drew from previously developed patterns of government. For example, Solon had instituted the Council of Four Hundred; Cleisthenes formed The Council of Five Hundred of elected candidates drawn from ten *demes* or tribal wards. Demesmen of each ward elected a number of candidates, each over thirty years of age, who came from middle and upper classes, the criteria being wealth and birth. The elected officers of the tribal groups making up a ward, then drew by lot the names of fifty of the elected candidates. Those chosen could serve for only one year. After screening by retiring councilors, the membership of the Council of Five Hundred was fixed for the year. No one could be elected to the Council more than twice.

For one tenth of the year, the councilors of one tribe sat continually as an executive committee of the Council dealing with day-to-day business. They were empowered to call the entire Council into session should the need arise. Of course the Council did meet from time to time for state occasions. Within the executive council, a chairman was chosen by lot each day. The secretary, also chosen by lot, served one year.

The election process controlled law — nine magistrates were elected to hold office for one year. The election process also affected the military. Each tribal assembly elected a commander to control the tribal forces, so that there were ten generals, each tenured for one year, in charge of the various aspects of defense. Consecutive terms were permitted.

The reorientation of the political life of Athens did not go unchallenged. Members of the Spartan Alliance prepared to attack, but Athenian forces prevailed and democratic Athens now felt prepared to withstand opposition from any and all comers. Herodatus commented:

> So Athens grew; and it shows, not in one incident only but throughout, what a noble thing is democracy; for the Athenians when under the tyrants were no more than a match in war for their neighbors, but when they were quit of tyrants they were by far the best. This shows therefore that when they were under a master they did not do their best, as working for him, but when they were freed every man was zealous to do the best for himself. (quoted in Burn, p. 190)

Not every person could participate in the democratic process. Only a man over 18 years of age could be recognized as a citizen, and then only if his father had been a citizen before him. In 546, this ruling had been made more stringent and citizenship was limited to men whose father and whose mother's father had been citizens. Of course this produced a very limited democracy. Out of some 300,000 residents of Athens, only about 45,000 were recognized as citizens. Women, married or single, and children, who constituted some 145,000 members of the population, had no political rights and were not considered to be citizens. The 35,000 or so foreigners in Athens were protected by Athenian law but, despite the fact that many were craftsmen, artisans and business men, they had no vote and could not hold public office. The remainder of the population was composed of slaves who were without vote and who could not choose their work. Many were captives from wars; some who entered slavery through poverty could, if they earned enough, purchase their freehom. What is most important is that the seeds of democracy had been sown and taken root. It was to take more than 2000 years for the plant to blossom.

The Philosophers, Pericles, and Freethought

In a world where in almost every country the practical needs of everyday life were overshadowed by superstitions and beliefs in the supernatural, the Greeks stand apart in the development of rational, critical thinking. As Edith Hamilton noted, "The Greeks were the first intellectualists. In a world where the irrational had played the chief role, they came forward as protagonists of the mind." (p. 10f) Like the other peoples we have encountered, the Greeks answered the question, "What is the origin of life, the universe and all that it contains?" in terms of mythology. But they did not stop there. They went beyond this question and asked "What is the primary nature of all that exists and how do we test what we know?" The response to these questions lay not in mythology but in philosophy and in the beginnings of scientific or rational inquiry.

This inquiring mind-set appears to have originated in Ionia in the sixth century B.C.E. The Persian conquest of Asia Minor at the end of the sixth century had dealt a damaging blow to the Greeks inasmuch as it meant the loss of the Greek cities along the coast of Asia Minor. Greeks driven from Ionia found a welcome for their ideas in Athens. Consequently, Athens was to become a center for free and open discussion. As N.G.L. Hammond has written:

> The reaction of the Athenians to the influx of Ionian freethinkers seems to have been guided at first by Pericles, who was himself a man of brilliant intellect and a powerful speaker. He became the center of the intellectual circle in Athens because he was a close friend of Anaxagorus, Zeno and Protagoras, and he had as his mistress a Milesian woman, Aspasia, who was famous for her free-thinking and free-living. (p. 132)

Pericles (c. 490-429 B.C.E.) was born in Athens, the son of a niece of Cleisthenes. He was just a boy when the Persians were about to invade Athens and he joined those who fled the city. Xerxes' armies destroyed the city. As a scion of an aristocratic family, Pericles was in a position to exert authority within the city. Having secured the support of the masses, he committed himself to making Athens "free, powerful and glorious" (Stobart, p. 137). He stressed freedom of opportunity and freedom of action or behavior for every citizen, without reference to social class or financial status. Within these freedoms, Athenians not only obeyed state laws but observed the principle of common decency. Athenians were confident of the democratic process and of their own ability. Decisions were made by the community following free and open discussion rather than being delegated to some commission. Pericles' speech, as recorded by Thucydides, contained no reference to the gods. His words reflect a noble expression of humanism, in which man is the sole measure of society.

But within the policy of freedom for citizens there were those who remained slaves. Moreover, within the environment of openness and tolerance, there was a political willingness to attack and destroy. From this negative spirit not even Pericles was immune, nor was Phidias, the greatest sculptor of ancient Greece, whose magnificent works adorned the Parthenon. Both became victims of political intrigue, despite the fact that their combined efforts contributed to the glory of Athens. Phidias was compelled to leave Greece about 437 B.C.E., accused of embezzlement. Pericles' last years were darkened by his helplessness in the face of a plague, and by the attacks made on what was perceived to be the weakness of his strategy during the Peloponnesian War (431-405 B.C.E.) in which Athens battled Sparta.

Nor were the philosophers completely free. Anaxagoras, the close friend of Pericles and the first Greek philosopher to migrate to Athens, was sent into exile on charges of atheism, heresy or impiety. He died at Lampsacus on the Hellespont about 428 or 427, one year after Pericles died. Not many years later, in 399 B.C.E. at age 70, Socrates was put to death on charges of impiety and that he corrupted the youth of Athens. Thus within Athenian democracy there was the potential for political bigotry and destructiveness. The Peloponesian War marked "the fatal convulsion of old Greece" (Bowra, p. 187). Athens was defeated, and Athenian democracy was abolished as the Spartans revived rule by tyrants. By 403 B.C.E., the Athenians had forced out the tyrants and introduced a stormy time in Athenian politics. But something of the soul of Athens survived, and a new age of philosophers was to come into being. Stobart reflected on the age of Pericles:

> . . . there was freedom in Athens such as no state in history has ever enjoyed, freedom in thought as well as in politics. This has been denied but the attacks made upon Phidias and Pericles, and upon the philosophers Anaxagoras and Socrates, may all be explained on political grounds. We have only to look at the plays of Aristophanes to see what amazing liberty of speech prevailed at Athens. Moreover, it was a privileged and educated equality. We must never forget that thousands of slaves whose cruel toil in mines and factory rendered the brilliant society possible at such an early stage in history nor that it was aided by revenues of an Empire. It must not be forgotten that Greek liberty and communism was that of an aristocracy, however democratic might be the relations between its members. Thus you have at Athens a citizen body living a very full social life in the open air, with everything to stimulate intellectual interests — the daily speeches and debates in the law-court and Assembly, the continual festivals and dramatic exhibitions, the endless conversations in the agora, the palaestra, and the various colonnades, the daily coming and going of ships from all quarters, constant embassies from the cities of the League, visits from all the talent of Greece, just sufficient intercourse with Egypt and the East — everything to stimulate the intelli-gence and make the "common man" a sharer in cultural pre-eminence. (Stobart, pp. 139-140)

The Ionians and the Beginnings of Philosophy

Sometime before 1000 B.C.E., a migration out of Greece had settled migrants along the coasts of Asia Minor and on adjacent islands. It is probable that the Dorian invasion contributed to the movement of peoples. It was in Ionia that Greek philosophy was born.

Based on our earliest records, Greek philosophy appears to have begun sometime in the sixth century in an Aegean Ionian community located on the coastal fringe of Asia Minor. There were three centers: Miletus, Colophon and Ephesus. The Dark Ages, ushered in by the Dorian invasion, appear to have left this region relatively untouched, and therefore open to the input of ideas through trade with Phoenicia and the Mediterranean countries in general. Consequently, insights from Egypt and the Near East touched the lives of these people. During the fifth century, the Persian conquests of Asia Minor encouraged many Ionians to leave.

Early Ionian philosophers chose the natural order of existence over the supernatural. They moved outside of Greek mythologies and stories about events that occurred according to the whims of the gods to search for naturalistic explanations without appeal to the supernatural. Walter Kaufmann has written that:

> . . . the pre-Socratics stand opposed to all theology. None of them condoned traditional religion or any popular beliefs or cults. Some were scientists, but their world was not devoid of mystery — on the contrary. They neither denied mystery, nor did they try to expound it to the point where it might cease to be mysterious. They were exuberant in their reliance on reason, and they wrote poetry about it, or superbly fashioned aphorisms. They delighted in the light of sane thought but always retained a profound sense of the outer darkness, the unexpected, and the uncanny. (p. 2-3)

Miletus was the home of Thales, Anaximander and Anaximenes. Xenophanes came from Colophon and Heraclitus from Ephesus. The Milesians sought to understand the basic stuff or substance of existence and to evoke an ultimate principle or explanation for what existed. They were, in a sense, materialists, in that they sought to explain their universe materialistically.

Thales (625?-542? B.C.E.) was an astronomer and mathematician. On the basis of our very limited knowledge of him, he appears to have initiated the idea that to solve problems one must understand the underlying principles. In this spirit, he sought to solve the problem of the nature of the world. He is reported to have argued that the primordial stuff of the universe was water upon which the earth floats. Of course, his claim that water was the basic element of the universe was not new; it reflects ideas that had been developed and were current in Babylon and in Egypt where Thales is reported to have spent some time. Whether he borrowed the notion from Egypt or, as Aristotle was to suggest, he drew his conclusions from the observation that all life was dependent on moisture and that the life-generating semen is moist, cannot be known. His naturalistic approach recognized that humans were composed of the same substance as other things, and along with other animate creatures were part of the material world. His claim that "all things are full of gods" should not be taken as polytheism but rather as reflecting the notion of "the *power* in things, which he held to be divine" (Wilbur and Allen, p. 35). In other words, Thales saw the world as alive and animated.

Thales was followed by others who suggested different primary substances. Anaximander (610?-546/545? B.C.E.) used the word *apeiron* to signify the basic stuff of the universe out of which everything came. The term implied a natural principle that is the indefinite or the boundless. He taught that the *apeiron* is without beginning and is without end and is immortal and brought the cosmos into being out of necessity, implying that the creative process was destined. Anaximander's notions of cosmic origins border on the metaphysical and move away from the concrete elemental substance put forth by Thales. On the other hand, when Anaximander talked about the origins of humans, he taught that all life forms emerged from water and that humans were, on first emerging, similar to fish. What is most interesting is that Anaximander also introduced into his *apeiron* thesis a moral dimension with the notion of "justice," which could be applied to the idea of established boundaries for human behavior.

Anaximenes (c. 545) chose air, which he appears to have assumed to be unlimited, as the primal stuff of the universe. In other words, he concretized the *apeiron* of Anaximander. Whether or not his idea was related to "breath" as the source of life, or whether he drew his notion from the appearance of the all-surrounding nature of air, cannot be known. What is clear is that in his teachings humans are part of the natural world. This unity of humans and nature was basic to Ionian thought.

Xenophanes (c. 560-478 B.C.E.) left or was banished from his native Colophon about the time the city fell to the Persians (c. 546 B.C.E.) and spent most of his life in Sicily. He appears to have been the first to comment on the anthropomorphizing of gods, and he mocked the antics of the gods as described in Homer and Hesiod. He pointed out that gods are simply projections by humans of humans themselves:

> But mortals think the gods are born and have the same clothes and voices and appearances as themselves. But if oxen or horses or lions had hands and could draw with their hands and create works of art like those fashioned by men, the horses would draw the forms of gods like horses, and the oxen of gods like oxen, and each would give them bodies like its own. Ethiopians say their gods have snub-noses and black hair, the Thracians that their's have blue eyes and red hair. (Fragments 14-16)

For him the basic stuff of the universe appears to have been both earth and water — a conclusion that may have been based on the fossils he saw embedded in the marble quarries at Paros, which suggested that great geological changes had occurred in the past.

Heraclitus was a citizen of Ephesus about 500 B.C.E. "Everything," he claimed, "is in a state of flux." He saw continuous change in the world patterns — such as day giving way to night, birth to death, hunger to satiety, heat to cold, evil to good. Nevertheless, within the seeming disunity there was unity. The uniting essence or the basic stuff of the universe was fire. Heraclitus' fire was in a constant state of change or tension, moving from going out to rekindling and including the consuming and transforming of itself. The ordering principle of unity in disunity he designated by the term *Logos* — the law or universal reason or rationality which gave order to the universe. Of course fire and logos were not to be accepted as personal gods. He could state:

> This world that is the same for all, neither any god or any man shaped it, but it ever was and is and shall be ever-living Fire that kindles by measures and goes out by measures (quoted in McClure, p. 121).

Indeed, Heraclitus rejected the claims of the mystery religions and mocked blood rituals and prayers before statues. At the same time, although he rejected the notion of personal gods, he did not deny the existence of the gods.

The Pythagoreans

Pythagorus (c. 580-500 B.C.E.) was born on the island of Samos in Asia Minor where he would probably have been influenced by Ionian thought. On reaching manhood, he migrated to the Greek colonies in southern Italy and founded the Pythagorean school — "a quasi-religious sect" (Kaufmann, p. 12) that appears to have been concerned with moral reform and the development of ethical culture. Pythagorus recognized three classes of men: those who sought knowledge, those who sought fame and honor, and those who sought gain. He stressed moderation in all things, belief in the transmigration of souls and the kinship of humans and animals. Pythagorus is best known for the mathematical formula that bears his name: the square of the hypotenuse of a right angle triangle is equal to the sum of the squares on the other two sides. Although Pythagoreans focussed on numbers and mathematics, these interests were related primarily to moral theory. Later they were to move more into scientific inquiry. What evolved out of the mathematical study of the cosmos was the concept of the earth as a sphere around which the planets revolved — an idea that was to lie dormant until the time of Copernicus and Galileo.

The Atomists

Leucippus of Miletus, and Democritus of Abdera in Thrace (c. 460-370), initiated the atomic theory of the universe. The teachings of Leucippus (who was Democritus' teacher) have perished. Reports about his teachings indicate that he postulated the existence of "indivisible units called atoms (*atoma*, or uncuttable things), infinite in number within infinite 'space' (*kenon* or void)" (Hammond, p. 128). An eddy of air brought the atoms into collision and, as a consequence of the interaction of atoms of different size, shape and constituency, each of which behave in accord with fixed patterns, everything came into being.

Democritus, too, postulated the existence of atoms in ceaseless motion as the basic stuff of the universe out of which all phenomena emerged. The atoms were self-generated and self-sustaining, therefore there was no need for a prime mover. Sensations and perceptions resulted from the contact of non-bodily atoms with those of the body. Inasmuch as the proximity of other objects, which also give off atoms, may distort the sensation, the person's perception of objects is not necessarily accurate or true. His theory of perceptions and sensations raises questions about how we know anything and how we can test what we think we know.

One of Democritus' followers, Anaxarchus, shared with his teacher the notion that sense perceptions were often contradictory. For example, the stick that looks bent when thrust into water can be perceived as straight when one runs one's fingers along it. But Anaxarchus' real interest was in the acquisition of happiness and good living; consequently he became known as "the Happy Man."

Socrates

Socrates (470?-399 B.C.E.), the son of Sophroniscus, a sculptor and Phaenarete, a midwife, was versed in geometry and astronomy, was a soldier in the Peloponesian War, was married and had three sons. We know about him primarily through the writings of his pupil Plato (428/7-348/7 B.C.E.). Plato stated his estimation of Socrates as "of all the men of his time whom I have known, he was the wisest and the justest and best" (*Phaedo*: 118). Such an evaluation did not protect Socrates from mockery by the playwright Aristophanes in the play *The Clouds*; nor did it protect him from conviction by a jury of 700 Athenian citizens for neglecting the gods and corrupting youth. The term *asebeia*, which was used in the indictment against Socrates, meant impiety or disrespect for the gods. *Asebeia* could extend from acts of desecration of holy places or objects, to denial of the existence of the gods.

What did Socrates believe or do? His student Plato is the most important source of information. It is possible that when Plato was still a child he met Socrates. Plato's uncle Charmides, brother of his mother, Perictione, was prominent in the oligarchy that ruled Athens at the end of the Peloponnesian war. Perhaps through this relationship, Plato, the boy, made his first contact with the great philosopher. But it was as a young man that Plato came under the spell of his teacher, and his moving description of Socrates' death in the *Phaedo* indicates he did not lose contact.

According to Plato's *Apology*, in which Socrates defends himself before the men of Athens, the old philosopher claimed that, when he learned that the oracle at Delphi had said that he, Socrates, was the wisest of men, it became his life work to prove the oracle wrong. He, therefore, consulted with men of power, wealth, influence and learning to find those who were wiser than he. His system of inductive reasoning employed questioning, cross-examining, and the use of rational inquiry, and demonstrated time and again that the persons whom he consulted were not really wise. His methodology attracted young men who began to use his techniques, much to the annoyance of those who preferred to hide behind the mask of reputed wisdom. Socrates further claimed that from childhood he had been guided by voices that never commanded him to do anything, but did forbid certain actions, one of which was going into politics. He argued that his effort in testing the oracle at Delphi was a demonstration of his belief in the gods, and that what the young men gained from him was a technique for testing claims of knowledge and wisdom. His arguments were not persuasive and he was sentenced to death.

As we examine his teachings it is clear that Socrates related knowledge to virtue. Knowledge was essential for virtue and virtue, or the excellence of a thing, was to be desired. The Socratic search for knowledge utilized a cross-examination process with the effect that the inquiry was recognized as important in and of itself. The Socratic method involved a pattern of free inquiry that provided resistance to dogmatism because it questioned philosophically held tenets, beliefs, and principles.

Socrates' death did not end his influence. His pupil, Plato, founded The Academy, a school in Athens that was to last for 900 years until it was closed in 529 C.E. by a Christian emperor, Justinian (527-565). In 367 B.C.E., Aristotle (384-322 B.C.E.) entered Plato's Academy and remained there until after Plato's death. One of Aristotle's pupils was the Greek king, Alexander the Great. Beyond the immediate effects of Socrates' thinking and teaching and the writings of his pupil Plato is his continuing impact throughout western philosophic history. The Socratic method of inquiry continues to be a magnificent tool for open inquiry and freethought.

The Sophists

The Sophists marked a change of focus in Greek thought from materialism and natural science to socio-political issues and ethical problems. Sophists were paid, itinerant, professional teachers, who sought to be disinterested inquirers after truth related to the control of life. They did not try to find the basic substance of the universe; their interests were practical and based on an amalgamation of information garnered from different countries, cultures and experience. They taught rhetoric — an essential for political life — and virtue, which focussed on the right way to win a just cause. But they were also skeptics who attacked old teachings, thereby unsettling the thinking of their students.

Protagoras (c. 490-420 B.C.E.) was born in Abdera in Thrace where he studied under Democritus. He came to Athens about 450 B.C.E. His best known teaching is "Man is the measure of all things, of things that are that they are, of things that are not that they are not." This would appear to make the opinion of one individual as valid as that of another on any and all subjects. However, he is also supposed to have taught that "whatever practices seem right and laudable to any particular State are so for that State, so long as it holds by them." He called for the wise man to substitute sound practices in place of the unsound. His emphasis was on the development of behavior codes by thinking humans, rather than the acceptance of such regulations simply because they have been handed down. Concerning the gods he said:

> I have no means of knowing either that they exist or that they do not exist, for there are many things that hinder such knowledge, both the obscurity of the subject and the shortness of human life. (Fragment 4)

Surely such a statement would place him among today's agnostics or perhaps even igtheists! In any case, at age 70 Protagoras was accused and convicted of atheism and forced to leave Athens.

Critias (c. 480-403 B.C.E.) too was an Athenian Sophist. He argued that laws were devised by men to regulate behavior during what had once been a disorderly and lawless period. Then humans began to violate the laws secretly to avoid punishment. At that point:

> a wise and clever man invented fear (*of the gods*) for mortals, that there might be some means of frightening the wicked, even if they do anything or say or think it in secret. Hence he introduced the Divine (*religion*), saying that there is a God flourishing with immortal life, hearing and seeing with his mind, and thinking of everything and caring about these things and having divine nature, who will hear everything said among mortals, and will be able to see all that is done. And even if you plan anything evil in secret, you will not escape the gods in this; for they have surpassing intelligence. In saying these words, he introduced the pleasantest of teachings, covering up the truth with a false theory. (quoted in Wilbur and Allen, p. 258)

Even as laws evolve out of human situations and are devised and formulated by humans, so fear of the gods, who are supposed to have given the laws and who are supposed to enforce them, is likewise a human creation.

The Cynics

The Cynic school of philosophy was founded by Diogenes of Sinope (c. 400—c. 325 B.C.E.). Because he lived according to nature and rejected all social conventions he became known as "the dog" (*ho kuan*). Although they never formed a school and did not work out a formal philosophical system, their concern was focused primarily on ethics and finding virtue through simple and independent living. Freedom from divine and human controls was attained through reason (*logos*) and by renouncing all material possessions and social entanglements. They were indifferent to death and held no beliefs in an afterlife.

The Skeptics

The desire to know and understand the universe could not be left to philosophical conjecture. How do we know anything? Can we trust our senses? What are the tests of knowledge or fact? These questions raise doubts and result in skepticism.

Skepticism thrived in the Greek world between the fourth and third centuries B.C.E. The Greek word *skeptikoi* originally meant "questioners," "inquirers" or "investigators" but ultimately came to be associated with "doubt." The founder of the skeptical movement was Pyrrho of Elis (c. 360-270 B.C.E.). He had been a pupil of Anaxarchus, had marched with the armies of Alexander the Great to the Indus river and, when Alexander died in 323, Pyrrho returned to Elis where he became a high priest and an honored philosopher.

Pyrrho's concern was with the attaining of practical wisdom that would produce *ataraxia* or a tranquility of mind characterized by "the absence of fanaticism concerning matters that cannot be proved" (Hallie, p. 11). What was accepted were called "appearances" which included "sense impressions we act on involuntarily, but also the guidance of nature, the laws of one's country, traditional values, instruction in the arts, and so on" (Hallie, p. 11). In other words, Pyrrhonic Skepticism tended to be conservative and traditional in outlook, seeking only to provide the happiness to be found in quietude. By challenging philosophical concepts or beliefs concerning that which is not apparent and by focussing on "appearances" in a non-dogmatic way, the Skeptic is relieved of the mental unrest occasioned by dogmatic positions and the need to defend them, thereby attaining quietude, tranquility or happiness. The suspended conclusions regarding the ultimate nature of things avoided the tendency found in some philosophical systems to proclaim an ultimate "truth."

Among Pyrrho's followers were: Timon (320-230 B.C.E.); Arcesilaus (c. 315-240 B.C.E.) who became a critic of Timon and who assumed leadership in Plato's academy; Carneades (213-128 B.C.E.); and finally Sextus Empiricus, whose teachings we shall examine when we consider skepticism in Rome (pp. 186-87).

The Epicureans

Epicurus (c. 341-270 B.C.E.) was born in Samos, but moved to Athens when he was eighteen years of age where he ultimately founded his school. Unfortunately, most of the 300 writings attributed to him have been lost to us. He accepted Democritus' theory of atomism, but rejected the notion of a fixed pattern. He believed that there was a happenstance factor at work by which deviations in the atomic patterns occurred, breaking the fixed mould and enabling human freedom of choice. Epicurus taught that nothing proceeds from nothing and nothing passes into nothingness. Our bodies are composed of pre-existing atoms and death simply marks a resolution into the basic atoms of which our bodies are composed.

While he did not deny the existence of the gods, he argued that the gods did not interfere in the lives of humans and that there was no afterlife. The gods, who were also composed of atoms and formed like humans, dwelt in tranquility (*ataraxia*) in their own world, eating and drinking and speaking Greek with no concern or thought for human affairs. By freeing men's minds of fear of the gods and concern about the afterlife, Epicurus sought to bring peace to the human spirit. Death, he taught, brought extinction. There was no afterworld and no judgment of the dead. Indeed, he advised, "Death is nothing to us, for the body, when it has been resolved into its elements, has no feeling, and that which has no feeling is nothing to us." (Diogenes Laertius 10.139)

His concern was with ethical issues and the quality of human life. He taught that life's focus should be on the here and now, on the attainment of individual happiness through friendship, affection, and by using wisdom to face the harsh realities of existence. He did not mean what so many interpret Epicureanism to be — a desperate pursuit of sensual pleasures. The philosopher noted that not all pleasures are worthy or equal, therefore one should exercise reasoned choice. Debauchery and drunkenness do not contribute to the continuance of pleasure for they produce unpleasant results and thus are not worthy of being chosen. What the Epicurean sought was health of body and tranquility of spirit — not the excess that is often, mistakenly, associated with the philosophy. Great stress was laid on friendship as contributing to the secure and tranquil life. The Epicurean image of the life of the distant gods provided a model for humans who should, like the gods, seek a lifetime of happiness in tranquility and freedom from stress.

The Stoics

The Stoics had much in common with the Epicureans for they also believed that the aim of philosophy was happiness according to virtue. However, whereas the Epicureans sought to free themselves from nature's law, the Stoics sought to submit to it. Virtue was interpreted as living in harmony with the formative and guiding principle in the universe which is the impersonal *logos* or reason. The efforts to interpret this concept resulted in a formidable philosophical system that embraced physics, logic and ethics. As with Socrates the focus was on knowledge and morals in the belief that informed persons would not err in the matter of morals.

The school originated with Zeno of Citium (335-263 B.C.E.) who had been taught by Crates, the Cynic philosopher.

The End of Greek Freethought

Greek freethought philosophy came to a virtual end when Christianity assumed power in the state. During the reign of Emperor Theodosius I (379-395 C.E.), non-Christian worship centers were demolished and rituals outlawed, often by Christian monks. Christians saw themselves as a people apart. Marriages between Christians and Jews were regarded legally as adultery (Latourette, p. 181). In the Greek city of Alexandria, Egypt, the Serapeum, the great temple of Serapis, was desecrated and turned into a Christian church.

Cyril, Bishop of Alexandria, a fanatical Christian, determined to purge his bishopric of all non-Christian influences during the reign of the mild-mannered emperor Theodosius II. In 415, Cyril assembled a Christian mob that attacked Jewish synagogues, turning the buildings over to the Christians. Jews were expelled, half-naked, from the city and their property was pillaged by the Christians.

Next, encouraged by Cyril, the Christian fanatics directed their fury against the celebrated woman philosopher, Hypatia (370-415 B.C.E.). Hypatia of Alexander "had charmed the world by her profound science, her eloquence and her purity" (Graetz, p. 619). Scholasticus Socrates wrote of her:

> Such was her self-possession and ease of manner arising from the refinement and cultivation of her mind, that she not infrequently appeared in public in the presence of the magistrates, without ever losing in an assembly of men that dignified mod-

> esty of her deportment for which she was conspicuous, and which gained her universal respect and admiration. (p. 148f)

Hypatia, the famous Neoplatonist philosopher and educator, was brutally murdered, her body virtually torn to pieces. Ironically, Cyril was later made a saint of the church!

In 435, the famed library of Alexandria was attacked by another group of Christian fanatics. Here were stored the half million manuscripts that had been gathered from all over the known world. Although the library was later burned (about 624), scholars believe that it had been so violently ravaged by the Christians that there was but little left to destroy.

When the Emperor Justinian (527-565) made himself master of the Eastern church, it was his intent to eradicate all vestiges of what he perceived to be heathenish thought. He closed down the schools of philosophy in Athens. Athens, that had once been the center of freethought and the open exchange of ideas, now joined the rest of the Christian world in turning from philosophy to theology, wherein discussion focussed on the idea of Jesus as world saviour. During the seventh and eighth centuries, Islam swept across the Mediterranean world; but by that time, according to Sohm, the Greek nation had lost its powers of life.

> It was a nation more richly endowed than any that has been before or after it; where the very porter in the streets philosophized; where the barber's shops and the taverns echoed to sounds of dispute about the mysteries of faith; where not only religion, but theology, was made popular, and stirred the multitude itself to wild excitement; where intellectual life, to which the conquering force of the whole nation contributed, seemed inexhaustible in its energy — this nation, the richest, the most glorious and wonderful of all nations, was overthrown, trodden down and trampled under foot, never more to rise up again. In the East, in the place of Hellenic culture, there appeared Arabian culture, itself an intellectual power far beyond the middle ages in mathematical and physical science, and in philosophy, and which had a powerful influence on the Western world in bringing forth medieval Scholasticism; a culture which, for all its sober subtlety of intellect, and the radiant glamour of Oriental poetry which surrounded it as with an imperishable glory, was yet a culture of the second order only, not worthy to be compared with that of ancient Hellas, destitute as it was of

> purity of form, of the Promethean force of genius, and, above all, of that sense of history which gives to investigation its spur, its freedom, its power of vision and an unbounded field of view.

The work of the Renaissance, at the end of the Middle Ages, was to deliver us from a medieval culture strongly influenced by Arabia, and to awaken the science and the culture of our own time. The Greek nation was no more; it never recovered from that fearful blow. With the Greek nation there fell the Greek Church. . . . The Greek Church of today, as we see it before us in Russia, and in the bordering countries of the Balkan Peninsula, is the Church of the seventh century turned to stone (Sohm, pp. 75-75, 77).

Sic transit gloria!

References

Bowra, C.M., *The Greek Experience*. New York: The World Publishing Company, 1957.

Bronowski, J, and Bruce Mazlish, *The Western Intellectual Tradition*. New York: Harper and Row, 1960.

Burn, A.R., *Persia and the Greeks*. New York: Minerva Press, 1962.

Chadwick, John, *The Mycenaean World*. Cambridge: Cambridge University Press, 1976.

Copelston, Frederick, S.J., *A History of Philosophy*. Vol. I, Westminster, Maryland: The Newman Press, 1946.

Duruy, Victor, trans. Joel Rosenthal, *The World of the Greeks*. Geneve: Minerva, 1971.

Graetz, H., *History of the Jews*. Philadelphia: The Jewish Publication Society of America, 1893. Vol. II.

Graham, James Walter, *The Palaces of Crete*. Princeton, New Jersey: Princeton University Press, 1962.

Grant, Michael, *The Ancient Mediterranean*. New York: Charles Scribner's Sons, 1969.

Grant, Michael, *The Rise of the Greeks*. New York: Charles Scribner's Sons, 1987.

Hadas, Moses, and Morton Smith, *Heroes and Gods*. New York: Harper Harper and Row, 1965.

Hallie, Philip P., and Sanford G. Etheridge, *Scepticism, Man and God.* Middletown, Conn.: Wesleyan University Press, 1964.

Hamilton, Edith, *The Greek Way to Western Civilization*. New York: Mentor Books, 1954. (Reprint of the W. W. Norton & Company, Inc. 1930 edition).

Hammond, N.G.L., *The Classical Age of Greece*. London: Weidenfeld and Nicolson, 1975.

Hatch, Edwin, *The Influence of Greek Ideas on Christianity*. New York: Harper and Row, 1957. (Harper torchbook edition of the 1888 Hibbert Lectures.)

Hopper, R.J., *The Early Greeks*. London: Wiedenfeld and Nicolson, 1976.

Kaufman, Walter, edit., *Philosophic Classics*. Vol. I., Englewood Cliffs, N.J.: Prentice Hall, 1961.

Lamont, Corliss, *The Philosophy of Humanism*. New York: Frederick Unger Publishing Co. Sixth edition, 1982.

Latourette, Kenneth Scott, *The First Five Centuries*. New York: Harper & Brothers, 1937.

McClure, Matthew Thompson, *The Early Philosophers of Greece*. New York: D. Appleton-Cokesbury Co., 1965.

Nilsson, Martin P., *A History of Greek Religion*, trans. by E.J. Feldon. Oxford: Clarendon Press, 1949.

Noss, John B., *Man's Religions*. London: MacMillan Company, 1969.

Otto, Walter F., "The Meaning of the Eleusinian Mysteries," *The Mysteries: Papers From the Eranos Yearbooks*. New York: Pantheon Books, 1955. Bollingen Series XXX 2, pp. 14-31.

Plutarch, *Life of Lycergus, The Dryden Plutarch*, revised by A.H.Clough. London: Everyman's Library, No. 407, 1929 VI.

Robertson, J.M., *A History of Free Thought*. Vol. I, London: Watts & Co., 1936.

Socrates, Scholastics, *History of the Church*. London: George Bell, 1874.

Sohm, Rudolf, *Outlines of Church History*. Boston: Beacon Press, 1958 (trans. by May Sinclair from the 1895 edition).

Stobart, J.C., *The Glory That Was Greece*. New York: St. Martin's Press, 1961.

Ulich, Robert, edit., *Three Thousand Years of Educational Wisdom*. Cambridge, Mass.: Harvard University Press, 1947, 1954.

Veyne, Paul, trans. by Paula Wissing, *Did the Greeks Believe in Their Myths?* Chicago: University of Chicago Press, 1983.

Wilbur, James B., and Harold J. Allen, edits., *The Worlds of the Early Greek Philosophers*. Buffalo, New York: Prometheus Books, 1979.

Winspear, Alban D., *The Genesis of Plato's Thought*. 2nd ed rev. New York: Russell and Russell, 1956.

9

Rome

Rome: the Fiction

A romantic tale, with many variations, grew up around the founding of Rome. According to legend, Rome was founded in 753 B.C.E. by Romulus. The life story of the founder echoes motifs that regularly appear in hero stories. Romulus and his twin brother Remus were miraculously conceived. Their mother was Rhea Silva, daughter of a deposed king named Numitor. Rhea was a Vestal Virgin, whose consecration to Vesta, the goddess of the hearth, would have begun when she was between six and ten years of age. According to legend, she was impregnated by the god Mars, who is best known to us as the Roman god of war. When it became known that the virgin princess had given birth to twins, the infants were placed in a basket and floated down the Tiber river. The basket came to rest at the foot of the Palatine hill, close to the site of a grotto-shrine, called the Lupercal, with its nearby holy fig tree (*Ficus ruminalis*). The crying of the infants attracted a she-wolf (Latin: *lupus*), an animal sacred to the god Mars, who suckled them. Shortly afterward, a shepherd named Faustulus found the twins and brought them to his wanton wife, Acca Larentia, to be raised. The young men grew to manhood among shepherd folk, became rustlers who plundered nearby estates, were caught, and brought to trial. It was then that their royal descent was made known.

Next, the twins decided to found a colony near the place where they had been rescued. Remus favored the Avantine hill, Romulus the Palatine. To determine which was the proper site, one night the brothers agreed to await a sign from Jupiter. At dawn, Remus saw six vultures flying overhead and claimed victory. However, shortly afterward, Romulus saw twelve vultures. Romulus' site was chosen and the city was named Rome after him. During the period of rivalry, Romulus killed Remus.

If the birth story was characterized by miracle, the story of Romulus' death is no less miraculous. One day, in 716 B.C.E., while performing a public act in the Campus Martius, the field of Mars, a violent storm broke, producing total darkness. When the light returned Romulus had disappeared; he had ascended into heaven where he joined the gods. Later he was identified with Quirinus, a Sabine war god. The exaltation of Romulus is therefore connected to the cult of Mars, both through his divine-human (virgin) birth, through the site of his ascension and through his divine status as a war god.

Scholars have had little difficulty in discerning the relationship of the myth to local settings. It seems that the Aventine hill was at one time called Remora or Remona, which might account for its choice as the site of a city by Remus. The Lupercal grotto was related to the festival of Lupercalia, a fertility celebration held each year on February 15. The relationship between the Latin name for wolf (*lupus*) and the name of the site probably accounts for the legend of the she-wolf that nurtured the twins. The account of the rescue by the shepherd whose wanton wife raised them may have been an effort, made at a later time, to move the account away from the wolf-story, inasmuch as the Latin name for a wanton woman or whore is *lupa*. But the wolf story was popular and, in 296 B.C.E., two Roman magistrates dedicated a statue of the wolf and the twins at the Lupercal. Finally, the play on words is also related to the most ancient name of the Tiber river which was Rumo, from whence came the name Romulus which simply means "Roman." ("The Myths of Ancient Rome," p. 150)

In this legend, we encounter familiar hero motifs — including the impregnation of a virgin by a god, the exposure of the infants employing the familiar basket-in-the-river pattern, the miraculous rescue of the endangered children, the subsequent rise to fame and, in the case of Romulus, the ascension into heaven.

History and the Origins of Rome

When we examine what is known of the history and founding of Rome, we seek to move away from legend. Unfortunately, no written accounts about the beginnings of the city were penned before the third century B.C.E. Even what remains is limited. For example we have about one-half of the major writings of Tacitus (c. 55-c. 120 C.E.) and only 35 of the 142 books by Livy (59 B.C.E.-17 C.E.). This means that the probe into Roman origins relies heavily on the finds and interpretations of archaeologists and their colleagues.

As in Greece, the Italian peninsula was sparsely occupied in the Paleolithic and Mesolithic periods. Neanderthal remains have been uncovered at various sites and the familiar clay female figurines have also been found. From North Africa by way of Spain, a neolithic group known as Ligurians entered Italy and settled the coastland around what is today Genoa. In the third millennium, Bronze Age people invaded from the north, and with their superior weapons soon were able to establish their encampments. Although writing and advanced culture was well developed in Mesopotamia and Egypt, the inhabitants of Italy were still in a pre-literate state and dwelt in squalid villages. Indo-European tribal groups moved down from the north into Italy proper and settled along the Tiber river during the second millennium. These people came to be known as the Latins and their territory was called Latium. Still another group of Bronze Age newcomers settled near what is today Bologna in northern Italy. Because evidence of their settlement was first uncovered near the town of Villanova, these people are called Villanovians.

Sometime after the tenth century B.C.E., a people of non-Indo-European tongue migrated from the eastern Mediterranean into northern Italy in an area that encompassed Villanovian territory. Exactly where they came from and how they arrived is still under debate, but the area in which they settled is known as Etruria and the settlers were called Etruscans. They were skilled metal workers employing iron weapons and tools and they soon gained control over most of northwestern Italy. Unlike the earlier inhabitants, the Etruscans were highly civilized. Concerning their beliefs, we know little because their writing has not yet been deciphered. Some information is drawn from their tomb art where statues memorializing the dead and depicting funeral feasts are accompanied by short inscriptions. Little is known about what occurred within their temples but it is known that they practiced divination. Their social structure followed the familiar city-state pattern, but because there was never a fusion of independent enclaves, no centralized governmental pattern emerged.

In the south, Greeks fleeing Greece during the Dorian invasion established settlements between the tenth and eighth centuries. So many Greek colonies sprang up that the area was known as *Magna Graecia* or Great Greece and, to this day, from a region 100 miles south of Rome to the tip of the Italian peninsula, the region is dotted with the remains of Greek Doric temples.

Thus it was that, by the eighth century, the Latins found themselves between the Etruscans on the north and the Greeks on the south. To add to the pressures, during the eighth century, another migration of Indo-Europeans, the Sabines, moved into the Tiber region.

The Growth of Rome

Rome began as one of the lesser Latium towns. It was not until the sixth century that the city grew in power and importance. At that time, the independent communities located on the seven famous hills of Rome were merged and enclosed by an encircling wall. Rome now began to reach out and take control of nearby towns. By the third century B.C.E., Rome controlled Italy.

The precise details of this growth in power are lost in a mixture of legend and history. Romulus is supposed to have been succeeded by a Sabine named Numa Pompilius who ruled until 673 B.C.E., and he linked the deified Romulus with the Sabine war god Quirinus. It was under his successor, Tullus Hostilius, that Rome began to incorporate nearby communities. Although the government was monarchal, the king was advised by an assembly of one hundred, representing the elders of the various clans. This assembly was known as the Senate (from the Latin term *senex* meaning old). Because their advisory role was seen as parental and like that of fathers, they were identified as *patricians* (from the Latin term *pater* for father). These important persons rapidly acquired a monopoly of both secular and sacred offices as well as control of the business ventures of the city.

Tullus was succeeded by Ancus Martius who welcomed migrant tribal groups. The newcomers were not accorded the status of the older residents and were identified as *plebeians* (from a Latin term *plebs* meaning "common people"). Ultimately, as we shall see, the company of plebeians grew and developed a movement to break the exploitative power of the rich. Plebeians were to achieve the full rights of citizenship and opportunity to hold high office for all Roman citizens.

During the sixth century B.C.E., expanding Etruscan power north of Rome posed a threat. Etruscan territorial claims were expanding even as Etruscan trade reached out into the western Mediterranean. At this point legend and history merge. About 575 B.C.E., Etruscan rulers began a 66 year reign in Rome. Tarquinius Priscus, Servius Tullus and Lucius Tarquinius Superbus successively occupied the throne. Under their strong leadership, a sewer system, still in use today, was built to drain swamps, new buildings were erected, and the Roman Forum was developed for the meetings of the Senate and the debating of business. Rome moved from village status to a new role as a powerful city. Soon all of central Italy was to submit to the power of Rome. Servius Tullus introduced a policy of forming alliances with neighboring powers including Carthage. Indeed, during the sixth century the combined Roman and Carthaginian forces defeated the Greek armada, and

Carthage gained possession of Sardinia and the Etruscans got Corsica. Tarquinius Superbus, the seventh and last Roman king, followed a different policy. He was a tyrant and forced the subservience of tribal groups in southern Italy. He ignored the Senate and terrorized the populace, which finally rose against him in 509 B.C.E. and sent him into exile. He was the last to bear the title of "king" in Rome.

Now a republican form of government came into being. The people elected leaders, known as consuls, who were advised by the Senate. Although both plebeians and patricians could vote, only patricians could hold political, religious or military office, so obviously they controlled both power and wealth. Some plebeians did become wealthy, but most others were poor — some so poor that they entered into debt bondage, which meant that the debtor became the servant of the person to whom money was owed. As a servant, the debtor could not earn enough to repay the debt, thus debt bondage became lifetime servitude. Excluded from the right to vote were slaves, who were generally war captives, and women, whose rights were severely limited.

In 494 B.C.E., the plebeians formed their own assembly, known as the Council of Plebeians. Their elected officials were called tribunes. Now, the plebeians called for law reform and underscored their demands by refusing to work or serve in the military. Up to this time only the king and the priests knew the law inasmuch as law was part of religion. The king alone was judge of public and private rights, although he could summon a council of advisors. Now, the plebeians demanded that the laws should be written and made known to all. Consequently, in 450 B.C.E., twelve bronze tablets, engraved with the new laws, were displayed in the Forum where they could be read by all. But the set forms of words in which pleadings were conducted remained in the hands of the patricians and it was not until about 140 years later, in 312 B.C.E., that these forms were made public.

The Twelve Tables, as they were called, provided the foundation on which Roman law was to rest. From the fragments that have survived, it is clear that efforts were made to maintain the caste system and plebeians were forbidden to intermarry with patricians. What did emerge was a fact-oriented legal pattern that laid stress upon a citizen's duty and upon fidelity (*fides*) to one's promise with little concern for abstract justice. It was not until 287 B.C.E. that the plebeians were able to finally achieve their demands for equality under Roman law.

Even as Rome was learning the politics of government, it was developing a powerful fighting machine. The concept of duty embodied in the Twelve Tables encouraged citizens to respond to calls for defense of the country. In 282 B.C.E., a part of the Roman fleet violated the territorial waters of the Greek city of Tarentum which was located in the instep of the heel of Italy. The Greeks, led by Pyrrhus, reacted with fury and viciousness and butchered the sailors. Pyrrhus then decided to move on Rome. He led a force of "20,000 infantrymen of the phalanx, 2000 archers, 500 slingers, and 3000 cavalry. Moreover, he had twenty Indian war-elephants. . . The simple Romans had never seen an elephant before; they called them 'snake-hands' and 'Lucanian cows,' and their horses were even more alarmed than they." (Stobart, p. 41)

Pyrrhus defeated the Roman troops and marched on toward Rome, expecting Roman villagers to join his forces. But cities shut their gates against him and Roman soldiers continued to harry his troops so that he was forced to return to Tarentum for the winter. He dispatched a courier to make terms of peace to Rome, but the Senate rejected the overture and established a basic doctrine that Rome would "never listen to terms while there were foreign troops on Italian soil" (Stobart, p. 42). Pyrrhus next drove the Carthaginians from Sicily, and finally returned home to Greece. Rome was now in charge of all of Italy and was recognized as a Mediterranean power.

But Pyrrhus had not crushed Carthage and Carthaginians now engaged Rome in a territorial battle for Sicily, Sardinia and Corsica. The first Punic war lasted from 264 to 241, the second from 218 to 200 B.C.E. It was in the second Punic war that Rome was confronted by the brilliant Carthaginian general Hannibal, who moved his troops through Spain, through Gaul, and across the Alps to attack Italy from the north. Frightful battles took place during the seventeen years, but Rome was able to withstand the invader. In 146 B.C.E., Rome sacked the city of Carthage.

Meanwhile, in Greece, military action under the leadership of Philip of Macedon and his son, Alexander the Great, had contained Persian power. Under Alexander and his successors, the Hellenization of the Mediterranean and Near Eastern world had blossomed. Greek was the language of trade and commerce. Greek art, Greek thought, Greek religion, and Greek philosophy permeated culture after culture, including that of Rome. But Roman military growth was such that, by the middle of the second century, Rome was mistress of the seas and the power of Roman gods and men was acknowledged everywhere.

The wealth of the empire now poured into Rome. Roman estates were tended by slave labor. A single Roman coinage replaced the individual coins produced by individual communities. New roads were built that helped to unify Italy, as did the development of a common citizenship. The Roman theater enacted plays written by Roman and Greek authors. The Roman gymnasia, like the Greeks before them, exalted the body. Power struggles within the nation were ultimately to yield to the leadership of Julius Caesar. Caesar, having risen through the ranks, entered into a pact with fellow triumvirs Pompey and Crassus in 59 B.C.E. This pact was known as the First Triumvirate. The pact was renewed in 56. When Crassus was killed in 53, a struggle for power began between Pompey and Caesar. Pompey was defeated in 48 and put to death and Caesar was in control. Factional fights were now over and the Roman empire was under the control of a dictator. Roman provinces were governed by responsible officers, who owed loyalty to the emperor.

On 15 March, 44 B.C.E., Caesar was murdered by a group of senators. Marcus Antonius, a loyal collaborator of Caesar, took control, but his leadership was challenged by C. Caesar Octavianus (Octavius), who had been adopted by Julius Caesar. By the year 30, the Roman empire was united under a single ruler. Octavius refused the role of dictator and retained his office as supreme commander of the armies and controller of finances. But the Senate, now convinced of the need for one-man leadership, gradually transferred more and more power to Octavius who assumed the name Augustus. In 12 B.C.E. Augustus was recognized as Pontifex Maximus, truly the supreme ruler.

Even as Rome maintained its hold on its vast empire through the army, in Europe dramatic cultural growth was underway. The fierce tribes in Germany and Austria had been held in check. In Gaul, Augustus sought to initiate the Dea Roma cult and the emperor cult alongside of the native religion. Magnificent roads were built, schools were opened and the Gauls entered into the cultural advantages with enthusiasm. But no such advances took place in Germany. Numerous independent tribal groups remained independent of Roman influence. Control of these people, who were only a one-week march distant from Rome, required the presence of Roman legions.

Roman Gods

Rome abounded in gods. Each of the peoples who moved into Italy brought their own deities. As a result, there were numerous minor gods — like Janus, the god of good beginnings, who gave his name to the month January; Portunus, a god of gates, who was recognized at portals; and Terminus the boundary god, whose presence was recognized each February 23rd when boundary stones were reverently oiled, garlanded and honored by sacrifice. Priapus was in charge of fertility, Sylvanus was associated with plowing and woodcutting. These gods were among the many *numina* or "powers" whose presence appeared to be everywhere. Divine powers were also associated with the dead: the Manes were spirits of the good dead, the Lemures were spirits of the wicked dead. Pluto, who was borrowed from the Greeks, was the god of the underworld. In addition, every Roman family had a Lar. The Lares were spirits of ancestors. Families also had Penates, gods of the hearth and guardians of storehouses.

A diversity of priesthoods developed during the early years of the Republic. There were two major colleges. The *pontifices*, with the *pontifex maximus* at their head, were concerned with sacrificial rites and with control of the Vestal Virgins who guarded the sacred hearth of the community. The *augures* sought to ascertain the will of the gods by studying such omens as the flights of birds. These two colleges were controlled by the patricians. Plebeian religion focused on the cults of Ceres (the Roman Demeter), Liber Pater (the Roman Dionysus) and his consort Libera.

Of greater significance were the great gods, whose myths have come down to us, so influenced by their Greek counterparts that their original nature is hard to discern. Here are their names with their Greek counterparts bracketed: Jupiter (Zeus), Juno (Hera), Neptune (Poseidon), Vesta (Hestia), Saturn (Cronus), Mars (Ares), Minerva (Athena), Venus (Aphrodite), Mercury (Hermes), Diana (Artemis), Vulcan (Haephestus) and Ceres (Demeter). Only Apollo retained his Greek identity upon entering the Roman pantheon. As the Greek gods were Romanized, they brought with them echoes of Greek mythologies which now became Roman property.

The shrine of Apollo at Cumae, on the Bay of Naples, was famous for its Sybil or prophetess. Apollo, god of music, archery, prophecy, healing, and the care of animals was, without question, one of the most attractive and inspiring of ancient deities. The Sibyl, having been endowed by Apollo with the gift of prophecy, was in charge of the Sibylline Books, the nine volumes of prophecy which were supposed to have been given at different times by various sibyls. In times of crisis, these volumes were consulted to determine what might be done to appease the angry gods. For example, during a famine in 493 B.C.E., the Cumae sibyl called for the erection of a shrine to Ceres, Liber, and Libera below the Aventine, thereby introducing Rome to the Eleusinian mysteries which we discussed in chapter 8 on Greece. In 349 B.C.E., during a pestilence, the sybil's advice was to institute pageants as an antidote. In the third century, during the Punic wars, when the old state religions failed to bring peace, the Sybilline books were consulted and the pageants were expanded into the vicious, cruel, and brutal gladiatorial games in which human slaughter was glorified. In 205 B.C.E., the sibyl provided an oracle that said that, although Hannibal was defeated, Hannibal would leave the country if Cybele, the mother of the gods, the great Asiatic goddess of fertility, was brought to Rome. Cybele was a Phrygian goddess whose power was embodied in a small black stone. Apparently the Roman ambassadors were able to persuade the Phrygians of the importance of moving the goddess. In April of 205, Cybele left Pessinus in Phrygia and arrived in Rome where she was welcomed with great joy. It would seem that the goddess went to work immediately, for Hannibal left Italy and an abundant harvest was attributed to Cybele's power.

But Cybele did not arrive alone. She brought with her Attis, her associate, who was the dying-rising god of vegetation, together with his devotees. Their festival was celebrated in Rome about the time of the vernal equinox. According to one Attis myth, the young god had castrated himself (hence, it is not surprising to find that his followers, emulating their god, became eunuchs). According to another myth, he was killed by a wild boar (which provided a basis for the cultic prohibition of eating pork). The rituals which took place between March 22nd and March 27th were characterized by barbarous, orgiastic behavior, frenzied dancing, self-gashing and self-castration, as well as symbolic representation of the death and resurrection of Attis. The rites also included sharing a sacramental meal and baptism in the blood of a bull. The behavior so shocked the Romans that the Senate forbade any Roman citizen to participate.

Another orgiastic religion which the Senate proscribed in 185 B.C.E. was the worship of Bacchus (Dionysus). This cult of the god of wine came to Rome through prisoners of war from Etruria or from the Greek colonies. The celebrations were characterized by young satyrs with fawnskins draped over their shoulders dancing to the music of flutes, and by drunken Silenus and wild female Baccantes and centaurs engaging in wine-soaked revelry. The action of the Senate may have had some dampening effect, but it was clear that the influence of the old gods of Rome was weakening, and that many Romans were attracted to the gaiety and revelry that separated participants from the problems and troubles of daily life and gave them, through the sacred rites, communication with a god. As we will see, the educated turned from religion to philosophy.

With such a variety of deities, each with his or her own area of specialization, Rome never developed any sense of a divinely ordained pattern for life. There was no list of commandments, no single savior god, no set of "revealed" scriptures. The closest that Rome came to anything of that nature was in the cult of the emperor and the notion of *Dea Roma*.

Efforts to centralize Roman religion began when Octavius became emperor of Rome. According to Cassius Deo (LII,36), Maecenas, a senator, provided the young Octavius with the following advice:

> . . . do you yourself worship the divine power everywhere by every means, in accordance with the traditions of our fathers, and compel others to honor it too. Hate and punish all who try to introduce innovations in this regard, not only for the sake of the gods . . . but because those who introducc new divinities persuade many to change their thoughts and practices; and from this there spring up conspiracies, revolts and factions . . . Do not tolerate atheists or magicians . . . and keep your eye on philosophers too.

Obviously, such attitudes and action precluded diversity or any toleration of freethought.

To commemorate peace, Octavius, now Augustus, erected in 13 B.C.E. the *Ara Pacis*, the altar of peace, symbolizing the *Pax Romana* (Roman peace) which he had established. He restored ancient temples, erected altars to the Lares (ancestral spirits) at crossroads, reintroduced forgotten festivals such as the Lupercalia, and introduced compulsory worship of emperors who were deified at their death. His father (by adoption) had already been declared a god by the Senate in 42 B.C.E. Now, at death, all Caesars became gods. Augustus himself was considered to be a living god in Asia, Spain, Gaul and Germany — but not in Rome, where the best that could be accomplished was an emphasis on the ruler's protecting genius which was recognized in shrines erected for that purpose. This was the beginning of emperor worship, which became mandatory in the provinces as a sign of loyalty to the Roman imperium. Some emperors refused to wait until death to be recognized as divinities, and Caligula (ruled 37-41 C.E.) and Domitian (ruled 81-96 C.E.) demanded worship during their lifetimes. Vespasian (ruled 70-79 C.E.) apparently took the honor with some humor and, as he lay dying, commented, "My goodness, I think I am turning into a god!"

Nevertheless, as Pontifex Maximus or Chief Pontif, Augustus was head of a national religion. The deification of the city of Rome as Dea Roma received some recognition within the city itself, but was never a factor in the unification of the nation or the empire. Even the Emperor cult was to fail in that respect. As we shall see, it was with the adoption of Christianity that a national cult was to develop.

Philosophy in Rome

It must be remembered that the Greeks who migrated to the Italian peninsula brought with them their own traditions. Nor did they lose contact with their homeland. It is not surprising to discover that the Romans were deeply indebted to the Greeks for philosophic thought. Cicero (Marcus Tullius Cicero, 106-43 B.C.E.) translated Plato's *Timaeus* into Latin, wrote treatises comparing various Greek schools of philosophy and provided a series of his own philosophical statements reflecting the Stoic emphases on practical reason. His teachings embraced the Roman ideal of *humanitas* (a term which he coined) which exalted human decency, nobility of action, morality and respect as the qualities that make for civilized living. During the Renaissance, *humanitas* was to become a central element in European culture where it impacted on the aristocracies by calling for both restraint and generosity. Education, according to Cicero, was not limited to intellectual pursuits but also embraced the moral:

> All literature, all philosophy, all history, abounds with incentives to noble action, incentives which would be buried in black darkness were the light of the written word not flashed upon them. How many pictures of high endeavor the great authors of Greece and Rome have drawn for our use, and bequeathed to us, not only for our contemplation, but for our emulation. (*Pro Archia Poetica*, p. 23)

Cicero accepted the existence of gods and argued that men and gods each possess the quality of reason, the highest of attributes, from which come ideas of law and justice. (*De Legibus*, p. 311f)

Lucretius (Titus Lucretius Carus: 96?-55 B.C.E.) was a rationalist who embraced the philosophies of Epicurus and Democritus. His Epicureanism led him to write of the wonder and beauty of the spirit soaring to freedom and knowledge. From Democritus he drew the notion of spontaneous natural creation from atoms, including both the human body and soul. His profound appreciation of the beauty and grandeur of nature and his atomistic philosophy led him to write *On the Nature of Things* (*De Rerum Natura*). In this philosophic poem he discussed origins of the earth, and of the earth-begotten plants, animals and humans. His materialistic universe was composed of an infinity of immortal atoms that meet, merge, separate, dissolve and change in accord with absolute laws. The soul, which is formed of atoms of wind, fire and air plus a fourth element, is diffused throughout the body, so that when the body dissolves, so does the soul.

He taught that the harshness of life was modified through the creation of the family, the state, language and technical and artistic discoveries. Religion, he argued, was invented because of human ignorance of the real causes of cataclysms — which were attributed to the wrath of the gods — a conclusion which produced fear. In his view, the first step to freedom from fear is to realize that nothing is ever begotten out of nothing by the divine will.

> Fear forsooth, so constrains all mortal men, because they behold many things come to pass on earth and in the sky, the cause of whose working they can by no means see, and think that a divine power brings them about. Therefore when we have seen that nothing can be created out of nothing, then more rightly after that shall we discern that for which we search, both whence each thing can be created, and in what ways all things come into being without the aid of gods. (Lucretius I, 183)

Lucretius was discounted by his fellow countrymen and, much later, during the Middle Ages, Christian monks consigned him to hell as the devil's disciple. However, when the scientific revolution began in the seventeenth century, his poem was given high praise and recognition, particularly for the doctrine of atoms.

Juvenal (Decimus Junius Juvenalis, (55?-140? C.E.) the Stoic satirist, viewed the foibles of Roman life with sarcastic amusement and expressed his reactions in pithy statements of ironic wit. As a Stoic, Juvenal interpreted deity as Fortune or Destiny, Nature and Reason, but he was ambivalent in his attitude towards these god concepts (Green, p. 38). He concluded Satire X with this comment:

> Fortune has no divinity, could we but see it: it's We ourselves, who make her a goddess, and set her in the heavens.

He mocked the gods of the empire: Jupiter, Mars, Saturn, and Juno — all of whom exhibited human weaknesses. He derided those who prayed to Jupiter for long life but who receive with their longevity all the physical and mental deprivations associated with age (Satire X: 190f). He scoffed at those who believed in the afterlife of Hades:

> Today not even children — except those small enough
> To get a free public bath — believe all that stuff about ghosts
> Or underground kingdoms and rivers, or black frogs croaking
> In the waters of Styx, or thousands of dead men ferried
> Across by one small skiff. (Satire II:146-150).

He scorned diviners, whether they were Chaldean astrologers or whether they represented the Mother Goddess or Osiris or the Jewish faith — each was a fraud seeking money (Satire VI:510-550). All the while, teachers and professors labored for a pittance and earned in one year the amount a jockey was paid for a single race (Satire VII:243). And as for oaths taken before one god or another — they are empty of meaning for the gods were silent:

> How can you listen to such lies, O Jupiter? Won't you even
> Open those lips of yours? Who cares if they are marble or bronze?
> You ought to say *something*. (Satire XIII:13-16)

Prayers revealed the greed of the prayer:

> The most popular, urgent prayer, well-known in every temple, is for wealth. *Increase my holdings, please make my deposit account the largest in town!* (Satire X:23-25)

Juvenal scorned the transparent phoniness of the social life of his time. He exposed the sexual proclivities of those who posed as normal, moral citizens but who were involved with pimps, whores, mistresses, courtesans, adultery and a multitude of deviant behaviors. He revealed the shallowness of relationships in business, government, love and marriage. No one escaped his barbed comments, not even emperors or priests or politicians or others in positions of power. Like other Stoics, he upheld the virtues of wisdom, reason, logic and morality. He denied or perhaps ignored the power of the irrational to hold some humans to moral behavior. He favored a rational morality that grew out of humans embracing good thoughts, good deeds and a good or moral life. It is not surprising to learn that he was exiled for a period of about five years to Egypt. Negative portrayals of national deities and of the lives of those in power, no matter how accurate, seldom reap rewards.

M. Aurelius Antoninus, Emperor of Rome (121-179 C.E.) was also a Stoic whose personal life was committed to Stoic values of reason, virtue and self control. He wrote of the insights he gained from his family and teachers including the importance of abstinence from evil, simplicity in living, freedom of will, steadiness of purpose, benevolence, love of family and of justice and truth, as well as mildness of temper and acceptance of that which cannot be changed. He also learned "not to give credit to what was said by miracle-workers and jugglers about incantations and the driving away of daemons and such things" (Thoughts I:6). He accepted the reality of the gods:

> To those who ask, Where hast thou seen the gods and how dost thou comprehend that they exist and so worshippest them, I answer, in the first place, they may be seen even with the eyes. In the second place, neither have I seen even my own soul, and yet I honor it. Thus then with respect to the gods, from what I constantly experience of their power, from this I comprehend they exist and I venerate them. (Thoughts XII:28).

The visibility of the gods reflects the Stoic doctrine that the universe, which Antoninus claims may be composed of atoms (Thoughts X:6), is a god and even the celestial bodies are gods. But gods were also the embodiment of the rational and it was through the rational that the gods touch the lives of humans: "With his intellectual part alone he [the god] touches the intelligence only which has flowed and been derived from himself into these bodies" (Thoughts XII:2). Prayer to the gods should entertain the rational:

> Either the gods have no power or they have power. If then they have no power, why dost thou pray to them? But if they have power, why dost thou not pray for them to give thee the faculty of not fearing any of the things which thou fearest, or of not desiring any of the things which thou desirest, or not being pained at anything, rather than pray that any of these things should not happen or happen? For certainly if they can co-operate with men, they can co-operate for these purposes. But perhaps thou wilt say, the gods have placed them in thy power. Well, then, is it not better to use what is in thy power like a free man, than to desire in a slavish and abject way what is not in thy power? And who has told thee that the gods do not aid us even in the things which are in our power? Begin then to pray for such things and thou wilt see. One man prays

> thus: How shall I be able to lie with that woman? Do thou pray thus: How shall I not desire to lie with her! Another prays thus: How shall I be released from this? Another prays: How shall I not desire to be released? Another thus: How shall I not lose my little son? Thou thus, How shall I not be afraid to lose him. In fine, turn thy prayers this way and see what comes. (Thoughts IX:40)

The Stoic acceptance of what cannot be changed and the Stoic search for control of desires and of life itself are reflected in the prayers. It takes no psychologist to recognize that what Antoninus is suggesting in his presentation of proper prayer constitutes a mental strengthening of the qualities that are dear to the Stoic through wishing for or through willing support from the deities.

Because it was both expedient and wise for the emperor to give recognition to beliefs entertained by the various factions within his realm, it is not surprising to find that M. Aurelius Antoninus was initiated into the Eleusinian mystery cult. The act does not imply that the ruler was uneasy or superstitious regarding the various faiths, but rather he did what was prudent, even though today the very act might be interpreted as a violation of the personal integrity of the man. But such is politics!

Perhaps the greatest ancient authority on Skepticism was Sextus Empiricus (late second century to 210 C.E.), from whose name the term "empiricism" is derived. According to Sextus Empiricus in his *Outlines of Pyrrhonism*, the Skeptic's desire was for "quietude in respect of manners of opinion and moderate feeling in respect of things unavoidable" (Hallie, p. 10). The skeptical tool was "doubt" which

> washes itself away along with the dubious unprovable claims it works on, and it does so, according to our Sceptical physician, "just as aperient drugs do not merely eliminate the humours of the body, but also expel themselves along with the humours." The ultimate purpose of scepticism is to make doubting unnecessary, to let the customs of our country, our needs for food and drink and so forth, and our plain everyday speech take over direction of our thought and life after doubting is done. (Hallie, p. 7)

Perhaps the most important writing by Sextus Empiricus, so far as freethought about the gods is concerned, is found in his *Against the Physicists, Book One*, where he discusses "the doctrine of gods." His analysis of varying arguments for the existence of gods or a god, and his presentation of the arguments of those who deny the existence of gods, is long and inclusive. Indeed, practically every argument which modern day theologians employ is included. Each argument is evaluated and found wanting. The conclusion to the exhaustive study is as follows:

> Well now, such are the arguments attempted on both sides for the existence of gods and for the non-existence of gods. Their logical consequence is the Sceptic's suspension of judgement, especially since in addition to them there is also the diversity of views on the part of ordinary people about gods. For different people have differing and discordant notions about them, with the result that it is possible neither to believe all of them, as they are conflicting, nor to believe some of them, on account of their being of equal force. Further confirmation of this is furnished by the myth-making of the theologians and poets, which is full of all kinds of impiety. Hence Xenophanes too, in his criticism of Homer and Hesiod, says:
>
> > Homer and Hesiod have ascribed to the gods everything
> > That is, with men, disgraceful and blameworthy:
> > Stealing, adultery, and deceiving one another.
> > (Hallie, p. 215)

Does Sextus Empiricus support the belief that gods exist or that there is a supreme God? The wise skeptic suspends judgment; there is no conclusive proof either way. This means that the subject remains in doubt and therefore, since an ultimate truth cannot be known, the issue does not impinge on the life of the skeptic. Such detachment from futile bickering and debate preserved the quality of living for those who "loved life too much to let it be ruined by arbitrary assertion." (Hallie, p. 28)

Confrontation With Judaism and Christianity

Augustus ruled Rome for forty-five years after the Battle of Actium, from 31 B.C.E. to 14 C.E. It was he who consolidated Roman power to form the Roman Empire that embraced the Mediterranean basin including Spain, North Africa, the Near East to the Euphrates river and in the north to Gaul and Rhine-Danube rivers. His kingdom was run by professionals — officials who were responsible for tax collection and maintaining the well-being of the provinces. Roman law was the law of the land, and under that law, religious and cultural differences were recognized and accepted. However, loyalty to Rome was a prerequisite. The Dea Roma cult which Augustus established was designed to give the empire, but more particularly the city of Rome, divine status and recognition as a spiritual entity.

In some parts of the empire, Augustus was treated as a god incarnate; at home he was *princeps* or leading citizen to the public and *imperator* or commander-in-chief to his troops. He did control the imperial cult, but in Rome, it was not until after his death that he was declared divine. He established the *Pax Romana* and maintained peace by stationing segments of the army throughout the empire

The conquest of the Mediterranean world placed the Romans in direct confrontation with the monotheism of Judaism, both in Palestine and in Alexandria, Egypt. The Roman empire had granted permission to the different peoples they conquered to worship their own gods, providing recognition was also given to the gods of Rome. For most nations, the inclusion of a few extra gods posed no problem. However, the pattern changed when Rome was confronted with the claims of Jews and later, Christians. These groups not only insisted on the right to worship their own deity but declared that the gods of Rome and of other cultures were not gods and refused to recognize them. Further, every Roman who was converted to Judaism and Christianity became an apostate to Roman religion.

The first reaction to the Jewish refusal to worship the Roman deities was marked by impatience, intolerance and persecution, particularly under Caligula. The Jews were seen as atheists who denied the validity of the Roman deities. However, when Claudius was Caesar (41-54 C.E.), he "extended his goodwill to the Judaeans of the entire Roman Empire, granting them complete religious freedom, and protecting them from the interference of the pagans." (Graetz, II, p. 191)

At first, Christians enjoyed the same exemptions, inasmuch as they were recognized as a Jewish sect. However, as conflict between Jews and Christians escalated, it became clear that Christianity was a religion in its own right and, therefore, not protected under the provisions exempting Jews from emperor worship. Christians were considered to be atheists and for a short period were subject to persecution. Here, atheism did not constitute a denial of the existence of a god or gods, but the refusal to worship Roman gods.

As Christianity came to be known among the Romans, there were those who opposed its teachings, preferring to retain belief in the numerous gods of Rome. One such person was Marcus Cornelius Fronto, the tutor of Marcus Aurelius. His work is now lost to us, hence we cannot know what arguments or what approach he may have employed. However, about 200 C.E., an African Christian convert, a lawyer named Marcus Minucius Felix, presented a dialogue between himself and two other lawyers: Octavius Januarius, a Christian, and L. Caecilius Natalis, who championed belief in the Roman gods. Of course, the account is made to end with the conversion of Caecilius; but in the presentation of Caecilius' opposition to Christianity, we are able to catch a glimpse of the way in which sophisticated Romans may have responded to Christian claims. It is possible that the arguments represent those which Minucius faced in his defense of Christians.

While accepting the reality of Roman deities, Caecilius did not hesitate to employ rationalism in his attack on Christian beliefs. He pointed out that even the Jews, "The lonely and miserable nationality" with their worship of "one God, and one peculiar to itself," worshiped openly in temples with ceremonies. Christianity had not yet reached the point of acquiring public buildings and hence worshiped in secret. He continued:

> But the Christians, moreover, what wonders, what monstrosities do they feign! — that he who is their God, whom they can neither show nor behold, inquires diligently into the character of all, the acts of all, and, in fine, into their words and secret thoughts; that he runs about everywhere, and is everywhere present: they make him out to be troublesome, restless, even shamelessly inquisitive, since he is present at everything that is done, wanders in and out of all places, although being occupied with the whole, he cannot give attention to particulars, nor can he be sufficient for the whole while he is busied with particulars.
>
> What! because they threaten conflagration to the whole world, and to the universe itself, with all its stars, are they meditating its destruction? — as if either the eternal order constituted by the divine laws of nature would be disturbed, or the league of all the elements would be broken up, and the heavenly structure dissolved, and that fabric in which it is contained and bound together would be overthrown. And not content with this wild opinion, they add to it and associate with it old women's fables: they say they will rise again after death,

> and ashes, and dust; and with I know not what confidence, they believe by turns in one another's lies; you would think that they had already lived again. It is a double evil and a twofold madness to denounce destruction to the heaven and the stars, which we leave just as we found them, and to promise eternity to ourselves who are dead and extinct — who, as we are born, so also perish! . . . Deceived by this error, they promise to themselves, as being good, a blessed and perpetual life after death; to others, as being unrighteous, eternal punishment . . .
>
> Behold, a portion of you — and as you declare, the larger and better portion — are in want, are cold, are labouring in hard work and hunger; and God suffers it, He feigns; He either is not willing or not able to assist His people; and thus He is either weak or inequitable. Thou who dreamest over a post-humous immortality, when thou art shaken by danger, when thou art consumed with fever, when thou art torn with pain, dost thou not then feel thy real condition? Dost thou not then acknowledge thy frailty? . . . Where is that God who is able to help you when you come to life again, since he cannot help you when you are in this life? Do not the Romans, without any help from your God, govern, reign, have the enjoyment of the whole world, and have dominion over you? (Felix, pp. 467-468)

Attacks on Christianity continued. In the eyes of many, Christianity was characterized as an illicit religion that could not be trusted in that its members would not swear by the *genius* of the Emperor. But the attacks were for the most part not organized and were sporadic. On the other hand, the Christian church had learned one thing from Roman government, namely the importance of organizational structure. The episcopal pattern tended to elevate men with management skills to positions of leadership. Despite the on-going theological battles within its ranks (see chapter 10 on Christianity), it encouraged its members to remain firm in the face of pressure from without. Tertullian (Quintus Septimus Florens Tertullianus) of Carthage (c. 155—c. 230 C.E.), a lawyer who converted to Christianity, raised the battle cry of defiance against persecution — "the blood of the martyrs is the seed of the Christians" — that helped to convert martyrdom into a weapon of propaganda for the faith.

The Roman government was in process of change. In 284 C.E., Diocletian became emperor. Under his guidance the old republican form of government was slowly transformed into an autocratic monarchy. Senatorial influence waned. The huge empire was subdivided and placed under the control of military leaders who would carry out Diocletian's wishes. As he and his colleagues observed the growth of the Church, they confronted Christians with the requirement of emperor worship and recognition of the old gods of Rome. Efforts were made to rid the palace and the army of Christians. The destruction of churches, the confiscation of sacred literature, the imprisonment of clergy and the use of torture were sanctioned. Once again there were many martyrs for the faith. After Diocletian's death persecutions waned. By 311, an edict gave toleration to Christians on the condition that they did nothing "contrary to discipline," to use the words of the church historian, Eusebius.

By 323, Constantine had overcome rivals and was in complete charge of the Roman empire. Christianity was more than tolerated. Little by little privileges were granted to the growing Church that eased its burdens socially, politically and financially. In 319 private non-Christian sacrifices were prohibited. Because of the influx of new money, churches were erected in Rome, Jerusalem, Bethlehem and elsewhere under the auspices of the emperor. Constantine moved the capital from Rome to Constantinople and the bishop of Rome was left in a position of high authority and power. Through all of this change, Constantine remained *pontifex maximus*, the high priest of the old Roman religion. Despite this role, he accepted Christianity and was baptized in the year that he died in 327 C.E.

The church had become a powerful business corporation; the emperor had favored its growth and encouraged its unity. In 325, the Council of Nicaea made it possible for bishops from various parts of the empire to assemble at government expense to struggle with theological issues. Constantine's sons, his immediate successors, followed his lead and gave varying degrees of support to Christianity. However, when they died and Julian became emperor (361-363), he returned to the old religions, thus earning for himself the designation of "Julian the Apostate." It is important to know that the religion he endorsed called for high ethical principles and laid stress on morality and on the duty of kindliness and charity. But his was the last official sanction of the old gods of Rome. By the fifth century, the empire had become Christian.

When Constantine accepted Christianity, Rome's borders extended from India to England. Although Rome had developed the world's greatest military organization, it lacked a genuine unifying principle to bind the nation. The notion of Dea Romana and the worship of Roman deities proved insufficient to unify the wide-spread nation.

Even emperor worship had failed. Christianity was to provide the unifying principle. Of course, ultimately, this too failed, and Rome fell to the barbarians. After Christianity was accepted by the crown, it failed to provide for free will acceptance, therefore it was not adopted by the subject people by choice, but through the compelling use of force. Interestingly enough, when the power of Rome was broken (the first cracking of frontiers began about 406) and the city fell to the Visigoths (in 410) and the Barbarians assumed control of Europe, Christianity was to become the religion of the western heritage.

References

Antoninus, M. Aurelius, *The Thoughts of the Emperor M. Aurelius Antonius*. Trans. by George Long. Boston: Ticknor and Fields, 1864.

Cicero, *De Legibus*. Trans. by Clinton W. Keyes. New York: Putnam, 1928 (Loeb Classical Library).

Cicero, *Pro Archia Poetica*. R.H. Watts, edit. Cambridge, Mass.: Harvard University Press, 1961 (Loeb Classical Library).

Felix, Minucius, *Octavius*, in *Ante-Nicene Christian Library*. Alexander Roberts and James Donaldson, edits. Edinburgh: Clark, 1869. Vol. XIII, pp. 467-468.

Graetz, H., *History of the Jews*. Philadelphia: The Jewish Publication Society of America. 1893, Vols. I-IV.

Green, Peter, "Introduction," Juvenal: *The Sixteen Satires*. Baltimore, Maryland: Penguin Books, 1976.

Hallie, Philip P., *Scepticism, Man, and God*. Middletown, Conn: Wesleyan University Press, 1964.

Juvenal, *The Sixteen Satires*. Trans. by Peter Green. Baltimore, Maryland: Penguin Books, revised edition, 1976.

Lucretius, *De Rerum Natura*. Edit. and trans. by Cyril Bailey. Oxford: Clarendon Press, 1947, Vol. I.

Stobart, J.C., *The Grandeur That Was Rome*. New York: St. Martin's Press, 1987.

"The Myths of Ancient Rome" in *Encyclopedia of World Mythology*. New York: Galahad Books, 1975.

10

Christianity

According to the Gospel traditions, the founder of Christianity was Jesus, who was raised in Nazareth as the son of a carpenter named Joseph and his wife, Mary. The Gospels refer to his sisters and to brothers named James, Joses or Joseph, Judas and Simon (Mark 6:3, Matt. 13:55). Jesus' purported statement that "a prophet is not without honor except in his own country, and among his own kin and in his own house" (Mark 6:4) suggests that the brothers and the family did not, at first, support Jesus' ministry.

As in the other religions we have discussed, here too we find the familiar motifs associated with heros. A virgin is impregnated by a deity and a miraculous birth results. The infant is threatened by hostile forces (in this case King Herod) and must be put in a place of safety (Jesus and his family flee to Egypt). The hero overcomes death and ascends to heaven. The mythic interpretations did not cease with the New Testament stories. The Apocryphal New Testament, most of which was composed during the second century C.E., contains an abundance of wonder tales. One story provides the basis for the immaculate conception dealing with Mary's birth and childhood, which she is supposed to have spent in the temple. Another tale seeks to verify the continual virginity of Mary by proving that Mary's hymen was not torn by the birth of Jesus. Some accounts tell of Jesus' magical powers as a child, including his ability to animate clay birds. Still others deal with Mary's assumption to heaven. These apocryphal tales indicate the continual mythologizing of Jesus and Mary in the early church. The historical evidence is different.

Christianity, the religion, began during the first century C.E. as a Jewish sect. According to the biblical tradition, shortly after the beheading of John the Baptizer, Jesus of Nazareth, who had been baptized by John, gathered a group of followers and began what was to become the Christian movement. Jesus was active for perhaps one year and no more than three years (based on three Passovers mentioned in the Gospel of John) before he was convicted of sedition by a Roman court of justice and put to death by crucifixion along with two other condemned men. Following his death, his followers reported a series of what have been called "religious experiences," through which they became convinced that Jesus' physical body had been resurrected and that he had returned, bodily, to heaven which, in first century thought, was a place located immediately above the earth. They believed that he would soon return from heaven riding on a cloud (Acts 1:9-11) to establish the Kingdom of Christians. Among the early converts was a Jew from Tarsus named Saul who became the Christian apostle Paul.

The Christian sect shared beliefs held by other Jewish groups. For example, like the Pharisees, Christians believed in the resurrection of the dead. Like the Zealots they believed in the coming of a Messiah. Like the Essenes they believed that they were living in the last days and that the end of the world was at hand. Where they differed from these other groups was that they believed that in Jesus they had a concrete example of the resurrection, they believed that Jesus was the long expected Messiah, and they believed that the return of Jesus would mark the end of time and usher in the kingdom of the triumphant faithful — the Christians.

Christianity and the Mystery Religions

From the letters of Paul, which were written by the Apostle to Christian groups in various Mediterranean cities, we catch a glimpse of the movement of Christianity into the world of the Gentiles. We also become aware of the flexibility of the developing movement and the problems that independent thinking engendered. As Paul encountered the mystery religions (described in chapter 8 on Greece), he adapted the Christian faith and the language of the movement to the current religious environment. When he wrote to the Christians in the town of Colossae in Asia Minor, he described the Christian message as "the mystery (*musterion*) hidden for ages and generations but now made manifest to his saints (Christians). God chose to make known to them how great among the Gentiles are the riches of the glory of this mystery (*musterion*), which is Christ in you, the hope of glory" (Colos. 1:26f). In other words, the Christians were the true *mystae* who knew the secrets of the faith — secrets not known by others. Like the participants in the Eleusinian mysteries, Christians entertained the hope of glory in the afterworld. In Christianity, the mythic drama involved the death and resurrection of Christ, just as in the Eleusinian religion, the mythic drama involved the death and resurrection of Persephone. Reference to the *musterion* appears in the letter to the church at Ephesus where Paul wrote of his mission "to make men see what is the plan of the mystery (*musterion*) hidden for ages in God who created all things" (Ephes. 3:9). The same emphasis appears in Romans 16:25f; I Cor. 2:7-10; and Ephesians 1:8-10. For Paul, Christianity was the new mystery religion.

The Gospels which, to the best of our knowledge, were composed later than the letters of Paul, echo the same theme. In Mark 4:11, Jesus purportedly tells his twelve disciples, "To you is given the secret (*musterion*) of the kingdom of God, but for those outside everything is in parables." (see also Matt. 13:11; Luke 8:10). Only those initiated into the faith could understand the hidden meaning of the parables; to others, the meaning was obscured.

Does the Christian mystery differ significantly from Greek mysteries? Both are mysteries of revelation. Both offer salvation and rewards in the afterlife. Both present dying and rising deities. Both required baptismal cleansing. Both involve rituals in which sacred foods are partaken, symbolic of the life power of the saving figure. Both claim to have secret information which gives power to those who belong. Both present the figure of the mourning mother whose suffering and loss parallels those of humans everywhere. Both speak to human need for salvation from the evils of the world. What is different is the emphasis on the Christian savior, Jesus, as an historical figure despite the theology that reveals his divinity. The emphasis on Jesus as an historical person, as opposed to the mythic heros in other cults, became important as the developing church challenged current mystery religions with which it entered into competition for members.

Christianity and Judaism

An interpretation of Jesus' death, that differed from the emphasis in the mystery cult interpretation, employed imagery associated with Jewish temple ritual. The Jewish deity, Yahweh, demanded from his worshippers rites to purge a person who had violated any of the several hundred commandments of the faith. The ritual employed the blood of a slain bull (Lev. 4) by which an individual or an entire community could be purged. According to the writer of "The Letter to the Hebrews," Jesus' blood provided a far more significant sacrificial cleansing (Heb. 9:13-14). Whereas the Jewish rite had to be performed over and over again, Jesus' death provided a once-for-all-time sacrificial act of redemption (Heb. 9:12). The writer of the Gospel of John, placed the recognition of this redemptive role in the mouth of John the Baptizer: "Behold the Lamb of God, who takes away the sins of the world!"

(John 1:29). The lamb was the central sacrificial victim in Jewish ritual. It was associated with the Passover, (Exod. 12:11-12), with daily offerings (Exod. 29:38-42) and so forth. Thus, the interpretation of Jesus' death was presented with reference to Jewish doctrines of sacrificial purification as well as in terms of the mystery cults.

Dissension in the early Church

As Christian evangelists moved into the Roman world, they found receptive ears among some Jews and non-Jews. But almost immediately dissensions arose. For example, a question concerning conversion centered on whether or not it was necessary for non-Jews to become Jews (undergo circumcision) before becoming Christians. Jerusalem Christians argued that they must be circumcised; the Pauline group argued against the need for the intermediary step. The debate is echoed in Paul's letter to the Galatians (chs. 2, 5). Ultimately, the non-circumcision group were victors. A similar question was concerned with Jewish kosher diet. Were non-Jews who converted to Christianity compelled to follow a kosher diet? In Corinth, where the market place was overshadowed by the temple to Apollo, the god of merchants, food sold in the shops was consecrated to him and was obviously non-kosher. Once again, Paul was compelled to preserve the independence of Gentile Christians so that they would not have to conform to Jewish food regulations (see I Cor. ch. 8). It is clear that freedom to reinterpret doctrine was part of developing Christianity.

Decisions, like those just mentioned, served to move Christianity away from inclusion within the multi-faceted structure of Judaism and to establish itself as an independent religious organization. Thus, Christianity, which began as a sect within Judaism, became a religion that rejected Judaism — a rejection that was to bear the seeds of anti-Semitism that would manifest itself in century after century by persecution of Jews by Christians once the latter came into power.

The Growth of the Church

The first century C.E. was an advantageous time for Christian expansion. The Roman emperor Augustus had brought peace (*Pax Romana*) to the world, ensuring safe travel and engendering a growing cosmopolitanism. Expanded trade and commerce, facilitated by the network of Roman roads and the common use of the Greek language throughout the empire, encouraged the sharing of ideas, religions, and philosophies to which, for the most part, the Empire proper was indifferent. Because Christianity was, at first, recognized by the government as a Jewish sect, Christian envoys and missionaries enjoyed the unique protective status Rome had granted to the Jews — a privilege that prevailed until it became clear that Christians could be identified as a separate group. Evidence of their separate status came as early as 64 C.E. when they were persecuted by Nero.

Finally, it is important to remember that the traditional state and family religions of the Greco-Roman world were losing their hold on people. This situation produced a restlessness that made many open to information about new religious ideas. Justin Martyr, who wrote about 153 C.E., told of his personal journey through Stoicism, Aristotelianism, Pythagoreanism and Platonism before becoming a Christian.

Christianity and Rome

At first, the early Church clearly believed in the separation of church and state ("Render to Caesar the things that are Caesar's and to God the things that are God's" cf. Mark 12:17; Matt. 22:21; Luke 20:25). Indeed, as the Church began to grow, it experienced governmental prejudice, persecution and prosecution. Christians were perceived as an atheistic group in that they rejected the old gods of the empire and the church was viewed as a treasonable and anarchic organization in its refusal to participate in emperor-worship. The intensity and amount of oppression varied in different parts of the empire and under different rulers — under Nero, Trajan (111-113), Hadrian (117-138), Antoninus Pius (138-161), Marcus Aurelius (161-180) and Diocletian in 303 and 304.

When King Constantine embraced Christianity in 312 the door was opened for the Church to exercise genuine power in the Roman world. Gifford notes:

> there followed the famous edict of Milan, in 313, granting religious liberty throughout the Roman world, "that whatever heavenly divinity exists may be propitious to us and to all that live under our government." It was only a political device; but it soon made the Christian Church the favorite son of the State — a doubtful gift, though it seemed at the time a very great one. (p. 172)

By the middle of the fifth century Christianity had effectively outlawed the ancient state religion, made idolatry treasonable, and had either closed or destroyed or taken over the temples associated with the old religion. Only among the peasants, the *pagani*, was the old religion still alive. The separation of church and state was replaced by collaboration and, at times, by the belief that the state was subject to the church.

Divisions Within the Early Church

As we have noted, from the beginning, there were divisions within Christianity. Separate groups formed, each claiming to possess the correct identity of Jesus. Each independent expression of the new faith involved the rejection of the claims and interpretations of other Christian groups. For example, Christians known as the Docetists (from the Greek: *dokein*: to seem) argued that Jesus only *seemed* to have appeared in the flesh, but was in reality a heavenly ghost-like being, not a creature of flesh and blood. The controversy with the Docetists is reflected in I John (1:2-3, 2:22, 4:2-3) where readers were warned that the proclaimers of the Docetic doctrine were "the anti-Christ" (2:22, 4:3).

Another group, known as Gnostics (from the Greek *gnosis*: knowledge), also denied the full humanity of Jesus and explained his appearance either in Docetic terms or as a temporary in-dwelling of the spiritual Christ in the human Jesus. For them, salvation came through "knowledge" — "a mystical, spiritual enlightenment for the initiated which brings him into communion with the true realm of spiritual realities" (Walker, p. 52). The Gnostic teacher, Valentinus, who made a bid for leadership in Rome between 130 to 160 C.E., divided humans into three categories: the "spiritual" who could attain "knowledge," the "psychical" who "were capable of faith, and of a certain degree of salvation," and the "material" who were beyond redemption (Walker, p. 53). Neither the Docetists nor the Gnostics were able to prevail and hence the human Jesus as Messiah was not deprived of the faith traditions of incarnation, death and resurrection.

Marcion, an ascetic Christian from Asia Minor, endorsed Gnostic beliefs and rejected the Jewish God of the Old Testament as an inferior or evil being. Marcion went to Rome about 139 C.E. to point out the errors of Judaism and to seek to exclude any Old Testament material from the Christian teachings. He compiled a canon of scriptures which included only expurgated copies of the Gospel of Luke and the ten letters of Paul (omitting the Pastorals) from which he removed all suggestions that Jesus regarded the God of the Old Testament as his father. Marcion was expelled from the Church in 144 C.E., but his movement lasted into the fifth century.

As Christian groups were established in the various cities of the Roman world, rival centers of ecclesiastical power located in Rome, Alexandria, Egypt, and Constantinople, began to emerge. By the end of the first century, the congregation in Rome was not only the largest Christian group, but had expressed its sense of power and leadership within Christianity by addressing a letter of advice (ascribed to Clement, an elder in the Roman church, 93-97 C.E.) to Christians in Corinth with the expectation that it would be obeyed. When, during the second century, debates over the dating for the Easter observances occurred, Rome's choice won the day.

Christianity: the New "Mystery" Religion

As we have noted, as the Christian church moved into the Mediterranean world, it sought to challenge the claims of the mystery religions by arguing the superiority of the Christian "mystery." Sometime around the end of the second century or the beginning of the third, Clement of Alexandria (died c. 215), a presbyter in the Alexandrian Christian church, contrasted the Christian mysteries with those of the Dionysian cult. Hugo Rahner has noted:

> In his famous chapter on mysteries in his *Protepticus* he [Clement] addresses Hellenistic man as follows:
>
> Come thou frenzy-stricken one, not resting on thy wand, not wreathed with ivy! Cast off thy headdress; cast off thy fawn-skin; return to soberness! I shall show you the Logos, and the mysteries of the Logos, and I shall explain to you in images that are known to you. This is the mountain beloved of God, no longer the scene of tragedies, like Cithaeron, but devoted to the drama of truth . . . O truly sacred mysteries! O pure light! . . . I become holy by initiation. The Lord reveals the sacred signs, for He Himself is the hierophant. . . . And thou shalt dance with angels around the unbegotten and imperishable and only true God, and God's Logos shall join with us in our hymns of praise. . . .

And then, after describing the most important of the Dionysian cult rites, he continues:

> These are the mysteries of the atheists. And I am right in branding as atheists men who are ignorant of the true God . . But I wish to display to you at close quarters the gods themselves . . . in order that at least you may cease from error and run back again to heaven. "For we too were once children of wrath, as also the rest; but God being rich in mercy, through His great love wherewith He loved us, when we were already dead in trespass, made us alive with Christ." For the Word is living, and he who has been buried with Christ is exalted together with God. . . . We . . . are no longer creatures of wrath, for we have been torn away from the error and are hastening toward the truth. (Rahner, p. 355f)

The references are clear. The men clothed in fawn skins and wreathed in ivy are participants in the Dionysiac or Bacchus cult. Clement offers a new mystery and a new dance, separate and different from the Dionysiac revels, namely, a dance with angels.

The manner in which the emerging Christian church adopted the language of the mystery cults cannot be overstated. Christianity became the new mystery religion. "We impart God's wisdom in a mystery (*sophia en musterion*)" Paul wrote in a letter to the Corinthian Christians (1 Cor. 2:7). In Ephesians 5:32, he described Christ and the church as the "great mystery (*musterion mega*). As symbols were carried in other mystery cult processionals, so in the Christian mystery religion a symbol was elevated. The symbol of the Christian mystery, which is carried in processionals even to this day, is the cross which symbolized the tree of life and immortality, denied to humans in the Adam and Eve story (Gen. 3:22f). Now immortality was made available to believers through the cross — the secret Christian symbol of the tree of life. Immortality was available to those who had been cleansed by the blood sacrifice of Jesus (Rom. 3:25), which was, as we have noted, imagery based on the blood sacrifices of animals in the Jewish temple.

Christianity Confronts Mithraism

As Paul and other Christian missionaries moved into the Mediterranean world they came in contact with Mithraic belief, which was active in Asia Minor and was formally introduced to Rome during the reign of Emperor Nero (54-68 C.E.). Christian religious imagery now adopted new dimensions and writers could speak of believers being "sprinkled" with the blood of Jesus (1 Peter 1:2), just as in the Mithraic taurobolium believers were sprinkled with the blood of the bull (see below).

The religion of Mithra was the greatest rival to developing Christianity. Mithraism was spread throughout the Mediterranean world. Initially, Mithra was an Indo-Iranian sun god who crossed the heavens daily in a chariot of gold, forcing the powers of darkness ("Ahriman" in Persian Zoroastrianism) to flee. The religion had royal sanction and several Parthian monarchs bore the name Mithradates ("given by Mithra"). Indeed, it was Mithradates VI (c. 121-63 B.C.E.) who helped to spread the worship of Mithra throughout Asia Minor. In 66 C.E., the name of Mithra was introduced into the Roman court of Nero when visiting King Tiradates of Armenia addressed the emperor with "I come to you, my god, to worship you as I worship Mithra." Some 200 years later, in 274, Mithra as *Deus Sol Invictus Mithras* (The Invincible Sun God) was declared to be the official god of the Roman empire by the Emperor Aurelius. By that time, Mithraism was spread throughout the Roman empire. The god's birth day was declared to be December 25th, "the date then accepted for the winter solstice" (Finegan p. 211). After Constantine became king, this date became the natal day for Jesus, rather than January 6th as it was celebrated in the Eastern Christian communities.

Mithraic mysteries, like other mystery religions, introduced worshippers to both the god-myth and the rites of entry into the cult. The cult myth involved the conflict between good and evil (a pattern in Zoroastrianism which we previously noted) — a struggle with which every human could identify. Cleansing was attained through a baptism of blood in which initiates, standing beneath a grate over which a bull was slain, were sprinkled with the blood of the animal. The ritual was known as the "taurobolium."

Other sacred ceremonies included a love feast, commemorating a last supper that Mithra celebrated with the sun god before his ascension. A bas-relief portraying the cultic enactment, discovered in Bosnia (Cumont, Fig. 38), portrays two persons reclining on a couch. Before them, on a tripod, are four small loaves of bread, each marked with a cross. Initiates stand around them and one presents a drinking horn. The eating of bread and the drinking of wine appears to have been a substitute for an earlier Iranian ritual in which the bread was mingled with an elixir of the sacred intoxicating drug Haoma — a plant unfamiliar in the west. The intoxicating liquor was designed to have the effect we previously noted in the discussion of Dionysiac rites — to provide mental and physical vigor, wisdom, and the power to combat evil. Because drinking Haoma was a sacred rite, it conferred on the initiate immortality. There were a number of degrees of initiants within Mithraism and the highest bore the title "Father." The chief Mithra priest was called "Father of the Fathers." Priests served as intermediaries between humans and the god and were in charge of the administration of the sacraments. The details of the cult are far too extensive for further consideration here, but have been discussed by Franz Cumont in *The Mysteries of Mithra*.

Christianity and Neo-Platonism

Another rival faith system known as Neo-Platonism began in Alexandria. The founder was Ammonius Saccas (c. 245 C.E.), but the developer of the faith was Plotinus (205-270), who took the religion to Rome where it was carried on by Porphyry (233-304). Plato had "disparaged the life of the senses and praised the life of contemplation," but Neo-Platonism under Plotinus "went farther" (Gifford, p. 145). Neo-Platonism focused on human sin and salvation — a moral conflict that reflected the wider universal struggle between evil and good. Matter was deemed to be evil and the enemy of the spirit. Salvation, therefore, began with extermination of physical desires and emotions with a view to achieving a sense of oneness with the divine and entering into mystic communication. This kind of thinking impacted on Christianity, particularly in the thinking of Augustine.

Christianity Confronts Manichaeism

A third rival faith, Manichaeism, developed out of the preaching of Mani who was born in Persia in 216 C.E. He proclaimed his religion in Babylon in 244 and was martyred in 277. Mani, like Jesus (who Mani listed along with Zoroaster as one of the messengers of God), was the founder of a new faith. Like Jesus, he drew upon older faith traditions — in his case Zoroastrianism, Judaism, Gnostic Christianity and perhaps also Buddhism. Like the early Christians, he called for renunciation and austerity. As his faith began to spread, Mani, like Jesus, came under judgment by the Roman government and was martyred. He preached salvation through renunciation. He envisioned good and evil in an eternal struggle, which he likened to the contest between light and darkness. Because humans are involved in this struggle, the deity supplied messengers like Mani and Jesus to set humans free. Salvation was obtained through knowledge of the true nature of humans and by following a path toward the light, which incorporated an austere rejection of that which is of darkness, including physical desire. Manichaeism became a genuine rival of Christianity and, despite violent persecution under the emperor Diocletian (c. 300), the religion spread throughout the Roman empire and Europe and into Asia where it remained active in China until the seventeenth century (Latourette, p. 352). Before he became a Neo-Platonist and, finally, a Christian, Augustine was a follower of Mani for some nine years. The religion failed, ultimately, because it was unable to secure monarchical support and because of its lack of leaders with organizational skills.

Early Christian Writings

Clearly, early Christianity developed in an atmosphere of controversy. Some struggles originated within the movement; others came from without. Within, there were debates concerning which Christian writings were to be accepted as authoritative for faith and conduct. Coptic Christian texts found at Nag Hammadi, Egypt, include a number of Gnostic gospels and some are attributed to persons mentioned in the New Testament (Thomas, Mary, Philip). These gospels plus numerous other writings were, apparently, accepted as authoritative for faith and conduct by Egyptian Christians. The Apocryphal New Testament (the contents of which we noted above were from the second century C.E.) contains documents purporting to be letters by Jesus and other early Christians plus reports on the infancy and childhood of Jesus and his mother, Mary — all of which are clearly fictional, but all of which are products of various factions within the early Church (cf. M.R. James). Hennecke defines the New Testament Apocrypha as:

> writings which have not been received into the canon, but which by title and other statements lay claim to be in the same class with the writings of the canon, and which from the point of view of Form Criticism further develop and mould the kinds of style created and received in the NT, whilst foreign elements certainly intrude. (p. 27)

The New Testament canon was not closed until the end of the second century. Arguments developed concerning the authenticity and authority of certain books now accepted as part of the canon, including 2 Peter, Jude, and 2 and 3 John. Some early Christian writings were excluded from the canon including the *Didache* and the *Shepherd* by Hermas of Rome, both composed in the early years of the second century, plus a number of other documents in circulation among Christians (Grant, ch. 10). When these documents and early second century letters, such as those of Clement of Rome (c. 93-97), Ignatius of Antioch (c. 110-117) and Polycarp of Smyrna (c. 110-117), mention the "scriptures," they appear to be referring to the Jewish scriptures (the Old Testament) as sources of authority. When referring to Jesus' teachings, although their statements reflect gospel material, they appear to be quoting an oral, not a written, tradition. Obviously, the early Christian church was anything but a homogenous entity. Christianity embraced numerous dissenting and independent-thinking groups that learned with difficulty how to work together.

Eastern versus Western Christianity

The first major bifurcation of the Church took place in the eleventh century. By this time Christianity had spread throughout Europe and into North Africa and India. It had developed and absorbed diverse faith patterns ranging from ascetics and monastics to rich and powerful churchmen who were not above using their office to satisfy their greed and their lusts. Christian freethinkers had challenged basic doctrines and there had been debates and councils on all sorts of theological issues out of which had come creeds and dogmas. And there had remained a tension between the Eastern and Western churches, between Constantinople and Rome. In 1054, Eastern and Western churches went their independent ways with the schism producing the Eastern Orthodox and the Western Roman Catholic traditions.

Dissent continued in both the Eastern and Western segments of Christianity. However, an appeal from the eastern Christians for help against the Muslims in Palestine, the Holy Land, was responded to positively in the hope that perhaps the schism might be overcome. The result was the Crusades which were designed to wrest holy places from Muslim control. Consequently, from 1096 to 1272, Christians in Europe were engaged in what became a fruitless struggle for control of Palestine — a struggle that resulted in death and in plunder as well as in the exploitation of children who were sold into slavery by Christians during the so-called Children's Crusade (1212) — a struggle that enhanced the role of the Pope as "the greatest, the mightiest, and the highest military sovereign of the West" (Sohm, p. 114). Meanwhile, the schism between East and West remained.

The Persecution of Witches

During this same period, the Christian hierarchy became concerned with "witchcraft," with the revival of the simplistic pagan beliefs in powers that lay outside of the Church. In the eyes of some learned clergy the whole idea was nonsense, but the Church saw an opportunity to attack Jews and witches. For example, in the eleventh century Jews were accused of killing the Bishop of Treves by making a wax image and burning it so that the Bishop dropped dead during a baptismal ceremony (Williams, p. 83). In 1231, Pope Gregory IX gave directions to Conrad of Marburg (and subsequently to the prelates in Germany) that resulted in a maniacal persecution of sorcery (Summers, p. 470f).

The witchhunt proper was instigated by the Church in the late fifteenth century. There was no systematized cult of witches at that time. By 1484, when witch burning was already well under way, Pope Innocent VIII, at the urging of the Dominicans, issued the bull *Summis Desiderantes Affectibus* which increased priestly power to persecute witches. Two Dominican inquisitors, the Rev. Henry Kramer, who occupied the chair of theology at the University of Salzburg, and James Sprenger, the Provincial of the German provinces, published *Malleus Maleficarum* in 1449. This was a textbook on the cruel means used to identify witches and the proper torturous treatment to be employed at their trials. Witchcraft persecution spread like a fever throughout Europe and ultimately the infection crossed the ocean to America (Larue, 1990, p. 101f).

Christian "Orders"

The Crusade years were also marked by the revivification of monasticism and by the rise of mendicant orders. The monastics, encouraged by the teachings and political influence of Bernard of Clairvaux (1091-1153), reached into communities throughout Europe to spread the Christian faith along with agricultural techniques. Francis of Assisi (born 1182) sought to combine practical Christianity with monasticism and asceticism and developed the Mendicant Orders (Franciscans, founded in 1209; the Dominicans in 1215) that owned no property but existed on the alms provided by Christian believers.

Development of the Christian Church

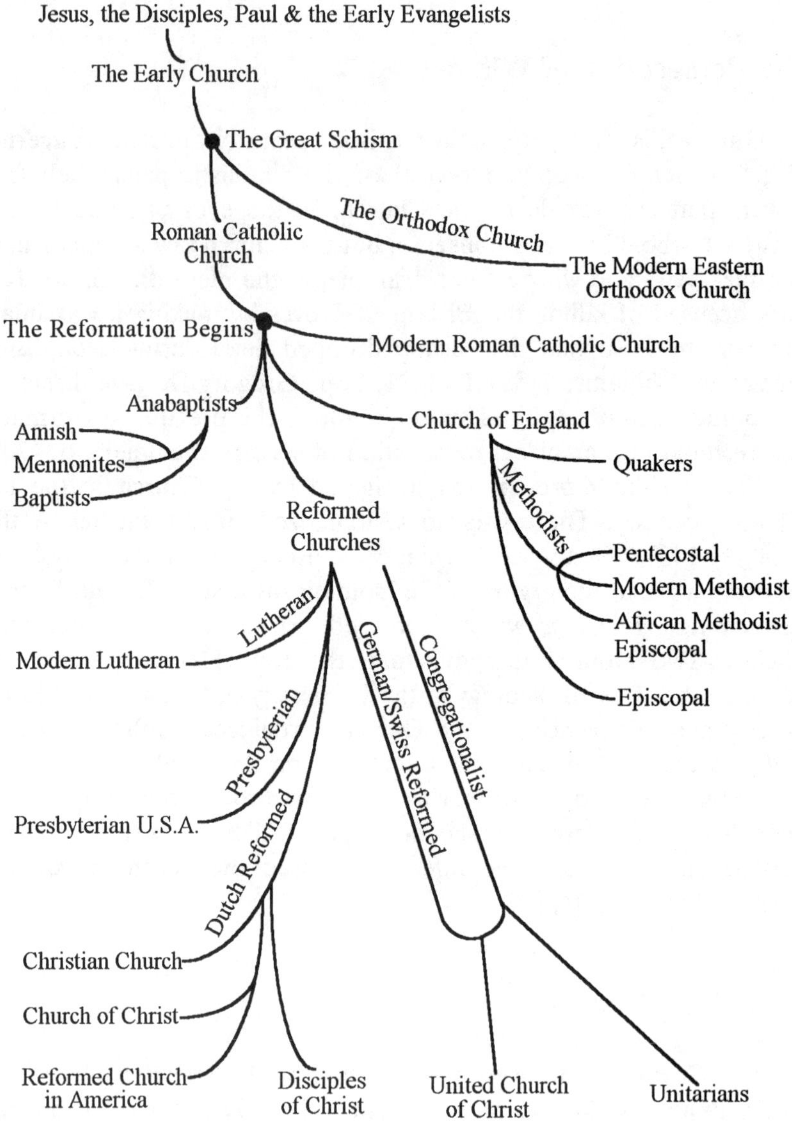

Forerunners of the Reformation

Meanwhile, Christian freethinkers continued to challenge the authority and claims of the religious hierarchy. In Lyons, France, Pierre Valdo or Waldes (d. 1197), upon reading translations of the Gospels, was moved to accept, literally, the words attributed to Jesus: "If you would be perfect, sell that which you have and give to the poor, and you will have treasure in heaven, and come follow me." Waldes gave away his possessions, founded an organization called "The Poor Brethren of Lyons." Without possessions other than the clothes on their back and wooden shoes, he and his followers went out, two by two, to preach the Gospel. Women were welcomed into the Waldensian organization as "sisters" and they, like the brothers, adopted a life of celibacy and poverty.

The Roman Catholic church reacted against the Waldensian's unauthorized preaching. Despite a decree issued by the Archbishop of Lyons prohibiting their activity, the Waldensian mission continued. The Waldensians were first excommunicated, then formally banned by Pope Innocent at the Fourth Lateran Council in 1215. The Waldensians had not attacked doctrine, although they rejected the Roman Catholic practices of selling indulgences and praying for the dead. Indeed, in an age of violence and crime, they sought to help their hearers live better lives. Their experience of freedom from hierarchical authority made it impossible for them to submit to a papal edict. The movement spread to Italy, suffered persecution under Dominican inquisitors, survived until the sixteenth century before being "largely absorbed into various Protestant bodies" (Gifford. p. 303).

In England, John (Wiclif, Wycliffe) Wyclif (1328?-1384), an eminent Oxford scholar (the University was later to expel him), reacted against the corruption of the Papacy and the clergy. He argued that the English king should have control over the Church in the nation just as he had over other institutions. He pointed out that bishops neglected their spiritual duties for engagement in politics. He rejected the doctrine of the Roman Catholic mass and called for a democratic clergy whose authority would be drawn from the scriptures, which Wyclif had translated into the language of the people. He went so far as to claim that the Pope was the Antichrist. He "rejected the Church's claim to power over the State, proclaimed war against the mendicant friars, enthroned the Bible as the only pure source of God's Word, and the only rule of ecclesiastical doctrine." (Sohm, p. 139)

In Prague, John Huss (c. 1369-1415), a priest, influenced by the teachings of Wyclif, declared that Christ, not the Pope, was the true head of the church, that the law of the church was the New Testament, and that the life of the Christian should be marked with Christ-like poverty, not papal wealth. Despite his initial success in Bohemia, he was condemned by the Council of Constance (1414) and burned to death for refusing to submit to its authority. About this same time, John Wyclif's body was disinterred and burned by the Church.

In Florence, Italy, Girolamo Savonarola (1452-1498), a Dominican priest, rose to great power. His efforts to purify local society met with opposition from the hierarchy. He reacted against the bribery by which Rodrigo Borgia had become Pope Alexander VI, (1492-1503) and against the Borgia pope's "unbridled immorality" (Walker, p. 283). He wrote:

> The scandal begins in Rome and runs through the whole clergy; they are worse than Turks or Moors . . . They buy preferments and bestow them on their children or brothers, who take possession of them by violence and all sorts of sinful means. Their greed is insatiable; they do all things for gold . . . They sell their benefices, sell the sacraments, traffic in masses . . . If a priest or canon leads an ordinary life, he is mocked and called a hypocrite (Gifford, p. 334).

Pope Alexander VI, whose evil character and misrule Savonarola denounced, had Savonarola excommunicated and in April 1498 "he was arrested, cruelly tortured, and on May 23 hanged and his body burned by the city government" (Walker, p. 285).

Desiderius Erasmus (1467-1536) was born in the Netherlands, but his excellent scholarship enabled him to move as a teacher into various centers of learning, such as Cambridge, Louvain, Venice, and Basel. His scholarship represented "that first flowering of New Testament exegesis, based on criticism and philology, through which the Renaissance . . . was to prepare the way for modern exegesis" (Bouyer, p. 493). At the same time he did not hesitate to mock "pilgrimages, rites, ceremonies, the tiresome disputes of the Scholastics, the personal character of many of the monks" (Gifford, p. 334). He was a Christian humanist (see p. 223) who stressed piety and charity as the heart of Christianity. He wrote:

> For this cause chiefly Christ was born and died, that he might teach us not to do as the Jews do, but to love. . . . Paul, when writing to the Corinthians, put charity before miracles and prophecy and the tongues of angels. And do not tell me that

> charity consists of going often to church, in bowing before the images of the saints, in lighting candles, in repeating the prescribed prayers. God has no need of these things. Paul meant by charity to edify your neighbors, to count all men members of the same body, to think of them all as one in Christ, . . . in short to employ all your wealth, all your effort, all your care, for this end, that in Christ you may be as useful as possible." (Gifford, p. 334)

He translated the New Testament from the original Greek, ignoring the Latin Vulgate. His work and his popularity made him an inspiration to other reformers.

The Roman Catholic Church itself was in disarray. There was papal involvement in national politics in Germany and France. There were regal attempts to determine who would be pope and that conflict produced more than one claimant to the papal throne. Popes were compelled to take up residence in Avignon rather than in Rome. These and other factors of religious decay combined to pave the way to the Reformation, the second major division in Christendom.

The Reformation

Christian freethinkers did not hesitate to challenge the authority of the Pope. In Germany, Martin Luther (1483-1546) refused to bow to the authority of Rome. Pope Leo X needed funds to support his extravagant habits and to complete the building of St. Peter's cathedral in Rome. He attempted to raise money by the sale of indulgences which promised those who purchased them letters of pardon guaranteeing freedom from punishment in purgatory for sins. The guarantee went even further and was extended to include loved ones who were already dead. Luther challenged whether papal power extended into purgatory and argued that the penitent would receive forgiveness for sins from God without the need to have in hand a papal letter of pardon. There were other issues including doctrines of salvation by works versus salvation by faith, the use of the Scriptures as a guide for life (Luther translated the Bible into German), the spiritual priesthood of all believers, which acknowledged that the laity have spiritual powers and faculties identical to those of the clergy and, consequently, the spiritual autonomy of the individual. These principles constituted a denial and rejection of the claims of the Roman Catholic Church and resulted in the establishment of a new religion — Protestantism.

In England, King Henry VIII (1491-1547) came into conflict with the papacy over marriage, papal revenues and over control of the church. The result was the creation of the Church of England with the monarch as the head. Once again, a new religion had come into being, still using the name "Christian" but distinct and apart from the Church of Rome.

In France, John Calvin (Jean Cauvin: 1509-1564), a student of law and the classics, influenced by the teachings of Luther and Erasmus and by what he found in the New Testament, converted to Protestantism. When the efforts to suppress Lutheranism began, he left Paris and ultimately moved to Basel, Switzerland, where Erasmus lived. With the publication of his *Institutes*, Calvin moved to Geneva and began the formation of the Reformed Church. As changes were introduced, including the replacement of daily Mass by a once-per-month observance of the Lord's Supper, a new Church was born.

The end result of these challenges to the Roman Church was the separation of the Roman Catholic Church from what has become the Anabaptists, the Reformed Churches (Lutheran, Presbyterian, Dutch Reformed and German/Swiss Reformed) and the Church of England with the faith systems that subsequently developed. Presently, it is estimated that there are some 22,000 different denominations worldwide, each with its own organizational structure and particular interpretations of the Christian faith and the Bible. (see chart on p. 206) Some are close enough in theology to pursue union or to engage in cooperative efforts (e.g. The National Council of Churches and the World Council of Churches); others continue to battle and move towards separation even within their own ranks (e.g. Southern Baptists.)

Inasmuch as the Christian faith is based, primarily, on the testimony of the Bible, the church has been compelled to respond to: the development of critical and analytical study of the Bible, the impact of modern science on biblical ideas, the findings coming out of archaeological research, and the study of folklore and comparative religions. The responses have varied. Some fundamentalist groups simply ignore or deny the validity of critical thinking and analytical research. They argue that the world was created in six days some 7,000 years ago. They reject the findings of modern paleontology, geology, astronomy, and so forth. They would place limits on the teaching of such research in the public schools. Some compartmentalize their thinking and keep their interest in modern studies apart from their personal religion. Some attempt to harmonize or reinterpret biblical thought in modern terms. Others recognize the impact of modern research and focus on those parts of the Bible which can be salvaged — particularly some ethical teachings — and observe with reservations the central festivals of Easter and Christmas. Still others have abandoned both the Bible and Christianity and have become freethinkers, agnostics, secularists and atheists. This development will be discussed in chapter 21 on Freethought in America.

Biblical Translations and Biblical Criticism

The Jewish scriptures (the Old Testament) were originally written in Hebrew (with a few passages in Aramaic). During thc 3rd century B.C.E., the Greek (Septuagint) version came into being to meet the needs of Greek-speaking Jews (principally in Alexandria, Egypt) who could no longer read Hebrew. The Greek translation included a number of writings whose authority was under debate among Jewish leaders, some of which were later excluded from the Jewish canon of scripture. The next major translation, the 4th century C.E. Latin Vulgate, contained the entire corpus of the Septuagint, or Alexandrian canon. This important translation, the product of the great Christian scholar, Jerome, played an important role at the time of the Protestant Reformation. There were other early translations of portions of the Jewish scriptures, including Coptic, Arabic, Syriac, Armenian, Slavonic versions, and so on, and parts of the Bible had been paraphrased into Anglo-Saxon.

John Wyclif's (1328?-1384) study of the Bible convinced him that the Bible, as the word of God, was the true law of the Church, and that the Church consisted of the whole company of Christians, not just the Pope, cardinals and other officers. Therefore it was important that the Bible, as the law of God, be given to the people in the English language. Wyclif's translation, based on the Septuagint, was proscribed in 1408 by Bishop Arundel and in 1414 a law was passed stating that those found reading the Bible in their own language "should forfeit land, catel, lif, and goods."

The second half of the 15th century introduced the period of change in Europe known as the Renaissance (the "rebirth") which was to last some two hundred years. This was a time of increasing awareness of "the world" occasioned by new inquiries and explorations by travelers, thinkers and scientists. It was the century of Columbus, Copernicus, and Leonardo da Vinci.

In 1453, Constantinople fell to the Turks and scholars from that great center of learning fled to Europe, bringing with them classical knowledge of the ancient world. The Jews were expelled from Spain in

Source and Translations of the Bible

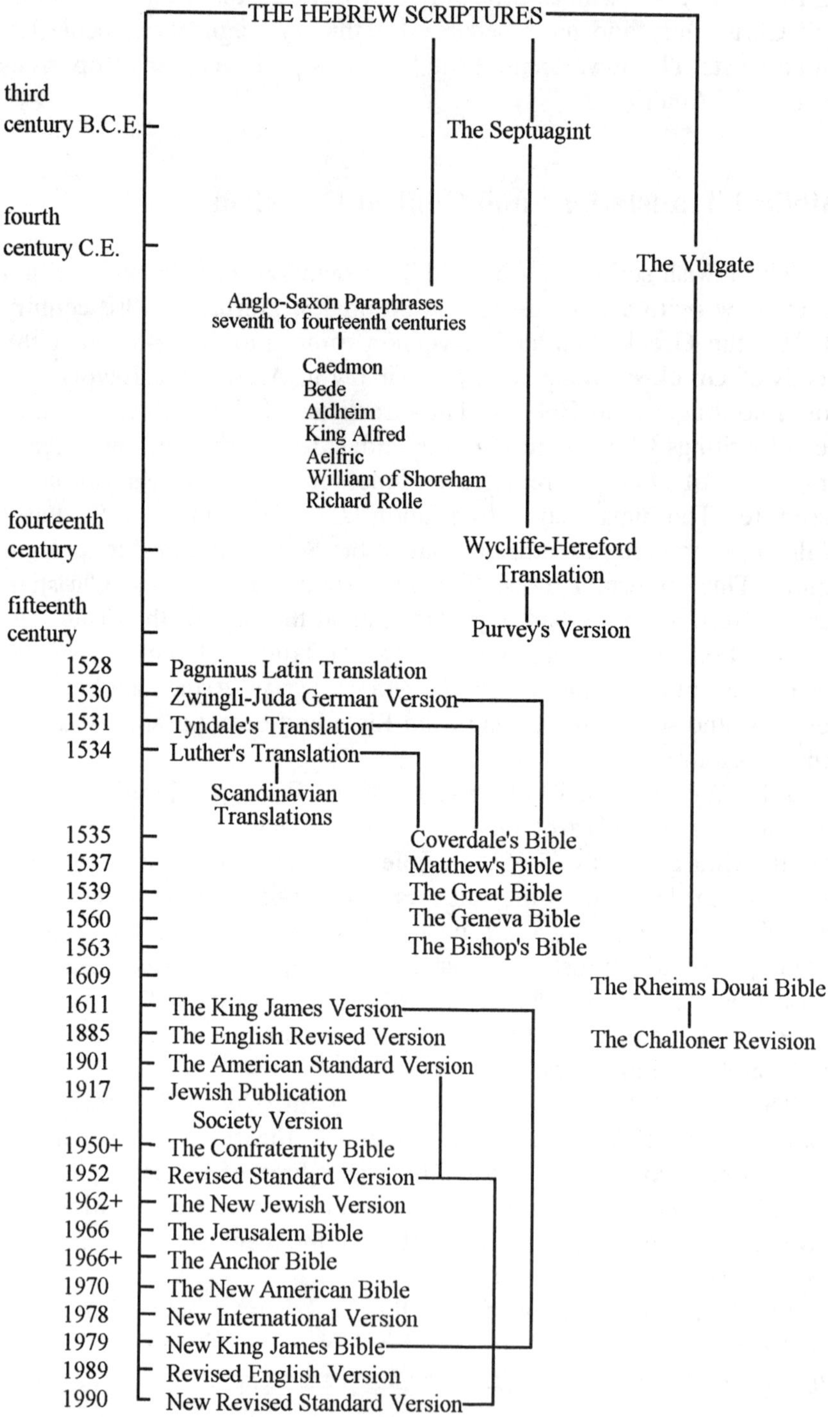

1492 and five years later from Portugal. They moved northward into Europe, revitalizing interest in the Hebrew scriptures and Jewish scholarship. This was also the era of the Protestant Reformation.

Most important for the literary world was the discovery of the means of printing using movable type. Now rapid and cheap reproductions of literary works became popular. In 1456, a Latin version of the Bible was printed by Henne Gensfleich, or as he is better known, Johann Gutenberg (Gutenberg was his mother's maiden name).

William Tyndale (1484-1536) grew up during this turbulent era of developing concepts. He was determined to translate the Bible into the language of the people and he expressed his intent to a clergyman, "ere many years I will cause a boy that driveth the plough shall know more of the Scripture than thou doest." His initial translations were of the New Testament, but by 1531 he had published a translation of the Torah and Jonah, based on the Hebrew text. Tyndale was arrested, imprisoned for 16 years, tried and executed by strangulation at the stake and burned. But his efforts bore fruit and his translation became the basis of subsequent English versions.

In Miles Coverdale's edition of the Bible (1535-6), the books of the Apocrypha (which are included as authoritative scripture in the Roman Catholic canon) were printed separately, between the Old and New Testaments, accompanied by this statement:

> Apocrypha, the books and treatises which among the fathers of old are not to be reckoned of like authority with other books of the Bible, neither are they found in the canon of the Hebrew.

Coverdale's Bible, which was dedicated to King Henry VIII, was widely accepted by both clergy and laity. It had now become clear that there was a thriving market for Bibles in the language of the people. There followed a series of new translations: The Matthew's Bible, the Great Bible, the Geneva Bible and the Bishop's Bible.

On April 8, 1546, at the Council of Trent, the Roman Catholic Church declared that the Vulgate (Latin) edition alone should be the official Bible of the Church and that "none should dare or presume to reject it under any pretext whatsoever." The proclamation was, of course, a reaction to the Protestant Reformation and to translations of the Bible into the language of the people (including the German edition by Martin Luther), which were not based on the Vulgate or Septuagint versions, but on the Hebrew, on the Jewish canon, and on the Greek New Testament.

The growing popularity of Protestant English translations led to a demand by Roman Catholic laity for an English version of their own. The result was the (1609) Rheims-Douai translation — so named because the original translation was begun at the English Roman Catholic College at Douai which later moved to Rheims. The title page noted that it was translated from "the authentical Latin," that is, the Vulgate.

As the number of English translations grew, a proposal was made to King James I, that a new version be undertaken. The so-called "King James Version" was the end product. Forty-seven scholars and clergymen were appointed to the translation committee (James' letter of authorization mentions fifty-four). The complete list of translators' guide rules, which can be found in the ninth edition of *The Encyclopaedia Britannica*, included the following:

1 The Bishop's Bible was to be followed and altered only where necessary.
2 Old ecclesiastical terms were to be retained.
3 No marginal notes were to be included except to give suitable alternative readings or to cite parallel passages.
4 Wherever Tyndale, Matthew, Coverdale, the Great Bible or the Geneva Bible, were closer to the original text, these translations were to be followed.

The translation was completed in 1611, but it was not perfect, and a revised edition appeared in 1613. Unfortunately, the Codex Alexandrinus (a 5th century C.E. Manuscript) had not arrived in England in time to be utilized, and eminent scholars were pressing for a new translation. There were further revisions, one in 1638, another more extensive one in 1762 and still another in 1769 which brought spelling and punctuation up to date. It is clear that the so-called "authorized version," the so-called "King James Version," which some mistakenly label the "*Saint* James" version, has no particular virtue in and of itself. It is simply one translation among others and as new manuscript discoveries are made, and better understanding of ancient languages is developed, more accurate translations will be forthcoming.

Translators are regularly challenged by the need to deal with scribal errors in the Hebrew scriptures. For example, the Hebrew text of Leviticus 20:10 repeats the first five words which read, in translation, "If a man commits adultery with the wife of, if a man commits adultery with the wife of. . ." The King James version dutifully included the dittography in the text. Present-day versions simply drop the second phrase to the footnotes and recognize it as a scribal error. The Hebrew text of I Samuel 14:41 contains what scholars label a "homoioteleuton," which means that the copier's eyes dropped from a line ending in one word to another line ending in the same word, thereby omitting all the intervening material. The missing portions of I Sam. 14:41, which are italicized below, are provided by the Septuagint version:

> Therefore, Saul said, O Yahweh, God of Israel
> *why hast thou not answered thy servant this*
> *day? If the guilt is in me or in Jonathan,*
> *my son, O Yahweh, God of Israel, give Urim,*
> *But if the guilt is in thy people Israel,*
> give Thummim.

The scribe's eyes dropped from the word "Israel" at the end of the first line to the word "Israel" at the end of the next-to-last line and omitted the italicized parts. The omitted words are included in modern versions.

Because there are in existence numerous manuscript copies of both Jewish and Christian scriptures, variations do occur, and sometimes the publication of variations can cause reactions among one or more of the many Christian denominations. For example, when the Revised Standard Version of the Bible was published in 1952, the genealogical table in Matthew 1:16 read: "and Jacob the father of Joseph the husband of Mary, of whom Jesus was born, who is called Christ." At the end of the verse was an italicized notation "e." The corresponding footnote read: "Other ancient authorities read: *Joseph, to whom was betrothed the virgin Mary, was the father of Jesus who is called Christ.*"

The reference was to the Sinaitic Syriac text, which, according to Sherman E. Johnson, "fits better with the original purpose of the genealogy" (Johnson, p. 253). However, so loud was the outcry of protest from ultra-conservative groups, who complained that the notation cast doubt on the virgin birth, that in subsequent editions footnote "e" was removed and in subsequent printings the textual notations moved from "d" to "f," thereby eliminating the troublesome reference. Obviously, there are those who believe that details of textual analysis, which reflect differing Christian appraisals of Jesus, should not be shared with the public.

Biblical writers, like their counterparts in surrounding nations, employed a variety of literary forms including myth (Gen. 1-2), legend (patriarchal narratives), history (the story of King David), fable (Judg. 9:8-15), legalistic writing (Deuteronomy), novella (Jonah), didactic materials (Proverbs), prophetic utterances, letters (Paul), tracts (Jude) and so on. In other words, the Bible is not a purely historical document. To understand it properly it is important to recognize the kind of literature one is reading and, insofar as possible, to know who wrote, when, where, under what conditions, and why. Then, and only then, can one begin to grasp what the writer intended to convey.

To be sure, there has been rebellion against this critical and analytical methodology by those who are interested only in what they label "the spiritual" message. Their approach often turns out to be a form of isogesis, which consists of reading *into* the Bible passage the meanings one wishes to take out of it. Scholars employ exegesis, which involves reading meaning *out of* the text by utilizing the best analytical tools available.

The development of critical methodologies by Christian and Jewish scholars took place over a considerable time period. Questions regarding the Mosaic authorship of the Pentateuch were raised in 1651 by Thomas Hobbes in *Leviathan*. As noted in our discussion of Israel, Baruch Spinoza in *Tractus Theologico-Politicus* (1670) found multiple literary strands representing different writers in the Torah and claimed that Ezra was the final editor. Such challenges to the traditional interpretations of the Bible were not easily stomached by church authorities. Many believed that Christianity had to be accepted as the true faith and the Bible as credible. A statute was enacted in England to the effect that anyone "who shall deny the Holy Scriptures of the Old and New Testament to be of divine authority" could not hold public office, and for a second offense could be sentenced to three years imprisonment. Indeed, in 1697 an eighteen-year-old man was hanged in Edinburgh because he said that Ezra wrote the Pentateuch and that Moses had learned magic in Egypt. (Neil, p. 241f)

In 1678, Richard Simon, a priest of the Congregation of the Oratory, found that the Pentateuch was a compilation of documents coming from differing dates. Jean Astruc, a French physician who was born into a Protestant family and who converted to Roman Catholicism, argued in *Conjectures on the Original Memoirs Which Moses Seems to have Used in Composing the Book of Genesis* (1753), that there were two major sources used in the writing of Genesis: an A source which used the name "Elohim" for God, and a B source which employed "Yahweh" as the personal name of the deity.

Other Christian scholars — both Catholic and Protestant — were to build on these foundations. For example, as a result of literary analysis, modern biblical research has demonstrated that the Pentateuch was not written by Moses, and that it is a composite document containing materials composed at various times between the tenth to the fourth centuries B.C.E. It has been shown that later editors made additions to the original words of the Hebrew prophets; that the Psalms attributed to David came from different eras; that Solomon did not write Ecclesiastes; that Jonah is a novella or teaching story and is in no wise history, and so on. The end result has been to raise questions about, and for some to destroy, the concept of inspired writings. As the German Christian theologian Curt Kuhl has put it:

> The Old Testament is not a book of revelation which descended from Heaven, as it were, as a whole and was thus presented by God to mankind. Written by men, it contains a collection of the most heterogeneous writings, which in our Bible are grouped together, in accordance with the New Testament arrangement, as books of history, instruction and prophecy. (p. 16)

Similar patterns have developed in New Testament research. Christian New Testament scholars have demonstrated that, of the synoptic gospels (Matthew, Mark, Luke), Mark is probably the earliest (compiled about 70 C.E.), and that the authors of Matthew and Luke used Mark's outline plus a collection of sayings attributed to Jesus which scholars label "Q" (from the German *quelle* meaning "source"). The Gospel of John is a late work, composed near the end of the first century. None of the Gospels are by Jesus' disciples. They are not by any means spontaneous writings or purely biographical. They are carefully constructed documents, produced by writers who had definite theologies to impart through their writings.

Some letters attributed to Paul are not his but are creations of unknown Christian writers (e.g. I and II Timothy). The letters attributed to Peter are not by the disciple, and so on. Recent analysis of sayings attributed to Jesus suggest that only about twenty percent can be assigned to him with any confidence. Out of the 111 sayings in the Gospel of Mark, only 17 are believed to be by Jesus — the rest are the creation of unknown writers in the developing Church (Sheler, p. 57f). Modern scholars discount the historicity of the birth and childhood narratives about Jesus. They also reject the resurrection accounts (for a summary, cf. Larue, Temple, 1991). Indeed, the analysis of the Jesus story raises so many questions that it has prompted some to question whether or not Jesus was a fictional, rather than an historical, figure (Wells, 1982).

Folklore, Comparative Religion and the Bible

Even as the literary genre of the Bible were being investigated, the relationship of literary forms to the same categories in other writings and faith systems was being explored. Biblical cosmologies and creation myths echo familiar motifs from similar myths found in Mesopotamia and Egypt. Genesis 1 can be related directly to the Babylonian creation account *enuma elish* (Larue, 1988, pp. 23-64). The flood story (the Bible has two versions) has Babylonian and Sumerian counterparts, indicating that biblical writers drew their accounts from a common theme. Proverbs 22:17-24:22 were drawn from the wisdom writings of Amen-em-ope of Egypt. Psalm 104 reflects a hymn to the sun written by the Egyptian Pharaoh Akhenaton. In other words, writers of Jewish scriptures did not hesitate to borrow words, themes and ideas from other cultures and religions.

Hero legends are found in most cultures. The motifs used in the presentation of biblical heros employed literary patterns which are no different than those employed by writers of the stories of non-biblical heros. For example, the hero often has a wondrous birth and may be seen as a divine-human figure, may be threatened by enemies at birth, is unrecognized until manhood, disappears and may be expected to return again when needed (Raglan). These common patterns can be recognized in part, in the Moses story, the Jesus story, the stories of Romulus and Remus (the legendary founders of Rome), right up to modern-day Superman and Lone Ranger depictions. Healing miracles attributed to Jesus are like those attributed to Aesclepius and other famous healers.

So omnipresent are the folkloric motifs that Sir James G. Frazier wrote a basic study titled *Folklore in the Old Testament*. His work has been up-dated in the light of more recent evidence by Theodor H. Gaster and titled: *Myth, Legend and Custom in the Old Testament*. These monumental reference works demonstrate the folkloric nature of many of the Bible stories.

Science and the Bible

Even as the literary and historical examination of the Bible was in full progress, the findings of modern science were also impacting on biblical studies. The astronomical theories developed by Copernicus and Galileo demonstrated that, despite the teachings of the Bible, the earth is not the center of the cosmos, but is a small planet circling a small star. Geology and paleontology have shown that the Genesis story of creation in six days is no longer tenable. Even the best efforts of church theologians to rescue the biblical account of creation, by suggesting that each biblical day might have measured several million years thereby harmonizing biblical creationism and scientific evolution, have failed. For example, plant life came into being on the third day while the sun was not created until the fourth day and, inasmuch as plant life requires sunlight, the botanical conflicts were impossible to reconcile. The references to night and day during the first three days of the biblical creation account make no sense without a sun. Of course, it is now known that the biblical account borrowed directly from the Babylonian *enuma elish*, where exactly the same pattern is found: references are made to day and night for three days prior to the creation of the sun — but the Babylonian account was not accepted in western culture as "the word of God" (Larue, 1988, pp. 23-64). (Obviously, present efforts by pseudo-scientists who call themselves "creation-science" proponents must ignore the analysis of the biblical and other ancient Near Eastern accounts as well as the findings of modern science. Their production of might-have-been "scientific" theories receives no acceptance in the scientific world.)

The fact that the exploration of the world was underway was to add another set of problems to the acceptance of the Bible as the infallible "Word of God." During the thirteenth century, the merchants of Venice, the Polo family opened new doors of communication and trade with China. In 1492, Christoforo Colombo (1451-1506) brought back news of his contacts with America. Travel produced questions about the Bible. For example, contact with America produced awareness of the existence of people unknown to the Europeans. If one accepted belief in the biblical account of a world-wide flood, and the biblical teaching that all humans were descended from the sons of Noah, how did these newly found people living in the Americas fit into the picture? There was no mention of them in the Bible. Sir Walter Raleigh (1552?-1618), the world traveler, was troubled by the discovery of new species of life he encountered in his voyages. He wondered: how could Noah fit all of these creatures and life forms into the ark? In his *History of the World*, published between 1613 and 1616, Raleigh estimated that by allowing for 100 different species, he could find room for all of them on the first floor of the ark. The second floor, he assumed, would be reserved for food storage and the third for birds and living quarters. However, the continuing discovery of new species soon made it clear that the ark could not possibly accommodate so many creatures (Larue, 1988, p. 150f).

Charles Darwin's *The Origin of Species* removed humans from the category of a special creation and placed them in the long evolutionary pattern that began with earlier and less sophisticated life forms. Neanderthal skulls, which were part of the early scientific evidence, have now been placed late on the evolutionary scale and may represent an evolutionary "dead-end." Today, through DNA studies, some anthropologists have suggested that perhaps all human life can be traced back to a single mother, whom they have named "Eve," who lived in sub-Sahara Africa some 200,000 years ago, as opposed to the biblical "Eve" who was supposed to have been created about 7000 years ago. Such scientific studies challenge biblical creationist ideas and render them inapplicable for the science of the modern world.

Archaeology and the Bible

Archaeology involves the unearthing of ancient sites using the most modern of scientific methods, equipment and means of analyzing, recording and interpreting. So-called "biblical archaeology" focuses on material remains that are directly or indirectly related to the Bible. Archaeology, as a scientific pursuit, is not designed to prove that the Bible is scientifically or historically accurate. At best, archaeological research provides a background against which the world of the Bible can be understood more clearly. Where evidence is uncovered that supports some statement within the Bible, that support is noted. Where the evidence is tangential or where it may not coincide with or support the Bible, that too is noted.

In many instances, the Bible provides helpful geographical data. Inasmuch as most ancient towns did not provide boundary markers as ours do today (one exception was the city of Gezer), biblical references to the locations of ancient cities often help excavators determine the identity of a site under study. Much of what is found in excavations are shards of broken pottery, which are important to the archaeologist, but which seem meaningless to the casual observer, apart from the fact that the fragments are old and come from a biblical site. Under the eye of the trained archaeologist, the shards provide important clues to dating, to cultural changes, to invasions and to local customs.

Some discoveries provide confirmations with biblical history. For example, in the excavation of the ancient site of Nineveh, the British archaeologist, Austen Henry Layard, uncovered huge inscribed stone slabs in the ornate palace of King Sennacherib of Assyria. One inscription provided an account of the submission to the Assyrians by the

Judean king, Hezekiah — a detail which is also reported in II Kings 18:14-16 (Pritchard, pp. 18-24, 156-159). Other discoveries provide important background material. The discovery of what is believed to have been an Essene colony at Qumran, Israel, together with what are now called the "Dead Sea Scrolls," provides valuable new insight into the religious and political environment of Israel at the time when Christianity came into existence. The Moabite Stone, discovered in 1868 at the site of ancient Dibon by the German missionary, the Rev. F.A. Klein, is a ninth century B.C.E. artifact that discloses a Moabite view of the encounters between Moab and Israelite Kings Omri (876-869 B.C.E.) and Ahab (869-850 B.C.E.). These conflicts were not mentioned by the biblical writer who was more interested in the religious struggles between the Canaanite religion of Ba'al and the Israelite religion of Yahweh (I Kings 16-22).

In other instances, some archaeological findings dispute biblical accounts. For example, it is now clear that the sweeping conquest of Palestine by the Hebrews as described in the book of Joshua never occurred. The claims of the biblical stories have been disproved by excavations of the so-called conquered sites that demonstrate that Canaanite life continued and there was no massive Hebrew invasion or conquest. The dramatic biblical account of the taking of Jericho simply never happened. It is true that archaeologists found that the walls of Jericho were in disrepair, perhaps as a result of an earthquake, but that earthquake occurred centuries before the coming of the Hebrews. At the time of the beginning of the Hebrew nation, there was no walled city of Jericho for the Hebrews to conquer. Furthermore, no matter how one may argue for miracles, huge stone city walls do not collapse when priests blow into rams' horns (*shofarim*), no matter how hard they blow. Archaeology and reason come together to support literary analysis which demonstrates that the Jericho story is simply a temple legend designed to convince Hebrew worshippers of the power of their god Yahweh and the importance of paying dues to the deity.

Sometimes archaeology fails to provide any evidence pertaining to biblical stories and one must use reason to evaluate accounts. There is absolutely no archaeological evidence to support the stories about the patriarchs (Abraham, Isaac, Jacob) or about Moses in Egypt, the plagues in Egypt, the miraculous crossing of the Sea of Reeds (Greek: Red Sea) by more than 1,000,000 fleeing Hebrews, and so on. It has been pointed out that such dramatic events would likely have been recorded in Egyptian documents, but so far no reference to such events has been found (see p. 84, first paragraph). Of course, arguments from silence prove nothing. Meanwhile these accounts are placed in the category of wonder-stories which are not to be accepted as history.

Demythologizing the New Testament

Literary analysis of the Bible and the recognition that the cosmological notions of early Christians, which had given rise to a mythologizing of the role and nature of Jesus, were absolutely wrong, produced scholarly efforts to demythologize the scriptures. Christian biblical scholars, in particular the German theologian Rudolf Bultmann, have sought to remove the mythic aspects from the Jesus story.

Bultmann recognized that the world view of the New Testament, with its three-story cosmos of heaven (the realm of God), the underworld (the demonic domain) and the earth (the place of humans where the divine and the demonic meet in conflict), is mythological. New Testament mythological accounts include theologies about Jesus' preexistence, birth, life, death, resurrection and the establishment of the Church. For example, it was obvious that the claims that Jesus descended into hell or ascended to heaven can have no validity if there is no subterranean hell and no heaven above and no life after death.

Bultmann's efforts could not be easily dismissed and some Christians sought to water down what was perceived to be the destructive harshness of his conclusions. What has happened is that, during the post-Bultmannian era, there has been a move away from "the emotionally charged term 'myth'" to preferred labels such as "narrative" or "story" (Kay, p. 327). Consequently scholars now safely engage in "narrative criticism" or "narrative theology" or "narrative ethics" or "narrative homiletics." The term "myth" is reserved for what Christians have termed the "pagan" world. Consequently, through such word-play, the New Testament and the Christian faith system are protected from the statements of those who would place the Jesus story on a literary par with that of other heros and deities.

How, then, do Christian believers, exposed to biblical analyses by Christian scholars like Bultmann, maintain faith in the light of such destructive criticism? For some, what has evolved is a faith system which argues that back of the mythological language is a "cosmic event" which the believer grasps, not through history but through a faith stance. Myth, it is explained, is not designed to present an objective view of the world but rather to enable humans to understand themselves in the world. As Burton H. Throckmorton put it, "Myths are to be interpreted not cosmologically, but anthropologically — or better still, existentially" (p. 23). Myth informs humans that they are not in control of the world. Whether or not they like it, they are subject to supernatural powers. Their earthly presence has meaning; they are here for a purpose. Myth informs humans about that purpose and provides means for deliverance from the external powers. So, it is argued that, although the New Testament message is couched in mythological language, the removal of the mythic framework does not in any way deny the validity of the message which must be grasped through faith.

The arguments which this approach has generated are far too detailed for discussion here. It is clear that the changes in labeling are protective devices designed to "keep the faith." Perhaps it is enough to suggest that, even as the New Testament is demythologized, basic New Testament theology is clung to and, for some, the theology is simply another form of myth.

Theistic Humanism

The roots of theistic or Christian humanism reach back to the fourteenth century and to the Renaissance, the re-birth that was marked by interest in nature, science, discovery, invention, the arts, literature and religion. The emphasis was on the discovery of the human, including human history and human achievements, as well as on the search for new knowledge through science. Christian Humanism began in Italy and, because it was not hostile to the Church, was endorsed and encouraged by Cardinals. The works of Dante Alighieri (1265-1321), who drew inspiration from Virgil and who included minute observations about nature in his writing, mark a beginning in Italian Humanism. Because of the corruption he observed in the Church, he did not hesitate in his "Divine Comedy" (*Divina Commedia*) to consign "several popes to hell, only one to heaven" (Gifford, p. 325). Francesco Petrarch's (1304-1374) lyric poetry expressed human sentiments. His collections of ancient manuscripts engendered museum inspiration that is alive today. His belief in the right to exercise a critical attitude toward all learning, including law, medicine, astrology and theology, marked his professional humanistic scholarship. Giovanni Boccaccio's (1313-1375) *Decameron* mirrored the world in its frank writing about humans and their affections. His celebrated *Three Rings* represented three religions: Jewish, Christian and Muslim. "Each believes itself to be the heir to revealed truth, but which one is right?" (Guignebert, p. 364)

Lorenzo Valla (1406-1457) ridiculed Christian ascetic vows of chastity, arguing that such vows could only result from superstition, and he attacked the temporal sovereignty of the Pope as well as papal tyranny (Guignebert, p. 366).

In France, Humanist alienation from medieval theology resulted in calls for reform of Christian life. Francois Rabelais (1494?-1553), who loved nature and life and who esteemed both human reasoning ability and science, faulted the church in its attempts to control human patterns of worship. In Germany the lives of the monks come under criticism.

It must be remembered that these criticisms came from men who remained Christian and who believed in God. Their influence was not to fade away and disappear; on the contrary it became part of the thinking that produced the Reformation and that stimulated critical examination of the Bible. Guignebert notes that these men, and this would include such dominant personalities as Luther and Bruno, still believed in all the enchantments of sorcery.

> . . . And yet these same men, almost without knowing it, are preparing and announcing the complete emancipation of the human mind and the triumph of reason over superstition. They continue plunged up to their neck and shoulders into the gloomy shadows of the Middle Ages, but their foreheads are aglow with the dawn of modern times (p. 382f).

The threads of theistic Humanism have been picked up again in modern times, perhaps in part as reaction to the growth of secular Humanism. For example, in 1952, in a lecture given in Pennsylvania and later revised and expanded in book form (1964), William Foxwell Albright of Johns Hopkins University, an internationally known and respected archaeologist and historian, suggested that there was a category of Humanism that could be called "theistic." His definition of "humanism" was that proposed by Christopher Dawson in 1952; "Humanism is a tradition of culture and ethics founded on the study of humane letters" (p. 3). The term "humane letters" refers to the branches of study (particularly literature, the classics, art, poetry, etc.) that are designed to make one more human and, perhaps, also more kindly disposed toward other humans and animals. For Albright, "Theistic Humanism," or as he sometimes calls it "Christian Humanism," is:

> the study and cultivation of our higher cultural heritage in the light of Judeo-Christian religious tradition. Since the term

> "higher culture" includes the accumulation of knowledge and art from the past, which vastly exceeds the additions of the present, this definition involves historically-centered consideration of our cultural heritage in the light of our religion, and conversely. The theistic humanist cannot be a mere historian, but must also be a philosopher; besides, he must be something of an artist in his sensitivity to cultural form. (p. 10)

Albright lauds the historian, Christopher Dawson, who presents "a Christian view of history, combining historical, philosophical and literary competence in an aesthetically satisfying whole" (p. 10). He discounts those who remain pure historians, as well as philosophers whose philosophy does not present a theistic interpretive emphasis. His definition cannot admit such religious giants as Reinhold Niebuhr and Paul Tillich and there is no room for Rudolf Bultmann in his circle of theistic or Christian Humanists. Albright's Theistic Humanism is comprised of an elitist group selected on the basis of his particular definition — and of course, he would include himself in this grouping.

Albright noted that in 1953 a symposium by "six distinguished American Catholic thinkers" met on the theme "Christian Humanism." He admitted that the contributions were excellent, devoted to philosophical and humanitarian issues "rather than to historical aspects of theistic humanism." He recognized the contributions to the symposium as forming "a complement and corrective to the emphasis" in his presentation (p. 3, f.n. 3).

Albright's Christian Humanism appears to have been no more than a passing comment or observation. No development of his theme has emerged and no movement known as Christian Humanism has developed.

The Death of God

The death of God emphasis within Christianity, like the death of God movement in Judaism, emerged in the 1960's. It is as though the findings of biblical, scientific and philosophical research reached a climax and it became apparent to many that the old ideas about God were no longer adequate. The old image of God was dead. This should not be taken as a complete denial of God, but rather that for some Christians a somewhat different concept of the divine-human relationship has emerged. For these Christians, God died on Calvary. God no longer matters to humans, but the Christian faith is still relevant.

Thomas J.J. Altizer wrote of his own struggle: "Since the summer of 1955 I had been torn between the interior certainty of the death of God in modern history and experience and a largely mute but nevertheless unshakable conviction of the truth of the Christian faith" (p. 301). William Hamilton put it this way:

> I am not here referring to a belief in the nonexistence of God. I am talking about a growing sense, in both non-Christians and Christians, that God has withdrawn, that he is absent, even that he is somehow dead . . . This feeling ranges from a sturdy unbelieving confidence in God's demise to the troubled believer's cry that he is no longer in a place where we can call upon him. (p. 43f)

What is the Christian response? Once again, it lies in a faith stance. Hamilton writes:

> . . . to be a Christian today is to stand, somehow, as a man without God but with hope. We know too little to know him now; we only know enough to be able to say he will come, in his own time, to the broken and contrite heart, if we continue to offer that to him. Faith is, for many of us, we might say, purely eschatological. It is a kind of trust that one day he will no longer be absent from us. Faith is the cry to the absent God; faith is hope. (p. 6)

The faith stance is further clarified by the belief in Jesus as "Lord," that is "the one through whom God meets us." He concludes:

> One thing is true. We have chosen to live with the dangers of the impotence or weakness of God rather than with the dangers of his power, for we believe that this was God's choice in the crucifixion. We have gained something, and we have lost something. We have gained the power to say: "because of Jesus the Lord, God is always emptying himself to meet us where we are. In joy and despair, he will never let us go." But if we have one kind of confidence along these lines, we have deprived ourselves of another kind, that kind which can say: "God's rule cannot be violated, his purposes for his creation are sure, his power stands sure over all earthly powers." We have chosen to stand with his lowly presence, but we have so defined power as weakness, that our life in that presence has

> lost much of the protective and serenity other Christians have known. (p. 96)

Altizer wrote:

> The Christian who chooses the ancient image of Christ as the Son of God, or who is bound to an epiphany of Christ in the long-distant past, must refuse the Christ who is actually present in our flesh. He wagers upon a purely religious image of Christ even at the price of forfeiting the actuality of our time and history. But the radical Christian wagers on a Christ that is purely profane. He bets upon the Christ who is the totality of the moment before us, the Christ who draws us into the fullness of life and the world. Finally, radical faith calls us to give ourselves totally to the world, to affirm the fullness and the immediacy of the present moment as the life and energy of Christ. Thus ultimately the wager of the radical Christian is simply a wager upon the full and actual presence of the Christ who is totally incarnate love. (p. 320)

The end result of such theology is the development of the so-called secular Christian, who seeks to combine a workable mixture of faith and secularism.

In 1966, R.G. Smith published a book titled *Secular Christianity* in which he recognized that the secular is in every man (p. 168). But, he argued, this modern secularism contains a *malaise* which is the confusion and lack of hope which modern science and philosophy have created together with a nihilistic bondage which robs man of his humanity. Rescue from this dilemma comes through the recognition of the *Homo religiosus* dimension of the human — a dimension recognized in secular Christianity. Because Smith never really defines "secular Christianity" but talks of its manifestation, it is difficult to summarize his position. He writes:

> But secular Christianity means the dialectical expression of the Spirit, which is the way of Christ in the world, in forms which can be neither objectively distinguished or enumerated. The form of Christ in the world is certainly a historical reality: it is *the* historical reality. It is the prolepsis of the End. But this historical reality cannot be pinned down. The theology of faith is a theology of the cross, and thus a *theologia viatorum*. It is a

> theology of a pilgrim journey which makes its own map as it goes. (p. 204)

Unfortunately, Smith's presentation lacks the clarity of other death of God theologians, hence his writing tends to become an example of theologians talking to theologians through which very little is conveyed to the laity.

The Unitarian Universalists

Unitarianism began as a revolt against the Christian Trinitarian formula which describes the deity in terms of Father, Son and Holy Spirit. Unitarianism envisions God as having a single being and nature and recognizes Jesus, not as God, but as a human being whose ethical teachings provided guides for life.

Unitarianism began during the Reformation. Michael Servetus (Miguel Serveto, 1511-1553), the Spanish physician who discovered the circulation of blood, argued that the Trinitarian formula as enunciated in the Nicene Creed was not found in the New Testament. His 1531 treatise, *Concerning the Errors of the Trinity*, was considered heretical and in 1553 he was burned at the stake (with Calvin's approval). Servetus wrote as an individual thinker, not on behalf of an organized religious group, but anti-Trinitarianism was alive and growing. A number of anti-Trinitarians suffered persecution and death for their beliefs at the hands of both the Inquisition and Protestants. The term "unitarian" appears to have been used first around 1600. In 1579, Faustus Socinus (Fausto Sozzini, 1539-1604), an Italian theologian who broke with the Roman Catholic Church, fled to Poland in 1579 to escape persecution for his views. Socinianism developed in Poland but ultimately was suppressed inasmuch as its break with the past was too great. The movement spread to the Netherlands and to England where the last two Englishmen to be burned at the stake for their faith were Unitarians (Bartholemew Legate and Edward Wightman), who died in 1612 under King James I.

The first Unitarian churches in America were founded in 1794 and 1796 by Joseph Priestly (1733-1804), the English chemist who discovered oxygen. The church grew in strength and in 1825 the American Unitarian Association was formed. A number of famous Americans were associated with the church, including Ralph Waldo Emerson, Thomas Jefferson, Oliver Wendell Holmes, Henry W. Longfellow, Julia Ward Howe, Susan B. Anthony and Daniel Webster.

The Universalist Church, which originated about 1770, was at first Trinitarian, but by 1850 most clergy had adopted Unitarianism. Universalists rejected the doctrine of eternal punishment and proclaimed ultimate salvation for all humankind. In 1961, the Universalists united with Unitarians to form the Unitarian Universalist Association.

A survey titled "The Quality of Religious Life in Unitarian Universalist Congregations" was conducted by the denomination in 1987. The results indicated that 7% listed themselves as Atheist, 3% as Agnostic-Skeptic, 7% as Feminist Humanist and 55% as Humanist-Existentialist. This last category referred to "a human-focused religiousness rooted in a sense of relatedness to trans-human cosmic process, not 'supernatural,' but continuous with humans and their universe." Not all Unitarian-Universalists have severed their roots with their Christian beginnings but the trend is clearly towards freethought. In the 1987 survey, 15% listed themselves as "Christian" and 4% as "Christian-Humanist," as opposed to the 43% who listed themselves as "Christian" in a 1967 survey. The degree of separation is further demonstrated by the finding that "UUs reject the concept of God or the divine as a superior or supernatural being: fewer than 4% would accept such a definition;" and further that, there was no agreement on what the term "God" meant, but there was general agreement "that the term stands for something that is not 'supernatural' in the old sense."

The New Christian Secularists

As a consequence of critical thinking and scholarly research, many who were raised as Christians have abandoned the faith. They have become secularists. They don't think about God or the Christian faith except in an abstract way. They live a secular life, which means that they live each day as fully as possible, without any expression of belief in God. They act with goodwill and kindness in their neighborhoods without hope of reward in some afterlife. They reach out to the suffering of the world to provide food, clothing, medicine and education without feeling they are compelled to act because of some divine commission. In other words, they fulfill their understanding of the noblest ethic of the Christian faith but without the church as a guide or a stimulant. They are simply good, decent human beings because that way of life provides the greatest personal satisfaction and because the secular philosophy provides fulfillment.

Some secularists may observe the Christmas season with a Christmas tree and the exchange of gifts. Santa Claus is really more important to their families than the Jesus birth story. Some may attend a church service and sing carols, but their approach is primarily secular. These persons may be unaware of the development of Christianity sketched above. They have moved away from Christianity on the basis of reason and logic. The faith no longer makes sense. Its world-view belongs to another age. These are moderns living in a modern world who refuse to have their thinking cluttered by beliefs in angels and devils, a wondrous birth from a divinely impregnated virgin, a descent into hell and a resurrection and ascension to a heaven, both of which they know do not exist. That mode of thinking belongs to the past. Yet, when they are asked on school forms to indicate religious preference, they may check off the traditional family faith system as Catholic or Protestant or, if the statement provides a space, "other." Few forms, as yet, include atheist or agnostic.

References

Albright, William Foxwell, *History, Archaeology and Christian Humanism*. New York: McGraw-Hill Book Company, 1964.

Altizer, Thomas J.J., edit., *Toward a New Christianity*. New York: Harcourt, Brace & World, Inc., 1967.

Bouyer, Fr. Louis, "Erasmus in Relation to Medieval Biblical Tradition" in G. W. H. Lampe, *The Cambridge History of the Bible*. Cambridge: The University Press, 1969, Vol. 2, pp. 492-505.

Bultmann, Rudolf, *Kerygma and Myth*. Edit. by Hans-Werner Bartsch, trans. by Reginald H. Fuller. London: Society for Promoting Christian Knowledge, 1953. Vol. I.

Bultmann, Rudolf, *Jesus Christ and Mythology*. New York: Scribner's, 1958.

Cumont, Franz, *The Mysteries of Mithra*. Trans. by Thomas J. McCormack. New York: Dover Publications, Inc. 1956. (Original was published by the Open Court Publishing Company in 1903.)

Dawson, Christopher, "Christianity and the Humanist Tradition," *Dublin Review*, 1952.

Finegan, Jack, *Myth and Mystery: An Introduction to the Pagan Religions of the Biblical World*. Grand Rapids, Michigan: Baker Book House Company, 1989.

Frazier, Sir James, G., *Folklore in the Old Testament*. London: Macmillan and Company, 1918.

Gaster, Theodor H., *Myth, Legend and Custom in the Old Testament*. New York: Harper and Row, 1969.

Gifford, William Alva, *The Story of the Faith*. New York: The MacMillan Company, 1946.

Grant, R.M., "The New Testament Canon" in P.R. Ackroyd and C.F. Evans, edits., *The Cambridge History of the Bible*. Cambridge: University Press, 1970. Vol. I, ch. 10.

Guignebert, Charles, *Ancient, Medieval, and Modern Christianity*. New York University Books, Inc., 1961.

Hamilton, William, *The New Essence of Christianity*. New York: Association Press, 1966.

Hennecke, Edgar, *New Testament Apocrypha*, edit. by Wilhelm Schneemelcher, trans. by R. Mcl. Wilson. Philadelphia: Westminster Press, 1963, Vol. 1.

Hobsbawm, E.J., *The Age of Capital, 1845-1875*. London: Weidenfeld and Nicolson, 1975.

James, M.R., *The Apocryphal New Testament*. Oxford; The Clarendon Press, 1953.

Johnson, Sherman E., "Introduction and Exegesis: Matthew," *The Interpreter's Bible*. Nashville: Abingdon-Cokesbury Press, 1951. Vol. 7, pp. 231-625.

Kay, James F., "Myth or Narrative?: Bultmann's 'New Testament Mythology' Turns Fifty," *Theology Today*, Vol. XLVIII, No. 3, October, 1991, pp. 326-332.

Kuhl, Curt, *The Old Testament: Its Origins and Composition*. Trans. by C.T.M. Herriott. Richmond, Vir.: John Knox Press, 1961.

Larue, Gerald A., *Ancient Myth and Modern Life*. Long Beach, Calif: Centerline Press, 1988.

Larue, Gerald A., *The Supernatural, the Occult and the Bible*. Buffalo, New York: Prometheus Books, 1990.

Larue, Gerald A., "'Who do Men Say That I Am?' — An Appraisal," *The Humanist*, Vol. 51, No. 3, May/June, 1991, pp. 5-6.

Latourette, Kenneth Scott, *The First Five Centuries*. New York: Harper & Brothers, 1937.

Neil, W., "The Criticisms and Theological use of the Bible, 1700-1950" in *The Cambridge History of the Bible: The West From the Reformation to the Present Day*, edit. by S. L. Greenslade. Cambridge: University Press, 1963, pp. 238-293.

Pritchard, James B., *Archaeology and the Old Testament*. Princeton, New Jersey: Princeton University Press, 1958.

Raglan, Lord, *The Hero*. New York: Random House, 1956.

Rahner, Hugo, "The Christian Mystery and the Pagan Mysteries," *The Mysteries: Papers From the Eranos Yearbook*. New York: Pantheon Books, 1955. Bollingen Series XXX 2, pp. 337-401).

Richardson, Cyril Charles, *The Church Through the Centuries*. New York: Charles Scribner's Sons, 1950.

Robinson, James M., *A New Quest for the Historical Jesus*. London: S.C.M. Press, Ltd., 1959.

Sheler, Jeffery, L., "What Did Jesus Really Say?", *U.S. News and World Report*, July 1, 1991, pp. 57-58.

Smith, Ronald Gregor, *Secular Christianity*. London: Collins, 1966.

Sohm, Rudolf, *Outlines of Church History*. Trans. by May Sinclair, Boston: Beacon Press, Inc., 1958 (reprint of 1895 edition).

Summers, Montague, *The Geography of Witchcraft*. Secaucus, New Jersey: The Citadel Press, 1965, 1975.

Temple, Kerry, "Who Do Men Say That I Am?", *The Humanist*. Vol. 51, No. 3, May/June, 1991, pp. 7-14.

Throckmorton, Burton H., *The New Testament and Mythology*. London: Barton, Longman & Todd, Ltd., 1960.

Walker, Williston, *A History of the Christian Church*. New York: Charles Scribner's Sons, 1959.

Wells, G.A., *The Historical Evidence for Jesus*. Buffalo, New York: Prometheus Books, 1982.

Williams, Charles, *Witchcraft*. New York: Meridian, 1959.

11
Islam

❖

A Westerner, in discussion with a merchant in a Near Eastern country, may be startled when conversation is interrupted for prayer. The businessman may reach beneath a counter, pull out a prayer rug, and with a word of explanation for the break in conversation ("it is time to pray") turn his attention from business to religion. He is a Muslim, "one who submits" to the teachings of "Islam" (*al-islam* in Arabic), a word which means "submission." To submit signifies "to accept" or "to believe in" or "to commit oneself to," and involves not only mental or inward acceptance of a faith system but the outward expression of that submission through a way of life. Today nearly one billion people are adherents of the multi-ethnic faith system known as Islam.

In the minds of its followers, Islam constitutes a new revelation — one that moves beyond Judaism and Christianity. It constitutes a rejection of those two faiths as being earlier divinely-revealed faith systems that are now superseded, rendered obsolete and replaced by what God (Allah) revealed to Muhammad, his chosen prophet. As a new, separate, and distinct religion, Islam provides an example of independent religious thinking and responding; it reflects aspects of the human capacity to reflect, to choose, to discard and to create in matters of religion.

Beginnings

Islam, a monotheistic faith, had its beginnings in Arabia during the 7th century C.E. The founder, Muhammad (570?-632 C.E.), was born in the trading center, Mecca (Makkah), into the Hashim clan (the same group identity as that claimed by the Hashimite King of Jordan) of the Quraysh tribe. His father was 'Abdallah and his mother Amina. Unfortunately, the earliest biographical material about the founder was not written until some 125 years after his death. Traditions pertaining to his earliest years are laced with the kind of legendary tales typical of hero accounts, including wonder stories about his birth and childhood.

His birth date is not known; he was born between 570 and 571 C.E. According to tradition, he was orphaned at an early age — his father died before his birth and then, when he was six years old, his mother died. He became a ward, first, of his grandfather, 'Abd el-Muttalib, then of his uncle, Abu Talib. He was raised in the area of Mecca and Medina and his early years were marked by poverty. It was not until he married the wealthy widow, Khadija bint Khuwaylid, that his fortunes were reversed.

When he was about forty years old, Muhammad began to experience "revelations." It was his habit to spend time each year during the month of Ramadan in a desert cave on top of a mountain near Mecca. On one particular night in 610 C.E., he was awakened by a voice that commanded him to "Read," to which he responded that he was unable to read. Again he was told: "Read: In the Name of thy Lord, who created all things, who created man from a clot of blood. Read: And it is thy most beneficent Lord who teaches man by the pen that which he did not know" (Surah 96:1-5). The voice identified itself as that of the angel Gabriel who, in both Jewish and Christian thought, was believed to be the messenger between God and humans.

At first Muhammad believed he was possessed by a demon, but when he returned to his home, his wife Khadijah assured him that his behavior was such that Allah would not permit a harmful spirit to afflict him. It was her hope that he would become a prophet. She took him to her cousin Waraqa ibn Naufal, an elderly man familiar with Jewish and Christian scriptures. Waraqa ibn Naufal informed Muhammad that the heavenly messenger was none other than the one who, in earlier times, had come to Moses. Muhammad was told that he had been chosen as the prophet for his people.

Muhammad continued to receive revealed information up the time of his death. The revelations were collected and preserved in the holy book of Islam, *Al-Qur'an*, which means "the Readings" or, perhaps, "the Recitings" of him who could not read. These revealed words are separated from the *Hadith* (sayings) or *Sunnah* (practices and tradition) of the prophet, which are the collected words of Muhammad gathered and edited during the 9th century C.E.

During the first few years, Muhammad preached only to his family and friends. On the whole, Meccans believed him to be somewhat addled or mad. His first converts included his wife Khadijah, his cousin Ali, his servant Zayd, his friend Abu Bakr, plus some of Abu Bakr's slaves and dependents. When he was commanded to "arise and warn" (Surah 74:2), he began his public ministry in Mecca, speaking against local gods and infuriating his fellow members of the Quraysh tribe who mocked and threatened him inasmuch as his "new religion" endangered their economic and social domination in Mecca. By his actions, Muhammad could be identified as an independent thinker, spokesman for a new faith system, and one in rebellion against traditional beliefs.

Obviously, Islam did not develop within a religious vacuum. In the environs of Mecca and Medina, where Muhammad was raised, Jewish, Christian and Persian Zoroastrian monotheistic faiths existed along side of an Arabian religious heritage rich in gods, goddesses and seers or *kahin* (a word linked to the Hebrew *kohen*, "priest"). The *kahin* claimed to experience visions or become possessed by spirits who spoke through them (compare the claims of modern "channelers") enabling them to locate lost camels or to foretell the future (cf. I Sam. 9-10). In addition, there was popular belief in spiritual powers known as *jinns*, some of which were benign, others malignant. Different deities were worshipped in different Arabian pilgrimage centers. For example, in Mecca and Medina, Allah was recognized as a supreme deity, the creator of the world, but the faith was not monotheistic. Allah had three daughters: Allat (the "goddess") who may have been personified by the morning star (Venus); 'Uzza (the all-powerful) who may also have been identified with Venus; and Manat (goddess of fate) who possessed power over life and death. Belief in these deities is reflected in Surah 53, although the verses have been altered so that, rather than indicating Muhammad's acceptance of these female children of Allah, they now imply rejection. According to Rodinson (p. 106f) the original statement read:

> Have you considered Allat and al-Uzza
> And Manat, the third, that other?
> They are the Exalted Birds
> And their intercession is desired indeed.

Later, it was revealed to Muhammad that he had been deceived by the devil, and the reference to the "Exalted Birds" and the benefits of their intercession was changed, so the last two lines (which reflect then current attitudes regarding preference for male children) now read:

> Do you have male children and God female?
> That is surely an unjust arrangement.
> They are no more than empty names,
> which you and your fathers have created.
> Allah has revealed nothing concerning them to authorize their
> worship.

In Mecca, Muhammad's tribe, the Quraysh, were guardians of the holy shrine, a cube-shaped structure called the Ka'bah (the word means "cube"). Embedded in one corner was a sacred black stone of meteoric origin. Other sacred stones, some idols and even some Christian pictures were also preserved in the Ka'bah, so that the shrine had meaning for many groups. For example, Hubal, the city god, was depicted in an image made of red carnelian (Rodinson, p. 16). Indeed, it is estimated that by 500 C.E. the Ka'bah housed more than 360 idols representing the deities of various tribes. The Quraysh also controlled the sacred fresh water well of Zamzam, which made Mecca an important stopping point on the trade routes. So important was Mecca to the Quraysh business interests that, during a four month period each year, fighting was prohibited near Mecca and the Ka'bah, to encourage and enable pilgrimages by tribal groups that would on other occasions be hostile to one another. Fees imposed by the Quraysh upon pilgrims and traders (a familiar pattern combining business and religion) insured Quraysh tribal wealth.

Traders from different parts of the European and Near Eastern world had brought with them beliefs in non-Arabian religions. For example, the presence of a close-knit society of Jewish artisans and merchants in Mecca and Medina provided a source for information about the basic tenets of monotheistic Judaism. Traders and merchants belonging to various Christian sects, though not as well organized as the Jews, were able to share basic Christian beliefs. These religious groups were known to Muhammad but how much they may have contributed to the development of Muhammad's monotheism can be debated. Although Muhammad sought to reach out to Jews and Christians, they, for the most part, rejected his overtures. In return, the prophet dismissed them. Surah 25 of the Qur'an, which records the prophet's dismissal, begins:

> In the name of Allah, the merciful, the beneficent. Blessed is He who has revealed the Criteria (of right and wrong) to his servant so that he might be a proclaimer to all creatures of Him to Whom belongs the kingdoms of heaven and of earth, to Whom belongs the sovereignty of the heavens and the earth, Who has begotten no son, and Who has no partner in His kingdom, Who created all things and arranged them according to His will. Yet they have taken other gods beside Him: which have created nothing but are themselves created, and are able neither to avert evil from, nor produce good for themselves,

> and who possess neither the power of death nor of life, nor power to raise the dead.
>
> Those who disbelieve say: This Qur'an is nothing but a lie that he has invented, and others have helped him with it; but they utter slander and a lie. And they also say: These are fables of the men of old which he has had written down and they are dictated to him morning and evening.

The quotation reveals the attacks on his faith by Christians, and Muhammad's rejection of claims such as Jesus' divine sonship, his anticipated role in the divine kingdom that was to come, his ability to reanimate the dead and his personal resurrection. Although Muhammad accepted the validity of the revelations given to Moses, the prophets and Jesus, he denied the divinity of Jesus and warned his followers to stay aloof from both Jews and Christians:

> O true believers, do not take Jews or Christians as friends. They are friends to one another. He who take them for friends is one of them. Truly Allah does not guide evildoers. (Surah 5:51)

The Surah continues with excoriations of Jews and particularly of Christians:

> They are truly infidels who say, "Behold Allah is Christ, the son of Mary" . . . They are truly infidels who say that Allah is one of three for there is no Allah beside Allah . . . Christ, the son of Mary is no more than a messenger, other messengers preceded him. His mother was a good woman. Both ate (earthly) food. Behold how we declare to them the signs of Allah's unity, and behold how they turn away from the truth. (Surah 5:72, 73, 75.)

Although Muhammad's early converts were mostly among the humbler people, little by little persons of rank and power moved to his side, much to the consternation of the Quraysh, who saw their business threatened. Their efforts at compromise failed as did their attempts to have Muhammad killed. Meanwhile, men from Yathrib (Medina), an oasis city two hundred miles from Mecca, accepted him as the expected prophet they had been told about by the learned Jewish rabbis who lived among them. An attempt on Muhammad's life caused him to flee from Mecca to Yathrib in 622 — a flight known as the Hegira and which constitutes the beginning of the Muslim lunar calendar. Moreover, it marked the transition of Muhammad from the role of a preacher to the ruler of a small state which was ultimately to grow through war and conversions and unite the disparate tribal groups in what was to become the empire of Arabia.

Although, as we have noted, Islam constituted a rejection of all other existing religious systems, the claim of being a receptor of divinely revealed information placed Muhammad directly in a long line of those who claimed their words came from a deity — a line that extends back to Sumerian times and includes Moses, the Hebrew prophets and Jesus, and forward to include Joseph Smith, Mary Baker Eddy and a host of others. Muhammad's first messages focussed on the oneness of God, Muhammad's appointment as God's messenger and belief in the day of judgment. He was rejected outright by Jews and Christians of Medina. Some mocked him. Some were skeptical of his claims. As his followers grew and resorted to military exploits, Muhammad's claims of divine protection and guidance were enhanced. Wealth came through the looting of fallen foes. Those who rejected the prophet were recognized as "Doubters" or skeptics (*munafiqun*) and as persons of little faith. Their presence is mentioned in the Qur'an (Surah 3:133-135, 160-162; 59:11-14).

Within one hundred years after Muhammad's death (632), the religion he created and which, at first, enrolled only family members and friends, had spread by military force throughout the Middle East, across north Africa and into Spain. Its militant growth was stopped in 732 by the Franks at the battle of Tours and Poitiers. In subsequent years Islam expanded throughout the Mediterranean world, into India, the Orient and ultimately to all parts of the globe. Muslims not only absorbed ideas and patterns from conquered cultures but developed their own magnificent centers of art, science and learning. For example, their presence in Spain left a lasting contribution in the magnificent architecture which can be seen today. They were expelled from Spain in 1492 after the marriage of Isabella of Castile and Ferdinand of Aragon provided enough Roman Catholic power to defeat the Muslims.

Today, Islam is endorsed by one-fifth of the world's population, and the words which the prophet claimed were conveyed by Gabriel are enshrined in Islam's holy book, the Qur'an, which consists of 6200 verses in 114 chapters (Surahs) of unequal length. The Qur'an was put together some 20 years after Muhammad's death from various scraps of writing combined with the memorized texts of professional "reciters." It serves as the core of Islam and, in Muslim thought, is believed to constitute the completion of the earlier revelations of the Old Testament prophets and Jesus. Muhammad is the final prophet.

We have noted that the term "Islam" means "submission;" therefore Muslims, as adherents of Islam, are those who submit to the "will of God (Allah)" as revealed through his prophet Muhammad and as preserved in the Qur'an. Every praying believer recites the Islamic creed (*Shahadat*: testimonies), which, prefaced by the phrase "I bear witness to" (*ashhadu inna*), is followed by *la ilaha illa 'Llah; Muhammadun rasulu 'Llah* — which means "There is no god but God (Allah) and Muhammad is the messenger (mouthpiece) of God (Allah)." Muhammad is not considered to be divine, nor the son of God, as Christians claimed Jesus was. Muhammad was simply a prophet — a category into which, as we have noted, Muslims place Jesus and Moses along with the Old Testament prophets. There is only one deity in Islam: Allah.

All Muslims are expected to follow the Five Pillars:

- *shadah*: a declaration of belief that "There is no god but Allah" and that Muhammad is Allah's prophet.
- *salat*: prayers offered five times a day while facing Mecca: at dawn, noon, mid-afternoon, sunset and before retiring.
- *sawm*: fasting during the month of Ramadan: no food or drink are permitted between dawn and sunset (the ill are not under obligation). Food is eaten after sunset or before dawn.
- *zakat*: charitable giving or almsgiving (which has been interpreted as paying a 2 1/2 % tax on capital to be used for the needs of the community). The Qur'anic text reads:

> Show kindness to parents, near kindred, orphans and those in need, to the neighbor who is kin to you and to the neighbor who is not kin, to the fellow-traveller, the wayfarer and the slaves who you own. Truly Allah loves not the proud and the boastful who hoard their wealth and who advise covetousness in others and who hoard that which Allah has given them (Surah 4:36-37).

- *hajj*: a pilgrimage to Mecca at least once during one's lifetime if finances and physical conditions permit. The pilgrimage is important in that it enables the worshipper to come into direct contact with the most sacred icon of Islam, the black meteorite encased in the Ka'bah. Ibn Jubayr who, in 1183, in repentance for having drunk wine, made the pilgrimage from Valencia, Spain, recorded his impression of the stone:

> The blessed Black Stone is encased in the corner (of the Ka'b-ah) facing east. The depth to which it penetrates is not known, but it is said to extend two cubits into the wall. Its breadth is two-thirds of a span, its length one span and a finger joint. It has four pieces, joined together, and it is said that it was the Qarmata — may God curse them — who broke it. Its edges have been braced with a sheet of silver whose white shines brightly against the black sheen and polished brilliance of the Stone, presenting the observer a striking spectacle which will hold his gaze. The Stone, when kissed, has a softness and a moistness which so enchants the mouth that he who puts his lips to it would wish them never to be removed. (translated by J.C. Broadhurst in Kritzeck, p. 215)

The Qarmata were a Shiite sect who seized control of Mecca and removed the stone to al-Bahrayn. It was returned in 911 by the Caliph al-Mansur. In addition to adhering to the Five Pillars, Muslims are expected to live according to a strict diet code which forbids the consumption of alcohol, illicit drugs, pork or any meat that is not *halal* (killed according to a coded procedure, much like Jewish *kosher*).

Fazlur Rahman notes that "Muhammad's monotheism was, from the very beginning, linked up with a humanism and a sense of social and economic justice whose intensity is no less than the intensity of the monotheistic idea" (p. 12). He substantiates his claim with a quotation from the Qur'an (107):

> Did you see the one who repudiates the Faith? He it is who maltreats the orphan and does not exhort (others) to feed the poor. Woe betide those who (although they) pray, are (yet) neglectful of their prayers; those who (pray for) show and (even) refuse (the use of) utensils (to needy people).

In other words, rejection or abandonment of the humanistic dimensions of Islam is the equivalent of repudiating the faith. The statement may reflect Muhammad's memories of his personal experiences as an impoverished orphan.

Muhammad's personal life appears to have had its ups and downs. Early rejection by those to whom he attempted to convey his message distressed him. When his first wife, Khadija, who was his greatest supporter, died, and when shortly afterward his uncle Abu Talib, who though loyal was not converted to Islam, also died, the prophet's courage faltered. Subsequent victories revitalized him and he took other wives.

Muhammad died in 632 in Medina, the second holiest city in Islam (the third is Jerusalem) and was buried in a chamber of a house next to the first mosque of Islam. His successors were members of the Quraysh tribe. The first, Abu Bakr, one of the prophet's fathers-in-law (father of Muhammad's wife, A'isha), who had been his military chief and close ally, became Caliph ("successor"). A second father-in-law, 'Umar ibn al-Kattab (father of Muhammad's wife, Hafsa), is said to have been the one to suggest gathering together the prophet's sayings. When Abu Bakr died in 634, 'Umar assumed command and, by the time of his death in 644, the armies of Islam had defeated the great power of the Persian empire and had stripped a number of provinces from the Byzantine rule.

So long as Muhammad was alive, he was the sole guide for faith and behavior for his followers; after his death sectarian divisions arose and collections of words attributed to the prophet were set down by his companions. In the ninth century, six of these collections or *Hadith* (the word means "narratives") were accepted as authoritative. Today there are differences in opinion as to how many of these collected sayings are actually Muhammad's words. There are critical analysts who argue that portions of the Hadith can be recognized as efforts to accommodate Islam to new situations and conditions that occurred after Muhammad's death.

Divisions in Islam

As in other faith systems, divisions developed in Islam. Although there is a sense of "family" underlying the varying expressions of the faith, tensions do arise between factions. Each division must be recognized as unique and separate, representing a kind of independent thinking that has, in turn, become solidified and locked in by theology. What Muhammad established was a religion; his followers engaged in developing theologies, doctrines and, most important, religious systems.

The Kharijites

The Kharijites (the "seceders" or "rebels"), a militant sect, came into being shortly after Muhammad's death. They rejected the current belief that the office of the Caliph, the post of successor to Muhammad, must be held by member of Muhammad's tribe, the Quraysh. Instead, they insisted upon absolute equality, arguing "that any Muslim whose character was unimpeachable was eligible for this office even though he be 'a black slave'." (Rahman, p. 169-170) This puritanical group made the *jihad* (the Arabic word means "striving" or "holy killing") the sixth Pillar of faith and on the basis of this notion justified killing any Muslim who failed to live up to their ascetic standards. They believed in free will and argued that a Muslim who sinned did so out of his own choice and thereby automatically could become a victim of the *jihad*. Men were to be judged "not only by the intensity of their faith but the quality of their work, their deeds" (Christopher, p. 105). In other words, they rejected the concept of justification by faith alone.

The Sunnis

Sunni Muslims, who constitute 80 percent of today's Muslims, see themselves as the orthodox, deriving their customs from the teachings of Muhammad as revealed in the Qur'an and the Hadith or Sunnah. The term "Sunni" is derived from the Arabic word *sunnah*, which means "custom" or "rule" or "tradition" based on the way the Prophet lived his life. The central rules are the five pillars, but there are numerous other rules covering diet, marriage, divorce, business contracts, and ethical conduct including the prohibition of murder or theft. The Sunnis see themselves as traditionalists who follow the revealed rules. Therefore, when questions arise and problems need solution, issues are resolved by referring to these basic sources. They consider their leaders (the caliphs) to be mere men who are, perhaps, more pious than others.

The Shi'ites

The Shi'ites, who are largely centered in Iran, are in a sense, opposed to the Sunnis and are, perhaps, the "anti-traditionalists." They claim to be the legitimate followers of the prophet. Their leaders (imams) are believed to be divinely inspired, thereby enabling them to deal authoritatively with changing conditions and new issues. In other words, for the Shi'ites, inspiration is not restricted to the past, to the sayings of Muhammad, but is a continuing reality. They believe that Muhammad intended that his successors should be members of his immediate family, not persons democratically elected to office. Therefore, Muhammad's cousin and son-in-law, Ali, "and Ali's two sons Hasan and Husein, who ruled as caliphs briefly are regarded as the legitimate heirs of a semi-divine authority" (Bahm, p. 329). Indeed, the name "Shi'ite" means "to be a follower of," and the sect began with those who followed Ali. Abu Bakr and 'Umar are regarded as usurpers. Inasmuch as the twelfth "legitimate" caliph disappeared in 878 C.E., the infallible authority has remained hidden and will continue to be hidden until the appearance of the Mahdi, the divinely appointed leader, who will come to restore Islam to the truth, conquer the world and reign for a millennium (Bahm, p. 330).

The Shi'ites have tended to be syncretistic, borrowing concepts from other faith systems including gnosticism. Divisions developed within Shi'itism including the "Twelvers," the Zaidis, the Ismailis, the *hashishin* or Assassins, the Alawis, the Druzes, and finally, the Baha'is (discussed below). A mystical group known as the Sufis emphasized ascetic practices and within this group Dervishes sought unity with the deity through ecstasy. Additional groups resulted from the impact of Greek philosophy.

The Mutazilites

The notion that man was a free and responsible agent was adopted by a sect known as the Mutazilites (the "neutralists" or "religious moderates"). They were not truly freethinkers but they did attempt to introduce a kind of rationalism into Islamic theology. They sought to de-anthropomorphize the Qu'ranic image of Allah, insisting that the divine transcendence or pure essence of the deity was free from limiting qualities. Inasmuch as they denied the quality of speech to Allah, the Qur'an had to be a created work (Rahman, p. 90). They believed reason was equal to revelation in determining religious truth, but since "they held reason to be the essential constitution of God, a purely Greek idea, the net result was to put reason above revelation" (Rahman, p. 90).

The only place where the Mutazilites appeared to place limits on the deity was in the concept of justice. "Borrowing from Stoic philosophy, they argued that the natural law of morality implanted in the universe by God obliged him to reward the virtuous and punish the wicked. This doctrine was sometimes called that of *promise and threat*: God had to make good his promise of heaven and threat of hell; he had to preserve men's free will, their capacity to choose between good and evil courses" (Christopher, p. 107). Of course, this doctrine made God subject to human standards of justice and automatically denied his omnipotence. A story of the refutation of this kind of thinking is attributed to the master Abul Hasan al-Ash'ari (873-935), who began as a Mutazilite and then used their theology against them to develop a closer harmony with Sunni thinking:

> Let us imagine a child and a grown-up in Heaven who both died in the True Faith, but the grown-up has a higher place than the child. And the child will ask God, "Why did you give that man a higher place?" And God will answer, "He has done many good works." Then the child will say, "Why did you let me die so soon that I was prevented from doing good?" God will answer, "I knew you would grow up to be a sinner, therefore it was better that you should die a child." Thereupon, a cry will go up from those condemned to the depth of Hell, "Why, O Lord, did you not let us die before we became sinners?" (Rahman, p. 91; Christopher, p. 109)

The Baha'is

In 1844, in Iran, Siyyid 'Ali Muhammadan, who became known as the Bab (the Gate) and who is considered the forerunner of the Baha'i faith, announced that God would make manifest a divine messenger. As we shall see, the messenger turned out to be a certain Baha'u'llah whose name means "The Glory and Splendor of God" and his followers are the Baha'is ("Followers of the Glory").

The Bab's announcement did not receive a kindly hearing in Shi'ite Iran, inasmuch as it ran counter to standard Muslim orthodoxy that taught "since the twelve Imams, The Gate of Knowledge is closed" (Robertson I, p. 300). Nor was his command that the Shah, his followers, and indeed all the rulers of the earth follow him, welcomed. He was arrested, imprisoned, and sentenced to die by a firing squad. His remains are presently buried in a shrine on Mount Carmel in Haifa, Israel.

Many of his followers were also put to death. One, Mirza 'Ali, Prince of Nur, was imprisoned and during incarceration had a visionary experience that proclaimed him to be the expected messenger. He became known as Baha'u'llah. On the order of the Shah, he was expelled to Baghdad and there the new faith prospered and some of the central Baha'i writings came into being. He went to Constantinople and was expelled, spent time in the prison in what is now Acre, Israel, and finally died at age seventy-six. His movement continued to grow despite opposition from Islamic protesters and soon became a world-wide religion. When, in 1978, the Shi'ite Muslims overthrew the Shah and took control of Iran, Baha'is became targets for persecution and death. Fundamentalist Muslims in Iran did not tolerate this religion that sprang from their loins, for the Baha'i faith is recognized as a rejection of Islam.

Muslim Skeptics and Freethinkers

Although modern studies in Islam tend to place emphasis upon the faith perspectives, from the earliest times there were skeptics and freethinkers and those who either refused to accept, or who questioned the legitimacy of, Muhammad's claims. Concomitant with the emergence of the various manifestations of Islamic faith was the development of philosophy and science. Some Muslim writers in these fields stressed the humanistic and social aspects of the faith; others questioned doctrine and expressed their skepticism in poetic form.

Nor did all Arabic tribes accept Muhammad as a genuine prophet. For example, although two Awsite clans and 'Abdallah ibn Ubayy of the Khazraj clan abandoned the worship of Manat (the goddess of fate who was believed to be one of Allah's daughters) and accepted Muhammad's teaching, other Medina clans belonging to the Aws tribe rejected both the prophet's monotheistic claims and his mission. A centenarian named Abu 'Afak, a man of the Medina Khazraj clan, wrote:

> I have lived a long time, but I have never seen
> Either a house or gathering of people
> More loyal and faithful to its allies, when they call on it,
> Than that of the Children of Qayla [the Aws and the Khazraj]
> as a whole.
> The mountains will crumble before they submit.
> Yet here is a rider come among them who has divided them.
> [He says] "This is permitted; this is forbidden" to all kinds of
> things.

> But if you had believed in power
> And in might, why did you not follow a *tubba'* [a South
> Arabian ruler]? (Rodinson, p. 157)

The Medina poetess 'Asma bint Marwan scornfully addressed the men of the Medina tribes who followed Muhammad:

> You obey a stranger who does not belong among you,
> Who is not of Murad, nor of Madh'hij [Yemenite tribes].
> Do you, when your own chiefs have been murdered, put your
> hope in him
> Like men greedy for a meal when it is cooking?
> Is there no man of honour who will take advantage of an
> unguarded moment
> And cut off the gulls' hopes? (Rodinson, p. 157f)

Whenever Muhammad heard these verses he would say, "Will no one rid me of this daughter of Marwan?" It is not surprising to learn that the woman was murdered. 'Umayr ibn 'Adi, a member of her clan, announced to Muhammad that he had stabbed the poetess to death as she lay sleeping with her children beside her. Rodinson comments:

> Assassination, like the war which is an extension of it, is the pursuit of political ends by different means. 'Umayr's exploit is listed by the chroniclers among Muhammad's "expeditions." (p. 171)

Ar-Razi (c. 865-923), the Persian physician, mathematician and philosopher, drew from Greek thought to produce his own freethinking, rationalist, anti-religious teachings. As a rationalist, he placed reason above religion, arguing that reason was God's greatest blessing "without which our state would be the state of wild beasts, of children and lunatics." When cataracts produced blindness, his detractors assumed that the loss of sight was Allah's punishment for Ar-Razi's impiety (Christopher, pp. 108-110).

Other philosophers, such as Avicenna (Ibn-Sina, 980-1037) and Averroes (Ibn-Rushd, 1126-1198), sought to harmonize philosophy and Islamic faith, while still others were closer to the Sufi, Al-Ghazali (1058-1111), who refuted the claims of philosophy in his work "The Incoherence of the Philosophers." He believed that only through personal experience of the truth that God places in the heart could one verify the validity of the claims of revelation and the dogmatism of theology.

Islamic physicians, like ar-Razi, were pioneers in the developing field of medicine but some among them were also astrologers and alchemists. The historian, philosopher and sociologist, Ibn-Khaldun (1332-1406), mocked these non-medical interests as irrational. Concerning astrology, he wrote:

> The worthlessness of astrology from the point of view of religious law, as well as the weakness of its achievements from the rational point of view, are evident. In addition, astrology does harm to human civilization. It hurts the faith of the common people when an astrological judgment occasionally happens to come true . . . Ignorant people are taken in by that and suppose that all other astrological judgments must be true. (quoted in Christopher, p. 128)

Ibn Khaldun rejected the claims of alchemists that they could transmute one substance into another and convert a base metal into gold or glass into emeralds:

> As to the claims of the alchemists, it must be clearly understood that it is not in their power to bring about any true changes of species. They can, however, produce excellent imitations, dyeing the red metal white so that it resembles silver, or dyeing it yellow so that it closely resembles gold. They can, too, dye white metal any color they desire, until it bears a close resemblance to gold or copper; and they can free the leads from most of their defects and impurities. Yet in these dyed metals the essential nature is unchanged. (quoted in Christopher, p. 129)

Independence from religious regulations was often expressed by Islamic poets. Disregarding the prohibition of alcohol, poets extolled the virtues of wine which, despite the claims of some, does not appear to be unfermented grape juice. Walid II, who was Caliph in Damascus from 743 to 744, has been recognized as something of a libertine. He boasted:

> I am Walid, the leader of Islam,
> In the pomp and glory of royalty;
> But I listen to the melodious songs of the beautiful maidens,

And when I walk proudly to the chamber of my beloved
I do not care what is said of me.
The real joy of life
Is to have music
And to drink wine
And to enjoy the ecstasy of intoxication;
I enjoy this life,
Rather than wait for Paradise. (Ullah, pp. 39-40)

Abul-'Ala al-Mar'arri (973-1057), the blind Syrian poet-philosopher, did not deny the existence of God but his concept of God seems to have been associated with the notion that everything is governed by blind fate. He rejected belief in resurrection or divine revelation. For him, religion was a human product that was simply accepted without debate through habit and education. He wrote:

Now this religion happens to prevail
Until by that one it is overthrown;
Because men will not live with men alone,
But always with another fairy tale.
(quoted by Robertson, I, p. 287)

Despite his agnostic stance, he was respected as a freethinker who challenged the claims of revealed religion:

Muslims, Christians, Jews and Magians
Are following the path of error.
In reality humanity is divided into
Intelligent ones who doubt faith,
And ignorant ones who are faithful. (Ullah, p. 68)

Perhaps the best known Persian freethinker is the poet, Omar Khayyam (died, 1132). His Arabic name is Omar ibn Ibrahim al-Khayammi ("al-Khayammi" means "the tent-maker" which seems to point to his occupation). His poem *The Rubaiyat* has become familiar to the western world through the Edward Fitzgerald translation. Whether or not the poem in its entirety is the work of Khayyam is debated by scholars. His work is characteristic of Arab agnostics and, where the concept of God enters, it is presented almost casually, reflecting no great depth of belief. Certainly, he places his freethinking above creed and he is no conformer to Muslim regulations. The poet's love of wine is threaded throughout the poem. He speaks to his lover:

Here with a little Bread beneath the Bough,
A Flask of Wine, a Book of Verse — and Thou
Beside me singing in the Wilderness —
Oh, Wilderness were Paradise enow! (Quatrain xii)

He challenges the validity of revealed truth:

The Revelations of Devout and Learn'd
Who rose before us, and as Prophets burn'd,
Are all but Stories, which, awoke from Sleep
They told their fellows, and to Sleep return'd (Quatrian lxviii)

Oh threats of Hell and Hopes of Paradise!
One thing at least is certain — *This* Life flies:
One thing is certain and the rest is Lies;
The Flower that once is blown for ever dies. (Quatrain lxvi)

And, as he encourages his readers to seize life and live it now, he ignores the prohibition of wine and denies belief in an afterlife:

Ah, make the most of what we yet may spend,
Before we too into Dust descend;
Dust into Dust, and under Dust, to lie,
Sans Wine, sans Song, sans Singer, and — sans End!
(Quatrain xxvi)

Some poets focused on the humanistic and humanitarian dimensions of Islam. Saadi of Shiraz (1185-1292) believed that "To worship God is nothing other than to serve the people" (Ullah, p. 297). In *Gulistan* (The Flower Garden), he wrote:

All men are members of the same body,
Created in one essence.
If fate brings suffering to one member
The others cannot stay at rest.
You who remain indifferent to the burden of pain of others
Do not deserve to be called human. (Ullah, p. 299)

The hypocrisy of the priesthood also came under attack. The Persian poet, Shams-uddin Muhammadan, known as Hafiz (13th century), expressed his love of wine even as he warned against the pietistic judgment by the righteous:

Censure not, pious man, in the purity of your soul, the lover of
wine, for in your book of account will not be written the sins
of others.
Whether I be good or bad, go your own way:
everyone will reap finally the seed that he has sown.
Make me not hopeless, on account of the past, of the benignity
of the Eternal One;
what do you know, who, beyond the veil, will be judged to be
good or evil? (Ullah, p. 307)

The 20th century Turkish poet, Nazim Hikmet, was the first known communist poet of Turkey. He did not hesitate to attack capitalism and censure the treatment of the poor. In his poem "The Old Book of the World" he surveyed what he perceived as "the fiction" of religious scripture. He concluded:

The heavens dispensed neither salvation nor mercy,
And the slaves who toiled, Jesus, Moses and Muhammadan,
Gave simply a vain prayer and incense;
And showed the way to the paradise of tales.
We are always the slaves, and we have our masters;
And always a wall, the damned stones of which are covered with no moss;
Bestowed two sorts of destinies to the children of earth,
In calling some of them masters and some others slaves.
May the masters, saints, the eremites
Be drowned in the depths of eternal darkness.
On the routes of law there exists
But a single religion, a single law, and a single right —
The work of workers. (Ullah, p. 413)

One of the best known and perhaps the most loved poets of Islam was the Lebanese, Khalil Gibran (1883-1931). His writings have been translated into more than 20 languages, and his best known work, *The Prophet*, sold over a million copies. In this book, Gibran comes through as a naturalist. He believes that one's daily life embraces that which is both temple and religion and one's achievements are testimony to how one enters into life as a religion, giving it one's all. To find God, one looks at playing children, or into space or at the wonders of nature: "You shall see Him smiling in flowers, then rising and waving His hands in trees" ("On Religion"). God is the self for "God listens not to your words save when He Himself utters them through your lips." Even the mountains and trees and seas utter prayer, and if one listens, in silence, one may hear them saying, "Our God, who art our winged self, it is thy will in us that willeth." (On Prayer) In other words, the divine, the sacred, is inherent in life, so that life becomes an utterance of the infinite. Recognition of the sacral nature of all that exists is an expression of naturalistic humanism.

In addition to the poets, pictorial artists have refused to be bound by Muslim dictates concerning art. Calligraphy has always been held in high esteem as an educational tool and Arab calligraphy reached decorative heights. Muhammad is supposed to have said:

> Read: by thy most beneficent Lord, who taught the use of the pen, who teaches man that which he does not know (Surah 96:3-5).

Therefore, inasmuch as writing was associated with the communication of divine revelation and was treated as a divine gift, "the profession of the calligrapher was one of honor and dignity because he was engaged in copying the Qur'an, and his labours thereby received a religious sanction" (Arnold, p. 3). It is not surprising to find that the decorations at the sacred mosque in Jerusalem are made up entirely of beautifully calligraphed quotations from the Qur'an. On the other hand, the depiction of the human body and of living things was deemed inappropriate because it was considered to be imitative of the divine creativity of Allah. Nevertheless, Muslim artists were at work. Some portrayals represent religious tales including the legendary story of Muhammad's miraculous journey to heaven on the back of the wonder horse Buraq, depictions of the legends of the prophet's birth and so on. Others show scenes from folk tales or show people, structures and activities. Some private homes and some public baths portrayed erotic scenes. James commented:

> However, despite the heavy hand which time has laid on Arab and Persian painting, despite the inherent dislike of many Moslems for any kind of representational art, and the inaccessibility of much of what is left, it is possible to assert that erotic elements were present, and have, in fact, played a quite substantial part in Islamic art throughout the whole of its existence. (James, p. 203)

Some artists, even those who in devotion to Islam portrayed scenes relating to the faith, became freethinkers, along with the Muslim poets and philosophers.

Contemporary Islamic Issues

There is no room in traditional Islam for the secularism and atheism expressed by Muslim writers. In his discussion of the Muslim in the Arab world, Wilfred Cantwell Smith has pointed out that "the secularist attack is foreign" (p. 112) and, he notes:

> The Westerner who finds his religion no longer tenable is being challenged to adopt a different set of his society's values. The Arab in a similar condition is being challenged to abandon his society's values. In a civilization as singly religious, Islamic, as the Arab's has been, to abandon Islam is seen as abandoning one's community. (p. 113)

Within the closed society there is no place for a secular voice. The Ayatollah Ruhollah Khomeini of Iran made this position clear in 1979:

> Familiarize the people with the truth of Islam so that the young generation may not think that the men of religion in the mosques of Qum and al-Najaf believe in the separation of church from state, that they study nothing other than menstruation and childbirth and that they have nothing to do with politics. The colonialists have spread in school curricula the need to separate church from the state and have deluded people into believing that the ulema [religious experts] are not qualified to interfere in the political and social affairs. The lackeys and followers of the colonialists have reiterated these words. In the prophet's time, was the church separated from the state? Were there at the time theologians and politicians? At the time of the caliphs and the time of Ali, the amir of the faithful, was the state separated from the church? Was there an agency for the church and another for the state?
>
> The difference between the Islamic government and the constitutional governments both monarchic and republican, lies in the fact that the people's representatives or the king's representative are the ones who codify and legislate, whereas the power of legislation is confined to God, may He be praised, and nobody else has the right to legislate and nobody may rule by that which has not been given power by God. This is why Islam replaces the legislative council by a planning council that works to run the affairs and the work of the ministries so that they may offer their services in all spheres.

> Christian, Jewish and Baha'i missionary centers are spread in Tehran to deceive people and to lead them away from the teachings and principles of religion. Isn't it a duty to destroy these centers? (quoted by Menendez and Doerr, p. 56f from *Islamic Government*, New York: Manor Books, 1979)

When these same Muslims move into the world of pluralism and democracy and the free expression of ideas, the security of their closed system is threatened. There is little room for deviation in modern Islam. Those Muslims who retreat from the tenets of the faith tend to remain quiet about their change of beliefs rather than embarrass their families and, perhaps, endanger their safety.

The publication of Salman Rushdie's *The Satanic Verses* endangered his life and placed him on an Islamic "hit list" when in 1989, Khomeini issued a *fatwa*, or religious edict, imposing a death sentence. Hitoshi Igarashi, assistant professor of comparative Islamic culture at Tsukuba University, Japan, who translated Rushdie's work into Japanese, was stabbed to death and the Shinsen Company, publishers of the translation, received many threats when the book first appeared. Ettiore Caprioli, who made the Italian translation, was stabbed by a Pakistani; and Gianni Palma, the promoter of the Italian version, had a "death sentence" pronounced on him by the head of the Pakistani Association of Japan (Helm).

But despite threats and violence, some liberal expressions are published. According to Kim Murphy (1992), when Alaa Hamid, a Cairo Muslim, wrote *The Man Inside the Triangle*, his book was condemned as a threat to fundamental Islamic societal beliefs and an incitement to atheism and apostasy. Hamid wrote:

> Until this day, it has not been made clear to humanity that God answers man's prayers, or that He has sent food to the hungry, or that He has sent a million pounds of gold to a poor man . . . Why has the sending of prophets and messengers stopped suddenly? Why doesn't God send a roast lamb like he did to Abraham? Why are there no more miracles?

Hamid was arrested for blasphemy, demonstrating once again that there is no room for freethought within orthodox Islam.

On June 9, 1992, Farag Foda, a Cairo newspaper columnist was murdered by a member of the Islamic Jihad, the Islamic extremist group responsible for the murder of Anwar Sadat in 1982. Fouda was an outspoken secularist and critic of militant Islam. He had just announced plans to form a new movement to unite Egyptians of all religions. (*Los Angeles Times*, June 10, 1992)

Feminist voices, protesting against certain Islamic customs, can be silenced politically. For example, Dr. Nawal Saadawi, a Cairo novelist and head of the Arab Women's Solidarity Association, has condemned the practice of female circumcision, the right of husbands to take a second wife without the permission of the first wife (Islamic law permits a man to have up to four wives), the limiting of wives' ability to work or get a passport without the husband's permission, as well as other customs supported by religion and law. Consequently, the publication of Solidarity's monthly magazine *Al Noon* was halted by the government because it "criticized allied Arab governments for their policies toward women" (Murphy, 1991) and the national chapter of the organization (Solidarity has branches in seven Arab countries) was dissolved. The primary issue defined as criticism of foreign intervention in the gulf crisis was the basis for the closure, according to the Cairo Ministry of Social Affairs, which pointed out that, according to Article 3 of the Statute of Organizations, "It is not permitted for any institution to discuss politics or religious affairs" (Murphy, 1991).

Despite the closure and despite the objections to free expression by conservative Islamic women, it is clear that the trend towards open discussion can only temporarily be stifled and that, as more Islamic women are educated abroad, other voices will protest the patriarchal restrictions. Jean P. Sasson records the struggle facing the women of Islam in her book, *Princess: A True Story of Life Behind the Veil in Saudi Arabia*. The voice of a Saudi princess, a prisoner behind the black veil, demonstrates that despite her royal rank she has no voice, no vote, no value in society other than that of bearer of sons. The identity of the princess is, of course, kept secret and she is referred to only as "Sultana." Her story resounds with accounts reflecting the restrictions placed on human rights and the roles of women and the enforcement of rigid Islam by the *mutawas*, the so-called "religious men," who do not hesitate to use physical punishment and imprisonment to compel conformity.

Secrecy of identity is essential when women publish their protests against Islamic restrictions. "Fatima B." is the pseudonym for a 22-year-old Algerian woman who has dared to object to the Algerian Islamic fundamentalist demands that all women must wear the veil (*hijab*). She states that "Scarcely a day goes by when a teacher, a journalist, a labor leader, a lawyer is not murdered, not to mention ordinary working people who show signs of freethinking." (Fatima B., p. B11) The silence imposed on freethought is so great that even "The secular, democratic parties will not come out to back us." Nor is there any support coming from France, the United States or any Muslim country. She appeals to the United States:

> I have to believe that you Americans do not understand us or the full importance of our problem. Those whom you supported or still support in Afghanistan and Saudi Arabia are full of scorn for you. They believe that American women are filthy whores. I do not believe this and neither do my friends. We do not want to be like you, but we want to live in a country where we can be like you if that is what we please, or be ourselves, or even wear a veil if we want to. But the Islamist terrorists, after they have turned Algeria into another Iran, will not give us any choices at all. (B11)

In May 1993, a group of Saudi Arabian scholars formed a "Committee for the Defense of Legitimate Rights;" within ten days they attracted some 10,000 supporters. Concern for human rights, including the rights of women and sectarian minorities, was the basis for the formation of the group. However, by the end of the month the movement "was dead. Its spokesman was jailed, its office telephone disconnected, its leaders dismissed from their jobs, their houses searched and monitored by secret police." (Murphy, May, 1993) It is clear that the House of Al Sa'ud has no intention of relaxing its control of the kingdom and the most conservative interpretation of Islam supports that intent.

Nasr Hamid abu Zaid had been a professor of Arabic literature for 22 years in the prestigious Cairo University. When he came up for promotion to full professorship, two colleagues recommended him highly; but a third was disturbed because Abu Zaid had suggested that the texts of the Qur'an "should be studied in the light of the men who interpreted them." (Murphy, 1994) He was denied promotion, denounced as a heretic and then subjected to a most unusual form of harassment and punishment. He was served with divorce papers, not by his wife, but by a fellow professor at the university who argued that a Muslim woman should be protected from marriage to an apostate. Abu Zaid is reported to have reacted with:

> Before the court case, I thought we were living in a modern civil society. When we heard about the case, my wife and I were shocked. We thought it was some form of a black joke. We were amazed to learn something like this is permitted un-

> der the Egyptian legal code. Now we realize the whole issue is intended to make me stop writing and teaching . . . To make me silent — whether by this deprivation of promotion, or by the loss of my wife, or by death. The intention is to stop the critical mind — a battle intellectuals thought was won 100 years ago. (Murphy, January, 1994)

Once again, the dangers to freethought that arise out of the alliance of church and state are illustrated. This problem is recognized by Mohammed Sid Ahmed, an Egyptian, who is quoted as saying:

> Intellectuals are placed in a very difficult situation. Either they espouse Enlightenment philosophies and then feel they are not on the wavelength of the people — who are caught up in the problems of joblessness, economic problems, deep frustration, the feeling of being manipulated rather than being master of your fate — or else they try to rationalize the Islamic movement . . . which is not an intellectual movement at all. It is a religious movement that has become a source of ideology, *faute de mieux* [for want of something better]. Enlightened intellectuals, if they are honest, they are torn apart. (Murphy, January, 1994)

Indeed, in Muslim countries around the world, those who support freethought or express any criticism of fundamentalist Islam are often attacked or murdered or have their lives threatened. Some now carry weapons or seek other means to protect themselves. Naguib Mahfouz, a Egyptian Nobel Prize-winning novelist was stabbed in the neck because he was seen as an apologist for Zionism and a protege of America and the west. When Riafaat Said, head of Egypt's leftist Tegamu Party, who had not hesitated to ridicule the excesses of Islamic fundamentalism, began to receive death threats, he began to carry a gun and travel with six machine-gun-armed bodyguards.

In Algeria more than two dozen journalists have been assassinated. Algerian pop singer Cheb Hasni was shot and killed in the western city of Oran after religious leaders reportedly issued a *fatwa*, or religious ruling, ordering the death of any singer considered vulgar.

Bangladeshi writer Taslima Nasrin was under the protection of 1,200 police officers assigned for her visit to France following her flight from Muslim fundamentalist death threats at home early in 1994. Nasrin has been ordered to stand trial for blaspheming Islam and has said she will eventually agree to serve a prison sentence if convicted, on condition that the government can guarantee her safety in prison. (Murphy, Nov. 28, 1994)

In non-Muslim countries, Muslims enjoy and support the advantages of a secular state wherein they are free to pursue their own religion, without the isolation or prejudice which non-Muslims experience within a Muslim controlled environment as in Iran. For example, at the All India Conference of Forward-Looking Muslims, held in Delhi, December 4 and 5, 1971, concern was expressed at the possible erosion of secularism in India:

> The Conference of Forward-Looking Muslims views with grave concern the growing tendency on the part of eminent public men, political groups and Government to water down the concept of secularism by defining it merely to mean non-communalism, thereby implying that the state is entitled, if not bound, to foster, to facilitate and encourage the growth of all religions and the religious outlook on life. This tendency has to be resisted in the interest of the material and cultural progress of the people of India. This Conference, therefore, restates and reaffirms the concept of the secular state, which is expected to adopt a position of neutrality not only among various religions but also between religion and non-religion. As such the state should not encourage any religion nor, for that matter, associate itself with religious activities in any form whatsoever. The state has to steer clear of all religious activities and must not give rise to the impression that it belongs to or is appropriated by a group following a particular religion. At the same time, the state shall not interfere with the freedom to profess and practice any religion except in the interest of public order and morality, public welfare, social reform and the universal human values enshrined in the preamble to the Constitution of India and Human Rights Charter of the United Nations. A secular state of this kind is a pre-condition for the survival and growth of a free democratic society in India. (Rao, p. 37)

The concerns expressed in this statement continue to haunt India. Strong orthodox Hindu groups call for an India in which Hinduism is recognized as the official religion. Memory of the persecution of Hindus in 1947 in Pakistan, when that Muslim country came into being and declared its independence, are fresh in the minds of many. Territorial conflicts over temple locations keep hostile feelings alive. The Muslims in India have reason to be concerned.

In Pakistan, Christians feel threatened by the 1991 mandatory death penalty for anti-Muslim blasphemy which includes all prophets accepted by Islam, not only Muhammad. This means that any critical evaluation of Noah, for instance, who could be described as a drunkard (Gen. 9:21) or of King David, who was an adulterer (2 Sam. 11), could result in prosecution. A Christian school teacher who was reported to have spoken an insulting word against Muhammad was stabbed to death. (Dahlburg) Prime Minister Benazir Bhutto, who espoused "a tolerant and liberal interpretation of Islam" when she was elected to office, remained silent in the face of the growing militancy of fundamentalist Islam.

Today, in the United States there are some 4 million adherents to Islam, nearly a third of whom are Black Muslims. This is not surprising in view of the fact that one in five African slaves shipped to America was a Muslim. With the influx of families from the Middle East, India, and parts of the Orient and with numbers converting to Islam, it is said to be one of the fastest growing faiths (Sheler, p. 71). But the free, open, democratic environment of America, which provides the freedom to practice Islam openly and without interference, simultaneously threatens the security of the Muslim family. Even when children are sent to Muslim schools where Muslim dress is the norm and Muslim customs and faith are stressed, these same children cannot escape the impact of the outside world which filters into their consciousness through radio, television, literature and social contact.

In University settings, where young men and women from different parts of the Muslim world come to study, genuine conflicts can occur. Some foreign students are so disturbed and unsettled by what they encounter that they return to their homeland. Others seek to maintain their identity by limiting their associations to fellow Muslims, insofar as possible. Still others, attracted by the openness to free inquiry, begin to question traditional beliefs. Some fall in love with non-Muslims and marry outside of their faith, much to the consternation of their families, who are encouraged by friends to excommunicate the freethinker and the non-Muslim mate and offspring, all the while wrestling with feelings of love and familial bonding. Life for an Islamic non-conformist can be very difficult.

Students in higher education may tend to pursue technical careers such as engineering, computer science, architecture and so on, which do not impact directly on faith concepts, rather than humanistic studies. Hence they are never led to question the authority of Muslim claims such as divine revelation, the validity of the story of the famous night journey where the prophet was magically transported from Mecca to Jerusalem and then through the seven heavens to the presence of Allah while riding the woman-headed horse Buraq, as well as other legends. Critical thinking in one field does not insure critical thinking in others.

It is important to remember that Islam does not recognize separation of church and state when Islam is the dominant religion. Orthodox Islam prescribes pattern of dress and conduct that do not allow for free expression. However, not all Muslims are fundamentalists and in Pakistan, a Muslim state, it was possible to elect a woman as Prime Minister. But the election of a woman has nothing to do with freedom of expression. When Salamat Missah, a twelve-year-old illiterate Christian was accused, along with two others, of writing derogatory phrases on the walls of a mosque, the cry from the orthodox was for the death penalty (Griffin, p. M2). They ignored the fact that Salamat was illiterate!

Many of the values espoused by Muslims are like those endorsed by other religions and by secularists, such as kindness, understanding, honesty, justice and so forth. However, none of these human virtues really need a faith system to justify their significance. As human beings everywhere have discovered, these ethical standards have validity in and of themselves. They are most freely practiced in a democratic society, as has been made clear by Maher Hathout, Senior Advisor to the Muslim Public Affairs Council, Los Angeles, and the Council's Director, Salam al-Marayati, in their article "The Tyranny of Brotherhood." They point out that:

> Today, Muslims in much of the world are under military dictatorships, occupations or theocracies — even subject to genocide — suffering human rights violations under Muslim and non-Muslim rulers . . . Muslims in America enjoy their freedom, but until Muslim countries allow their citizens to think freely and write without fear of retribution, as the Sharia (Islamic law) mandates, let us not deceive ourselves by claiming that those countries are part of our dream. No, they are part of our nightmare.
>
> The problem in Muslim societies is rooted in authoritarianism, which burdens practically every community, mosque and family. . . Muslims continue to suffer because of the abject failure of the religious Establishment to live up to the standards of human decency set by Islam . . . . When the Koran, for example, stipulates, "There shall be no compulsion in religion" (2:256), there is no excuse for religious police patrolling Muslim streets. This form of repression pushes people to the

> margins of civilized society, because the voice of reason, which plays a vital role in Islamic jurisprudence and in opposition politics, along with the spirit of the Koran, is silenced — jailed, exiled or dead. . . .
>
> The controversies surrounding Salman Rushdie and Taslima Nasrin . . . are symptoms of a larger problem engulfing the Muslim world — the erosion of Islamic ethics. The death threats levied against the two writers should be condemned. . . Today, the Muslim world is held captive by clergy and governments that promote intolerance and oppose cooperation with other religious groups. . .
>
> It is time to redefine Muslim culture based on true Islam, and perhaps a new beginning in the West. Then, the public could understand how Islam is concerned with secular affairs and balances the concerns of this world with concerns of the hereafter, the temporal with the eternal; how reason is also a cornerstone of Islamic jurisprudence, and how the will of the people is inseparable from the will of God. . . .
>
> One can practice Islam in America without worrying about secret police dragging people out of bed in the middle of the night. Women can pray and lecture in American mosques rather than suffer exclusion from society. In America, one can criticize the government and feel patriotic. It is not an issue of being anti-secular or anti-religion, but of being anti-oppression and anti-exploitation.

The redefinition of Islam that Dr. Hathout calls for may presently be taking place — not in the West as he suggested, but in Iran, Egypt, Tunisia and Algeria. Abdol Karim Soroush, Dean of the Faculty at the Research Institute for Human Sciences in Tehran, Iran, is a key figure in what some have suggested is the beginning of a movement akin to the Reformation in Christianity. Soroush is joined by Rashid Gannouchi of Tunisia (who has recently been forced into exile in Europe), Hassan Hanafi of Egypt, and Mohammed Arkoun of Algeria, in questioning traditional beliefs and practices and in proclaiming that it is possible to be Islamic without being fundamentalist.

Soroush is quoted as saying:

> Islam and democracy are not only compatible, their association is inevitable. In Muslim society, one without the other is not perfect . . I have given two bases. The first pillar is this: To be a true believer, one must be free. To become a believer under

> pressure or coercion will not be true belief. And this freedom is the basis of democracy. The second pillar in Islamic democracy is that the interpretation of religious texts is always in flux. Those interpretations are also influenced by the age you live in. So you can never give a fixed interpretation. . . No one group of people has exclusive right to interpret or reinterpret religion. That is something to be abolished. (Wright, p. A10)

It is obvious that, as Sorush argues that each person is free to make personal interpretations of the sacred text, some interpretations will be produced by scholars and clerics, others by lay persons. However, no one interpretation will be automatically authoritative. Soroush's solution moves away from totalitarian theology and ideology. Indeed, he recommends that the ideal Islamic republic is that ruled by secularists, not by mullahs or sheiks.

His interpretation of *Sharia* or Islamic law is concerned with its potential expansibility and flexibility without contradicting the concept of Islam as "submission." He argues:

> If you surrender or submit, this does not mean that you have sacrificed your freedom. You should be free as well to leave your faith. It is a contradiction to be free in order to believe — and then afterward to abolish that freedom. (Wright, p. A11)

Soroush's concepts are echoed by Gannouchi who

> advocates majority rule, protection of minorities, full women's rights and equality of all secular and religious parties. "Freedom," he pronounced, "is superior to Islam." (Wright, p. A11)

Mohammed Reza Bouzari, a Tehran businessman who agrees with Soroush, has commented:

> He is finding ways to reconcile Islam and modernism for educated Muslims who have had problems with traditional Islam. He shows how understanding changes day by day, year by year. This is the only way to save Islam in the modern world. (Wright, p. A11)

Obviously, Soroush and his colleagues are not plotting to overthrow or destroy Islam; rather they seek to make changes from within that will enable Islam to become reconciled with the modern world. To help actualize this ideal, Soroush lectures in the Tehran University School of Theology and makes his thinking known through the bimonthly publication *Kiyan* (which means "soul" or "source"). *Kiyan* was founded in 1991 and is widely read is Asia, Europe and the Americas. Time alone will tell whether or not the efforts to free Islamic theology from control by traditionalists and fundamentalists will bear fruit, but the seeds of freethought are being sown and beginning to take root.

References

Arnold, Sir Thomas W., *Painting in Islam*. New York: Dover Publications, Inc., 1965.

Bahm, Archie, J., *The World's Living Religions*. New York: Dell Publishing Company, 1964.

Bishai, Wilson B., *Islamic History of the Middle East*. Boston: Allyn and Bacon, Inc., 1968.

Christopher, John B., *The Islamic Tradition*. New York: Harper and Row, 1972.

Cragg, Kenneth, *The House of Islam*. Belmont, Calif: Dickenson Publishing Company, Inc., 1969.

Dahlburg, John-Thor, "After Attacks, Christians Feel Threatened in Pakistan," *Los Angeles Times*, April 25, 1994, p. A4.

De Boer, T. J., *The History of Philosophy in Islam*. New York: Dover Publications, Inc. 1967.

Fatima B., "Wearing the Veil, Under Penalty of Death," *Los Angeles Times*, April 1, 1994, p. B11.

Gabrieli, Francesco, *Muhammadan and the Conquests of Islam*. New York: McGraw-Hill Book Company, 1968.

Gaver, Jessyca Russell, *Baha'i Faith*. New York: Universal Publishing and Distribution Corporation, 1967.

Gibran, Khalil, *The Prophet*. New York: Alfred A. Knopf, 1962, based on the 1923 edition.

Griffin, Jennifer, "Is It a Mosque or a State? A Boy Forces Pakistan to Debate Identity," *Los Angeles Times*, March 20, 1994, p. M2.

Guillaume, Alfred, *Islam*. Baltimore, Mar.: Penguin Books, Inc., 1968.

Hathout, Maher, and Salam Al-Marayati, "The Tyranny of Brotherhood," *Los Angeles Times*, September 18, 1994, p. M5.

Helm, Leslie, "Translator of 'Satanic Verses' Slain," *Los Angeles Times*, July 11, 1991.

Hitti, Philip K., *Islam, A Way of Life*. Chicago: Henry Regnery Company, (Gateway edition), 1970.

James, David, "Islam", *The Erotic Art of the East*. Philip Rawson, edit., New York: Prometheus Press, 1968, pp. 205-275.

Kritzech, James, edit., *Anthology of Islamic Literature.* New York: Holt, Rinehart and Winston, 1964.

Menendez, Albert J. and Edd Doerr, *The Great Quotations on Religious Freedom*. Long Beach, Calif.: Centerline Press, 1991.

Murphy, Kim, "Speaking Her Mind on Women's Rights," *Los Angeles Times*, August 27, 1991.

Murphy, Kim, "Muslim Voices Joining Mideast's Press Chorus," *Los Angeles Times*, August 11, 1992, p. H6.

Murphy, Kim, "Saudi Arabia's First Human Rights Group is Outlawed Within a Month," *Los Angeles Times*, May 21, 1993, p. A5.

Murphy, Kim, "A Fight to Keep Their Voice Alive," *Los Angeles Times*, January 27, 1994, pp. A1, 9, 10.

Murphy, Kim, "Arab Militants Fight Symbols of Secularism," *Los Angeles Times*, November 28, 1994, pp. A3, 8.

Rahman, Fazlur, *Islam*. New York: Holt, Rinehart and Winston, 1966.

Rao, G. Ramachandra (Gora), "Secularism Defined," *The Atheist*, Vijayawada, India, March-April, 1972, p. 37.

Robertson, J.N., *A History of Freethought*. London: Watts and Co., 1936, Vol. I.

Rodinson, Maxime, *Muhammad*. Trans. by Anne Carter. New York: Pantheon Books, 1980.

Sasson, Jean, P., *Princess: A True Story of Life behind the Veil in Saudi Arabia*. New York: William Morrow and Company, Inc. 1992.

Schuon, Frithjof, *Understanding Islam*. Trans. by D.M. Matheson. Baltimore, Mar.: Penguin Books, Inc., 1972.

Shah, Indries, *Tales of the Dervishes*. New York: E.P. Dutton and Co., Inc., 1970.

Shah, Indries, *The Way of the Sufi*. New York: E.P. Dutton and Co., Inc., 1970.

Shah, Indries, *The Sufis*. Garden City, New York: Doubleday & Co., 1971 (Anchor paperback).

Sheler, Jeffery L., "Islam in America," *U.S. News & World Report*, October 8, 1990, pp. 69-71.

Smith, Wilfred Cantwell, *Islam in Modern History*. Princeton: Princeton University Press, 1957.

Ullah, Najib, *Islamic Literature*. New York: Washington Square Press, Inc. 1963.

Warraq, Ibn, *Why I am Not a Muslim.* Buffalo, New York: Prometheus Books, 1995

Wright, Robin, "Islamist's Theory of Relativity," *Los Angeles Times*, January 27, 1995, pp. A1, A10-11.

12

Africa

Just when the people of Africa began to develop philosophical and religious ideas about themselves and their environment is not known. There are no written records so our knowledge of the beliefs of the earliest Africans can only be based on anthropological and archaeological research, folklore and comparative studies, all of which have conjectural components. What is clear is that, long after *Homo erectus* began to move out of Africa (some 1 million years ago), both within and without Africa, *Homo sapiens* was to evolve (about 400,000 years ago). Ultimately, within the continent proper, several great nations were to develop, each with its own identity and life patterns. The greatest of these was Egypt.

Because Egypt impacted on the western world in a unique way, and because we have a long written history reflecting Egyptian history and beliefs, Egypt's religion and freethought are presented separately in chapter 6. However, Egypt must be recognized as a product of Africa, and efforts by some to separate Egypt from Africa proper are no longer acceptable. Further, arguments attempting to prove that Egyptians were Caucasians are invalid. Nor are Egyptians any longer considered to be "Hamites" — a label based on biblical folklore about the flood. According to the biblical flood myth, all humans descended from Noah. The Egyptians were supposed to have been descendants of Noah's son, Ham (as were the Canaanites). This folkloric notion belongs to the time when it was written — nearly 3,000 years ago. It contributes nothing but confusion and misconception to our present day studies. Therefore, although the chapter on Egypt is separate, it is still important to remember that Egyptians were, primarily, Africans.

We know that over the millennia, through cycles of droughts that may have lasted for centuries and which were followed by rainy periods, all life forms in Africa learned to adapt to survive. African *Homo sapiens* mastered the use of fire, the making of weapons and hunting tools including the harpoon and bow and arrow, and the manufacture of pottery and artifacts for household use and for decoration. Sometime, during the long period between 35,000 and 8,000 B.C.E., burial of the dead was initiated — a practice that suggests that Africans developed a humanistic respect for family members similar to that which we have seen elsewhere. Not only were the bodies of the deceased interred to protect them from wild animals but the practice may also reflect some form of belief in an afterlife.

As we have noted, there were migrations out of Africa into Europe and Asia, beginning about 1 million years ago, but reverse migrations also occurred, starting near the close of the Mesolithic era, perhaps between 12,000 and 10,000 B.C.E. Thus, even as Africans continued to move into Europe, Europeans (Caucasoids) came to North Africa to settle along the coastline and mingled with the Negroid population.

Some early Africans continued hunter-gatherer patterns of existence and tended to be migrant. Others, during the Neolithic or New Stone Age period (after 8,000 B.C.E.) settled in villages, and developed agricultural and pastoral skills to augment the products of hunting and fishing. As early as the fifth millennium B.C.E., artistic statements were painted or engraved on rock surfaces, depicting animals, hunting scenes and dancers. It was not until the nineteenth century of our era that writing was widely introduced into Africa. Therefore, unless an African community produced written literature, as they did in Egypt, we are compelled to depend for information about beliefs and customs on archaeological and anthropological studies, on reports by outsiders such as traders or missionaries, and on theories based on studies of present life patterns. Unfortunately, many early reports reflect a prejudicial sense of the social and religious superiority and the distance between what was called "civilized" culture and what was labelled "savage" or "primitive" or "naive" beliefs. African religion constituted what "those people" believed as separated from what "we" believe and, of course, "our" beliefs are superior!

The Bible has contributed to prejudicial attitudes that block appreciation of African, Negroid and Black culture. As noted above, Egyptians or Africans were believed to be descendants of Ham, and Egyptian culture was labelled "Hamitic." Ham was cursed in the biblical story for seeing his drunken father lying naked, so it was assumed that Negroid or Black people were the cursed descendants. Dark skin pigmentation was often interpreted as a sign of the curse and, frequently, it was assumed that dark-skinned people were, somehow, less than human. The notion that dark skin coloration is the result of a divine curse is still present in the literature and in the thinking of some religious groups. Also, the notion that dark-skinned people are members of some kind of sub-culture continues to surface (unfortunately) from time to time among the uninformed who are ignorant of the fact that the idea has been completely discredited. The biblical claim that the descendants of Ham would be slaves provided scriptural sanction for the cruel and inhuman slave trade developed by Christians and Muslims. Finally, because Africans were assumed to be a sub-human species, discoveries of human progress found in Africa were automatically written off as products of African contact with non-African peoples!

Modern anthropologists and researchers have changed their approach. African religion is recognized as a reasonable and legitimate human response to life and existence. Today, western scholars learn tribal languages, live for years among the people and seek to report on African culture with understanding — writing, as it were, from the "inside," rather than judgmentally from the "outside." Moreover, recent research has moved away from the descriptive labels such as "animism" and "animatism" employed by early writers with reference to African religion. Also abandoned is the notion that developing religions move according to some sort of a progression from primitive spirit-infested worlds, to polytheism, and finally to monotheism which, in the western world, is accepted as the highest form of religion. The new descriptive patterns are those which we will use for the discussion of African religions. There will be no pejoratives and older anthropological clichés are avoided.

Geography and Life in West Africa

The Sahara is a great desert that stretches across northern Africa from the Atlantic Ocean to the Red Sea. At one time, before 5000 B.C.E., this area had flowing rivers, forests and meadow land. Ancient inhabitants recorded their impressions of their life and the environment in cave paintings. About 4000 B.C.E., the climate underwent change. Lack of rainfall and a rise in temperatures transformed the vast region into a desert, so the people moved southward and westward.

Today, only one river, the Nile, cuts across this desolate area. Drawing from headwaters in the Mountains of the Moon in Central Africa, the Nile flows northward to empty into the Mediterranean Sea. Its mighty stream is augmented by the Blue Nile that emerges out of Lake Tana in Ethiopia and by the Atbara River which also comes out of Ethiopia. These two streams join the Nile immediately below Khartoum above the fifth cataract. On the western side of the continent, near the Atlantic coast, the Niger River rises in the mountains of Sierra Leone and the Ivory Coast, flows northward, away from the Atlantic ocean, into the Sahara to Timbuktu, before turning southward to meet the Atlantic at the Gulf of Guinea in Nigeria.

It should not be assumed that African deserts are sand-locked spaces, empty of life. Desert geography is varied and in some places scrub growth occurs and oases are fed by underground springs. Despite the forbidding nature of the vast Sahara wasteland, over the centuries traders, adventurers and invaders have challenged the desert's austere environment. Camel caravans linked the Mediterranean coast of North Africa with West Africa, and the Atlantic coast with the kingdoms of the Nile.

Today, the deserts are part of the territorial claims of various African states or nations. For example, parts of the Sahara are possessed by Mauritania, Algeria, Mali, Liberia, Niger, Chad, Egypt and Sudan. Each nation has outposts of one kind or another located in what might seem to be the most forbidding locales. Perhaps the pattern can be understood when one considers the ways in which the desert areas of Southern California, Arizona and Nevada are populated.

In West Africa, long before the coming of the Europeans, African people mined gold and silver, smelted and cast iron and sculpted in bronze, wood, clay, stone and ivory. They developed their own codes of law. Their medical practitioners' skill in healing and the use of natural medications is still being investigated (Barrett, p. 184). In other words, the pejorative terms traditionally used to describe Africans, which implied that they were mentally, spiritually and culturally backward or deficient, simply do not hold water.

It is believed that the use of iron was introduced to West Africa from the north by traders. With the coming of the iron age came the development of the early empires of the western Sudan. By 450 B.C.E. a people, who had settled near the present-day city of Nok in Nigeria since about 900 B.C.E., learned to smelt iron. For reasons presently unknown, these people had moved away by 300 B.C.E. Some migrated to a place known as Jenne-jeno on the delta of the river Niger near the present city of Jenne in the Republic of Mali. Here they developed a thriving city culture. Each year, as the river overflowed the delta, it deposited rich sediment that supported rice farming. Fishing and cattle raising augmented local diet. The abundance of food and a vigorous trading industry helped to swell the population to some 10,000 people. Archaeologists Susan and Roderick McIntosh have unearthed iron tools, gold and copper jewelry, and clay animals that testify to the skill of local artists and artisans. For reasons still unknown, this site was abandoned about 1400 C.E. Nearby, the cultures of Ife and Benin came into being. These people, too, left evidence of high artistic skill in sculpting in clay and bronze.

Over the centuries, iron-using people moved southward, employing superior weapons to overcome those who were still in the stone age. Thus, between the third and sixteenth centuries C.E., iron-age culture spread, ultimately reaching the southern tip of Africa. As territories were conquered, new social organizations and more complex patterns of government evolved.

Between 500 and 1400 C.E., powerful independent African states and empires were created:

> Among them were Ghana, Mali, Songhai, Kanem-Bornu and the Housa states, which were clustered along the southern frontier of the Sahara. Still further south, between these states and the forest region, arose the Mole-Dagbane states and the Mossi states. Finally, in the forest and coastal zones of Guinea emerged the states of Takrur and Wolof in the region of the Senegal and Gambia rivers, or Senegambia; the Akan, Fante and Ga states in the area of modern Ghana; and the states of Ife, Oyo and Benin in Nigeria. (Boahen, p. 177)

So far as we can tell, the business of the empire was conducted according to a word-of-mouth plus a memory-of-agreements system. There were no written records. Much of what is known of these kingdoms rests in oral tradition, with the first written reports coming after the incursion of Islam during the 8th century. Communication within and between kingdoms was important for trade and was made possible by well-kept roads. Law and order prevailed within the separate states, and early reports indicate that the people were prosperous, comfortable and well-fed. Prosperity and well-being gave rise to increased populations. Caravan trade made some who lived in cities at the edge of the desert immensely wealthy and simultaneously avaricious. The coming of Islam with its own doctrines of law, justice, taxation, its different architectural designs and its own religion, language, and scholarship produced an educated bureaucracy, which disrupted old patterns. New metropolises came into being and the boundaries of kingdoms underwent change. But beneath the surface of the new, much of the old prevailed, just as it still does today.

One of the great ancient kingdoms, called Ghana (not to be confused with the modern state), was located in what is today Mali (the name means "Where the king lives"). By the ninth century C.E., Ghana had developed into an important trading center. It happened this way: around 300 C.E. nomadic Berbers, whose origins lay in the Middle East, settled in ancient Ghana and developed a vast trading empire.

They were displaced in 780 by the Soninke people who began the conquest of surrounding communities, employing the iron weapons which were superior to those of the other peoples. By 1000 C.E., they had subjugated a number of smaller states and were masters of 100,000 square miles of territory and thousands of subject people. They exported gold dust to North Africa and Europe and, because trade routes passed through their territory, they supplemented their income by taxation revenues derived from itinerant merchants. Koumbi, the capital city, became the most powerful market center in West Africa.

When Muslim traders moved into Ghana, in order to keep the Muslim faith separate from local religion, Koumbi was divided into two sections linked by a six-mile-long boulevard. Muslim structures, including twelve mosques, were of stone. Soninke dwellings were constructed of wood and clay with straw roofing, except for the royal palace which was of wood and stone.

In 1324, Mansa ("emperor") Kankan Musa, who had ascended the throne in 1307 and who was a devout Muslim, made a pilgrimage to Mecca. His retinue included:

> 12,000 slaves, all dressed in brocade and Persian silk. Mansa Musa himself rode on horseback. . . . Directly preceding him were 500 slaves, each carrying a staff of gold weighing about 6 pounds. Then came Mansa Musa's baggage — a train of 80 camels, each carrying 300 pounds weight of gold dust. (Hutchinson, p. 23)

On his return to Mali, the emperor invited Arab scholars and traders to visit. From these visitors, Europe first learned of the existence of centers of learning and culture in cities like Niana and Timbuktu. The rulers who succeeded Mansa Musa lacked his leadership skills and a weakened kingdom turned to Portugal for help. Ultimately the kingdom was enslaved to Portugal and other European countries.

Perhaps it is unnecessary to state the obvious, but is important to remember that all Africans do not look alike. Some are dark-skinned, some are light skinned, some are very tall and lean, some are short. And, it should not be surprising to discover that different life styles with unique cultural patterns developed within the various zones of this massive continent. People adapted their way of life to their environments, drawing from the soil, the water and the animal life, food to sustain existence and materials for housing and clothing, tools and weapons. For example, central Africa lies along the equator and is largely hot and rainy all year round. In this humid environment, the Twa people who were formerly called "pygmies" live.

The Twa

Deep in the rain forests of the Congo river in Central Africa, the Twa, the "little people," whom westerners called "pygmies," have lived for millennia. Until the middle of the nineteenth century, they were almost unknown to the western world and, since that time, contact with the "outside" world has affected the life patterns of some groups.

The Twa represent a separate human ethnic strain with its own long history. Males average about four feet, four inches, in height, females are somewhat shorter. They have long torsos and arms, but short legs, and their skin coloration has been described as "earth brown" (Hays, p. 285). They have adapted to life in a part of Africa that was, until more recent times, seldom entered. However, their presence was not unknown. A VIth Dynasty inscription in the tomb of Harkhuf, an official of the court of Pharaoh Neferkare Pepi II (c. 2300 B.C.E.), records a trip deep into Nubia/Punt. Harkhuf received a message from his young master urging him to return immediately to the royal court and to:

> bring with you this pygmy whom you have brought from the land of the horizon-dwellers live, hale, and healthy, for the dances of the god, to gladden the heart, to delight the heart of King Neferkare who lives forever! When he goes down with you into the ship, get worthy men to be around him on the deck, lest he fall into the water! When he lies down at night, get worthy men to lie around him in his tent. Inspect ten times at night! My majesty desires to see this pygmy more than the gifts of the mine-land [Sinai] and of Punt! (Lichtheim, p. 27)

Just how this particular Twa came to be in the region of Nubia/-Punt cannot be known, but it is clear that he was considered to be an oddity and something of a treasure for the amusement of the pharaoh and his court. Perhaps he had been taken captive by the Nubians who treated him as an article for barter.

To the best of present knowledge, despite intrusions by other African groups and by Westerners in search of large game and ivory, the Twa represent one of the last few groups of humans who have pursued a simple, semi-nomadic way of life for millennia, reaching back into the Paleolithic period. Game and wild vegetable products have always been readily available, therefore there has been no need or drive to engage in agriculture or to establish settled villages and towns. Their tools and weapons were primarily products of the stone age until, some 2,000 years ago, their territory was, for the first time, encroached upon by African groups from the north. The encroachment introduced iron but the Twa did not become iron-workers. Indeed, they did not bother to create pottery, which they do not really need, although pots could be acquired through trade. Their climate does not call for excessive clothing (daytime temperatures range from a steamy 80 to 90 degrees Fahrenheit), and thus loin coverings are all that are usually worn. No doubt their way of life will be intruded upon more and more as Africans and other outsiders seek to exploit the Congo's wealth.

Twa religion is relatively uncluttered. The creator god, called "Mungu" (although he has several different names), is the all-powerful lord of the wood, animals, life and death. Other supernatural creatures are recognized, but there is no formalized theology. Rituals seek to invoke power, control storms and appease the powers. Tribal shamans employ primitive magic to discover thieves, murderers and so forth. Simple puberty rites mark transitions from childhood to adulthood. Young women are fully developed by age nine and thus, at what western society would label an exceedingly young age, become wives and mothers.

The San

The Kalahari desert lies south of the Zambesi river and extends from the Indian Ocean to the Atlantic. It is penetrated on the north by the Zambesi River whose varied sources flow southward out of Angola into the desert, then to the east to empty into the Mozambique Channel which is part of the Indian Ocean. The western edge of the desert lies unbroken along the Atlantic. Between March and December, the hot sun bakes the land. In December, when the rains come, the region blossoms briefly, water holes are filled, grasses and scrub brush are lush, animals are plentiful. By August, all has changed — the water holes are dried up, the plants are dry, the land is sere.

In this rugged, demanding, environment the San, whom westerners called "Bushmen," survived for millennia as hunters and gatherers. They hunted the antelope, the eland, the hartebeest as well as other animals. They dug for roots and gathered the wild melons that provide liquid nourishment during the drought periods. Their way of life can be traced back to the Paleolithic period and facets of their most recent life-style reflect patterns depicted on rock paintings that are between 8,000 and 10,000 years old. Indeed, the San have been called "one of the oldest people still living in the world." (Hays, p. 269)

Until recent times, San society was composed of roving bands, each of which operated in a specific territory. The coming of European (particularly the Dutch) settlers with their apartheid policies, not only meant the loss of hunting grounds for the San, but also resulted in their being treated as less-than-human creatures. To avert starvation, the San killed the settlers' cattle. This poaching led to a war that not only enslaved many San, but reduced their numbers to fewer than 50,000.

Like the Twa, the San are small in stature, with males seldom being taller than five feet, and the women shorter. Their skin color has been described as "yellowish brown" and their hair tends to form tight, kinky ringlets. Traditionally, the men wore only a skin pouch to cover their genitals, while the women wore an apron that covered them both in front and behind. In cold weather they donned skin cloaks.

Their religious patterns have been poorly reported, but it is clear that they lack cult centers and dogmatic faith patterns. The moon is said to be important in some rites; in others, the star Canopus, also known as the "Bushman's Rice," is prayed to for food. On occasion a burning stick is pointed starward in a plea for warmth during the cold season (Hays, p. 274).

The mantis has been personalized as a supernatural being called the Kaggen. According to San lore, this insect's head resembles that of the hartebeest, hence it is recognized as a protector of animals. Other myths have grown up around the baboon, the elephant, and some birds. The shamans or doctor-magicians, who engage in sorcery, are believed to have special powers affiliated with the Kaggen. Certain San dances are designed to have magical potential and some are concerned with animal procreation and with hunting. Other dances are engaged in for the pure joy of dancing or are associated with courting rites.

San burials reflect patterns that, according to anthropologists, echo Paleolithic customs. For example, sometimes the dead are buried in a sitting position. Among the Khoi (formerly called "Hottentots"), the close neighbors who live to the south of the San at the tip of South Africa, the dead are buried in a flexed position and weighted down with two large stones — a pattern found in Paleolithic burials. The San do not think of death as natural. They believe it is caused by evil spirits or by magic. At burials, mourners remain upwind of the grave lest the evil spirit be blown toward them and do harm. Some San put red ochre on the head of the corpse, reminding anthropologists of the red coloring used in Paleolithic burials.

Contact with European modernism has eroded San customs and life patterns. Nevertheless, the life style of these people continues to include echoes of the most ancient past.

The Kingdoms of Northeast Africa.

Although, in the discussion of Africa, most attention is given to the kingdom of Egypt, largely because of its relationship to the Mediterranean world, it is important to note that, as tribal groups grew in size and perhaps combined with other groups, tribal leaders often assumed the roles of kings or emperors. How far back this pattern goes is hard to estimate. There is clear evidence of trade, warfare and rivalry. To appreciate this reality we will look at other powerful African kingdoms that existed in the proximity of Egypt.

Punt

Egyptian records tell of trade and/or warfare with the kingdoms that lay to the south. Just when contact with these southern states began is hard to determine. No doubt there was a continual migration from central Africa by those who followed the Nile river on its northward journey. Egyptian fleets reached "the land of Punt" during the fifth dynasty in the time of the Pharaoh Sahura (c. 2458-2541 B.C.E.). In the XVIIIth dynasty, during the ninth year of the reign of Queen Hatshepsut (1496 B.C.E.), a fleet of five Egyptian ships journeyed to Punt to trade for myrrh, ebony, ivory, gold, cosmetics, animals and slaves — an expedition that was recorded in the queen's beautiful temple at Deir el-Bahari. Punt has been identified as modern Somalia which borders the Gulf of Aden and the Indian Ocean. How this lush agricultural land was governed, or the forms of the belief system, cannot be known. Egyptians titled the goddess Hathor "The Lady of Punt," just as she was titled "Lady of Byblos" in the shrine erected to her in Byblos, Lebanon, and "The Lady of Turquoise" in the shrine dedicated to her in the Sinai from which the turquoise came (Montet, pp. 151-152). What is clear is that an organized empire was functioning in Punt from earliest times — an African empire that engaged in trade with other cultural centers. It is not impossible that their divinities were like those recognized in Egypt.

Nubia

Nubia (or Cush) was located south of the Aswan (first) cataract of the Nile. This territory embraces parts of modern Ethiopia. An inscription discovered in 1914:

> makes it reasonably certain that the Ethiopians designated their country, or at least a goodly part of it as the land of Qevs (Kesh). The discovery and transliteration of these inscriptions marked a very important advance in the study of Nilotic and Oriental history, for according to the authorities named [Dr. A.H. Sayce and Mr. G.L. Griffith of Oxford University], the Ethiopian word Kesh may be identified with the Egyptian word Kush and the Hebrew word Cush . . . (Harris, pp. 8-9)

Because the Nubians did not develop a written form of their language until the 7th century B.C.E., their history is known only from archaeological research and from references in Egyptian and other literature. Excavations indicate that the area was sparsely occupied from the paleolithic to the neolithic period, but by the time of the first dynasty in Egypt (3rd millennium) the population appears to have grown considerably.

On the basis of tomb exploration, it has been surmised that the culture bore similarities to Egypt. This is not surprising because Egyptian penetration into Nubian territory began early. During the third millennium, just after the union of Upper and Lower Egypt, First Dynasty rulers, Hor Aha and Zer, pushed Egyptian boundaries far into Nubia. Rock-cut inscriptions record that Egyptian armies reached the second cataract during the reign of Hor Aha. It is clear that Nubia suffered greatly at the hands of Egypt. Sneferu, the last king of the third Egyptian dynasty (c. 2600 B.C.E.), took 7,000 prisoners and 200,000 head of cattle. Lower Nubia was exploited for its copper, its gold and the fine diorite stone used for statuary. For years, going back at least until the VIth dynasty, this region was a source of dark-skinned warriors and laborers for Egypt and it is clear that Egyptian life and thought impacted directly upon the Nubians. Efforts to maintain control of Nubia and its rich gold mines during the reigns of Pharaohs Amenemhat I (1991-1962 B.C.E.) and Sesostris I (1971-1928 B.C.E.), made it necessary to maintain Egyptian control up to the second cataract. Excavations of the huge royal Nubian burial mounds from this period have demonstrated that servants and members of the ruler's harem were buried alive (Smith, p. 75). Perhaps the sacrificial deaths were designed to provide the dead leader with accustomed services in whatever afterlife may have been imagined. The sacrificial pattern continued up to and into the Byzantine period (6th century C.E.), indicating that the Nubians maintained primitive customs long after similar patterns had been abandoned in Egypt (Emery, p. 86).

During the coronation of Thutmosis I (1525-1508 B.C.E.), reference was made to the "Viceroy of Nubia," indicating that Egyptian control of Nubia had assumed a distinct form with an appointed governorship. Nevertheless, Thutmosis found it necessary to mount an expedition during his second year of rule — an expedition that pressed as far south as the fourth cataract of the Nile.

Contact with and strict control of Nubia was important for Egyptian trade and commerce, and for a time the Nubians appear to have been little more than a separate Egyptian colony. However, following the decline of Egyptian power during the Middle Kingdom, the Nubians broke away and established their own independent kingship. Depictions of royal receptions picture the dark-skinned royalty of Cush or Nubia magnificently outfitted and attired.

During the eighth century B.C.E., Nubian kings, Kashta and Piye (Piankhi), who are now called Ethiopians, ruled Egypt from Napata, just above the third cataract. They established the XXVth Egyptian (Cushite/Nubian/Ethiopian) dynasty (751-656 B.C.E.). As worshippers of the Egyptian god Amun, they recognized Amun as the supreme deity of the empire.

Their rule was not appreciated because they were Nubians and their reigns were marked by extreme cruelty. Excavations have demonstrated that their burials in unique pyramid tombs followed Osirian rituals and the royal records employed Egyptian hieroglyphics. Their dynasty collapsed when the Assyrians invaded Egypt in the seventh century B.C.E.

Later, with the coming of the Christians, Nubians were controlled by Christian princes. On the island of Philae at Aswan, Christian icons and shrines replaced those of the Nubian god, Mandilis, and those of the Egyptian goddess, Isis. During the Middle Ages (12th century C.E.), Muslims, led by Saladin, took control of the southern Nubian kingdom. The Coptic Christian monastery of St. Simeon at Aswan was abandoned and Nubians worshipped in the mosques of Islam. Presently, the nation is largely Muslim with a much smaller Christian population.

Ethiopia

From the discussion of Nubia, it is clear that the area that we know as Ethiopia appears to have emerged out of ancient Nubia or Cush. The XXVth dynasty in Egypt (751-656 B.C.E.), which can be labelled either the "Ethiopian Dynasty" or the "Nubian Dynasty," collapsed when the Assyrians invaded Egypt. In 671 B.C.E., Esarhaddon of Assyria sacked Memphis. Although Esarhaddon could boast that he had captured the queen, the harem, the family, and the heir of the Ethiopian Pharaoh Taharqa (690-664), and that he tore the root of Cush out of Egypt so that no one escaped submission to him, the report was only partially accurate. In truth, Pharaoh Taharqa had escaped and within a year retook Memphis and forced the Assyrians out of the Egyptian delta. Taharqa ruled Egypt unmolested for three years before the Assyrian army returned. Once again, Memphis was taken and Taharqa retreated to Thebes. Egypt's delta region was under Assyrian control.

Taharqa died in 664 and his nephew Tanutamon (664-653) assumed the throne in Thebes. He marched on Memphis and put down the resistance of those Egyptian rulers in the delta who were loyal to Assyria. King Ashurbanipal of Assyria, who had succeeded Esarhaddon, reacted and in 663 an Assyrian army entered Egypt. Tanutamon fled, and the delta princes paid homage to Ashurbanipal. Thebes was taken and sacked. Wah-ib-ra, who became the most powerful among the delta princes, controlled Egypt as Pharaoh Psamtek I (663-609). Thus, for a time, there was an overlap between the XXVth Ethiopian Dynasty (751-656) and the XXVI dynasty (663-525). Psamtek I expelled the Assyrians between 658 and 651 B.C.E.

The loss of control over Egypt did not mark the end of the Ethiopian monarchy. The capital was moved from Napata to Meroe but kings continued to be buried at Napata. When Persian power exploded during the fifth and fourth centuries, Persian influence impacted on Egypt. Ethiopia was less directly affected, despite the fact that Cambyses' (528-522) Persian troops did penetrate the country. Monotheistic Persians mocked the multi-god religions of both Ethiopia and Egypt.

Now the social, intellectual, cultural and spiritual power of Egypt, that had long fed Ethiopia, began to wane even as ancient religious patterns continued to thrive. During the fifth century, the Greek historian Herodatus wrote about what he had learned of the existence at Meroe of a temple to the god Amun and of a sun temple with a Table of the Sun:

> This Table of the Sun is said to be a meadow, situated in the outskirts of the city, where a plentiful supply of boiled meat of all kinds is kept; it is the duty of the magistrates to put the meat there at night, and during the day anybody who wishes may come and eat it. Local legend has it that the meat appears spontaneously and is the gift of the earth. (III, 17, 18)

The sun temple seems to have been a stone structure marked with the sun disc set on a brick platform (could this have been the Table?).

From the time of Alexander the Great to the Roman occupation of Egypt, the Ethiopians maintained independence. Efforts to resist the Romans at Philae resulted in a Roman pillage of Ethiopian territory up to the fourth cataract despite an appeal from the Ethiopian queen Candace (it should be noted that in Nubia, all queens were called "Candace" and the proper identity of this particular queen is Amanesh-akhete). Meanwhile, divisions were developing and a new Ethiopian kingdom, to be separated from the Nubian, was coming into being with its center at Axum.

What has become increasingly clear is that Ethiopia/Cush not only looked to Egypt for trade and commerce, but sent ships into the Red Sea, the Indian Ocean and perhaps even made contact with China during the Han dynasty (first century of the Common Era). These out-of-Africa contacts could only have served to enrich the culture of Ethiopia and ultimately of Egypt.

The Ethiopia best known to the western world emerged after the conversion of the Aksumite King Ezana to Christianity during the fourth century C.E. (probably around 330 C.E.). Today, it is primarily a Christian nation, although other religions, including Judaism and Islam, are also represented. In more recent times, particularly during the reign of Haile Selassie, efforts were made to reinforce the legendary link between Ethiopian kingship and ancient Israel. The legend, repeated over and over again in both literature and art, identified the Queen of Sheba who visited King Solomon (I Kings 10) as an Ethiopian queen named Makeda. She became pregnant by Solomon and the son she bore (named Menelik) was sent back to Jerusalem to be educated by his father. According to the legend, Solomon presented his offspring with the Ark of the Covenant and the tablets of the ten commandments which are supposed to be housed in the Ethiopian Christian Church of Mary of Zion at Axum. Thus Solomon is supposed to have been a progenitor of the Ethiopian monarchy (cf. Isaac, pp. 80-83).

Today, the Ethiopian monarchy has disappeared. The young people who were part of its overthrow never believed the monarchical legend and, in any case, disregarded it. The rebels, some of whom I met, were not Christians; they were secularists. Their experiences under a Christian monarchy had been characterized by cruel treatment, the suppression of freethought, and the need to get a modern education elsewhere — often in places like the American University in Beirut. The social confusion that now exists in Ethiopia results from opposing forces seeking control and expressing little interest in human values.

Libya

The settlement of parts of Libya go back to the paleolithic period when north Africa was still a fertile, rain-washed land. With the decrease in rainfall, human habitation was centered on the numerous oases. Libyan oases were important for caravan travel and thus Libyan-Egyptian relationships and interchange of persons and products resulted. Small kingdoms or enclaves of power centered around oases were developed under Libyan chiefs.

The brown-skinned Libyans were closely related to the Nile-dwelling Egyptians and shared some of the same god concepts. For example, according to myth, the god Horus was rescued from potential enemies and suckled and raised by the cow-goddess Sekhet-Hor or Hathor. The goddess, guardian of cattle, was recognized both in Egypt and Libya. Cattle-raising was an important industry in Libya and Egyptian records boast of the number of heads of cattle taken as booty from Libya. During one period (11th century B.C.E.) the high priests of the god Amun in Thebes were descendants of Libyan chieftains and these priestly overseers ruled their offices like feudal lords.

The Libyan kingdom developed along the north coast of Africa to the west of Egypt and during much of Egyptian history constituted a threat. In the early dynastic period of Egypt (c. 2980), portions of the Egyptian delta that had been held by Libyans came under Egyptian control. From that time onward, there was both tension and intermingling between the two kingdoms. In the 16th century B.C.E., Libyan tribes overran much of the delta region and Amenhotep I was compelled to repel them and establish a western fortress to protect the area. Thutmose III (15th century B.C.E.) conquered Libya. Libyan rulers sat on the throne of Egypt during the XXII and XXIII dynasties (c. 945-718 B.C.E.)

Other African Empires

Among the Swazi of north-eastern South Africa, memories of past rulers may go back thirty generations (Parrinder, p. 119). Whatever historical data such memories may contain can be so intermingled with legend and folktale that real events can scarcely be documented.

It is obvious that under tribal leadership huge building projects were undertaken. For example, in Zimbabwe, massive conical stone towers, constructed between the ninth and fifteenth centuries C.E., guard entry ways into the ancient city in which there are more stone structures. There was a time when western prejudice overrode reality and it was assumed that Africans could not have engineered the construction of these monuments. That notion has been abandoned as hundreds of other stone ruins have been found throughout the area, as well as similar structures in Nigeria on the opposite side of the continent. Some ruins have been identified as shrines or temples, but just what they represented or what ceremonies may have taken place within the sacred enclosures cannot be known.

Another African state, Songhai, was an empire that grew out of what had been part of Mali, Hausa, and Kanem Bornu. Such independent entities were self-governing but were always influenced by the teachings of Islam.

What is important for our purposes is to recognize that the people of Africa had developed their own high cultures before the coming of the Europeans. The wide variety of life patterns included farmers, herdsmen, miners and smelters of ores and fashioners of utensils, tools, weapons and jewelry from these various metals. Those who lived along the coastlines built ships and engaged in trade. In other words, the peoples of Africa were not what many prejudiced writers described them to be. They were, like other human beings, people with the same skills, talents, reasoning abilities and concern for meaningful life and living.

African Religion

There are more than three thousand tribes in Africa. Each has its own distinct religion, so of course there is no single "African religion," there are only "African religions." Many belief systems exhibit parallels, overlaps and similarities, but there are also differences. Our focus will be, primarily, on fundamental similarities, on that which is common and shared, rather than seeking to embark on the difficult and tremendously involved task of differentiating between the social groups and their individual faith systems. African traditional religions tend to be communal rather than personal. A person exists as a member of a group and the religion of that group permeates all aspects of life. As John S. Mbiti has noted:

> Wherever the African is, there is his religion: he carries it to the fields where he is sowing seeds or harvesting a new crop; he takes it with him to the beer party or to attend a funeral ceremony; and if he is educated, he takes religion with him to the examination room at school or in the university; if he is a politician he takes it to the house of parliament . . . it . . . accompanies the individual from before his birth to long after his physical death. (p. 2)

There is no way a person can become detached from the group religion and remain a member of the group. This means that African religion exists, in a sense, in ways that are apart from our western technological way of life. Religion is not associated with a structure (synagogue, church or mosque) nor with attendance at once-a-week gatherings. The whole of the life of the African is permeated with religion.

Nor are there dogmas or formulated creeds. There are no religious founders, nor missionaries seeking to convert and compel others to accept some creedal statement. There are no reformers seeking to upset or challenge long-accepted beliefs and customs. There may be revered memories of heros and leaders who can be seen as role models or even elevated to some sort of semi-divine status, but there are no single saviors or redeemers. In an address before the Economic Symposium held in Blantyre in 1962, the late Dunduzu K. Chisiza, former parliamentary secretary in Malawi's ministry of finance, said:

> Unlike Easterners who are given to meditation or Westerners who have an inquisitive turn of mind we of Africa, belonging neither to the East or to the West, are fundamentally observers, relying more on intuition than on the process of reasoning. Our field is not that of spiritualism which is the domain of the East nor that of science and technology which is the hobbyhorse of the West, but that of human relations. . . With us, life has always meant the pursuit of happiness rather than the pursuit of Beauty or Truth. We pursue happiness by suppressing isolationism, individualism, negative emotions, and tension

> on one hand; and by laying emphasis on a communal way of life, by encouraging positive emotions and habitual relaxation, and by restraining our desires on the other . . . Our attitude to religion has more often than not been determined by our habitual desire for change. We adhere to a religious faith only so long as it is the only faith we know. If some other faith comes our way we do not isolate ourselves against its influence . . . That we behave in this way is no indication that we are fickle; rather it is an indication of the fact that in each one of the religious faiths which we encounter there is an element of divine truth whose fascination we fail to resist. And this is as it should be for religion is one. (quoted in Wallerstein, p. 519)

Chisiza then continued to expand on the humanistic essence of African religions, which emphasize family relations, communal relations, care for one another, humor, tolerance, generosity, forgiveness, kindness, love of music, rhythm and dance and "a strong dislike for imposing our beliefs on other people." (p. 521)

A child is born into and soon assimilates communal religious beliefs and practices. Should life conditions alter, he or she simply adapts the religion or way of life to those changes. African tribal religion tends to be oral not written, lived not analyzed. It does not separate the physical and spiritual, therefore the notion of an afterlife embraces physical concepts. There are no concerns about heaven or hell or about some closer walk with God, no messianic or apocalyptic dreams. The religion is practical, utilitarian, human-centered.

Because African religion is anthropocentric or human-centered, all dimensions of religion are seen in the context of their relationships to the human community. The world view is dynamic. Religion embraces the total place-world or topocosm of the tribal or social group and the individual. Everything is interrelated and everything is interpreted anthropocentrically. Basically, there is an awareness of an underlying energy or life force that permeates all that exists. The source and controller of this power is God, but God is not that energy or power. God is an important part of anthropocentric religion because God generates and sustains all that is, including humans. God is both omnipresent and omnipotent. Natural forces such as wind and rain are in his control. God is transcendent, above all that exists and dwelling in the sky. But he is also imminent, near and reachable through ritual acts such as offerings, incantations and prayers. The concept is not pantheistic, for God retains his otherness and is not present in the objects of the topocosm. He is thought of in spirit-form, accompanied by other divinities or spirit-forms. Good fortune, crop and animal fertility can be attributed to him, but misfortunes are also the work of God, coming as punishments or as a result of divine anger. In other words, Africans tend to conceive of God's personality and moral values in terms of themselves. It was this dimension of African religion that confronted Pope John Paul II when he visited Contonou, Benin in February, 1993.

The Associated Press report noted that Pope John Paul met with worshippers and priests of *verdun*, "as the ancestral gods are known in the Fon language." The believers in voodoo accept the idea of one god, but also accept lesser deities and practice rituals that involve the use of snakes and fetishes. The Pope sought to convert these people to Christianity by pointing out that, just as they drew upon ancestors for their faith system, so Christians revere "ancestors in the faith, from Apostles to missionaries." Because the ancestors of the missionaries had their own faiths before becoming Christian and lost nothing by converting, so, according to the Pope, the followers of voodoo would not betray their traditional faith by converting to Christianity. (Assoc. Press) If such conversions should take place, one can speculate that what will happen is what has happened in numerous other cultures: the old religion will continue under a veneer of Christianity, resulting in a shallow, pasted-on, label of "Christian."

The basic humanistic nature of African religion has been commented on by Kenneth Kaunda who was President of Zambia:

> To a certain extent, we in Africa have always had a gift for enjoying Man for himself. It is at the heart of our traditional culture, but now we see the possibility of extending the scale of our discovery by example to the whole world. Let the West have its Technology and Asia its Mysticism! Africa's gift to world culture must be in the realm of human relationships! The Colonialists may talk condescendingly about the things they have taught us, yet I honestly believe that we have been all the time nearer to the heart of things that really matter than our Western teachers. After all, don't the scientists tell us that Africa was the cradle of Man? The way things are going, Africa may be the last place where Man can still be man. . . . I believe that the Universe is basically good and that throughout it great forces are at work striving to bring about a greater unity of all living things. It is through cooperation with these forces that Man will achieve all of which he is capable. (quoted by Booth, p. 7)

In other words, Kaunda would reverse the papal invitation and suggest that the Christian world would not lose anything by accepting the humanistic dimensions of African religion!

African religion abounds with spirits. The Yorubas recognize 1,700 spirits (Mbiti, p. 75); other groups have smaller numbers. The spirits may be in charge of death, or disease, or war or healing or weather and so forth. Natural features like lakes or mountains or rivers may be said to be associated with spirits. Consequently, cultic groups have grown up around certain of these powers. Some spirits are identified as extra-human beings that were created; others are the spirits of those who died a long time ago or are, perhaps, exalted human heros. These spirits are important because they may have access to the basic underlying energy of the topocosm. They also provide an explanation about human destiny for, as we shall see, every human being at death becomes a spirit, maintaining identity and personality. Spirits may manifest themselves in dreams and to shamans. Their manifestation may take any form including human, animal and plant. They are unpredictable and may act maliciously.

Humans are important because they are at the center of existence, at the core of being. Some few gifted individuals appear to have the ability to manipulate or tap into the primal energy. These are the shamans, the rainmakers and those who can use power for good or evil. Such individuals assume tremendous power in a community. They are sought out for advice, for interpretation of dreams, for healing, for alleviation of what are presumed to be the effects of evil spirits. Some engage in medical cures for a variety of illnesses, using roots and herbs that have been part of the secret healing practice for centuries. Today, modern communication techniques have greatly expanded the outreach and the wealth of these *sangomas* or witch-doctors. They use the telephone in much the same way that so-called seers or psychics use the call-in pay-by-the-minute 900 number in America (Kraft).

But there is, in African religion, a pervasive sense of ecological wholeness. Plants, animals, indeed all life forms are important because they provide the basic needs for existence and, together with non-living objects and phenomena, constitute the topocosm or the place-world for humans. It is possible to establish a mystic relationship with the natural world. African religion embraces a multifaceted pattern and requires that all parts be recognized, harmonized and kept in balance.

This human-centered religion finds an eternal rhythm in nature that relates directly to the individual. This rhythmic pattern includes birth, puberty, initiation, marriage, procreation, aging and old age, death, entry into the community of the departed and ultimately into the company of the spirits. Within this rhythm, key transitional moments for the individual may be marked by ceremonials. For example, to become a full human being one must have gone through a naming ceremony, puberty and initiation rites, marriage and sometimes parenting. Marriage and family have important implications for the dead. When a person dies, individual existence goes on in the community of the dead. In other words, the individual still exists as part of the human family. That aliveness or existence is manifested in the memories and in the customs of those who participate in symbolic familial communal rites by pouring out beer or milk and setting forth food for the dead. Familial rituals guarantee a kind of personal immortality so that the dead may be remembered up to four or five generations. Obviously, large families assume importance, for the more relatives the dead person leaves behind, the better are the chances of being long remembered. To die and not be remembered is as if one had never existed. It has been pointed out that such practices do not constitute ancestor worship, but are statements of familial community. When the time comes when the individual is no longer remembered, he or she enters into the community of the spirits where the spirit acquires a kind of collective immortality (Mbiti, p. 26).

Of course, not all family spirits are believed to entertain benevolent attitudes toward the living, nor do the living always entertain benevolent memories of the dead. As one young Ghanaian told me, "In our village we bury the dead with their feet pointing away from the village so that when the spirit rises it goes away from us."

On the community level, the natural rhythm is manifested in the seasonal cycle and the activities associated with hunting or sowing and reaping. Nature itself can interrupt the harmony by eclipses, drought, insect invasions and so forth. Responses to these intrusive events may involve communal religious response.

It is important to remember that traditional tribal or societal religions have been affected by the incursions of Middle Eastern and Western religious thought, including Islam and Christianity. Muhammad's first African convert was an Ethiopian slave, Bilal (Hadzrat Bilal ibn Rahab), who became the prophet's muezzin. When Islam swept across North Africa, black populations were both converted and enslaved. North African Moors participated in the invasion and conquest of Spain. From that time on, Islam moved deeper and deeper into Africa, producing a kind of national unity through a common language and faith.

But even where "outside" religions like Christianity and Islam have been adopted, a central core of the ancient beliefs remains active and influential. Changes in circumstances, such as migration resulting from famine, have resulted in assimilation of concepts, but even so, the core of the tribal religions remain constant.

The Loss of Freedom

What was lost in Africa by the incursion of Western power, business and government was freedom. Loss of freedom resulted, in part, from the slave trade which began as early as Roman contacts with Africa. North African captives were considered by Romans to be lesser human beings. The slave trade continued through the early Christian period and was greatly expanded by the incursion of Arabs and Islam. The greatest enslavement occurred when, having "discovered" America, the Spanish and Portuguese needed workers to till the fields and work in the mines in the Americas. The decimation of the native American Indian population by disease and warfare increased the need for men and women who could be forced to work for mere survival benefits.

That need was supplied by the capture and enslavement of people from Africa — a practice that was legalized by the Spanish crown (Boahen, p. 315). Portuguese, Spanish, Dutch, English and French all joined the inhuman business. Indeed, Africans themselves participated. Criminals, persons captured from neighboring tribes, prisoners of war and domestic slaves were offered for trade by their African captors. Up until 1929, when the last officially recorded slave caravan occurred, an estimated 100,000,000 men, women and children had been taken out of Africa by Christian and Muslim slave traders during the almost 500 continuous years of wars, manhunts and forced marches (Wellard, p. 144). Of these, it is estimated that more than 11,000,000 Africans were exported to the New World before slavery was to end (Boahen, p. 316).

Accounts of the ways in which Africans were captured and transported in slave ships stagger the imagination and produce horror images of the brutal savagery which the traders, both Christian and Muslim, inflicted on helpless captives. For example, during the seventeenth century, some "300,000 Negroes were exported to Jamaica alone after being packed like sardines into the stinking holds of slave ships . . ." (Wellard, p. 150). In good weather, the slavers hoped to deliver 90% of their human cargo. In foul weather, where sea-sickness and dysentery spread among the captives, two out of three died. Those who arrived in the Americas went from the ships to the auction block to the plantations where treatment varied from master to master.

To Africa, the Europeans brought missionaries and disease. Missionaries sought to impose their faith systems on the African peoples, often assuming that baptism was equal to conversion. Diseases such as smallpox decimated tribal groups like the Hottentots, those light-brown skinned Africans who were among South Africa's oldest settlers. As the Europeans settled in the land, occupying and working soil long held by the Bushmen and as part of the Bantu kingdoms and city states, they were met with fierce opposition which resulted in the decimation of tribes. Native Africans were, in the minds of the Europeans, a lesser people, suitable for services as slaves, unable to rule properly.

Presently, Africans are reasserting themselves. Few Westerners are aware that much of the present confusion in African life stems from the acquisition of freedom from the Colonial powers that controlled the various states. This freedom, which has been won during the past 40 or so years, has created struggles for power within the various states, the development of militant groups as new patterns of culture growing out of western technology clash with traditional modes of living, and so forth. The following listings may help to demonstrate the extent of control in Africa by Colonial powers. Former Colonial designations are provided in the parentheses; where more than one power exercised control, square brackets are used to indicate combinations (based on Ungar, pp. 479-502).

France: Benin (Dahomey); Burkina Faso (upper Volta); [Britain] Cameroon (French and British Cameroons); Central African Republic (Ubangi-Shari); Chad; Comoros; Congo (French Congo); Djibouti (French Somaliland); Gabon; Guinea; Ivory Coast; Madagascar (Malagsy Republic); Mali (French Sudan); Mauritania; Niger; Senegal; [Britain] Seychelles.

Great Britain: Botswana (Bechuanaland), Gambia; Chad (Gold Coast); Kenya; Lesotho (Basutoland); Malawi (Nyasaland); Nigeria; Sierra Leone; [Italy] Somalia (British/Italian Somaliland); Swaziland; Uganda; Zambia (Northern Rhodesia); Zimbabwe (Southern Rhodesia).

Germany: [Belgium] Burundi (Urundi); [South Africa] Namibia (South-West Africa); [Belgium] Bwanda; [Britain] Tanzania (Tanganyika and Zanzibar); [Britain, France] Togo (Togoland).

Portugal: Angola; Cape Verde Islands; Guinea-Bissau; Mozambique; Sao Tome and Principe.

Holland: [France, Britain] Mauritius; [Britain] South Africa (Union of South Africa).

Spain: Equatorial Guinea; Western Sahara (Spanish Sahara).

Egypt: [Britain] Sudan (Anglo-Egyptian Sudan).
Belgium: Zaire (Belgian Congo).

Each nation introduced its own language which was layered, so to speak, over the varieties of local tongues. Each established its own businesses, built its own schools and established its own religious institutions. But under the overlay of Western culture, African culture was alive and well, and beneath the surface of Christian religion indigent African religions thrived. It is this reality which enabled the African spokesmen quoted above to speak and write as they have. At the same time, it is important to realize that the coming of Islam and Christianity provoked a challenge to previously held beliefs. Africans had to engage in critical thinking. Some who did convert retained old patterns in the home or in group meetings apart from mosque and church. Even where the old religion was abandoned, the humanistic spirit was retained.

African religion was imported to the Americas through slave trading. Although the Spanish government insisted that slaves be inducted into Roman Catholicism, beneath the ritual of baptism and compulsory worship, African religion survived, particularly in a form known as Santaria.

Santaria

Santaria is a form of the Yoruba religion which was dominant in Nigeria and surrounding areas. The religion recognizes a supreme deity known as Olodumare, the encompassing creative spirit in whom everything — past, present and future — rests. The incarnation of Olodumare is a world force called *ashe* which represents Olodumare's power directed toward health, life and righteousness. To tap that power, Santaria engages in a variety of religious expressions that embrace magic, prayer, dance and sacrifice. The blood rituals that call for the sacrifice of animals and birds, recognize that all human life preys on other life-forms and that the *ashe* also requires blood. The flesh is eaten by the worshippers. Hence there is in the religious rites a divine-human sharing of body and blood that has been severely criticized by Christians.

Santaria developed first in Cuba and there Roman Catholic saints and Yoruba ancestral figures tended to merge. It was imported into America and, although the following is relatively small, it has come under fire, largely from those fundamentalist Christians who are convinced that it is somehow related to a Satanist conspiracy which they, without any concrete evidence, insist is active throughout the United States. In actuality, Santaria is little more than a carry-over of African religion. It has undergone alterations and reform under pressure from Roman Catholicism and modern American life. Santaria efforts to bring spiritual power and healing into the lives of participants through dance, through offerings, through blood sacrifice and so forth are little more than expressions of faith that parallel aspects of Pentecostal religions.

Freethought in Africa

Today, many parts of Africa are in chaos. There is a search for new answers. Many have moved away from the notion of a spirit-infested world and from the belief that good fortune and misfortune are engendered by supernatural forces. Many oppose Islamic and Christian supernaturalism. With better scientific education and the educational emphasis on rational thinking, some are moving toward secularism. Norm Allen has reported that a Rationalist Center has opened in Ghana. There are secular Humanists in Nigeria. In the Ogun State, Emmanuel Kofi Mensah heads the Action for Humanism group and a newly formed Humanist Friendship Center has been started in Imo State. Other groups are in process (Allen, p. 7). Freethought and secularism are beginning to make inroads. When humanistic ideals of freethought meet the humanistic ideals of African religion, the possibilities of educational and compassionate outreach are enhanced.

At least two African ritual observances come under strong protest from freethought groups. These involve male and female circumcision. It is true that the circumcision of male infants is widely practiced in the western world, partially on the basis of Jewish religious tradition, partially on the basis of certain highly questionable health claims, but largely because the custom has become culturally embedded. In other words, circumcision, or genital mutilation, is what one does to one's infant male children.

In Africa, male circumcision is a puberty rite, designed to ritually move a boy to manhood. The young male is compelled to stand upright, sometimes against a tree, while a local elder or juju practitioner removes the child's foreskin. The boy is encouraged to be brave, to show no sign of pain or flinching in this ceremony that makes him a man. The ritual is painful and, despite the packing of the penis with herbal preparations, often results in infection. Circumcision rites are the occasion for celebrations.

Protestations by westerners against the inhumanity of this practice have little effect inasmuch as the same pain-filled custom is observed in western society, albeit the victim is an infant. Protestations within African society face the weight of tradition, but rational thinking and humanistic concerns are beginning to have some impact.

What is more upsetting to westerners is the widespread practice of female circumcision. This ancient custom involves young women, usually from the age of nine or ten to the time of the first menstruation. The ritual removal of the inner labia of the vagina and, in some instances, the clitoris, is performed by a female elder or "wise woman" assisted by other women in the community. The young girl is held down by women and the painful operation is performed. After the healing of the wounds (although some result in infection and death), the victim is ready for marriage and intercourse. As with male circumcision, celebrations accompany the mutilations. (Ploss, et al. pp. 141-143)

References

Allen, Norm, Jr., "Humanism and Religion in West Africa," *Free Inquiry*, Vol. 11, No. 3, 1991, p. 7.

Associated Press, "Becoming Christians Won't Betray Their Faith, Pope Tells Voodooists," *Los Angeles Times*, Feb 5, 1993, p. A12.

Barrett, Leonard, "African Religion in the Americas: The 'Islands in Between'" in: Newell S. Booth, Jr., edit., *African Religions: A Symposium*. New York: NOK Publishers, 1977, pp. 183-215.

Boahen, A. Adu, "Kingdoms of West Africa" in *The Horizon History of Africa*. New York: American Heritage Publication Co., 1971, pp. 177-208.

Boahen, A. Adu, "The Coming of the Europeans" in *The Horizon History of Africa*. New York: American Heritage Publication Co. 1971. pp. 305-51.

Booth, Newell S., Jr., "An Approach to African Religion" in: Newell S. Booth, Jr., edit., *The Horizon History of Africa*. New York: American Heritage Publication Co., 1971, pp. 1-11.

Davidson, Basil, "Africa: the Face Behind the Mask" in *The Light of the Past,* published by the American Heritage Foundation. New York: Simon and Schuster, Inc., 1967, pp. 190-210.

Davidson, Basil, *Africa in History*. New York: Macmillan Publishing Company. Revised edition, 1991.

Emery, Walter B., *Egypt in Nubia*. London: Hutchinson & Co., 1965.

Fagan, Brian, "All About Eve," *Archaeology*, November/December, 1992, pp. 18-24.

Fage, J.D., and R.A. Oliver, edits., *Papers in African Prehistory*. Cambridge: University Press, 1970.

Harris, Joseph E., edit., *Africa and Africans as Seen by Classical Writers*. Vol. II, Washington, D.C.: Howard University Press, 1977.

Hays, H.R., *In the Beginning*. New York: G. P. Putnam's Sons, 1963.

Hutchinson, Louise Daniel, *Out of Africa: From West African Kingdoms to Colonization*. Washington, D.C.: Smithsonian Institution Press, 1979.

Isaac, Ephraim, "Is the Ark of the Covenant in Ethiopia?" *Biblical Archaeology Review*, Vol. 19, No. 4, July/August, 1993, pp. 60-63.

Karp, Ivan, and Charles S. Bird, *Explorations in African Systems of Thought*. Bloomington, Ind.: Indiana University Press, 1980.

Kraft, Scott, "'Dial a Witch Doctor' Promises Fast Relief for Illnesses, Bad Sex," *Los Angeles Times*, August 25, 1992, p. H/6.

Lichtheim, Miriam, *Ancient Egyptian Literature*. Vol. I. Berkeley, Calif.: University of California Press, 1975.

Mair, Lucy, *African Kingdoms*. Oxford: Clarendon Press, 1977.

Mbiti, John S., *African Religions and Philosophy*. Portsmouth, New Hamp.: Heinemann Educational Books, Inc., 2nd edition, 1990.

Montet, Pierre, *Eternal Egypt*. New York: The New American Library (a Mentor Book), 1964.

Murphy, Joseph M., *Santaria: An African Religion in America*. Boston: Beacon Press, 1988.

Parrinder, Geoffrey, *African Traditional Religion*. Westport, Conn.: Greenwood Press, 1954.

Parrinder, Geoffrey, *African Mythology*. London: Paul Hamlyn, 1967.

Ploss, Herman H, Max Bartels and Paul Bartels, *Femina Libido Sexualis*. New York: The Medical Press, 1965.

Samkange, Stanlake, *African Saga*. Nashville: Abingdon Press, 1971.

Smith, William Stevenson, *Ancient Egypt*. Boston: Museum of Fine Arts, 1960.

Ungar, Sanford J, *Africa: The People and Politics of an Emerging Continent*. New York: Simon and Schuster, 1985.

Wallerstein, Immanuel, "Africa for the Africans" in *The Horizon History of Africa*. New York: American Heritage Publishing Co. Inc., 1971, pp. 496-528.

Wellard, James, *Lost Worlds of Africa*. New York: E.P. Dutton & Co., Inc., 1967.

13

India

As in the river civilizations of Egypt and Mesopotamia, so in India, the earliest centers of settled life have been found at 4th and 3rd millennium river sites. But it is not until cities come into existence that we are permitted a glimpse of the magnificent societal structure that emerged.

The earliest inhabitants of India are known as the Proto-Dravidians — a mixture of peoples who entered the sub-continent in a series of waves between 4000 and 2500 B.C.E. Although some forty sites have been discovered, it is from the excavation of two major Indian river cities (in what is now Pakistan), Mohenjo-daro and Harappa, that we get the clearest picture of the quality of life that developed. From these two sites, each more than three miles in circumference, we learn that, by the middle of the 3rd millennium B.C.E., the Indian river people had developed a high degree of architectural and city planning.

Mohenjo-daro was surrounded by massive baked-brick walls with well laid-out streets paved with bricks. The inhabitants had developed the two-wheeled ox-cart which is still used in parts of India today. They engaged in farming (they grew wheat, barley, field-peas, melons, sesame and dates), husbandry (they bred cattle, buffalo, camels, horses and asses), pottery-making, metal-working and trade with surrounding areas including Mesopotamia.

Sophisticated levels of specialization and cooperation were clear from the architecture, which ranged from individual homes with central atriums to huge burnt-brick and timber granaries and storage structures. The use of one huge building, measuring 87 by 64-1/2 feet with five sunken conical pits, is unknown but provides insight into the problems archaeologists face as they attempt to decipher the past. For example, it has been suggested that the structure may have been part of a dyeing industry, or perhaps it was part of a public restaurant. A huge bath, 39 by 23 by 8 feet with accompanying cells for private bathing, might have been used for ritual cleansing (as in present-day Hindu ceremonials), or it could have marked the beginning of the baths or tanks found in India today (Wheeler, pp. 235-36). On the other hand, the great bath might also have been associated with fertility rituals, where women committed to the service of the mother goddess engaged men devotees in sexual rites. Such women were not permitted to marry or have a settled family life. Chosen for their beauty, they were trained in luring songs and dances designed to entice the males. Figurines have been found depicting females, wearing heavy bird masks that completely covered their heads, representing the goddess who presided over births and death (Kosambi, p. 68). As we shall note later, this ancient custom has its modern counterparts with frightening overtones for the status of women and for health in India.

Artists modeled animals in terra cotta and human figures in bronze. Others engaged in sculpting and the manufacture of seals carved in stone. Jewelry was made from faience, steatite, carnelian and gold. There is evidence of the beginning of writing, but as yet the symbols have not been deciphered.

The mighty city of Mohenjo-daro was destroyed in the middle of the 2nd millennium B.C.E., probably by the Indo-European Aryans who invaded India in the name of their fierce war god Indra, known as a "fortress destroyer." Unfortunately, Harappa was plundered for its bricks before archaeologists excavated it and part of the site is covered by a Buddhist monument from the second century C.E. Even so, clear evidence of sophisticated city life and culture remained for archaeologists.

The religious beliefs of the pre-Aryan city-builders cannot be known. Humans were interred with pots, but there is no way of knowing whether the grave furnishings might be associated with a belief in afterlife. Because they were primarily an agricultural people, it is natural to expect that fertility themes would dominate their religion. Female figurines (mother-goddess images?) may imply concern for procreation. Some scholars believe that the Hindu god Shiva might be prefigured in one of the seals; the figure has three faces with perhaps a fourth on the far side, and is seated in a yoga position with heels together and attended by a tiger, elephant, buffalo and rhinoceros. It is possible that some elements of their religion may be found in the Hindu doctrine of *karma* and the notion of reincarnation, neither of which were part of the religion of the Aryan invaders and which are not mentioned in the Vedas.

The Coming of the Aryans

The light-skinned Aryans (as opposed to the dark-skinned Dravidians) were, like most European people, of Indo-European stock. Their language (Sanskrit) is related to Greek, Latin, German and English. They were a cattle-herding people, organized in tribes, each under the leadership of a *rajah* (king). With their horse-drawn chariots and their herds, they swept into northern India in the middle of the 2nd millennium B.C.E., pushing the dark-skinned Dravidians southward.

Hinduism

Hinduism is the oldest and one of the largest in membership of all present-day religions. Basically, it is composed of aspects of the faith systems of both the ancient Dravidians and the Aryan invaders, which have been modified and enhanced over the centuries. Aryan beliefs are predominant. The religious scriptures comprise a complex collective work, known as Vedanta, which reveal a process of continuing interpretation over centuries. The four Vedas (sacred knowledge) are the oldest parts and provide information about the Indo-Aryan gods. But the Vedas have been supplemented by Brahmanas, which instruct in ways to use the hymns and prayers of the Vedas in ritual. The Brahmanas were, in turn, supplemented by Forest Books that explain how those who lived in the forests made magical use of the hymns and prayer. And the Forest Books were supplemented by the Upanishads, which are philosophical discussions. Consequently, because the Hindu scriptures of India were developed over a long period of time, they are both complex and lengthy. For example, the oldest portion, the Rig-Veda consists of over a thousand hymns and prayers in ten volumes.

From these ancient writings, which form the basis of Hinduism, we learn of the gods and demons that infested the religion of the Aryans. Indra, the war god, associated with an intoxicating drink called *soma*, was called the "obstacle defeater." It was he who killed Vritra, the demon of cosmic waters who was recognized as an inhibiting power. Sometimes the drink Soma is presented as a deity in itself. Agni was the fire god (cf. Latin: *ignis*, English: ignite) and could be recognized in varying forms including the sun, lightning, the family hearth and sacrificial flames. Dyaus, the sky god (cf. Latin: Deus, Greek: Zeus), was called Dyaus Pitar (Father Sky) and was often associated with Prithivi (Mother Earth). But there were other sky deities: Varuna who presided over cosmic law, and Surya who was identified with the sun. The list continues with the identifications of various natural forces and elements as gods or demons. Gods such as Vishnu and Shiva, who were originally minor figures, assumed important roles in the developing system.

By 600 B.C.E., the Aryan invaders had settled into a number of principalities. Some were ruled by hereditary rajahs and some by clan organizations led by representative chieftains. A caste system had developed. At the top were the light-skinned Aryans, at the bottom, the dark-skinned Dravidians. There were four distinct social groupings: the Kshatriyas (nobles), the Brahmins (priests), the Vaisyas (Aryan common people and peasants) and the Sudras (enslaved non-Aryan dark-skinned people). The three upper groups kept themselves apart from the Sudras on the basis of *varna* (color-based caste) with everything from inter-marriage to sharing a meal forbidden. Finally, there developed a class known as "the untouchables," who were considered unclean and consisted of those who had no hope of advancement on the social scale.

Belief in reincarnation or the transmigration of souls (*samsara*) may originally have been part of the ancient Dravidian religion. Under Aryan influence the concept developed to become part of Hinduism. The belief was that at death, the soul would be reborn into another existence and, after the death of that existence, would again be reborn — over and over again and not necessarily in the same dimension. A rebirth could be in animal, vegetable or human form or consist of a time in any one of a series of heavens or hells. The rebirth could move the soul to a higher or lower existence according to the law of *karma*. *Karma* means "deeds" and implies "that one's thoughts, words, and deeds have an ethical consequence fixing one's lot in future existences. Looked at retrospectively, *karma* is the *cause* of what is happening in one's life now." (Noss, p. 107) Therefore, whether one is born into a Brahmin caste or as an untouchable is due to what occurred in a previous incarnation. In other words, the caste system that relegates one person to the rank of a Brahmin and another to the status of an untouchable is based on the Hindu religious belief in *karma*.

Liberation from the cycle or wheel of *karma* comes with the loss of identity (*atman*: self) through absorption into or becoming one with Brahma, who is universal, uncreated energy, or Being itself — the All, the Ultimate, the Absolute. Clearly, the purpose and intent of Hindu religion is escape from the bondage of this world. The escape can be a step by step process through the caste system, but the opportunities for emancipation are, according to Hinduism, open to all:

> even those who belong to the lower castes — women, Vaisyas and Sudras too — can reach the highest spiritual realization, if they will take refuge in me. Need I tell you, then, that this is also true of the holy Brahmins and pious philosopher-kings? . .

> Fill your heart and mind with me, adore me, make all your acts an offering to me, bow down to me in self-surrender. If you set your heart upon me thus, and take me for your ideal above all others, you will come into my Being. (Bhagavad-Gita 9.32,33)

As in other faith systems, divisions developed. Each group might focus on a separate or particular aspect of the primal Hindu mythology. However, quite often dissenters continued to be part of the Hindu faith system. Ancient skeptics who expressed doubt regarding the powers of certain deities, including Indra (Rigveda VIII, 100.3) or on divine omniscience (Rigveda X, 129), were still considered to be Hindus.

When dramatic shifts in the faith system occurred, the innovators were sometimes outlawed, at other times simply acknowledged as their new group remained a part of Hinduism. For example, the Ajivakas, who were followers of Makkali Gosali (6th century B.C.E.), were freethinkers and, essentially, atheists. They dismissed the notion of *karma* in favor of *niyati*, which refers to the happenstance nature of events and happenings. This group, which disappeared after the 13th century C.E., rejected beliefs about sin and punishment. They explained the occurrences of life in terms of accidental relationships of time and place. (Bharati, p. 316)

The Samkhya and Mimamsa schools of Hinduism, each of which came into being perhaps as early as 400 B.C.E., and the Vedanta system formulated in the 8th century C.E. by the teacher Samkaracarya, are each avowedly atheistic, but are still considered part of Hinduism (Bharati, p. 317f). This does not imply that their ideas were not attacked. Indeed, the beliefs of the Samkhya, like those of the Charwaka and Lokayata schools of thought, are known only through details provided in their condemnation and vilification by Hindu detractors. Warnings against deviation were given in the *Code of Manu* which stated:

> If a person with greater confidence in logic disregards the vedas and Dharma Sastra, he is to be considered a disbeliever (Nastika). Even if such a person be a Brahmana he must be thrown out of society. (Bhatty, p. 35)

These freethinkers were atheists, rationalists and philosophical materialists who believed that physical matter in its movements and modifications is the only reality, and that all thought, feeling and so forth can be explained through physical laws. Samkhya "had its roots in pure philosophic speculation . . . without any reference to . . . god," but gradually theists introduced the notion of deity. (G. S. Rao, 1976,

p. 129) The Mimamsa followers "swore so much by the Vedic ritual that they felt no need for a god. They believed that the chanting of mantras would produce certain effects. So, for them the *devas* of the Vedas had only verbal significance and no separate existence." (G. S. Rao, 1976, p. 129) The fourteenth century yogi, Vemana, criticized creedal religion, superstition and blind belief. He taught morality without reference to gods or punishment or reward in the afterlife. His ethical principles, expressed in part in poems, reveal his role as a humanist and a philosopher to the Telugu people. (G. S. Rao, 1970, p. 5)

Obviously, Hindu religion is not a single faith system. There are many gods, dozens of religious books, hundreds of temples reflecting regional influences, and a multitude of sects with competing deities, texts, rituals and so on, and varying social customs. It is quite possible for a "good Hindu" to be an atheist or an agnostic, to ignore rituals, to be a vegetarian or to eat beef, because the hallmark of Hinduism is tolerance.

But there are also the intolerant Hindu groups which developed during the colonial age. The Arya Samaj (Aryan Society), founded in the mid-19th century, is what might be called a "fundamentalist" sect that has designed rituals and ceremonies to win back Hindus who converted to Christianity and Islam (which they regard as enemies of India). A more militant anti-Muslim group, the Rashtriya Swayamasevak Sangh (RSS) or National Volunteer Corps, is nationalistic and committed to a theocratic state. Clearly, the term "Hindu" is inclusive. One does not cease to be a Hindu if one is an atheist. One ceases to be a Hindu only when one joins another faith system such as Buddhism, Jainism, Christianity or Islam.

In present day India, the ethnic, religious and linguistic diversities make it imperative that only a secular political government can meet the needs of all citizens — including Hindus of all castes as well as Muslims, Sikhs, Christians, Buddhists and Jains.

Jainism

Jainism, a religion completely separated from Hinduism, constitutes a rejection of Hinduism. Jainism developed in India during the 6th century B.C.E. when the Hindu caste system was being formulated and when the Brahman caste was making claims of spiritual superiority. Jainism is an ascetic philosophy advanced by Nataputta Vardhamana (599-527 B.C.E.), who is better known as Mahavira (The Great One).

According to Jain tradition, Mahavira was born near modern Bihar, into the family of an immensely rich and powerful rajah. When he was thirty years old, his parents died, and Mahavira, who was obviously an independent thinker, gave away his riches, retained only a robe as his one earthly possession, and joined a group of monks. Shortly afterward, he discarded the robe and went about nude, clad only in "atmosphere." After a long period of wandering, seeking always to be rid of the cycle of birth, death, and rebirth, he became convinced that only through the most severe asceticism could the soul be purged, and that the maintenance of a purified soul required the practice of *ahimsa*, or non-injury to any living thing. He begged for his food, always being sure that no living life form (including everything from insects, insect eggs, sprouts, etc.) was in the food. As he walked, he carried a soft broom with which to sweep away any insects that might inadvertently be in his path. He is said to have been impervious to harsh weather conditions, to injury, and to the pain inflicted by those who mocked him. After thirteen years, while in deep meditation, he achieved *nirvana* — the transcendent realm of true being and freedom. For the next 30 years he taught, finally dying by self-starvation at age 72.

Although Jainism is a faith system completely separated from Hinduism, it shares the same concern over the relationship between human salvation and the law of *karma*. Jains recognize different factors affecting *karma*, including the length of one's life, one's given mental and physical characteristics, caste, capacity for pleasure and pain, and attitudes of faith or doubt. The efforts to achieve freedom from these mental, physical and material factors receive no help from a god or world soul, which Jains do not believe exists, nor from higher spiritual beings or gods. These inanimate creatures are themselves in need of redemption and are, therefore, concerned with their own rebirths. All release must be self-attained, without help from other humans, including priests. Salvation lies within the self. It is achieved though self-control which purifies the soul from dependence upon animate or inanimate dimensions of the world.

The freeing regulations include *ahimsa* and the renunciation of deceit, anger, greed, mirth-making, sexual pleasures, or any emotions that might betray one into falsehood. These hard demands are relaxed for the laity. The Jain first pledges never to knowingly take the life of a sentient creature. This promise automatically outlaws tilling the soil or any form of butchery. Consequently, Jains tend to succeed in the world of business. Jains also pledge never to lie or steal or be unfaithful (the pledge of marital fidelity). They promise to be on guard against that which encourages sin and to meditate regularly, to observe periods of self-denial, to give alms to support ascetics, and to spend a period of time as a monk.

There are sects within Jainism. The Digambaras believe that any monk who wears clothes or owns property cannot reach Isatpragbhara, the place of supreme bliss where the soul is no longer subject to rebirth. Women are accorded secondary ranking, and thus Jainist religion does not contribute to changing the status of women in India. Men are warned: "Do not talk to a woman. Do not look at a woman. Do not dwell in a house where any woman is living" (Ajniat, p. 145). Women are excluded from temples and monastic life on the basis of Mahavira's teaching that women are "the greatest temptation in the world" and "the cause of all sinful acts." Women can only achieve salvation through being reborn as men (Noss, p. 120). During December, 1993, hundreds of thousands of Jain pilgrims gathered before the 57 feet tall monolithic statue of a naked Jain ascetic, Lord Bahubali, located at Shravanabelagola in the southern India state of Karnataka.

In a ritual that occurs only every twelve years, devotees watched as water from nearby sacred tanks were poured over the giant figure, followed by buckets of sugar cane juice, then milk, and finally pasty mixtures of herbs. The message of the chief clerics stressed the familiar Jain theme of happiness through non-violence and peace through renunciation (Dahlberg). Bahubali's legend follows the familiar hero pattern of a son of a king who, believing that pride and desire produced misery, abandoned his royal station to seek spiritual happiness in the forest. He became a "siddha" or one that achieved salvation. The statue was erected in 981 C.E.

The Sthanakvasis sect have neither idols nor temples and practice meditation wherever they may be. The Shvetambarass monks admit women to their order and assume they can achieve salvation (*moksha*).

Finally, Jainist philosophy avoids absolutes. Every question has both a positive and a negative answer since no proposition is either absolutely false or true. It is estimated that today there are some two million Jainists in India, most of whom live in the Bombay region (Noss, p. 122).

Buddhism

Like Jainism, Buddhism represents a rejection of Hindu doctrine. Indeed, Buddha was regarded as an atheist (*Nasthika*) by orthodox Hindus, inasmuch as he opposed Vedic rites and animal sacrifices. (G.S. Rao, 1988, p. 98) Without question, he was a freethinker.

Siddhartha Gautama (Siddhatta Gotama, in the Pali dialect), the founder of Buddhism, was born in 563 B.C.E. in northern India in Kapilavastu in the district of Nepal. Until recently, the locale of the city was unknown and some scholars questioned whether Siddhartha had ever lived. Excavations, undertaken during the 1970s, located the lost city and recovered material remains associated with Buddhism from the 5th and 4th centuries B.C.E. The excavations indicated the site was first occupied in the eighth century B.C.E. and continued to be occupied until the fourth century C.E.

When Siddartha died in 483 B.C.E., his body was cremated and, according to legend, a one-eighth share of his ashes remained in Kapilavastu; the remainder went to various shrines. Whether or not the actual remains of Siddartha have been found cannot be determined, but certainly there is solid evidence that cremated remains of adherents of Buddhism have been found, some dating back to the fifth century B.C.E. (Dart) While this evidence does not prove the existence of Buddha, it does lend credibility to his life by demonstrating that Kapilavastu did exist and that shortly after Buddha's death it became a shrine associated with his birth, life and death.

What can be questioned are the legends surrounding the birth of Siddartha. As with other hero figures, the miraculous and the magical came to be associated with him. According to tradition, sometime in his late twenties he abandoned his princely, Kshatriya caste family (his father was a petty chieftain in the Sakya clan), including his wife and child, to become a religious mendicant in a search for salvation.

Buddha first examined Brahmin teachings and became a disciple of two Brahmin ascetics. Having become convinced that the Brahmin way could not lead him to salvation, he tested the asceticism of Jainism, becoming emaciated through his self-mortification. This path also failed. Enlightenment came some six years later as he was meditating at the foot of a fig-tree. There, having been tempted by Mara, the god of desire and death, to forsake his search and enjoy life, and having been physically tortured by demons, he experienced enlightenment (*bodhi*). Now, purged of sensual desires and thoughts, he became "aware" and entered a state devoid of both satisfaction and dissatisfaction. He had moved beyond the requirement of rebirthing and experienced an earthly foretaste of *nirvana*. He had become the Buddha, the Enlightened One. The next 45 years of his life were spent in "preaching, teaching and constructive planning" (Noss, p. 132). He died at age 80 in 483 B.C.E. Following his period of meditation, the Buddha set forth Four Noble Truths, through which one might realize *nirvana*. They are, in summary:

1. Human life is characterized by suffering and sorrow. He is reputed to have said: "Birth is suffering, decay is suffering, illness is suffering, death is suffering. Presence of objects we hate is suffering; separation from objects we love is suffering; not to obtain what we desire is suffering."

2. The cause of suffering lies in human desire and greed for power, pleasure and possessions. He spoke of a threefold thirst for pleasure, existence, and prosperity as the causes of human misery.

3. Suffering and sorrow are overcome through deliverance from the three thirsts by destruction of desire and the absence of passions.

4. The way to the cessation of suffering is the eightfold path which leads to no desire and which consists of:

Right Belief (that is, belief in The Four Noble Truths)

Right Aspiration (that is, the renunciation of sensuality and misery-inducing desires, the entertaining of the right love for others and the resolution to do no harm to living beings)

Right Speech (that is, not engaging in hurtful talk)

Right Conduct (that is, expressing love for all creatures through word and deed)

Right Means of Livelihood (that is, the proper use of one's time and energy to earn a living in keeping with Buddhist principles)

Right Endeavor (that is, the continuous expending of mental effort to distinguish between wise and unwise desires or attachments)

Right Mindfulness (that is, mental discipline geared toward focusing on helpful themes)

Right Meditation (that is, the attainment of trance states which mark the advanced stages on the road to becoming an arahat [an enlightened one], and the assurance of a transition from death to *nirvana* marking the end of rebirth).

The goal is *nirvana* and, should one die before having reached that status, the person is reborn or reincarnated into another living form. In the reincarnated state, the person once again strives toward gaining enlightenment. The *karma* principle teaches, that how one lives in this life determines the life form to be inhabited in the next, and that the status of one in this life has been determined by a previous life. In other words, one's social situation does not come about by the happenstance of being born into a certain caste. The Sutta Nipata (Discourses) puts it this way:

No Brahmin is such by birth.

No outcaste is such by birth.
An outcaste is such by his deeds.
A Brahmin is such by his deeds. (de Bary, p. 143)

The Sangha or Order which the Buddha established initially drew members from his own caste, the Kshatriya, but also attracted Brahmins and those from lower castes. At first, the Order was composed only of males, but ultimately women were admitted as nuns, but in a status below that of the males. The attitude towards women and the importance of avoiding them is reflected in the Mahaparinibbana Sutta, Chapter V (Ajniat, p. 145):

Anand: How are we to conduct ourselves with regard to womankind?
Buddha: By not seeing them, Anand.
Anand: But if we should see them, what are we to do?
Buddha: By not talking to them, Anand.
Anand: But if they should speak to us, Lord, what are we to do?
Buddha: Keep wide awake, Anand.

Obviously, the new Order required guidelines, and these came in the form of the Dhamma (Law or Truth or Doctrine) and Vinaya (the Discipline). Ten Precepts were formulated to create "the Middle Way" between the extremes of self-indulgence and of asceticism. The first four Precepts parallel those embraced by Jainist monks and, together with the fifth Precept, were obligatory for lay-members or for those who approved of the Buddhist ideals but remained attached to non-ascetic life. The Five Precepts (summarized) are:

1. The principle of *ahimsa* which forbids the destruction of life (principle of non-violence)
2. Do not take what is not given (no theft)
3. Abstinence from unchastity (for the monks this signified celibacy)
4. Refusal to lie or deceive
5. Abstinence from intoxicants

Monks were expected to observe the remaining Precepts:

6. Eat moderately and not after noon
7. Abstinence from dancing, singing, music, and dramatic spectacles
8. Avoid the use of ornaments, garlands, scents, unguents
9. Do not sleep on high or broad beds
10. Do not accept gold or silver

The Buddha's teachings were intensely practical. He avoided philosophical discussion and theological speculation. Questions concerning whether or not the world is eternal, or whether the soul has an identity apart from the body and whether or not the soul is immortal, whether or not gods and goddesses exist, he dismissed as queries that did not "edify," thereby signaling that they were irrelevant and meaningless.

Buddha rejected religious devotion to a god as a way of salvation. He accepted a practical atheism, which is to say that "He believed that the universe abounded in gods, goddesses, demons and other nonhuman powers and agencies, but all without exception were finite, subject to death and rebirth" (Noss, p. 134). For him there was no supreme deity in charge of the universe, directing human destiny, waiting to judge, reward or punish humans in some afterlife. He rejected the Hindu pantheon and the authority of the Brahmin priesthood.

Instead, he taught his disciples how to rely on themselves and their own power and potential to obtain salvation though spiritual discipline. Each individual must use his or her own strength and resources to achieve *nirvana* inasmuch as no other resources are available. This strict form of individualistic humanism would seem to differ from modern humanism which calls for team effort, the principle of sharing and helping one another maximize potentials for meaningful living in this world (without anticipation of rebirth). However, as Noss points out in his discussion of the role of the *arahat* or "Buddhist saint":

> One of his outstanding qualities is benevolence. He is the Buddhist ideal of what one may become and ought to be. He is magnanimous; he overflows with good will . . . Although fundamentally the Buddhist seeker is bent on his own self-cultivation, his own blessedness, and is often encouraged, in the words of the Buddha himself, to "wander alone like a rhinoceros," forsaking houses and lands and kindred because they hinder him, nevertheless he is charged to love all mankind without exception. That the Buddha himself possessed the quality of compassion for all men is evident in a life devoted to preaching and teaching. Though he strove to sunder every personal tie to particular individuals based on emotion, on the ground, as we have seen, that any such tie is misery-producing, he charged his disciples to love all mankind with a mother's love. (Noss pp. 141-142)

Interestingly enough, it was this tension between the search for personal salvation and the need to love all humans that contributed to the fundamental bifurcation of Buddhism into the Mahayana and the Theravada (Hinayana).

The Growth of Buddhism

Buddha's followers increased rapidly — first in the Ganges river basin and then throughout the sub-continent. Missionaries travelled to Ceylon (Sri Lanka), then to China, Korea, Japan and throughout Southeast Asia. Others moved westward into Syria. Buddhist tradition relates that, three years after the death of the Buddha, an assembly or Council of some 500 Buddhist monks was held at Rajagaha in 480 B.C.E. This was the first of a series of such gatherings.

Initially, the Buddha's teaching were transmitted orally, and at the first Council at Rajagaha the monks were said to have recited the complete canon of scripture. It wasn't until the Fourth Buddhist Council, held at Matale, Ceylon (Sri Lanka), in 25 B.C.E., that the oral tradition was finally put into writing — in Pali, rather than in Sanskrit, to further symbolize the rejection of Hinduism. The writings were divided into "three baskets" or the Tripitaka: the Vinaya Pitaka (the basket of monastic rules), the Sutta Pitaka (the basket of Discourses or narratives and teachings), and the Abhidhamma Pitaka (the basket of supplemental philosophy).

The second Council, held at Vesali in 380 B.C.E., was characterized by disputes concerning discipline. By the time of the third Council (240 B.C.E.), dramatic political changes had occurred in India.

During the last third of the 4th century B.C.E., the Greek forces of Alexander the Great had established bastions in India. Many of these Greek strongholds were routed by the Indian leader Chandragupa of Magadha, who then went on to conquer the rest of India. His grandson, Asoka, who became ruler in 273 B.C.E., converted to Buddhism. Asoka tried to legislate key Buddhist concepts, such as the Dharma ethic, which included familial responsibility, the principle of *ahimsa*, courteous behavior, and proper treatment of others including slaves, servants, teachers, ascetics and Brahmins. His awareness of tensions that developed during the second Council led him to discourage schisms and to stress inter-Buddhist harmony. Under his leadership Buddhist missionaries went to Egypt, Greece and the Middle East. Mahinda, a close relative (brother or son), went to Sri Lanka (Ceylon), which was to become a center of Buddhist learning and tradition. There can be little question that, through the influence of Asoka, early Buddhism was transformed from what might have been classified as a philosophy into something approaching a religion. Asoka visited sites associated with the Buddha. He saw to the erection of stupas, which are architectural monuments housing sacred relics or marking sacred locations. He built shrines and chapels with accompanying living quarters for monks and encouraged the development of rituals and pilgrimages.

Of course, Chandragupa had not completely eliminated the Greeks. In Northwest India, the Greco-Bactrian king, Menander, continued to extend Greek influence from his headquarters at Sagala (modern Sialkot). Because he was interested in education, he entered into dialogue with a learned Buddhist named Nagasena. The conversations which are supposed to have led to Menander's conversion are known as *The Questions of King Milinda* (Milinda = Menander) — "a Buddhist historical romance which must have originated not too long after Menander's death" (Finegan, p. 276).

Asoka's efforts to ease the tensions within the Buddhist movement were not successful. In Sri Lanka, the Theravada ("Song of the Elders"), or as it is sometimes called, the Hinayana ("The Small Vehicle") sect of Buddhism prevailed. They claim to be in the direct line of the Buddha, conserving both the oldest texts of Buddhism (in Pali) and holding to the tenets of early Buddhism. Theravada Buddhism denies the existence of the *atman* (self), views the world as a transient place, constantly in flux wherein all forms of life exist in sorrow and misery, and has *nirvana* as its goal. For them, the Buddha does not exist inasmuch as he has entered *nirvana* and therefore "he is at peace, and knows nothing any more of becoming and ceasing to be" (Noss, p. 152). There have been Buddhas before Gautama and there is in process the next Buddha who is presently a Bodhisattva. He is the Maitreya or Buddha to come, awaiting the proper time to be manifested when he will achieve enlightenment and accomplish for his time what Gautama did in his.

Mahayana Buddhism ("The Large Vehicle"), which developed in northwest India, transformed the human Buddha into a glorified superhuman, a divine being who came to earth at the request of the gods. This teaching gave rise to wondrous birth stories (in Sanskrit), which the Mahayana sect claim as part of the original canon, but which scholars recognize as later creations. The mythology continued to develop.

Now there were pre-Gautama Buddhas, some of whom had come to earth as teachers (Manushi Buddhas); having performed their task, attained enlightenment and realized *nirvana*, they were removed forever from the outreach of humans. On the other hand, there were Bodhisattvas who remain in heaven and, out of compassion for suffering humanity, postpone their entrance into *nirvana*. They may respond to the prayers of those who call upon them and at times will descend to earth as ministering angels to aid in the ransoming of suffering mortals. Dhyani Buddhas exist in the heavens and they too postpone their entrance into *nirvana* to minister to human needs. They are the contemplative Buddhas whose statuary symbolizes their calm composure. Salvation, in Mahayana Buddhism, was no longer an individualistic matter; now there were a multitude of compassionate super-beings eager to help.

Buddhism's outreach gave it anchorage in the Far East when, after the seventh century C.E., it began to decline in India. Several causes for decline have been suggested. One contributing factor may have been the invasion of northern India by the White Huns, which resulted in the destruction of Buddhist centers and disrupted normative Buddhism. Perhaps the lack of intellectual development within Indian Buddhism weakened the movement. Perhaps the fact that Hinduism adopted the Buddha as an incarnation of Vishnu drew people away from Buddhism, while adding strength to Hinduism which already had a popular following because of rituals that touched human life from birth to death. Certainly the coming of Islam played a part in Buddhist decline. As a consequence, Buddhism was weakened and its strength was transferred to the Orient.

Judaism

There was a time when it was suggested that the Jewish presence in India could be traced back to the time of Solomon in the 10th century B.C.E. This idea rested on attempts to relate biblical Ophir, a city with which Solomon traded (I Kings 9:28; 10:11), to the city of Supara, north of Bombay, India. The basis for this notion rested on a statement in Josephus (*Antiquities* VIII. vi.4) which describes the destination of Solomon's fleet as "Aurea Chersonesus which belongs to India." This relationship is no longer accepted (Van Beek, p. 605f).

Although small colonies of Jews fleeing persecution in Persia by the Magians were established in India during the late 5th century C.E. (Graetz, II, p. 629f), merchant contacts go back more than 2000 years. Jewish communities have tended to consist of relatively small enclaves and have had little impact on life and thought in India as a whole.

Christianity

According to legend, Christianity was introduced into India during the first century C.E., by the doubting disciple, Thomas. According to a second century C.E. account included in the Apocryphal New Testament and titled "Acts of the Apostles," Thomas received a divine command to go to India:

> At that season all we the apostles were at Jerusalem, Simon which is called Peter and Andrew his brother, James the son of Zebedee and John his brother, Philip and Barthalomew, Thomas and Matthew the publican, James the son of Alphaeus and Simon the Canaanite, and Judas the brother of James; and we divided the regions of the world, that every one of us should go unto the region that fell to him and unto the nation whereunto the Lord sent him. According to lot, therefore, India fell unto Judas Thomas. (James, p. 365)

At first, Thomas refused to go, but eventually he made the journey. Local tradition says that he died a martyr's death at Mylapore, near Madras in 78 C.E. A small chapel is supposed to mark his burial place. In 1522, the Portuguese moved what were believed to be his bones to the Church of St. Thomas in Goa (Paul, p. 16). Whether or not there is any truth in the legend cannot be known, but a representative from the church in India is supposed to have attended the Council of Nicaea (325 C.E.).

When the Portuguese came to India at the beginning of the 15th century, they were surprised to find a flourishing community of Syrian-Indian Christians in Malabar who had no knowledge of Roman Catholicism nor of the papacy. The Portuguese Christians exploited and used the Indian Christians in a variety of immoral ways.

In 1542, Francis Xavier, a missionary zealot of the Clerks Regular of the Society of Jesus, an order initiated by Ignatius Loyola, arrived in Goa where, in three years of preaching and teaching, he is said to have converted 700,000 to Christianity. His embalmed body lies on display (only the head and shoulders can be seen) in the Bom Jesus Basilica in Goa, missing only two big toes said to have been bitten off by female fanatics, and an arm that was sent to Rome at the request of a pope.

Protestant Christianity entered India in 1706 though the efforts of King Frederick IV of Denmark as part of the efforts of the Dutch East India Company to establish colonies. These first missionaries were German Lutherans. The British followed in 1784 when Baptist and

Anglican missionaries arrived. During the nineteenth century Lutherans and Anglicans and Baptists were supplemented by Congregationalists, Presbyterians, and Methodists. Christian missionary programs have continued and the Christian Church has established itself with some twenty million adherents in India.

The missionaries introduced dramatic changes. Their main purpose was to convert the people of India. To accomplish that purpose they built schools, mission hospitals, organized conferences and fed the hungry with missionary funds sent from their home countries. Of course, many of those who converted were "rice Christians" whose need for food, rather than the persuasiveness of the faith, was the prime attraction. The introduction of better farming techniques by the missionaries helped to produce better harvests.

Rajaiah Paul has claimed that:

> it was with the gradual permeation of Christian ideas that a new reverence for womanhood came to be, till, at the moment, both in the eyes of the law and in social convention, all disabilities under which Indian women have been suffering for untold ages have been removed. Today a woman can be the Governor of a province, the Minister of a state or a member of the state legislatures. Women can and have become leaders in public life. The idea of home life of a type very different from the ancient Hindu model is also directly the creation of Christian ideas. (p. 88)

Not everyone would agree with Paul. There are Indian women who believe that Christianity has contributed little to the changing of the lives of women in India. The New Testament letters of the Christian missionary Paul contain edicts on the status of women that are in harmony with standard Hindu teachings. For example, in his letter to the Christians in Corinth, Paul wrote "neither was the man created for women, but the woman for the man" (1 Cor. 11:9) and "Let your women keep silence in the churches, for it is not permitted them to speak; and if they will learn anything, let them ask their husbands at home for it is a shame for women to speak in church" (14:34,36). Narayanan Periya claimed that the Asian Christian Peace Conference, held at Kottayam in 1974 "admitted in a resolution that Christianity was responsible for the slavery of Asian Women" (p. 150).

Female enslavement continues, with the exploitation of women, some as young as eight or nine years of age, in a prostitution industry that not only degrades and demeans women, but is the source of the spread of virulent diseases including AIDS for which there is no present cure. (AIDS is acquired immune deficiency syndrome, which is a deficiency in the human immune system due to infection with HIV, human immunodeficiency virus.)

It is quite possible that there is some truth in both claims. Rajaiah Paul would also argue that:

> The new respect for human personality, the present eagerness to deal fairly with workers and the lower classes in general is also to be attributed to conceptions borrowed from Christianity, which has done more for the elevation of Indian society in the one century than its predecessors did in all the ages of their respective dominion." (p. 88f)

It must be admitted that, due to the British presence and control, Christianity and European cultural patterns have had a permeative effect. As young Indian scholars went abroad for their education, they returned with new perspectives about how life could be lived. These new ideas were not necessarily drawn from association with Christian churches, but were absorbed through secular channels and through living in the more sophisticated educational world of the west.

As we shall see, much of the social activism pressure for change was not and is not the product of the Christian church. Rather, vocal secularists, who do not work according to ecclesiastical administrative patterns, have insisted on change. They have had their levels of awareness raised through the reading of the works of writers whom we will discuss under the developing European and American scene and from their knowledge of ancient Greek rationalists. They continue to demand a different way of life for secular India — a way in which caste systems and customs and regulations growing out of ancient Hindu doctrine will no longer be in control.

Zoroastrianism

Indian Parsees (named after the Iranian province of Pars) are those followers of the religion of Zoroaster who fled from persecution by Muslims in Persia around 766 C.E. They constitute a small community of some 10,000 believers living in the area around Bombay. Their fire ritual involves the giving of a piece of sandalwood to the priest who then, with appropriate prayer, places it on the fire which is the symbol of the god Ahura Mazda (see chapter 5 on Mesopotamia). The worshipper then rubs the ashes on his or her forehead, receives a priestly blessing and leaves. Funerary practices involve exposing the body of the deceased on a platform on top of a tower of silence (*dakhma*) where vultures devour the flesh. The skeletal remains are then deposited on a stone floor to disintegrate, thus protecting the earth from defilement.

Because membership in the religion is hereditary as is membership in its priesthood, the secular nature of much of Indian life is tending to reduce the number of Zoroastrian adherents. The religion has had little impact on Indian life.

Islam

Although Islam had reached India as early as the seventh century C.E., it was not until the eleventh century that its militant expansion occurred. At that time, Muslim Sufis made Islam, like Christianity, a proselytizing religion and this resulted in large scale conversions to the monotheistic faith system. By the twelfth century, after converting many Hindus, especially those from the lower castes, Islam dominated northwest India. From this well-established base, Islam pressed southward to gain control over the entire nation.

Islam challenged the validity of multi-god Hindu faith, denied the validity of rituals, mocked the imagery, and discarded some of the Hindu food laws and the social caste system. The challenge was not without results and millions converted to the new faith. Although Islam did not open doors to freethought, it did force the Hindu religion into a defensive stance that resulted in spiritual ossification and social isolation (G. S. Rao, 1976, p. 130). In 1947, with the demise of British control over India, some 90 million Indian Muslims demanded a separate autonomous state, and as a result the state of Pakistan was created. Today, Islam remains a powerful force in India.

Sikhism

The impact of Islamic monotheism with its rejection of images and statuary and ceremonials prompted some Hindu reformers to try to purge Hinduism of certain beliefs and practices. For example, Ramananda in the 14th century C.E., rejected both the caste system and meat-eating restrictions. His disciple, Kabir (1440-1518), was raised by Muslims, was a monotheist and, like the Hindu poet Namdev who lived a generation earlier, mocked the notion that gods could live in idols. "He took no satisfaction in the external forms of religion — rituals, scriptures, pilgrimages, asceticism, bathing in the Ganges, and such like — if these are unaccompanied by inward sincerity or morality of life" (Noss, p. 235). He taught that freedom from *karma* came through the love of God, and freedom from the Brahmins came through teachers who were spiritual leaders (gurus). His sect, which exists today as Kabirpanthis, was a forerunner of Sikhism (which means "student" or "disciple").

Nanak, the founder of Sikhism, was born into a Hindu family in 1469 C.E. in the village of Talwandi in the Punjab region. His school teacher was a Muslim. The religion he founded drew from both Muslim and Hindu sources. Nanak's religious experience led him to express himself in a statement that is repeated each day by Sikhs:

> There is but one God. He is the True Name.
> He is the creator, devoid of fear and enmity.
> He is everywhere pervading the universe.
> He is immortal, unborn, and self-existent.
> He is great and bountiful.
> In the beginning was the True name,
> And when time began, there was the True Name,
> And the True Name is now and evermore shall be.

After extensive evangelism (which included musical interpretations of his faith) and travel (he visited Mecca), his following grew in the Punjab region. Before his death, Nanak appointed a successor named Angad to continue his teaching and his efforts to develop a faith system that bridged the gap between Hinduism and Islam. He had taught, "There is no Hindu and Musselman."

Nanak accepted the transiency of the world, the transmigration of souls and *karma*. Salvation was not found in the Muslim paradise, but through absorption in and loss of individuality in the True Name. The True Name, he taught, was not the transcendent other, but was to be found in the human heart and in the Guru's teachings. Ritual, pilgrimage and asceticism were replaced with the repetition of the divine name, compassion and ethical behavior.

Nanak's teachings, together with those of gurus who followed him, plus wisdom from Hindu and Muslim teachers, have been gathered in the Adi Granth. The ethical code of Sikhism emphasized a casteless society, the rejection of both the veil for women and of *sati*, the funereal sacrificial burning of widows on the pyre of their dead husbands.

In time, a militant community emerged — a development that was used by the British in the colonial period to their own advantage. They found that the Sikhs made excellent soldiers. The Punjab remains the central state of the Sikhs in India.

Freethought

It is clear that, as far back as we can go in Indian history, there were those who rejected the religious claims of Hinduism. Some were atheists and freethinkers such as Ajivakas and the schools of Samkhya and Mimamsa schools, which were discussed above. But these non-believers remained within Hinduism. The clear breaks and the formation of secular societies was to come later.

During the British colonial period, English education systems were introduced and opened to the low-castes. When the non-Brahmin Justice Party came into power in 1919, initial steps towards compulsory education were taken. However, from 1937 to 1939, and from 1952 to 1954, when a Brahmin became Chief Minister of Madras, efforts were made to introduce programs that would have limited education among non-Brahmins and in particular among the lower classes. The plan was upset when K. Kamaraj of the Justice Party with the support of Periyar (see below) became Chief Minister (1954-1962).

Through the British and through liberal Indian educators, Indian youth were introduced to world history, to the rise and fall of tyrannical systems and to the writings of thinkers like John Locke, Sir Francis Bacon, Thomas Paine, and Voltaire (Innaiah, p. 344). These powerful writers provided encouragement for the development of Indian secularist and atheist freethought societies. These groups initiated systematic and open challenges to the customs and value teachings of Hinduism, including those pertaining to the status of women and the caste system, both of which had religious and political dimensions.

Few outside of India are aware of Hindu scriptural teachings about women. The negative comments are many. For example, in the Rig-veda (8/33/17) it is stated that "women have little wit" and that "with women there can be no lasting friendship. Women's hearts are the hearts of hyenas" (10/95/15). "A girl is a storehouse of sorrow" (Aiteraya Brahman 7/3/1). In the Manu Smriti (code): "it is the nature of women to seduce man in this world" (2/214); "By a girl, by a young woman, or even by an aged one, nothing must be done independently, even in her own house" (5/147); "In childhood, a female must be obedient to her father, in youth to her husband and when her 'lord' is dead, to her sons. A woman must never be independent" (5/148); and "women have impure desires, wrath, dishonesty, malice and bad conduct" (9/17). Other sources label women as "the abode of all sin" and state that "women and animals are equal. Both of them should be beaten." (Ajniat, p. 146)

The Hindu Freethought Union, formed in 1875 in Madras, challenged the teaching of the *Code of Manu* (a code of rules produced about 200 B.C.E.) which stated that "A husband must be constantly worshipped as a god by a faithful wife" and which forbade widow remarriage. Indeed the widow should "never mention the name of another man" and the widow "who from a desire to have offspring, violates her duty to her dead husband, brings on herself disgrace in this world" and in the next will "enter the womb of a jackal" (Noss, p. 194). By contrast, the Freethought Union advocated widow remarriages and the rehabilitation of child widows.

In South India, the Self Respect movement, led by E.V. Ramaswami (1879-1973), who was affectionately called "Periyar" (the great one), was openly atheistic. Like other rational movements, the Self-Respect group looked to modern science and the use of reason and logic to test concepts and to question the naive belief in the magical power of the many Hindu gods, the reverence for cow dung and cow urine, and the reliance upon religious magic to solve human problems. It questioned the validity of the Hindu scriptures, of the Manu Dharma Sustra which expounds as law, inequality and the fixing of avocations for the different castes. Periyar E.V. Ramaswamy expressed his disdain for these teachings by publicly burning the Manu Dharma Sustra.

In his 94th birthday message, which was reprinted in the *Periyar Memorial Souvenir*, Periyar described the Hindu scriptures as "things made some two thousand to three thousand years ago when human civilization was nothing short of barbarism. That period lacked scientific knowledge and the people were ignorant of the very sense of growth and development." (Janarthanam) In challenging the validity of the caste system, which he properly traced to the Hindu religious system, he is reputed to have said: "Man is disgraced by caste and caste is disgraced by religion. How can we destroy one keeping the other alive?" (Hansen)

Professor M.K. Subramanian, of the Chikkaiah Naicker College, Erode, commented on Periyar's atheism:

> According to Periyar, progress in human society could have been many times greater, faster, and superior, had man effectively used his critical intelligence all through human history

> brushing aside the wasted efforts in the realization of God and in the attainment of salvation through the so-called spiritual and emotional means. Thus Periyar's atheism, besides being a denial of the existence of God at a high intellectual level, serves in society as a dynamic force to kindle the reasoning power so that man's critical intelligence can effectively operate without constraints of what are called fear in God and faith in religion, fructifying at every stage of human progress in innovative correctives to the defective and obsolete part of social mechanism and innovative techniques for further improvement in terms of efficiency in the already operational part of social mechanism. Periyar's atheism is, after all, a technique of social dynamism.

With regard to the Self-Respect movement, Subramanian writes:

> Self-Respect philosophy is based on reason, critical intelligence, analytical intellect, empirical evidence, statistical verification and scientific approach. There is nothing negative in the Self-Respecter's box of tools which is used to unravel the charm, internal consistency and rationality of the universe and also aesthetically to enjoy the dazzling beauty of nature at its sublime best and to establish and verify the reality in the context of the social set-up we live in.

It should be noted that Periyar was active in the Indian Congress. His deep concern for human rights, particularly those of the Dravidians and the Tamil Indians, resulted in efforts to enhance their position, to protect their language and culture against the imposition of the Hindi language, to provide education and to help to prevent exploitation of their weakness. In other words, Periyar's atheism was not simply an academic or intellectual posture; it was linked to social reform and social action and to the welfare of the people of India. The Self-Respect movement has been a primary factor in the emancipation of Tamil women who were so demeaned that in some villages they were not permitted to wear blouses to cover their breasts.

The spirit of open inquiry and scientific rationalism was pioneered in India by M.N. Roy (1887-1954), who produced a journal called *Independent India*, founded the Radical democratic party and taught that ethics and morals need not be based on religion and superstition. Rajah Ram Mohan Roy fought against *sati*, the Hindu practice of throwing the widow of a deceased male on her husband's funeral pyre.

The basis for this primitive life-destroying custom is explicitly stated in the *Code of Manu*: "She must on the death of her husband allow herself to be burnt alive on the same funeral pyre; then everybody will praise her virtue." Although, today, the custom is forbidden by law in India, on occasion widows still sacrifice themselves.

The world's first Atheist Center was established in 1940 at Mudunar by Gora (Goparaju Ramachandra Rao, 1902-1975) and Mrs. Saraswathi Gora. In 1947, it was moved to Vijayawada. The Center provides marriage counseling and guidance on raising children and condemns the caste system by providing for inter-caste marriage and inter-caste dining. The Center seeks to expose the superstitions of witchcraft and sorcery through the work of teams of psychiatrists, social workers, medical doctors, scientists, magicians and trained hypnotists, who critically examine the claims of supernatural events. Gora pointed out that:

> Hindus are divided into castes, not because they understand the principles of the division of labor which is the ostensible reason put forth to justify caste divisions, but because they are trained by tradition and are bound by convention. . . .
>
> So, untouchables are untouchables by traditional faith in *karma*. They lie reconciled to their lot, however miserable it may be, as they consider their plight inevitable. The forbearance kills initiative and deadens rebellion against an obvious injustice. Therefore, Hindus are sentimentally idealistic but virtually wicked on account of outdated and unfair caste distinctions. Otherwise neither would the untouchables have lain low for so long, nor would the non-untouchables have callously allowed the inequalities and indignities to continue . . .

As Gora contemplated the problems of Indian society and the caste system, he wrote:

> Only atheism stirs the Hindus from this magnificent stupor and impotent complacency. It dismisses their faith in *karma* and rebirth as a myth and a hoax and thereby demolishes the foundations of the caste system. The atheistically awakened untouchables open their eyes and see that they are humans like any others. Atheistic awakening breaks traditions of caste rules, and converts all castes into one humanity. Nothing short of the adoption of atheism can abolish untouchability and restore human justice. (Rao [Gora] 1975, p. 132)

When the Atheist Center was awarded the 1986 International Humanist Award at Oslo, Norway, by the International Humanist and Ethical Union, Mrs. Mythri, who accepted the award on behalf of the Center, echoed Gora's call for positive atheism in her acceptance speech:

> The world needs a positive alternative to religion. Like theism, atheism is a way of life, an alternative to religion. Let us develop a non-religious way of life for a post-religious society . . . let us not be satisfied with the separation of religion and politics . . . Let us alleviate human suffering, dispel superstitions, wipe out illiteracy, fight racial discrimination. Injustice anywhere is a threat to justice everywhere. Let us wage a relentless war against poverty, injustice and inequalities . . . Let us all work unitedly to make the world a better place to live in — free from poverty, war, injustice and superstition. (*The Atheist*, 1986, p. 92f)

The Indian Secular Society, begun in 1959 by A.B. Shah (1920-1981), challenged the inequities between men and women in Hindu society, for while Hinduism admonishes men to honor women, the honor is that "bestowed by superiors upon those who serve them well" (Noss, p. 194).

The Rationalist Association, formed in Bombay in 1930, is one of several such groups operating in Madras and Calcutta and in Sri Lanka. Through magazines such as *The Radical Humanist* and *Samiksha*, Atheist and Humanist groups continue to wage intellectual battles against what they recognize as Hindu superstitions, and against systems that deprive women and those still marked by caste regimentation of social equality (Innaiah, p. 345f). In 1970, the Indian Rationalist Association in Madras began publishing *Freethought* which was advertised as "The Largest Circulated Rationalist Monthly." Other Rationalist groups were formed in Sri Lanka, and throughout India in districts, towns and provinces.

These groups enlisted scientists and teachers to challenge popular superstitions. For example, in 1963, Dr. Abraham T. Kovoor (1896-1978), who became President of the Sri Lanka Rationalists, offered a reward of 100,000 Rupees to anyone who could demonstrate supernatural or miraculous powers. No one was able to claim the money. Dr. Kavoor had been a college science professor. In his passion for removing unfounded fears of the occult from people, he challenged the claims of astrologers, miracle performers, numerologists, necromancers and others, going so far as to sleep in so-called haunted houses and wandering in cemeteries where ghosts were supposed to have appeared. After Dr. Kavoor's death, Mr. A. Suryanarayana, who was then General Secretary of the Association and who had participated with Dr. Kovoor in four All India Divine Miracle Exposure Campaigns, renewed the offer of 100,000 Rupees and was able to retain control of the money.

The Indian Science and Rationalists Association with 86,000 members in 300 branches has since 1949 exposed fraudulent "godmen" who deceive the gullible public by "religious trickery." When Hindu believers in September 1995 flocked to temples to witness the "miracle" of religious idols drinking milk, the "guru busters" demonstrated that porous stones absorb many liquids by capillary attraction. Raised in numerous religions, most of the rationalists are now atheists and attack India's worst mystics in a broader assault on all religions, including Christian evangelists, while India resists rationalism. (Burns)

The Indian Humanist Union began publishing *Humanist Outlook*, a quarterly journal, in 1974. Its published aim was concern "with the promotion of the scientific attitude, ethical values, social reform and communal harmony." The Union, centered in Lucknow, is a member of the International Humanist and Ethical Union which has headquarters in Utrecht, Holland, and world-wide membership.

The Humanists, with their emphasis on the value of each individual human life, are also confrontative when infant females are killed. Females are considered to be of less value to the family than males inasmuch as males are better able to support their parents in old age. Furthermore, when the daughter matures and marries, her attention must be turned toward her husband's family. The pattern is also prevalent in China and it is estimated that there are 60 million fewer women in India and China than would be expected normally. The primary cause of this shortage is believed to be the result of female infanticide (Maugh).

In India, when a woman bears a female infant, the unwanted child is often murdered by her parents. Presently, easily accessible ultrasound clinics make it possible for physicians to determine the sex of a four months or older fetus. As the C.B.S. 60-Minutes program reported on Sunday, June 13, 1993, when it is determined that the fetus is female, it is usually aborted. The Humanists of India struggle to abolish such unethical and barbaric attitudes and practices.

The denigration of females is also manifested in the more than 5,000 deaths-by-burning of young married women. As we noted above, the bride becomes part of the husband's family. When money becomes a crucial issue, the bride is often pressured by her husband and her in-laws to find some way to increase the dowry. Failure can result in the young woman being doused with gasoline or other inflammable liquid and being set afire. At times, the bride will pour the flammable liquid on herself and commit suicide. In the rural villages, female infanticide is not uncommon. Some baby girls are smothered, some have poisonous liquids such as the sap of the oleander mixed with castor oil forced down their throats, some have their necks broken (Dahlberg, 1994). Why? Because it costs money to raise a girl who, when she marries, will require a dowry and will contribute nothing to her parental family. Threats of prosecution and government programs designed to aid families when girls are born have had only limited success. Nor have Christian field workers had much impact. The ancient Hindu teachings about the value of a female when combined with dire economic situations negate the impact of humanistic teachings about the worth of all humans — male and female.

Women are consigned to the most menial forms of drudgery. Those of us who have witnessed rural life in India, have seen village women, up to their elbows, mixing clay and sacred cow dung (which every articulate Indian guide will label "holy shit") to form, for example, basins for watering animals. Or the woman might carry on her head a load of sacred cow droppings which are to be added to the stack of manure patties near her residence. Gandhi may have been right in his time to employ household yarn-making and weaving in the battle against colonial industrial patterns. In our age of high technology it is disturbing, to those committed to human dignity and freedom, to find women working for endless hours at tasks that could be accomplished in minutes by machine, thus freeing the women from tedious bondage. On the other hand, it is important to note that many Indian women are well-educated and hold important posts in industry, government and education. They are not bound by ancient traditions.

One of the most serious and most destructive attitudes towards women is related to the prostitution industry — some of which is condoned and carried out under the aegis of the temple and the priesthood in the name of Hindu goddess worship (Drogan). Today, the increase in AIDS through prostitution has become a serious health threat in India — particularly in Bombay and Madras. Secular health authorities battle ignorance, indifference, dismissal of health claims and profiteering by business men and Hindu priests as they seek to stem the rising tide of life-threatening infections. Children who are victims of rape or incest are exiled from rural villages and end up as captive prostitutes, held in cages by their captors. Some are victims of kidnapping or have been sold into bondage by their parents. Ruthless Hindu priests compel *devadasi*, the female devotees to the Hindu goddess of fertility, to become common prostitutes for hire. In return, the women receive little more than food, clothing and a place to sleep. The AIDS epidemic, which was in its early stages in 1992-93, is spreading rapidly through sexual contact into the homes of business people and workers who frequent the prostitutes. The number of medical practitioners trained in dealing with AIDS is limited and some have deep concerns for their own health as they seek to treat the disease. Once again, the Humanists of India, with their desire to change the continuing demeaning of women, face an overwhelming enemy in the greed of profiteers as well as in ancient customs, beliefs, and religion.

In the northern state of Bihar (between Calcutta and New Delhi), the authority of Hindu theology is being challenged and the ancient caste hierarchy is beginning to crumble. The Untouchables, who prefer to be called Dalits or the Oppressed and who constitute 18 percent of India's 870 million population, are in armed revolt. Over the centuries, as victims of a divine slavery ordained by Hindu rebirth theology, they have been subjected to barbaric violence and degrading practices by members of the upper classes. Sons have been sold and wives and daughters violated. Employment opportunities have been limited to such humiliating tasks as toilet cleaning and corpse burning. Wages earned have been denied. The caste war that has been building in full ferocity in Bihar, as the Dalits act in self-defense, is now spreading to neighboring states. (McGirk)

Challenging and rejecting the notion, that the status of Untouchables is ordained and determined by misdeeds in a previous life, is no longer limited to Indian humanistic movements. As the Dalits think for themselves, they are beginning to experience the liberating power of freethought. Perhaps their rebellion will move India's constitution, which bans discrimination based on untouchability, from legal language to living reality. However, only time will tell whether Dalit freethought and challenge to Hindu authoritarian theology will achieve their emancipation from degradation.

References

Ajniat, Surendra C.I., "Status of Women in Hindu Scriptures," *Freethought*, Vol. 5, Nos. 11-12, November-December 1975, pp. 144-46.

Arvon, Henri, *Buddhism*, trans. by Douglas Scott. New York: Walker and Company, 1964.

Auboyer, Jeannine, *Daily Life in Ancient India from 200 B.C. to 700 A.D.* London: Weidenfeld and Nicolson, 1961.

Bharati, Agehananda, *The Ochre Robe*. Garden City, New York: Doubleday & Company, Inc., 1970 (Anchor Book).

Bharati, Agehananda, "Hinduism and Unbelief" in: Gordon Stein, edit., *The Encyclopedia of Unbelief*. Buffalo, New York: Prometheus Books, 1985, Vol, I, pp. 314-321.

Bhatty, M.R., "Book Review: *Old Testament of Indian Atheism* by Prof. Surndra Ajnat," *Freethought*, Vol. IX, No. 1, January 1979, p. 29.

Burns, John F., "'Guru Busters' Debunk India's Holy Charlatans," *San Francisco Chronicle*, October 11, 1995, p. C1.

Dahlberg, John-Thor, "India Pilgrims Gather to Annoint Statue," *Los Angeles Times*, December 20, 1993, p. A7.

Dahlberg, John-Thor, "Fight to Save India's Baby Girls," *Los Angeles Times*, February 22, 1994, pp. A1, 14.

Dart, John, "Home of the Buddha: Diggings May be Lost City," *Los Angeles Times*, October 17, 1976.

Davids, T.W. Rhys, translator, *The Questions of King Milinda*. New York: Dover Publications, Inc., 2 vols, 1963.

de Bary, W.T., edit. *Sources of Indian Tradition*. New York: Columbia University Press, 1961.

Drogan, Bob, "Bombay - Epicenter of Disaster," *Los Angeles* Times, November 26, 1992, pp. A1, 10.

Finegan, Jack, *The Archeology of World Religions*. Princeton, New Jersey: Princeton University Press, 1952.

Graetz, H, *History of the Jews* (six volumes). Philadelphia: The Jewish Publication Society of America, 1893.

Hansen, Bent Smidt, "In Respect for Periyar Ramaswami" in Janarthanam, edit., *The Periyar Memorial Souvenir*. Madras: Arooran Printers, 1973. (n.p.)

Hesse, Hermann, *Siddharta*, trans. by Hilda Rosner. New York: New Directions Publishing Corporation and Bantam Books, Inc., 1978.

Hoffmann, Yoel, *The Sound of One Hand*. New York: Basic Books, Inc., 1975.

Innaiah, N., "India, Unbelief in" in: Gordon Stein, edit., *The Encyclopedia of Unbelief*. Buffalo, New York: Prometheus Books, 1985, Vol, I, pp. 343-346.

Ions, Veronica, *Indian Mythology*. London: Paul Hamlyn Limited, 1967.

James, M.R., *The Apocryphal New Testament*. Oxford: The Clarendon Press, 1953.

Janarthanam, A.P., *The Periyar Memorial Souvenir*. Madras: Arooan Printers, 1974.

Kirk, James A., *Stories of the Hindus*. New York: The Macmillan Company, 1972.

Kosambi, D.D., *Ancient India: A History of its Culture and Civilization.* Cleveland, Ohio: The World Publishing Company (A Meridian Book), 1969.

Mahathera, Narada, *Buddhism in a Nutshell.* Honolulu, Hawaii: First Chinese Buddhist Association, 1973.

Maugh II, Thomas H., "Researchers Find Widespread Infanticide of Girls in India," *Los Angeles Times*, February 9, 1992, p. A12.

McGirk, Tim, "India's Caste Conflict Turns Radical," *San Francisco Examiner*, February 5, 1995, p. C-10.

Newbigin, Lesslie, *A South India Diary*. London: S.C.M. Press, 1951.

Noss, John B., *Man's Religions*. London: Collier-Macmillan, 1969.

Paul, Rajaiah, *The Cross Over India*. London: S.C.M. Press, Ltd, 1952.

Periya, Narayana, "Religion—the Enemy of Woman," *Freethought*, Vol. 5, Nos. 11-12, November-December, 1975, p. 150.

Rao, G. Ramachandra, (Gora), *An Atheist With Gandhi*. Ahmedabad: Navajivan Publishing House, 1951.

Rao, G. Ramachandra, (Gora), "Untouchability—Problem and Solution," *The Atheist*, Vijayawada, India, November-December, 1975, pp. 129-134.

Rao, G. Sambasiva, "A Critical Survey: The History of Atheism in Andhra," *The Atheist*, Vijayawada, India, January, 1970, pp. 5-8.

Rao, G. Sambasiva, "Atheism in India—Ancient and Modern," *The Atheist*, Vijayawada, India, December, 1976, pp. 129-132.

Rao, G. Sambasiva., "Do I have a Soul?" *The Atheist*, Vijayawada, India, October-November, 1988, pp. 91-100.

Renou, Louis, *Religions of Ancient India*. New York: Schoken Books, 1968.

Subramanian, M.K. "Creative Destruction in Self-Respect Philosophy," *The Periyar Memorial Souvenir.* Madras: Arooran Printers, 1974.

Van Beek, G.W., "Ophir," *The Interpreter's Dictionary of the Bible*. Nashville: Abingdon Press, 1962, Vol. 3 (K-Q) pp. 605-606.

Waghorne, Joanne Punzo, Norman Cutler, Vasudha Narayanan, edits., *Gods of Flesh/Gods of Stone*. Chambersburg, Pennsylvania: Anima Publications, 1985.

Wheeler, Sir Mortimer, "Ancient India" in: Stuart Piggott, edit., *The Dawn of Civilization*, New York: McGraw-Hill Book Company, 1961, pp. 229-252.

Wheeler, Sir Mortimer, *The Indus Civilization*. Cambridge: Cambridge University Press, 3rd, edition, 1968.

14
China

❖

Beginnings

About 1,700,000 years ago, according to dating by Chinese prehistorians, what may be the earliest specimen of *homo erectus* in China lived in caves in Yunnan in South China. This Yuan-mo Man, as he has been labelled, produced primitive stone tools. Archaeologists have also found evidence from 600,000 years ago of hominids who lived in the Lan-t'ien district. Lan-t'ien Man (*Sinanthropus lantienensis*) was a hunter and tool-maker dwelling in small communities. Some 100,000 years later, this hominid line appears to have died out and was replaced by Peking Man (*Sinanthropus pekinensis* or "Chinese Man of Peking"), a cave-dwelling tool-maker and hunter who controlled fire. About 200,000 years ago, Neanderthal type humans inhabited what today is the Hubai province and still later, about 100,00 years ago, the Guangdong region (Elisseeff, 9. 13). Although there are still large gaps in the history of humans in China, it was about 50,000 years ago that modern man (*Homo sapiens*) appeared. His physical remains, found in the so-called Upper Cave Man deposits at Chou-k'ou-tien, suggest that he was the physical equivalent of modern races (Watson, 1974, p. 18f), as well as being one of the ancestors of the modern Chinese.

The Neolithic period in China began about 10,000 years ago. The excavation of Neolithic villages of the Yang Shao culture on the Yellow River in Honan and South Shansi indicates that, although hunting (they used the bow and arrow) and fishing were still part of the culture, the tilling of the soil to produce millet, and the raising of pigs, cattle and goats provided for survival needs.

Only limited archaeological evidence of belief patterns have survived from this early period, but images found on painted pottery suggest that there was belief in supernatural powers that could affect survival. For example, schematic patterns combining human faces and fishes suggest that "Behind these drawings lies fisherman's magic, intended to increase the catch, the human face representing perhaps a god particularly concerned with this branch of fertility" (Watson, 1974,

p. 27). Crescent-shaped stones found with other grave gifts in human interments appear to be forerunners of those later described in written sources as symbols of the heavens. The worship of the heavens and the earth, apparently well established by this time, was the forerunner of what was to become a central part of later Chinese religion as evidenced in the great Altar of Heaven in Peking (Ellwood, p. 153). The discovery of burned scapulae of sheep at K'ai-jui-chuang gives evidence of the practice of scapulimancy, which is divination by means of interpreting cracks that appear in shoulder blades scorched by fire (Chang, p. 100). Just what rituals may have been involved or how interpretations were made cannot be known, but perhaps this was the beginning of the use of oracle bones (described below).

About 3000 B.C.E. in the Middle Neolithic period, the Lungshan culture developed in northeast China. These people were farmers growing millet and wheat and raising cattle, sheep, pigs and dogs. They also hunted and fished. They had learned to harvest the silk from silkworms from which they wove fabrics. According to legend, it was from this group that the first Chinese dynasty, the Xia, developed.

Chinese written history purports to record dynastic history back to the Xia Dynasty in the late Neolithic period — about 2000 to 1500 B.C.E., depending upon which of three ancient chronological systems is accepted; but it is not until the Bronze Age, with the coming of the Shang dynasty, that a correlation between archaeology and historical tradition can be established. According to traditional chronology, the Shang dynasty is dated 1766-1122 B.C.E.; but according to the chronology of "The Annals of the Bamboo Books" (which may have originated during the third century B.C.E. but were discovered in a tomb from 281 C.E.) the dates are 1558-1050 B.C.E., and in the revised chronology of the Bamboo Books, 1523-1027 B.C.E. (Finegan, p. 321)

In any case, Chinese culture had entered the Bronze Age. Most of the people were farmers who lived in villages. Walled cities had come into being, suggesting the presence of engineers and authorities who organized massive labor gangs. Among the important artifacts from the period found at Anyang in northern Honan were the so-called "ritual bronzes." These vessels, decorated with theomorphic patterns, were used in ancestor cult rituals. Inscriptions often contain the name of a parent and express the wish that the vessel might be used for thousands of years. Weird and fantastic figures are also displayed, suggesting that beyond the worship of ancestors some echo of fears of powerful, non-human forces are being depicted.

The discovery of "oracle bones," some of which can be dated to the 13th century B.C.E., give insight into the practice of consulting the spirits of dead ancestors. Although more than 100,000 oracle bones have been found and some 37,000 have been studied, many were permanently lost during the 19th century C.E. when they were popularly labeled "dragon bones" and were believed to have magical medicinal powers. Consequently, they were ground up and sold in apothecary shops.

Oracle bones consisted of pieces of oxbone or tortoise shell inscribed with questions. The inscribed bones had been subjected to heat to produce a T-shaped crack which, apparently, could be read or interpreted as giving either a positive or negative answer. Just how responses were determined is not known. The questions, which would always be simple and answerable by a simple "yes" or "no," included queries about wars, farming, illness, trips and sacrifice. In addition to the questions, the names of ancestors and the identities of elemental powers such as the north or the south, earth, wind, and so on, were inscribed. Specific deities are named, including Shang Ti, who was associated with rain and war and fortune. In the Zhou period, which followed the Shang period (1122-221 B.C.E), Shang Ti was united with the Zhou god of heaven, T'ian, to become the chief deity (Finegan, pp. 321-329). The references to various diseases and maladies, for which the unseen powers were consulted for advice and guidance, "shows the extent to which ancient Chinese medicine was also imbued with the notion that diseases were sent by gods and demons." (Thorwald, p. 234)

Shang monarchs consulted ancestral spirits as well as the gods of the Four Quarters and the supreme god, Shang Ti. Animal and human sacrifices were made to encourage response. Some oracle bones depict scenes of human sacrifice. A decoration on a Shang bronze axe depicts one man holding a dagger-ax across the throat of another. The axe also pictures the steamer that was used with oracle bones along with an inscription meaning "to sacrifice." The discovery at Anyang of the mass burials of decapitated persons provides evidence of human sacrifice (Finegan, p. 329). Excavation of the burial pits of the rich and powerful reveal that, when these persons were buried, retainers and animals were sacrificed and buried with them, perhaps to serve them in some afterlife. The presence of useful artifacts in graves may also be interpreted as representing the need for such objects in a life beyond death.

In 1027 B.C.E., an invasion from the north by the Zhou people ended the Shang period. Subsequently, the country was divided into feudal states and, by the beginning of the 8th century B.C.E., there were some 200 independent principalities, each controlled by nobility, worked by serfs, and each owing loyalty to the monarch. Tensions and rivalries developed and the continuing state of warfare which ensued was condemned by philosophers, including Confucius (see below). Watson claims that the state religion "centered on sacrifice to Heaven and Earth. Its chief instruments were still the bronze vessels in which meats and wine were offered to cosmic and ancestral spirits" (Watson, 1961, p. 272). It was during the Zhou period that the concept of the *Yang* and the *Yin*, the interacting energy forces of the cosmos, came into being.

The term *Yang* means "the bright side of the hill" and is described as masculine in character — active, procreative, warm, dry, bright and strong. Examples of Yang include the heavens, summer, joy and life itself, and Yang is manifested in anything containing heat such as fire. *Yin*, on the other hand, means "the dark side of the hill" and is described as female, and denotes life in a lower or slower energy mode. It has the qualities of the dark, cold, wet, mysterious, secret, fertile and negative in nature. It is seen in shadows, the quiescent, the dormant. A single object may manifest both qualities. A dead piece of wood, rotting on a dark forest floor reveals the Yin but, when placed in a fire to burn, manifests the Yang. The concept is not limited to inanimate objects. Humans in various interactions manifest both Yin and Yang. When these basic energy-modes are translated into the field of ethics, they can be recognized in positive or perhaps "good" behavior (Yang) and negative, or evil behavior (Yin).

In 221 B.C.E., the country was united. The feudal principality of Qin, run by a single family, had become so powerful that it was able to take control of China (the name China is derived from Qin). Now the nation was sub-divided into 36 provinces or states, each ruled by a military defender and a governor. The uneasiness of the rule is reflected in the introduction of literary censorship. Books had to deal with medicine or agriculture or farming and could not in any sense be critical of the government; otherwise they were labeled "useless" and were consigned to the fire. It was at this time that the 1500-mile-long great wall of China with its 25,000 watch towers was constructed as a bulwark against the encroachment of nomads from the north. Among those sentenced to the labor gangs were authors of forbidden books or those who refused to turn over so-called "useless" writings.

Confucianism

The name "Confucius" is a Latinized version given, by sixteenth to seventeenth century Jesuit missionaries, to the great teacher the Chinese know as K'ung-fu-tzu (551-479 B.C.E.), the Master of the K'ung family. The most reliable source of information about Confucius is found in the *Analects*, a collection of his sayings made by his disciples.

Later tradition, most of which cannot be substantiated, has provided the following biographical details. Confucius was born (about 551 B.C.E.) into a poor family of aristocratic refugees who had fled from the province of Sung to Lu (Shantung) following a political revolution. Shortly after his birth, his father died. His mother, despite straitened circumstances, saw that her son received education befitting a gentleman. Confucius' interests included classical music which he played on a lute, poetry, Chinese history and sportsmanship. His mother died when Confucius was in his mid-twenties. By this time he had already served as a local tax collector for the Lu government and had married and fathered a son. Following the death of his mother, he observed the required 27 months of mourning, but when, at the end of that period, he took up his lute, he found he could not play. Therefore he extended the mourning period an extra five days, thus becoming a classical model of filial devotion.

Now, he began his career as a teacher with a band of disciples, some of whom were sons of influential families. He taught poetry, history, music, propriety, divination and government, insisting that his principles could affect change only if he and his followers entered government service. One tradition asserts that, when he was 50 years old, Confucius served the Duke of Lu in a series of offices ranging from public works, through the ministry of justice to the rank of prime minister when, due to intrigue, he "lost face" and resigned (Noss, p. 278). Subsequently, he and some of his disciples roamed from state to state for thirteen years, giving advice to and being entertained by the feudal lords, but with no real support for his teachings. Indeed, like other great teachers, he is supposed to have been persecuted and scorned. Finally, in 484 B.C.E, when he was sixty-seven years of age, he was invited to become an occasional consultant to the court of Lu.

His last years were spent in retirement during which, according to a late and rather shaky tradition, he compiled the Confucian classics: The Book of History (*Shu Ching*), the Book of Poetry (*Shih Ching*), the Book of Rites (*Li Chi*), The Book of Music (*Yueh*) which is now Chapter ten of the *Li Chi*, The Book of Changes (*I Ching*), and the Annals of Spring and Autumn (*Ch'un Ch'iu*). There is substantial evidence to demonstrate that the basic materials in these sources were in existence and used in the education of nobility before Confucius. If we can accept the tradition that Confucius drew upon these sources, then his originality consisted in editorial changes and in culling from them the guiding principles which he made the property of the common man. He defined his own role as that of a student who loved the classics and as a transmitter of their wisdom. He died in 479 B.C.E. Many of his sayings and aphorisms were collected by his followers in the *Lun-Yu* or, as the Jesuits were to label the work, "The Analects," which is a purely secular work.

In the *Lun-Yu*, Confucius taught that individuals should act in the right way because of the inner moral law (*tao*) and the concept of *i*, which constitutes a categorical imperative. That is to say, that humans are to act morally in accord with the inner law, not to gain some advantage (*li*), nor with regard to success or failure, but simply because of *i*. Such action is the proper way to behave. The result or consequence of the act is determined by fate (*ming*), over which humans have no control.

Confucius lived when the power of the Zhou dynasty was weakening — a period marked by chaos with increased lawlessness and social disintegration and uneasiness as traditional customs and modes of behavior were breaking down. From ideas current in his day, Confucius sought to create for the ruling class a system of ethics with values that would provide moral guidance for the populace. He was indifferent to metaphysics and logic, and taught that "Moral integrity, loyalty and fearless advocacy of just and selfless rule are the distinctive characteristics of the Chuntzu, the 'superior man'" (Watson, 1961, p. 273). At first, his principles were accepted only by a group of disciples and it was not until some two centuries later that his teachings were widely recognized. Unfortunately, by that time changes had been introduced that transformed his value system "From a cry for human righteousness . . . to a plea for social regimentation" (Browne, p. 209).

Confucius was a humanist. His central concern was for human well-being. He believed that humans alone were responsible for solving societal problems. He was an agnostic in that he acknowledged "ignorance as to the gods and indifference toward religious rites" (Browne p. 210). He was an atheist in that he directed his teaching toward life without acknowledging the influence of gods. He was a practical teacher in that he could use the common, popular verbiage, even if it reflected religious beliefs, to convey his message. For example, in discussing the function of the ruler in the Li-Ki, he acknowledged:

> Heaven produces the seasons. Earth produces the sources of wealth. Man is begotten by his father and instructed by his teacher. The ruler correctly uses these four agencies, and

> therefore he stands in the place where there is no error. (Browne, p. 226)

The references to heaven and earth could be understood theologically as a reference to Shang Ti, but in Confucius thought they reflected nothing more than the implication of "a rational cosmic order with which rulers and subjects must passively conform in the interests of peace and welfare" (Watson, 1961, p. 273).

At the core of his ethical teachings is the concept of *jen*, a word written with two Chinese characters: the first representing "man", the other "two." *Jen* has been translated as "human-heartedness" and it is a term that pertains to the relationship between two people and signifies one individual's will to seek the good of the other. As one recognized the worth of another, no matter what the person's status, that recognition was expressed in kindly behavior. The *Li Chi* lists five basic relationships that developed out of Confucius' concept of reciprocal relationships (*shu*): they are between father and son, older brother and younger brother, husband and wife, elders and those younger, ruler and subject. The kindness expressed by the father is reciprocated by filial piety in the son. The gentility of the older brother is balanced by humility and respect from the younger. Proper behavior in the husband is responded to by wifely obedience. Elders should show consideration for others while juniors should defer to the old. Rulers should be benevolent, and ministers and subjects should be loyal. The foundation of these relationships is *jen*, which incorporates sincerity, loyalty and mutual respect, and which, when combined with *li*, calls for propriety or the observance of proper relational behavior. The fact that the first three of the relationships are familial underscores the importance of family in Chinese culture — a culture in which even today several generations may share a common home. Confucius is reputed to have said:

> In ministering to parents, a child may on occasion gently disagree with them. When it is clear that their will is not to heed the argument, the child should, nevertheless, continue to show them reverent respect, never obstinacy. And should this cause distress, let it be borne without murmuring. (Analects, IV)

As with other teachers, Confucius was confronted with a request for a simple formula. His disciple Tzu-kung wanted one single word to serve as a guide for the ethical life. Confucius chose *shu*, the principle of reciprocity, which involves mutual respect, adding in explanation, "What you do not want done to yourself, do not do to others" (Analects, XV.23).

Confucian ethics, when applied to those in power, called on rulers to first regulate their own families, which required the sincere development of personal values. These same values would then be extended into government. His idealistic belief in what Noss has labeled "government by moral example" prompted him to say: "Guide the people by law, keep them in line by punishment, and they may shun crime, but they will be shameless. Guide them by mind, keep them in line by courtesy, and they will learn shame and grow good." (Noss, p. 288)

Confucius was not hostile to and did not oppose the religious beliefs of his time; rather he appears to have accepted them as a social reality that impacted but peripherally on his life. He could speak of acting in accordance with the "will of Heaven," but such a phrase cannot be taken as anything more than expressing his feeling of being on the right track in terms of current thought. He had no opinion or was agnostic concerning prayer and an afterlife. Certainly, secular ethics was at the core of the movement he founded.

Following Confucius' death, his disciples appear to have scattered, but within a few years established their own independent schools. Among those who continued the Confucian tradition was Tzu Ssu, the founder's grandson. The work of Confucius' disciples also involved the collection of the master's sayings and the compilation of the Confucian Classics listed above.

The Confucian philosophy was developed toward a "less exclusive humanism" by Meng K'o, who is better known as Mencius (372-289 B.C.E.). A legend associated with Mencius' childhood reflects his teaching that environment affects human life. According to the story, his father died when Mencius was a child. He lived with his mother near a cemetery. When she discovered that he had developed a propensity for playing games associated with attending funerals, she moved to a house near a market. Now Mencius began to play at being a merchant and at buying and selling. His mother again moved, this time near a school. As she expected, Mencius began to behave like the students and teachers.

Mencius became a student in a school led by disciples of the Tzu Ssu. Like Confucius, he became an itinerant teacher, wandering from state to state seeking to persuade rulers to follow the way of Confucius. When his mission failed, he retired to his home town of T'sou where he taught and wrote until his death.

Mencius' teachings started from the idea that human nature is intrinsically good. All humans have within the self four inborn fundamental qualities. These are humanity or human compassion, right action or the shame of not doing the right thing, propriety or the sense of respect, and wisdom or moral awareness. Humans have, therefore, the responsibility to develop these qualities to produce human goodheartedness to govern social relationships. In other words, within each person is the innate predisposition toward moral order. Although he would not have endorsed rebellion against a corrupt ruler, he did state that the will of heaven in the choice of a successor to the Zhou kingship would be declared through the voice of the people, by which he meant the ruling class, the literati and the land owners.

Hsun-tzu (c. 298-238 B.C.E.) rejected Mencius' notion on innate human goodness and denied that Heaven had anything like a personal concern for human affairs. He taught that man was evil by nature and only became good through being taught goodness. He endorsed ceremonials and rules of proper conduct and taught that the state should enforce *li* education upon the people. Without a proper teacher, the human disposition is towards violence and disorder. Through education, humans learn to discern between the good and the evil and between truth and falsity.

So far as Heaven (Ti'en) was concerned, Hsun-tzu taught that it had nothing to do with the ways of human life. To pray for rain and get rain was a useless action, because it was going to rain anyway. The coming of the rain had nothing to do with the prayers. Prayers were meaningless rites, because Ti'en had no power to affect the well-being of human life. Natural events occur because of natural law. Divination and supernaturalism were meaningless activities for neither the gods nor demons nor ancestral spirits exist. Rites associated with funerals might have beneficent effects in that they evoke emotions associated with memories which might have a societal cathartic effect. Sacrificial ceremonies might be beneficial as expressions of human feeling and might induce responses of loyalty, reverence, awareness of love and beauty. Hsun-tzu saw these as expressions of propriety and perhaps as endorsing patterns of proper conduct, all of which could have benefits if not carried to wasteful extremes, such as the burning of the carriages that carried the dead and the burial of objects of value with the dead. But, apart from the aesthetic and moral values, there were no supernatural benefits to be acquired through these rituals.

It was not until the Han dynasty (206 B.C.E. to 220 C.E.), that it became apparent that government did not function well when structured solely on legalistic grounds. The first Han emperor, Han Gaozu, was uneducated and among those he appointed to governmental office were Confucian scholars. As we have noted, during the Qin dynasty, a ban on books had been ordered. In 191 B.C.E., Gaozu lifted this ban and some Confucian texts were rewritten from memory. Subsequently, it was found that there was a need for legalism and hence legalism and Confucianism, although seemingly opposite, were linked. Confucian scholars were placed in charge of the training of officials in a government-sponsored program and thereby initiated a two-thousand-year pattern of influence in social and governmental life.

Of course changes did occur. As we have noted, legalism was introduced as bureaucratic patterns developed. The image of Confucius underwent change and he became, in public thought, something more than a mere human. The teachings of Mo-tzu (see below) crept into the system with the argument that, to succeed, the government needed the approval of Ti'en, the Heavens above, as well as that of the spirits.

In 630 C.E., the Emperor T'ai Tsung decreed that every prefecture in China must raise a temple to Confucius. In the eighth century, images of Confucius and portraits of his followers were officially placed in the halls of state temples. With these changes Confucian religion achieved the status of a state cult and the temples began to look more and more like their Buddhist counterparts. In 1530 a reaction developed and the Ming emperor, Chia Ching, reversed the trend and returned Confucian temples to something approaching their earlier simplicity.

With the advent of modern education in the twentieth century, the Confucian cult began to languish. Temples were abandoned. The Kuomintang or Nationalist Party that came into being after the 1911 revolution was committed to no religious group. Confucian values were endorsed including loyalty, correct attitudes, benevolence, fidelity, filial piety, humanitarianism, harmony, and peace. Even after Chiang Kai-shek became a Christian and inaugurated the New Life Movement in 1934, Confucian values were incorporated, including *Li* or courtesy, *I* or justice, *Lien* or integrity and *Ch'ih* self-respect. Where once Confucian portraits had been displayed, now there were pictures of Western heros including Pasteur, Newton, Galileo, Benjamin Franklin and others — all symbols of the new emerging China.

But all of this was to change with the coming of the Communist government. Confucius was honored for his innovations in private education, but for little else. It is estimated that strains of the Confucian ethic remain in the lives of modern Chinese people, combined with the official atheism reflected in the writings of Mao Tse-tung.

Taoism

Taoism (which means "the Way"), like Confucianism, originated in the late Chou period. Its origin is attributed to Lao-tzu ("The Old One") who is believed to have lived between 604 and 524 B.C.E., although there are those who question whether he ever existed. Like other culture heros whose ancestry is unknown, legends concerning his miraculous birth developed. From the best evidence available, and that is very limited, as an adult Lao-tzu appears to have lived a simple life, perhaps even a solitary life. The Confucian writings indicate that Confucius once sought out this older contemporary, and the record of the visit suggests that Confucius was baffled by Lao-tzu.

Only one writing is attributed to Lao-tzu: *Tao Te Ching* which translates as "The Way and Its Power." Most scholars question Lao-tzu's authorship of this one work and argue that it was composed in a later period. According to the legend associated with this document, Lao-tzu, disillusioned by his failure to persuade men to cultivate natural goodness, rode westward, on the back of a water buffalo, toward what is today Tibet. When he came to the Hankao Pass, a gatekeeper sought to dissuade him from leaving the country. Lao-tzu refused his request, but was persuaded to compose a record of his beliefs for those he was leaving behind. The result was the 5000 character *Tao Te Ching*. So ended the story of the life of Lao-tzu, the founder of Taoism.

What is the Tao? According to the *Tao Te Ching* it is undefinable ("hidden without a name"). The one who attempts to define it, does not know it, and the one who does know it, does not define it. Tao represents the undefinable mystical harmony that underlies all that is and, so far as humans are concerned, is expressed in action, in relationships and in the sense of unity and harmony with the universe. The one in harmony with the Tao will not seek fame or power or domination of others but will live in harmony with nature. The result will be one who, in life, expresses kindness, sincerity, simplicity, love of others and humility. The acquisition of these virtues does not come from the worship of the Tao, but through meditation. There is no place for war or violence in Taoism; rather there is a vision of international altruism.

In a sense, early Taoism was a form of escapism. Human society was evil and therefore one should abandon it and the chaos of its struggle. One should seek places of solitude in the mountains or other natural environments. At least this was the teaching of the fourth century thinker Yang Chu, whose teaching focussed on the self and the need to avoid injury and preserve life.

The emphasis on simplicity separated Taoists from Confucianists, and indeed, there is some evidence of rivalry. While there was a parallel in basic values, Confucian acceptance of ritual was offensive to Taoists. The Confucian focus on humanity and organized society was not adequate for Taoists, whose emphasis was on the natural world and natural simplicity which extended beyond humans.

During the succeeding centuries, Taoism was transformed by the introduction of magic. In the second century C.E., when Buddhism impacted most strongly in China, Taoism imitated the Buddhist pattern and became a religion. Soon temples were erected. Taoist writings were canonized and Lao-tze was divinized along with an acceptable group of associates. During the eleventh century C.E., there was added the notion of heaven and hell as well as a number of Chinese folkloric gods, including the popular Eight Immortals. Presently, the religion no longer exists in a formal sense, although its magical notions still continue to find expression in the thought and practice of many Chinese.

The Mohists

Shortly after the death of Confucius, Mo-tzu or Mo-Ti (c. 479-381 B.C.E.) developed a philosophy in opposition to that of Confucius. Although his school died out, he represents an important example of free, independent thinking, and a contributor to Chinese thought.

It appears that in his early life he was influenced by Confucian teachings, but he broke away to develop a more democratic perspective of relationships. He argued that Confucian ethics were harmful to society and rejected the Confucian notion of graded relations as the basis for society. As a substitute, he called for the conception of an all-embracing love. This love is not emotional affection but an intellectual and utilitarian love. He believed that familial affection should be extended to unite all in an altruistic fellowship devoted to common welfare. In other words, universal love combined with a commitment to pacifism were recognized as the cure-all for human woes. He believed that battles between states, families and individuals arose out of a lack of mutual love and mutual aid. The cure, which he claimed was not only in harmony with what Heaven desired for humans but was of practical benefit for all, was as follows:

> It is to regard the states of others as one's own, the houses of others as one's own, the person of others as one's self. When

feudal lords love one another, there will be no more war; when heads of houses love one another there will be no more mutual usurpation; when individuals love one another there will be no more mutual injury. When ruler and ruled love each other they will be gracious and loyal; when father and son love each other they will be affectionate and filial; when elder and younger brother love each other they will be harmonious. When all the people in the world love one another, then the strong will not overpower the weak, the many will not oppress the few, the wealthy will not mock the poor, the honored will not disdain the humble, and the cunning will not deceive the simple. And it is all due to mutual love that calamities, strifes, complaints, and hatred are prevented from arising. (Quoted in Noss, p. 295)

Mo-tzu accepted the idea of a supreme god who loves all humans and whose will is that humans should love one another. After his death, just as he anticipated, Mo-Tzu's philosophy was attacked by Confucianists and Taoists as impractical.

Buddhism

Buddhism, which began in India during the sixth century B.C.E., entered China during the Han dynasty (first century C.E.) through traders and missionaries who travelled the Silk route, the famous road that linked China to the Middle East and Europe.

As the Han dynasty moved toward a troubled end (3rd century C.E.), the Confucian emphasis on proper conduct, duty, and the virtues of public or familial service seemed empty. Buddhism promised escape from the cycle of life with its suffering by way of following the paths of meditation that led to enlightenment and peace. By the fifth century C.E., despite opposition from Confucian followers, Buddhist temples and monasteries were thriving and Buddhist centers became rich in property in China.

The imported religion brought representatives of both Hinayana and Mahayana Indian sects. Ultimately, several main Chinese sects evolved. *T'ien t'ai* or Heavenly Terrace Buddhism was founded by Chih-k'ai in the sixth century C.E. and received its name from the mountain where the chief monastery was located. It combined an emphasis on meditation and a philosophy, drew from both Hinayana and Mahayana sects to produce a rationalist approach and argued that the Buddha taught differently at different stages of his life. The fullest revelation came in the *Lotus of the Good Land*, where it is revealed that Buddha is the manifestation of an all-pervading cosmic principle. All beings, from the tiniest to the largest can manifest their Buddha nature and become Buddhas ultimately. Thus the relativity, the contingency and the internal contradictions of all things imply a ladder of ascent. There is a simple truth for those who accept the reality and values of the material world; a higher level of truth for those who, in confusion, seek to live a spiritual life in a material world; and a third level for seekers who employ meditation to discern the truths of Buddha's teachings.

Pure Land Buddhism (*Ching-tu*) stresses faith, rather than works, as the means of entry to a western-concept paradise as taught by Amitabha Buddha. Faith in Amitabha and the repetition of his name in the formula "Hail, Amitabha Buddha" (*Namu Omito Fo*) are all that is required. According to tradition, the sect was founded in 402 C.E. as The White Lotus Society by Hui-yan. Its expansion appears to have begun through the work of T'an-luan (476-542 C.E.), a convert from Taoism.

The *Ch'an* or Meditation school was imported from India, probably in the sixth century. The school rejects the validity of insight that comes out of lectures, reading, and good works, although these aids are used. True insight comes from meditation that results in insight or awakening. In Japan, the Ch'an sect became known as Zen Buddhism.

The True Word School (*Chen yen*), derived primarily from Indian Tantric Buddhism, arrived in China early in the eighth century. It emphasized the magic of incantations, formulas, charms, charts or mandalas, gestures, and liturgies and rites (including exploding firecrackers), plus belief in the efficacy of a pantheon of male and female Buddhist saviors to produce a good life, cure disease, control weather and so forth. Although the school still exists in modern China, it is really not approved by the Communist government. Indeed, Buddhism is officially looked at as a "foreign religious import" that led its followers to deny the reality of the work-a-day world.

Christianity

In 1514, the first Portuguese ships reached China and by 1557 the Portuguese had established a coastal colony at Macao. Soon Jesuit missionaries opened missions to convert the Chinese. Because they introduced European mathematics and astronomy, they drew some people to their centers. It was not until the conversion of Chiang Kai-shek in 1934 and the inauguration of the New Life Movement, that Christianity received any sort of real recognition in China. This recognition was short-lived. With the coming-to-power of the Communists in 1949 and the death of Chiang Kai-shek, who with his generals abdicated to Taiwan, the influence of the Christian church faded to what is believed to be a mere handful of families who secretly cling to their beliefs.

Materialistic Communism

Materialistic Communism dominates the life of China. History, including the history of the religions in China, has been rewritten to show the negative contributions of faith systems and the very few positive contributions they may have made. The teachings of Mao Tse-tung (1893-1976) have replaced those of Confucius. While one can have no argument with the right of a people to choose any form of government they may desire, the fact that Chinese Communism is an imposed and harshly controlling system denies any potential for choice. Atheism imposed by dictatorial decree is no more acceptable than Islam or Christianity or any other belief system that is imposed on a people.

Recent events have indicated that there is a stirring within the huge nation for a democratic voice in the system. Should this small voice for free choice be heard, should change come and should a democratic system of government finally emerge, there can be little doubt that some of the traditional religions of China will find a new voice — a voice vastly changed in a world that is committed to science and freethought. There can be no question that atheism will remain as a vital part of Chinese thought — an ethical atheism, one would hope, inspired by a modern value system that grows out of the teachings of Chinese seers like Confucius and that embraces a free and open democratic political system.

References

Browne, Lewis, *The World's Great Scriptures*. New York: The Macmillan Company, 1946.

Chang, Kwang-Chih, *The Archaeology of Ancient China*. New Haven, Conn.: Yale University Press, 1963.

Creel, Herrlee G., *What is Taoism?* Chicago: University of Chicago Press, 1970.

Elisseeff, Danielle and Vadime, *New Discoveries in China*. Secaucus, New Jersey: Chartwell Books, Inc. 1983.

Ellwood, Robert S., *Many Peoples, Many Faiths*. Englewood Cliffs, New Jersey: Prentice-Hall, Inc., 1976.

Finegan, Jack, *Archeology of World Religions*. Princeton, New Jersey: University of Princeton Press, 1952.

Hutchinson, John A., *Paths of Faith*. New York: McGraw-Hill Book Company, 1981.

Legge, James, Translator, *The Texts of Taoism*. 2 vols. New York: Dover Publications, Inc. 1962.

Noss, John B., *Man's Religions* (Fourth edition). New York: The Macmillan Company, 1969.

Thorwald, Jurgen, *Science and Secrets of Early Medicine*. London: Thames and Hudson, Ltd., 1962.

Watson, William, "A Cycle of Cathay" in: Stuart Piggott, edit., *The Dawn of Civilization*. New York: McGraw-Hill Book Company, 1961, pp. 253-300.

Watson, William, *Ancient China*. Greenwich, Conn., New York Graphic Society, 1974.

15

Japan: Land of the Rising Sun

Myths of Beginnings

According to Japanese mythology, as told in the *Kojiki* (The Record of Ancient Tales) written in 712 C.E., in the beginning there was chaos, symbolized as an ocean of mud. Out of chaos came three *kami*, the invisible spiritual powers. Then came others, in pairs, male and female, and in particular two *kami* who are mentioned in the *Nihongi* (The Chronicles of Japan) written in 720 C.E.: *Izanagi* (the male who invites) who became the sky father, and *Izanami* (the female who invites), who became the earth mother. These two were commissioned to create the world. Descending the Floating Bridge of Heaven, which may have been a rainbow, and using a jeweled spear, Izanagi thrust the spear deep into the oceanic mud. As he withdrew the spear the droplets fell from the tip to become the island Onogoro ("self-coagulating"). This account "is one of the earliest suggestions of phallicism in Japanese mythology" (Piggott, p. 15).

After they had erected a palace and a pillar, Izanagi and Izanami descended to the island and made it their home. Then Izanagi asked Izanami, "How is thy body formed?" She replied, "My body grows in all parts, except one." Izanagi said, "Mine also grows in all parts but in one especially. It is good that we should join this part of my body with that part of thine which does not grow. In this way we will engender countries." His sister replied, "Truly it would be good." He then proposed that they should go around the pillar of their house in opposite directions. This they did and found themselves face to face and Izanami exclaimed, "Oh! What a fine man!" and Izanagi said, "Oh! What a beautiful woman!" and they were united. Now the fact that the first words had been spoken by a woman signified a breach of ritual. Izanagi said, "I am a man, and by right I must speak first. How is it that thou, a woman, spoke first? This brings bad luck!" Therefore, they produced several islands and deities. One of the offspring was an ugly, puny boy named Hiruko. He was placed in a basket and abandoned to the waves of the ocean. Subsequently, they repeated the ritual and this time Izanagi spoke first and the error was corrected. Before her death Izanami gave birth to numerous *kami* of the sea, the waves, mountains, the islands of Japan and so on.

The myth continues with Izanagi's visit to Izanami in the underworld. On his return he created Amaterasu, the sun goddess, from his left eye and from his right eye he brought forth Tsukiyomo-no-Mikoto, the moon god. From his nose came Susanowo, the storm god. Obviously, the myth is more than an explanation of creation. It has social overtones in that it clearly gives the female secondary status. In addition, it provides the basis for the belief that nature is *kami*-infested — an idea that is most important in Japanese religion.

During the subsequent struggle for power among the gods, the sun goddess, Amaterasu, animated the world, giving life to everything. Her jealous brother, the storm god, wrought destruction on the growing things. In distress, Amaterasu took refuge in a cave, and consequently, with the disappearance of the sun, all was in darkness. To coax her from the cave, the *kami* presented her with a mirror and a string of sparkling jewels. After she emerged, the cycle of day and night was regenerated and she related the reasons for her disappearance. Her brother, Susanowo, was banished to earth and became the progenitor of the Japanese people.

Not everything pertaining to Susanowo is negative. In one account he is said to have killed an eight headed dragon that had eaten a minor female goddess each year. This he accomplished by stupefying the dragon with eight bowls of *sake* which, according to one version, was poisoned. In the tail of the dragon Susanowo found an iron sword which was to become part of the imperial regalia.

Much later (according to pious tradition), when Amaterasu sent her grandson Ninigi to take control of the islands of Japan, she presented him with the symbols of divine power: the mirror, the jewel and the iron sword. Her charge to Ninigi was: "The Luxuriant Land of Reed Plains is a country which our descendants are to inherit. Go, therefore, Our Imperial Grandson, and rule over it! And may Our Imperial lineage continue unbroken and prosperous, coeternal with heaven and Earth!" Ninigi conquered the descendants of the storm god and became the first emperor. Thus was born the legend of the divinity of the emperor of Japan — a legend that existed for centuries until it collapsed after World War II, when the Emperor admitted that he was not divine and that therefore the myth was nothing more than a religious concoction.

Beginnings

The real beginnings of human life in Japan were in the Neolithic period, some 10,000 years ago, with the immigration of a Caucasoid people. About 8,000 B.C.E., other migrants came, probably from Korea. The discovery of fishhooks, harpoons, discarded shells, together with animal bones and stone objects such as axes, scrapers, picks and knives suggest that the newcomers were primarily fishers and hunter-gatherers, although they may have practiced some simple hoe-culture agriculture. Handmade pottery vessels were decorated by pressing twisted cords into the wet clay to produce a design called "jomon" or "rope-pattern" which provided the name for the culture: Jomon. Clay figurines, called *dogu*, combine human and animal forms and may have been used for magico-religious purposes.

It is believed that the remnants of the Jomon culture are today represented by the aboriginal Ainus who live on the northern isle of Hokkaido. The religion of present-day Ainus may reflect earlier belief patterns. These people are animists and worshippers of nature. Almost every object is believed to be inhabited by some personal intelligent life. The highest celestial deity is the sun; the most important earth deity is the fire or hearth goddess called "Fuji" which means "ancestress." Perhaps, because the famous Japanese volcanic mountain is also called Fuji, it was once an object of worship. (Finegan, p. 42) Over against the beneficent powers in the clouds, seas and vegetation, are demonic spirits that can be exorcised.

The Jomon culture gave way to the Yayoi (200 B.C.E.-250 C.E.) which was initiated by invaders from Korea. The Yayoi soon developed settled agricultural wet-rice communities located on the Yamato plain and the island of Honshu. They had domesticated animals, including the horse, and it is supposed that mounted warriors armed with weapons made of iron and bronze easily uprooted the primitive stone age Jomons. In their huge dolmen-type graves, metal artifacts which included swords, spears, bells, mirrors and crowns, wheel-made pottery together with terra-cotta figurines of armor-clad warriors, suggest that perhaps the culture was governed by a male, supported by warriors. Other clay figurines consisted of cylinders surmounted by the bust of a male or female. According to chronicles written by ancient Chinese visitors to Japan, following a period of turmoil in the third century C.E., a woman named Pimiko assumed power. "She was a shaman who lived in seclusion with a thousand female attendants and a single male, who mediated between her and the outside world; this sorceress-queen remained unmarried and 'bewitched the populace.'" (Ellwood, p. 30)

In the sixth century C.E., Japan looked to Korea and, ultimately, to China for cultural and technological advancement. Along with the important social contributions, it received Confucian ideas and moral concepts including the emphasis on filial devotion. Ancestor worship, which had been part of earlier Japanese culture, now emerged with new vigor, accompanied by the mythic notion that the emperor was descended from the sun-goddess and that all Japanese were descendants of related deities. Thus was laid the basis for the divine status of the emperor and the belief that the entire nation was of a single divine family — truly a nation of gods and under a god.

Buddhism

Buddhism was introduced during the sixth century C.E. when Emperor Kimmei Tenno received from the king of Korea a gold-plated copper statue of Buddha together with some sacred writings and artifacts. While it was politically correct to welcome this gift from a neighboring monarch, there was some uneasiness that the *kami*, the ancient or traditional native gods of Japan, might be offended by the introduction of a new religion. To test the hypothesis, the Buddha image was presented to the head of the Soga clan. When they experienced an outbreak of pestilence, it was assumed that the *kami* were, indeed, angered. The statue was discarded. Later, a second Korean monarch dispatched Buddhist priests, sacred texts and artisans to Japan. With the support of the Soga clan and in the spirit of diplomatic courtesy, permission was granted to construct a Buddhist temple. Once again, pestilence broke out and it was argued that this was surely evidence that the *kami* were upset. The Sogas, however, reversed the argument. They suggested that it was the Buddha who was upset by the lack of welcome. By the end of the century, through the efforts of Shotoku Taishi, a devout Buddhist who was a nephew of the Empress Suiko, Buddhism had been accepted by members of the Japanese royal court. Buddhist temples were built throughout the land and many common people became followers of the Buddha.

When Prince Shotuko (573-621) accepted Buddhism, he not only encouraged the building of Buddhist shrines, but also lectured and wrote treatises urging the Japanese to reverence Buddhism. His teachings also embraced Confucian ethics and ideals. The influence of the Chinese was also acknowledged in the adoption of the Chinese calendar and the Chinese hierarchical court system (Hutchinson, p. 245).

Buddhism developed rapidly within Japan during the centuries after Shotuko, particularly in the capital city of Nara. Toward the end of the eighth century, Buddhist monks began to interfere in governmental affairs, so a new capital was founded in 794 at Heian, the site of present-day Kyoto.

In 804, two Japanese monks visited Buddhist centers in China: Saicho (762-822), who became known as Dengyo Daishi; and Kukai (773-835), who was called Kobo Daishi (the term "daishi" means "great teacher"). Saicho returned to Japan with the doctrine of a Buddhist school that had been founded two centuries earlier on Mount Tendai in south China and which based worship on the Lotus Sutra and favored esoteric forms of Buddhism. This sect, which still flourishes in Japan today, has subdivided into some twenty different groups. Among these are Pure Land, Nichiren and Zen, each of which has its roots in the Tendai system.

Kukai, or Kobo Daishi, also spent his time in China in a Buddhist monastery. When he returned to Japan in 807, he founded the Shingon sect or "the Sect of Formulas," which drew from Tantric Buddhism (named after the *tantras* or canons in which formulas were recorded). Kukai located the Shingon monastery on Mount Koya. The use of symbols, spectacular rituals and art helped to popularize Buddhism. Indeed some of the folk deities that emerged in the sect included the popular Kwan-yin and Jizo, the Bodhisattvas dedicated to helping wanderers and women and children. Mystical or magical rites helped the priests achieve reputations as healers and diviners.

By the close of the twelfth century, which ends what is known as the Heian period (1192), the two sects were engaged in violent conflict. This was a time of social disruption marked with deep pessimism. The next period, called the Kamakura which continued until 1333, was also a time of pessimism. As if in response, Pure Land, Nichiren and Zen Buddhism came into prominence.

Belief in the saving power of Amida Buddhism had already developed within the Tendai sect. They taught that it was impossible for most humans to obtain enlightenment without help from the Buddha. Therefore, the individual would first have to be reborn in the Pure, Blessed Land of the West (*Gokuraku-jodo*) where the Amida Buddha preached. According to the zealous monk Honen (1133-1212), humans in their helpless depravity could not save themselves. The way to enter the pure land was to endlessly repeat the name of its Buddha: Namu Amida-butsu ("Glory to the Buddha Amida"). Honen's enthusiastic efforts to propagate the faith resulted in the formation of the Jodo sect and also earned him enemies. He was exiled with a group of disciples to northern Japan.

Shinran (1173-1262) was Honan's disciple. When he took a wife, he was exiled for violating the monastic vow of celibacy. He founded the Shin sect of Buddhism and with his followers argued that marriage brought them closer to the people they sought to influence. Shinran's teachings differed from those of his master. He focussed on inward faith. Name recitation was not essential. All that was needed was inner faith and belief in Amida's vow of salvation. It was this notion that gave rise to the Shin sect, whose appeal to the average layman was the movement away from the monastic ideal of earlier Buddhism.

The Nichiren sect was created by the monk Nichiren (1222-1282). He chided the Amida group for their devotion to a Buddha from a foreign land and for the neglect of the Japanese Buddha Sakyamuni, whose doctrines were drawn primarily from the exalted Lotus Sutra. In place of the homage paid to the Buddha of the west, the Nichiren Buddhist formula called for "Glory to the marvelous law of the Lotus Sutra." Hence the Lotus Sutra itself rather than the Buddha became an object of worship. The present day sect has some 35 groups and the largest following of Buddhists in Japan.

Zen, or the School of Meditative Buddhism, began in China in the Ch'an sect. When it was brought to Japan in the twelfth and thirteenth centuries, it encountered hostility. It was developed through Dogen, who started as a Tendai monk, and Essai who studied in China.

Dogen moved toward strict monasticism with an emphasis on discipline requiring concentration on each act and each moment of life, and the practice of meditation. For Dogen, enlightenment was earned gradually. His monks were taught to sit facing a bare wall, focussing on breathing and posture. From such a discipline, the believer hoped to discover the basic essence of nature, free from entangling awareness of self.

Essai was more flexible and did not focus on any particular scripture. Monks meditated facing one another, seeking the same experience. Unlike Dogen, Essai taught sudden enlightenment, that is that nirvana could be attained in a single lifetime. A tea drinking ritual emphasizing control and harmony with nature was introduced as a way of health. Zen ethics were drawn from Confucius. Zen also focussed on a work ethic teaching farmers, "One day no work, one day no food." (Hoffman, p. 9) Essai's Zen Buddhism posed puzzles (*koans*) as a way to sudden enlightenment. Questions were asked such as "What is the sound of one hand?" and students were taught how to respond. (Hoffman, p. 28)

With Buddhism came the rich cultural heritage of China that resulted in improved harbors, irrigation canals, reservoirs, roads and humanitarian outreach. Buddhism prospered in Japan and developed various schools. During the eighteenth and nineteenth centuries (the era of the Tokugawa Shoguns) when a revived Shinto religion challenged the people to return to the native belief system, Buddhism suffered a serious relapse. About this same time, Christian missionaries also sought to win converts from Buddhism.

Since World War II, the Nichiren group has spawned a new organization: the Soka Gakkai ("Value Creating Society") which has become the largest of the Nichiren sects. Like Tenrikyo, Soka Gakkai is classified as a "new religion." It appeals to the masses and is largely a layman's movement. It is this-worldly and involves believers in chanting, which is supposed to enable the individual to achieve results in the here-and-now.

Shinto

The earliest known use of the term "Shinto" is found in the *Nihongi* or "Chronicles of Japan" which were compiled and written in 720 C.E. The *Nihongi* purports to carry Japanese history back to 660 B.C.E., but scholars reject this date and suggest the earliest date should be about 40 C.E. In any case the text states that, during the reign of Tomei Tenno, the second successor of Kimmei:

> "The Emperor believed in the Law of Buddha and reverenced the Way of the Gods (Shinto)." The phrase "Way of the Gods" is a literal translation of "Shinto," *shin* (Chinese, *shen*) meaning "gods" and *to* (Chinese *tao*), "way." . . . The equivalent in pure Japanese of the basically Chinese name Shinto, is Kami no Michi. (Finegan, p. 436)

The title Kami no Michi means "The Kami Way" and therefore implies that Shinto is a symbolic representation of the Japanese way of life. As we have noted, the Ainu believed that all of nature was imbued with *kami*, the supernatural power and potency of the divine. The animistic religion embraced ritual magic either to induce beneficent responses from the spiritual powers or to ward off or exorcise evil. This religion, which permeated Japanese life, was without a theological structure and fed upon folk-tales and local myths.

With the coming of Confucianism and Buddhism, the desire to record and systematize prevalent Japanese myths arose. About 806 C.E., the *Kogushui* or "Gleanings from Ancient Stories" was written. Celestial *kami* and terrestrial *kami*, present in rocks and trees, were recognized. For example, the god of the Yamato area was Yamato-no-o-kuni-dama, "The Spirit of the Great Land of Yamato."

In the early myths, the sword, the jewels and the mirror had great significance. The mirror, the symbol of the sun goddess, Amaterasu, and the jewels, both originally gifts to Amaterasu, were deified. The legendary sword, called Kusa-nagi-no-tachi, "The Herb Quelling Great Sword," supposed to have come from the middle tail of an eight-headed serpent that had terrorized earth deities, was also a gift to Amaterasu. When it became time to build shrines to house these divine symbols, the original structures were little more than small, one-room huts for there were no congregational gatherings or rituals. Individual worshippers simply stood outside of the structure to pay homage or to present prayers and offerings to the *kami*.

According to the Nihongi, there was a plague during the reign of Sujin Tenno (230-258 C.E.). The emperor was uneasy about the proximity of the shrines of Amaterasu and Yamato-no-o-kuni-dama, both of which were located in the palace precincts. Therefore Amaterasu's shrine, together with the sacred mirror, the jewels and sword, was relocated at the village of Kasanuhi and the emperor's daughter was installed as high priestess. The shrine was later moved to Ise where it was thenceforth connected with the imperial house.

Simple Shinto shrine structures underwent change with the coming of Buddhism and Confucianism. They began to incorporate Buddhist temple designs with "complex symmetrical plans, southward orientation, surrounding walls and colonnades and gate buildings, painting, gilding, sculptural decorations, curving roof lines" (Finegan, p. 437). There was also a mingling of Buddhist thought to the point that *kami* and Buddhas were equated. For example, in the Shingon school of Buddhism, founded by Kobo Daishi, it was taught "that the Buddhas and Bodhisattvas appeared as various gods in different countries and had also appeared in Japan" (Noss, p. 322). Thus Shinto and Buddhism could be viewed as a single faith. Priests of some Buddhist sects reported visions in which Amaterasu was identified as a manifestation of the Buddha Maha-Vairocana (Noss, p. 322). Despite the tendency toward fusion, Shinto with its thirteen sects has remained a separate and distinctive religion in Japan.

Tenrikyo, (*tenri* = divine wisdom; *kyo* = religion) a sect of Shinto, was founded by a woman, Nakayama Miki (1798-1887). In 1837, she experienced a trance in which it was revealed that the divine resided in her and that she was to be used as an instrument to save the world. Following a pattern so familiar in oriental religions, she abandoned wealth for poverty. She engaged in a faith-healing ministry and introduced ecstatic dancing. She moved away from traditional Shinto in her emphasis on a single deity known as the Father-Mother God. After her death her teachings were gathered to become the canonical basis for the faith. The center of Tenrikyo is Tenri City, where the central shrine is said to include an area believed to be the originating place of the human race and to which all will return. The emphasis in the religion is positive. It denies sin and the idea that humans are born in sin. Only ignorance or illusion keeps people from being free and happy. The focus is on living a happy, fulfilled life here and now, free of disease and suffering. Despite the emphasis on this life, the notion of transmigration is still present. (Thomsen, p. 33f)

Tenrikyo is classified by researchers among the "new religions" of Japan, in that its syncretistic approach has attracted a number of post-World-War-II Japanese youth. Personal involvement in the cultic activities contrasts sharply with the impersonality of present day technological Japan and with worship at the traditional shrines. The emphasis on so-called "positive thinking" helps to move followers away from the despair and negativism of modern society.

Christianity

Catholic Christianity was first brought to Japan in 1549 by Francis Xavier and Jesuit missionaries. Franciscans followed soon after. Efforts to convert the Japanese met with success until 1600 when Tokugawa came to power. Then Christians were persecuted and tortured, and every effort was made to stamp out the religion. Nevertheless, when in 1868 Roman Catholic missionaries again came to Japan, they discovered that in some towns and villages *kakure Kirishtan*, "hidden Christians," had kept alive vestiges of the faith.

Post-World-War-II Japan

Recent events have impacted on traditional Japanese religion. In 1945, after the Americans dropped atomic bombs on the cities of Hiroshima and Nagasaki, the Japanese government acknowledged the first defeat of the nation in recorded history. On New Year's Day, 1946,

Emperor Hirohito issued an Imperial Rescript denying both his own purported divinity and the pre-war notion of the superiority of the Japanese over other people and nations. Political despotism was replaced with a democratic framework.

In November of that same year the Japanese Constitution provided for the complete separation of Church and State. No religious organization could receive any privilege from the State or exercise any political authority. The State could not engage in any religious education or engage in any religious activity, nor could public monies or property be used or appropriated for the benefit or use or maintenance of any religious institution or group.

Now, Japan was wide-open to the continuing impact of western culture, science, reading and philosophy. As a result, a growing disrespect for the claims of traditional religion developed. At one time, to have entertained doubts about the divinity of the emperor would have constituted blasphemy, impiety and a political crime. Today, those who may cling to any vestige of the idea that the emperor is descended from the sun or has any aura of divinity are considered to be clinging to outmoded ideas. Thus, for learned young Japanese attending one of the many recently founded universities, the claims of traditional religion belong to the past, not to the present or future. Imported traditional Christianity has little to offer. Its cosmology and creation mythology are out of touch with modern science, and its claims for a divine-human Jesus are considered to have no more validity than the Shinto exaltation of the emperor as a divine human. Buddhist discipline does not interest them.

According to the *World Christian Encyclopedia*, it estimated that, of the approximately 125,000,000 people of Japan, only about 40% affirm any affiliation with a religious organization or belief system. Buddhists claim about 16,450,000 followers, Shinto some 3,520,000, Christians about 3,000,000 and new religions (including Sect Shinto and new denominations of Buddhism) about 26,330,000. On the other hand, according to a poll taken by the prestigious daily press *Mainichi Shimbun*, January 4, 1986 and the Japanese Broadcasting Corporation in 1984, more than 85% of the Japanese have indigenous and basic religious sentiment — a sentiment that keeps many from any rigid personal commitment to a particular faith system, deity or dogma.

What has emerged is what Winston Davis has identified as a form of "civil religion." At one time the people were self-identified as descendants from the gods with a divine emperor which produced "the mystery of the ineffable National Essence (*kokutai*)" (Davis, 1992, p. 269). Today, the national character (*kokumin*) has replaced *kokutai*, and the uniqueness of Japanese society is set forth in "symbols, values, and imagery, produced by the literature of Japan theory." (Davis, *loc.cit.*) The ancient "way of the warrior" is replaced by the way of the international salaryman. The development of Japanese technology arises from the competitiveness of free market economy. Davis concludes his fascinating study with:

> The self-images we see emerging in contemporary Japan theory are not the finished products of a new ideology, but an ongoing search for a new national identity by a people whose economic enterprise has recouped what generals, gods, and a divine emperor previously lost. Although I have described Japan theory as a secularization of a civil religion, because secularization itself is not inevitably a one-way or irreversible process, it is conceivable that Japan theory, under new historical circumstances, will give birth to a new religious self-understanding, or perhaps even to a new civil religion. (p. 270)

Some aspects of the national identity have centered on the Yasukuni Shrine where more than 2,500,000 Japanese soldiers are interred. The shrine was initially established in the nineteenth century as a place sacred to the memory of those who were killed in the service of the emperor or the state. The memorial service held there, usually attended by an official of state including the emperor (who was God in the flesh), sought to invoke and appease the souls of the dead, but in time also enshrined the dead warriors as guardian deities of the state. Debates concerning the involvement of the state in the religious recognition of the dead warriors arose from the post World-War-II constitution with its emphasis on the separation of Church and State, because State involvement in any way at the shrine might be interpreted as endorsing Shinto as a state religion. Hence, it was suggested that, although state officials may visit the shrine as private individuals to honor the dead, they may not participate in any official way or seek to use public monies for the shrine. However, the rising nationalist spirit in Japan has moved away from this notion, and presently there is public honoring of the dead on every August 15th — a date that commemorates the termination of the Pacific War in 1945.

It is important to note that the spiritual gap that developed through the discarding of traditional faith systems, which had given identity, meaning and direction to life, did open the door to some unique developments. Following the war and during the 1960s new faith systems came into being. They drew from Buddhism, Shinto and

Christianity. These religions, which are new in the sense of recombining elements of the old, embraced modern evangelical presentational techniques and often developed new rituals. Like the youthful expressions of the 1960s in the western world, they stressed optimism, hope and joy. They reject negativism such as the idea of humans being sinners. Their colorful dances, ceremonies and celebrations were geared toward expressing the potential of peace and meaning in the here-and-now, rather than in some mythical future. They were dedicated to saving the world by conquering disease, expressing unity and concern for humanity. Some introduced the magical overtones of faith-healing. Heaven was to be found on earth, not in the sky. These "new religions" include Tenrikyo and Soka Gakkai, discussed above.

More recently, Japan has been exposed to western New Age occultism. Channelers, psychics, crystal therapists and faith healers from America seek to capitalize on the religious void. These persons claim to be channelers for everything from extra-terrestrials to Jesus Christ and dolphins (Larue, pp. 36-42). The influence of the animism of ancient Shinto has made it possible to woo some Japanese to these bizarre claims of spiritual authority. The complexity of life in overcrowded cities, with the stress of business and survival needs, have pressed some Japanese to look for magical answers to problems — answers that come through magical thinking. The rigidity of Japanese social teachings, and the lack of emphasis on personal self-worth, have provided ready listeners to the pop-psychology of so-called channelers. These individuals call for the freeing of self from whatever limits self-creativity. They talk vaguely about planetary and inter-planetary love as the solution to personal problems. New Age religion, with its emphasis on each person being a god-in-the-self, accords with the ancient Japanese religious teaching of a god-descended race.

New Age teachings have attracted a relatively small number of adherents — numbered in the hundreds of thousands in a nation of 125 million people. But the outreach is growing, much to the delight of channelers whose bank accounts soar with the excessive payments made by Japanese devotees. Unlike America, where New Age religion is challenged by Christians who label it Satanic, and by rationalists who label it nonsense, in Japan it is without serious challenge. An Osaka group, headed up by "Danny Manheim, an Israeli doctor of Chinese medicine, and Nobuhiko Sato, a Japanese real-estate baron," plans to build a series of New Age metaphysical resorts "combining vacation-like leisure with studies in nutrition and meditation, healing and channeling" (Watanabe, A13). New Ageism in Japan gives promise of becoming a lucrative business.

Skepticism in Japan

Skepticism in Japan is not a recent development. Indeed, each time a new development occurred in Shinto or Buddhism, that change represented a skeptical appraisal and rejection of other religious expressions. Now, with the advent of the so-called "new religions," the rejection of the old and the turning to the new reflects a skepticism of that which is traditional. At the same time, there are those who give token acknowledgment to tradition. On festive occasions, such as the new year, they go to the traditional shrines and embellish their homes with decorations. But there is no commitment. Such behavior reflects "this is the thing to do." They are much like many western families who may attend synagogue at Rosh Hoshannah or go to church on Easter Sunday, but avoid religion during the rest of the year. Some retain a magico-religious attitude. They consult mediums about weddings or business deals. They wear amulets that are designed to ensure good luck or that are supposed to help in finding a mate. Sometimes new cars are magically blessed by a Shingon priest. It is important to note that all of these activities are this-worldly — they are associated with getting something here and now. They represent the efforts to bring in magical help to acquire benefits for life and living.

Modern disbelief or complete rejection of religion appears to have had its beginnings early in this century. According to Charles Braden, a census taken in the University of Tokyo in the 1920s showed that, out of a total of 4,608 students, 2,989 listed themselves as agnostics, 1,511 as atheists and only 118 as adherents of Christianity, Buddhism or Shinto (p. 169). Unbelief has been augmented by recent events. What is lacking is a freethinker movement or center to provide unity and direction for these persons.

One other dimension of Japanese rejection of traditional religions needs to be mentioned. Progress in the Japanese educational system rests primarily upon memorization and regurgitation of prescribed materials. Little attention is given to critical thinking or to the encouragement of personal evaluation of life patterns. Further, the stress on technological innovation removes many young Japanese from associations that would invite introspection, philosophical examination, critical thinking or involvement in social concerns. The result is that many young, educated, financially successful Japanese are centered in a search for immediate satisfaction of the desire for personal happiness. They live primarily for "the day" so that entertainment and excitement become the keys to release from the work-a-day world. In the minds of some Japanese thinkers, these young people represent another dimension of New Ageism in Japan.

One residue from the past that continues to impact on Japanese society is the concept of *burakumin*. *Burakumin* is the practice of discrimination against persons based on the birthplace of ancestors. The term itself simply means "village people" but the implications are that these people are some sort of sub-species or even "non-human." The social rejection of *burakumin* rests in the ancient feudal ideology associated with Buddhism and Shinto together with a "philosophy of bloodline," according to Akinobu Tanimoto, general affairs director of the Buraku Liberation League (Jameson, p. A28). During the feudal period, the *burakumin* performed the "unclean" work for the warrior, farmer, artisan and merchant classes. This work included tasks such as butchering of animals and tanning of hides, which were considered beneath the dignity of the hereditary classes. As a consequence, the districts in which the *burakumin* lived were deprived of such amenities as properly paved roads and sanitation.

In 1871, the class system was abolished, but family registers continued to list "class origin" entries. Following World war II, the United States occupation forces ordered an end to the listing. Consequently, "the 'non-humans' of the feudal era became the 'new ordinary people' — a phraseology that suffered no loss of clarity in identifying *burakumin* origins." (Jameson, p. A29) It was not until the 1970's that the elimination of class origin entries on old family registers was completed. Nevertheless, the bias remains, affecting marriages, employment and education opportunities. The Buraku Liberation League, a secularist organization, seeks to have the government abolish the system of family registers, which trace family trees back for centuries and which enable the identification of *buraku* communities. However, the importance of the family as a social institution in Japan has thwarted this effort. Consequently, the *burakumin*, out of shame or embarrassment for their heritage, fail to participate in traditional family gatherings at family birthplaces, held at the time of the Japanese New Year or during the *o-bon* festival (a Buddhist, late summer, festival when the spirits of dead ancestors are believed to return and rejoin the living). Thus, class discrimination, rooted in ancient religious beliefs, continues to defy and inhibit the new humanism being manifested in Japan.

References

Braden, Charles S., *Modern Tendencies in World Religions*. New York: The Macmillan Company, 1933.

Clarke, Grahame, *World Prehistory: A New Outline*. Cambridge: University Press, 1969.

Czaja, Michael, *Gods of Myth and Stone: Phallicism in Japanese Folk Religion*. New York: Weatherhill, 1974.

Davis, Winston Bradley, *Toward Modernity: A Developmental Typology of Popular Religious Affiliation In Japan*. Cornell University East Asia Papers. Ithaca, New York: Cornell University, 1977.

Davis, Winston, *Japanese Religion and Society: Paradigms of Structure and Change*. New York: State University of New York Press, 1992.

Earhart, H. Byron, *Japanese Religion: Unity and Diversity*. Belmont, Calif.: Dickenson Publishing Company, Inc. 1969.

Earhart, H. Byron, *Gedatsu-Kai and Religion in Contemporary Japan*. Bloomington, Ind., Indiana University Press, 1989.

Eliseev, Serge, "The Mythology of Japan" in *Asiatic Mythologies*. New York: Crescent Books, 1963, pp. 385-448.

Ellwood, Robert S., Jr., *An Invitation to Japanese Civilization*. Belmont, Calif.: Wadsworth, Inc., 1980.

Finegan, Jack, *Archaeology of World Religions*. Princeton, New Jersey: Princeton University Press, 1952.

Hoffmann, Yoel, *The Sound of One Hand: 281 Zen Koans with Answers.* New York, Basic Books, 1975.

Hutchinson, John A., *Paths of Faith*. New York: McGraw-Hill, 1981.

Jamieson, Sam, "Japan's 'Untouchables' Suffer Invisible Stain," *The Los Angeles Times*, January 2, 1992, pp. A28-29.

Larue, Gerald A., *The Supernatural, The Bible and the Occult*. Buffalo, New York: Prometheus Books, 1990.

Mainichi Shimbun, Jan. 4, 1986 (Japanese Newspaper).

Noss, John B., *Man's Religions*. Toronto: The Macmillan Company, 1969.

Packard, Jerrold M., *Sons of Heaven*. London: Queen Anne Press, 1988.

Piggott, *Japanese Mythology*. New York: Paul Hamlyn, 1969. Public-opinion Poll Department of the NHK, edit., *Nihon-jin no*.

Saunders, E.D., and B. Frank, "Japan: Cults and Ceremonies" in: Pierre Grimal, edit., *Larousse World Mythologies*. Secaucus, New Jersey: Chartwell Books, Inc., 1965, pp. 293-333.

Shukyo Ishiki (Religious Consciousness of the Japanese). Tokyo: Japan Broadcasting and Publishing Corporation, 1984.

Thomsen, Harry, *The New Religions of Japan*. Westport, Conn.: Greenwood Press, 1963.

Watanabe, Teresa, "Japanese Buy American . . . Gurus, That Is," *The Los Angeles Times*, July 6, 1992, pp. A1,12,13.

16

Americans Before Columbus

Myths of Beginnings

As we begin our discussion of the development of religion and freethought in the Americas, it is important to consider and dismiss the imaginative and fictional claims made by theologians, psychics and others concerning the beginnings of life in the Americas. For example, when the Spanish first made contact with humans in the Western hemisphere, the problems raised for the European world were not primarily scientific, but theological. Because the Spanish were committed to the biblical world-view, it was necessary to fit the native people of America into this picture. Where were they mentioned in the Bible? If all human life had been destroyed by the Flood, from which of Noah's sons were the peoples of the Americas descended?

The question was answered in the 1569-1573 edition of *Biblia Poliglota* where a note indicated that the people of America descended from Shem, the son of Noah. Modern archaeology and literary research have produced solid evidence to show that the biblical flood story is religious fiction or a teaching story, related to and perhaps drawn from older Babylonian and Sumerian flood myths. Geologists have demonstrated that there is absolutely no geological evidence of a world-encompassing flood. Logic and reason have pointed out that, should the earth ever have been covered by waters to the depth of the tops of mountains, there is no reasonable explanation of where the waters went. Theological efforts to link life in the Americas with the Hebrew Bible fail because, like their Near Eastern contemporaries, the ancient Hebrews had no knowledge of the existence of the Americas.

Edgar Cayce is reputed to have been a "psychic" and was known as "the sleeping prophet." In Readings 364-3 and 440-5, he claimed that the ancient Atlantis lies beneath the waters of the Gulf of Mexico (Ferro and Grumley, p. 124f). Therefore, the ancient Greeks would have had contact with America. The notion is simply nonsense and is not accepted by any reputable scientist or scholar. Atlantis, as described by Plato in the *Critias* and the *Timaeus*, was an island lying outside the gates of Hercules. According to the legend, the ancient Atlanteans had developed a high culture before they offended the gods and were swallowed up by the sea. At present, the island of Santorini (Thera) in the Mediterranean is under excavation and some archaeologists cautiously venture the suggestion that this might be the place that Plato had in mind when he referred to Atlantis. As yet, no definite city landmarks or inscriptions have been found to support this hypothesis. Furthermore, the island is in the wrong place. According to Plato's description, Atlantis was to the west of the gates of Hercules which would put it in the Atlantic ocean; Santorini is to the east of the gates of Hercules and in the Mediterranean.

Nor was there ever a land called Mu, inhabited by Lemurians. Imaginary Mu was supposed to have existed in the Pacific ocean and to have included Australia, New Zealand and parts of the west coast of North America from Baja California to Southern Alaska. This particular non-historical aberration was created in 1936 by a Chicago homeopathic doctor, Robert D. Stelle. He was supposed to have received information about this mythical land through revelation.

Fiction science created by Swiss writer Eric Von Daniken suggested that extra-terrestrials visited the Americas and introduced unique cultural developments to the early inhabitants. For example, Von Daniken interpreted the lines in the earth created by humans at Nazca, Peru, as evidence of primitive airports where his imaginary non-earth beings from another galaxy could land their spacecraft. His theories have been thoroughly discredited and his writings should be read for entertainment, not as science or history.

Nor are the claims of the Book of Mormon concerning the migration of Hebrews to America at the end of the seventh century B.C.E. supported by archaeological and historical research. This particular theory is based on words which Joseph Smith, who founded the religion, is said to have translated from golden plates he is alleged to have found during the 19th century C.E. Other theories about the relationship of the Americas to Europe and Asia will be discussed later.

Our best information does not come from psychics or those who claim information received by inspiration or revelation. Nor does it come from writings that, like the Bible, are between 2000 and 3000 years old. Our most reliable source for understanding the past is based on careful historical and archaeological research. Archaeology utilizes proven technologies and the best scientific equipment, together with the skills of experts from various fields (anthropology, botany, chemistry, anatomy, physics, geology, medicine, etc.), to analyze and date material remains. Theories formulated by anthropologists and historians to explain how ancient Americans lived must fit the findings and the evidence. Such claims are always tentative; new discoveries may call for alterations in early theories.

What archaeological research has demonstrated is the magnificent adaptability of *Homo sapiens* in America. Various groups of people produced their own weapons, tools and equipment and learned to add agriculture to hunting and fishing to meet survival needs. Some developed massive communal projects and evolved their own cultural expressions in art, pottery, weaving and religion. The greatness that was ancient America is still being uncovered.

Beginnings: The Coming of the First Americans

Human life in America did not follow the long evolutionary patterns that can be traced in Europe, Asia and Africa. Sometime, perhaps as far back as 50,000 years ago or more, groups of human beings (*Homo sapiens*) began to follow the food chain of migrating animals from Northern Asia across the Bering Straits into North America. These migrations were made at different times during the ice age when the Bering straits were still a land bridge (called Beringia by some scholars), perhaps as wide as the state of Alaska (Haag, p. 270). The evidence indicates that the earliest arrivals in America are to be linked to the people of Asia.

The newcomers were Stone Age people who, with their primitive weapons, hunted the woolly mammoth, the American mastodon, the bison, the tapir, the camel, the peccary and the giant sloth in competition with other carnivores including the dire wolf, the saber-toothed cat and the American lion. Through corridors left by receding and advancing ice fields, they came in succeeding waves, moving ever southward into Central America. Perhaps, as has been suggested, some may have travelled by boat and followed the coast line.

The Amerindians, as they have been called, have proved to be of different Mongoloid affinities, including "the strong-featured Indians of the central plains and the smaller and highly specialized peoples who developed the Eskimo cultures" (Burland, p. 12). They did not come as conquerors or invaders, but as migrants to a land rich in game and wild edible plants. As they moved into the continent, some followed river valleys to become the Plains Indians. Evidence uncovered by Richard S. MacNeish of the Andover Foundation for Archaeological Research in Massachusetts indicates that around 30,000 years ago some of these people lived in caves in the proximity of Fort Bliss in New Mexico (Rensberger). Others pressed into Central and South America and ultimately founded the great cultures of the Mayans and Aztecs and Incas. It is known that by 10,000 B.C.E., the migrant humans had reached Monte Verde in Chile where they built hide-covered log huts. Evidence of human activity from the same period has been found elsewhere in South America — at Taima Tiama in Venezuela by Alan Bryan of the University of Alberta, Calgary; at Tequendama, El Abra and Tibito in Columbia by excavators from the National University of Bogota; at Los Toldos near Santa Cruz in Argentina by Augusto Cardich from the University of La Plata; and from even earlier periods, perhaps as far back as 50,000 years ago, at Pedra Furado in Brazil by archaeologist Niede Guido. (Long, 1994)

Free from the influences of Europe and Asia, the newcomers developed their own varied societal patterns. It was not until about 3,000 B.C.E., when the Alaskan climate was maximizing its warming period, that the last migrants from Siberia came and remained in the far north to become known as the Inuit (Eskimos). By 1000 B.C.E., they had spread across the Arctic from Alaska to Labrador, creating "a relatively comfortable way of life based on foraging from the natural bounty of the area" (Maxwell, p. 34).

It has been postulated that the true ancestors of North American Indians arrived about 11,500 years ago when the ice fields began to recede. Archaeologists have called these skilled New World hunters the Clovis people after their flint bi-facial, fluted, projectile point (the Clovis point) first discovered at Clovis, New Mexico. When used with a spear-throwing device known by its Aztec designation as the *atlatl*, the Clovis people were able to kill the giant mammoths (a similar device was used by Cro-Magnon man in France about 12,000 B.C.E. and is still used by aborigines in Australia). Indeed, the Clovis people have been accused of being responsible for wiping out these giant animals, although changes in climate must also have played a part.

Within a few hundred years superior weapons were manufactured. The finely worked, razor-sharp Folsom-type flint projectile points (first found near Folsom, New Mexico) became the new hunting tool. Hunters roamed the country in family-sized groups from Alaska to Chile and from the east to west coasts. They moved into the forests, the prairies and the deserts, existing on meat, fish, wild fruits and vegetables.

Dramatic climatic changes, marked by the end of the ice age, contributed to the extinction of numerous wild creatures that had served as food for humans. Gone were the woolly mammoths, mastodons, giant sloths, the American horse, and the camel (although relatives of the camel still exist in the Andes mountains as llamas, alpacas, guanacos and vicunas). When game became scarce, some groups turned to agriculture.

Of course, early Americans had already discovered and used wild agricultural products. Carbon dating of materials found in Danger Cave in southwest Utah, indicates that around 8000 B.C.E. these desert dwellers harvested and ground wild seeds, nuts, bulbs and acorns and wove baskets from plant fiber, and many anthropologists believe that these findings mark agricultural beginnings. Certainly, the evidence from the Cochise Culture of Arizona demonstrates that, within a few millennia, the skills of growing and harvesting corn, squash and beans had been fully developed. Excavations at the Bat Cave in Catron County, New Mexico, revealed that, between 3000 and 1750 B.C.E., the inhabitants had learned to manipulate genetically the size and quality of corn (maize). Similar evidence comes from Meso-American cave explorations. For example, the people who lived in caves near Tehuacan, Mexico, had a diet that included plant food such as steria grass seeds, wild avocado, prickly pear fruit, and so forth, as early as 5000 B.C.E.; and within a few millennia, they too were engaged in agriculture.

The earliest pottery made in the Western Hemisphere has been found at Taperinha, near the Amazon River in the Santarem region of Brazil. Anthropologist Clark Erickson of the University of Pennsylvania has dated the ceramic finds between 8,025 and 7,150 B.C.E., several thousand years before pottery was used elsewhere in the Americas. He believes that the Amazon residents first came about 12,000 years ago, having migrated south after crossing the Bering Straits. Their descendants remained in the area until the coming of Europeans. (Maugh, "Rain Forests")

As early as 4000 to 5000 B.C.E., tools and weapons were, for the first time, made of copper. Over the centuries, metalsmiths perfected their skills to produce finely-crafted awls, spearpoints, knives and so forth as well as decorative ornaments. Jewelry was made from shell, polished stone and bone. By now, some had moved from the hunting-gathering way of life to a sedentary existence in complex societies.

As settlements developed in select locales, territorial claims and interests developed. Leaders and specialists emerged within the groups. Sometimes independent tribes lived in harmony with one another, at other times they battled. In other words, like humans in all other cultures, indigenous Americans formed their own groups with unique social patterns, attitudes and relationships. It is estimated that several hundred distinct linguistic groups existed.

The First North Americans

By the time the Spaniards came to the Americas, the Indians of North America had developed three different ways of living that sometimes overlapped. Along the Pacific Coast from Oregon northward into Alaska and along the shores of the Gulf of Mexico from Texas to Florida, the primary means of subsistence was fishing. This is not to deny that some groups, like the Chumash in southern California, also engaged in hunting, but survival energy was, for the most part, directed toward the exploitation of the rivers and the sea. The greatest part of North America was occupied by hunter-gatherers. Inland, extending northward from the Gulf of Mexico in Texas, through most of Arizona and California to Alaska and the Northwest territories, and eastward across Canada to the Atlantic ocean, and in the United States from Northern California to the Great Lakes, the land was occupied by migratory tribal groups. Some groups remained in one area. For example, the Hopi of Arizona have occupied the mesas of the Southwest for more than 2,000 years. They built no permanent housing, but followed the movements of herds of game animals and the seasonal ripening of wild crops.

For centuries, the Great Plains had been sparsely populated due to drought. The climatic changes that occurred in the fifteenth century prompted migratory tribes to move into the area. For example, the Navajos moved into the Hopi lands at the Four Corners region of Arizona between 1500 and 1700. Settled village life tended to be limited to the fertile lands of the great river basins of the Mississippi and its tributaries. Here agricultural centers flourished. Pueblo villagers in Arizona and New Mexico also engaged in farming where some built dwellings of adobe, while others, like the Hopi, used native stone. A variety of crops resulted from the innovative adaptation of farming techniques to particular locales.

What archaeological research has demonstrated is that these first Americans, wherever they were located, exploited the natural environment, not for wealth or profit, but for survival. For example, the desert people utilized desert plants for fibers for weaving, local clays for pottery making and the sculpting of figurines. Settlers in the Great Lakes area discovered how to smelt copper and shape the metal into useful tools and weapons. Local timbers were carved into dug-out canoes. Shelters ranged from natural caves to structures built of adobe or stone, or dwellings made from branches and leaves and perhaps covered with animal skins. The creative talents were unlimited.

Tribal groups manifested a singular lack of individual possessiveness. Territory belonged to the tribe, not to the individual. The welfare of the tribe was the responsibility of each member. Tribal leaders were selected for their wisdom and ability to guide, but decisions were made in councils. Where tribal confederations existed, a common language, trade and intermarriage linked groups. But even where there was no such linkage, it is clear that extensive trade and barter were carried on among peoples separated by many hundreds of miles.

Unfortunately, for those who would trace Indian history, no written records of tribal migrations and development exist. The Iroquois kept wampum belts composed of shells strung in strands that could be used as mnemonic devices. The Ojibway pictorially recorded sequences of events on bark paintings. Totem poles carved and erected by the northwest Indians signaled the tribal totem and perhaps incorporated some facets of the local mythology. These sources, while useful, are inadequate for tracing social, cultural and religious development. Of course, archaeologists use modern tools for establishing dates, including tree ring dating and carbon 14 dating, but these techniques do not provide a history of events.

Some information comes from the excavation of graves. The ways in which bodies were prepared for burial reflect aspects of beliefs. Objects placed in the tombs provide evidence of trade. Developmental changes can be discerned in interment patterns. For example, the huge earthen burial mounds in the Ohio river valley, built by villagers between 500 B.C.E. and 350 C.E., are representative of the many thousands of prehistoric earthworks that dot the eastern half of the United States. These earthen creations rise to heights of 60 or 70 feet in some places and vary in form and structure from flat-topped pyramids to flowing outlines of animals. Exploration of the Ohio mounds has provided insight into the ways in which these structures developed.

The Adena people, who inhabited the Ohio Valley between 500 B.C.E. and 250 C.E., lived in circular houses made of poles lashed together with branches and which, with their thatched roofs, must have looked like inverted baskets. Adenas buried their dead in clay-lined pits over which they raised conical mounds. Sometimes the bodies had been exposed to the air prior to interment and only skeletal remains were buried.

The earliest graves were small and individual. They contained copper and clay artifacts and in some cases a headdress adorned with elk antlers. The mound above the grave was composed of multicolored clays which appear to have been brought from different locales —

perhaps in small containers — for deposit on the burial place. What these contributions of earth from different sites may have signified cannot be known, but obviously the custom had significance — perhaps religious, associated with the sacral nature of the earth; or perhaps territorial, related to tribal boundaries. In time the grave artifacts became more elaborate and included copper beads and bracelets, tubular stone pipes, wolf masks, mica ornaments and tablets with intricate engraved designs. Some males, perhaps those of high rank in the community, were buried in log crypts with elaborate grave goods including finely carved effigies.

Over time the mounds grew larger and larger until they become hillocks composed of numerous burials, layered one above the other, indicating long use of the site. Occasionally several small mounds were incorporated to become a larger mound. Some of the enlarged mounds were circular in shape. One, known as The Great Serpent Mound, was in the form of a huge uncoiling serpent, 1200 feet in length from tail to head.

As the Adena culture developed, great circular enclosures were constructed around some of the mounds. These appear to have been designed for ceremonial purposes which are, as yet, not understood. Adena culture spread southward from the Ohio valley but, for some unknown reason, began to go into decline during the first century C.E.

The Hopewell Mounds, constructed between 100 B.C.E. and 200 C.E. in the heartland of the Adena culture, ranged in size from 160 to 470 feet in length and from 20 to 32 feet in height (Prufer, p. 222). The excavation of these mounds provided archaeologists with treasures of finely crafted figurines made from stone, mica, clay, obsidian and copper.

> A single grave in the Turner mound group of Hamilton County, Ohio, yielded 12,000 pearls, 35,000 pearl beads, 20,000 shell beads and nuggets of copper, meteoric iron, and silver, as well as sheets of hammered gold, copper, and iron beads. From a mound at the Mound City group near Chillicothe came hundreds of pipes, copper figurines of birds, turtles, and humans, a mask made from fragments of a human skull, and a copper-covered wooden effigy of the death cup mushroom. In the Seip Mound in Ross County, excavators uncovered a copper ax weighing 28 pounds, a set of copper breastplates, more thousands of pearls, and a skull adorned with an artificial copper nose. (Maxwell, p. 40)

What beliefs might have prompted these people to envelope a corpse from head to foot with freshwater pearls or copper plate? What concepts were associated with entombment of the variety of artifacts extending from artistic statements to practical, everyday tools? Was the meaning of a headdress made from pieces of animal hide attached to a human skull related to shamanism? What was the significance of the square, circular or octagon shaped enclosures, some one-quarter mile in diameter, enclosing 20 or 30 conical mounds? Were the artifacts in the graves simply gifts to important persons? Were the items for use in some conjectured afterlife? Were the pearls and copper the possessions of the dead person infused with his or her personality or spirit? Why were the mounds constructed? Did they represent the community of the dead where spirits could commingle? Because no written records were made, there are no answers to these questions. Although the beliefs behind their attention to the burial of the dead cannot be known, the patterns point to complex belief systems. Archaeologists and anthropologists can only read their own interpretations and speculations into the finds. From the evidence, we can ascertain that the Hopewell people engaged in extensive trade and apparently lived peacefully in their communities.

In subsequent centuries, agriculture, particularly the growing of corn (maize), spread throughout the Mississippi valley and the southwest. Some of the agricultural communities were in existence when the Spanish, led by Hernando de Solo, visited the area between 1539 and 1547.

One of the largest agricultural communities was located at Cahokia, just north of East St. Louis, Illinois. In the early stages of development, this site embraced more than six square miles of fertile soil. Between 900 and 1250 it expanded and with satellite communities covered an area of 125 square miles. Over 100 mounds were built, some 26 of which now lie in downtown St. Louis. Extensive cornfields are believed to have supported a population of more than 20,000 people. Ultimately, forests were stripped and the land lost its fertility. When French settlers arrived during the 18th century, all that remained of the once magnificent culture were weed-covered mounds.

The largest Cahokia mound is Monk's Mound, named after the Trappist monks who lived there between 1809 and 1813. This mound, which covers 18 acres of land, was completely man-made and was constructed in 14 stages over a period of 300 years between 900 and 1250. It has four terraces and rises a hundred feet above the flatlands. The builders had no domesticated beasts of burden and one can only imagine the tremendous amount of human labor that must have been required to move an estimated 22 million cubic feet of earth. The huge pits from which the earth was taken are now lakes. On the top level was a large building (104 x 48-1/2 feet), which may have been used as a council chamber or perhaps was the residence of the leader. Smaller buildings on lower levels may have housed lesser officials or may have been used for administrative purposes. Below was a huge plaza area, perhaps designed for ceremonials or recreation. Beyond the plaza were smaller mounds. Houses were constructed of poles and branches and topped with steeply pitched thatched roofs. Interior walls were coated with mud and sometimes painted. Each dwelling had a central firepit for warmth, and it is assumed that cooking was done outside.

The rich assortment of artifacts provides evidence of the presence of skilled craftsmen who worked in clay, flint, metal, and stone to create weapons, tools, effigies and jewelry. Traders, hunters, fishermen and food gatherers made Cahokia a cultural and religious center.

Little can be known for certain about religious practices. Archaeologists have interpreted the location of certain wooden posts as part of an observatory by which an astronomer priest mights determine sunrises, solstices and equinoxes. This person would then decide the proper times for planting and harvesting of crops, for seasonal ceremonies and for rituals related to fertility and productivity.

The cultural heirs of the Cahokia were the Nachez. According to their traditions, the Cahokia ruler was a priest-king with absolute powers of life and death over his subjects. It was he who presided over games, rituals and special religious ceremonies. Beneath him was a cohort of priests and administrators. The excavation of Mound 72 revealed the burial place of one chief (although it is surmised that two others were buried nearby) who had been interred with a rich horde of grave goods. What was more significant was the uncovering of other entombments of which more than half were young women between 15 and 25 years of age, all of whom had been sacrificed. These women may have been the wives or concubines or servants of the deceased chieftain. What can be conjectured is that the religious beliefs were associated with agriculture, that the rituals may have been in part seasonal, and that the burial of men of power was accompanied by human sacrifice.

The religion of the Plains Indians can best be described as pantheistic. There was a general belief in a power or a Great Spirit that directed affairs on earth. In some tribal mythology, the Great Spirit was the creator, in others some other being did the creating having been delegated to do so by the Supreme Spirit. But spiritual powers were everywhere. The world was infused with the supernatural. Natural land configurations, celestial bodies, animals — all had spiritual dimensions that could affect the world of the human. For example, among the Ogala of the Teton division of the Dakota Indians, the infusing spirit was called *wakan*. Beyond the *wakan* of natural objects were eternal *wakan* beings to whom humans could turn for help. The Great Spirit was called *Nagi Wakan* and was associated with the sky (Walker, pp. 152-153). Among the Delaware Indians the great spirit was *Mani*, the creator, who lived above the earth (Harrington, pp. 18-19).

It was essential to live in harmony with these powers who could react to wrong behavior with punishment. What developed was a unique reverence for nature, for powers inherent in nature and for the ways in which human beings related to their environmental surroundings. The Plains Indians did not exploit the land and nature, but sought to live in harmonious relationship with their environment.

At puberty, through rituals of fasting, smoking tobacco and the experience of a vision, males acquired spirit guardians. The encounter with the supernatural might be manifested through something as environmentally normal as a bird or a lizard or by that which seemed to be unusual in nature — perhaps spectacular cloud formations. Men might also carry a pouch containing items believed to have magical power — bits of bark, pebbles, or perhaps some tribal token. Tribal rituals, led by a shaman, included sun dances, rain dances and war dances. Much of the information about tribal religion comes to us through the written records of traders, missionaries, military men, early newspaper accounts and anthropological/archaeological research.

Some sites have provided unusual data pertaining to the culture of certain groups. For example, the 600-year-old Mogolian Indian village called Casa Malpais, located at the 7,000 foot level in the White Mountains near Springerville, Arizona, provided archaeologist John Hohmann with architectural remains that reveal the builders' skills in design and in the use of local materials (Maugh, "Time Vaults"). The 50 foot square Great Kiva or ceremonial center, surrounded by a ten-foot-high wall made of closely fitted rocks and stones, was equipped with benches along the walls and a fire pit in the center. Here, for 150 years before their disappearance around 1400 C.E., the Mogolians held their religious celebrations. Close-by was a pueblo or multi-storied living complex with some 58 conjoined rooms plus many single-room structures. What is most fascinating is the way the Mogolians used a natural fissure in the basaltic lava as a repository for their dead. They partially reworked natural chambers to form what Hohmann has labelled "catacombs" where the dead were placed together with various artifacts. What cannot be known are the rituals performed in the kiva and the beliefs associated with the dead.

Nor can we know the rites employed by the Anasazis who constructed Pueblo Bonita in Chaco Canyon, between 920 and 1400 C.E. and the magnificent cliff dwellings at Mesa Verde, New Mexico between 700 and 1400 C.E. Both settlements were abandoned, perhaps because of drought, leaving only the buildings and artifacts for archaeologists to interpret. New pueblos were established by the Anasazis along the Colorado and Rio Grande Rivers. These were discovered by the Spanish as they moved northward from Mexico during the 16th century. Today, the descendants of the Anasazis are known as Hopi, Keres, Tanos, and Tewas (Dozier, pp. 113-137).

What is eminently clear is that there is no single "American Indian religion" — there are too many variations to make such an inclusive statement. To discuss Indian beliefs thoroughly would require the presentation of individual tribal concepts — a task far too extensive for consideration here. It is enough to note that there was a general idea that nature was infested with spiritual powers. It was an era of human history characterized by superstition and supernaturalism.

It is equally important to recognize the dramatic changes that took place with the coming of the Europeans. It has been argued that European biblical religion entertained a completely different attitude regarding the relationship of humans to the ecosystem. Europeans had been taught, on the basis of the Genesis creation myth, that humans were to exploit the earth, to "subdue" it. This notion, which has been challenged, conflicted with the reverential attitude towards the earth embraced by the Indians. During the nineteenth century, drastic changes took place, engendered by the coming of the railroad, the killing off of the buffalo, the introduction of the horse and European weaponry, products, disease and lust for territory. American Indian religion today is the diverse and variegated remnants of what once existed, comingled with the imported European Christianity. Efforts to maintain the validity of Indian religion in a technical age add further difficulties to the continuation of ancient faith observances.

The First Meso-Americans

The beginnings of human occupation in Meso-America paralleled those of northern America. However, in the broad strip of land that links North and South America, strong and independent cultural patterns were to emerge.

The Olmecs

During the period scholars label the Formative Period of Meso-American culture (1500 B.C.E. to 300 C.E.), people who today are called Olmecs laid the foundations for a new world civilization. One of their centers was located to the east of Mexico City and close to the Gulf coast near present-day San Lorenzo. Between 1200 and 900 B.C.E. huge blocks of basalt, some weighing as much as twenty tons, were hauled down the mountainsides and perhaps floated on rafts to the locale. Some were used in the construction of temples; others were carved into the now famous nine colossal heads. These huge, helmeted sculptings may have represented priest-rulers. Why they were made or what they signified we cannot know.

At its peak, the population of the rich Olmec agrarian culture may have numbered in the tens of thousands with territory embracing an area of more than 6,000 square miles. There appears to have been social stratification with peasant workers at the bottom, artisans and craftsmen in the middle, and above them the elite class composed of architects, town planners and governmental administrators who worked under the priest-rulers. Sometime around 900 B.C.E., San Lorenzo's prosperous era came to an abrupt end, evidently by violent destruction of the site.

Meanwhile, a new Olmec center, apparently with the same social structure, had come into being at La Venta, an island near the coast. The La Venta Olmec community began about 1000 B.C.E. and lasted until 300 B.C.E. Here crops, including gourds, squash, beans, maize, peppers and avocados were raised in accordance with a calendric system. Diet also included fish, crocodiles and aquatic birds from the rivers, plus wild forest animals such as monkeys, deer, wild pigs and pheasants. Like the San Lorenzo site, La Venta's end appears to have embodied violence, but a gradual decline can also be recognized.

Artifacts reveal the importance of the jaguar, the rain god. "Two sculpted monuments show a woman coupling with a jaguar." The cat-faced jade statuettes of plump babies — all with jaguar-like features — may represent the offspring of the sexual union, "the half-human, half-divine spirits of the rain." (Maxwell, p. 46) Along with the jaguar rain-god, the Olmecs worshipped the plumed serpent known as Quetzalcoatl who was later to become a central figure in Mayan religion.

The Quetzalcoatl myth, as it developed over time, is both varied and complex. Part of the name comes from the *quetzel*, which is a rare, seldom-seen bird with green feathers that lives in the treetops in Guatamalan highlands. The bird is unique in that it has only two front toes on each foot and almost no claws. The second part of the name, *coatl*, is the Nahua word for snake, but *coatl* is composed two terms: *co*, which means snake, and *atl*, which means water. The mythological Quetzalcoatl is a composite figure. He is at once water, serpent (which may signify earth) and bird (air). He is the messenger of the gods and the wind god. He can be linked to the planet Venus or to the sun. It was he who discovered maize and gave the gift of that life-sustaining food to humans. Indeed, the maize god, Cinteotl, is but another aspect of Quetzalcoatl.

Quetzalcoatl became a god-man. According to one myth, his mother is Coatlicue, the goddess of the skirted serpent, who was both mother of the sun and the sun's wife and sister. Having swallowed a feather (an emerald in another account), she became pregnant and gave birth to the Quetzalcoatl. Myths tell of his miraculous conception and birth, his childhood, his temptation, his yielding to becoming intoxicated with wine and the resulting carnal relationships with his sister. Having tarnished his ascetic purity, Quetzalcoatl repented, cast himself on his funeral pyre and was cremated. His heart rose to heaven to become the star Venus.

At a certain moment in history, Quetzalcoatl was believed to have become incarnate. In his human form, he was the compassionate and kind great lawgiver who civilized humans. As a god-man of peace, he could not hurt or harm any living creature and he refused to indulge in human sacrifice. In this role he became the earliest American role model of the highest humanistic ethic, evidencing concern for his fellow creature. Those who later became his priests were supposed to live humbly and in chastity. They were to be at peace with all and were to show compassion to all. Quetzalcoatl provides yet another version of the myth of a god incarnate.

The Mayans

Much of our knowledge of pre-Columbian culture and religion is owed to the Mayans, for about 50 C.E. these people began to produce the earliest writing in the Americas. From carved inscriptions on stele and from four sacred bark codices, historians have learned much about Mayan history and beliefs. The names of rulers like Pacal of Palenque, Bird Jaguar of Yaxchilan and Yax-Pac of Copan, among others, have been deciphered from monuments. One sacred text called Popul Vuh ("Book of Advice") was compiled in the dialect of the Quiche branch of the Mayans and preserved in Latin. This complex document embraces historical data intermingled with religious myth in a non-systematic fashion. For example, the creation myth begins with preexistent spiritual powers pervading the chaos. These beings establish the corners of the earth, the three layers of the sky with its thirteen heavens, the earth, the underworld with its seven hells, and the council of the seven solar gods who created by "word." Mayan cosmology pictured the world as a flat disc supported in a lily-strewn lake on the back of a giant crocodile. The sky above was held in place at its four corners by the gods. The gods began creation with vegetation, then went on to birds, serpents, and mountain spirits that were to be guardians of the plants. Finally, human beings were created to be worshippers of the gods.

Archaeological research suggests that Mayan farming may have begun in the lowland areas of central Mexico as early as 1800 B.C.E. In time, small farming villages came into being. The culture spread to embrace areas from the Pacific ocean to the Gulf of Mexico. In the rainy forest region of the Yucatan peninsula, Mayan civilization flowered. The earliest Mayan city known so far was located at Nakbe in northern Guatemala. Archaeologist Richard Hansen from the University of California, Los Angeles, believes that the city came into being as early as 630 B.C.E. when Mayans worked together to overcome harsh environmental conditions. Rainwater was funnelled into huge reservoirs because the nearest potable water was several hours away. To traverse the swamps massive causeways were constructed; some were 6,000 feet wide. Monumental architecture began around 300 B.C.E. with the construction of huge pyramid forms featuring sophisticated sculpting (Maugh, 1992). Elsewhere, between 100 B.C.E. and 200 C.E., some of the Mayan villages became small cities with palaces and pyramids. The so-called golden age of Mayan culture extended from about 250 to 900 C.E. — a period which scholars label "Classic." At least 40 cities with populations of more than 20,000 people each came into being. Estimates of Maya population in this period range from one million to three million. Somewhere about 900 C.E. the civilization collapsed — just why, no one really knows, but perhaps from internecine warfare, perhaps from over-exploitation of the ecosystem, perhaps from overpopulation together with the disintegration of the agricultural system and consequent malnutrition. When the Spanish arrived in the 16th century, the population had greatly diminished. Today, about 2 million people in Guatemala and Mexico speak assorted Mayan languages.

More than a dozen Mayan sites have been explored and many others are marked for future investigation. The city of Tikal was probably the grandest Mayan city. The remnants of its more than 3,000 structures, which include six huge temple pyramids (the tallest was over 200 feet) and seven temple palaces with their highly ornate decorations, plus the man-made reservoirs and ball courts, reflect the glory that was once the Mayan culture.

Seven separate Mayan calendars were based on astronomical observations. At a time when Europeans were still fixated with biblical calculations that placed the creation of the world and the beginning of time at 4004 B.C.E., Mayan computations extended back over millions of years. Their solar calendar of 365 days had 18 months of 20 days each with 5 intercalendric days. The five transition days, which characterized the death of the year, were marked by societal death symbols that included fasting and refraining from usual activities. In the 260 day religious calendar, each day was shown to be under the aegis of two gods. The calendar revealed which gods controlled any given day. Another calendar determined favorable days for planting, hunting and the performance of religious ceremonies. These calendars were controlled by the priests.

Like their Olmec predecessors, Mayans operated on a class system largely supported by peasant labor but augmented by extensive trade for the disposal of surpluses of foodstuffs, ornaments and so on. The top echelon included the priests and rulers who administered communal and religious affairs covering everything from astronomical observations to architectural styles, town planning, labor allocations and taxes. The support of the theocratic state, with its need for temples built to glorify kings plus the maintenance of a large priesthood, must have placed heavy economic demands on the populace.

The close relationship of religion and nature is reflected in the use of tobacco, in the burning of resin for incense and in the use of hallucinogenic mushrooms and peyote cactus in worship rites. These products of nature put the user in contact with the deities through visions and ecstasy. Blood rites were of great importance and included the torture of captives. Some prisoners were compelled to engage in a ball game in which the heads of losers could be used for balls. On important occasions, Mayan aristocrats drew their own blood in rituals, designed to nourish the gods or to inspire hallucinations of serpents through which they contacted the gods and the dead. Before going to war, for example, the king would puncture his penis with a stingray spine, while his wife drew a thornbarbed rope through her tongue. The Mayas believed such activities were vital for sustaining the universe. (Eckholm, p. 334)

The Toltecs

In the Post-Classic period (900-1500), sometime between the tenth and eleventh centuries, the Nahuatl-speaking people came from the north to central Mexico. One of their branch groups, the Toltecs ("Master-craftsmen"), under the leadership of Mixcoatl ("Cloud Serpent" = The Milky Way), became a dominant power between the tenth and twelfth centuries. These people, who glorified war and human sacrifice, founded Tula, a military and religious center, and Culhuacan, which became the capital. When they occupied the ruins of Teotihuacan, they adopted the worship of the god Quetzalcoatl ("Plumed Serpent").

The city of Teotihuacan ("City of the Gods") had begun as a collection of small separate farming settlements between 600 and 700 B.C.E. Sometime during the first two centuries B.C.E., these independent groups united to form an urban center. It was at this time that construction began on two of the largest structures in the city — the pyramids of the Sun and of the Moon — as well as a number of other buildings. By 350 C.E., 100,000 people lived in the city and, through conquests and trade, the eight square mile city became not only a commercial and religious center but a place where people from outside areas came to live. It was a hub of activity for artists and craftsmen and builders. As its fortunes grew, so did the population which reached 200,000 by 650. During the next century, the city began to fail and by the ninth century many of the buildings had been burned and were in ruins. What caused the devastation is not known.

The Toltecs were awed by the majestic ruins of Teotihuacan. They believed that the first gods, the Sun and the Moon, had been created there. When their leader, Mixcoatl, was murdered by his brother, Mixcoatl's widow was pregnant and bore a son Topiltzin ("Our Prince"), who became known as Ce Actl Topiltzin ("One Reed" — the year of his birth — "Prince"). He is described as having black hair and fair skin. In 965 he established his capital at Tula. Having been raised in the Quetzalcoatl cult, he adopted the name of the god, became the high priest and was regarded by many as Quezalcoatl incarnate — the god in flesh. When, as priest-king, he abolished human sacrifice and offered only animal sacrifices, he incurred the wrath of the followers of the fierce god Tezcatlipoca ("Smoking Mirror") whose cult supported human sacrifice. He was driven from Tula, but promised to return.

With a faithful retinue, Topiltzin travelled to the Yucatan, subjugated numerous cities, including Chichen Itza, and introduced Toltec traditions to Mayan culture. Mayan traditions speak of the arrival of

Kulkulcan ("Feathered Serpent") from the west and, inasmuch as Kulkulcan is a Mayan translation of Quetzalcoatl, it is assumed that the reference is to Topiltzin. Of course, the king did not return to Tula. The mythology stated that he set sail on a raft of entwined serpents, but that he would return to rule in the year Ce Actl (One Reed), the anniversary of his birth.

The tale has overtones of myths found in almost every culture. Like the Egyptian god Osiris, Topiltzin carried Toltec culture abroad. Like Jesus, he promised to return and rule at a later date. As we shall see, Mayan mythology was to have devastating results for the people when the Spaniards arrived.

The Aztecs

Disastrous droughts and famines triggered social upsets early in the 12th century. Nomadic Chichemec ("wandering") tribes from the north, invaded and destroyed what remained of Toltec hegemony. These Mexica (pronounced mesheeca, according to Thomas), whom the Spanish were to label "Aztecs" (because, according to legend, they came from a place called Aztlan — "Heron Place"), claimed that they moved into Toltec country because of a vision. About 1168 C.E., their patron deity, the fierce tribal war god Huitzilopochtli ("Hummingbird of the South"), appeared to a priest and demanded that the people migrate to a place where they would find an eagle perched on a cactus. There they were to build a city which would make them lords and kings. For a century and a half, the Mexica (Aztecs) wandered. Then, in the year 4-Coatl (1325), on an island in the middle of Lake Texcoco, they espied an eagle perched atop of a prickly pear cactus with a snake in its talons. This was accepted as a divine sign for the location of the city. The god told them to divide the city into four quadrants with his temple at the center.

On this twelve square mile piece of land, they began to build their empire. They drained and cultivated much of the marshy island and built the city of Tenochtitlan ("Cactus Rock"). Mud from the swamps was used to construct dwellings. To farm the area around the city, floating gardens or chinampas were built. The chinampas consisted of raised strips of land, 300 feet long and from 15 to 30 feet wide, completely surrounded by canals. The gardens, tended from canal boats, produced corn, squash, beans, tomatoes and chili peppers. Long causeways (one was over five miles long) formed land-links with surrounding islands. Soon, Tenochtitlan became a thriving city of some 250,000 people. This center of culture drew a multitude of visitors.

> Artists came seeking commissions from the nobility. Warriors came to win fame and fortune. Traders carried exotic treasures to its markets. Dignitaries paid visits of state. Priests and pilgrims visited its sacred shrines. Thieves, performers, tourists and prostitutes filled its busy streets. As the center of the empire, it was eulogized in Canteros Mexicanos, a collection of Aztec poetry:
>
> > Proud of itself is the city of Mexico-Tenochtitlan
> > Here no one fears to die in war.
> > Have this in mind, oh princes,
> > do not forget it.
> > Who could conquer Tenochtitlan?
> > Who could shake the foundations of heaven? (Day, p. 47)

From this island beginning, the Aztecs were to venture forth with their armies. By 1428, their empire extended from the Pacific to the Gulf of Mexico and they were the dominant power in Mexico. Aztec communities, called calpullis, were composed of families of different social ranks. On the lowest level were the slaves who were war captives, Aztecs who had fallen into debt, or those who had committed crimes. Above them were the serfs who worked the land they could not own. The majority of the population was composed of commoners who farmed the fields, wove the cloth and paid taxes in goods and services. On the top level were the officials and the nobles whose offices and ranks were inherited. These were the governmental officers, the priests and the warriors who lived off the tribute paid by those on lower social levels. Male children were educated in history and religion in local schools.

Between 1486 and 1502, the Aztec military emperor, Ahuitzotl, led Aztec armies through Mexico and Central America. In 1487, he dedicated the great temple to the war god Huitzilopochtli. To meet this deity's unquenchable thirst for human blood, some 20,000 prisoners of war were sacrificed in a ritual that lasted for eight days and nights. Indeed, these annual religious ceremonies made the Aztec rites among the most bloody in human history. Living victims were cut open and their hearts, still beating, were removed and held aloft for the blood-hungry gods. There is also some evidence pointing to cannibalism.

When the emperor Montezuma (Moctezuma) ruled (between 1502 and 1520), the Aztecs controlled some 5,000,000 people living in 80,000 square miles in central and southern Mexico.

Like the Mayans, the Aztecs produced literature written on bark pages and preserved in codex or book form. Spanish conquerors destroyed many of the codices; others were allowed to mildew and perish in the humid climate. From the few that remain, translators have been able to provide insights into the Aztec culture.

The Aztecs absorbed much of the Toltec patterns and religion including the Quetzalcoatl legend. Quetzalcoatl became revered as the inventor of the calendar and books, the teacher of craftsmen and agriculturalists. The Aztecs described this god to the Spaniards as a wise, kind-hearted, blue-eyed, gray-bearded, fair-skinned celibate, who had come from the east in a winged ship wearing a black robe bordered with white crosses. Ultimately he disappeared in the eastern ocean on a raft formed by entwined serpents. He was to return and establish a new era. Of course, this Aztec Quetzalcoatl is a composite figure combining imagery drawn from the mythology of the ancient feathered serpent god of Meso-America with the story of the Toltec priest-king Ce Acatl Topiltzin Quetzalcoatl who lived in the 10th century.

The descriptions of Quetzalcoatl and the garments he was supposed to have worn have provided ammunition for those who insist that Meso-American culture was impacted on by Europeans before the arrival of the Spaniards. Attempts to identify this contact, unsuccessful so far, have suggested that Quetzalcoatl was a Christian missionary, perhaps, St. Brendan, but there is no evidence to support this conjecture.

The First South Americans

In South America, in the Andean mountains of Peru, another unique, independent, center of American civilization developed 1,000 years earlier than those in Central America. Excavations in the Flea Cave, located between Lima and Cuzco in the Ayacucho valley, have revealed evidence of stone-tool-making people around 20,000 B.C.E. Bones of animals hunted by these early inhabitants include the ground sloth and the horse. The cave presented an evolutionary pattern with tools becoming more sophisticated over the centuries.

By 8500 B.C.E., peppers and gourds were cultivated in Peru. Five thousand years later, by 3,500 B.C.E., the llama had been domesticated. Within 500 years, although fishing was the main industry, farming communities had sprung up along the coast and in the Andean highlands. Fish nets and fish bones and shells give clues to a diet supplemented by sweet potatoes and beans. Indeed, researchers have found intact 5,000-year-old bits of cloth, potatoes and seeds, wonderfully preserved because of Peru's arid climate.

The Peruvian stone monuments that dot the coast and highlands were constructed around 3,000 B.C.E. The dozen or so structures at the coastal site of El Paraiso contain over 100,000 tons of quarried stones, and it is estimated that it required more than one million person-days of labor to build. Between 2100 and 800 B.C.E., settlements moved further inland along the river valleys. New irrigation technologies were developed along with new methods of pottery making and weaving. The larger and more sophisticated buildings maintained the rounded corner "U-shaped" structures common in the coastal areas. The largest prehistoric monument in the new world, a pyramid at the valley site called Sechin Alto, was 12 stories high and nearly 1,000 feet wide at the base. Yale University archaeologist Richard Burger, who is excavating Cardal, believes that monument making reflected a religious response arising out of fear of the gods, rather than out of royal power as in Egypt (Allman, Schrof, p. 50).

Between 800 and 100 B.C.E. a group of migrants from Mexico settled near the mouth of the Chicama river. They introduced the worship of a feline deity — the jaguar or the puma. They may also have associated divinity with the condor and the snake. Evidence for support of what has been called the "Chavin cult" is sparse. The cult idea rests partially on the interpretation of objects found in the elaborate graves, which might point to a belief in some sort of afterlife. The spread of the group's power, demonstrated by discoveries of their highly stylized relief carvings, also suggests the growth of a cult-centered people.

In the high, flat plateaus where water is scarce, the nights cold and the days very hot, the Tanawakans made their homes. Their culture flourished between 300 B.C.E. and 1200 C.E. and extended over a 1500 square mile territory that embraced the plateaus of Peru and Bolivia and the coast of southern Peru and northern Chile. Potatoes and grains were grown. Inventive agricultural techniques were developed. Fields were carefully prepared. First, a cobblestone base was laid. Over this base, gravel was poured in three levels, each level using finer material than the last. Finally, the bed was covered with a thick layer of soil. Water, channeled from nearby lakes, flowed around these raised beds, providing protection from night frosts through the warming of the water by absorption of sun heat by day.

Villages were connected by a network of roads built by laborers under the command of rulers. Over these roads llama pack-animals carried potatoes, grains, woven textiles and jewelry for trade. From Bolivia, the Tanawakans imported exotic bird feathers, monkeys, woods and tropical fruits. From Chile and Peru came sea products, corn, peppers, copper and gold. Caravans were protected by patrols.

Tiwanak was the holy city and the commercial hub of Tanawakan culture. Here, pilgrims came to pay homage at the Gateway of the Sun. On the basis of many carvings, archaeologists have come to believe that the condor was honored as the protective spirit of the city. The bird may also have been associated with priest-kings believed to be able to influence the gods.

Sometime between 1100 and 1300 the city was abandoned. Perhaps the irrigation system failed through drought or through the overflowing of Lake Titicaca, or perhaps invaders forced evacuation. By 1400 all that remained were ruins in the Andes highlands.

Along the arid Pacific coastline and in the stark, barren foothills of northern Peru between 100 and 700 C.E., Moche culture developed. By constructing mud aqueducts, the Moche conveyed water to their fields from the small rivers that flowed down from the Andes mountains to the Pacific ocean. One channel was 70 miles long. In addition, these people terraced slopes to grow corn, peanuts, beans, squash and hot peppers. Their vegetable diet was augmented with fish from the rivers, shellfish from the ocean and flesh of llamas and guinea pigs.

All structures were built of the local mud mixed with straw to form adobe bricks. It is clear that this was no egalitarian setting. Class distinctions were observed between the food producers (farmers, fishermen and hunters), and the elite (that included artisans, engineers, warriors and priests).

The richest tomb ever found in the Americas was uncovered at Moche, the religious center, located in the midst of irrigated fields near the coast in northern Peru. Here, amid the ruins of temples and pyramids built of adobe, the grave of a gold-bedecked warrior-priest was found. This important figure had been entombed together with several men and women, who may have been servants, and a pet dog. The man appears to have died in his mid-30s; the treasure-trove that accompanied his entombment contained "feathered headdresses, gold, silver and copper ornaments, earrings, bracelets and face masks, a gold rattle, a gold armor plate, dozens of exotic seashells, fine cloth and various weapons" (Allman, Schrof, p. 53). The presence of others in the tomb points to ritual sacrifice associated with the death of a leader.

Between 1493 and 1527 C.E., the Inca empire was at its peak. The country was united under the rule of Huayna Capac, whose empire extended over 2000 miles from Ecuador to central Chile. His subjects numbered 10,000,000. The ruler was called the Inca (which meant "Prince") and he was worshipped as a descendant of the sun god called Inti in Quechua. The earthly symbol of Inti was gold, which was highly revered. The capital, founded by the first Inca, Manco Capac, was at Cuzco, two miles above sea level. Under the divine control of the Inca, skilled engineers built roads, aqueducts and magnificent buildings.

After Huanyna Capac's death, his empire was equally divided between his two sons, who soon engaged in a bitter struggle for complete control. The conflict weakened the empire. When the Spanish conquistadors arrived in 1532, the Peruvians were unable to withstand their attacks. Ten years later Peru was declared a viceroyalty of Spain.

Did any of the Incas dare challenge or question the belief system? A most interesting report has been preserved by the 16th century Jesuit historian and translator of Quechua, Father Blas Valera. Apparently Topa Yupanqui, the grandfather of Atahualpa, questioned the validity of deifying the sun. Father Blas Valera reports this freethinker as saying:

> Many say that the Sun lives and that He is the maker of all things. Surely, he who makes a thing assists in its creation, but many things are made when the sun is absent. Therefore, He is not the maker of all things. And it may be concluded that He does not live, because he makes so many revolutions, and yet is never tired. If he was a living thing, He would become tired as we do, and if He was free He would visit other parts of Heaven which he never reaches. He is like a tethered beast that always makes the same round, or like a dart which goes where it is sent, and not where it wishes. (quoted in Hyams and Ordish, p. 112)

Before Columbus: The Asiatic Connection

When overland migrations from Asia across the Bering Straits ceased, the Americas were free to invent and develop their own unique cultural patterns separate from the developing civilizations in Asia and Europe. In recent years, however, a number of archaeological finds have been interpreted as indications that from time to time groups from Asia may have landed in America, not to demonstrably affect or change the existing culture but long enough to leave evidence of their presence.

In 1986, on the coast of Ecuador near the fishing village of Valdivia, an amateur archaeologist found 5,000-year-old pottery fragments of a type not found elsewhere in the New World. Based on the shell fishhooks and pebble weights found at the site, native Valdivians appear to have been simple fishers and food-gatherers. Suddenly, amid this rather primitive cultural setting, appeared pottery representing artistic variety and high development. Archaeologists Betty J. Meggers and Clifford Evans examined the pottery fragments and found that they were close replicas of unusual pottery forms developed on the Japanese islands of Kyushu and Honshu during the same time frame — about 3000 B.C.E. (Meggers, Evans, p. 97) Although the development of this pottery type can be traced back over the one-thousand-year Jomon period in Japan, no such evolutionary pattern can be found in America. How would this Japanese pottery form get to Ecuador?

Meggers and Evans speculated that a Japanese fishing boat, caught in a typhoon, drifted with the Japanese current down the coast of North America to the bulge of South America. Because there was no way for the newcomers to return home, they settled. The pottery they produced and left behind provides an archaeological reminder of their brief encounter with the New World. Another possible explanation is related to a volcanic eruption on Kyushu during the same time period. The eruption, which caused volcanic ash to be spread over the entire island, perhaps forced the people to evacuate. In either case, because the pottery is so unique and reveals so many parallels to the Japanese pottery, diffusionists are convinced that these similarities cannot be explained by coincidental development. However, it is important to note that there are archaeologists who do not accept this hypothesis.

Other suggestions of Asian-American contacts are based on ancient Chinese literary travel accounts and parallels in art and toys. For example, according to Chinese records from the Liang Dynasty kept by the historian Li Yen (9th century C.E.), a fifth century C.E. Buddhist priest named Hui-Shen, together with four other monks, sailed eastward from China on a voyage of 20,000 li or approximately 7,000 miles, to a land he called Fu-Sang. If he followed the Great Circle route, that journey would land him in Mexico in the area around Acapulco. His detailed description of people, food, customs, agriculture and animals appear to match to some degree what is known of American culture in

Mexico or perhaps Southern California in the first millennium C.E. However, once again, the validity of the claim of a China-America contact is under dispute. Some archaeological finds suggest that, perhaps during the Han dynasty (second century B.C.E. to second century C.E.), contact was made with America by the Chinese. Similar arguments have been made for contacts by Cambodians. Thus, all claims remain *sub judice* — under judgment.

Before Columbus: The European Connection

Is it possible that Egyptians or Phoenicians might have made contact with the Americas as far back as 1000 B.C.E.? Dr. Barry Fell, Professor Emeritus of Biology from Harvard University, is convinced that not only Egyptians and Phoenicians, but also Celts and Arabs made contact with America more than a millennium before Columbus. He points to the Davenport Tablet found in Iowa in 1877, and claims he can decipher three languages inscribed on it: Egyptian hieroglyphics, Iberian Punic and Libyan, plus Celtic Ogam. His theory has been attacked. Actually, the so-called "inscriptions" can be recognized as the results of natural erosions, suggesting that Dr. Fell has "read into" the erosion marks his own convictions. Furthermore, what he has perceived as evidence of early settlements has been described as "root cellars" only a few centuries old. His theories are not treated as valid.

A more controversial inscription is the Paraiba Stone, discovered in 1872 on a Brazilian Plantation near the Paraiba River. It is in ancient Phoenician and purports to record the journey of Phoenician sailors. Could some nineteenth century scholar have produced the tablet as a hoax? Dr. Cyrus Gordon of Brandeis University has examined the four pieces of the broken tablet and concluded that it is unlikely to be a forgery inasmuch as it contains expressions and grammatical forms that were not known to linguists of the nineteenth century. The translation reads:

> We are sons of Canaan from Sidon, from the city where a merchant (prince) has been made king. He dispatched us to this distant island . . . We sailed from Ezion-geber into the Red Sea and voyaged with ten ships. We were at sea together for two years around Africa. Then we got separated by the hand of Ba'al and we were no longer with our companions.

Dr. Gordon dates the inscription to the 6th century B.C.E. reign of King Hiram III of Tyre. Of course, there are scholars who dispute the hypothesis and Dr. Gordon acknowledges that there are, as yet, "too many unanswered questions." This "ancient inscription" may not be ancient and certainly cannot be accepted as evidence of Phoenician contact with the Americas.

In 1899, a Smithsonian scientist uncovered nine burials in a mound at Bat Creek, Tennessee, which were assumed to be Cherokee. Among the grave furnishings was a small engraved stone which had been placed beneath one skull. At first, it was assumed that the stone contained a Cherokee message. When Dr. Cyrus Gordon examined the inscription, he found it had been viewed upside down and that it was really in Hebrew and reads either "for the Judeans" or "for Judea." Apparently the grave had not been tampered with so the authenticity of the find is not questioned. Carbon 14 dating of wood artifacts from the grave provide a date for a mass burial between 32 and 769 C.E. Despite the 700 year span in the carbon dates, the period covered is pre-Columbian. The Hebrew is comparable to that found on Jewish coins from around 100 C.E., and bracelets found within the grave are made from a metallic brass like that produced by Romans between 40 B.C.E. and 200 C.E. It is Gordon's hypothesis that Jews, seeking escape from Roman oppression, sailed across the Atlantic, into the Gulf of Mexico and upriver in the Tennessee valley to Bat Creek. (Jackson, pp. 78-79). The hypothesis has not had wide acceptance; indeed, for the most part it is completely rejected. Therefore, like other suggestions of a Near East-America contact, it remains under judgment (cf. McCullough, pp. 47-53; McCarter, pp. 54-55).

The *possibility* of some connection with Egypt was demonstrated by Thor Hyerdahl who, in 1970, sailed in a reed boat across the Atlantic from Safi to Barbados. He demonstrated that such a journey *could* have been made by the Egyptians. However, there is absolutely no evidence that what *could* have been done actually was done.

Irish folktales about St. Brendan from County Kerry, who may have made contact with America in the fifth or sixth centuries C.E., lack hard evidence to back up the wondrous story. Nor are the accounts of fair-skinned, blue-eyed Indians in the Dakotas, whose language and customs paralleled those of the Welsh, accepted as evidence of the pre-Columbian discovery of America by the Welsh. The fair skins and blue eyes are most likely to be traced to intermarriage between Indians and early colonists (Jackson, p. 81). On the other hand, archaeological finds in Newfoundland provide solid evidence that Norsemen arrived before Columbus, perhaps as early as the journey by Bjarni Herjolfsson in 986 C.E. Then Lief Ericsson may have landed in Greenland and Newfoundland and perhaps even in the Boston area. (Jackson, p. 81f)

Accounts of the early discovery of America by Europeans and Asiatics long before the coming of the Spaniards and Christopher Columbus cannot be taken seriously. The legends from the Orient, like those from Ireland, and even the inscriptions, must be taken with a grain of salt. What is equally important is the recognition that, should these almost casual relationships between Asiatic and European cultures have taken place, they, together with the few America coastal settlements, left no real residuals such as those that marked the dramatic changes that occurred after the end of the 15th century. Some Caucasians seem to have difficulty in recognizing creativity in other peoples. Where magnificent cultural patterns develop, there seems to be the attempt to demonstrate that somehow, in some way, that greatness was affected or triggered or conditioned by Caucasian input.

See pp. 475-481 for References of chapters 16-21.

17

Europe "Discovers" America

Obviously, America had been "discovered" long before the coming of Columbus. As we have seen, migrations over the Bering straits had populated the land and enabled the development of magnificent cultures independent of both Asian and European influence. Thus, during the 16th century, the Spanish, Portuguese, and other Europeans entered a land that had been lived in for millennia. They encountered American cultures that had developed unique and rich heritages that were different and apart from the cultures of Europe. Simultaneously, the Americas were to enter a new age that would bring them to what are, for us, "modern times."

The Conquest of "New Spain"

The colonization of the Americas began at the end of the 15th century. On August 3, 1492, Christopher Columbus (Italian: Christoforo Columbo; Spanish: Cristobal Colon) left Spain with a fleet of three ships. He failed in his intended goal to reach India by sailing westward from Spain. But he returned to Spain with information about the existence of what was to become known as the Americas. Information about this exciting "discovery" opened a new world for European commerce and colonization. Columbus pointed the way; others would imitate his daring example. The Spanish and the Portuguese moved quickly in adventurous exploitation of the new continents. Farther north, the English and the French began colonization.

When Columbus made contact with the New World, it is estimated that as many as 90 million people were resident in the Americas. Of these, about ten million lived in what is now the United States and Canada, the rest resided south of the Rio Grande river. Columbus, believing he had made contact with India, named the people, *los indios*, hence the name Indians. The people he met referred to themselves as Taino, their word for "good" or "noble." (Sale, p. 97) They were distantly related by language and culture to the Arawaks who occupied the South American mainland from whence they had migrated (Sale, p. 97).

The Tainos had much in common with mainland Indians. They were friendly and curious. They greeted the Spaniards with food, water and gifts. Columbus soon recognized the Tainos pattern of living harmoniously with each other: "They are very gentle and without knowledge of what is evil; nor do they murder or steal," he wrote (Sale p. 100). He could only have been impressed by the way their lives harmonized with their environment and by their spacious homes (which contrasted with the crowded dwellings in the Spaniards' homeland), the excellence of their boats (canoes) made from single trees, their home furnishings, which included hammocks and chairs, and their agricultural products such as the sweet potato, squashes and beans. In his journal, Columbus noted that they were naked, that their bodies were painted and that they would make fine servants. Because they had no iron and were simply armed, he observed that they could easily be overcome. He was also convinced (wrongly) that they had no religion and could easily be converted to Christianity. He formally possessed and claimed the Tainos land in the name of the King Ferdinand and Queen Isabella of Spain.

Columbus recognized in these people a ready source of slave labor. He informed the king and queen that he was prepared to ship as many slaves as were requested. In a statement sent to the royal house of Spain in 1493 he commented on the native population of Puerto Rico and San Domingo as follows:

> Seeing how necessary here are cattle and beasts of labor for the maintenance of the people who will be here, and for the good of all these islands, your Highnesses may give license and permission to a sufficient number of caravels to come each year and bring those cattle and other goods and things for settling the country and benefitting from the land, and at the prices reasonable to the costs of those who would bring them, which things can be paid them in slaves from these cannibals, people so rough and willing and well proportioned and of very good understanding, which, taken from that inhumanity, we believe will be better than any other slaves . . . . (quoted in Hutchinson, p. 39)

Thus was slave trade introduced to the New World by Columbus. It was a system that was to expand as the settlers needed workers to till the soil.

But there was still another reaction, namely greed. Persuaded by the trinkets and objects of gold given to him by the Tainos, Columbus assumed that there were local mines of gold to be exploited. When this information was presented to the court in Spain, lust for gold vied with the lust for land and with the desires to Christianize the heathen Indians and to colonize what was recognized as New Spain. The result was an invasion by Spaniards who saw no beauty in the Indians of America and who viewed them as some lower species of humans to be subdued, enslaved and used.

Within a few years, Columbus and others were busily engaged in the buying and selling of people for whom they held no respect. In 1502, a Spanish Dominican missionary, Bartolome de Las Casas (1474-1566), noted that the Spaniards:

> . . . made bets as to who would slit a man in two, or cut off his head at one blow; or they opened up his bowels. They tore the babes from their mother's breasts by their feet, and dashed their heads against the rocks . . . . They spitted the bodies of other babes, together with their mothers and all who were before them on their swords.

Selected Tainos were hung from a gallows frame:

> . . . just high enough for their feet to touch the ground, and by thirteens, in honour and reverence for our Redeemer and the twelve Apostles, they put wood underneath and, with fire, they burned the Indians alive (quoted in Sale, p. 157).

It is not surprising that within twenty years after Spain began to colonize, Tainos numbers had been reduced by slaughter, enslavement, and by imported disease from about 250,000 to 20,000. Later, diseases brought from Europe, including smallpox, were to result in the death of thousands more native Americans. The Spanish had set the tone for conquest that other nations would emulate — some providing even worse treatment of the American native population.

In 1502 Spanish-born Blacks were exported to Hispanolia as slaves. These were the sons and daughters of those first kidnapped Africans who were sold to the Spaniards in the fifteenth century by the Portuguese. Within the next two decades trade in African slaves was to grow into an important business.

The Situation in Spain

At this point, it is important to recall what had been happening in Spain. Neither Spain nor Portugal experienced a Reformation such as that which occurred in central Europe. In both countries, the power and authority of the Roman Catholic Church was unchallenged.

Two developments were instrumental in linking the Church and the monarchy. The first was the establishment of the Spanish "Holy Office" in 1480 by Queen Isabella of Castile and her consort, King Ferdinand of Aragon. The second, which accompanied the first, was the inauguration of the Spanish Inquisition with Tomas Torquemada (1420-1498) as Inquisitor-General. Religious orthodoxy and patriotism were conjoined. As an institution of the State, "The Holy Office" utilized the services of civil servants in carrying out its mission to repress heresy and dissent. Ten thousand accused persons were burned to death and one hundred thousand imprisoned. Jews and Muslims were persecuted, and those who did convert to Christianity were held suspect.

In January, 1492, the city of Granada, the last stronghold of Islamic power in Spain, surrendered to Queen Isabella and King Ferdinand. Between March and August, 1492, all Jews of whatever age or station were expelled from Spain. It is estimated that between 120,000 and 150,000 were compelled to flee, abandoning holdings that had been in their families for generations. Nor were Jews permitted to take with them any jewels or gold or silver or currency; these properties went to the crown. Finally, the independent power of the nobility was broken, the royal treasury was enriched and religious medievalism became the characteristic way of life and thought for the Spanish church.

Rivalry between Roman Catholic religious orders served only to increase the zeal of each in converting numbers to the faith. Therefore, the religion brought to the New World by the Spanish and the Portuguese provided no room for doctrinal challenge or questioning. Religious dogmatism and intolerance of dissent reflected the authoritarian nature of the church-state combination. There was no place for free-thought. In this spirit of religious intolerance and superiority, the conquistadors sought to convert the resident Americans and exploit their resources.

It was not until much later, when the Napoleonic wars shook the Spanish monarchy, that rebellion against Spain and Portugal was to develop in the Americas. Men like Simon Bolivar, Jose Miguel de Carrera, Jose de San Martin and Bernardo O'Higgins led early 19th century revolts against royalist authority, which were to give rise to independent nations in the parts of the New World that had been seized by Spain.

The Coming of Cortes

Among those intrigued by Columbus' reports was Hernando Cortes, a student of law at the University of Salamanca. Cortes led the Spanish expedition to Mexico, landing in what is now Veracruz early in 1519. On November 8, 1519, with a bedraggled company of 300 soldiers, he entered the magnificent Aztec city of Tenochtitlan where he and his men were received with honor by the Aztec ruler Montezuma II. The Spaniards were stunned at the beauty of the magnificent city located on an island in the midst of a lake, resplendent with its shining towers, pyramids, gardens, parks, and boat-filled lagoons.

Aztecs religious traditions had made the people most vulnerable. According to the Aztec calendar, 1519 was the year "One Reed," when it was believed that Quetzalcoatl would return. The European newcomers fitted the mythic description of the divine-human hero. They were fair-skinned. They arrived in tall ships from the Eastern Sea. The pattern was close enough to Aztec religious mythology to prompt Montezuma II to greet the newcomers with open hospitality. Some twenty women were presented to Cortes for his pleasure. One named Malinche, a Tabascan Indian who served as Cortes translator, produced a son (Martin). Martin was to become the symbol of the *mestizo*, the new mixed-blood race that formed a marginal people in the new caste system that developed.

Montezuma's relaxed openness to the Spaniards backfired, the Aztec ruler ending up as a prisoner and hostage in his own city. It happened like this. In the spring of 1520, a Spanish expedition under the leadership of Captain Baneful de Narvaez arrived in Mexico from Cuba. He had been commissioned by Cortes' enemy, Governor Velasquez, to arrest Cortes and take him prisoner back to Cuba. Cortes set out to confront Narvaez, leaving Pedro de Alvarado in charge at Tenochtitlan. Cortes attacked by night, defeated Narvaez and persuaded Narvaez' defeated soldiers to enlist in his own army.

Meanwhile, back at Tenochtitlan, during an Aztec religious ceremony, de Alvarado ordered his troops to open fire on the people. The Aztecs fought back. Cortes returned to find his garrison under siege. Aztec attacks decimated his troops and Cortes and his men fled for their lives. A year later (1521), having gathered a small army of Spaniards and disaffected Indian vassals of the Aztecs, Cortes attacked and took possession of the city. Much of Tenochtitlan had previously been reduced to rubble by Spanish canon fire, and a plague of smallpox brought to the Americas by the Spanish killed many Indians. Cortes began the building of a new city on the site of the old which he named Mexico City. Later, Cortes, with his Spanish comrades and native Indian supporters, ravaged the remains of the Aztec city.

By 1522, by order of King Carlos I of Spain, Cortes had been appointed Governor and Captain General of New Spain, as Mexico was then called. Carlos was the grandson of Ferdinand and Isabella, but he was more than a Spanish monarch. He was also King Charles V, the Holy Roman Emperor, whose dominions embraced Spain, Germany, Austria, Hungary, the Netherlands, and most of Italy. Now his territorial claims were being extended to the Americas. His emissary, Cortes, the conqueror (*conquistador*), was placed in charge of the first great Spanish American possession — a territory that extended from the Caribbean to the Pacific ocean. What Cortes had set in motion by his conquests was a pattern to be copied by others who would come to conquer, to plunder, to enslave and to control.

After Cortes

Even before Cortes began his adventure in Mexico, another Spanish explorer, Vasco Nunez de Balboa, was active in Panama. He led a party of Panama Indians and armed Spanish soldiers through a dense wilderness across the isthmus. On September 25, 1513, he stood on a peak in Darien and became the first European to view the Pacific ocean from America. He called the waters *El Mar del Sur*, the South Sea. Later, a Portuguese navigator, Ferdinand Magellan, in making a round-the-world journey on behalf of Spain, called the ocean, which he found to be peaceful, "Pacific."

In 1519, the city of Panama was founded and Francisco Pizarro, an uneducated swineherd from Trujillo, Spain, who had accompanied Balboa, was named mayor and magistrate. Pizarro had heard tales about a golden kingdom to the south and lusted after finding it. In 1526, following an earlier abortive effort, he finally reached the edge of Inca territory which he named Peru. Later, in 1531, he journeyed from Panama City to Peru with three ships carrying about 180 men, 30 horses and some light cannon. When he landed in June 1532, he established his base and named it San Miguel de Piura.

This was a propitious time for Pizarro. The Incas, weakened and divided by war between the rival brothers, had recently come under the control of Atahualpa, the younger son of Huayna Capac. On November 16, 1532, after an arduous journey up the slopes of the Andes, Pizarro and his men arrived at the city of Cajamarca where Atahualpa was encamped with his army. The Indians were awestruck by the fair-skinned humans and their horses — animals unknown in the Western Hemisphere. They made no move to take up arms against the newcomers.

The discussions that followed the arrival of the Spanish were often marked with theological instruction. The Incas listened to the Dominican priest Vincente de Valverde (who later became bishop of Cuzco). They were told about Christian beliefs and that the Pope, as the vice-regent of the apostle Peter, had ordered the Spanish king to "conquer and convert" the people of the New World. The Incas were not persuaded. Atahualpa is supposed to have said:

> I will be no man's tributary. I am greater than any prince upon the earth. Your emperor may be a great prince; I do not doubt it, seeing that he has sent his subjects so far across the waters; and I am willing to hold him as my brother. As for the Pope of whom you speak, he must be mad to talk of giving away countries that do not belong to him. As for my faith, I will not change it. Your own god, as you tell me, was put to death by the very men he created. But my god still looks down upon his children. (quoted in Hyams and Ordish, p. 222)

When Atahualpa asked on what authority Valverde made his demands, he was handed a Bible. He glanced at a few pages then threw it in the dust, thereby enraging the Spanish and providing them with the very excuse they needed to attack. This they did without warning and more than 2,000 of Atahualpa's followers were massacred. Atahualpa was taken prisoner. To buy his release, he promised to fill a room 22 feet long and 17 feet wide with gold to a depth of as high as a man could reach. In addition he promised to fill another, smaller room, twice over with silver. Pizarro agreed. Within two months this magnificent treasure was collected. On August 29, 1533, the Inca leader was baptized a Christian and then publicly strangled to death by order of Francisco Pizarro. Pizarro was now in charge of the Inca empire.

In September 1533, Pizarro moved southward to Cuzco. After beating off Indian resistance, he found himself in control of a city virtually laden with gold and silver. Cuzco was looted and, with the exception of a few buildings and walls, reduced to rubble. A new city was begun on the site of the old — this one employing Spanish colonial design with churches replacing Inca temples. In compliance with Pizzaro's wishes, Manco Capec, a half-brother of the deceased Atahualpa, was enthroned as a puppet ruler.

In 1535, Pizarro began construction of a seaport city on the banks of the Rimac river. He named it Ciudad de los Reyes — City of Kings. It became the new capital of Peru (today it is called Lima, a corruption of Rimac). Using this new city as a base, Spain was able to expand its conquest of South America.

In a desperate move, Manco Capec attempted to throw off the Spanish yoke. As a result, from February to August in 1536, Cuzco was besieged by the Spanish. Capec fled with a band of followers and took refuge in a mountain city located on a plateau half a mile above the sacred Inca river, the Urubamba, some 50 miles northwest of Cuzco. There Manco Capec died in 1571 and the city of refuge was abandoned and became lost to the world. It was rediscovered in 1911 by Dr. Hiram Bingham of Yale University, who called it Machu Picchu ("Old Peak") after a nearby mountain.

In 1585, Guaman Poma de Ayala (born about 1535), a native Peruvian, began a long letter (1,118 pages) addressed to the Spanish monarchy, complaining about Spanish rule. Guaman Pomo knew a great deal about European culture for he had served as a notary and translator for the Spanish. The letter, which was completed in 1615, not only described in detail the Andean civilization as it had been before the coming of the Spanish, but defended it and offered suggestions for improved government of the area. Pomo described the brutality and incompetence of the conquistadors and by drawings portrayed the cruel treatment of native people by the Spanish — one sketch portrays a writhing Andean being trampled by a Spanish horseman. There is no evidence that King Philip III of Spain ever received or read it. Poma was later branded a subversive by the Spanish because he taught native Peruvians to write legal claims for their lost land.

Between 1535 and 1536, a rival of Pizarro, named Diego de Almagro, began the conquest of Chile (named from the Indian word *Tchili*, meaning "snow") which he named "New Toledo." As governor of New Toledo, Almagro claimed a strip of land between Chile and Peru and in 1537 he seized Cuzco. Thus began a civil war among the Spaniards. Almago's efforts to conquer Chile failed. Pizarro responded to this failure and in 1540 commissioned a soldier, Pedro de Valdivia, to conquer and colonize the country.

Despite opposition from the Atacama Indians, Valdivia pushed southward and in 1541 founded Santiago del Nuevo Extremo (Santiago of the New Frontier) in Chile's central valley. By 1546, by conquest, he had pushed Spanish boundaries to the Bio-Bio river. In 1549, as he attempted to go beyond the river, he was confronted by the brave, renowned, Araucanian Indian warriors, nearly one million strong. The struggle was fierce and, in 1553, Valdivia was captured and put to death — according to legend by being forced to drink molten gold. The Spanish were spared further advances by the Araucanians due to an outbreak of smallpox in the Indian forces. However, Indian resistance in Peru continued into the 19th century and the Spanish were held at the BioBio river. Pizarro was killed in his palace in Lima on June 26, 1541. In 1542, Peru along with Panama and almost all of Spanish South America except Venezuela became a viceroyalty of Spain.

The acquisition of Aztec and Inca gold infected others with gold fever. A legend told of South American rituals in which great quantities of gold, silver and jewels were cast into a lake as offerings to the gods. The chieftain of this wondrous place was known as "El Dorado," "the Golden One." Jiminez de Quesada (1500-1579), a lawyer and writer, was determined to find him. In 1556, he set out with 800 men and 100 horses to explore the highlands of Colombia. On a high plateau, he encountered the Chibchas Indians — a group whose existence was based primarily on agriculture. Chibchas craftsmen were expert goldsmiths. Quesada burned their temples, enslaved the people and seized their gold and emeralds. Near the site of the Chibchas capital city called Bacata, he founded another capital which he called Santa Fe de Bacata (Santa Fe after his birthplace in Spain). Today, it is the city of Bogota. He did not find El Dorado, but the area he conquered he labelled New Granada and it became and remained part of the viceroyalty of Peru until 1718.

Gonzalo Pizarro, the half-brother of Francisco Pizarro, hunted for El Dorado in Ecuador. As Pizarro and his men ascended the Andes, he sent his lieutenant, Francisco de Orellana, ahead to find food. Orellana proceeded down the eastern side of the Andes but was unable to bring his boat upstream against the strong current. Instead, he moved with the current and became the first European to navigate the great river that he eventually called the Amazon, on the basis of an encounter he had with female warriors who called to his mind the Amazons of Greek mythology.

Spain and Portugal were also colonizing the eastern shores of South America. In 1526, Sebastian Cabot (Cabato), an Italian navigator working for Spain, sailed into a wide estuary in Argentina. Impressed by the sunlight glinting on the surface of the water, he named it *Rio de la Plata* ("the Silver River"). Ten years later, Don Pedro de Mendoza founded the Spanish colony of Buenos Aires ("Good Airs"), which faltered under Indian attacks and was abandoned in favor of the town of Asuncion located on the east bank of the Paraguay River. Buenos Aires was re-established in 1580.

In 1500 the Portuguese commander, Pedro Alvarez Cabral, took possession of Brazil in the name of the Portuguese crown. By 1530, colonies were being established along the coast, and in 1565 Rio de Janeiro ("River of January") was founded. As the Portuguese pressed into the interior they discovered redwoods similar to Oriental brazilwood, hence the country was called "Brazil." The Portuguese settlement of the area was relatively peaceful in contrast to the ruthless and brutal methods commonly employed by Spaniards.

By the end of the seventeenth century, South America was almost entirely under the control of Portugal and Spain. The one exception was the Guiana area which was parceled out between England, France, and the Netherlands. The Spanish and the Portuguese introduced Roman Catholic Christianity. Franciscan, Dominican, Augustinian and Jesuit missionaries Christianized large portions of the Indian population. During the next century, tens of thousands of immigrants poured into the Portuguese and Spanish New-World territories. Ships conveyed precious cargo in gold, silver, copper, tropical woods, sugar, tobacco, cacao, cotton, vanilla and medicinal plants back to Spain and Portugal. From Spain and Portugal came household furnishings, clothing, tools, hardware, olive oil, wine, mules, horses and, of course, immigrants. In addition, slaves captured in Africa were shipped to America to augment the slaves taken from Indian groups.

Early conquerors and settlers brought few women with them from Europe. Many chose mates from among the conquered Indians. These *mestizos* (Spanish) or *mamelucos* (Portuguese), as they were called, were looked down upon by those of unmixed parentage. But class discrimination existed even among the "pure" Spanish families. Those born and bred in Spain were the *peninsulares,* who were awarded the highest offices by the Spanish government and the church. Those of Spanish descent born in America were the *criollos*, who were generally excluded from high offices in the government or the church. The same discrimination was observed by the Portuguese. Portuguese-born officials, known as *reinois*, were considered to be upper class. Lower than the *mestizos* and *mamelucos* were the *mullatoes,* who were of mixed European and black parentage, and the *zambos* who represented those of mixed African and Indian descent. At the foot of the social ladder were the full-blooded Indians and imported Africans.

Spanish colonies were under the direct control of the monarch. The king held a monopoly on colonial trade through the Casa de

Contratacion ("House of Trade"), which acted as the Crown's agent with complete jurisdiction over every aspect of trade. Colonies were considered to exist for the benefit of the mother-land. Colonists were told what and where they could trade. Mining companies were compelled to pay the king's *quinto*, the royal fifth, of all mineral wealth extracted. Agriculture flourished, based on Indian methods which were improved by the Spanish. New crops were introduced. Great estates or *haciendas* came into being. Ranching and livestock raising produced great profits for wealthy Spaniards.

Similar patterns developed in Portuguese Brazil. Huge plantations called *fazendas*, worked by imported African slaves, produced sugar and cotton. Gold and diamond mining added to the immense wealth of the few.

The role of the Roman Catholic Church in developing colonies cannot be overestimated. As noted previously, there was from the beginning an alliance between the Church and the Spanish crown. Roman Catholic clergy arrived with the Spanish and Portuguese invaders of the Americas. Franciscan friars journeyed with Columbus on his second voyage. Jesuits arrived in 1572. It comes as no surprise to find that the Roman Catholic Church was a beneficiary of the colonization program. In the New World, the Church provided important services in the consolidation of holdings. The clergy established frontier missions, opened schools, hospitals and orphanages. Clerics were active in mapping and exploring interior areas. As a consequence, they were awarded huge land grants. By 1800, fully half of the private land in the colonies was owned by the Church.

Because the vast majority of native residents had no voice in government, there was little opportunity for the development of self-governing communities and even less chance for democratic procedures to emerge. Indians were viciously exploited and many were reduced to slavery. Threatened with punishments, including the lash, they were compelled to labor long hours in the fields and in the mines. The Christianity of mine owners did not include concern for the safety or well-being of enslaved workers.

Some clergy enriched themselves at the expense of the Indians by charging for every service. Concubinage, using Indian women, was common among priests and monks. But there were some who sought to help the Indians. Bartolome de Las Casas, the Dominican missionary, disturbed by the cruel treatment as well as the suffering and harsh living conditions of the native Americans, dedicated his life to bringing about change. He earned the title "Protector of the Indians" and "Apostle to the Indians." He appealed to the Spanish monarchy on behalf of the native Americans. In 1542, the Spanish Crown issued a set of New Laws, designed to eliminate the wrongs inflicted on the Indians. Spanish colonists opposed the laws, most land owners ignored them, and local officials usually failed to enforce them. The wretched condition of the enslaved Indians continued unchanged.

In 1608, the Jesuits were authorized by King Philip III of Spain to Christianize the Indians of the upper Parana and Uruguay rivers. They introduced the concept of *reduciones* or settlements. The settlements, designed to facilitate conversions, served to protect the Indians from the slave hunters. The inhabitants were taught useful skills including weaving, carpentering, tailoring, sculpting and printing. In something over 100 years there were 30 large *reduciones* operating as independent theocratic states embracing about 150,000 Indians within the Spanish-American empire. By 1767, it is estimated that some 700,000 Indians had been baptized. The system was not favored by white settlers. Between 1759 and 1760, the Portuguese, fearing the growing power of the Jesuits, expelled them from Portugal and Brazil. In 1767, King Charles III of Spain ordered the Jesuits expelled from the Spanish colonies. The abandoned Indians scattered or were taken into slavery.

Spanish conquest was not limited to Central and South America. Spanish influence spread northward and eastward from Central America through North America. Spanish colonies were located along the coast of the Gulf of Mexico and into the Florida panhandle.

Of course, even as the native Americans accepted the Christian faith, they retained many facets of their own beliefs. Some religious elements were absorbed and given new meaning by the Roman Church. For example, the Basilica of Our Lady of Guadaloupe in Mexico City is located on a site of the Aztec shrine once dedicated to the earth and corn goddess known as "The Little Mother." The choice of this site by the Church has been justified by a legend of the miraculous appearance of the Christian goddess, Mary, to Juan Diego in 1531. Appropriately, the face of "Our Lady of Guadaloupe" is that of a brown Indian with black hair. The Spanish religious leaders simply took an existing Aztec religious symbol and transformed it into a Christian statement. (Larue, 1990, p. 162)

Spanish invaders of the New World had three interests: gold, land, and the conversion of the resident Americans to Catholicism. They pursued these goals with a viciousness born of greed, intolerance of local religious and cultural viewpoints, and with the dogmatic fanaticism of zealots. There was little or no respect for the persons of the resident Americans. Columbus had noted that they ought to make good servants and be easily converted, inasmuch as "they had no religion." He noted, too, that the people were kind, honest and happy, although he did not hesitate to describe them as being "like beasts" in their willingness to share (Sale p. 100). The negative image was to be expanded to justify cruel exploitation. For example, during the mid-sixteenth century, the Dominican monk Tomas Ortiz wrote:

> They are more given to sodomy than any other nation. There is no justice among them. They go naked. They have no respect for either love or for virginity. They are stupid and silly. They have no respect for truth, save when it is to their advantage. They are unstable. They have no knowledge of what foresight means. They are ungrateful and changeable . . . . They are brutal . . . . The older they get the worse they become. About the age of ten or twelve years, they seem to have some civilization, but later they become like real brute beasts. I may therefore affirm that God has never created a race more full of vice and composed without the least mixture of kindness or culture. Sale, pp. 201-202)

The consequence of such attitudes was the justification of the enslavement of multitudes of people, the spread of diseases that decimated the population, the stripping of New World shrines of their treasures, and the imposition of Roman Catholicism on the subject people. There was no appreciation of the magnificent cultures developed by the resident Americans, who were looked at and treated as sub-humans. Indeed, it has been estimated that the results of the "discovery" of the Americas initiated the greatest genocide the world has ever known; some 50 million native American people are believed to have died.

See pp. 475-481 for References of chapters 16-21.

18

The Conquest of North America

The eastern coast of North America has a different history of colonization. Even as the Spanish and Portuguese were moving into Central and South America, English, Portuguese and French navigators were exploring the coast of North America.

Indian Life

As Europeans began to move into the eastern coastlands, they encountered scores of well-organized Indian tribal groups. Coastal, lake and river tribes harvested a bounty of fish. In the fertile woodlands and eastern prairies, most tribes sustained themselves by hunting, gathering and agriculture. Algonquin-speaking tribes predominated in numbers and territory; the lesser number were Iroquois-speaking.

The Algonquin-speaking people were widely scattered from the eastern seaboard to the Mississippi. They were known by a number of tribal names, such as the Abnakis of Maine, the Micmacs of Acadia, the Montagnais above the St. Lawrence River, the Ojibways to the north of Lake Superior, the Ottawas and Potawatomis around Lakes Michigan and Huron, and the Crees in the Far West. It is estimated that they numbered about 90,000 when the Europeans first arrived. As European trade in furs and hides developed, Algonquins became important contributors to that growing market. Their love of freedom made it impossible for them to submit to the restraints of European life. As Europeans intruded more and more into their territories, the Algonquins withdrew further and further west.

The earliest democratic system in America was not that introduced by European immigrants. Indeed, as we shall see, the newcomers brought with them all the intolerance and bigotry that was characteristic of life in Europe. The first American democratic system was in existence among the Iroquois long before the coming of the Europeans.

The Iroquois were located south of Lake Ontario between the Hudson River and Lake Erie. They were sometimes called the "Five

Nations" because they had formed a league that consisted of five nations or tribes — Mohawks, Oneidas, Onondagas, Cayugas and Senecas. Later, around 1714, when they were joined by the Tuscaroras, the confederacy was known as the "Six Nations." Unlike the European systems in which power was held by individuals, whether monarchs or feudal lords, in the Iroquois Confederacy, government was representative, democratic, and not burdensome to the people.

According to legend, the Confederacy grew from a vision by Degan-widah (or Dekanawidah), a holy man who had been born to a virgin mother. According to his vision, the Iroquois were to end the constant warring among themselves and unite under the sheltering branches of the "Tree of Great Peace." A Mohawk named Hiawatha spread the message and the League was born. What developed, perhaps as early as 1450, was a form of democratically-run representative government (Johansen, p. 22).

Each Nation sent male representatives from its sub-tribes to form the fifty-seat Council. For example, the Mohawks sent nine members representing the Dekarihokenh, the Ayonhwathah, the Shadekariwadeh, the Sha-renhowaneh, the Deyoenhegwenh, the Orenregowah, the Dehennakarineh, the Rastawenseronthah and the Shoskoarawaneh groups. Nine seats were allotted to the Oneidas, 14 to the Onondagas, 10 to the Cayugas and 8 to the Senecas (Maxwell, pp. 128-129). Meetings were held beneath a great white pine, known as the Tree of Great Peace, in Onandaga territory at what is presently Syracuse, New York. There the Great Council Fire was lighted and intertribal matters were considered. All resolutions required the unanimous support of the fifty representatives. Otherwise, each nation took care of its own business and governed itself with little or no League interference.

The Confederacy was governed by a constitution known as The Great Law of Peace, which was not recorded in English until 1880. Prior to that time its contents were retrievable from the codes preserved in patterns woven in Iroquois wampum belts. The Great Law opened with the planting of the Great Tree of Peace and notes that:

> Roots have spread out . . . One to the north, one to the west, one to the east and one to the south. These are the Great White Roots and their nature is peace and strength. If any man or nation outside the Five Nations shall obey the laws of the Great Peace and shall make this known to the statesmen of the League, they may trace back the roots of the tree. If their minds are clean and they are obedient and promise to obey the wishes of the Council and the League, they shall be welcome

> to take shelter beneath the Tree of Long Leaves. (quoted by Johansen, pp. 23f)

The Confederacy did not discriminate on the basis of differing religious beliefs, and no efforts were made at conversion.

Within the tribes, women possessed unique authority. Women owned and tended the longhouses, raised the children, planted and harvested the fields, and owned the agricultural tools. At marriage, a man moved into his wife's longhouse. Within each longhouse, the eldest woman was recognized as the central authority figure. Men were warriors and hunters who supplemented the diet of corn, squash, beans, sunflower seeds, nuts, berries and apples with meat from elk, moose, deer and beaver. At first the chiefs who participated in the Great Council were elected by the women, although later they came to be selected on the basis of leadership qualities.

Although the Iroquois were famous as savage warriors, it is estimated that at no time could they have mustered a force of over three thousand fighting men. Through warfare, the strength of the Five Nations was reduced constantly, but numbers were maintained by a curious adoptive custom. When a warrior was killed, his wife or relatives might adopt into their family one of the prisoners brought in by the war parties. The newly adopted, grateful for having been saved from cruel and vicious torture and ultimate death, became one with his captors and later fought beside them, even against his own kinsmen. Captured children and women were often brought into the tribe. Quite often Europeans, both French and English, became members of an Indian tribe through capture. Delighting in the freedom of life among the Indians, many refused to return to their native culture even when they were able to do so.

The Sioux, who lived west of Lake Superior, were so like the Iroquois that they were known as the "Little Iroquois of the West." The Hurons dwelt south of the Georgian Bay between Lake Huron and Lake Simcoe in thirty-two villages and numbered about 30,000. Like the Iroquois, they lived in settled communities and raised corn as the main source of food. One of their most unique religious ceremonies was associated with the dead.

The dead were believed to live in a shadowy world that paralleled that of the living. Dead men went on hunting and fishing expeditions; dead women tended crops and nursed dead children. Cemeteries were located near the villages. Every so often, sometimes in periods separated by ten years, the Feast of the Dead was observed. Each village exhumed their dead, removed and burned the funeral wrappings together with any remaining flesh on the corpses. The bones, having been cleansed, were transported to the site of the Feast for ritual burial in a common pit (Maxwell, p. 138).

Indian religion was, as we have noted, spirit-filled; their world was spirit-inhabited. Some spirits were dangerous and could cause disease. Fortunately, malevolent powers could be thwarted by medicine men who were able to use the very powers that caused illness to effect cure. It was important to remain in good favor with the spirits of the woods, the streams and the lakes which yielded the gifts of food that sustained life. Europeans were amazed to discover that an Indian might make a long speech of apology to a wounded bear. There was no concept of a supreme deity, but the Indian word *Manitou* signified the universal presence of power that was outside of the human realm. Dreams played important roles because Indians believed that, through dreams, they gained knowledge of the cure of diseases, the haunts of game and the plans of enemies.

The Coming of the Europeans

In Europe, the news of Columbus' discovery spread rapidly. Among those fired with zeal by the reports were John Cabot and his son Sebastian. The Cabots were of a Venetian family that had moved to England and settled in Bristol. In 1497, John Cabot received a charter from Henry VII granting trading privileges. His ambition was twofold: "to bring back so many fish that England will have no more business with Iceland" and to find a north-west passage to India.

Cabot's first venture took him to the coast of Labrador or perhaps Newfoundland. On the second voyage, accompanied by his son Sebastian, he moved down the American coast towards Florida which was under Spanish control. The third expedition was led by Sebastian alone. Needless to say, the Cabots failed to find the north-west passage, but they opened up for England a rich source of cod in the Newfoundland shoals. After the death of the Cabots, Henry VII abandoned the Atlantic adventure. In June, 1897, the Royal Society of Canada placed a plaque in Halifax honoring John Cabot. It read, in part:

> This tablet is in honour of the famous navigator, JOHN CABOT Who under the authority of letters patent of HENRY

> VII, directing him *to conquer occupy and possess* for ENGLAND all lands he might find *in whatever part of the world they be* sailed in a BRISTOL Ship THE MATTHEW and first planted the flags of ENGLAND and VENICE on the 24th of June, 1497 on the northeastern seaboard of NORTH AMERICA and by his discoveries in this and the following year gave to ENGLAND a claim upon the Continent which the colonizing spirit of her sons made good in later times.

His recognition in England was more modest. From the king he received ten pounds, given to "Hym that founde the new ile."

In 1500, Miguel Cortes Real, representing Portugal, visited the coasts which the Cabots had traced. He returned to Lisbon with some 50 Newfoundland Indians who were destined to become slaves. In 1524, Verrazano, under orders from the King of France, explored the North American coastline from Carolina to Nova Scotia. He brought back more than 50 Indians from Maine.

In 1534, Jacques Cartier left St. Malo, France, with two small ships. He was commissioned to visit the lands reported by Verrazano and take possession of them in the name of France, to seek minerals and furs and, if possible, to find a passage to China (Cathay). He sailed up the St. Lawrence River, entered what he labelled La Baie de Chaleur (the Bay of Heat), encountered a colony of Indians which he estimated would be easily converted, and engaged in trade with them. Later, at Gaspe, he erected a huge cross emblazoned with the inscription, "Long Live the King of France." On this voyage he took ten Indian prisoners back to France.

In his second voyage with three ships, Cartier visited the Indian village of Stadacona, which consisted of a cluster of wigwams on what is today the site of Quebec city. Further up the river, he came to the Indian community of Hochelaga, situated on the present site of Montreal. Here some fifty longhouses, each about 150 feet long and 45 feet wide and each accommodating several families, had been built around a public square. The entire community was surrounded by fortifications consisting of triple rows of tree trunks. After a miserable winter, during which 25 of Cartier's party died, he returned to France, this time with ten Indians.

During the third voyage (1541-1542), an attempt was made to establish a colony called Charlesbourg Royal. The French constructed a huge manor house complete with great halls, kitchens, chambers and workshops, spacious enough to house the entire colony. Shortage of provisions and disease resulted in abandonment. This time, two more Indians were taken to France.

Nor were the first English ventures more successful. Captain Martin Frobisher's exploits in Baffin Land in 1576 and 1578 were not aimed at settlement but at the acquisition of gold. He had found gold in black rock on his first trip, but on his subsequent journeys, the rocks with which he loaded his ships were not ore bearing. He did bring back with him four Inuit captives. In 1583, Sir Humphrey Gilbert took formal possession of Newfoundland in the name of Queen Elizabeth and made the first attempt to plant an English colony in the New World, but this effort was soon abandoned. Although seamen continued to fish the eastern coastline, interest in the interior of what is now Canada and the northern United States virtually ceased during the 16th century.

In 1603, the task of exploration was taken up by Samuel de Champlain — a service that won for him the title "Father of the New France." He discovered that changes had occurred in the St. Lawrence area. Whereas in Cartier's time bands of Indians had peopled Stadacona and Hochelaga, now only a few wandering Algonquins remained.

In 1604, Sieur de Monts obtained permission from the French court to colonize Acadia which includes today's provinces of Nova Scotia and New Brunswick and the state of Maine. He was granted a monopoly on fur trading and was given the commission to Christianize the Indians. Soon the newcomers were comfortably established at Port Royal. The colony was abandoned in 1606 when they lost the fur trading charter. When it was revived in 1607, Jesuits set about the task of converting the Indians, but a new danger was to threaten the community.

In 1607, Jamestown, an English settlement had been founded on the banks of the James river in Virginia (named for the virgin queen). Its mission was "to digg, mine and search for all manner of mines of goulde, silver and copper," and to find a passage to Asia. In 1613, Samuel Argall of Jamestown was cruising the waters of the Bay of Fundy when he discovered the French colony of Port Royal. He destroyed the place and it was many years before the French again attempted to develop settlements in Acadia. That battle can be seen as a symbol of the rivalry and outright warfare that was to develop between the French and the English, particularly in what was to become Canada.

The Jamestown settlement had come into being under the aegis of the Virginia Company of London which was organized by English investors in 1606. The Company's intent was to establish colonies in America. In terms of religion, the colonists were conforming members of the Anglican church with strong "anti-popish" attitudes. They tended to embrace the severely restrictive attitudes of Calvinism so that whatsoever smacked of Roman ritual was suspect. At first, the Anglican church in England paid little heed to what was taking place in Jamestown and the colonists tended to develop their own religious patterns. But when the Virginia Company lost its charter in 1624, Virginia became a Crown colony and conformity to the Church of England was required. Within fifteen years a narrow bigotry was asserting itself. There was persecution of Roman Catholics and of those who embraced Calvinistic concepts. As a result, many non-conformists migrated to Maryland and New England (Bridenbaugh, p. 66). When Quakers began to arrive in 1656, they were treated harshly and imprisoned as members of a "most pestilent Sect."

After the death of King Henry VIII, whose break with Catholicism had brought the Church of England into being, English religious life went through a series of disruptions. Edward VI, the boy king who succeeded Henry, died after a brief reign. He was followed by Mary, a Roman Catholic, who married King Philip II of Spain. Her zealous efforts to undo the results of the Reformation in England and to restore Catholicism earned her the label "Bloody Mary." When she died in 1558, her half-sister Elizabeth (daughter of King Henry and Ann Boleyn) was crowned. She ruled for 45 years until 1603 in a period of growth and richness for England that came to be called "the Elizabethan Age." It was a time of exploration, excitement, scientific growth and navigational achievement.

Sir Francis Drake explored the west coast of America and circumnavigated the world. As a crown-endorsed pirate he plundered Spanish merchant ships of their gold and silver. In a confrontation with the Spanish Armada, Drake defeated the forces of Philip II, thereby dealing a serious blow to Spanish influence and power. Meanwhile, Sir Walter Raleigh explored and colonized Virginia. He introduced potatoes and tobacco from America to England.

The spirit that was so alive in the Elizabethan Age underwent change at her death in 1603. Because she had never married and produced offspring, James I of Scotland, a Calvinist in theology, assumed the throne. James' belief in the "divine right of kings" put him into conflict with the English Parliament, and for seven years (1614-1621) James ruled without that organization being called into session.

The Puritans

In England in 1608, under threat by James I to "harry them out of the land," a small group of religious dissenters fled from England to Holland. These people were known as "Separatists" because they wished to sever all ties with the Established church. In 1620, another group of dissenters known as Puritans set sail from England on the ship the Mayflower. This group chose to remain within the Church of England, seeking to purify it from within. In November, they sighted Cape Cod. Some passengers from Southhampton and London appeared disruptive; therefore, before landing, 41 Pilgrims met and drew up what is known as the Mayflower Compact. In this document, which was to become the newcomers' first written constitution, they pledged themselves to the development of "just and equall lawes, ordinances, acts, constitutions and offices."

When they finally set foot on land in the Fall of 1620, they were greeted in English by a Wampanoag Indian named Squanto. Squanto was one of the Indians who had been kidnapped and taken to England in 1614 by the Virginia Company. He had rapidly learned the language before being returned to what was being called "New England." Squanto assisted the newcomers to survive the winter, and it was the Indians who provided the wild turkeys that were enjoyed at what was to become known as the first Thanksgiving feast. Squanto has been called a "Pilgrim father" by virtue of his role in assisting the Pilgrims to adjust to their new environment (Johansen, p. 4).

It should not be imagined that the Puritans were religious liberals or concerned with democracy. Indeed, the Reverend John Cotton declared that democracy was "not fit government either for church or commonwealth." (Meltzer, p. 4) When a company of the Puritans founded the Massachusetts Bay Colony at Boston in 1630, their intent was the establishment of a commonwealth in which their "purified" church would prosper. Within ten years some twenty-five thousand persons were living in Massachusetts, making it the largest English settlement in America.

There were some who rebelled against the rigid rules of the Puritan leaders. The Reverend Nathaniel Ward was assigned the task of preparing the Massachusetts Body of Liberties which was adopted in 1641. The document affirmed such human rights as equal justice, but a democratic system of government was not yet in vogue. In fact, Roger Williams, a Separatist who advocated religious liberty and a more tolerant government, was in 1635 ordered to leave Massachusetts.

The Continuing Struggle

Meanwhile, further north, Champlain continued his explorations. He sided with Hurons in their continuing warfare with the Iroquois. He founded the city of Quebec. In 1627, Cardinal Richelieu assisted in the formation of a new corporation of the One Hundred Associates, sometimes called the Company of New France. The French crown granted this group a virtual monopoly on fur trade and other commerce for New France which included Canada, Acadia, Newfoundland and even Florida. They were commissioned to immediately settle and support several hundred settlers and within fifteen years raise that number to four thousand.

In 1629, the English defeated Champlain and took possession of Quebec, but the English hold on Canada was short-lived. Charles I, desperate for money, sold the country to France for $240,000. Once again, the Company of One Hundred, with Champlain at its head, controlled Quebec and eastern Canada.

Life patterns imported to the New World from France were modelled after the feudal system which flourished in France from the eleventh through the thirteenth centuries. The theory back of this system was that the king received his land from God as a fief or feud — hence the term "feudalism." In reality, the crown held the land by the power of the sword. The land was divided among the nobles who supported the king's wars. Each noble sublet the greater portion of his fief to his followers. The noble was the lord or suzerain or liege, the grantees were liegemen, vassals or retainers. The lord gave protection, the vassal provided service. It was this system that Cardinal Richelieu introduced with the charter of the One Hundred Associates. His objective was two-fold — to create a New World aristocracy and to establish an easy way of dividing land among the settlers. The suzerain received the fief from the monarch and became his vassal. The seignior or suzerain was required to clear the land and put it to use. In turn his retainers, called *habitants* in Canada, cleared the land, cultivated the soil and paid rent — partially in money but also in produce such as wheat, live fowl, eggs and so forth.

Not everyone fitted into this social pattern. The fur trade was so lucrative that many young men ventured into the woods to acquire the choicest hides from the Indians. Enamored by the freedoms they experienced, they rebelled against settled life and as *coureurs de bois* (runners-of-the-woods) consorted with the Indians and at trading time engaged in unrestrained revelry. So popular did this way of life become that it is estimated that at one time it engaged approximately one-twelfth of the population.

Tradesmen did not hesitate to exploit the weakness of the Indians and introduced the tribal groups to brandy ("firewater") so that, rather than trading with governmental agents, the Indians took their furs to those who would provide them with alcohol. When homemade liquor was exchanged for goods with the Northwest Chinook Indians, their name for the alcoholic beverage was "Hootchenoo" — hence the slang expression "hootch."

It was an uneasy time. In 1670, King Charles II of England granted a charter to "The Company of Adventurers of England trading into Hudson's Bay." Consequently, the Hudson's Bay Company was drawing off fur trade from the northern tribes. Between 1648 and 1649, the Iroquois destroyed the Huron nation, thereby ending the work of the Jesuits among these people. Battles between Iroquois and French settlers and between French and English in Acadia unsettled the land. The Treaty of Utrecht, signed in 1713, made the Iroquois British subjects, and ceded Hudson Bay, Newfoundland and Acadia to Great Britain. Nevertheless, the struggles continued with intermittent war and shaky peace treaties.

The Treaty of Paris, 1763, marked the end of French rule in Canada. Canada was formally ceded to Great Britain. Not everyone accepted the agreement. Western Indians opposed British rule. French-Canadians insisted that their traditional patterns of justice be recognized. Protestants rejected what they perceived as Roman Catholic tyranny. The French of Acadia were forced to leave their homeland (a story that has been made familiar in Longfellow's poem "Evangeline"). They resisted British efforts to incorporate them in the British colonies on the Eastern seaboard. Rebuffed by colonial governors in Virginia and elsewhere because of their Catholicism, the Acadians sought refuge in the French colony of St. Domingue, which was known to the inhabitants as Haiti. In 1765, some 230 Acadians-in-exile hired a ship and sailed from Haiti to southern Louisiana, which was at that time a Spanish territory under a French caretaker government. At first the newcomers worked on the large cattle ranches, but soon claimed land on their own. By 1785, news of available land and religious toleration prompted a migration to the area of 4,000 former Acadians, some former French soldiers and a large group of freed African-American slaves. This mixed group of refugees melded to develop the famous Cajun culture that was to spread across the southern state.

George III's short-sighted, obstinate approach to the colonists resulted in the American Revolutionary War. The Treaty of Paris, 1783, recognized the independence of the thirteen colonies. As a consequence of the struggle between 1783 and 1784, some forty or fifty thousand persons, who came to be known as the United Empire Loyalists, moved out of Maine into Quebec, Cape Breton and Nova Scotia. The final struggle between the United States and Canada was the war of 1812-1814, which was settled by the Treaty of Ghent.

For a long period the Roman Catholic Church had been without a rival in the effort to Christianize the Indians. But the Loyalists who came from Britain wanted their own clergy and forms of worship. In 1782, the first Methodist minister preached in Halifax. Two years later, the Anglican church began its work and in 1786 the first Protestant church was erected among the Mohawks in Upper Canada. By the close of the century Anglican, Presbyterian and Methodist churches were functioning in the Canadian provinces.

The pioneers who settled most of what is now the United States and Canada were not Spanish or Portuguese and their thinking was not controlled and dictated by the Spanish church and crown. Some newcomers from central Europe brought with them elements of freethought that had developed out of rebellion against the authority of the church and the crown. There were also those who had been influenced by the scientific thought that had been developing in Europe. What was equally important were the opportunities for personal ownership of land rather than employment as servants to the rich and powerful. Indeed, jumps from servant status to freeman status, enhanced by the Protestant work ethic, resulted in attitudes that limited or made impossible European feudal or manorial tenant-farmer systems.

The American Colonies Discover "Democracy"

The democracy that became America did not happen all at once. There can be no question that the Magna Carta, the Reformation and the Enlightenment provoked feelings of independent thought and the rights of people to freedom and justice. As we have noted, language reflecting these ideas was part of the Mayflower Compact. But there was little tolerance of differing points of view, and there were those convinced that government should be in the hands of persons of certain religious persuasion. How then did democracy come into being?

It was not long after the coming of the Pilgrims that feelings of being separated and perhaps different from Europeans began to develop. Among the newcomers were exiles and fortune seekers, many of whom had hoped to return one day to their homeland. However, new generations who had never known England or Europe were born. And, as the colonists continued to learn by experimentation and from the Indians how to live in the New World, the sense of being a distinct people grew. Ultimately, they identified themselves as "Americans" — a label that was, at first, reserved for Indians.

The colonists occupied a narrow strip of land along the Atlantic seaboard; the Indians were spread across a continent of forests, rivers and plains, so broad that its dimensions were unknown. For survival, it became important to seek alliances with the native inhabitants. The British sent representatives to work through agreements with the Iroquois. Now, the new Americans came into direct contact with an Iroquoian system of democratic government — a government of the people, by the people and for the people — in which various groups sent representatives to the Great Council to serve their best interests. Iroquois officials were servants of the people as opposed to the European pattern where the people were servants of overlords and monarchs.

As the colonies developed and trade with the Indians increased, new problems arose. Indians protested both the encroachment of the new Americans on their ancestral lands and the sale of alcohol to their people. These protests resulted in dialogue and treaties. It is clear from the records that the eloquence of the Iroquois matched that of the colonists. The man most responsible for printing the treaty agreements was Benjamin Franklin of Philadelphia.

Franklin was a Deist who had moved away from the Puritan restrictiveness of Boston to the Quaker city of Philadelphia. So impressed was he by the Iroquois organizational pattern that when, in 1774, the idea of a unified Colonial military command was discussed (the idea had been suggested by the Iroquois for some seven years), he wrote:

> It would be a very strange thing if Six Nations of Ignorant Savages should be capable of forming a Scheme for such a Union and be able to execute it in such a manner, as that it has subsisted Ages, and appears indissoluble, and yet a like union should be impracticable for ten or a dozen English colonies. (quoted in Johansen, p. 66)

In 1753, Franklin was appointed by the Pennsylvania government to be one of the colony's commissioners to participate in a meeting with the Six Nations. This appointment, which began Franklin's diplomatic career, provided him with greater appreciation for the Iroquois system of government. In 1754, he and others proposed that "the British American colonies be federated under a single legislature and a president-general to be appointed by the Crown." (Johansen, p. 71). The plan called for a Grand Council to be composed of 48 representatives with each colony providing a number based on population and contributions to the military force. The impact of the Iroquois system is clear both in the name and the organizational pattern. But the time was not ripe for such a scheme and the plan was turned down by the colonial legislatures.

Two decades later, the atmosphere was different. In 1774, in fury over the Stamp Act of 1765 and the insistence that the colonies contribute to the Crown's war debts, colonists, dressed as Indians, dumped tea into the Boston Harbor. The colonists declared that taxes could only be levied by colonist legislatures, not by the British parliament. In Carl N. Degler's words, "the colonists suddenly realized that they were no longer wards of Britain, but a separate people, capable of forging their own destiny." (Degler, p. 78) As war with the British was at hand, commissioners from the recently united colonists smoked the peace pipe with the representatives of the Six Nations. Before the new nation could emerge, the shackles of the old had to be discarded.

When the time came to write the Declaration of Independence and Benjamin Franklin was invited to compose the statement, the seventy-year-old man declined. He was willing to join the drafting committee and he did become Thomas Jefferson's major editor. Jefferson was thirty-three years old in 1776 and the final writing of the Declaration echoed principles that Franklin, Jefferson and Adams had observed among the Iroquois, including human equality, the pursuit of happiness, government by the consent of the governed and the power of public opinion to condition morality. But there were other powerful sources for the ideas of freedom and democracy. These sources constitute the rich European heritage. The founding fathers were not prepared to establish a new nation without careful study of earlier and existing forms of government. Nor were they unaware of the intellectual and social movements in Europe.

See pp. 475-481 for References of chapters 16-21.

19

The European Heritage

Long before their sailors began to travel to the American continents, central Europe had been engaged in exciting intellectual growth and debate. Scientific thinking and rationalism had challenged religious belief systems and the authority of the Roman Catholic Church. The developing European spirit of freethinking became an American heritage that made democracy possible.

As early as the 12th century, Adelard of Bath studied in Muslim countries, where he learned to follow reason rather than authority (Durant, p. 1004). In the thirteenth century, the Oxford Franciscan, Roger Bacon (c. 1214-1292), stressed the importance of testing in scientific experimentation and called for "the empirical investigation of nature" (Heer, p. 247). Freethinking, which did not hesitate to draw information from Jews and Muslims, was not the way to popularity. After all, in 1215, the Fourth Lateran Council had ordered Jews to wear a "yellow patch, horned cap and other emblems of Cain (which) invited the hostility of those who saw Jews as 'murderers of Christ'" (Heer, p. 255). Bacon died in prison.

William of Ockham (?-1349?), an Oxford scholar and a Franciscan, entered into debate with Pope John XXII (1316-1334). Efforts to relax the strict rules of poverty endorsed by the Franciscan Order had been vigorously opposed by those who were known as "Spirituals" and who insisted that Christ's poverty was absolute. The Pope opposed the concept of absolute poverty; Ockham supported the Spirituals. He defied a sentence of excommunication and declared Pope John XXII to be a heretic. His published statements defended the independence of the state from the authority of the church and argued that secular rulers had jurisdiction over material property in the hands of ecclesiastics, so that the kings of England had the right to tax church property. The true Church, he maintained, consisted of the whole community of the faithful as opposed to a formally constituted body headed by an ecclesiastical hierarchy. His thinking was to influence reformers like Luther.

The Renaissance

The Renaissance (14th to 17th centuries) was born in Italy. Lacking a centralized government, independent city-states, which had come into being after the collapse of feudalism, were ruled by wealthy families in some cases and by tyrants in others. Often ruling families used their power and wealth to beautify their city. Many turned to the works of ancient Greeks and Romans for guidance in art. At the same time, Greek and Roman classics and philosophies introduced humanistic ideals. The developing humanism clashed with Roman Catholic Christianity.

Whereas the Church viewed human beings as sinful, humanists emphasized their dignity, worth and ability to achieve. From Virgil and Socrates came ideas of individual worth. From Pericles and Cicero came the image of men devoted to public service. From men like Archimedes, who was a scientist, an inventor and a mathematician, came a vision of the unlimited possibilities that could be called forth from individuals. The ideal of the person well-rounded in knowledge became popular and gave birth to the concept of the Renaissance man. The result was a flowering of art, science, and independent thought. Renaissance thought, which was primarily humanistic and often secular in nature, presented challenges to current Christian thought.

Early Christian Humanists did not hesitate to look critically at the Church and condemn or make sport of its doctrines and its leaders, even as they remained within the church. Some of these from poor families had entered religious orders to gain an education.

Desiderius Erasmus (1467-1536), the Dutch Christian Humanist, was just 25 years old when Columbus landed in America. He had come out of poverty and joined the Augustinians to pursue higher learning. Troubled by church leaders who engaged in immoral behavior and by learned clergy who engaged in ridiculous doctrinal arguments, he wrote his satirical *The Praise of Folly*. He mocked pilgrimages, church rituals and the boring disputes among church scholars, and exposed the immoral life of the monks. His Christian humanism, described in the *Enchiridion*, focussed on humans and stated that the essence of Christianity was charity (love). This charity was not expressed in church attendance, bowing before images, lighting candles and reciting prescribed prayers. Rather, it was directed towards one's neighbors, seeking their well-being. Even as he focussed on human dignity and worth, he retained many standard church doctrines. For example, he reminded his readers that rewards and punishments in the afterlife were based on acts performed during this earthly existence. Like other

Christian Humanists, he continued to be concerned for the welfare of the church. This was a time of exchange of ideas and Erasmus was influential in bringing the Renaissance to England. The number of informed persons was on the increase, thanks both to the invention of movable type, which enabled the spread of information, and to the establishment of universities that were open to others beside the clergy.

The church itself provided Desiderius Erasmus with ample evidence to legitimize his condemnations. The Roman Catholic papacy had been in turmoil. From 1309 to 1377, the Popes had lived in France, removed from Rome by schisms and family feuds. When they returned to Rome the feuds continued. Then in 1378, Pope Gregory IX died and the cardinals elected Urban VI. Urban's anti-French stance provoked hostility and four months later the cardinals chose Clement VII as pope. Clement immediately took up residence in Avignon, while Urban remained in Rome. Now the Church had two popes. In Rome, Urban was succeeded by Boniface IX (1389-1404) and Boniface by Innocent VII (1404-1406) who was followed by Gregory XII (1406-1415). In Avignon, Clement VII was succeeded by Benedict XIII (1394-1417).

In 1409, at the Council of Pisa, an effort was made to heal the schism. The Council declared both popes deposed and chose a new pope who became Alexander V. In actuality, the Council worsened the situation, for now there were *three* claimants to the papal throne and each pope was supported by different nations! Alexander died in 1410 and was replaced by John XXIII. In 1414 at the Council of Constance, John XXIII was imprisoned, Gregory XII submitted his resignation and Benedict XIII was declared a heretic. The problem was not resolved until 1417 with the election of Martin V who received universal approval. It was this same Council of Constance that ordered John Huss burned to death as a heretic and commanded that the bones of Wyclif be exhumed, burned and scattered to the winds.

Political machinations in the church did not cease with the election of a single pope. Pope Sixtus IV (1471-1484) was a militant whose greed for power involved him in financial abuses. He promoted a policy whereby indulgences could be sold to release the souls of those in purgatory. His successor, Innocent VIII (1484-1492), sold church offices. After him, Alexander VI (1492-1503), who was Rodrigo Borgia, bribed his way into the papacy, and under his rule the papacy sank to its lowest spiritual and moral level. It has been estimated "that there were at least 6,800 courtesans in the Holy City." The pope and his cardinals consorted openly with their mistresses and did not hesitate to acknowledge their bastard offspring even to the point of enriching them with riches stolen from Church coffers (Stillman, p. 91). Borgia, like his papal predecessors, was essentially an Italian prince. Although these immoral popes often expressed high literary and artistic tastes, their political ambitions involved them in intrigue, murder and debauchery. It was partly out of protest against Church abuse that the Reformation was born.

The Protestant Reformation

The Protestant Reformation was to some extent a move toward religious freethought. It was marked by the critical thinking of men and women who saw themselves as devout Christians but who, on the basis of their analysis of Christian Scripture, as well as on the basis of their observation of the abuses in Roman Catholicism, were prepared to stand against the authoritarian posture of the Roman Church. Obviously they were not prepared to critically evaluate the biblical claims. Their concerns remained within the boundaries of the Christian faith, and their protests came out of deep faith commitments and out of social concerns.

Martin Luther (1493-1546), a key figure in the Reformation, was just nine years old when Columbus arrived in America. By the time Luther died, he had founded a new, non-Roman Catholic Christian religion, free of papal control and dogma. Luther was an educated monk, profoundly influenced by Christian humanistic thinking and deeply disturbed by what was occurring within Roman Catholicism. In a moment that was to trigger the Reformation, he posted ninety-five propositions on the door of the *Schlosskirche* in Wittenberg on October 31, 1517. These statements, which were designed to reform the church from within, included attacks on the sale of indulgences by which Pope Leo X was seeking to raise money to complete the building of St. Peter's cathedral in Rome. Within a fortnight Luther's theses, as they came to be called, had spread throughout Germany and within a year throughout Europe.

Of course his claims did not go unchallenged. Other Roman Catholic theologians were prepared to debate with him. When Luther was called to account in Rome, he refused to go and continued to publish volumes that now called for changes in doctrine as well as in practice. On June 15, 1520, Pope Leo X issued a bull — a papal statement — which not only condemned and excommunicated Luther but banned his works. Luther publicly burned the papal bull that excommunicated him and responded to it with a treatise titled *On the Freedom of a*

Christian Man. He called on the nobility to support his doctrinal argument for a priesthood of all believers, by which no individual could have the kind of authority that made possible the papacy. His argument that believers receive salvation through faith, not through an intermediary whether priest or church, and that all Christians are priests and can approach God through the one mediator, Jesus Christ, flew in the face of the teachings of the Roman Catholic Church.

In 1521, Luther was summoned to Worms by Charles V, the Holy Roman Emperor, who guaranteed him safe conduct. On April 17th he appeared before the Emperor and refused to recant. He rejected the authority of popes and councils, choosing to rely instead only on the Scriptures for his stand. He was not truly a freethinker for he actually substituted one authority (the Bible) for another (the papacy). He was placed under a ban and ordered to surrender. The reading of his books or the providing of shelter for him was forbidden. Fortunately for Luther, he had the support and protection of Frederick the Wise, Prince of Saxony, by whom he was hidden away and protected from harm.

In 1525, Luther married a former nun, Katherine von Bora. His translation of the Bible into the German language in 1534 (which could be quickly printed and distributed because the printing press had been invented in 1450) enabled Germans to read for themselves the bases for Luther's teachings. Luther had both followers and opponents throughout Germany. Even though the German empire was composed of divisive elements, the Lutheran Church was able to come into being through support of believers in separate sections of Germany. The 1529 *Protestio*, which protested the right of the Roman Church to worship in Lutheran lands, was defeated but gave rise to the term "Protestant" as a designation for the Lutheran party.

It should not be imagined that Luther was either always a supporter of the underdog or always a man of peace. German peasants protested feudal extractions by the German lords and the laws that barred them from forests and stream. They based their claims on Scripture. They pointed out that, since Christ had redeemed all, they should not be serfs. Since God had given men dominion over the earth, they should not be barred from the forests and streams. At first, Luther responded with a document titled *An Exhortation to Peace* in which he condemned oppression by the nobility whom he labeled "overlords," but at the same time he declared serfdom to be in accord with Christianity. He recommended arbitration. When the peasants revolted, Luther called them "pigs" and other grosser names and urged that they be ruthlessly suppressed by the sword. The uprising, known as "The Peasants' Revolt," was put down with frightful bloodshed.

Luther's anti-Semitism was revealed in his vicious lashing out against the Jews. He believed Jews were damned and depraved parasites who exploited honest Germans workers and then sat around enjoying themselves with monies fleeced from Germans. In 1543, he set forth his program for dealing with Jews. He exhorted Germans to set fire to synagogues, to destroy Jewish homes and scriptures, to take away Jewish possessions, to deny Rabbis the right to teach on pain of death, and to grant no safety to Jews on highways, all to the end that they be driven like mad dogs from the land (Luther, 47:135, 258, 266-292). This scurrilous attack was widely distributed in pamphlet form right up to the time of the Nazi holocaust and no doubt contributed to the cruel treatment of Jews by the Nazis.

Luther was not alone in his separation from the Roman Catholic Church. The spirit of the Reformation spread throughout Europe, adding "to the confusion and uncertainty of an age in which men and states were tugging unwillingly and unwittingly at the anchors that had so long held Europe." (Churchill, II, p. 6)

In Switzerland, Huldreich Zwingli (1484-1531), a contemporary of Luther, was engaged in reformation, but from a humanistic and intellectual angle of vision, rather than from a consideration of human religious needs. He, too, broke with the Catholic Church (1524). Among his own people he sought to eliminate as many outward forms of worship as possible. He refused to have images in the church. In his rejection of mysticism, he interpreted the Lord's Supper simply as a bread and wine memorial rite. At this point, he came into conflict with Luther, who claimed that partakers received mystically the true body and blood of Christ. Because Zwingli rejected infant baptism and called on those who had been so baptized to be rebaptized as consenting adults, the rebaptized were called Anabaptists (the Greek term means "to baptize again"). Those baptized for the first time as adults were known as Baptists. Seven years later (1531), Zwingli died in battle against Swiss Catholic cantons.

The Anabaptist movement spread into Moravia and into Germany where Strassburg became a center. With its growth came persecutions, deaths and subdivisions. Jacob Hutter's followers in Austerlitz gave rise to the Hutterite Brethren sect. In the city of Munster, Jan Bockelson of Leyden proclaimed himself the Anabaptist king and Messiah and predicted the coming of the biblical apocalypse. In keeping with the biblical command to increase and multiply, males were encouraged to take many wives. Debauchery ensued. Following the Diet of Worms in

1535, forces were mustered against the city of Munster and this fanatical form of Anabaptist religious extremism was eliminated. Jan Bockelson of Leyden, after having been subjected to cruel and vicious torture, was put to death (Stillman, p. 95).

Zwingli's work was continued in Geneva by John Calvin (1509-1564). The doctrine of predestination became a characteristic of the faith together with rigorous Puritan discipline. With regard to the Lord's Supper, Calvinists believed that, although mere bread and wine were ingested, the believer also received the spiritual body of Christ. The Calvinist movement became the basis of the Reformed Church. As distinct from Lutheranism, it spread across France (where it gave rise to the Huguenots), to the Netherlands, and into Britain (where its influence was most strongly felt in Scotland). Calvin, not Zwingli, came to be regarded as the founder of the Reformed Church. In Scotland, John Knox (1505?-1560), who had been a disciple of Calvin, helped the Presbyterian Church come into being.

In England, King Henry VIII (1509-1547), through his unhappy marriages, laid the basis for the Reformation in that country. Twenty years before his death, he forced the papacy out of England. Roman Catholic monasteries and properties were seized. Ecclesiastical power that had once belonged to the papacy was transferred to the monarch. The Crown became the head of the church, and the Church of England came into being.

Not everyone believed in the union of church and state. A group of independents, who became known as Congregationalists, sprang up in the late 17th century. Although they were heirs to the Anabaptists, unlike the Baptists they believed in infant baptism. About this same time, the Society of Friends (Quakers), which stressed the mystical experience of the "inner light," began in England, initiated by George Fox (1624-1691). They believed that because God gave each individual the "inner light," each person was charged with the responsibility to respond and follow; therefore a professional ministry was not needed. The emphasis was upon personal commitment: to truth, making oaths unnecessary; to peace, which led to rejection of war; and to humility, which denied the significance of titles and status. A century later, at the beginning of the industrial revolution, the Methodist Church came into being. Methodism originated within the established church as an urban movement reaching out with missionary zeal to those whose spiritual needs were unmet. The prime movers were John Wesley (1703-1791) and his brother Charles (1709-1788).

It was this mixture of diverse religious beliefs and commitments that was to characterize the religious beginnings of the colonies in

North America. Unlike the homogeneity of nationality and religion that marked the European colonization in Central and South America, North American colonization was represented by a variety of national origins and religious preferences. This heritage encouraged a kind of spiritual freethought bounded by the walls of religious doctrines. Although there was no encouragement to move out of the Christian tradition, the mushrooming of new faith statements in everything from store front missions to splits within traditional denominations resulted in a wide variety of Christian "churches." At the same time, the desire for an educated clergy exposed young theologians to secular and critical thought that often challenged traditional beliefs. One of the contributors to higher education was the Enlightenment.

The Enlightenment

What was even more important than religious pluralism to American democratic beginnings was the influence of the Enlightenment, which was characterized by a revolt against authority in the interest of science and critical thinking. Enlightenment knowledge was not based on authority, scriptural or otherwise, but on openness to new theories, along with openness to testing and scientific experimentation. Knowledge was empirical, derived from the experiences of the senses, and was subject to measurement, logic and testing by critical examination. The final authority was not revelation nor the authoritative proclamations of the church. Reason, which was possessed by all, was the final authority. Where truth could not be tested by science, as with the spiritual claims of religion, each religion must be free to go its own way without entering into battle. Each person must be free to follow his or her own reasoning and choose the religion that made sense to him or to her. Out of this thinking developed an optimistic view of human potential. Human obligation did not derive from axioms proclaiming what God required, but rested on the basis of what human beings could accomplish. The stress on the individual invited men and women to seek their own fortunes, to exploit their own abilities, to adventure into fields that would advance their personal interests.

The spirit of the Enlightenment was fed by the implications of the developing science of astronomy. The role of Copernicus has been previously noted. It was Giordano Bruno of Nola (1548-1600) who related Copernican cosmology to philosophy, openly rejected the Ptolemaic geocentric theory and declared the infinity of space. His arguments flew in the face of accepted theological beliefs. Trained as a

Dominican, Bruno, through his studies and research, was led to abandon the clerical role.

It was a dangerous time to be classified as a heretic. Europe was engaged in bitter religious struggle through the Reformation and counter-Reformation. Ignatius Loyola had formed the Jesuit organization to confront and undo the work of Calvin and Luther. The Council of Trent had charged the Jesuits "to erase with fire and sword the last traces of heresy." The Inquisition was set at work to eliminate heresy.

Suspected of heresy, Bruno fled from Naples to Rome. His accusers followed him and again Bruno fled. For the next sixteen years he became an itinerant lecturer. He went to Geneva, a city noted for its hospitality to religious reformers. There he discovered that Calvinists could be as intolerant as Roman Catholics. He lectured in Paris and then in England. When he presented his findings on the Copernican theory at Oxford, he was coldly received by scholars who had turned Aristotelian philosophical concepts into a dogma. Because he had received an appointment as secretary to Castelnau de Mauvissiere, the resident French ambassador, he was a frequent visitor at the court of Queen Elizabeth. This relationship with English royalty was later used against him, inasmuch as the Protestant queen was considered to be a heretic by the Roman Church. When Castelnau was recalled to France, Bruno returned to Paris where he lectured and made a fruitless attempt at reconciliation with the Catholic Church. He taught in Germany and then returned to Venice where he was arrested. He was tried in the Venetian Inquisitorial courts and condemned as a heretic and blasphemer. After seven years imprisonment in Rome, during which he was denied visitors, writing materials and books, he was tortured and burned alive at the stake as an impenitent heretic. The injustice of his cruel treatment for being a freethinker has never been acknowledged by the Roman Catholic Church. Rather, any reconsideration of Bruno's case ends up somehow justifying the punishments he received.

Bruno was more Deist or perhaps pantheist, than atheist. Imerti, the translator and editor of the English version of Bruno's *The Expulsion of the Triumphant Beast*, which was the writing most often used against Bruno in his trial, notes that Bruno "lashes out against the pedants in religion, in science, philosophy, and letters." (Bruno, p. 22) Bruno's view of the boundless universe removed God from a place above the earth. His pantheistic philosophy linked God and nature. He taught that facets of belief such as the virginity of Mary, the significance of the crucifixion and the relevance of the mass were meaningless. He was truly a martyr of freethought in a time when Christianity, both Protestant and Catholic, could not tolerate intellectual challenge to biblical beliefs.

But the age was alive with the spirit of exploration and the adventure of reaching out to new lands. As we noted in chapter 10, between 1613 and 1616, Sir Walter Raleigh (1552?-1618), who was truly a world traveler, wrote his *History of the World* in two volumes. In it he expressed his concern for the biblical story of Noah's ark. As he continued to learn of new species of animals he wondered how all the creatures could be confined in a wooden ark that was some 450 feet long (300 cubits), 75 feet wide (50 cubits) and 45 feet deep (30 cubits). With three floor levels it would only provide a floor space of 101,250 square feet. He estimated that, allowing for 100 different species, he could crowd all the animals into the first level, reserve the second for food storage and house the birds on the third floor. The continuing discovery of new creatures soon made the ark overcrowded. The question as to how Noah would know the differing kinds of food required for each animal was also raised.

Although Raleigh was accused of being an atheist, he was in reality a Deist. Perhaps his association with Christopher Marlowe, whose derision of biblical beliefs was widely known, contributed to the label. Raleigh's essay "The Skeptick" noted that "the skeptick doth neither affirm nor deny any position; but doubteth of it, and applyeth his Reason against that which is affirmed, or denied, to justifie his non-consenting" (quoted by J.M. Robertson, II, p. 545). Marlowe was killed in 1593. Raleigh, who at first enjoyed good favor with the crown during the reign of Queen Elizabeth, fell out of favor during the time of James I of Scotland. It was during his imprisonment for treason for thirteen years in the Tower of London that he wrote his *History of the World*. He was beheaded on October 29, 1618. Because he smoked a pipe before going to the block, there were those who thought that the belief that he was an atheist was confirmed (Bronowski/Mazlish, p. 137).

One of Raleigh's companions, the mathematician-astronomer Thomas Hariot, was critical of biblical concepts. He rejected the biblical creation story which, according to the interpretation of that time, espoused the *creatio ex nihilo* (creation out of nothing) notion. He quoted Lucretius: *Ex nihilo, nihil fit* ("out of nothing, nothing comes") which is the basis of scientific materialism. His death from cancer was interpreted by some as a divine punishment for his heresy.

Hariot was not alone in his questioning of the claims of religion. There is considerable evidence that suggests that the spirit of the Renaissance was alive in England and that open inquiry in science cast doubt on the interpretations of religious orthodoxy. This, coupled with the excitement of what humans could accomplish, developed an intellectualism that negated the need for God (Buckley).

In France, Michel Eyquem Montaigne (1533-1592), who was raised as a Roman Catholic, became intrigued with the philosophy of doubt that originated with Pyrrho and was explicated by Sextus Empiricus. Whether or not Montaigne ever abandoned the Catholic concept of deity and revelation has been debated. What is clear is that he was no religious fanatic and perhaps, like the ancient skeptics, he accepted the laws and customs of his community including Catholicism. His skepticism did challenge the dogmatism of faith positions and, inasmuch as final truth was not attainable, he could point out the folly of the endless theological arguments of his time. Montaigne influenced what Popkin has labelled "the theological crisis" of his time which challenged the rule of faith. Montaigne also touched the "humanistic crisis of knowledge" ("how can we possibly tell which theory is true?") and "the crisis of scientific knowledge" ("the reliability of sense knowledge, the truth of first principles, the criterion of rational knowledge, our inability to know anything except appearances, and our lack of any certain evidence of the existence or nature of the real world"). (Popkin, pp. 52-53) His writings impacted on the thinking of the seventeenth-century world.

When Rene Descartes (1596-1650) became aware of the number of falsehoods that he had accepted as true when he was a child and as these once accepted "truths" proved to be unreliable and false, he sought for a way to establish foundations that would be stable and lasting. He was aware of the new Pyrrhonism that was current and was familiar with the writings of Montaigne. But as he sought to find his own way, he became impressed by the diversity in accepted behavior from nation to nation. He became aware of the fact that what one people accepted as right and proper, another group would reject. He realized that we could be deceived by perceptions, so that a tower that appeared round in the distance might be perceived as square from a closer view. Therefore the senses are untrustworthy criteria for truth. Dreams too were puzzling, for how could he be sure that at any given moment he was not dreaming? How can dreams be distinguished from reality? Finally he wondered whether or not some evil demon might not be deceiving him. Not only did he doubt the thinking of earlier philosophers and writers but he doubted his own reasoning.

Out of this struggle came the famous affirmation *Cogito, ergo sum!* — I think, therefore I am! His very doubts were recognized as a form of thinking. To think was to be, to exist. He could not doubt his own existence. This assertion became the first principle of his philosophy.

For him, the method of doubt became the cause of the acquisition of knowledge. This awareness, he believed, came as a result of a continuous act of divine intervention, so that the *cogito, ergo sum* not only provided a basis for the development of philosophy, but for the recognition of other truths, including metaphysical truths.

It has been argued that Descartes' skepticism "showed the way to the certain knowledge sought by dogmatists; he saw himself as the first philosopher to *overthrow* the doubts of sceptics." (Hookway, p. 41) But his efforts are not convincing: "His proofs of God's existence do not carry conviction." At least part of his legacy lies in "a realization of how powerful skeptical arguments can be." (p. 43)

Baruch Spinoza (1632-1677) drew upon the skepticism of Pyrrho, Sextus Empiricus, and Descartes to develop his own critical approach. He began by investigating the claims of the Judeo-Christian-Islamic tradition and worked his way through the Bible and through current theology. While he could admit that philosophically God existed, he could also argue that the existence of God was not self-evident and that the God concept was diffuse and devoid of clarity. Spinoza's God concept left no room for revelation or supernaturalism and could only be inferred. So far as the Bible was concerned, he evaluated its various teachings and ideas on the basis of rationalism and what we know about nature. His methodology transformed the Bible from a source of knowledge to an object of knowledge which could be critically examined (Popkin, p. 234). His examination of the teachings of biblical prophets convinced him that they not only held conflicting opinions, but could not be relied upon for either natural or spiritual knowledge. He questioned the authenticity of the claims for miracles. Indeed, as a result of his investigations, he argued that philosophy and theology should be separated. He scorned attempts to reinterpret the Bible to make its teachings coincide with rational thought — a methodology he found in Maimonides and his followers. His skepticism concerning the values of the biblical world and their relevance for rational human beings in the seventeenth century, and his skepticism regarding the teachings of theology, led to the denial of the worth of revealed religion.

Spinoza was deeply committed to principles of free speech and freethought. He could state in *Tractus Theologico-Politicus*:

> It follows, plainly . . . that the ultimate aim of government is not to rule, or restrain, by fear, nor to exact obedience, but, on the contrary, to free every man from fear, that he may live in

> all possible security; in other words, to strengthen his natural right to exist and work without injury to himself or others.
>
> No, the object of government is not to change men from rational beings into beasts or puppets, but to enable them to develop their minds and bodies in security, and to employ their reason unshackled; neither showing hatred, anger, or deceit, nor watched with the eyes of jealousy and injustice. In fact, the true aim of government is liberty.

Enlightenment thinking postulated that the role of the state was to enact enabling laws enhancing human freedom rather than enacting legislation that placed religious impositions on humans. The state was to look to the safety of all and the freedom of all. Religious affiliation and belief were matters for personal, individual choice. Churches represented the gathering together of those who had voluntarily made similar choices. The fundamental social emphasis of the Enlightenment was a toleration that enhanced human freedom. The way in which that toleration and freedom could best be preserved was through the separation of church and state.

In 1685, John Locke (1632-1704), living at the time in Holland because of his fear of imprisonment in England for participating in revolutionary political activity, wrote *A Letter Concerning Toleration*. The *Letter* was written in Latin, published in Holland in 1689, then translated by William Popple and published anonymously in England. Locke called for the separation of church and state and for religious toleration:

> . . . I esteem it above all things necessary to distinguish exactly the business of civil government from that of religion, and to settle the just bounds that lie between the one and the other . . . . If a Roman Catholic believe that to be really the body of Christ which another man calls bread, he does no injury thereby to his neighbor. If a Jew do not believe the New Testament to be the Word of God, he does not thereby alter anything in men's civil rights. If a heathen doubt of both Testaments, he is not therefore to be punished as a pernicious citizen. The power of the magistrate and the estates of the people may be equally secure whether any man believe these things or no. I readily grant these opinions are false and absurd. But the business of laws is not to provide for the truth of opinions, but for the safety and security of the commonwealth, and of every particular man's goods and person. And so it ought to be. For the

> truth certainly would do well enough is she were once left to shift for herself. She seldom has received, and I fear never will receive, much assistance from the power of great men, to whom she is but rarely known and more rarely welcome. She is not taught by laws, nor has she any need of force to procure her entrance into the minds of men. Errors indeed prevail by the assistance of foreign and borrowed succors. But if truth makes not her way into the understanding by her own light, she will be but weaker for any borrowed force violence can add to her.

During the eighteenth century the notion began to grow that perhaps government under a king, who seemed to be more interested in the nobility and the rich, was unjust and oppressive. Why, it was asked, should so many work so hard to support the few? Was the divine right of the kingship really a divine scheme? Contributing to the questioning was the development of science.

Galileo died in 1642. He had aroused the interest and support of Francis Bacon, who was not a scientist but a writer. In his two popular and powerful volumes, *The Advancement of Learning* and *Novum Organum*, Bacon argued that the learning of theologians and philosophers was no longer profitable and that humans would benefit most through the study of nature. His ideas struck a responsive chord. The people were wearied by wars that were largely based on religious conflict — the Thirty Years' War in Germany and the Civil War in England — that really settled nothing. Influential thinkers were turning toward science, and one of these was Newton.

Isaac Newton was born the year that Galileo died (1642). Although Newton's scientific discoveries related to the relationship between light and color, and the effects of the force of gravity, his book *Principia* (1686) was to propose a new notion about the universe. Under the influence of the Catholic church and the teachings of Thomas Aquinas, it was taught that humans were naturally disposed to evil and that civil authority was divinely bestowed on kings and leaders who should be obeyed as they sought to regulate human behavior, education and belief. These same ideas were embraced by Luther and the reformers. But under the influence of Copernicus, Bruno, Galileo and now Newton, a different concept was emerging. Belief in a creator God remained, but it was pointed out that, since the world and the universe were believed to have been designed according to a rational plan, humans had been endowed with a rational mind for understanding nature. Reason was the key to understanding the universe and, with understanding, human problems could be solved. In other words, human beings were to be masters of their own fate. They were capable, through the use of reason, to increase knowledge and make progress. When the ideas of human potential were applied to religion and to government, the power of the church and of rulers began to weaken. If knowledge rested on reason, then it was reasonable that political and religious authority should rest on consent.

Newton died in 1727, but the ideas he and others espoused had taken root. Francois Marie Arouet, who took the name Voltaire (1694-1778), became a champion of reason and tolerance. After persecution in France for his biting wit, Voltaire bought his freedom from imprisonment by volunteering to go to England in 1726. He attended Newton's funeral and was impressed by honor bestowed on this ordinary professor of mathematics. He was delighted with the freedom of speech enjoyed in England and wrote *Lettres philosophiques*, a book that was eagerly read by the public in France when he returned in 1734. In it he criticized the intolerance of the French government and praised the freedom he found in England where "The English, as a free people, choose their own road to heaven." He was disgusted with the fact that only in England, Holland, Germany and Switzerland could a Frenchman speak his mind about politics and religion. Of course, his book was condemned by those in power.

His more influential book, dealing with history from the earliest times, showed that the greatest advancements in knowledge and civilization took place when there was the greatest freedom of thought. Positive examples were drawn from Greece, Rome, the Renaissance; negative examples from the "Dark Ages" when, through the power of the church, the greatest restrictions on learning resulted in periods of ignorance and unhappiness. Voltaire was not an atheist, but he was a bitter enemy of the suppressive power of the Catholic Church in France. "Natural law," he claimed, "is that which teaches all men. . . . Human rights should be founded, in all cases, on the law of nature."

However, Voltaire was more than a writer who produced delightful plays like *Candide* or books on science like *The Philosophy of Newton*. He was also an activist who did not hesitate to act on behalf of the oppressed. When, in 1761, Mark Anthony Calas, the son of a Huguenot shopkeeper committed suicide, a rumor claimed that his father Jean Calas and Mark's brother had murdered him to keep him from converting to Catholicism. Despite the fact that there was no evidence to support the rumor, Jean Calas was tortured and broken on the wheel, his two daughters and son were compelled to enter monastic life, and all the Calas property was confiscated. Voltaire studied the case and found that the vicious punishment of an innocent man rested in religious hatred and bigotry. After three years, during which time he published a statement of the facts and encouraged his friends to use their influence with officials, he had the case reopened. The verdict was reversed. The children were set free, Madame Calas was brought to Paris, and Voltaire helped to raise money for care of the family. By the time he died in 1778, most people in France no longer believed in divine right of the state or the church to impose controls over the education and the freethinking of people.

Even as Newton was drawing conclusions about the world and humanity through his scientific pursuits, John Locke wrestled with principles of government. The theory of the divine right of kingship implied that rebellion against the monarchy was tantamount to rebellion against God. Locke sought to produce a new concept of government and to defend the right of the citizenry in the dethroning of James II in 1688. In 1690, he published *Two Treatises of Government*. His theory was as follows:

- All men have certain natural rights including the right to life, liberty, and the fruits of their own labor
- So that men might know their natural rights and devise a government to protect them, God gave man reason
- Having established government, men owe obedience to that government so long as it protects their basic rights.
- When government fails to protect these rights it can be overthrown.

Locke's essay was read by the leaders of the American revolution. It is clear that in writing the opening to the Declaration of Independence, Thomas Jefferson employed Locke's ideas:

We hold these truths to be self-evident:

- that all men are created equal;
- that they are endowed by their creator with certain inalienable rights
- that among these are life, liberty, and the pursuit of happiness;
- that to secure these rights, governments are instituted among men, deriving their just powers from the consent of the governed;
- that whenever any form of government becomes destructive of these ends, it is the right of the people to alter or to abolish

> it, and to institute new government, laying its foundation on such principles and organizing its powers in such a form as to them shall seem most likely to effect their safety and happiness.

Obviously, a major thrust of the Declaration was freedom — a freedom that had, at least, six basic dimensions or aspects. These were:

1. **Freedom of expression**, which includes freedom of speech, freedom of the press and the freedom to petition.
2. **Freedom of action**, which embraces the rights of political assembly and vote plus the right to move freely.
3. **Freedom of thought**, which includes the right to make decisions.
4. **Freedom to consent**, which is the right to convert opinion or thought into a statement by means of a vote. This right to participate in decision-making is echoed in the Declaration of Independence statement that government derives "their just powers from the consent of the governed."
5. **Freedom of dissent**, which is the right to protest, to be heard in open recognition that the majority is not always right, and that minority groups must also have a voice and a part in decision-making.
6. **Freedom to promote public welfare**, by which expression for the public good can be made.

The Preamble to the Constitution includes the intention to "promote the general welfare" in order to "secure the Blessing of Liberty to ourselves and our Posterity." In other words, the freedoms embodied in the statements of both the Declaration of Independence and the Preamble to the Constitution are not limited to some specific group in some specific time, but belong to all Americans throughout time.

See pp. 475-481 for References of chapters 16-21.

20

Freethought Expands Freedoms

These were heady times in America. Enlightenment emphasis on human equality, civil rights and freedom enhanced the immigrants' growing awareness that they were in the process of creating new ways of life that were separate and different from their European heritage. Even as Europe continued to be governed by tyrants or kings and queens, America was learning how to combine Enlightenment challenges to the monarchy with what they had learned from the Iroquois regarding the way a democracy could be fashioned.

Traditional roles were questioned. If, as the Enlightenment teaching insisted, all human beings were created equal, then were Indians and slaves equal to Europeans and their white slave owners? While religious leaders taught that the Bible provided a guide and defined roles for family living, American women began to question those notions. Freethought became a moving force in expanding human freedoms in America.

Freedom for Women

From the beginning, women accompanied the men from Europe as they began to colonize America. They too had endured persecution in Europe. When the Pilgrim Fathers boarded the Mayflower, eighteen were accompanied by their wives. Every privation and threat to existence experienced by the Pilgrim Fathers was shared by the Pilgrim Mothers. As the men sought to develop a self-sustaining colony, the women worked with them, helping to build, planting gardens, maintaining a home and raising children. No one can question the important role that women have played in the development of Western culture.

Some men came to America in the hope of making a quick fortune and then returning to Europe. The dream was not easily nor quickly fulfilled. Those who were married and could establish a home soon found that their interests and dreams for the future were tied to their new homeland and not to Europe. Children born in America had no longing for a European homeland, apart from that imparted by parental nostalgia — their homeland was America. Some Europeans married Indian women and raised families whose heritage was both European and American Indian. Those without wives were without family life and were often lonely and homesick. It became clear that human longing and need for sex, love, companionship and a home were as pressing as the need for material goods and equipment. Members of the London Company acknowledged "the Plantacion can never flourish till families be planted and the respect of wives and Children fix the people on the Soyle." In 1619, members of the first legislative Assembly agreed: "In a newe plantation it is not knowen whether man or women be more necessary." (Bridenbaugh, p. 125) The European governments attempted to respond.

In 1620, the Emigration Company imported ninety young English women to Jamestown. A potential husband was required to pay one-hundred-and-twenty pounds of tobacco for a bride should the young woman choose to accept him. Shiploads of available young women followed and the development of the Jamestown colony grew. In 1706, twenty young women were sent to Louisiana by King Louis XIV and in 1721, eighty more arrived (Beard, pp. 13-15). Of course, not all of the women found happiness in their new homeland. The work of survival was demanding and home life was often unpleasant. It is not surprising to find that some women did not remain faithful to their husbands, and hence a set of legal punishments that included the public "ducking stool" were developed for wayward wives (Bridenbaugh, p. 125f). But for the most part, the women labored with men in laying the foundations for what was to become a developing nation. Because the governmental processes were male-dominated, the contribution of the female has not always been recognized.

Despite the example set by the Iroquois, the status of colonial women was never equal to that of the men. Religious teachings emphasized the inferiority of women and social patterns taught that women's place was in the home. Women imported as servants were often maltreated and placed on the same level as slaves. Such women were subject to the whims of their masters and mistresses, and could be used and abused as objects rather than as persons.

Some women worked the land on their own after a husband died. Some managed shops and other businesses. Some sold garden produce or the baked goods that they prepared. A few attained reputations in botany. (Beard, p. 31f) When the conflicts with Britain began to develop, a group of women organized the Daughters of Liberty, an organization to parallel the male Sons of Liberty. They curtailed imports by producing textiles. They wrote letters and cheered at gatherings. During time of war they tended the injured and did all they could to support the soldiers.

Because institutions of learning were closed to them, many educated themselves; others resorted to private tutors. Women whose spouses were in positions of power exercised a behind-the-scenes influence in both business and politics. Letters written by Abigail Adams (1744-1818) to her husband resound with political concerns. In 1776, at the time of the framing of the Constitution, she wrote:

> In the new Code of Laws which I suppose it will be necessary for you to make, I desire you would Remember the Ladies, and be more generous and favourable to them than your ancestors. Remember all Men would be tyrants if they could. (Butterfield, p. 121)

In a subsequent letter she warned that in time women would not only free themselves but also "subdue our Masters." (Butterfield pp. 123, 127) In a letter dated July 31, 1777, she reported on an uprising by women in Boston who, during a shortage of sugar and coffee, became convinced that merchants were hoarding these products:

> It was rumored that an eminent, wealthy, stingy merchant (who is a bachelor) had a hogshead of coffee in his store which he refused to sell to the committee for under six shillings per pound. A number of females, some say a hundred, some more, assembled with cart and trucks, marched down to the warehouse and demanded the keys, which he refused to deliver. Upon which one of them seized him by his neck, and tossed him into the cart. Upon his finding no quarter, he delivered the keys, when they tipped him out of the cart and discharged him; then opened the warehouse, hoisted the coffee themselves, put it into the trucks and drove off. (quoted in Beard, p. 70)

Concern for women's rights prompted Mary Wollenscroft (1759-1797) of England to publish in 1792 what has been called the first "considered statement of feminism" which she titled *A Vindication of the Rights of Women*. Her book, a response to and an expansion of ideas set forth in the 1790 edition of *A Vindication of the Rights of Men*, pointed out that, inasmuch as there cannot be society among unequals, there must be equal rights for all without regard for differences of sex. Women, "educated in worse than Egyptian bondage," were not given the opportunity to develop their rational skills, which had given rise to beliefs in the inferiority of women. Her work inspired others, including those who lived in America.

The Bible, as interpreted in Puritan thought, exercised a most restrictive power in the developing colonies. As the communities grew in size and security, some women were educated and did not hesitate to publish and make known their thinking about issues in religion and politics. Hannah Adams, raised in Massachusetts in the last half of the eighteenth century in an environment of Puritan dogmatism, began the study of religions. Impressed by the ways in which one denomination would denigrate the teachings of another, she sought to determine, without bias, exactly what each group thought and what was the basis for their teachings. Ultimately, despite many difficulties, she published her *View of Religions*. Exercising her freedom to choose, she became a Unitarian.

During this same time period Lucretia Mott (1793-1880), a Philadelphia Quaker, used the public platform to express her convictions and helped to further the right of free expression. She advised that:

> . . . while reading and studying the Scriptures, let the *general tenor* of these invaluable writings govern thy conclusions, making all due allowance for the time and circumstances in which they were written; but do not puzzle and perplex thy mind with inferences from isolated passages here and there, which are contrary to the spirit of the whole, and do violence to the noble gift of reason, divinely bestowed upon us . . . while thou holds fast to that excellent sentiment that no text of Scripture however plain can shake thy belief in a truth which thou perceives by intuition, or makes thee believe a thing which is contrary to thy innate sense of right and wrong, it will lead thee to frequent introversion, and thou wilt know "of whom thou learnest these things" and wilt not have need that any man should teach thee . . . (quoted in Beard, 185)

She did not accept the dogmas of the Puritan church leaders, and she, like other courageous women, moved closer and closer to freethought.

Lucretia Mott was also involved in the efforts to abolish slavery, and in 1833 became secretary of the Philadelphia Female Anti-Slavery Society. In 1840, at a meeting of the World Anti-Slavery Society Convention in London, she met with Elizabeth Cady Stanton. At this particular meeting, women were not allowed to participate, but were granted permission to listen in a room curtained off from the main assembly. These two women, Mott and Stanton, together with others, later laid plans for the first Women's Rights Convention in human history, which was held in July, 1848, in the Methodist church in Seneca Falls, New York, where Elizabeth Stanton lived. The meeting was attended by three hundred women and some men. Out of that meeting came a Declaration of Principles, signed by sixty-eight women and thirty-two men. It employed language made familiar in the Declaration of Independence:

> When in the course of human events, it becomes necessary for one portion of the family of man to assume among the people of the earth a position different from that they have hitherto occupied . . .
>
> We hold these truths to be self-evident: that all men and women are created equal; that they are endowed by their Creator with certain inalienable rights; that among these are life, liberty and the pursuit of happiness. . . .
>
> The history of mankind is a history of repeated injuries and usurpations on the part of man toward woman, having in direct object the establishment of an absolute tyranny over her. To prove this, let facts be submitted to a candid world. . . .

Stanton recorded her memory of the event in her *Reminiscences*:

> These were the hasty steps of "the most momentous reform that had yet been launched on the world — the first organized protest against the injustice which had brooded for ages over the character and destiny of one-half the race." No words could express our astonishment on finding, a few days afterward, that what seemed to us so timely, so rational, and so sacred, should be the subject for sarcasm and ridicule to the entire press of the nation. With our Declaration of Rights and Resolutions for a text, it seemed as if every man who could wield a pen prepared a homily on "woman's sphere." All the journals from Maine to Texas seemed to strive with each other to see which could make our movement appear the most ridiculous. The anti-slavery papers stood by us manfully and so did Frederick Douglass, both in the convention and in his paper, *The North Star*; but so pronounced was the popular voice against us, in the parlor, press, and pulpit, that most of the ladies who had attended the convention and signed the declaration, one by one, withdrew their names and influence

> and joined our persecutors. Our friends gave us the cold shoulder and felt themselves disgraced by the whole proceeding.

Obviously, the male-dominated world was not ready for free-speaking and independent-thinking women. Despite the reactions, other conventions followed in Ohio, Indiana, Massachusetts, Pennsylvania and New York City and these laid the groundwork for further women's rights activities. In 1866, Mott and Stanton formed the National Women's Suffrage Association, and in 1868 Mott became president of the Philadelphia Peace Society and served on the executive committee of that organization until her death.

In 1881, Elizabeth Cady Stanton with others edited the masterful *History of Woman Suffrage*. She recorded her remarks at Lucretia Mott's memorial service, that this was "a woman emancipated from all faith in man-made creeds" and that "Nothing was too sacred for her to question, as to its rightfulness in principle and practice." She recalled Mott's comment on dancing, a practice which was frowned upon by the church: "I regard dancing as a very harmless amusement. . . . The Evangelical Alliance that so readily passed a resolution declaring dancing a sin for a church member, tabled a resolution declaring slavery a sin for a bishop." (Beard, p. 183)

Other women who fought for the abolishment of slavery and the emancipation of women included Lucy Stone, Anna Dickenson (at age twenty-one she was invited to address Congress on the issue of slavery), Julia Ward Howe, Susan B. Anthony, Victoria Woodhull and so many others. Although the Constitution was concerned with freedom for all, the traditionally subjective role of women was never politically confronted or seriously considered. This was not because there was no outcry for equal rights. Women and men who refused to be bound by biblical and Puritanical tradition cried out for liberation. John Stuart Mill was among the men who acknowledged the ability of women to contribute to mature thought which would have positive influence in the world. In the moving dedication to *On Liberty* (1859), he recognized his wife (Harriet Taylor) as both "the inspirer, and in part the author of all that is best in my writings." Despite such statements, the notion that women could only indulge in frivolous or trivial thought prevailed. During this same period, Marian Evans (1819-1890) was compelled to publish such literary masterpieces as *Adam Bede*, *The Mill on the Floss*, *Silas Marner*, etc. under the male pseudonym of George Elliot.

It was not until 1920 that American women received the right to vote. By that time they had proven themselves over and over again as persons worthy of the full rights of citizenship. They had worked in the factories, replacing male workers during war time; they had truly "kept the home fires burning" during a time of national crisis. They had expressed themselves in writing and on platforms. Finally, their voices were heard, and the right to vote was passed. But emancipation was not complete.

The right of women to engage in jobs and services that have been limited to males is still an issue. Each time barriers have been broken, women have proven their ability to compete on equal terms with men. Discrimination still exists in the market place where salary differences are based on sex, where promotions are based on sex, where eligibility to join certain "old-boy-networks" that provide inside information to males is still to be achieved.

Emancipation has brought new freedom to women. The traditional image of the wife-at-home-raising-the-children is giving way to new images of marriage and the family and to new perspectives on the capacities of women to fulfill themselves as freethinking, independent, and self-possessed individuals. Liberated women have been vital contributors to freethought movements.

Freedom for the Indians

As indicated in chapter 18, the democratic patterns practiced by the Iroquois Confederacy appear to have made some contribution to the development of democracy in America. However, the democracy that was developed did not embrace the Indians. High-sounding statements, proclaiming that humans were created equal with certain basic rights, were not extended to the Indians. Those who for centuries had lived in harmony with the land were ruthlessly deprived of their territories, were lied to, cheated, and humiliated by the Europeans who treated them as nonpersons. During this twentieth century, our awareness of genocide in history has been heightened by the Nazi holocaust which resulted in the deaths of some thirteen million people including six million Jews, most of the Gypsies in Europe, and others who did not fit the Nazi prototype of the ideal Aryan. Sensitivity to, and awareness of the genocide of the native American Indians has been slow in coming and is still dormant in the minds of most. Nevertheless, the decimation of the native Indian population by diseases imported from Europe, by violence perpetrated by men and women hungry for the land the Indians inhabited, by forced migrations, and by military attacks approved by the government, must constitute one of the most, if not the most, infamous genocide in human history.

It is important to remember that, although some Europeans came to America to escape persecution and in the search of freedom, others came seeking wealth, power and land. In both cases the focus was on personal interests; concern for Indian welfare was minimal.

One of the commitments of the Europeans was to Christianize "the heathen" Indians. In other words, there was little or no respect for Indian religious beliefs and traditions. In 1583, Humphrey Gilbert came with orders to convert to the faith "poor infidels, it seeming probable that God hath reserved the Gentiles to be introduced to Christian civility by the English nation." The charter granted to the Virginia Company in 1606 by King James called for "propagating the Christian Religion to such people, as yet live in darkness and miserable ignorance of the true knowledge and worship of God." Governing authorities were required "to provide that the true Word, and Service of God be preached, planted, and used, not only in the said colonies, but also, as much as might be, among savages bordering among them, according to the rites and doctrine of the Church of England." (Wood, p. 18) Obviously, there was little room left for appreciation of Indian culture and beliefs.

Indeed, from the beginning, the attitude of the migrants from Europe concerning the Indians was that of superiors dealing with inferiors. The Indian way of life seemed primitive, despite the fact that the Iroquois Confederacy had enjoyed a mature democracy that was to impact on the developing American democracy. In general, Indians were viewed as a "heathen" people and targets for conversion to European Christianity. Indian social customs, which were based on kinship, were foreign to Europeans whose alliances were often political. Indian concerns were for the welfare of the group, rather than for greed or the personal accumulation of possessions and power. To the Indian, European patterns came through as selfish and marked by a lack of concern for others. Nor were the Indians considered mature enough to be given a voice in the developing nation that was to become America.

Of course there were conversions — a great number of them — but beneath the acceptance of Christianity there was the retention of native Indian religion. At times Indian logic challenged the claims of the Christian missionary. The Christian statement about monotheism appeared in conflict with Christian factionalism:

> The insistence that religion was relative was also the point of Red Jacket's complaint to the missionary Cram. "Brother! You say there is but one way to worship and serve the Great Spirit," the Seneca chief asserted, "yet you Christians constantly disagree among yourselves," . . . (Wood, p. 23)

Nor was it clear to the Indian why, if all were children of one father God, that same father provided only the whites and not the Indians with knowledge of the Ten Commandments. Christian teachings about the crucifixion and resurrection left the Indian "dumbfounded by a faith whose omnipotent being allowed his own son to be killed. What kind of omnipotence was that? It just did not make sense." (Wood, p. 24) Christian impatience with and intolerance of Indian religion mythology was also puzzling:

> After listening to a Swedish missionary relate the Genesis account of Adam and Eve, a group of Susquehanna Indians concluded, according to a story told by Benjamin Franklin, that "It is indeed bad to eat apples." When the Indians then related their own legend about a beautiful woman who had descended from the clouds and helped them find maize, kidney beans, and tobacco, the missionary ridiculed their story as "mere fable, fiction, and falsehood." Offended because they believed the "rules of common civility" obliged him to believe their story as they had his, they criticized him for his insolence and bad manners. Condemning the Indian's myths as "nonsense and rank superstition," the Christian saw no similarity between the supernatural events of the Indian's religion and his own biblical "miracles." (Wood, p. 16)

Furthermore, although Christianity taught the importance of all persons before God, Christians continued to make distinctions and the Indians were relegated to second-class status. Deprived of their homes, their patterns of livelihood, their rights; subject to broken treaties and exploitation by the more powerful Caucasians; and finally isolated on reservations, the Indians were viewed as a social nuisance and embarrassment.

During the 19th century the flow of migrants from Europe greatly increased and the occupation of Indian lands pressed further and further westward. Over and over again treaties with the Indians were violated. Indians who protested were killed. Under President Andrew Jackson, the Indian Removal Bill was introduced and under his successor, President Martin Van Buren, seventy thousand Indians who lived east of the Mississippi were forced westward. Those who resisted were decimated by American troops. At every turn the Indians were thwarted and discriminated against.

The Cherokees in Alabama, Georgia and Tennessee began to adapt their way of life to the European pattern and many became artisans, farmers, and tradesmen. Their life style began to emulate that of the resident whites. Their decision-making councils became more like the white man's. President Jackson rejected their efforts to form an independent government and ordered them to move beyond the Mississippi. The discovery of gold in the Cherokee territory in Georgia in 1829 engendered an invasion by thousands of speculators who used every dishonest and violent means at their disposal to take advantage of the Indian land owners. The list of violations of human rights and of treaties went on and on until the Indians were relegated to designated areas, some completely foreign to the environments they knew. Perhaps the forced migration of 1838, known as the "Trail of Tears," epitomizes the maltreatment. Authorized by Congress, the movement of seventeen thousand Cherokees, from their lands east of the Mississippi to territories on the western side, resulted in some 4,000 deaths from sickness, drought, and exposure to heat and cold.

Of course there were protests against the cruel and hateful treatment of Indians. Many came from Indian leaders, some came from clergy who had been impressed with the quality of Indian life, and some came from powerful writers like Ralph Waldo Emerson. But to no avail. Greed, lust for land, and the dehumanization of the Indian as a person, led to genocide and territorial rape.

In the late twentieth century, voices of protest are again being raised against the sad situation of many Indian groups. It is clear that some Indians seek to reclaim their own religious heritage. Some have adopted what is now perceived as the "normal" way of American and Canadian life. They have engaged in business, merchandising native handicrafts. Others have received higher education and have become professionals in law, medicine, education, government, and so forth. The struggle for identity continues. Recognition as full citizens is still in the future as a paternalistic government continues to treat them as children needing supervision and control.

Freedom for the Slaves

Slave trade was introduced by the Spanish shortly after the arrival of Columbus. It began in the Puritan colonies, perhaps as early as 1624, but certainly by 1638. In that year, Captain William Pierce docked his ship, the *Desire,* in the Boston harbor with a cargo of salt, tobacco, cotton and slaves. Although the initial status in New England of these men and women imported from Africa is not clear (they may have been bound to masters for a specified period of years), in 1641 the "Body of Liberties" was enacted in Massachusetts. This document proscribed bonded slavery in the colony "unless it be lawfull Captives taken in just warres, and such strangers as willingly sell themselves or are sold to us." (Franklin, p. 102-103) Thus slavery was made acceptable. To justify owning slaves, a slave owner or trader needed only to argue that his slaves were captives taken in war, or that they had willingly sold themselves into bondage, or that they had been purchased from another slave owner.

Of course, trade in slaves was already a thriving business in the Caribbean and South America. At the time when the Jamestown settlement was just getting started, there were more than one million slaves in the Spanish and Portuguese colonies. By the end of the seventeenth century, slavery had achieved legal recognition in New England and the slave trade began in earnest. As the plantation system grew, more and more slaves were needed to tend the fields. It was not long before a vast slave population developed, particularly in the south. By 1700, the 6,000 slaves in Virginia comprised one-twelfth of the population; by 1763, there were 170,000, comprising one-half of the population.

At first, control of the slave-trade industry was in the hands of the English, the Dutch, the Portuguese and the Spanish. African slaves were brought to the West Indies and then transported by ship to New England. By the end of the eighteenth century the monopolies had been broken, and New England slave traders imported "black gold" directly from West Africa. Because these captive human beings were treated as a commodity, both Massachusetts (1705) and Rhode Island (1711) imposed an import tax on each slave.

How many slaves were imported into the colonies? Franklin reports as follows:

> It has been estimated that in 1700 when the total population of the New England colonies was approximately 90,000, there were not more than one thousand Negroes in the region. The

> eighteenth century witnessed a substantial increase in the Negro population. Massachusetts . . . led the other New England colonies . . . In 1715, its Negro population was estimated at 2,000. In 1735, when the white population of Massachusetts was 141,400, there were 2,600 Negroes. By 1764 there were 5,235 Negroes as against 218,950 whites. In 1776 the negro population was 5,249, while the white population was 343,845. Connecticut . . . took the lead . . . just before the War of Independence . . . in 1774, Connecticut had 6,464 Negroes and 128,212 whites in the colony. (p. 104)

These numbers appear to be small. Indeed, the total number of imported Africans in New England never exceeded 20,000, and only in Rhode Island did the African American population constitute as much as 5 per cent of the total population. But for the individual men and women who had lost their identity as persons and had become slaves in America, head count was not the key. What was important was treatment and the dream of freedom. And of course there were those who fled from their masters in the search for freedom.

Slavery was important for economic growth and security for the Colonists. Here was a source of cheap labor and, as migrants continued to arrive from Europe, the need for laborers increased. Laws were passed to sustain slavery. To maintain control of slaves, and to limit the possibility of flights to freedom in the West Indies or other mainland colonies, movement of slaves was limited. Some slaves plotted ways to achieve freedom, often by entering into alliances with enslaved Indians. Therefore, in most New England colonies slaves were not allowed to be on the streets at night. Slaves were not permitted to defend themselves against abuse nor to bring charges against white persons. The use of the lash served to control, humiliate and punish disruptive slaves. Children of slaves could be bought and sold. Slaves could not serve in the military.

As some African American slaves assumed responsibilities as clerks and recorders, it was important that they be taught to read and write. As Franklin has noted, in such important business roles they worked with rather than for their masters (p. 106). Ultimately, it was the New England respect for education that led to efforts to teach slaves to read and write.

What was completely ignored, even among those who were to protest slavery, was the African's concept of the self. As we have noted in the discussion on Africa, African identity was, like American Indian identity, linked to the community. To break with community, to seek personal wealth and personal power after the European pattern was to violate basic precepts of belonging. In African thought, one who was outside of the kinship group was a nonperson. Thus, uprooted from the kinship bonds, cut off from customs and rituals that linked the person to the group, the African American was, in a sense, socially dead. Only by finding ways to relate with others in his or her predicament was a slave able give some meaning to personal existence. Those who adopted European customs, largely through enlistment in one of the Christian churches, began to lose the essence of their heritage. As the Africans quoted in our discussion of Africa have noted, singing and dancing have been an integral part of African response to life and to the world. Now, in America, Christian dogma looked on dancing as sinful and even as evidence of demon possession; therefore dancing was not permitted among converted slaves. Professor Forrest G. Wood, in his powerful book *The Arrogance of Faith*, has quoted the 1864 statement of Mancure Conway of Virginia, a Methodist minister:

> The impression has gone around the world with ubiquitous sable minstrels that the slaves are a merry, singing, dancing population, far removed from the cares that gnaw the hearts of more civilized classes. In all the twenty-three years of my life in the land of Slavery, I never saw a Negro-dance, though in those years I have heard of a few in our neighborhood. The slaves of the Border States are almost invariably members of Baptist and Methodist societies, which are particularly rigid in denying them such amusements. On the large plantations of the far South, dances are encouraged, and formerly were frequent; but of late years they have become infrequent, through the all-absorbing tendencies of the Negroes toward religious meetings. (Wood, p. 183)

Not all Africans brought to America to be slaves submitted easily to servitude. Some rebelled, some ran away, some resorted to violence, some conspired against their owners, some sought ways to avoid work and, of course, some submitted. It was to the slave owner's advantage to break the spirit of the enslaved person and to teach the African his or her "proper place." Consequently, violations were severely punished. The lash was employed for some violations. More serious infringements, particularly those that involved loss of property or of life, were treated by mutilation (lopping off ears) or by death by hanging or burning.

Where were the protests against the enslavement of fellow human beings? Not in most churches, which gave support to the economic needs of the colonists. Sermons were preached to prove from the Bible that the black race was cursed and that slavery brought them "within the reach of God's grace" (Franklin, p. 105). At first, conversions to Christianity were not openly welcomed by slave owners. They feared that converted slaves might spend too much time away from work studying the Bible or attending religious services. They were not convinced that baptism might not be interpreted as conferring freedom. If baptism and conversion made the slave a member of a congregation, might they be able to exercise voting power within the church? As these fears did not materialize, active efforts at conversion began during the eighteenth century. Religion was recognized as a tool for control. (Zinn, p. 173) Marriages among African Americans followed the customs required of white marriages, including the publishing of bans and the recognition of marriage as a legal contract. They were required to obey the strict "Sabbath" laws.

In the long run, slaves in New England were not subjected to the harsh treatment so many experienced in the south. They had their own dwelling places where they could express themselves, tell and retell African tales, and in many ways perform as independent people. They associated freely with one another and with the friendly Indians. There were intermarriages between Indians and African Americans and between African Americans and whites, although these latter unions often came under severe condemnation.

Human sexuality was a frequent subject for discussion in the Christian churches. Original sin was linked to sexuality and, according to Christian doctrine, every human came into the world tainted with Adam's sin. In Puritan teaching, sexual gratification was not in and of itself evil or sinful, but because human depravity led to excessive sexuality all aspects of sex had to be circumscribed. Because both African slaves and native American Indians were considered to be of a lower status and more akin to animals, great concern was expressed for the sexual appetite of these peoples:

> Thomas Jefferson believed that black men and women possessed sexual appetites that had nothing to do with love or tenderness but, rather, were simply manifestations of their primitive animal natures. Male slaves were "more ardent after their females," he wrote in *Notes on the State of Virginia* (1787), "but love seems with them to be more an eager desire, than a tender delicate mixture of sentiment and sensation." Jefferson,

> who would certainly have to be considered one of the most enlightened men of his time, also assumed that black men preferred white women for much the same reason, as he put it, the "Oran-ootan" in Africa pursued black women, although he never stipulated what that reason was. Consequently, he was convinced that freeing the slaves would unleash hordes of sex-crazed black men who would lust after the helpless white female population. (Wood, p. 198)

Such negative, unfounded, and poisonous attitudes gave rise to sermons, pamphlets and books denigrating the slaves. At the same time, slave owners indulged their sexual appetites with female slaves, producing large numbers of children who came to be labeled "mulattos." These children were accepted into the black community, but were ignored or rebuffed by the white community.

By the middle of the eighteenth century, slavery was an accepted part of American life. Of course, there had been protests against the custom. Initially, the American concern for human rights did not include the slaves. Among those who felt that trade in human flesh was not in accord with their religious principles were the Mennonites of Germantown, Pennsylvania. On February 18, 1688 they adopted a resolution which challenged the trade in "black gold." The resolution drew upon the Golden Rule and asked if those engaging in the trade would like the treatment they gave to African captives. Quakers challenged the right of one person to hold another in bondage. Abigail Adams objected to the plundering of those "who have as good a right to freedom as we have." (Franklin, p. 128f)

When conflict with England developed, it was argued that American efforts to end slavery had been blocked by the British. Of course, this was not true. The colonists were actively engaged in slave trade and in some of the southern colonies there was strong approval of slavery. In the formulation of the Declaration of Independence, even as Jefferson made specific charges against the crown, he chose to ignore what was really taking place in the colonies. His charge against the king was:

> He has waged cruel war against human nature itself, violating its most sacred rights of life and liberty in the persons of a distant people who never offended him, captivating and carrying them into slavery in another hemisphere, or to incur miserable death in their transportation thither. This piratical warfare, the opprobrium of *infidel* powers, is the warfare of the

> Christian king of Great Britain. Determined to keep open a market where men should be bought and sold, he has prostituted his negative for suppressing every legislative attempt to prohibit or to restrain this execrable commerce; and that this assemblage of horrors might want no fact of distinguished die, he is now exciting those very people to rise in arms among us, and to purchase that liberty of which he deprived them, by murdering the people upon whom *he* also obtruded them; thus paying off former crimes committed against the *liberties* of one people, with crimes which he urges them to commit against the *lives* of another. (quoted in Franklin, p. 130f)

The Southern delegation at the Congressional Congress found these statements unacceptable and they were removed from the Declaration. The final formulation of the Declaration of Independence noted that all men were created equal and were endowed with certain inalienable rights, one of which was liberty. But there was no place in the document for anti-slavery statements nor for the enactment of freedom for the slaves. In 1787, the famous Northwest Ordinance barred slavery north of the Ohio river and sought to protect Indian rights. The Fugitive Slave Law of 1850, which made it easy for slave owners to recapture slaves, was signed by President Fillmore and supported by Senator Daniel Webster. That law, which was severely criticized by northern African Americans, inspired Harriet Beecher Stowe (1811-1896) to write *Uncle Tom's Cabin* which, despite recent criticism, was actually a powerful analysis of current racism, and contributed to the national resistance to slavery which led to the Civil War — a fact which Lincoln himself recognized.

One of the most powerful voices on behalf of the slaves was that of Frederick Douglass. He had been a slave in Baltimore, where somehow he learned to read and write. In 1838 he escaped to the northern states where he became a writer, editor and lecturer. In 1854 he spoke at a northern conference of Negroes, saying ". . . it is emphatically our battle, no one else can fight it for us. . . . Our relations to the Anti-Slavery movement must be and are changed. Instead of depending upon it we must lead it." (Zinn, p. 180) He was not alone. Other powerful voices joined his, including Sojourner Truth and Harriet Tubman. Insurrection by Nat Turner and John Brown added to the developing turmoil. In 1857, the Supreme Court ruled that Dred Scott, a Negro slave, could not sue for freedom because he was not a person but property. In 1863, President Abraham Lincoln, who had earlier refused to denounce the Fugitive Slave Law, signed the Emancipation Proclamation:

> That on the 1st day of January, AD 1863, all persons held as slaves within any State or designated part of a State the people whereof shall then be in rebellion against the United States shall be then, thenceforward and forever free. . . .

But real liberty was still in the future. The freedom envisioned in the Emancipation Proclamation was thwarted for years by segregation laws and practices. African Americans were still looked at and treated as a sub-species of humans. They had to live in areas apart from white residents. They were segregated in buses and other forms of transportation. They could not drink from certain public water fountains, eat in white-controlled restaurants, obtain rooms in white-controlled hotels and so on and on. Children were forced into segregation in schools, playgrounds, swimming pools and other recreational facilities. Everything possible was done by the ruling white majority to keep African Americans in their proper place. Violation of these social patterns often resulted in violence. It was not until late in the twentieth century and after civil rights demonstrations that desegregation was abolished and doors were opened to educational institutions, public parks, swimming pools, golf courses, theaters, bus terminals and other facilities for all persons no matter what their race or skin coloration.

Throughout the long years of persecution, the men and women who had been imported from Africa and whose ancestors had come as slaves, remained loyal to their new American homeland. When hostilities against Britain broke out in the eighteenth century, African Americans joined the colonists in battle against British forces. But even fighting for their homeland was not enough to bring recognition as full human beings to Americans of African descent. In the *Atlantic Monthly*, January 1901, Woodrow Wilson wrote:

> An extraordinary and very perilous state of affairs had been created in the South by the sudden and absolute emancipation of the Negroes, and it was not strange that the Southern legislatures should deem it necessary to take extraordinary steps to guard against the manifest and pressing dangers which it entailed. Here was a vast "laboring, landless, homeless class," once slaves; now free, unpracticed in liberty, unschooled in self control; never sobered by the discipline of self-support; never established in any habit of prudence; excited by a freedom they

did not understand, exalted in false hopes, bewildered and without leaders, and yet insolent and aggressive; sick of work, covetous of pleasure — a host of dusky children untimely put out of school.

Some 15 years later, in 1916, he was elected President of the United States. When on April 6, 1917, Congress declared war on Germany, Wilson declared that "The world must be made safe for democracy." Whether or not he included in this concept of democracy the idea of civil liberty for the former slaves he had so patronizingly described as "a host of dusky children" is not clear. Nevertheless, some 367,000 African Americans were called into active service. In subsequent wars they have faithfully served the country that imported their ancestors as slaves. Slowly, slowly, they are moving into full citizenship and are asserting their abilities and potentials as leaders in business, the professions and in government.

Religious Freedom in America

Religious freedom did not come easily in America. It grew with protest and conflict out of ideals of freedom and human rights that developed in the Enlightenment. The concept of separation of church and state had been introduced in America in the seventeenth century by William Penn and Roger Williams. Penn (1644-1718), a Quaker, founded Pennsylvania as a place of refuge for the persecuted of all countries. He wished to secure freedom from oppression that Quakers had been denied in England. This was accomplished by The Toleration Act of 1689 which granted freedom of worship to all. Consequently, no other colony was composed of so great a diversity of religious bodies.

Roger Williams (1604?-1683) was a Puritan minister who classified himself as a "Seeker" after the true church. He left England in 1631 when pressures on dissent became too great to tolerate. In Massachusetts, he found that authorities were equally hostile to dissent. Williams claimed that the British crown had no right to give grants of land that rightfully belonged to the Indians. He opposed the Reverend John Cotton's concept of a theocratic state and was soon regarded as a dangerous agitator. Cotton's "An Abstract of Lawes of New England" left no room for compromise with dissenters:

> 1. First, Blasphemy, which is cursing of God by Atheism or the like, to be punished with death.

> 2. Idolatry to be punished with death.
>
> 3. Witchcraft, which is fellowship by covenant with a familiar Spirit to be punished with death.
>
> 4. Consulters with Witches not to be tolerated, but either to be cut off by death, or by banishment.
>
> 5. Heresie which is the maintenance of some wicked errors, overthrowing the foundation of Christian Religion, which obstinacy if it be joyned with endeavour, to seduce others thereunto to be punished with death: because such an Hereticke no less than an Idolator seeketh to thrust the soules of men from their God.
>
> 6. To worship God in a molten or graven Image, to be punished with death.
>
> 7. Such members of the Church as doe willfully reject to walke after due admonition, and conviction, the Churches establishment, and their Christian admonition and censures, shall be cut off by banishment.
>
> 8. Whosoever shall revile the Religion and Worship of God, and the Government of the Church as it is now established, to be cut off by banishment.

Each of Cotton's statements was supported by scriptural references.

Roger Williams was banished but escaped before the authorities could seize him. As he made his way through the Narragansett woods, he was befriended by Indians. Having learned their language, he was impressed by their tolerance which fed his own concerns for liberty. He founded Providence and the colony of Rhode Island. When the Massachusetts colony attempted to assume control, Williams returned to England and on March 14, 1644, won a charter for Rhode Island. While he was in England, he wrote a pamphlet, titled "The Bloudy Tenent of Persecution," in which he argued that all individuals and religious bodies, including Jews, Catholics, Protestants and pagans, had the natural right of religious liberty:

> It is the will and command of God (since the coming of his Son the Lord Jesus) a permission of the most paganish, Jewish, Turkish, or antichristian consciousness and worships, be granted to all men in all nations and countries; and they are only to be fought against with that sword which is only (in soul matters) able to conquer, to wit, the sword of God's Spirit, the Word of God.

He went on to state that any attempt to enforce "uniformity of religion" was in conflict with Christian principles and that freedom of religion could only result in "a firm and lasting peace."

In 1776, Virginia disestablished the Anglican Church by suspending the payment of tithes. In 1777, Jefferson drafted a bill to establish religious freedom as part of a revised code of laws designed to transform Virginia from a royalist into a democratic state. The bill was introduced into the General Assembly in 1779 when Jefferson was Governor. It declared that "our civil rights have no dependence on our religious opinions any more than our opinions in physics or geometry." It met with bitter attack and was shelved. Six years later, in 1786, the Virginia Statute of Religious Liberty, which had been drafted by Jefferson, was passed. It enacted:

> That no man shall be compelled to frequent or support any religious worship, place or ministry whatsoever, nor shall be enforced, restrained, molested, or burthened in his body or goods, nor shall otherwise suffer on account of his religious opinions or belief; but that all men shall be free to profess, and by argument to maintain, their opinion in matters of religion, and that the same shall in no wise diminish, enlarge or affect their civil capacities.

Freedom in the American colony had moved a long distance from life in fifteenth century Spain. Jefferson wrote, "It is honorable for us to have produced the first legislature who has had the courage to declare that the reason of man may be trusted with the formation of his own opinions." (Menendez and Doerr, item 206) At the same time, shocked by the religious intolerance he saw all about him, Jefferson wrote in 1776:

> Why have Christians been distinguished above all people who have ever lived for persecutions? Is it because it is the genius of their religion? No. Its genius is the reverse. It is the refusing of toleration to those of different opinion which has produced all the bustles and wars on account of religion. (Bedell, Sandon, Wellborn, p. 449)

Bitter rivalry and persecution remained among Christians. On August 11, 1834, the Roman Catholic Ursuline convent in Charlestown, Massachusetts, was burned down. The men accused of the arson were acquitted and afforded hero status among Boston Protestants. Shortly after, in 1849, a secret society called the Order of the Star-Spangled Banner, came into being. Only American-born Protestants who had no Roman Catholics in their families were admitted. The Society began to enter into the political scene. When questioned about aspects of the society, members would reply "I know nothing," thus giving rise to the label the Know-Nothing Party. As the Know-Nothings were successful in several elections in Massachusetts, President Lincoln was led to comment regarding the Declaration of Independence:

> When the Know-Nothings get control, it will read: "All men are created equal except negroes, foreigners and Catholics. When it comes to this I should prefer emigrating to some country where they make no pretence of loving liberty — to Russia, for instance, where despotism can be taken pure, and without the base alloy of hypocrisy. (Menendez and Doerr, item 265)

The Know-Nothing party came to an end in 1856 as the slavery issue came to the fore and the Republican Party came into being. Unfortunately, the religious bigotry espoused by the Know-Nothings has not completely disappeared. In chapter 21, we will see evidence of progress toward elimination of religious bigotry in the United States.

See pp. 475-481 for References of chapters 16-21.

21
Freethought in America

American deviation from religious orthodoxy represented a statement of freedom that embraced both liberation from the control of Europe and the rights of freethinking individuals who challenged the authority of the Bible and the Church. The development of religious diversity affirmed the reality that no single religion could be accepted as the one true faith for the emerging nation. The right to challenge religious authority that marked the Reformation and the Enlightenment opened the door for the expression of the results of critical thinking and open inquiry. Religions *per se* could be analyzed, evaluated and attacked or religions could be ignored. When Gottlieb Mittelberger, a visitor from Germany, visited Pennsylvania in 1750, he wrote that there were "many hundreds of adult persons who have not been and do not even wish to be baptized . . . Many do not even believe there is a true God and Devil, a Heaven and a hell, salvation and damnation, a resurrection of the dead, a judgment and an eternal life; they believe that all one can see is natural." (quoted in Degler, p. 54)

Some Pioneering Freethinkers

Only some of those who challenged religious authoritarianism and who analyzed the Bible and the role of the church can be discussed in this overview. But these persons of influence have contributed greatly to the magnificent freedom to think independently and creatively and to exercise critical judgment and critical thinking that is ours today. Because our educational system encourages critical thinking, these pioneers and contemporary thinkers deserve recognition.

Ethan Allen (1737-1789) was truly a freethinker. According to Timothy Dwight, a 19th century president of Yale University, the 1784 publication of Ethan Allen's *Reason the Only Oracle of Man, or a Compenduous System of Natural Reason* was "the first formal publication in the United States openly directed against the Christian religion" (Koch, p. 30). Koch has described Allen as a "speculative frontiersman" and a "fighter for freedom." Although Allen was unable to receive a college education, he engaged in preparatory studies through which he came into contact with English freethought. Allen read, studied, pondered and questioned ecclesiastical authority, the prevalent theologies and the theory of the divine inspiration of the Bible. He did not challenge the existence of God but he did question the various theological doctrines concerning the deity.

His belief in human moral freedom led him to assert that, with the freedom to choose between good and evil, the moral person, the religious person, will choose the good which, he believed, to be the essence of religion. He saw the Bible as a fallible document, not divinely inspired, and argued that, rather than the Bible controlling human reason, human reason ought to control the Bible. His attacks on the Bible led him to reject those of the Ten Commandments that did not accord with the laws of nature. For example, he dismissed the keeping of the Sabbath as an "arbitrary imposition of Moses" (Koch, p. 37). As for Jesus' mission as the destroyer of the works of the devil and the redeemer of fallen man, he wrote:

> We cannot be miserable for the sin of Adam, or happy in the righteousness of Christ, in which transactions we were in no way accessory or assisting as accomplices, or otherwise concerned; and are not at all conscious of those ancient matters . . . What have those old and obsolete matters to do with our virtues or vices, or with our consciousness of righteousness or wickedness, happiness or misery, reward or blame? (quoted by Koch, p. 39)

Interestingly enough, he did not reject the notion of immortality. He believed that the design of the universe reflected the nature of the deity and, because the purpose of creation was

> to exalt and happify the moral world, that human life is but a presage and pre-requisite existence for an introduction into another more dignified in the order of being; those vain and idle mistrusts of our immortality will vanish, and our minds will be established in a firm alliance on God, that in the order of nature and course of his providence, (however inconceivable to us) he has secured our immortality. (quoted in Koch, p. 42f)

For those who lived sinfilled lives, he postulated a kind of redemptory purgatory through which one might be made acceptable for immortal life. At this point he became an Universalist, rejecting the Calvinist belief in hell and eternal torment for sinners and trusting in the divine redemption of all.

Allen's God was nature's God and knowledge of nature provided the revelation of God. He described himself as generally "denominated a Deist, the reality of which I never disputed, being conscious I am no Christian, except mere infant baptism makes me one; and as to being a Deist, I know not strictly speaking, whether I am one or not, for I have never read their writings . . ." (Koch, p. 40)

Thomas Paine (1737-1809), one of the great contributors to American freethought, continues to impact on the thinking of those who read his writings. He was born into a Quaker household in England. In 1774 he came penniless to the American colonies, just one year before the first shots of the American War of Independence from Britain were fired at Lexington. A letter of introduction from Benjamin Franklin, who was then the London agent of the colonies, got him the job of editor of the *Pennsylvania Magazine*. In January, 1776, Paine published a pamphlet titled *Common Sense*, which sold 120,000 copies in the first three months. The pamphlet issued a plea for total independence from Britain and immediately plunged Paine into political battles. These were times in which momentous events were occurring. Between June 10th and June 28th, Thomas Jefferson wrote a rough draft of the Declaration of Independence. As we noted in chapter 20 in the discussion of slavery, it opened with a statement of governmental principles, and went on to indict the British Crown for violations of these principles. It concluded with a statement that the colonies would now be free and independent. On July 4, 1776, Congress adopted the Declaration of Independence and the thirteen states constituted a new nation founded on democratic principles.

Paine joined the remnants of George Washington's army and was part of the retreat to Delaware in 1776. The army had been reduced in numbers by disease and desertion. Morale was low. Washington appealed to Paine to use his fiery rhetoric, which had helped to inspire independence, to reenergize the troops. In December of that same year, Paine published "The *American* Crisis." The essay with its famous opening lines, "These are the times that try men's souls," was read to the troops and it renewed their zeal for the high mission of American independence. A few days later, on Christmas day, 1776, the Delaware was crossed and the next day Washington's troops defeated the Hessians at Trenton. That victory renewed the faith of those who had begun to believe that the American cause was lost. In England, Paine wrote his pamphlet, *The Rights of Man* (1791-1792); its attack on English institutions led to his prosecution for treason and flight to Paris, where he was later imprisoned for his part in French affairs.

His book *The Age of Reason: An Investigation of True and Fabulous Theology* (1794-95), extended Paine's political ideals to address the entrenched biblicism which he recognized as the basis for Christian opposition to social and political reform. It should be remembered that, by the time of the seventeenth century, a number of Christian scholars had wrestled with issues such as the Mosaic authorship of the Pentateuch (the first five books of the Bible). For example,

> Carlstadt, a leader of the Reformation in Germany, wrote a pamphlet in 1520 arguing that Moses did not write the Pentateuch, for the style of writing in the verses reporting Moses death (Deut. 32:5-12) was that of the preceding verses. In 1574, A. Du Maes, a Roman Catholic scholar, suggested that the Pentateuch was composed by Ezra, who used old manuscripts as a basis. Thomas Hobbes, the English philosopher, concluded in 1651 that Moses wrote only parts of Deuteronomy (*Leviathan* III:33). In *Tractus theologico-politicus* (1677), Baruch Spinoza, the Jewish philosopher, recognized as one of the founders of modern biblical criticism, reached a conclusion much like that of Du Maes, that Ezra compiled Genesis to II Kings from documents of varying dates. Shortly afterward, Richard Simon, a Roman Catholic priest, often called "the father of biblical criticism," gathered together the substance of critical analysis up to his time and raised the problem of literary history, thus opening the door to the application of techniques used in the study of non-sacred literature to the Bible. (Larue, 1968, p. 28)

In other words, even as Paine was evaluating the Bible from the point of view of a freethinker and rational Deist who was grounded in the emerging astronomical science, biblical scholars were critically investigating and commenting on the Bible as they struggled within their faith positions.

Paine was no scholar and some of his biblical analyses made him vulnerable. Fundamentally, his approach to the Bible bluntly raised the same questions of authorship and authority that Church scholars were confronting in Europe. Paine went further than they. He pointed to the hostility of some parts of the Bible to the emerging American concepts of ethics and justice. He rejected both the divinity of Jesus and the resurrection. He recognized the Bible as the product of human beings, not as a divinely inspired book. Paine was a Deist who wished to harmonize a religious belief with emerging science and reason. The fact that the *Age of Reason* has maintained its importance for freethinkers, is due in part to the way in which it serves to jolt those who have been raised in traditional religions and who have doubts about their faith, into a fresh analysis of the Bible by directing thinking to rationalism and freethought.

Elihu Palmer (1764-1806) also contributed to freethought in America through his anti-Christian Deism. Palmer graduated from Dartmouth College and, after studying divinity, became a Presbyterian preacher. His career was doomed from the start. His first sermon, preached on Thanksgiving Day, failed to dwell on sinful humans but instead exhorted parishioners to enjoy themselves in the festivity of the occasion. So he joined the Baptists but once again fell into disfavor. He became minister of the Universal Society which had been founded by John Fitch, the inventor of the steamboat. Encouraged by the liberal spirit of that group, he denied the divinity of Jesus. He studied law, but during the 1793 plague of yellow fever lost his wife to the disease and he himself went blind. Of course, some of his religious opponents found the affliction to be a just punishment by a righteous God.

Palmer's studies led him to deny the divine authority of the Bible. Even considering it as a human compilation, he found that its merits had been highly overrated. He wrote:

> The obscurity, incredibility and obscenity, so conspicuous in many parts of it, would justly condemn the works of a modern writer. It contains a mixture of inconsistency and contradiction; to call which the *word of God*, is the highest pitch of extravagance: it is to attribute to the deity that which any person of common sense would blush to confess himself the author of. (quoted by Koch, pp. 61-6 from Palmer's *Principles of Nature*, p. 6)

Palmer dismissed prophecies as irrelevant, vague and as so indifferent that they could not properly be applied to any event or person. Miracles were called "specimens of that miserable and disgusting extravagance with which this *Holy Bible* is everywhere replete" (Koch, p. 62). He found the scheme of salvation to be absurd and contradictory. With regard to Jesus' virgin birth story he wrote:

> This story of the virgin and the ghost, to say no more of it, does not wear the appearance of much religion; and it would not, it is presumed, be difficult in any age or country, to find a sufficient number of men who would pretend to be ghosts, if by such pretensions they could obtain similar favours, especially with the consoling reflection superadded, of becoming the progenitors of the pretended Saviour of a wicked and apostate world. How absurd and contradictory are the principles and the doctrines of this religion? In vain do its advocates attempt to cover this transaction with the machinery of ghosts and supernatural agents. The simple truth is, that their pretended Saviour is nothing more than an illegitimate Jew, and their hopes of salvation through him rest on no better foundation than that of fornication or adultery. (quoted by Koch p. 64 from Palmer's *Principles of Nature*, p. 19)

Sin, he believed, lay in the exploitation of belief in human depravity. Evil did not lie in man, but in corrupt institutions. Hell was an invention. If despotism and superstition were destroyed, reason and education would accelerate progress toward a moral human race.

It is important to remember that Allen, Paine and Palmer were products of the Christian Church. Allen's and Palmer's criticisms began within the Church and were based on a solid grounding in theology and biblical studies. Freedom of inquiry, the right to look critically at writings considered to be sacred, opened the way for rational thinking and open challenge to the authority of the Bible and the Church.

Robert Green Ingersoll (1833-1899) has been described as a patriot, civil libertarian, lawyer, agnostic, humanist and a colonel in the Illinois 11th Cavalry — all of which describe, in part, this spokesman for freethought. His public lectures reached thousands of people long before the age of radio and television; his written articles touched thousands more and through the responses of newswriters he attracted audiences. He was no biblical scholar — at least not in the technical sense — but his thoughtful reading of the Bible and his knowledge of its teachings enabled him to become a powerful practical interpreter of its content. As a result, he became an opponent of the teaching of religion in public schools. He wrote:

> I want to free the schools of our country. I want it so that when a professor in college finds some facts inconsistent with Moses he will not hide the fact; that it will not be worse for

> him for having discovered the fact. I wish to see an eternal divorce and separation between church and schools. The common school is the bread of life; but there should be nothing taught in the schools except what somebody knows, and anything else should not be maintained by a system of general taxation. I want its professors so that they will tell everything they find; that they will be free to investigate in every direction, and will not be trammeled by the superstitions of our day. What has religion to do with facts? Nothing. Is there any such thing as Methodist mathematics, Presbyterian botany, Catholic astronomy or Baptist biology? What has any form of superstition or religion to do with a fact or with any science? Nothing but to hinder, delay or embarrass. I want, then, to free the schools; and I want to free the politicians, so that a man will not have to pretend he is a Methodist, or his wife a Baptist, or his grandmother a Catholic; so that he can go through a campaign, and when he gets through will find none of the dust of hypocrisy on his knees. ("Mistakes of Moses")

Ingersoll defined himself as a naturalist in that he recognized nature as the source of all knowledge. He wrote:

> Man never had an idea; man will never have an idea, except those supplied to him by his surroundings. Every idea in the world that man has, came to him by nature. Man cannot conceive of anything, the hint of which you have not received from your surroundings. You can imagine an animal with the hoof of a bison, with the pouch of a kangaroo, with the wings of an eagle, with the beak of a bird and with the tail of a lion; and yet every point of this monster you borrowed from nature. Every thing you can think of — every thing you can dream of, is borrowed from your surroundings — everything. And there is nothing on earth coming from any other sphere whatever. Man has produced every religion in the world. ("Hell")

He set forth his humanistic stance in terms of the criticisms he received from clerics:

> Now my crime has been this; I have insisted that the Bible is not the word of God. I have insisted that we should not whip our children. I have insisted that we should treat our wives as loving equals. I have denied that God — if there is any God —

> ever upheld polygamy and slavery. I have denied that God ever told his generals to kill innocent babies and tear and rip open women with the sword of war. I have denied that, and for that I have been assailed by the clergy of the United States. ("Skulls")

His joy in his discovery of a naturalistic frame of reference was unbounded and gave birth to his commitment. He wrote:

> When I became convinced that the universe is natural — that all ghosts and gods are myths, there entered into my brain, into my soul, into every drop of my blood, the sense, the feeling, the joy of freedom. The walls of my prison crumbled and fell, the dungeon was flooded with light, and all the bolts and bars and manacles became dust. I was no longer a servant, a serf, or a slave. There was for me no master in all the wide world — not even in infinite space. I was free — free to think, to express my thoughts — free to live my own ideal — free to live for myself and those I loved — free to use all my faculties, all my senses — free to spread imagination's wings — free to investigate, to guess and dream and hope — free to judge and determine for myself — free to reject all ignorant and cruel creeds, all the "inspired" books that savages have produced, and all the barbarous legends of the past — free from popes and priests — free from all the "called" and "set apart" — free from sanctified mistakes and holy lies — free from the fear of eternal pain — free from the winged monsters of the night — free from devils, ghosts, and gods. For the first time I was free. There were no prohibited places in all the realm of thoughts — no air, no space, where fancy could not spread her painted wings — no chains for my limbs — no lashes for my back — no fires for my flesh — no master's frown or threat — no following another's steps — no need to bow, or cringe, or crawl or utter lying words. I was free. I stood erect and fearlessly, joyously, faced all worlds.
>
> And then my heart was filled with gratitude, with thankfulness, and went out in love to all the heroes, all the thinkers who gave their lives for the liberty of hand and brain — for the freedom of labor and thought — to those who fell on the fierce fields of war, to those who died in dungeons bound in chains — to those whose bones were crushed, whose flesh was scarred and torn — to those by fire consumed — to all the

wise, the good, the brave of every land, whose thoughts and deeds have given freedom to the sons of men. And then I vowed to grasp the torch they had held, and hold it high, that light might conquer darkness still.

Modern Education, Freethought and Religion

The aim of every caring, dedicated and thoughtful educator is to provide for his or her students the best and finest knowledge we possess concerning the universe and the life forms within it. The hope of every parent is that his or her children will be provided with the most up-to-date information concerning on-going research about our world and our responsibilities in it. The desire of every school child is that he or she will be put in touch with the great minds that shape our awareness of ourselves in relation to the cosmos and that some understanding of who we are and how we came to be will be provided for us.

It is clear that we can no longer rely on textbooks that were written centuries ago to inform us. We are in a different time and place. Our scientists, our poets, our psychologists and philosophers, our thinkers and our dreamers continue to make us aware of that reality.

Psychology, Freethought and Religion

It is important to recognize the impact of psychological research and analysis on religion and belief systems. Not every psychotherapist has written on the subject, but many have. We will consider only a few theorists and practitioners whose names have become household words, so to speak. One of these is Sigmund Freud.

Sigmund Freud (1856-1939) wrote of conclusions he reached concerning the origins of religion in *Totem and Taboo* which was published in 1912, and in *Moses and Monotheism* which appeared in 1939. For his study he drew primarily on the research and conclusions of Charles Darwin, J.J. Atkinson and the famous Semitic scholar Robertson Smith to arrive at his conviction that the god idea was invented in the process of the discovery of the totem. While his ideas have been largely abandoned today, the impact of the words of the father of psychoanalysis were considerable in their time. He wrote:

> From Darwin I borrowed the hypothesis that men originally lived in small hordes; each of the hordes stood under the rule of an older male, who governed by brute force, appropriated all the females, and belaboured or killed all the young males, including his own sons. From Atkinson I received the suggestion that this patriarchal system came to an end through a rebellion of the sons, who united against the father, overpowered him, and together consumed his body. Following Robertson Smith's totem theory, I suggested that this horde, previously ruled by the father, was followed by the totemistic brother clan. In order to be able to live in peace with one another the victorious brothers renounced the women for whose sake they had killed the father, and agreed to practice exogamy. The power of the father was broken and the families were regulated by matriarchy. The ambivalence of the sons towards the father remained in force during the whole further development. Instead of the father a certain animal was declared the totem; it stood for their ancestor and protecting spirit, and no one was allowed to hurt or kill it. Once a year, however, the whole clan assembled for a feast at which the otherwise revered totem was torn to pieces and eaten. No one was permitted to abstain from this feast; it was the solemn repetition of the father-murder, in which social order, moral laws, and religion had had their beginnings. (*Moses and Monothesm*, p. 168)

According to Freud, the god hypothesis was invented by humans to meet human needs. Religion originated in human feelings of helplessness in the face of the external forces of nature and the internal feelings within. It begins at a time when humans do not use reason as the tool to confront and deal with either external or internal forces. Thus, in the childhood of human development, humans developed what Freud has called "illusions" which represent the regression to childhood needs for protection by a strong father who is the embodiment of love and wisdom, courage, strength and protection. Humans cling to this outmoded idea because they remain "infantile," need protection even when fully grown and therefore cannot bring themselves to relinquish the notion of god-support (p. 165). So far as his personal beliefs were concerned, Freud wrote:

> I do not believe that one supreme great God "exists" today, but I believe that in primeval times there was one person who

> must needs appear gigantic and who, raised to the status of a deity, returned to the memory of men. (*ibid.* p. 166)

For the Freudian, God could have no external reality in that the concept was the product of a traumatized psyche.

C.G. Jung (1875-1961), one of Freud's disciples, studied myths in various cultures and developed the theory of what he called a "collective unconscious." To his way of thinking, God is a collective archetype, an unconscious psychic image, and through the use of such specialized language Jung neither affirms nor denies the existence of God. God statements are human statements. They stem from the psyche from whence they have entered consciousness through dreams, images, ideas or intuitions and are then expressed in myths and other belief statements. The cause of these images cannot be known. However, in his discussion of mythic thinking he wrote:

> Has mankind ever really got away from myths? Everyone who has his eyes and wits about him can see that the world is dead, cold and unending. Never yet has he beheld a God, or been compelled to require the existence of such a God from the evidence of his senses. On the contrary, it needed the strongest inner compulsion, which can only be explained by the irrational force of instinct, for man to invent those religious beliefs whose absurdity was long since pointed out by Tertullian. In the same way one can withhold the material content of primitive myths from a child but not take from him the need for mythology, and still less his ability to manufacture it for himself. One could almost say that if all the world's traditions were cut off at a single blow, the whole of mythology and the whole history of religion would start all over again with the next generation. Only a very few individuals succeed in throwing off mythology in epochs of intellectual exuberance — the masses never. Enlightenment avails nothing, it merely destroys a transitory manifestation, but not the creative impulse. (Jung, p. 25)

But are the mythic notions fact or truth? For Jung the idea is *psychologically* true because it exists in the human mind. Therefore in Jung's analysis the religious experience is an emotional experience involving surrender to a higher power, whether that higher power is conceived of as existing outside of the self and called God, or whether it is an internal power called the unconscious. In other words, as

Fromm has put it, "Jung reduces religion to a psychological phenomenon and at the same time elevates the unconscious to a religious phenomenon." (*Psychoanalysis and Religion*, p. 20)

One of the more recent developments in psychology is *humanistic psychology*. Here the focus is on human beings and their potential for self-achievement, for self-actualization, for the integration of the self. Its proponents have moved away from earlier religious and psychological evaluation of human beings as inherently evil and find in all humans the propensity for good.

Erich Fromm (1900-1980) can write of the importance of rational faith which is to be distinguished from irrational faith. He wrote:

> While irrational faith is rooted in the submission to a power which is felt to be overwhelmingly strong, omniscient, and omnipotent, in the abdication of one's own power and strength, rational faith is based upon the opposite experience. We have this faith in a thought because it is a result of our own observation and thinking. We have faith in the potentialities of others, of ourselves, and of mankind because, and only to the degree to which, we have experienced the growth of our own potentialities, the reality of growth in ourselves, the strength of our own power of reason and of love. *The basis of rational faith is productiveness*; to live by our faith means to live productively and to have the only certainty which exists; the certainty growing from productive activity and from the experience that each one of us is the active subject of whom these activities are predicated. (*Man for Himself*, p. 208)

Like other humanistic psychologists, Fromm sees religion as a human expression and points out that:

> "Do you believe in the existence of God?" has been made the crucial question of religionists and the denial of God has been the position chosen by those fighting the church. It is easy to see that many who profess the belief in God are in their human attitude idol worshippers or men without faith, while some of the most ardent "atheists," devoting their lives to the betterment of mankind, to deeds of brotherliness and love, have exhibited faith and a profoundly religious attitude. Centering the religious discussion on the acceptance or denial of the symbol God blocks the understanding of the religious problem

> as a human problem and prevents the development of that human attitude which can be called religious in a humanistic sense. (*Psychoanalysis and Religion*, pp. 113-114)

As we look back on our effort in chapter 2 to come to terms with the struggle to define religion, it is clear that Erich Fromm chooses to embrace the term in a humanistic rather than a supernaturalistic way. For him, religion is a symbol of human efforts to come to terms with meaning and the development of values.

The Sciences and Freethought

Bertrand (Arthur William) Russell (1872-1970), the 3rd Earl Russell, was a mathematician, philosopher, winner of the Nobel Prize in Literature in 1950, a pacifist active in disarmament and anti-nuclear testing movements and a skeptic dedicated to a life of reason. In the Preface to *Why I am Not a Christian*, Russell wrote:

> I think all the great religions of the world — Buddhism, Hinduism, Christianity, Islam, and Communism — both untrue and harmful. It is evident as a matter of logic that, since they disagree, not more than one of them can be true. (p. v)

The "harm" that Russell found in religions was the need to have a conviction that could not be shaken and therefore the corresponding need to keep the believer from any information that might challenge the faith or present contrary evidence. The result is a stunting of the mind which avoids the importance of basing conclusions on evidence rather than on unfounded dogmas. A further consequence is the tendency to encourage the development of virulent fanaticism and hostility among believers who cannot understand or tolerate the fanaticism and hostility of those who have different beliefs.

So far as harm is concerned, Russell recognized that within the different religions are tenets that "do definite harm." Among these are Roman Catholic attitudes towards birth control, the Hindu sacralization of the cow and the belief that "it is wicked for widows to remarry," and the Communist acceptance of dictatorship. In contrast Russell describes his vision of a more acceptable world:

> The world that I should wish to see would be one freed from the virulence of group hostilities and capable of realizing that

> happiness for all is to be derived rather from co-operation than from strife. I should wish to see a world in which education is aimed at mental freedom rather than at imprisoning the minds of the young in a rigid armor of dogma calculated to protect them through life against the shafts of impartial evidence. The world needs open hearts and open minds, and it is not though rigid systems, whether old or new, that these can be derived. (p. vii)

With regard to whether he was an atheist or an agnostic, he wrote:

> Therefore in regard to the Olympic gods, speaking to a purely philosophic audience, I would say that I am an Agnostic. But speaking popularly, I think that all of us would say in regard to those gods that we were atheists. In regard to the Christian God, I should, I think, take exactly the same line. There is exactly the same degree of possibility and likelihood of the existence of the Christian God as there is of the existence of the Homeric God. I cannot prove that either the Christian God or the Homeric gods do not exist, but I do not think that their existence is an alternative that is sufficiently probable to be worth serious consideration. Therefore, I suppose that on these documents that they submit to me on these occasions I ought to say "Atheist," although it has been a very difficult problem, and sometimes I have said one and sometimes the other without any clear principle by which to go. When one admits that nothing is certain one must, I think, also add that some things are much more nearly certain than others. (quoted by Seckel, p. 85)

Albert Einstein (1879-1955) expressed his beliefs as follows:

> The most beautiful thing we can experience is the mysterious. It is the source of all true art and science. He to whom this emotion is a stranger, who can no longer pause to wonder and stand rapt in awe, is as good as dead: his eyes are closed. This insight into the mystery of life, coupled though it be with fear, has given rise to religion. To know that what is impenetrable to us really exists, manifesting itself as the highest wisdom and the most radiant beauty which our dull faculties can comprehend only in their most primitive forms — this knowledge, this feel-

> ing, is at the center of true religiousness. In this sense, and in this sense only, I belong in the ranks of devoutly religious men.
>
> I cannot imagine a God who rewards and punishes the objects of his creation, whose purposes are modeled after our own — a God, in short, who is but a reflection of human frailty. Neither can I believe that the individual survives the death of his body, although feeble souls harbor such thoughts through fear or ridiculous egotism. It is enough for me to contemplate the mystery of conscious life perpetuating itself through all eternity, to reflect upon the marvelous structure of the universe which we can dimly perceive, and to try humbly to comprehend even an infinitesimal part of the intelligence manifested in nature. (pp. 6-7)

> I do not believe in the immortality of the individual, and I consider ethics to be an exclusively human concern with no superhuman authority behind it. (Dukas)

Julian Huxley (1887-1975), a British research scientist, expressed his views as follows:

> I do not believe in the existence of a god or gods. The conception of divinity seems to me, though built up out of a number of real elements of experience, to be a false one, based on the quite unjustifiable postulate that there must be some more or less personal power in control of the world. We are confronted with forces beyond our control, with incomprehensible disasters, with death; and also with ecstasy, with a mystical sense of union with something greater than our ordinary selves, with sudden conversion to a new way of life, with the burden of guilt and sin and ways in which these burdens may be lifted. In theistic religions, all these elements of actual experience have been woven into a unified body of belief and practice, in relation to the fundamental postulate of the existence of a god or gods.
>
> I believe this fundamental postulate to be nothing more than the result of asking a wrong question, "Who or what rules the universe?" So far as we can see, it rules itself, and indeed the whole analogy with a country and its ruler is false. Even if a god does exist behind or above the universe as we experience it, we can have no knowledge of such a power; the actual gods

> of historical religions are only the personifications of impersonal facts of nature and of facts of our inner mental life.

Edward O. Wilson (1929-), a sociobiologist who is professor of entomology at the Museum of Comparative Zoology at Harvard University, is deeply concerned with the relationship between science, evolution and ethics. In a recent interview, reported in *Free Inquiry* magazine (Vol. 13, No. 2, Spring 1993, pp. 28-31), he said,

> . . . we can understand human nature best and in greatest detail by viewing ourselves as evolutionary products in which the mind, although undeniably unique in the history of evolution, nevertheless has biological roots that can only be understood by references to the deep genetic history of humanity and of our pre-human ancestors. The relationships we develop toward each other are based on that long history of genetic socialization, and our ethics has arisen from that deep history as well. Therefore a sound ethics has to take into account our biology and our genetic history, both of which are far more complex and difficult to understand than hereto appreciated within the traditional venues of moral reasoning. Once deep history has been penetrated and better understood, it should allow a much more objective evaluation of moral codes. This naturalistic approach, which is certainly not new to me but goes back to evolutionary biologists of the nineteenth century, has special applicability in our approach to the environment. It inclines us to recognize that our humanity evolved in close association with other life-forms and has the innate tendency to affiliate with them, by the multifarious aesthetic pleasure they provide and the environments — places to live and search — we innately regard as optimal. This affiliation I've called "biophilia." . . It means "love of life" . . .

Andrew Dickson White (1832-1918), a New York State Senator, and a founder of what became Cornell University (he served as its first president, 1867-85), developed the idea of a university detached from all sects and parties and free to pursue truth without deference to dogma. He was one of the first educators to use the system of free elective studies. Cornell was nonsectarian and the charge of "godlessness" was made against it. Continuing controversies over the antagonism between the theological and scientific view of the universe and of education in relation to it led White to write his monumental *A History of the*

Warfare of Science with Theology in Christendom. As a practicing Episcopalian, White maintained that freedom was beneficial to religion. He said:

> In all modern history, interference with science in the supposed interest of religion, no matter how conscientious such interference may have been, has resulted in the direst evils both to religion and to science, and invariably; and, on the other hand, all untrammeled scientific investigation, no matter how dangerous to religion some of its stages may have seemed for the time to be, has invariably resulted in the highest good both of religion and of science. (Vol. I, p. viii)

Concerning the detrimental influence of theology on modern science, he wrote:

> The establishment of Christianity, beginning a new evolution of theology, arrested the normal development of the physical sciences for over fifteen hundred years. The cause of this arrest was twofold. First, there was created an atmosphere in which the germs of physical science could hardly grow — an atmosphere in which all seeking in Nature for truth as truth was regarded as futile. The general belief derived from the New Testament Scriptures was, that the end of the world was at hand; that the last judgment was approaching; that all existing physical nature was soon to be destroyed: hence, the greatest thinkers in the Church generally poured contempt upon all investigators into a science of Nature, and insisted that everything except the saving of souls was folly.
>
> This belief appears frequently through the entire period of the Middle Ages, but during the first thousand years it is clearly dominant. . .
>
> Then, too, there was established a standard to which all science which did struggle up through this atmosphere must be made to conform — a standard which favoured magic rather than science, for it was a standard of rigid dogmatism obtained from literal readings in the Jewish and Christian Scriptures. The most careful inductions from ascertained facts were regarded as wretchedly fallible when compared with any view of nature whatever given or even hinted at in any poem, chronicle, code, apologue, myth, legend, allegory, letter, or discourse

of any sort which had happened to be preserved in the literature which had come to be held as sacred.

For twelve centuries, then, the physical sciences were thus discouraged or perverted by the dominant orthodoxy. . (Vol. I, pp. 375-76)

Modern Biblical Research and Freethought

Biblical research, conducted primarily by confirmed Christians and Jews, continues to enrich our understanding of this important document. Literary analysis, archaeological investigations, and comparative studies of the religious concepts of the ancient world outside of and within Palestine, provide new insights into biblical history.

The impact of modern biblical research and of literary and historical analysis have demonstrated the following:

- The Bible is a product of the time of its writing. That is to say that it reflects the world view, the notions and concepts that were prevalent some 2,000 to 3,000 years ago, before the development of modern science. It is not surprising to find that the biblical ideas about the world and humankind, like those of others who lived and wrote several thousand years ago, are not supported by modern science.
- The biblical creation accounts are myths and in no way reflect the way in which the earth, the planets and the solar system have evolved. Biblical creation mythology embraces notions similar to those found in the cosmological myths of Egypt and Mesopotamia. Indeed, the Genesis 1 account reflects patterns borrowed from ancient Babylon when Jews were captives in that city during the 6th century B.C.E. (cf. Larue, 1988, chapter 2)
- The stories of the patriarchs and of Moses have no basis in fact. The biblical tradition of the 40-year desert wanderings by some 1,000,000 or more Hebrews are religious fiction created by a temple priesthood in Jerusalem. Not only would it be physically impossible for such a multitude to survive in the desert, but there is absolutely no archaeological evidence that such an exodus ever occurred.
- The accounts of the conquest of Palestine by the Hebrews are also temple fiction. For example, the description of the fall of the city of Jericho, supposedly as the result of Hebrew priests blowing on the rams' horn trumpets (*shofarim*), is fiction. Careful archaeological investigations have demonstrated conclusively that the walls of Jericho had collapsed and the site was abandoned long before the coming of

the Hebrews. Indeed, there are questions concerning whether *any* invasion actually occurred. The Hebrews now appear to have been present in Palestine as part of the local population. Their coming to power under Kings Saul and David was like that of any other indigent group taking control of a government.

▪ There is some solid history within the Bible, such as that found in the early source of the story of King David. Like all historical accounts, the presentation of material is colored by a local bias — in this case a Jewish religious bias. Such a bias is to be expected inasmuch as the documents were produced by the royal courts and the temple priesthood. Furthermore, the earliest accounts which seem to have an historical basis have been overwritten by later writers who have inserted supernaturalistic material to heighten the theological aspects of the story.

▪ The Bible, critically studied, does present an evolution of Jewish theology. Early Jewish religion was monolatrous, which is to say that the Jewish god Yahweh was considered to be the god of the Hebrew people only, just as the Moabite god Chemosh was the god of the Moabite people only. This belief is echoed in the commandment "You shall have no other god before (beside) me." There is no denial of the existence of other gods; in fact, it is clear that the commandment recognizes that there were other gods demanding recognition. During and after the time of exile in Babylon (6th century B.C.E.), the idea of monotheism was developed in Judaism. Monotheism states that there is only one god and that all other claims are nonsense. The theme is set forth in chapters 40 to 55 of the book of Isaiah, which were composed by an unknown Hebrew prophet in exile in Babylon. It can be argued that the notion of monotheism was borrowed from Zoroastrian religion, although that cannot be proven conclusively.

▪ Christianity developed first as a sect of Judaism, employing ideas that were current in Jewish thought. As it expanded during its early years it borrowed ideas from the mystery cults and from philosophy.

▪ The biblical stories about Jesus' birth and childhood are religious fiction and contain motifs that are common to many ancient hero stories. Early Christians, including Jesus and Paul, were quite wrong in their anticipation that the world would end in their time.

▪ The notion of a resurrection of a dead body and the disposal of the re-animated corpse of Jesus by the theory of the ascension to heaven was possible only in first-century thought. In many current Near-Eastern myths, God-figures descended into the underworld, the place of the dead, and were resurrected. The idea of the ascension could be imagined because the people thought that heaven was a place just above the earth. Neither the idea of there being a realm of the dead existing beneath the surface of the earth, nor the idea of a realm of the gods existing above the earth, makes any sense in terms of modern geological and cosmological concepts.

- The book of the Revelation of John, the last book in the Christian New Testament, reflects early Christian beliefs in a coming apocalypse. This belief can only be sustained in modern times by clergy and other expositors, who continually reinterpret the colorful symbols and read into the thinking of the first century writer references to nations (such as the United States and Russia) concerning which people in those ancient times had no knowledge and which would make no sense to the original writer.

Unquestionably, these conclusions are troublesome and upsetting for those whose faith system is based on the belief that the Bible is the inspired, infallible word of God. It is not surprising to find that most educated clergy do not even begin to share these findings with their congregations. Even instructors in biblical studies in universities and colleges avoid presenting such conclusions to their classes. Why? The reasons are obvious! They do not wish to upset fundamentalists. They do not want to become involved in religious controversies that could affect the security of their position. Only when they are hard pressed do they share such information (cf. Temple). When asked to explain why, in the light of this knowledge, they continue to belong to church or synagogue organizations, some clergy will speak of an "ethnic" heritage; others will frankly confess "political" motives; while still others refer to familial, and financial, and social pressures.

Where does one find these excuses? These statements are difficult to document because they represent the results of dozens of private conversations over the years with men and women of the clergy and with academicians who teach in the field of religion. The extent to which such persons can be accused of "dishonesty" or of not being "up-front" must be balanced against survival needs. For example, one professor of New Testament Studies in a very conservative seminary, which requires that, annually, each instructor sign a statement to the effect that s/he believes the Bible to be the divinely inspired and infallible word of God, admitted that his research had led him to reject such a conclusion. To refuse to sign would cost him his job and at his age (early fifties) finding a new teaching post would be almost impossible. He had his family to think about — his children were in college and his aging parents needed his help and support. He knew that to sign was to dissemble. To protect his feelings of personal integrity while conforming to the demand, he told me that each year he signs "under protest."

A young New Testament scholar whose teaching post in a prominent private university was financed by his ultra-conservative denomination was compelled to find a teaching post that was not denominationally supported when it became clear that he no longer accepted the Bible as the divinely inspired word of God. The power of denominations to control the teaching of religion is primarily limited, of course, to those institutions where they have control or where they finance chairs or professorships.

However, even in a liberal, secular, private university, unsophisticated and uninformed believers can bring pressure to have their own points of view expressed in the classroom. I can personally testify to this kind of pressure. On one occasion, after I had lectured as a guest speaker in a class on human sexuality about the biblical attitudes towards sex, the professor in charge of the class was subjected to abusive phone calls from the parents of students who were upset by the lecture. On other occasions, University chaplains, joined by colleagues in the School of Religion, expressed deep concerns that my courses did not reflect faith positions. They met and tried to bring pressure on me to conform to their particular angle of vision. As a scholar, researcher and educator, I have always been convinced that it was my task to present the latest and the best findings available regardless of whether or not such material might support some given faith stance. I was teaching as an historian of religion, not as a minister or rabbi.

Biblical Creationism, Freethought and Modern Science

One issue that perennially confronts the school system is the argument that biblical creationism should be presented in science classes as an alternative theory to scientific evolutionism. Over and over again, modern scientists, including Nobel Prize winners, have taken their stand against the introduction of the non-scientific world-view of the Bible into science classes. The thesis needs some examination.

As we have seen, the biblical accounts of creation are to be numbered among dozens of similar accounts that were current when they were recorded. They reflect the limited observations and the limited knowledge of their time of writing.

In more recent times, James Ussher, Archbishop of Armagh in Ireland (1581-1656), sought to place creation in an historical time frame based on the Bible. Using the dates provided in the book of Genesis, he determined that Adam was created in 4004 B.C.E. and that the flood occurred 1655 years later in 2349 B.C.E. On the basis of Ussher's dating patterns, John Lightfoot of Cambridge, in 1642, stated that Adam had been created at precisely 9:00 a.m. on October 23, 4004 B.C.E! Between 1650-54, Ussher published his biblical chronology under the title *Annales Veteris et Novi Testamenti*. In 1703, the dates he proposed were inserted in the margins of the King James Version of the Bible — by whose authority, no one really knows. For many, these dates became as authoritative as the biblical text itself. Although some Bible-believers still attempt to argue that Ussher's dates have a basis in fact and seek to interpret or to create scientific evidence to fit their beliefs, no literate or informed persons will accept Ussher's dates nor the notion that the world is less than 10,000 years old. There is simply too much scientific evidence to the contrary. It is not surprising to find that present-day versions of the Bible omit these dates.

One of the bases for rejection of biblical chronology and creationist concepts developed from the research of Charles Darwin. In 1831, Captain Robert Fitzroy, at the urging Darwin's science teacher at Cambridge, John Stevens Henslow, invited Charles Darwin, a naturalist, to accompany him on the second voyage of H.M.S. Beagle. Out of the research and experiences of that five-year journey around the globe came the volume that was to challenge biblical concepts and present basic data that would lead to the theory of evolution. Darwin's *Origin of Species* appeared in 1859 and immediately the debate with religionists began. Darwin had assumed that his investigations were consistent with religion and in the final chapter of the book he wrote:

> I see no good reason why the views given in this volume should shock the religious feelings of anyone. . . . A celebrated author and divine has written to me that "he has gradually learned to see that it is just as noble a conception of the Deity to believe that He created a few original forms capable of self-development into other and needful forms, as to believe that He required a fresh act of creation to supply the voids caused by the action of His laws." (p. 466)

Darwin concluded the book with:

> There is a grandeur in this view of life, with its several powers, having been originally breathed by the Creator into a few forms or into one, and that while this planet has gone circling

> on according to the fixed law of gravity, from so simple a beginning endless forms most beautiful and wonderful have been, and are being evolved. (p. 474)

But his religious sentiments were to undergo change. Later, when Darwin was asked about his personal faith, he replied:

> What my own views may be is a question of no consequence to anyone but myself. But, as you ask, I may state that my judgment often fluctuates. . . . I think that generally, and more and more as I grow older, but not always, an Agnostic would be the more correct description of my state of mind. (quoted by Fridtjof Nansen, p. 93)

Darwin's theories energized problems that would not be explained away. He had set forth four fundamental concepts:

1. There was, in all of nature, a struggle for survival
2. The most adaptable forms were those that would survive
3. There is a constancy in heredity
4. The principle of variation

This naturalistic account of the progressive adaptation of organisms to their environment flew in the face of the theological notion of the providence and wisdom of God. Moreover, the evidence of violence and wastage in the natural processes appeared to invalidate Newton's idea of nature doing "nothing in vain," so that God, the perfect draughtsman, was shown to be something less than perfect.

When the British Association for the Advancement of Science met at Oxford in 1860, Captain Fitzroy, who had earned a reputation both as a navigator and meteorologist, angrily protested what he, as a conservative Victorian, rightly perceived as a violation of the teachings of the first chapter of Genesis. The controversies that raged over Darwin's theories are too extensive for discussion here. An excellent summary can be found in *Darwin*, edited by Philip Appleman (1979). But it should be noted that Bishop Samuel Wilberforce, who had challenged Darwin's protagonist, Thomas Henry Huxley, to a debate, failed miserably to sustain his arguments from scripture.

The creationist-evolution issue came to a head in educational circles in America in the famous Scopes trial. In 1925, the Tennessee legislature forbade the teaching of evolution in the public schools. John

Scopes, a science teacher in a Dayton High School, agreed to test the law. He was arrested and, supported by the ACLU, was defended in court by Clarence Darrow. William Jennings Bryan supported the fundamentalist religious point of view. Scopes was convicted, but the fundamentalist position was weakened. In 1926 and 1927, Mississippi and Arkansas passed anti-evolutionary teaching laws. However, the scientific evidence could not be ignored. Tennessee repealed its legislation in 1967, and the Arkansas law was declared unconstitutional in 1968 by the United States Supreme Court (cf. Appleman, p. 556f).

Textbook publishers have been compelled to exercise extreme caution in designing science books for use in public schools. Indeed, the word "evolution" has been almost entirely avoided to salve the concerns of fundamentalists. Recently, a high school teacher in San Clemente, California, decided to ignore his commitment to teach according to the program developed for California public schools. He introduced biblical creationism as "science" into the classroom. His action ignored the advice and the concern expressed by 19 Nobel Laureate Scientists in a letter to the California State Board of Education in 1972. These eminent scholars stated firmly that "Creation 'theory' is *not* based on science and does not belong in a science textbook" (italicizing theirs). (cf. Appleman pp. 382-384)

California education, like that in other civilized centers, seeks to provide students with the best, most reliable, most trustworthy and most proven information available. The ideas about nature and the development of life held by persons of the biblical era who lived in a non-scientific age have no place in a science class. Their notions would be suitable in a class on the history of ideas, presented together with the beliefs of other early people. In other words, creationist theories cannot be taught as "science" because they are not science, but are purely religious.

The well-known scientist J. Bronowski has commented on the conflict:

> The theory of evolution made literal church dogmas look as flimsy as four hundred years ago Copernicus had done. But at both times, against Darwin as well as against Copernicus, the established religions did not linger in defeat. They simply abandoned the ground on which they had once stood pat. The church which has humiliated Galileo found, with a great show of tolerance, that a belief that the earth is the center of the universe in not really cardinal to its doctrine. The bishops who thundered at Charles Darwin and John Tyndall were suddenly

> content to abandon the literal truth of the story of the Creation, and to endow it instead with a more shining splendor as some mystic parable to the evolutionary process.
>
> For this reason you will find no respectable church authorities today who are willing to challenge the proposition for which Buffon was once threatened with excommunication, that the crust of the earth carries the marks of past history. No sermons are preached by educated clerics against geology, the fossil record, and evolution. Indeed, no defense of church doctrine, outside Spain, the Republic of Eire, and some states of America, takes as its ground the factual truth of these doctrines. The issue of fact has been yielded to the experimental scientist. Whatever issue is now paraded, whatever kind of truth is now claimed for ancient dogmas, truth which is accessible to rational inquiry has been abandoned.
>
> It is of course annoying of the churches to shift their ground like this. For 1800 years and more, the dogmas laid down by the Christian churches, their predecessors, and their rivals were advanced as matters of literal truth. To fly in the face of Genesis was throughout the centuries held to be as outrageous as to fly in the face of gravity; and was in fact a great deal more dangerous. Now the great dignitaries tell us, with beatific charm, and with a smile of tolerance at our foolish materialistic obtuseness, that all this meant nothing. The churches have changed their mind. They no longer believe the biblical stories — indeed, some of them plainly find the existence of the Bible an embarrassment. And anyone who went to the stake for sharing this disbelief prematurely, as so many men did, may now in retrospect bask in their regrets . . . Religion as it existed up to and in the nineteenth century is dead. Nineteenth-century rationalism killed it . . . (Bronowski, 1977, pp. 250-251)

It is important that we look at other areas of research and recognize how scientific thought and freethought merge. Freethought provides the basis for investigating any area of human interest free of any authoritarian dogma that might dictate or influence conclusions. The scientific method involves critical examination and re-examination of data, employing the best tools available for analysis, and subjecting the results of research and inquiry to the critical examination and testing by others. Scientific conclusions are always tentative, because the development of better tools, new approaches and new findings may make necessary refinements, changes or even discarding previously held theories and concepts. In other words, both freethought and scientific thought seek to be on the cutting edge of inquiry. The result is excitement and exhilaration in open inquiry.

Geology, Freethought and the Bible

Perhaps the most dramatic clash between biblical creationism and science came in the field of geology. Before the end of the seventeenth century, John Ray argued that fossils were the remains of living organisms. Their presence revealed that the earth's surface had undergone dramatic changes that could not be reconciled with the Genesis account of creation. Something of the irritation generated in the minds of Bible believers by these geological inquiries was expressed by the poet William Cowper (1731-1800):

> Some drill and bore
> The solid earth, and from the strata there
> Extract a register, by which we learn,
> That he who made it, and revealed its date
> to Moses, was mistaken in its age.

Paleontologist Georges Leopold Cuvier (1769-1832) attempted to allay the fears of Bible-believers by suggesting that the earth had experienced a series of cataclysms that had destroyed its inhabitants, so that the idea of the Flood could be maintained. But the six days of creation continued to be a problem. Taylor Lewis, in 1855 sought to demonstrate that the Bible could be seen as being in accord with science. He argued that "the Bible does not teach that the creative days were twenty-four hours long, but leaves a great latitude in this respect, determining nothing about their duration except that they must be in harmony with the growths and processes assigned to each." (Lewis, p. 12)

British geologist, Sir Charles Lyell (1797-1875), published *Principles of Geology* (1830-1832) in which he tried to accommodate geological findings to the Genesis account. However, when in 1863 he published *Evidence of the Antiquity of Man*, he demonstrated convincingly the presence of humans long before the time allowed in biblical chronology.

Astronomy, Freethought and the Bible

When Copernicus and Bruno and the others who came after them proved unconditionally that the sun did not circle the earth, but that the earth circled the sun, new concepts evolved. Geocentricity, that placed the earth at the center of the universe, was gone forever. At first, the new focus was on heliocentricity, that placed the sun at the center of our planetary system. But then our growing awareness of the vastness of the universe plunged us into cosmic consciousness. In desperation to maintain our centrality, some turned to anthropocentrism by placing humans at the center of the universe as the most important life-form. However, as the great American astronomer Harlow Shapely was to comment, the "presumption of man's cosmic importance — our presumption that we are existing in a universe centered on the terrestrial genus Homo . . . " no longer holds and calls for the "abandonment of a one-planet religion and a one-planet deity . . ." (pp. 100, 105) Shapely would

> equate nature and God. The phrase, now almost too well known, is "All Nature is God and all God is Nature." Still shorter, and deeply meaningful, is "Nature is All." That last is the essence of natural piety. (p. 107)

He concluded this chapter, which he titled "Life and Hope in the Psychozoic Era," with these words:

> To me it is a religious attitude to recognize the wonder of the whole natural world, not only of life. Is not the creed of Schweitzer [Reverence for Life] too narrow, too selective? Why not revere also the amino acids and the simple proteins from which life emerged? Or why not go all the way and avow reverence for all things that exist, all that is touched by cosmic evolution, and reserve the greatest reverence for existence itself? (p. 123)

Harlow Shapely's Cosmic Naturalism coincides with the thinking of many other scientists. Reverence for nature — all nature — replaces adoration of the God of the Bible. For such scientists the biblical God image is too small, too narrowly defined, too limited by the mind-set of the peoples who developed it some 2000 to 3000 years ago. The divine no longer focuses on humankind — the divine is inherent in nature, in all that exists. Humans are important only to themselves, not to some divine entity that they have created or fantasized.

The distinguished astronomer and Humanist, Carl Sagan, has also commented on the relationship of the science of astronomy to religion. He has pointed out that "As we learn more and more about the universe, there seems less and less for God to do." (p. 286) He believes that:

> Religions ought to be subject to at least the same degree of skepticism as, for example, contentions about UFO visitations or Velikovskian catastrophism. I think it is healthy for the religions themselves to foster skepticism about the fundamental underpinnings of their evidential bases. There is no question that religion provides a solace and support, a bulwark in a time of emotional need, and can serve extremely useful social roles. But it by no means follows that religion should be immune from testing, from critical scrutiny, from skepticism. . . .
>
> Religion used to provide a generally accepted understanding of our place in the universe. . . . The way to find out about our place in the universe is by examining the universe and by examining ourselves — without preconceptions, with as unbiased a mind as we can muster. . If we look at the universe in the large, we find something astonishing. First of all, we find a universe that is exceptionally beautiful, intricately and subtly constructed. Whether our appreciation of the universe is because we are part of that universe — whether, no matter how the universe were put together, we would have found it beautiful — is a proposition to which I do not pretend to have an answer. But there is no question that the elegance of the universe is one of its most remarkable properties. At the same time, there is no question that there are cataclysms and catastrophes occurring regularly in the universe and on the most awesome scale. . . . We see a universe simultaneously very beautiful and very violent. We see a universe that does not exclude a traditional Western or Eastern god, but that does not require one either.
>
> My deeply held belief is that if a god of anything like the traditional sort exists, our curiosity and intelligence are provided by such a god. We would be unappreciative of those gifts (as well as unable to take such a course of action) if we suppressed our passion to explore the universe and ourselves. On the other hand, if such a traditional god does not exist, our

curiosity and our intelligence are the essential tools for managing our survival. In either case, the enterprise of knowledge is consistent with both science and religion, and is essential for the welfare of the human species. (pp. 288-291)

Anthropology, Freethought and the Bible

Some twenty-five years ago, I was fortunate enough to be in an intimate home-setting with Dr. L.S.B. Leakey (1903-1972), the famous explorer of the Olduvai Gorge in Tanganyika (now Tanzania). He was on a fund-raising tour in Los Angeles, and I was invited to share an evening with him in the home of one his contributors. This fine social anthropologist and naturalist and his second wife, Mary Leakey, had found the remains of what Leakey formally called *Zinjanthropus* or East African man (now known as *Australiopithecus-boisei*), who lived some 1,750,000 years ago. Leaky had been raised in a missionary compound in East Africa and he has recorded that his discoveries resulted in spirited conversations with South African missionaries who accepted the marginal notations in the Bibles with Archbishop Ussher's dates as authoritative (Leakey, p. 138).

I don't know whether or not he thought that because one of my areas of interest was biblical archaeology that I, or perhaps his hosts, might be disturbed by anything that challenged a literal approach to the biblical creation concepts (I was/am not, cf. Larue, 1988, p. 63f). In any case, he made a point of saying that his findings did not contradict Genesis, chapter one. He suggested that "we don't know how long a day was then" and that, therefore, a day might have been a million or more of our days in length. I was a guest and I did not argue the point, even though I thought the notion was simply nonsense. How would such a suggestion explain how, in Genesis, plant life came into being on the third day before the sun was created? How could there be "Day One" and "Days Two and Three" when the sun had not yet come into being? Finally, was God still "resting?" Obviously, Leakey was counting on me not to get technical. What is important in this anecdote, is that it represents one of the ways in which some researchers have tried to protect the authority of how the Hebrews conceived of the universe several thousand years ago.

The famous anthropologist, Sir Arthur Kieth — a man most tolerant of the place of religion in society — wrote:

> We who seek to explain the evolution of the universe and all that is therein, living and dead, must postulate certain conditions as axiomatic. We must postulate a universe already in existence — permeated and controlled by certain qualities and forces which were capable of evolving and changing until the universe assumed the state and form in which we now find it. How and why the universe came into existence is beyond our present reach. It is childish to say it is the work of a potter who stood outside his clay . . We humans are weak-kneed beings. Most of us still demand a God, cast in our own mold — one who can give succor when approached in prayer. An emotional need has called Him into being. (pp. 381-381)

Kieth, writing during the social cataclysm of World War II, was not prepared to throw away prejudicial feeling responses such as patriotism that "lead us to love our own land and our own people. I do not see, as the world now is, how man can throw away these crutches; without them he would have been still in the jungle. . . Our instincts, our feelings, our passions, and prejudices should serve us but not master us." (p. 382)

When the Jewish scholar, Nahum M. Sarna, produced his interpretive book, *Understanding Genesis*, he told his readers:

> It should be obvious that by the nature of things, none of these stories can possibly be the product of human memory, nor in any modern sense of the word scientific accounts of the origin and nature of the physical world.
>
> Biblical man, despite his intellectual and spiritual endowments, did not base his views of the universe and its laws on the critical use of empirical data. He had not, as yet, discovered the principles and methods of disciplined inquiry, critical observation or analytical experimentation . . . . Hence, it is a naive and futile exercise to attempt to reconcile the biblical accounts of creation with the findings of modern science. (p. 2f)

Poets, Writers, Singers and Freethought

Poets are often dismissed when one deals with scientific or philosophical issues. What is clear is that many poets, novelists, and singers are deeply involved in the study of ideas and social phenomena which they incorporate in their writings. For example, the English poet **Byron**

(1788-1824) was affected by the skepticism of Hume to the point of denying the basis for Christian redemption theories. In a letter to Francis Hodgson, written in 1811, he commented:

> . . the basis of your religion is *injustice*; the *Son of God*, the *pure*, the *immaculate*, is sacrificed for the *guilty*. This proves *His* heroism; but no more does away with *man's* guilt than by a schoolboy's volunteering to be flogged for another would exculpate the dunce from negligence, or preserve him from the rod.
> . . . I do not believe in revealed religion, because no religion is revealed; and if it please the Church to damn me for not allowing a *nonentity*, I throw myself on the mercy of the *"Great First Cause, least understood,"* who must do what is most proper; though I conceive He never made anything to be tortured in another life, whatever it may be in this.
> . . . And our carcasses, which are to rise again, are they worth raising? I hope, if mine is, that I shall have a better *pair of legs* than I have moved on these two-and-twenty years or I shall be sadly behind in the squeeze into Paradise. Did you ever read "Malthus on Population"? If he be right, war and pestilence are our best friends, to save us from being eaten alive, in this "best of all possible worlds." (quoted in Shadduck, pp. 70-71)

Mark Twain (Samuel Langhorne Clemens, 1835-1910) is best known for his masterpiece *The Adventures of Huckleberry Finn* (1835) — a book which often comes under attack when placed on public school reading lists. Twain's skepticism and freethought-humor is best revealed in the lesser known writing, *Letters From the Earth*, which was edited by B. de Voto and published in 1942. In 1909, when Twain wrote the *Letters*, he predicted that they would and could never be published, "because it would be a felony." After Twain's death, his daughter, Clara Clemens, refused to permit the publication of the *Letters*. She reversed her objections in 1940.

The *Letters* are a roguish examination of biblical stories, marked by Twain's satirical and humorous view of humans. It is clear that Twain had read his Bible. It is equally clear that he did not give it the exalted status it occupies in synagogue and church. Truly, Twain belongs among the freethinkers of America.

In 1986, at a meeting of the International Ethical and Humanist Union held in Oslo, Norway, I was introduced to a song entitled *Die Gedanken sind frei* — "The thoughts are free." The song dates back to the Peasants' Revolt of 1524-1526, discussed in chapter 19 in the context of the Protestant Reformation. Freethought Germans who formed the *Die Freien Gemeinden* or "The Free Congregations" imported the folksong to the United States in 1859 (see Hoops, pp. 248-249). The song reflects opposition to persecution for freethinking, speaks of the rights of a free people, and repeats the refrain *Die Gedanken sind frei*.

The huge number of freethought poems and songs are too numerable to mention. One collection, *We Sing of Life*, edited by Vincent Silliman, was published by the Starr King Press and distributed by the Beacon Press under the auspices of The American Ethical Union, and includes 172 different poems set to music. Although some poems utilize biblical motifs, the emphasis is deistic; most are non-theological.

Perhaps it is fitting to close this section with what is unquestionably the most memorable song by **John Lennon**, namely *Imagine*. If freethinkers indulged in prayer, the song could be recognized as a freethought prayer. In any case, it reflects a longing for universal peace and understanding, devoid of the divisions, religious and otherwise, that separate humankind into warring camps.

Imagine, by John Lennon

Imagine there's no heaven
Its easy if you try
No hell below us
Above us only sky
Imagine all the people
Living for today

Imagine there's no countries
It isn't hard to do
Nothing to kill or fight for
And no religion too

Imagine all the people
Living life in peace

Chorus
You may say that I'm a dreamer
But I'm not the only one
I hope some day you will join us
And that the world will be as one

Imagine no possessions
I wonder if you can
No need for greed or hunger
A brotherhood [and sisterhood]
of [woman and] man
Imagine all the people
Sharing all the world

Chorus
You may say that I'm a dreamer
But I'm not the only one
I hope someday you will join us
And that the world will live as one.

References

Allman, William F., and Joannie M. Scrof, "Lost Empires of the Americas," *U.S. News and World Report*, April 2, 1990, pp. 46-60.

Appleman, Philip, edit., *Darwin.* New York: W.W. Norton & Company, 1979.

Beard, Mary R., edit., *America Through Women's Eyes*. New York: The Macmillan Company, 1934.

Bedell, George C., Leo Sandon, Jr. and Charles J. Wellborn, *Religion in America*. New York: Macmillan Publishing Co., Inc., 1975.

Bernard, Victor, "Then a Miracle Occurs," *Free Inquiry*, Vol. 11, No. 3, 1991, pp. 31-37.

Brande, Scott, "Pandas Attack Science Education," *Free Inquiry*, Vol. 11, No. 3, 1991, pp. 28-31.

Bridenbaugh, Carl, *Jamestown, 1544-1699*. Oxford: Oxford University Press, 1980.

Bruno Giordano, *The Expulsion of the Triumphant Beast*. Trans. by Arthur D. Imerti. New Brunswick, New Jersey: Rutgers University Press, 1964.

Buckley, George T. *Atheism in the English Renaissance*. Chicago: University of Chicago Press, 1932.

Bronowski, J. and Bruce Mazlish, *The Western Intellectual Tradition*. New York: Harper & Brothers, 1960.

Bronowski, J., *A Sense of the Future*. Cambridge, Mass.: The MIT Press, 1977.

Bushnell, G.H.S., "The Crimson-Tipped Flower" in: Stuart Piggot, edit., *The Dawn of Civilization*. New York: McGraw-Hill Book Company, 1961, pp. 359-386.

Butterfield, L.H. et al., edits., *The Book of Abigail and John: Selected Letters of the Adams Family, 1762-1784*. Cambridge, Mass., 1975.

Churchill, Winston S., *A History of English Speaking Peoples* (four volumes). New York: Dorset Press, 1990 (reprint of 1956 edition).

Darwin, Charles, *The Origin of Species*. New York: Hurst & Company, n.d.

Day, Jane Stevenson, "A Walk Through Tenochtitlan," *Archaeology*, Vol. 45, No. 5, September/October, 1992, p. 47.

Degler, Carl N., *Out of Our Past*. New York: Harper & Row (Colophon edition), 1962.

Desmond, Adrian and James Moore, *Darwin: The Life of a Tormented Evolutionist*. New York: Warner Books, 1992.

Dillehay, Tom D. and Kathleen Deagan, "The Spanish Quest for Empire," *Antiquity*, Vol. 66, No. 250, Mar. 1992, pp. 113-119.

Dozier, Edward P., "The Hopi and the Tewa," *New World Archaeology*, San Francisco: W. H. Freeman and Company, 1974, pp. 132-137. (First published in *Scientific American*, June, 1957).

Dukas, Helen, and Banesh Hoffman, edits., *Albert Einstein: The Human Side*. Princeton, New Jersey: Princeton University Press, 1979.

Durant, Will, *The Age of Faith*. New York: Simon and Schuster, 1950.

Eckholm, Eric, "The Secrets of the Maya Decoded" in: Kevin Reilly, *Readings in the World Civilizations*. New York: St. Martins Press, Vol. 1, pp. 333-337.

Einstein, Albert, in *Living Philosophies*. New York: Simon and Schuster, 1931, pp. 3-7.

Ferro, Robert and Michael Grumley, *Atlantis: The Autobiography of a Search*. New York: Bell Publishing Company, 1971.

Franklin, John Hope, *From Slavery to Freedom: A History of Negro Americans*. New York: Alfred A. Knopf, Inc., 1967 (third edition).

Freud, Sigmund, *Totem and Taboo*. Trans. by James Strachey. New York: W.W. Norton & Company, 1950, paperback edition.

Freud, Sigmund, *Moses and Monotheism*. Trans. by Katherine Jones. New York: Vintage Books, 1967.

Fromm, Erich, *Man For Himself*. New York: Holt, Rinehart and Winston, 1964.

Fromm, Erich, *Psychoanalysis and Religion*. New Haven, Conn.: Yale University Press, 1967.

Gardner, Joseph, edit., *Mysteries of the Ancient Americas: The New World Before Columbus*. Pleasantville, N.Y., The Reader's Digest Association, Inc., 1990.

Gaspar, A. Tejera and E. Aznar Vallejo, "Lessons From the Canaries: the First Contact Between Europeans and Canarians c. 1312-1477," *Antiquity*, Vol. 66, No. 250, Mar., 1992, pp. 121-129.

Giammanco, Roberto, "Lest We Forget: Bruno, Galileo, and the Power to Define," *Free Inquiry*, Vol. 11, No. 3, 1991, pp. 16-19.

Gifford, William Alva, *The Story of the Faith*. New York: The Macmillan Company, 1946.

Haag, William G., "The Bering Strait Land Bridge," *New World Archaeology*. San Francisco: W.H. Freeman and Company, 1974, pp. 263-270. (First published in *Scientific American*, January, 1962.)

Harrington, M.R., *Religion and Ceremonies of the Lenape*. New York: Museum of the American Indian, 1921.

Heer, Friedrich, *The Medieval World*. London: Wiedenfelf and Nicolson, 1961.

Helms, Mary W., "Empire and the Hinterland in Lower Central America," *Antiquity*, Vol. 66, No. 250, Mar. 1992, pp. 191-203.

Hookway, Christopher, *Scepticism*. London: Routledge, 1990.

Hoops, Walter, "Die Freien Gemeinden" in: Gordon Stein, edit., *The Encyclopedia of Unbelief*. Buffalo, New York: Prometheus Books, 1985, Vol. 1, pp. 248-249.

Howard, Kathleen, *Mexico: Splendors of Thirty Centuries*. New York: The Metropolitan Museum of Art and Bullfinch Press, 1990.

Hutchinson, Louise Daniel, *Out of Africa*. Washington D.C.: The Smithsonian Institute Press, 1979.

Hyams, Edward, and George Ordish, *The Last of the Incas*. New York: Dorset Press, 1990 (reprint of 1963 edition).

Ingersoll, Col. R.G., *Complete Lectures.* Chicago: J. Regan & Co., n.d.

Isbell, William H., "The Prehistoric Ground Drawings of Peru," *Scientific American*, Vol. 79, 1978, pp. 140-153.

Jackson, Donald Dale, "Who the heck *did* 'discover' the New World," *Smithsonian*, September, 1991, Vol. 2, No. 6, pp. 76-85.

Johansen, Bruce E., *Forgotten Founders*. Ipswich, Mass.: Gambit, 1982. (Reprinted by Harvard Common Press, Boston, 1982.)

Jung, C.G., *Symbols of Transformation*. Trans. by R.F.C. Hull. Princeton, New Jersey: Princeton University Press, 1976.

Kayserling, M., *Christopher Columbus and the Participation of the Jews in the Spanish and Portugese Discoveries*. North Hollywood, Calif.: Carmi House Press, 1989.

Kieth, Sir Arthur, "I Believe" in: Clifton Fadiman, edit., *I Believe: The Personal Philosophies of Certain Eminent Men and Women of Our Time*. New York: Simon and Schuster, 1939, pp. 379-383.

Koch, G. Adolf, *Religion of the American Enlightenment*. New York: Thomas Y. Crowell Company, 1968.

Larue, Gerald A., *Old Testament Life and Literature*. Boston: Allyn and Bacon, Inc., 1968.

Larue, Gerald A., "Creationism: 500 years of Controversy," *Free Inquiry*, Vol. 2, No. 3, Summer 1982, pp. 9-14.

Larue, Gerald A., *Ancient Myth and Modern Life*. Long Beach, Calif.: Centerline Press, 1988.

Larue, Gerald A., *The Supernatural, the Occult and the Bible*. Buffalo, New York: Prometheus Books, 1990.

Leakey, L.S.B., *By the Evidence*. New York: Harcourt, Brace Jovanovich, 1974.

Lemonick, Michael D., "Secrets of the Maya," *Time*, August 9, 1993, pp. 43-49.

Lewis, Tayler, *The Six Days of Creation: or the Scriptural Cosmology with the Ancient idea of Time-Worlds, In Distinction From Worlds in Space*. London, 1855.

Ley, Willy, *Another Look at Atlantis*. New York: Bell Publishing Company, 1969.

Long, William E., "Just When Did people Get Here?" *Los Angeles Times*, March 1, 1994, pp. A1,10,13.

Luther, Martin, "On Jews and Their Lies" in: Jaraslav Pelican, edit., Luther's Works., St. Louis: Concordia Publishing House (1955-1975).

MacNeish, Richard S., "Early Man in the Andes," *New World Archaeology*. San Francisco: W.H. Freeman and Company, 1974, pp. 143-153. (First published in *Scientific American*, April, 1971.)

Mander, Jerry, *In the Absence of the Sacred*. San Francisco: Sierra Book Club, 1991.

Marriott, Alice and Carol K. Rachlin, *Plains Indian Mythology*. New York: New American Library (A Mentor Book), 1977.

Maugh, Thomas H., "Time Vaults," *Los Angeles Times*, September 9, 1991, p. B9.

Maugh, Thomas H., "Rain Forests Not as Fragile as Believed, Ancient Pottery Hints," *Los Angeles Times*, December 16, 1991, p. B9.

Maugh, Thomas H., "Archaeologist Finds Mayans' Largest, Oldest Sculpture," *Los Angeles Times*, March 6, 1992, pp. A. 3, 28.

Maxwell, James A., edit. *America's Fascinating Indian Heritage*. Pleasantville, N.Y.: Reader's Digest Association, 1990.

McCarter, P. Kyle, "Let's be Serious About the Bat Creek Stone," *Biblical Archaeology Review*, Vol. 19, No. 4, July/August, 1993, p. 54f, 83.

McCulloch, J. Huston, "Did Judean Refugees Escape to Tennessee?" *Biblical Archaeology Review*, Vol. 19, No. 4, July/August, 1993, pp. 47-53, 83.

McNiven, Peter, *Heresy and Politics in the Reign of Henry IV*. Suffolk: The Boydell Press, 1987.

Meggers, Betty J. and Clifford Evans, "A Transpacific Contact in 3000 B.C.," *New World Archaeology*. San Francisco: W.H. Freeman and Company, 1974, pp. 97-104. (First published in *Scientific American*, January, 1966.)

Milanich, Jerald T., "Native Societies and Spanish Empire in the 16th-Century American Southeast," *Antiquity*, Vol. 66, No. 250, Mar. 1992, pp. 140-152.

Mill, John Stuart, *On Liberty*. New York: Penguin Books Ltd., 1982.

Millon, Rene, "Teotihuacan," *New World Archaeology*, San Francisco: W.H. Freeman and Company, 1974, pp. 113-125.

Milones, Louis, "The Time of the Incas: The Colonial Indians' Quest," *Antiquity*, Vol. 66, No. 250, Mar. 1992, pp. 204-216.

Moctezuma, Eduardo Matos, "Imperial Tenochtitlan," *Mexico, Splendors of Thirty Centuries*. New York: Little, Brown and Company, 1990, pp. 212-234.

Nansen, Fridtjof, in *Living Philosophies*. New York: Simon and Schuster, 1931.

Nicholson, Irene, *Mexican and Central American Mythology*. London: Paul Hamlyn, 1968.

Osborne, Harold, *South America Mythology*. Feltham, Middlesex: The Hamlyn Publishing Group, 1968.

Pons, Frank Moya, "The Politics of Forced Indian Labour in La Espanola, 1493-1520," *Antiquity*, Vol. 66, No. 250, Mar., 1992, pp. 130-139.

Popkin, Richard H., *The History of Scepticism from Erasmus to Spinoza*. Berkeley, Calif.: University of California Press, 1979.

Porterfield, Amanda, "Witchcraft and the Colonization of Algonquian and Iroquois Culture," *Religion and American Culture*, Vol. 2, No. 1, Winter 1992, pp. 103-124.

Proskouriakoff, Tatiana, "The Death of a Civilization," *New World Archaeology*, San Francisco: W.H. Freeman and Company, 1974, pp. 127-131. (First printed in *Scientific American*, May, 1955.)

Prufer, Olaf H., "The Hopewell Cult," *New World Archaeology*. San Francisco" W.H. Freeman and Company, 1974, pp. 222-230. (First printed in *Scientific American*, December 1964.)

Raphael, David, *The Alhambra Decree*. North Hollywood, Calif.: Carmi House Press, 1988.

Raphael, David, *The Expulsion 1492 Chronicles*. North Hollywood, Calif.: Carmi House Press, 1992.

Raven, Charles E., *Science and Religion*. Cambridge: The University Press, 1953.

Rensberger, Boyce, "New Clues Put Humans in New World 28,000 Years Ago", *Los Angeles Times*, February 10, 1992, p. A21.

Richardson, Cyril Charles, *The Church Through the Centuries*. New York: Charles Scribner's Sons, 1950.

Russell, Bertrand, *Why I am Not a Christian*. London: George Allen & Unwin, Ltd, 1957. Reprinted by Simon and Schuster, New York, as a Touchstone paperback.

Sagan, Carl, *Broca's Brain*. New York: Random House, 1974.

Sale, Kirkpatrick, *The Conquest of Paradise*. New York: Alfred A. Knopf, 1990.

Sanders, William T., "Ecology and Cultural Syncretism in 16th Century Mesoamerica,"*Antiquity*, Vol. 66, No. 250, Mar. 1992, pp. 172-190.

Sarna, Nahum M., *Understanding Genesis*. New York: Schocken Books, 1966.

Seckel, Al, edit., *Bertrand Russell on God and Religion*. New York: Prometheus Books, 1986.

Shadduck, Gayle, *England's Amorous Angels, 1813-1823*. New York: University Press of America, 1990.

Shapely, Harlow, *Beyond the Observatory*. New York: Charles Scribner's Sons, 1967.

Schardel, Richard P., "The Archaeology of the Spanish Colonial Experience in South America," *Antiquity*, Vol. 66, No. 250, Mar. 1992, pp. 211-242.

Sheridan, Thomas, E., "The Limits of Power: The Political Ecology of the Spanish Empire in the Greater Southwest," *Antiquity*, Vol. 66, No. 250, Mar. 1992, pp. 153-172.

Silliman, Vincent, edit., *We Sing of Life*. Boston: The Beacon Press, 1955.

Sohm, Rudolf, *Outlines of Church History*. Boston: Beacon Press, 1958.

Stanton, Elizabeth Cady, *Eighty Years and More (1815-1897): Reminiscences of Elizabeth Cady Stanton*. London: T. Fisher Unwin, 1898.

Stillman, Edmund, "The Holy Terrors of Munster," *Horizon*, Summer 1967, Vol. IX, Number 3, pp. 90-95.

Strahler, Arthur N., "The Creationist Theory of Abrupt Appearances: A Critique," *Free Inquiry*, Vol. 11, No. 3, 1991, pp. 37-43.

Sykes, Egerton, *Atlantis, The Antediluvian World*. New York: Gramercy Publishing Company, 1949.

Temple, Kerry, "Who Do Men Say That I Am?" *The Humanist*, Vol. 51, No. 3, 1991, pp. 7-14.

Thomas, Hugh, *Conquest: Montezuma, Cortes and the Fall of Old Mexico*. New York: Simon and Schuster, 1994.

Thompson, Dick, "The Secrets of a Moche Lord," *Time*, September 26, 1988, pp. 77-78.

Ture, Kwame, and Charles V. Hamilton, *Black Power*. New York: Vintage Books, 1992.

Twain, Mark, *Letters From the Earth*. B. DeVoto, edit., New York: Harper & Row, 1962.

Walker, J.R., *The Sun Dance and Other Ceremonies of the Oglala Division of the Teton Dakota*. New York: American Museum of Natural History, Anthropological Papers, Vol. xvi, part II, 1917.

White, Andrew Dickson, *A History of the Warfare of Science with Theology in Christendom*. 2 volumes. New York: Dover Publications, 1960. (Reprint of 1896 edition by Macmillan and Co.)

Wood, Forrest G., *The Arrogance of Faith*. New York: Alfred A. Knopf, 1990.

Zubrow, Ezra B.W., Margaret C. Fritz and John M. Fritz, edits., *New World Archaeology: Theoretical and Cultural Transformations* (Readings From *Scientific American*). San Francisco: W.H. Freeman and Company, 1974.

22

Conclusion

As we conclude this study, we now look to the future. The importance of freethought, critical thinking and open inquiry in human history cannot be denied and, therefore, they demand recognition. Our children will reach maturity in the twenty-first century and they need role models and heroes to encourage them to utilize their critical capacities, to examine precepts openly and to press ahead freely in seeking to understand and explore everything from human nature to the cosmos itself.

We who are older have lived through the most horrendously brutal century in human history. Wars of extermination, based on racial and religious bigotry, have demonstrated conclusively that, when unquestioned dogma is perceived as truth, savagery of unimaginable proportions can be released in the name of ethnic purity or the fulfillment of God's will. The new tomorrows will move beyond these narrow, destructive notions and beliefs, only when ideas and pronouncements and dogmas and beliefs are open to question and challenge. Limitations imposed by racial, ethnic, religious, political, and sexual bigotry and dogma must not be allowed to limit the possibilities of a potential world of human harmony. Ancient teachings about humankind are marked and limited by territorial, theological, racial and sexual uncharitableness that are venomous and encourage virulence. Ancient beliefs about the cosmos and the relationships of human beings to their environments and to one another are non-scientific, limited in humanistic vision and in awareness of the interrelatedness of life forms on the planet earth. Such concepts are products of another time and place and, when introduced as fundamental truths, serve only to inhibit free inquiry and retard and frustrate the possibilities for the emergence of a new world marked with the values we all cherish, including peace, justice, freedom and concern for the well-being of all.

Freethought calls upon all of us and each of us to engage in the honorable role of educator — a role whose meaning is derived from the Latin root *educare*: to lead out. The educator (*educo*: I lead out) is one who leads his or her pupils out — beyond whatever walls confine and inhibit creative thought. While imparting respect for the rich heritage of the past, the educator encourages students to move beyond the limitations imposed by the past and to engage in thinking that will shape and determine their future.

Each generation leaves its own watermark on the sands of time. It is always a tragedy when a new generation accepts as final what has been done in the past, thus denying itself the right to explore and develop new paths, new insights, new responses to life and living. Today we witness the frightening potentials of religious neofundamentalism in Islam, Hinduism, Christianity and Judaism, each seeking to produce theocratic states where life, education and freedom are regulated by religious dogmas rooted in their particular ancient pasts. Such neofundamentalism displays a lack of faith in human beings and in our ability to work through and solve our own problems, develop our own ethics, enhance our own futures. Neofundamentalism's demand is to return to the supernaturalism of past generations and to yield the power to dictate our thinking, our science, and our approach to life itself, to men and women who lived at a time when the world was believed to be flat and the sun revolved around the earth.

Interestingly enough, as we look at the Islamic fundamentalist states with their restrictions on human rights and freedom, we note that those in power demand for themselves all the riches and benefits and freedoms that modern science has to offer, all of which have grown out of freethought and open investigation. We need only look to medieval Europe to witness the stagnation that ensued when religious dogmatists come to power. During that period, leaders in the church and state had no qualms about the use and abuse of others and about placing restrictions on the life and thought of others, all the while demanding freedom for themselves. In modern India, freethought is slowly bringing about the emancipation of women from the debasing and dehumanizing teachings of Hinduism, even as Hindu and Islamic fundamentalists seek to convert the country to their particular religious persuasions. In Ireland, in Lebanon, and in country after country, efforts to control and contain life according to religious dogma bring human beings into warring conflict and retard human progress.

At the same time, the limitations of political dogmatism cannot be ignored. Young people in Communist China are experiencing what generations experienced in Communist Russia — restrictions resulting from a dogmatic, undemocratic, political authority and tyranny that denies human rights and freedoms. Once again, outmoded policies are employed as final truths to restrict free and open inquiry and democracy.

Throughout human history, progress has come through the men and women who dared to challenge the precepts and dogmas that curtailed freedoms. Freethinking (which includes skepticism, rationalism, unbelief, atheism, agnosticism, humanism and so forth) has made great and lasting contributions to human freedom, human rights and human equality. But freethought cannot exist or survive where religions and governments are not separated. As we have seen, over and over again, whenever church and state enter into partnership, human freedom is restricted, intellectual growth is stifled, and education is formalized and routinized to exclude and smother innovation and creativity. Fortunately, in the United States and in other free and democratic countries, church and state are separated; therefore the rights, the freedoms, and the contributions to societal growth by freethought groups, including skeptics, atheists, doubters, seekers, questioners and open inquirers, are all given status equal to that of formalized religious groups and churches. Our First Amendment, with its provision for the separation of church and state, makes this possible inasmuch as it guarantees both freedom ***for*** religion and freedom ***from*** religion, thus protecting the most important freedom of all — the freedom of the mind or freethought. The freedom to think for oneself, and the right to be able to express one's freethought without fear of persecution or exclusion from the community, would not be possible without the separation of governments from religions. Thus the insights and ideas stemming from freethought are provided a standing — especially under law — equal to ideas and insights growing out of the multitude of religious beliefs.

Today, the democratic world that is slowly emerging has at hand a ready-made model in the existing free democratic countries of the western world, particularly in America. But even in America, the democratic model is still being shaped as barrier after barrier to human freedom is being brought down, while encouragement for the human spirit to rise to new and still unknown heights is being fostered. We dare not let those, with an agenda — religious or otherwise — that is designed to reduce free and open inquiry and to place education under the control of dogma, deny our children the right to knowledge about the heroic men and women who have suffered and died in the cause of freethought. The list includes names like Copernicus, Galileo, Bruno, John Wyclif, Sir Walter Raleigh and the host of others mentioned in this book. They represent part of our heritage of freethought that we must share with the men and women of the future.

We are in a world of changing and emerging values as freethought and the democratic process expand human knowledge through science and the scientific method and make us aware of ancient injustices and cruelties. During the last centuries, we have outlawed slavery as a cruel, unjust and inhuman pattern. We have liberated women — a process that is still developing — providing rights and opportunities denied to them by theologies that depicted women as the weaker sex, originators of sin in the world, and as life forms created to serve the needs of the male. We are still in the throes of the struggle to recognize the rights and freedoms of all persons regardless of sexual orientation. Battles are still to be fought and won to eliminate racial and ethnic disharmony which has, in the past, been fostered and maintained in large part through nationalistic and religious bigotry.

The answer to these problems lies in democratic freethought where ideas may be generated, challenged, and accepted or rejected on the basis of scientific examination and verification, and evaluated on the basis of the highest human values that emerge from the developing society.

One purpose of this book is to encourage the recognition of freethought and freethinkers throughout human history and to acknowledge the contributions they have made to human freedom and to human progress. Over and over again, they have demonstrated that the greatest advancements in knowledge and civilization have occurred when and where there was freedom of thought.

A second purpose is to encourage our young people — the citizens of tomorrow — to build on their heritage of freethought, to have the courage to explore their ideas, the energy to work towards a better world, and the joy of experiencing freedom to reach their greatest potential as human beings. Through them, our students, we will, in the words of the creators of Star Trek, "go where no one has ever gone before" toward the development of a new Age of Enlightenment.

Appendix
Freethought Organizations and Literature

❖

Worldwide there are more than 22,000 Christian denominations. To catalog these together with other faith systems is impossible. However, because this book is concerned with freethought, it is important to list some of those groups.

United States

Listed below are the principal membership organizations and sources of literature in the broad free-thought field in the U.S. After that are listed some of the organizations outside the U.S.

American Ethical Union, 2 West 64th Street, New York, NY 10023; 212-873-6500. Has individual members and local societies for promotion of humanistic ethics.

American Humanist Association (AHA), 7 Harwood Drive/POB 1188, Amherst, NY 14226-7188; 716-839-5080 and 800-743-6646. Has members and chapters for advancing humanism. Publishes a bi-monthly magazine, *The Humanist*; and a membership newsletter, *Free Mind*. Offers humanist books and audio tapes. Has World-Wide-Web site: @http://freethought.tamu.edu/ore/aha/

Americans for Religious Liberty, POB 6656, Silver Springs, MD 20916; 301-598-2447. A national membership organization dedicated to defending church-state separation, reproductive rights, and religious neutrality of public education, and opposing any and all public support of religious institutions. Publishes a quarterly newsletter, *Voice of Reason*. Produces books of "The *Essential* Church-State Library."

Americans United for Separation of Church and State, 1816 Jefferson Place NW, Washington, DC 20036; 202-466-3234. Has members and chapters for defending the "wall" separating religion and government. Publishes magazine, *Church and State,* monthly (except August).

Atheist Alliance, 3510 S. MacDill Ave., Tampa, FL 33629-8906; 813-839-7567. A democratic alliance of autonomous societies advancing atheism. Publishes a quarterly magazine, *Secular Nation*.

Biblical Errancy (monthly), 2500 Punderson Drive, Hilliard, OH 43026.

Center for Inquiry, P.O. Box 664, Amherst, NY 14226-0664; 716-636-7571. Branch offices in Los Angeles, Kansas City, KS, and Oxford, U.K. Major activities are: Council for Secular Humanism; The Academy of Humanism; African Americans for Humanism; Committee for the Scientific Examination of Religion (CSER); Alliance of Secular Humanist Societies (ASHS); and publication of a quarterly journal, *Free Inquiry*.

Committee for the Scientific Investigation of Claims of the Paranormal (CSICOP), POB 703, Amherst, NY 14226-0703; 716-636-1425. Publishes bi-monthly the *Skeptical Inquirer*, and serves an informal network of Skeptic groups.

Freedom From Religion Foundation (FFRF), POB 750, Madison, WI 53701-0750; 608-256-8900. Has members and chapters for advancing freedom from religion and the separation of church and state. Publishes a monthly newspaper 10 times annually, *Freethought Today*, and several freethought books.

Freethought History (quarterly), Box 5224, Kansas City, KS 66119.

Freethought Observer, The, "News and Views Concerning the Nation's Freethinkers;" and ***The Freethought Exchange***, "The Freethinkers' Bi-Monthly Journal of Correspondence." Both are published bi-monthly by The Gnostic Press, P.O. Box 202477, Arlington, TX 76006; 817-461-2145.

Hemlock Society USA, P.O.Box 101810, Denver, CO 80250; 800-247-7421. Has members and chapters for advancing death with dignity.

Institute for First Amendment Studies, POB 589, Great Barrington, MA 01230; 413-274-3786. Publishes: a monthly newsletter, *The Freedom Writer*, "A Hard Look at the Hard Right;" and a quarterly newsletter, *Walk Away*, "The Newsletter for Ex-Fundamentalists." Sells books related thereto.

North American Committee for Humanism (NACH), P.O. Box 191, 5901-5 Wyoming NE, Albuquerque, NM 87109; 509-821-7207. Operates the Humanist Institute, a graduate study program. Publishes *Humanism Today*, an annual journal.

Prometheus Books, 59 John Glenn Drive, Amherst, NY 14228-2197; 800-421-0351. Large catalog lists hundreds of books under many subject headings.

Rational Recovery Self-Help Network, a division of Rational Recovery Systems, Inc., Box 800 Lotus, CA 95651; 916-621-2667. Has members in groups for achieving recovery from addictions through self-help.

Rationalist Association, Inc., P.O.Box 994, St. Louis, MO 63188; 314-962-2917. Publishes bi-monthly *The American Rationalist* magazine, and operates a book store.

Secular Organizations for Sobriety (also known as Save Our Selves), 5521 Grosvenor Boulevard, Los Angeles, CA 90066; 310-821-8430. Has members in groups for achieving sobriety through self-help.

Skeptics Society, The, 2761 N. Marengo Ave., Altedena, CA 91001; 818-794-3119. Devoted to the investigation and promotion of science and rational skepticism. Publishes quarterly journal, *Skeptic*.

Society for Humanistic Judaism, 28611 W. 12 Mile Road, Farmington Hills, MI 48334; 810-478-7610. Has members and chapters for advancing humanistic Judaism. Publishes quarterly journal, *Humanistic Judaism*.

The Truth Seeker Co., Inc., 16935 W. Bernardo Road, Suite 103, San Diego, CA 92127; 619-676-0430. Publishes bi-monthly *Truth Seeker*.

Unitarian Universalist Association, 25 Beacon Street, Boston, MA 02108-2800; 617-742-2100. Has over 1,000 congregations and 200,000 members, most of whom are freethinkers.

Outside the U.S.
Sample of Freethought Organizations

International Association for Religious Freedom, 2 Market St., Oxford 0X1 3EF, England, UK. Members are about 60 organizations in 21 countries. Most members seem to be liberal religious churches, but also some humanist groups.

International Humanist and Ethical Union, Nievwegracht 69A, 3512 Utrecht LG, Netherlands. The IHEU is the world humanist organization with 84 member organizations in 32 countries. Individual memberships. Publishes a quarterly magazine.

International League of Non-Religious and Atheists, Postfach 880, D-12118 Berlin, Germany.

Humanist Institute for Cooperation with Developing Countries (HIVOS), Raamweg 16, 2596 HL Den Haag, Netherlands.

Action for Humanism, P.O.Box 91, Ilishan Remo, Ogun State, **Nigeria**.

Asociacion Iberoamericana Etico, 1120 Are. 7a bis, Costado este de la Casa Amarilla, 1000 San Jose, **Costa Rica**.

Assembly of Freethinkers, House No. 258, Road No. 1, Dhanmondi R/A, Dhaka 1205, **Bangladesh**.

Association for Humanism, c/o Prof. Dolowy, UL. Rackowiecka 39A M 10, 02-521 Warsaw, **Poland**.

Association of Irish Humanists, 25 Wolf Tone Square West, Bray, Co. Wicklow, **Ireland**.

Atheist Centre, Benz Circle, Vijayawada 520 006, **India**.

British Humanist Association, Bradlaugh House, 47 Theobald's Road, London WC1X 8SP, **UK**.

Bund Freireligioser Gemeinden Deutschlands, Ulmenweg 5, 63263 Neu-Isenburg, **Germany**.

Centre D'Action Laique, CP 236, Campus de la Plaine U.L.B., Boulevard du Triomphe, 1050 Brussels, **Belgium**.

Centro Coscienza, Corso di Porta Nuova, 16-20121, Milan, **Italy**.

Centro Positivista do Parana, Rua Comendador Araujo 531, 80420-000 Curitiba, Parana, **Brazil**.

Danish Humanist Debate, Bjaelkevangen 2 C, 2800 Lyngby, **Denmark**.

Ethical Dialogues, Moscow State University, Faculty of Philosophy, Department of Ethics, 119899 Moscow B-234, **Russia**.

Human Etisk Forbund I Norge, St. Olav's Plass 27, 0130 Oslo, Norway. Mailing address: Postboks 6744, 0130, **Norway**.

Humanism and Solidarity, B.P. 15849, Kinshasa, **Zaire**.

Humanist Association of Canada, P.O. Box 3736, Station 'C', Ottawa, Ontario, **Canada** K1Y 4J8.

Humanist Ethical Education Organisation (HVO), Plompetorengracht 21, 3512 CB Utrceht, **Netherlands.**

Humanist Society of New Zealand, P.O. Box 3372, Wellington, **New Zealand.**

Humanist Union of Finland, P.O. Box 793 00101 Helsinki 10, **Finland.**

Humanistisch Verbond Belgie, Lange Leemstraat 57, 2018 Antwerpen, **Belgium.**

Hungarian Humanist Association, Szemere Street 10, 1054 Budapest, **Hungary.**

Indian Rationalist Association: (1) S. Edaramuku, 779, Pocket-5, Mayur Vihar-1, New Delhi, 110 091 **India.** (2) M. Innaiah, A 60 Journalist Colony, Jubilee Hills, Hyderabad 500 034, **India.**

Ligue Francaise de l'Enseignement et de l'Education Permanente, 3, Rue Recamier, 75341 Paris Cedex 07, **France.**

Mexican Ethical Rationalist Association, Apdo 19-546, Mexico City, DF 0-3900, **Mexico.**

Prometheus Society, Osadna 3, 831 03 Bratislava, **Slovac Republic.**

Rational Centre, P.O. Box 01132, Osu-Accra, **Ghana.**

Study Group of the History of Western Humanism, The Library of Chinese, Political College of Young, Beijing, **China.**

> **NOTE:** *Freethinkers Directory* lists many freethinker societies by states, the USA, and International and non-USA, plus Computer Bulletin Boards and an Index. Many entries include useful descriptive information. Published by David Briars, Rt-1 B-45, Craftsbury, VT 05826; 802-586-9628.

Index